FRANK LLOYD WRIGHT

GARLAND BIBLIOGRAPHIES IN
ARCHITECTURE AND PLANNING
(General Editor: Arnold L. Markowitz)
Vol. 3

GARLAND REFERENCE LIBRARY
OF THE HUMANITIES
Vol. 294

Frank Lloyd Wright (circa 1950s). Photo by Obma Studio; courtesy of the State Historical Society of Wisconsin.

FRANK LLOYD WRIGHT
A Research Guide to Archival Sources

Patrick J. Meehan, A.I.A.
Architect

with a foreword by
Adolf K. Placzek

GARLAND PUBLISHING, INC. • NEW YORK & LONDON
1983

Library of Congress Cataloging in Publication Data
Meehan, Patrick Joseph.
  Frank Lloyd Wright : a research guide to archival
sources.

  (Garland bibliographies in architecture and planning ;
v. 3) (Garland reference library of the humanities ;
v. 294)
  Includes index.
  1. Wright, Frank Lloyd, 1867–1959—Archives—Catalogs.
2. Wright, Frank Lloyd, 1867–1959—Manuscripts—Catalogs.
I. Title. II. Series. III. Series: Garland reference
library of the humanities ; v. 294.
Z6616.W74M44 1983 [NA737.W7] 016.72'092'4 81–47448
ISBN 0–8240–9342–9

Printed on acid-free, 250-year-life paper
Manufactured in the United States of America

To my wife, Karen

CONTENTS

Part I: The Frank Lloyd Wright Archival Collections

Part II: The Frank Lloyd Wright Manuscripts

ILLUSTRATIONS

FOREWORD

The primary goal of this book, in the words of its dedicated and indefatigable author Patrick J. Meehan, is to provide an organized working guide to Frank Lloyd Wright archival material in the widest sense of the term. The research guide locates, records and describes original manuscripts, drawings, letters, documents, and, importantly, furniture, building fragments and other artifacts that are in collections accessible to the public. The research guide thus points the way to countless treasures which, though widely dispersed, often acquired accidentally or bequeathed fortuitously, and in some cases saved by chance or luck, can be found in a number of archives, libraries and museums across the country and even in two European collections. The very existence of many of these treasures was until now known only to a very few specialists; there are also some instances of objects or documents whose reputed existence could not be verified. In both respects, in tracking down the heretofore unknown and in setting the record straight on the fictitious, Mr. Meehan has performed a major service.

For many of the items listed and described in the research guide the term "treasures," that is, art objects, seems justified. There are, first of all, the original drawings to which the researcher is directed, and some will be found to be of extraordinary beauty. Then there are typescripts, numerous letters and artifacts such as chairs; there are designs for brochures; there are miscellanea. Frequently, even among minor items, there is that vitality and consistency of style and form, that esthetic sense which seems to inhere in everything Wright touched. The research guide of course is not concerned only with the esthetically significant treasures. It also leads to the nitty-gritty, to the basic stuff of original research: to letters concerning payment problems, to a note regarding the lighting in a living room, to documents like Wright's passport and his genealogy, to transcripts of speeches. By adding the original documents and artifacts, Patrick J. Meehan's research guide provides a powerful buttress to the great work already done in Wright bibliography, such as Henry-Russell Hitchcock's *In the Nature of Materials*, Edgar Kaufmann and Ben Raeburn's *Frank Lloyd Wright: Writings and Buildings*, William A. Storrer's *The Architecture of Frank Lloyd Wright, a Complete Catalogue* and Robert L. Sweeney's *Frank Lloyd Wright: An Annotated Bibliography*. It is a giant step forward in the mastery of the available material, a giant step consisting of countless small steps of unflagging effort, pursuit, painstaking detective work and ultimate discovery. The organization of the research guide—first by institution, then chronologically by individual item and finally by separate indexes—will be found both highly usable and logical.

What the research guide reveals to us is the magnitude of Wright's activity and output—written, sketched, typed, designed and even (recorded) talk. He hardly seemed to weary. However stymied, resisted or misunderstood he may have been, he never lost interest. He was always brilliantly, indeed dangerously, articulate. He was invariably master of the specific detail or problem, and however often he may have changed his mind, he never changed his belief, his objective and his single-minded devotion to a new architecture. He lived a very long life, a life which—as Goethe said about his own—was in itself a work of art. He created this life not only in glorious buildings, but in his social relationships, in his impact on his fellow humans, in his teaching, his pioneering, his loves, feuds, lectures and of course in the streams of his written words. It was a great and singularly productive life in the face of frequent adversity and occasional stark tragedy. All this comes through very clearly in the thousands of original items recorded in the research guide. It is made particularly dramatic and poignant through the exact chronological order in Part II (with the inevitable exceptions of the undatable items) in which Mr. Meehan has organized and presented the material: seven chapters, from the Early Years, through Turmoil, Innovation, New Forms to the Last Golden Years (to quote some of his apt headings).

What also comes through in the research guide, together with the wealth of material, is the wide dispersal of sources. Systematic researchers will of course have to start at Taliesin West, in

Scottsdale, Arizona, the fountainhead of all Wright research. They will then have to go not only to the Avery Library in New York and the Burnham Library in Chicago, but will have to travel the length and breadth of the country, with side trips to Amsterdam and London: many institutions are listed in the research guide, apart from Taliesin itself. They will encounter occasional difficulties of access, some disappointments and some thrilling discoveries. They will at first be overwhelmed by the sheer bulk of original Wright material facing them—even though the early years up to the 1920s yield strangely little material, and even though much original material must still be in private hands or must be lost. We know of course how terrible was the loss in the burning of Taliesin East in 1914. Even with these gaps, the researchers will feel overwhelmed—and then be profoundly grateful to this comprehensive and path-breaking guide which will direct and assist their search and research.

Adolf K. Placzek
Avery Librarian Emeritus
Columbia University

ACKNOWLEDGMENTS

Acknowledgments appear in many books and may seem to be full of clichés and rhetoric to most readers. My acknowledgments may fit this description. However, they are sincere, since it would have been impossible to put together such a research guide as this without the cooperation and assistance of many others. My wife, Karen, gave to the research project much of her time and energy and assisted in research, evaluation, and proofreading, as well as offering me encouragement. For all of this and more I thank her. If not for Karen this research guide would not have been realized, and I dedicate it to her. My parents, in-laws, and other relatives were very understanding at times when I was unapproachable, and I appreciate their patience.

I want to thank Bruce Brooks Pfeiffer, Director of Archives of the Frank Lloyd Wright Memorial Foundation, and Adrienne A. Carney, Assistant to the Director of Archives of the Frank Lloyd Wright Memorial Foundation, who were most helpful in dispelling the seemingly unfounded myth perpetrated by some scholars that access to the Frank Lloyd Wright Memorial Foundation archives was not possible, and for their suggestions which ultimately led to the title of this research guide. Through Mr. Pfeiffer's and Mrs. Carney's efforts and assistance, a clear and succinct policy statement appears here outlining scholarly access to the vast holdings of the Frank Lloyd Wright Memorial Foundation archives; the photographing and cataloguing of this archive was in progress as of 1983.

I am honored to have Adolf K. Placzek write the foreword to my work. Mr Placzek also assisted with access to the many Wright related materials housed in the Avery Architectural Library at Columbia University.

Professor Damie Stillman, formerly my professor of modern architectural history at the University of Wisconsin–Milwaukee (my twice Alma Mater), sparked my interest in the Prairie School in general and provided me with a good framework for the study of modern architecture. Professor Amos Rapoport of the School of Architecture and Urban Planning at the University of Wisconsin–Milwaukee, Michael Stancl, and Louise Weber gave their support for the research project in its early stages. Jean Gutkowski spent many hours typing the draft manuscript. Leigh A. Milner of *The Capital Times* of Madison, Wisconsin, assisted with access to their information on Wright.

Also, for their courteous and helpful cooperation, I gratefully acknowledge the following persons and institutions (none, of course, is responsible for any shortcomings of this research guide):

Barbara Ballinger, Head Librarian at the Oak Park Public Library, Oak Park, Illinois

Mary T. Bates, Assistant Dean, Business Affairs at the School of Architecture and Urban Planning of the University of Wisconsin–Milwaukee

Michael Birdsall, Assistant Curator to the Department of Decorative Arts of the Minneapolis Institute of Arts

John C. Borst, Manuscripts Curator of the Historical Resource Center of the South Dakota Department of Education and Cultural Affairs

John C. Broderick, Chief of the Manuscript Division of the Library of Congress

Lisa Calden, Registrar of the Elvehjem Art Center at the University of Wisconsin–Madison

Cecilia Chin, Head of the Reference Department at the Art Institute of Chicago

Jane Colokathis, of the Joseph Regenstein Library at the University of Chicago

David Crosson, Research Historian of the Archive of Contemporary History at the University of Wyoming

Carolyn A. Davis, Manuscript Librarian of the George Arents Research Library at Syracuse University

D.E. Dean, Librarian of the British Architectural Library of the Royal Institute of British Architects

Carol Falcione, Reference Librarian of the Avery Architectural Library of Columbia University

Shonnie Finnegan and Christopher Densmore of the University Archives of the State University of New York at Buffalo

John Frankland, Librarian for *The Milwaukee Journal*

Marilyn Fuss, of the Southern California Chapter of the American

Institute of Architects

Ann Goodfellow, Curator of the Arts Study Collections at Chicago Circle Campus

Peter L. Goss, Associate Professor of Architecture at the Graduate School of Architecture of the University of Utah, for his assistance with the Taylor A. Woolley Archives

Richard N. Gregg, Director of the Allentown Art Museum, Allentown, Pennsylvania

Donald Hallmark, Director of the Richard W. Bock Collection at Greenville College, Greenville, Illinois

Paul R. Hanna, Senior Research Fellow at the Hoover Institution of Stanford University and former Frank Lloyd Wright client

Dr. Josephine L. Harper, Reference Archivist of the State Historical Society of Wisconsin

Diana Haskell, Curator of Modern Manuscripts at the Newberry Library in Chicago

Thomas A. Heinz, Editor of *The Frank Lloyd Wright Newsletter* of Oak Park, Illinois

Randy Henning, formerly of Milwaukee, for pointing out the existence of the Harold M. Groves Papers at the State Historical Society of Wisconsin

Alyn W. Hess, formerly of the Wisconsin Architectural Archives of the Milwaukee Public Library, for providing me with photographs of the demolished Lake Geneva Hotel

Joanne E. Hohler, of the State Historical Society of Wisconsin

Susan Cosgrove Holton, Librarian of the American Institute of Architects

Jethro M. Hurt, III, Education Coordinator and Curator of the Chicago Architecture Foundation

Frank Jewell, Reference Librarian of the Chicago Historical Society

Donald Leslie Johnson, Senior Lecturer in Architectural History of the Flinders University of South Australia

Frances Follin Jones, Curator of Collections, The Art Museum of Princeton University

Donald Kalec, Architect, of the Frank Lloyd Wright Home and Studio Foundation at Oak Park, Illinois

Virginia Kazor, Curator, Municipal Arts Department of the City of Los Angeles

Katherine Lee Keefe, Curator of The David and Alfred Smart Gallery at the University of Chicago

Dr. Juro Kikuchi, Curator of the Museum Meiji-Mura, for his aid in obtaining photographs of the reconstructed and relocated Imperial Hotel lobby wing

Joe W. Koelsch, of Richland Center, Wisconsin

David Kopitzke, former Director of The Warehouse at Richland Center, Wisconsin

Robert H. Land, for his assistance at the Library of Congress in Washington, D.C.

William T. Lane, College Archivist, Milne Library of the State University College of Arts and Science at Geneseo, New York

Alan K. Lathrop, Curator of the Northwest Architectural Archives at the University of Minnesota

Elliott Maraniss, Executive Editor of *The Capital Times* of Madison, Wisconsin

Terry Marvel, of the Prairie Archives of the Milwaukee Art Museum (formerly the Milwaukee Art Center)

R. Russell Maylone, Curator of the Special Collections Department at the Northwestern University Library

Leela Meinertas, of the Department of Furniture and Woodwork at the Victoria and Albert Museum

R. Craig Miller, Assistant Curator of the Department of Decorative Arts at the Metropolitan Museum of Art, New York

Bebbe Klatt-Mooring and Stephen C. Mooring, for their assistance with the Edgar Kaufmann, Sr., Office at the Victoria and Albert Museum

Milo M. Naeve, Curator of American Arts of the Art Institute of Chicago

Kathryn Otto, of the State Historical Society of Wisconsin, for her assistance in searching through their numerous manuscript collections for Frank Lloyd Wright related materials

Clive Phillpot, Librarian, the Museum of Modern Art, New York

Steve Portch, of the University of Wisconsin–Richland Center, for his assistance with the Frank Lloyd Wright manuscripts housed in The Warehouse collections at Richland Center, Wisconsin

Alba Priore, Assistant Registrar of the Albright-Knox Gallery at the Buffalo Fine Arts Academy

Edith M. Prise, Assistant Manuscripts Librarian at the Maryland Historical Society

John D. Randall, Director of the American Architectural Museum and Resource Center, Buffalo, New York

Raymond D. Reed, Dean of the College of Architecture and Environmental Design at Texas A&M University

Mary Lynn Ritzenthaler, Assistant Manuscript Librarian of the University of Illinois at Chicago Circle Library

Carol Robbins, Assistant Curator of the Dallas Museum of Fine Arts

Christian Rohlfing, Curator of Collections at the Cooper-Hewitt Museum, New York

Christine St. Lawrence Taylor, of the Historic American Buildings Survey, Washington, D.C.
Samuel A. Sizer, Curator of Special Collections of the University of Arkansas Library at Fayetteville
Edward Skipworth, of the Special Collections Department of the Alexander Library of Rutgers, The State University of New Jersey
Caroline T. Spicer, Reference Librarian, Cornell University Libraries
Louis M. Starr, Director of the Oral History Research Office of Butler Library, Columbia University
Nan Sullivan, of the library staff of *The Capital Times* of Madison
George Talbot, Curator of Iconography of the State Historical Society of Wisconsin
Yoshiko Tanigawa, of Japan, for providing the author with data and Japanese publications on Frank Lloyd Wright
Deborah R. Temme, Graduate Assistant at the Graduate School of Architecture of the University of Utah, for her assistance with the Taylor A. Woolley Archives
Christa C.M. Thurman, Curator of the Department of Textiles at the Art Institute of Chicago
Christopher Wilk, of the Architecture and Design Study Center at the Museum of Modern Art, New York
Ann E. Williams, Curator of the Wright Collection of the Kenneth Spencer Research Library at the University of Kansas, for her investigation of the letters by Frank Lloyd Wright housed in that collection
Myrna Williamson, of the Iconographic Collections Department of the State Historical Society of Wisconsin
Wim de Wit, of Rijkdienst voor de Monumentenzorg Nederlands Documentatiecentrum voor de Bouwkunst
William E. Woolfenden, Director of the Archives of American Art at New York
Hortense Zera, Librarian at the American Academy and Institute of Arts and Letters, New York
John Zukowsky, Architectural Archivist of the Art Institute of Chicago.

Patrick J. Meehan, A.I.A.
Registered Architect
Milwaukee, Wisconsin
May 1983

INTRODUCTION

Purpose and Scope of the Research

The architecture of Frank Lloyd Wright has exerted a continuing influence on architectural design throughout the world. To date, however, a comprehensive documentation and research guide to Frank Lloyd Wright's original manuscripts, letters, drawings, furniture, building fragments, and various other artifacts housed at numerous institutions and libraries has not existed. The primary goal of this book is to provide an organized working guide to Frank Lloyd Wright archival materials, including original manuscripts, letters, drawings, furniture, building fragments, and various other Wright related artifacts housed in collections which are generally accessible to the scholarly researcher. The book provides a source of organized documentation of Wright's life and architecture through the many archival collections described. The existence of many of the Frank Lloyd Wright archival materials identified here has not been widely known. The documentation provided in this research guide, however, is not intended to serve either as a substitute or as a replacement for the study of the original Frank Lloyd Wright archival materials but should be used as a guide and a point of departure for more intense research and investigation into the various aspects of Frank Lloyd Wright's life and architecture.

Research Methodology

A literature search was conducted to identify those publications which contain information and data relating to existing Frank Lloyd Wright archives. The identification of these source materials was accomplished by consulting various indexes, abstracting journals, catalogues, periodicals, books, experts, and librarians. These provided initial contacts with several archives which eventually led to additional contacts with other archives over a period of about six years extending from 1974 through 1980.

In final efforts to locate and identify any additional Frank Lloyd Wright archival materials which may have been inadvertently overlooked the author placed queries in *The Newsletter of the Society of Architectural Historians*, Vol. 24, No. 1, February 1980, p. 4, and in *The Frank Lloyd Wright Newsletter* (Oak Park, Illinois), Vol. 2, No. 3, Second Quarter 1979, p. 18. Both queries listed the tentative title of the book as well as the types of Frank Lloyd Wright archival materials being researched by the author. This approach provided the author with the opportunity to locate some of the more obscure Frank Lloyd Wright archival collections and to be as thorough as possible in identifying the archives.

Organization of the Research Guide

The research guide is organized into two parts: Part I, The Frank Lloyd Wright Archival Collections, and Part II, The Frank Lloyd Wright Manuscripts. In addition to these two basic parts of the guide two related appendixes are included, as well as relevant indexes to further assist the researcher in identifying specific areas of study.

Part I, the guide to the Frank Lloyd Wright archival collections, identifies the Frank Lloyd Wright related archival contents of fifty collections housed in privately owned, publicly accessible archives, publicly owned archives, university libraries, art museums, historical societies, libraries, and other types of repositories. The types of materials identified in Part I include, but are not limited to, original manuscripts written by Frank Lloyd Wright, drawings from Wright's office, furniture and decorative arts related objects designed by Wright, and fragments from buildings designed by Wright. Collections belonging to private individuals are not discussed in this guide due to their very limited access.

Part II, the guide to the Frank Lloyd Wright original manuscripts, is intended to aid the researcher in the use of the manuscripts at their respective archives. The original manuscripts of Frank Lloyd Wright, including both published and unpublished letters housed in public archives, are catalogued and indexed in chronological order from 1894 (the year of the earliest discovered original manuscript) to 1959 (the year of Wright's death). Part II is divided into seven chapters or groupings of manuscripts, representing seven different time periods corresponding to significant stages of Wright's lengthy architectural career. Each of the over five hundred manuscripts catalogued is precisely indexed. Extensive bibliographic references are provided at the end of each of the seven chapters. Part II is extensively illustrated with photographs to augment the text.

Appendix A, an index to undated Frank Lloyd Wright original manuscripts, identifies those original manuscripts for which dates could not be determined. Appendix B, a compiled chronology of buildings, designs, and projects, provides a comprehensive listing of Wright's work with revised dates based upon an analysis of the manuscripts and other sources. The book is indexed by several methods, making it relatively easy for the researcher to locate materials at various archives and to identify needed data.

Access to Frank Lloyd Wright Archival Materials

Access to Frank Lloyd Wright archival materials at the various collections or archives depends on the policies adopted by the individual repository. In the case of private repositories, access can be limited on a highly selective basis, and equality of access among scholars and researchers may be almost nonexistent or so selective as to be exclusionary; but this may be justifiable in some instances, in order to maintain the protection of the contents of the archives. Public repositories, however, should permit access by scholars within the limits of protecting the actual archival materials from damage, loss, or theft. Unfortunately, equal access is not permitted by all the public archives housing Frank Lloyd Wright archival materials. In 1973 the Joint American Historical Association–Organization of American Historians–Society of American Archivists Committee on Historians and Archives, approved the "Statement on User Fees and Access" which stated for archives that "Proposals that access be limited to students and faculty of the institution where the materials are housed, thus turning the university's manuscript collection into a kind of private hunting ground for its own students and faculty . . . are out of harmony with those traditions of scholarship which have always opposed erecting walls around libraries and scholarly sources" (*The Society of American Archivists Newsletter*, January 1974, p. 1). This statement, unfortunately, seems to be ignored by several public archival repositories which hold Frank Lloyd Wright related archival materials, but perhaps this situation will change for the better.

The Society of American Archivists Committee on Reference, Access and Photoduplication has prepared "Standards for Access to Research Materials in Archival and Manuscript Repositories," which were endorsed by the Council of the Society of American Archivists in December of 1973. These standards were published in *American Archivist*, Vol. 37, January 1974, pp. 153–154, and in Sue E. Holbert's *Basic Manual Series: Archives and Manuscripts—Reference and Access* (Chicago: Society of American Archivists, 1977, pp. 28–29) and are reprinted here with permission from the Society of American Archivists:

1. It is the responsibility of an archival and manuscript repository to make available research materials in its possession to researchers on equal terms of access. Since the accessibility of material depends on knowing of its existence, it is the responsibility of a repository to inform the researchers of the collections and archival groups in its custody. This may be accomplished through a card catalog, inventories, and other internal finding aids, a published guide and reports to NUCMC where appropriate, and the freely offered assistance of staff members.

2. To protect and insure the continued availability of the material in his custody, the archivist may impose several conditions. (a) The archivist may limit the use of fragile or unusually valuable materials so long as suitable reproductions are made available for the use of all researchers. (b) All materials must be used in accordance with the rules of and under the supervision of the repository. Each repository should publish and furnish to potential researchers its rules governing access and use. Such rules must be equally applied and enforced. (c) The archivist may refuse access to unprocessed materials, so long as such refusal is applied to all researchers. (d) Normally, a repository will not send research materials for use outside its building or jurisdiction. Under special circumstances a collection or a portion of it may be loaned or placed on deposit with another institution. (e) The archivist may refuse access to an individual researcher who has demonstrated such carelessness or deliberate destructiveness as to endanger the safety of the material.

3. Each repository should publish a suggested form of citation crediting the repository and identifying items within the collection for later reference. Citations to copies of which the originals

are in other repositories should include the location of the originals.

4. A repository should advise the researcher that he and his publisher have the sole responsibility for securing permission to publish beyond fair use from unpublished manuscripts in which literary property rights are retained or from materials protected by statutory copyrights, or to publish extensive quotation (beyond fair use) from copyrighted works. A repository should, to the best of its ability, inform the researcher about known retention of literary rights.

5. A repository should not grant privileged or exclusive use of materials to any person or persons, or conceal the existence of any body of material from any researcher unless required to do so by law, donor, or purchase stipulations.

6. A repository should, whenever possible, inform a researcher of parallel research by other individuals using the same papers. It may supply names upon request.

7. Repositories are committed to preserving manuscript and archival materials and to making them available for research as soon as possible. At the same time, it is recognized that every public agency has certain obligations to guard against invasion of privacy and to protect confidentially in its records in accordance with law and that every private donor has the right to impose reasonable restrictions upon his papers to protect confidentially for a reasonable period of time. (a) It is the responsibility of the archivist to inform researchers of the restrictions which apply to individual collections or record groups. (b) The archivist should discourage donors from imposing unreasonable restrictions. (c) The archivist should, whenever possible, require a specific time limit on all restrictions. (d) The repository should periodically reevaluate restricted records and work toward providing access to material no longer harmful to individuals or to national interest.

The Society of American Archivists Committee on Reference and Access Policies further prepared a "Statement on the Reproduction of Manuscripts and Archives for Reference Use" which was approved by the Council of the Society of American Archivists in April of 1976. This statement was published in *American Archivist*, Vol. 39, July 1976, p. 411, and in Sue E. Holbert's *Basic Manual Series: Archives and Manuscripts—Reference and Access*, p. 29. It is reprinted here with permission from the Society of American Archivists:

1. It is the responsibility of a library, archives, or manuscript repository to assist researchers by making or having made reproductions of any material in its possession for research purposes, subject to certain conditions. Manuscript and archival materials may be reproduced if: (a) The condition of the originals will permit such reproduction. (b) The originals have no gift, purchase, or legal restrictions on reproduction.

2. In the interest in making research collections more generally available, the orderly microfilming of archives and entire manuscript collections, together with appropriate guides, is to be encouraged, within the available resources of the repository.

3. The price of reproductions shall be set by the repository, which should endeavor to keep charges to a minimum.

4. Copies should be made for reference use as follows: (a) Repositories which permit their manuscript and archival holdings to be reproduced in whole or in part must specify before the copies are made what restrictions, if any, have been placed on the use or further reproduction of copies. (b) Repositories may require that purchasers agree in writing to abide by any restrictions. (c) All reproductions should identify the source of the original manuscript collection or archival record group.

5. The repository should inform the researcher: (a) When and under what conditions permission to make extensive direct quotation from or print in full any reproduction must be obtained from the institution owning the originals. (b) That in the case of material under copyright, the right to quote or print, beyond fair use, must be obtained by the researcher from the copyright owner. (c) That the researcher assumes legal responsibility for observing common law literary rights, property rights, and libel laws. (d) Of known retention of literary rights.

6. A repository may decline to furnish reproduction when fulfilling mail requests requires subjective criteria for selection of material to be duplicated or the commitment of an unreasonable amount of staff time for extended research to identify the material.

7. In cases when researchers request the reproduction of large amounts of material which they have identified in the course of their research, the repository may prescribe a preferred method of copying (i.e., microfilm vs. xerox) and may provide for a reasonable time period in which to produce the copies.

Some public institutions and archives do not subscribe to the Society of American Archivists statement regarding the reproduction of manuscripts because of the possibility that they might lose whatever control they have over the use of the manuscript. The copyrights to all Frank Lloyd Wright unpublished manuscripts belong to his legal heirs. In cases where published manuscripts written by Frank Lloyd Wright had their copyrights vested in the publisher, the renewals of those copyrights have been vested in the legal heirs of Frank Lloyd Wright.* The rights of Frank Lloyd Wright's legal heirs should be respected with regard to manuscripts written by Frank Lloyd Wright. Serious research utilizing Frank Lloyd Wright unpublished manuscripts as source documents should begin with appropriate application to the Frank Lloyd Wright Memorial Foundation at Taliesin West as outlined in this research guide. The Frank Lloyd Wright Memorial Foundation houses the largest archive of materials related to Frank Lloyd Wright and is a logical first step for any in-depth research of him and his architecture which requires the use of primary data sources such as manuscripts and/or drawings. In this respect, and due to the voluminous content of the Frank Lloyd Wright Memorial Foundation archives, much of which is still to be catalogued by the Foundation, the Foundation archives are not represented here to the degree worthy of its importance to the study of Frank Lloyd Wright. The compilation of Frank Lloyd Wright archival materials contained here represents a beginning and is not complete.

*Personal correspondence to the author from Ms. Adrienne A. Carney, the Assistant to the Director of Archives of the Frank Lloyd Wright Memorial Foundation, dated August 9, 1979.

Part I
The Frank Lloyd Wright
Archival Collections

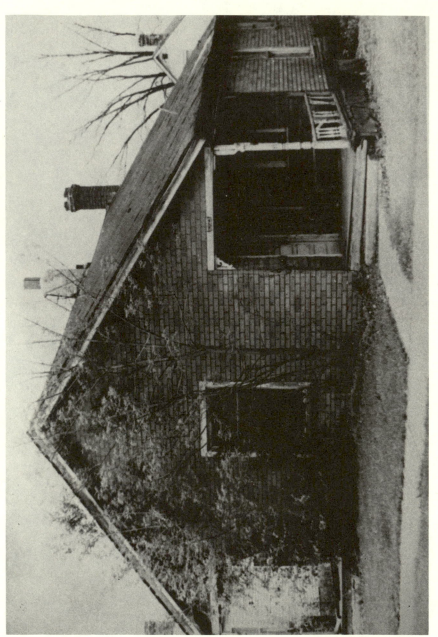

1-1.1   This house, which stood at 774 South Park Street, Richland Center, Wisconsin, is believed to have been the birthplace of Frank Lloyd Wright (circa mid-1800s; demolished early 1970s). Photo by Joe W. Koelsch.

Part I, the guide to the Frank Lloyd Wright archival collections, identifies the archival materials related to Frank Lloyd Wright in fifty collections housed in privately owned, publicly accessible archives; publicly owned archives; university archives and libraries; art museums; historical societies; public libraries; and other types of repositories. The types of materials identified here include, but are not limited to original manuscripts written by Frank Lloyd Wright, drawings from Wright's office, furniture and decorative arts related objects designed by Wright, and fragments from buildings designed by Frank Lloyd Wright. Photograph collections of Frank Lloyd Wright or of his buildings, and related types of materials, housed at various libraries and institutions for the most part have not been catalogued or indexed in this guide, except for the Oskar Stonorov Papers housed in the Archive of Contemporary History at the University of Wyoming Library because the significance of this collection--photographs prepared in conjunction with Wright's "Sixty Years of Living Architecture" exhibition of the early 1950s--warranted an elaboration of its contents.

Several archives which were reported to house collections containing archival materials related to Frank Lloyd Wright proved not to hold such materials. It is in the interest of assisting other researchers, and with the hope not to seem unnecessarily critical, that these references are pointed out here: James Muggenberg, in "Frank Lloyd Wright in Print, 1959-1970" (*Papers of the American Association of Architectural Bibliographers*, Vol. 9, 1972), pp. 85-132, reported that Frank Lloyd Wright related manuscripts were contained in the Ogden Smith Manuscripts Collection at Rutgers University. A search of the Ogden Smith Manuscripts Collection housed in the Special Collections Department of the Alexander Library at Rutgers did not uncover any Frank Lloyd Wright related manuscripts. The Ogden Smith Manuscript Collection materials were written during the period 1827 to 1862, predating Frank Lloyd Wright's birth in 1867. A further search of the index to manuscript holdings at the Alexander Library has shown that Rutgers does not house any papers or correspondence of Frank Lloyd Wright.

The Art Museum of Princeton University was thought to house a dining table and side chairs designed by Frank Lloyd Wright. However, these items were only on display at the museum in 1972 (see Robert Judson Clark, Editor, *The Arts and Crafts Movement in America, 1876-1916* [Princeton, New Jersey: Princeton University Press, 1972]). Similarly, the Olin Library at Cornell University was believed to be the holder of six drawings executed by Frank Lloyd Wright of his design for the Avery Coonley Residence at Riverside, Illinois, of 1907. The staffs of Cornell's Reference Library, Fine Arts Library, and Department of Manuscripts and Archives were unable to uncover the existence of these drawings in their respective collections at Cornell.

The College of Architecture and Environmental Design at Texas A & M University was reported to house two early Frank Lloyd Wright drawings (for photographs of these two drawings see "Wright Drawings"

[*The Prairie School Review*, Vol. 4, No. 4, 1967], inside back cover).
However, in a letter to the author dated May 30, 1979, Dean Raymond D.
Reed of the College reported that the University had returned the
two drawings to the Frank Lloyd Wright estate in 1969 or 1970.
    The *National Union Catalog of Manuscript Collections* reported
that archival materials related to Frank Lloyd Wright were housed in
the Carl Schmidt Collection of American Architecture, 1915 to 1972,
at the College at Geneseo Library of the State University of New York.
This collection does not house any archival materials other than a
set of photographic slides which Mr. Schmidt had taken of various
residences designed by Frank Lloyd Wright.
    The Frank Lloyd Wright Memorial Foundation collection is listed
first in this part because of its extreme importance as a research
source; the others are listed thereafter in alphabetical order. There
is a brief synopsis of the original Frank Lloyd Wright manuscripts
housed in each collection, listed by date, when known. In the case of
archives which house both original manuscripts and other types of
archival materials related to Frank Lloyd Wright, the manuscript
collections are discussed first. Other types of archival materials,
such as drawings, furniture, decorative arts related objects, fragments from Wright designed buildings, etc., are listed in chronological
order, using the dates in Appendix B, by building, design, or project
to which the archival material is attributed, and are not dated according to those on the archival material. Each archival item is described
from catalogues and indexes, since not all the items were personally
inspected by the author and give physical measurements in both inches
and millimeters, where known. Consequently, variations exist in the
method and style of indexing. In some instances, access policies are included but the researcher using this guide should bear in mind that these
policies may change considerably through time. Because of the abundance
of materials listed in this part of the guide, no photographs of the
archival items were included.

A1

The Frank Lloyd Wright Memorial Foundation
Taliesin West
Scottsdale, Arizona 85258
    The Frank Lloyd Wright Memorial Foundation is a tax exempt chari-
table organization whose purpose is to perpetuate and preserve the
works of Frank Lloyd Wright and to educate the public concerning his
important and unique contribution to architecture. The most extensive
collection of Frank Lloyd Wright archival materials, including more
than 19,000 Frank Lloyd Wright drawings, thousands of letters, hun-
dreds of original manuscripts, numerous photographs, as well as other
related materials, belong to and are housed by the Frank Lloyd Wright
Foundation. The Frank Lloyd Wright Foundation has permitted the Frank
Lloyd Wright Memorial Foundation access to the collection for the
purpose of cataloguing. This activity has yielded an extensive list
of the items in the collection and is still progressing. It is not

possible in this guide to list all the items; instead, a brief general discussion of each type of archival material in the collection is presented.

The Frank Lloyd Wright Foundation does not permit the study of the original material, except in very special instances. However, Mr. Wright's works are being photographed by the Memorial Foundation in both black and white and color. All items are reproduced on 4-in. x 5-in. (101.6-mm x 127-mm) color transparencies. The excellent quality of the transparencies can be sampled in *Frank Lloyd Wright: Selected Drawings Portfolio*, published by Horizon Press in New York, in 1977. The researcher utilizing the Frank Lloyd Wright Memorial Foundation's facilities can either study these transparencies or have 8 x 10 photographs made if he cannot pursue a course of study at Taliesin West. In November 1979 the cost of having the Frank Lloyd Wright Memorial Foundation provide 8 x 10 photographs was $25.00 per photo, on an eight-month loan basis.

Wright's letters were in the process of being catalogued by the Memorial Foundation in November 1979. Out of respect for and consideration to the correspondents and their heirs, one may not study the unpublished letters in the collection, except in special cases. The Memorial Foundation will, however, research the letters in order to answer scholars' questions.

The Frank Lloyd Wright Memorial Foundation is constantly discovering more manuscripts in the enormous files. They are being microfilmed and paper photoduplicates are being made, which researchers are permitted to use for study.

One may obtain access to the information and materials maintained by the Frank Lloyd Wright Memorial Foundation by requesting and receiving permission in writing from the Board of Directors. The requests should give a good and clear background to the proposed project and what will need to be studied. A reasonable lead time is required by the Memorial Foundation after the request is approved by the Board of Directors in order to prepare the materials for viewing. The fee for viewing the materials is based on the pre-research work and the time spent with the researcher when he is studying the materials pro-rated at the number of hours for each day's use. The fee may be modified by the type of request and the researcher's funds available from research grants and other sources. The Director of Archives or his assistant must be present with the researcher during the study period. The Memorial Foundation does not permit the researcher to photoduplicate any of its archival materials; however, notes may be taken and tape recording is permitted. Study is limited only to the months from October to May at Taliesin West, Scottsdale, Arizona.

All Wright's drawings and letters in the archives are copyrighted by the Frank Lloyd Wright Foundation. Publication of any materials in the Foundation's archives can be done only with their written permission. The first rights to any hitherto unpublished drawings, letters, and manuscripts, even when they are not in the possession of the Foundation, are also, by Federal Law, protected and vested in Mrs. Frank Lloyd Wright and the Frank Lloyd Wright Foundation. A general discussion of the archives has appeared in Bruce Brooks Pfeiffer's "The Archives of the Frank Lloyd Wright Memorial Foundation" (*The Frank Lloyd Wright Newsletter*, Vol. 4, No. 2, Second Quarter 1981), pp. 17-18.

A2

Allentown Art Museum
Fifth and Court Streets
P.O. Box 117
Allentown, Pennsylvania 18105

The Allentown Art Museum purchased the library room of the now demolished Francis W. Little Residence II, "Northome," of 1912, from the Metropolitan Museum of Art of New York. The home was originally located at Deephaven, Minnesota. A booklet by Deborah S. Haight and Peter F. Blume entitled *Frank Lloyd Wright: The Library from the Francis W. Little House*, published by the Allentown Art Museum in 1978, offers a complete description of the Frank Lloyd Wright designed library. A portion of this publication is reprinted here with permission:

> The library was located to the left of the entrance into the family quarters. The brick pier on the left as one entered the room was a continuation of the wall and brick piers flanking the exterior entrance. This asymmetrical entrance to the library was a repetition of the material of the outside wall which was again visible as one looked out to the terrace from the short windows to the left. Approaching the library from the entrance hall one looked south through the "leaded" glass windows to some large maples and spacious sloping lawn. The east wall, which looked onto the terrace, consisted of four windows, with the module adjusted to fit the space; the west wall was lined with white oak bookcases to the height of four feet eight inches, in soffited recess. The room was actually a small reception room; there was limited shelving for books. It was one of the few self-contained rooms in the house, though the spaces flowed into the entrance and billiard room beyond. The open transom at the entrance was only six and one half feet high, giving one an exaggerated sense of ceiling height and lightness when one entered the room proper. All of the basic architectural features described above have been retained in the transition to Allen-town; but a different kind of architectural setting has led to several changes in the appearance of the room. The library now fronts onto an enclosed sculpture terrace. The short approach to the room had to be eliminated and the transom closed. Both of these factors have altered Wright's concept of the flow of space but were inevitable changes with the demolition of the house.

> Edgar Tafel, the Allentown Museum's architect, felt that the room had never been finished according to Wright's intention and that the detailing had been neglected in the secondary rooms, perhaps due to Wright's absence from the building site at Northome. Following the style of the ceiling treatment in the living room, Tafel has included two strips of white oak molding around the double-sloping ceiling, and concealed indirect lighting in the light deck that follows the perimeter of the room....

> Closets were necessities that Wright frequently overlooked in the scheme of his designs to the general inconvenience of his clients. Little may have had this one added; it would have been the only closet in the vicinity of the entrance to the house.

The closet is not included in any of the floor plans which indicate a continuation of the bookcases around the small alcove. Curiously, the original flooring in the closet was raised two inches from the rest of the room suggesting [the] fact it may have been original. However, the wood of the sliding doors does not match the rest of the trim in the room in finish or age.

According to recollections of the Littles' daughter, Mrs. Raymond Stevenson, the library was furnished with an oak desk and chair, several wicker chairs, and two standing lamps. There were no curtains to detract from the windows and the view beyond. A dark red oriental rug covered the floor. On the south wall to the right of the windows was a Hiroshige woodcut.

It is impossible to identify specific pieces of furniture from the schematic drawing for the Little House that is in the Metropolitan Museum (New York) although one may assume that the floor lamps, referred to by Mrs. Stevenson and now in New York, were used in the library. With only these vague recollections and clues available, the room in Allentown is not an exact duplication of how it appeared at Wayzata (Deephaven), but represents Wright's taste in interior design as it might have been seen at Taliesin, a house that evolved over many years.

The chairs are reproductions of those designed in 1904 for the Martin House in Buffalo.

The design of the four wall-lighting fixtures was executed for the living room. At the time of demolition the wall lighting treatment in the library and other secondary rooms of the house was silk shades over light bulbs. This is not akin to Wright's usual lighting treatment. The oak fixtures installed at Allentown each consist of sixty-five pieces of wood. They were reproduced from those made for the living room.

The table was designed by Edgar Tafel for this room in the Wright manner of the late 1930's or early 1940's. Other incidental furnishings in the library reflect Wright's enthusiasm for Oriental art rather than the Little's collecting habits.... The Hiroshige print, mentioned by Mrs. Stevenson, was probably a gift from Wright, who was notably generous with his own impressive collection of Japanese prints....

The basic design of the windows seen here could be found, with modular adjustments, in all the rooms of the house. The glass is basically clear with small opaque white or sandblasted triangular panes. There is a small rectangle of red glass in the corner of each panel; this was Wright's trademark and appears on his drawings filled in with red when they were completed. The delicate vertical traceries are made of zinc electroplated with copper. This "leading" between the small panes of the glass does much to balance the strongly horizontal articulation of the woodwork.

The library room was put on permanent exhibition at the Allentown Museum in 1978 (see "Room from Wright Prairie House Goes on Permanent Exhibition at Allentown, Pennsylvania, Art Museum" [*Architectural Record*, Vol. 163, No. 7, June 1978], p. 35).

A3

Library
American Academy and Institute of Arts and Letters
633 West 155 Street
New York, New York 10032

The Correspondence Collections of the American Academy and Institute of Arts and Letters contains materials relating to the awarding
of the National Institute of Arts and Letters Gold Medal for Architecture to Frank Lloyd Wright in 1953. They include correspondence
from Douglas Moore, President of the Institute, to Frank Lloyd Wright
dated January 9, 1953, informing Wright of the Institute's selection
of him as the recipient of the award, and from Marc Connelly, another
President of the Institute, to Frank Lloyd Wright dated March 12,
1953, in which Connelly requests that Wright send him a copy of his
acceptance speech prior to the ceremony. There are also three letters
written by Frank Lloyd Wright: a letter to Douglas Moore dated January
22, 1953; a copy of a letter to Ralph Walker dated March 12, 1953;
and a letter to Marc Connelly dated March 16, 1953. The collection
also contains a five-page acceptance speech written by Frank Lloyd
Wright which was not used at the ceremony of May 27, 1953; a two-page
acceptance speech which was used at the ceremony; and the speech for
the presentation of the award to Frank Lloyd Wright by Ralph Walker
of the Institute.

Written application to the Institute must be made in order to obtain photoduplicates of any of the Frank Lloyd Wright related materials.

A4

American Architectural Museum and Resource Center
212 Prudential Building
Buffalo, New York 14202

The American Architectural Museum and Resouce Center, formerly
the Louis Sullivan Architecture Museum, was founded in 1974 by John
D. Randall, the director and owner of this private museum's artifacts.
The two-room museum is located on the second floor of the Louis
Sullivan designed Prudential Building. The museum houses the following
original pieces:

Sherman M. Booth Residence Project (1911)
Glencoe, Illinois
One colored pencil drawing on illustration board measuring
21-5/8 in. x 32 in. (533.4 mm x 812.8 mm).

Ravine Bluffs Development Plan for Sherman M. Booth (1915)
Glencoe, Illinois
One pencil on tracing paper drawing of a residence for lot
22 of the subdivision measuring 17 in. x 21-1/2 in.
(431.8 mm x 546.1 mm).
One tempera on illustration board drawing of the concrete
bridge measuring 22 in. x 28 in. (558.8 mm x 711.2 mm).
Various other drawings of site development, plans, presentation folios, working drawings, specifications, and renderings.

Sherman M. Booth Residence (1915)
Ravine Bluffs Development
Glencoe, Illinois
  One table and other accessories and fragments.
  One pencil on tracing paper drawing of the garage and stable
    which measures 12-1/4 in. x 28-1/4 in. (311.2 mm. x 717.6 mm).

Wallpaper and Fabric Designs for F. Schumacher and Company's
Taliesin Line (1955)
New York, New York
  Several items from these designs.

In addition to the items listed, the museum also houses a copper
vase, dated 1893-1902, designed by Wright, measuring 29-1/2 in. x
4-1/2 in. x 4-1/2 in. (749.3 mm x 114.3 mm x 114.3 mm). The museum houses
a small collection of general and early books, periodicals and reprints,
exhibition catalogues, guides, monographs, photographs, and several minor
original and copied manuscripts. Some of the materials are related to but
not authored by Wright. The museum is briefly reviewed in "A Sullivan
Building Houses a New Sullivan Museum" (*Architectural Record*, Vol.
166, No. 5, October 1979), p. 35.

A5

Archives Library
American Institute of Architects
1735 New York Avenue, N.W.
Washington, D.C. 20006

Photostats of thirteen sets of working drawings for thirteen of
Frank Lloyd Wright's most famous buildings are housed in the AIA
Archives. The 141 photostats measure 18 in. x 24 in. (457.2 mm x
609.6 mm). The following photostats of drawings are in this collection:

Frank Lloyd Wright Residence (1889)
Oak Park, Illinois
  Four sheets of blueprints which measure 18 in. x 17 in.
    (457.2 mm x 431.8 mm).

William H. Winslow Residence (1893)
River Forest, Illinois
  Nine sheets of blue line prints on linen which measure
    29 in. x 38 in. (736.6 mm x 965.2 mm).

Ward W. Willits Residence (1901)
Highland Park, Illinois
  Eight sheets which measure 32-1/2 in. x 39-1/2 in. (825.5 mm x
    1003.3 mm).

Unity Church (1905)
Oak Park, Illinois
  Eight sheets in ink on linen which measure 29-1/2 in. x
    42-1/2 in. (749.3 mm x 1079.5 mm).

Aline Barnsdall "Hollyhock" Residence (1917)
Los Angeles, California
  Eleven sheets in ink on linen which measure 36 in. x 39-1/2 in.
    (914.4 mm x 1003.3 mm).

Edgar J. Kaufmann, Sr., "Fallingwater" Residence (1935)
Ohiopyle, Pennsylvania
 Twelve sheets in pencil on tracing paper measuring 30 in. x
 36 in. (762 mm x 914.4 mm).

Paul R. Hanna Residence (1936)
Stanford, California
 Ten sheets in pencil on tracing paper measuring 36 in. x
 42 in. (914.4 mm x 1066.8 mm).

V.C. Morris Gift Shop (1948)
San Francisco, California
 Six sheets, pencil on tracing paper, measuring 36 in. x
 40 in. (914.4 mm x 1016 mm).

Unitarian Church (1947)
Shorewood Hills, Wisconsin
 Eleven sheets in pencil and ink on tracing paper measuring
 25-3/4 in. x 44-1/2 in. (654.1 mm x 1130.3 mm).

Harold Price, Sr., Price Company Tower (1952)
Bartlesville, Oklahoma
 Fifteen sheets in pencil on tracing paper measuring 36 in. x
 50 in. (914.4 mm x 1270 mm).

Solomon R. Guggenheim Museum (1956)
New York, New York
 Twenty sheets in pencil and ink on tracing paper measuring
 36 in. x 60 in. (914.4 mm x 1524 mm).

Beth Sholom Synagogue (1954)
Elkins Park, Pennsylvania
 Twelve sheets in pencil and ink on tracing paper measuring
 36 in. x 48 in. (914.4 mm x 1219.2 mm).

S.C. Johnson and Son Research Tower (1944)
Racine, Wisconsin
 Fifteen sheets in pencil and ink on tracing paper measuring
 36 in. x 39 in. (914.4 mm x 990.6 mm).

 The collection of drawings is available to view at the AIA
Archives in Washington, D.C. However, the drawings cannot be reproduced in any manner without the express permission of the Frank
Lloyd Wright Foundation. A detailed review of the circumstances
surrounding the acquisition of these drawings by the AIA is given
in Karl Kamrath's "Frank Lloyd Wright Drawings in the AIA Archives"
(*AIA Journal*, Vol. 42, July 1964), pp. 50-51. Kamrath's article
reproduces three of the drawings in the collection--an elevation of
the V.C. Morris Gift Shop, floor plans of the Beth Sholom Synagogue,
and wall sections through the dining room of the Ward W. Willits
Residence.

A6

Southern California Chapter
American Institute of Architects
Suite 510
Bradbury Building
304 South Broadway
Los Angeles, California 90013

The collections of the Southern California Chapter of the American
Institute of Architects include two stained glass windows from the
Aline Barnsdall "Hollyhock" Residence designed by Frank Lloyd Wright
at Los Angeles, California, in 1917. One of the two windows measures
26-3/4 in. x 12-5/8 in. (679.5 mm x 320.7 mm); the other window is
from the demolished original loggia of the residence.

A7

Office of the Director
Archives of American Art
41 East 65th Street
New York, New York 10021
and/or
Inter Library Loan Service
Archives of American Art
5200 Woodward Avenue
Detroit, Michigan 48202

The Emily Genauer Papers, 1930-1957 of the Archives of American
Art contains nine items relating to Frank Lloyd Wright on microfilm,
call number #NG 1. Three of the items are letters to Emily Genauer
dated May 5, 1953 (although this particular letter is addressed to
someone named Elizabeth not Emily Genauer); June 2, 1953; and January
7, 1957.
The other items in the collection include a signed copy of Frank
Lloyd Wright's "The Sovereignty of the Individual: In the Cause of
Architecture." This is a twenty-page reprint of Wright's preface to
his *Ausgefürte Bauten und Entwürfe von Frank Lloyd Wright*, published by
Wasmuth in Berlin in 1910, which served as the introduction to Wright's
Palazzo Strozzi Exhibition of his work in 1951. This reprint is dated May
25, 1951. There is a press release dated May 3, 1953, entitled "A Visit
with Frank Lloyd Wright," from NBC Television News; this release announced
Wright's famous interview with Hugh Downs telecast over NBC television
on May 17, 1953. The entire twenty-eight-page transcript of Wright's
interview with Downs for NBC television is also here; the actual
interview date was May 8, 1953. Also included is a three-page press
release from Carson-Ruff Associates of New York headed "Frank Lloyd
Wright to Receive National Institute's Gold Medal" (National Institute
of Arts and Letters) dated for release May 14, 1953. There are a four-
page transcript dated May 27, 1953, entitled "Speech by Frank Lloyd
Wright in Acceptance of the Gold Medal for Architecture," and an
eleven-page undated typed manuscript by him, titled "Frank Lloyd
Wright Speaks Up," in which he verbally attacks the "International
Style," modern architecture, and the Bauhaus Movement.
The microfilm may be borrowed through special request, using
interlibrary loan service; however, photoduplication of the manuscripts is not permitted without permission of the copyright owner
and the Archives of American Art.
The Archives of American Art also houses original drawings for
the Frank Lloyd Wright Taliesin Line of fabrics and wallpapers manufactured by F. Schumacher and Company in 1955. The drawings are based
on a collaboration between Frank Lloyd Wright and Schumacher's director
of design, Rene Carrillo (see "New Era for Wright at 86: The Market
Place Redeemed?" [*Architectural Record*, Vol. 118, October 1955], p. 20).

One of the drawings was reproduced on page 196 of David A. Hanks'
The Decorative Designs of Frank Lloyd Wright published by E.P. Dutton
at New York in 1979.
    F. Schumacher and Company had a catalogue, sample book, and sample
box of its Taliesin Line prepared as *The Taliesin Line of Wallpapers
and Interior Finishes*, published by E.W. Bredemeier and Company Sample
Books at Chicago in 1955. Copies of this catalogue can be found in
the collections of the Milwaukee Public Library, the Cooper-Hewitt
Museum, and the Art Institute of Chicago. A more detailed report on
the Taliesin Line designs can be found in this book in the discussion
of the Milwaukee Public Library.

A8

Special Collections
University of Arkansas Libraries
University of Arkansas
Fayetteville, Arkansas 72701

    The John Gould Fletcher Papers, 1881-1960 collection of the
University of Arkansas Library contains one letter written by Frank
Lloyd Wright addressed to Fletcher dated February 3, 1950, which is
a brief note inviting Fletcher to visit Taliesin West. Formal application for access to this letter must be made. Access is generally
limited to faculty and graduates of universities doing research in
connection with writing a graduate thesis, a scholarly book, or an
article for publication.

A9

Burnham Library of Architecture
The Art Institute of Chicago
Michigan Avenue at Adams Street
Chicago, Illinois 60603

    Six letters written by Frank Lloyd Wright are contained in the
Frank L. Smith Bank Collection at the Institute. These letters pertain to Frank Lloyd Wright's work on the Frank L. Smith Bank design
at Dwight, Illinois. They include three letters to Frank L. Smith,
one dated November 2, 1905, another January 29, 1906, and an undated
letter (1905 to 1907?); and three letters to Roland S. Ludington
dated July 6, 1906, November 26, 1906, and January 25, 1907. Among
the correspondence from Wright's office are letters signed by William
Drummond and Walter Burley Griffin. This collection also houses
several drawings attributed to Frank Lloyd Wright pertaining to the
Frank L. Smith Bank.
    The Herbert and Katherine Jacobs Frank Lloyd Wright Collection
contains nineteen letters and telegrams written by Frank Lloyd Wright
to Mr. and Mrs. Herbert Jacobs concerning their two residences which
Wright designed for them in the Madison, Wisconsin, area in 1936 and
1943. These letters are dated July 31, 1937; January 12, 1938;
November 9, 1938; January 19, 1939; September 13, 1939; October 9,
1939; October 16, 1939; fall 1939 or spring 1940; February 13, 1940;
December 7, 1940; April 8, 1943; December 11, 1943; December 30, 1943;
February 8, 1944; March 21, 1944; September 14, 1945; January 31,
1946; February 23, 1946; and July 25, 1946.

Other items in the Herbert and Katherine Jacobs Frank Lloyd
Wright Collection include:

A photocopy of Frank Lloyd Wright's passport dated February
9, 1905.

One copy of a letter to Catherine and Kenneth Baxter dated
February 7, 1921.

A building contract for architectural services dated November
15, 1936, for the first Herbert Jacobs Residence designed
by Wright.

A cancelled bank check dated November 28, 1936, to Frank
Lloyd Wright from Herbert Jacobs.

A cancelled bank check dated January 25, 1937, to Frank
Lloyd Wright from Herbert Jacobs.

An undated (1938?) ditto copy of a manuscript entitled
"Unconnected Notes on the Lecture on the Jacobs House by
Frank Lloyd Wright."

Questions and answers which are undated (1940s) concerning
the Unitarian Church at Shorewood Hills, Wisconsin.

A cancelled bank check dated November 28, 1948, to Frank
Lloyd Wright from Herbert Jacobs.

A cancelled bank check dated March 22, 1944, to Frank Lloyd
Wright from Herbert Jacobs.

A copy of a text of a speech entitled "Architecture as
Religion" dated August 21, 1951.

A memorandum to Herbert Jacobs dated March 18, 1957, regarding Frank Lloyd Wright's proposed Monona Terrace Civic
Center Project for Madison, Wisconsin.

Additional items in this collection include a variety of
correspondence with others rather than Frank Lloyd Wright, Taliesin
publications, twenty envelopes of photographs, eight boxes of photographic slides, many newspaper clippings, articles from periodicals,
and the many drawings of the first and second residences for the
Jacobs. Much of the material in the collection was used by Katherine
and Herbert Jacobs in the preparation of their book, *Building with
Frank Lloyd Wright: An Illustrated Memoir* (San Francisco: Chronicle
Books, 1978).

The Wrightiana Collection contains several manuscripts of significance, including a copy of a contract dated September 22, 1909,
between Frank Lloyd Wright and Herman von Holst; a copy of the text
of a speech, "Dinner Talk at Hull House," dated November 8, 1939;
recollections by Frank Lloyd Wright in the form of a letter entitled
"The Auditorium Building and Its Architects" dated July 10, 1940;
a copy of the text of a speech, "Address at Princeton University
Bicentennial Conference--Planning Man's Physical Environment," dated
March 5-6, 1947; the typed text of a speech entitled "In the Realm
of Ideas" dated October 5, 1948; and Christmas greetings to Dan
Catton Rich dated December 25, 1953.

The Burnham Architectural Library also houses prints, photostats,
and original drawings for ten of Frank Lloyd Wright's buildings. Nine
of these buildings are residences; one is a bank. The buildings and
drawings are:

George Blossom Residence (1892)
Chicago, Illinois
Eight black line prints made from the original drawings for
the residence. The original drawings were in the possession

of Mrs. Charles F. Hasetine, owner of the residence in
1940.

Frank L. Smith Bank (1905)
Dwight, Illinois
The following drawings are all photostats of the original
drawings and measure 18 in. x 24 in. (457.2 mm x 609.6 mm).
All are working drawings which Frank Lloyd Wright prepared
for construction of the building.
   Sheet 1--Foundation plan, dated July 8, 1905, revised
      August 28, 1905.
   Sheet 2--First floor plan, revised August 28, 1905.
   Sheet 3a--Street elevation/rear elevation; the street
      elevation of the building is shown as brick masonry and
      is undated.
   Sheet 3b--Street elevation/rear elevation; the street
      elevation is shown as stone faced and is undated.
   Sheet 4--Cross-section/longitudinal section, undated.
   Sheet 5a--Details/building sections; the details and sections
      show stone as the primary material and is undated.
   Sheet 5b--Details/building sections; the details and build-
      ing sections show brick masonry as the primary material
      and is undated.
   Three other drawings are also in the collection relating
   to the Frank L. Smith Bank. They include a small pencil
   sketch on paper of hanging lamps for the bank, probably
   by the hand of Frank Lloyd Wright, measuring 8-1/2± in. x
   5± in. (215.9± mm x 127± mm), dated November 16, 1905,
   and show the three hanging lamps in elevation. The second
   drawing, probably from Wright's office, is of the screen
   doors and frame and is dated May 1, 1906. It measures
   24± in. x 20± in. (609± mm x 508± mm) and is drawn in
   pencil and yellow colored pencil on tracing paper. The
   third drawing is of the plan, front, and side elevations
   of an ink well, probably sketched by the hand of Frank Lloyd
   Wright.
All the drawings relating to the Frank L. Smith Bank are
housed in the Institute's Frank L. Smith Bank Collection.

Frederick G. Robie Residence (1906)
Chicago, Illinois
One mylar copy of the Historic American Buildings Survey
   drawing of a table.
Three prints of floor plans and two interior perspectives
   of the Robie Residence alterations made for the Adlai
   Stevenson Institute.

Avery Coonley Residence (1907)
Riverside, Illinois
One drawing of the desk for the rear guest room in pencil,
   ink, and wash on tracing paper measuring 10-7/8 in. x
   15-1/2 in. (276.2 mm x 393.7 mm). The drawing was made by
   Niedecken-Walbridge Company of Milwaukee, Wisconsin, and
   drawn by George Niedecken.

E.P. Irving Residence (1909)
Decatur, Illinois
and

Robert Mueller Residence (1909)
Decatur, Illinois
   One sheet of planting plans drawn by Marion Mahony Griffin
      in ink on linen measuring 27-7/8 in. x 16-1/2 in. (708 mm x
      419.1 mm).

Joseph J. Bagley Residence (1916)
Grand Beach, Michigan
   The following sheets are all blueprints with the title block
   "Frank Lloyd Wright, Architect-Chicago" and each measures
   20± in. x 36± in. (508± mm x 914± mm). The drawings are
   probably from the set of working drawings used to construct
   the residence rather than a set of presentation drawings.
   They are:
      One sheet of the floor plan.
      One sheet showing the foundation plan.
      One sheet showing the street elevation and lake elevation.
      One sheet showing the court elevation and side elevation.

Edgar J. Kaufmann, Sr., Residence, "Fallingwater" (1935)
Ohiopyle, Pennsylvania
   The Herbert and Katherine Jacobs Frank Lloyd Wright Collection
   contains one blueprint for the standing lights used in the
   bedrooms of the Kaufmann Residence. The blueprint of the
   lights' working drawings is in Box 1 and is signed "F.L.W."
   It is undated and measures 20± in. x 28± in. (508± mm x
   711± mm).

Herbert Jacobs First Residence (1936)
Madison, Wisconsin
   The Herbert and Katherine Jacobs Frank Lloyd Wright Collection houses seventeen drawings, which vary from preliminary
   to final working drawings for the residence as well as the
   furniture and are:
      One sheet of a preliminary plan for the residence, unsigned,
         dated June 9, 1937, drawn in black and red pencil on
         tracing paper measuring 30± in. x 36± in. (762± mm x
         914± mm).
      One sheet showing four preliminary elevations, unsigned,
         and dated June 9, 1937, drawn in pencil on tracing
         paper measuring 30± in. x 36± in. (762± mm x 914± mm).
      One sheet of elevations, plans, sections, and construction
         details. The drawing is signed "F.LL.W." and dated, al-
         though the date cannot be easily read. The medium of the
         drawing is pencil on tracing paper and measures 30± in. x
         36± in. (762± mm x 914+ mm).
      Three blueprints of the first scheme of the residence which
         were submitted to Jacobs for his review, dated November
         15, 1936, and signed "F.L.W." in a square on each sheet.
         The first sheet is of the floor plan of the residence
         drawn at a scale of 1/4 in. = 1 ft. 0 in. and measures
         30± in. x 36± in. (762± mm x 914+ mm). The second sheet
         contains drawings, at a scale of 1/4 in. = 1 ft. 0 in.,
         of the east, north, west, and south elevations and
         measures 30± in. x 36+ in. (762+ mm x 914+ mm). The third
         sheet shows three building sections, drawn at a scale
         of 1/4 in. = 1 ft. 0 in., and also measures 30± in. x
         36± in. (762± mm x 914± mm).

Three blueprints of the second scheme for the residence,
the one which was eventually built. The first sheet is a
floor plan drawn to a scale of 1/4 in. = 1 ft. 0 in. and
measures 30± in. x 36± in. (762± mm x 914± mm). The second
sheet shows four elevations of the residence drawn at a
scale of 1/4 in. = 1 ft. 0 in. It measures 30± in. x
36± in. (762± mm x 914± mm). The third sheet is a wiring
diagram superimposed on a base floor plan drawing drawn
at a scale of 1/4 in. = 1 ft. 0 in. and measuring 30± in. x
36± in. (762± mm x 914± mm). These three sheets are undated.

One sheet of drawings, in red ink and pencil on tracing
paper, measuring 20± in. x 24± in. (204± mm x 609± mm),
of the front door and north door details drawn at a scale
of 3/4 in. = 1 ft. 0 in.

One sheet of full-size preliminary sketches of window details,
drawn in pencil and colored pencil on tracing paper,
measuring 18± in. x 24± in. (457± mm x 609± mm).

One sheet of preliminary working drawing sketches of fixed
glass at the south end of the living room, drawn at
various scales in colored pencil on tracing paper measuring 24± in. x 36± in. (609± mm x 914± mm). The sketches
are undated and are not signed.

One sheet of drawings of the fireplace detail/carport framing detail as constructed, drawn at various scales with
colored pencil on tracing paper. The drawings measure
24± in. x 36± in. (609± mm x 914± mm) and were preliminary
sketches for working drawings. The sheet is unsigned and
undated.

A one-sheet drawing of the ceiling panel detail done in
pencil on tracing paper with a red pencil grid system
defined lightly on the sheet. The drawing measures
30± in. x 40± in. (762± mm x 1016± mm). It is unsigned
and undated and probably drawn by Wright.

A one-sheet drawing of a section of the kitchen cabinets
drawn at a scale of 3/4 in. = 1 ft. 0 in. It measures
18± in. x 24± in. (457± mm x 609± mm) and is drawn in
pencil on tracing paper probably by the hand of Wright.

One sheet of kitchen details, drawn at various scales,
measuring 20± in. x 24± in. (508± mm x 609± mm). The
drawing has a preliminary character, is unsigned and
undated, and is done in pencil on tracing paper.

A one-sheet drawing of the twin beds and bedstand, drawn
at a scale of 1-1/2 in. = 1 ft. 0 in., on brown tracing
paper and measures 24± in. x 36± in. (609± mm x 914± mm).

Herbert Jacobs Second Residence (1943)
Middleton, Wisconsin

Thirty-three drawings of Wright's design for the Jacobs'
second residence are also in the Herbert and Katherine Jacobs
Frank Lloyd Wright Collection. Among these are two sets of
working drawing blueprints of Wright's first design for this
second Jacobs residence; these two sets include nine blueprint sheets each which are listed as follows:

Sheet 1-- Heating systems plan, with details drawn at a
scale of 1/4 in. = 1 ft. 0 in., measuring 20± in. x
36± in. (508± mm x 914± mm).

Sheet 2--Ground floor plan with detail section of the pool,
 drawn at a scale of 1/4 in. = 1 ft. 0 in., measuring
 24+ in. x 36+ in. (609.6+ mm x 914+ mm).
Sheet 3--Mezzanine floor framing plan, drawn at a scale
 of 1/4 in. = 1 ft. 0 in. (609.6± mm x 914± mm).
Sheet 4--Mezzanine floor plan, drawn at a scale of 1/4 in. =
 1 ft. 0 in., measuring 24+ in. x 36+ in. (609.6+ mm x
 914+ mm).
Sheet 5--Roof framing plan, with section through tower roof,
 measuring 24+ in. x 36+ in. (609.6 mm x 914+ mm), drawn
 at a scale of 1/4 in. = 1 ft. 0 in.
Sheet 6--Four elevations of the residence, drawn at a scale
 of 1/4 in. = 1 ft. 0 in., measuring 24± in. x 36± in.
 (609.6 mm x 914+ mm).
Sheet 7--Details and sections, drawn at various scales,
 detailing the fireplace and building sections along
 radiants U and H (Wright's plan radiates in a circular
 form and to ease construction detailing several radii
 were drawn and labeled). The drawing measures 24+ in. x
 36+ in. (609.6+ mm x 914+ mm).
Sheet 8--Sash schedule and details, drawn at a scale one-
 half full size, measuring 24+ in. x 36+ in. (609.6 mm x
 914+ mm).
Sheet 9--Details of the approach tunnel, including a plan
 and section through the tunnel, drawn at a 1/4 in. =
 1 ft. 0 in. scale and measuring 24+ in. x 36+ in. (609.6 mm
 x 914+ mm).
One set of refined design drawings of the second Herbert
Jacobs residence is also in the collection. The set consists
of eight sheets of working drawing blueprints drawn in much
more detail than the first set. Each drawing measures 22+ in. x
36+ in. (559+ mm x 914+ mm) and is detailed as follows:
Sheet 1--Mat plan and heating system, drawn at a scale of
 1/4 in. = 1 ft. 0 in.
Sheet 2--Ground floor plan, drawn at a scale of 1/4 in. =
 1 ft. 0 in.
Sheet 3--Mezzanine floor framing, drawn at a scale of 1/4 in. =
 1 ft. 0 in.
Sheet 4--Mezzanine floor plan at a scale of 1/4 in. = 1 ft.
 0 in.
Sheet 5--Roof framing plan at a scale of 1/4 in. = 1 ft.
 0 in.
Sheet 6--Four elevations at a scale of 1/4 in. = 1 ft. 0 in.
Sheet 7--Sections and details drawn at various scales including sections through radiants M and H. A portion of
 this blueprint has been cut from the upper right-hand
 corner.
Sheet 8--Sash details drawn at one-half full size.
The remaining six drawings of the second Herbert Jacobs
residence in the collection are:
A black ink pen rendering perspective drawing signed "FLLW"
 on heavy white paper dated October 10, 1944, which measures
 30+ in. x 36+ in. (762+ mm x 914 mm).
One sheet of a floor plan, drawn at a scale of 1/4 in. =
 1 ft. 0 in., and one sheet of the mezzanine plan with the

electrical plans for both drawings. Both drawings are done
in red colored pencil and black pencil on tracing paper.
These two drawings were probably used as the base drawings
from which Frank Lloyd Wright generated the working drawings
for the residence. Both drawings are signed "FLLW" in a
red sqaure and dated "'47."
One blueprint of the dining table in elevation and plan
signed "FLW" and dated "'48" in a square.
One blueprint sheet of a dining chair, drawn at a scale of
1/4 in. = 1 ft. 0 in., measures 36+ in. x 24+ in. (914+ mm
x 609+ mm), is signed "FLW," and dated "1940's" in a square.
One diazo blue line print on white paper of the cabinets in
the bedroom, drawn at a scale of 3/4 in. = 1 ft. 0 in.,
measures 28+ in. x 36+ in. (711+ mm x 914+ mm). It is dated
September 30, 1959.

Melvyn Maxwell Smith Residence (1946)
Bloomfield Hills, Michigan
   Eight photostats of the blueprints for the residence, each of
   which measures 17 in. x 20-1/4 in. (430 mm x 515 mm).

   In addition to the previously mentioned manuscripts and drawings
the Art Institute also houses many parts of buildings which were
designed by Wright, including several items of furniture. The following is a list of these items:
Robert W. Roloson Apartments (1894)
Chicago, Illinois
   One cast terra-cotta baluster measuring 17 in. (431.8 mm) in
   height.

Francis Apartments for the Terre Haute Trust Company (1895)
Chicago, Illinois
   Wrought iron entrance gate with attached post measuring
   99-9/16 in. x 47 in. (2528.9 mm x 1193.8 mm).
   A cast-iron circular ventilator cover measuring 38-3/8 in.
   (974.7 mm) in diameter.

Charles E. Roberts Residence and Stables Remodeling (1896)
Oak Park, Illinois
   Pedestal library table made of oak, with pine as a secondary
   wood, measuring 30-5/8 in. x 47-3/4 in. (777.9 mm x 1212.9 mm).

Larkin Company Administration Building (1903)
Buffalo, New York
   One upholstered oak chair measuring 40-1/4 in. x 15-7/8 in. x
   18-1/4 in. (1022.4 mm x 403.2 mm x 463.6 mm), with a seat
   measuring 18-1/2 in. (469.9 mm).
   One upholstered steel frame chair measuring 37-9/16 in. x
   14 in. x 16 in. (954.1 mm x 355.6 mm x 406.4 mm), with a
   seat measuring 19-1/2 in. (495.3 mm).

Darwin D. Martin Residence (1904)
Buffalo, New York
   A leaded glass window, depicting the "tree of life," measures
   41-1/2 in. x 26-1/4 in. (1054.1 mm x 666.8 mm).

Rookery Building Remodeling (1905)
Chicago, Illinois

A plaster cast impression tile measuring 10 in. x 11-3/4 in. x 1/2 in. (254 mm x 298.5 mm x 12.7 mm).

Avery Coonley Residence (1907)
Riverside, Illinois

A desk made of oak, glass, and metal measuring 45-1/4 in. x 40-1/8 in. x 28-1/16 in. (1149.4 mm x 1019.2 mm x 712.8 mm). This desk is the same one which appears on the original presentation drawing for this piece of furniture, which is also housed in the Art Institute of Chicago.

An upholstered oak side chair measuring 37-3/16 in. x 14-1/4 in. x 14-1/2 in. (944.6 mm x 362 mm x 368.3 mm) with a seat measuring 18-7/8 in. (479.4 mm).

An upholstered oak side chair for a child measuring 27 in. x 15-3/4 in. x 16 in. (685.8 mm x 400.1 mm x 406.4 mm) with a seat measuring 16-1/8 in. (409.6 mm).

A wood framed, leaded glass window with opaque white squares of glass, has an overall measurement of 43-3/4 in. x 19-5/8 in. (1111.3 x 498.5 mm).

Robert W. Evans Residence (1908)
Chicago, Illinois

One armchair made of oak, with upholstering, measures 34-1/8 in. x 30-1/8 in. x 23-7/8 in. (866.8 mm x 765.2 mm x 606.4 mm) and has a seat measuring 23 in. x 22-1/2 in. (584.2 mm x 571.5 mm).

An oak library table, with a two-shelf bookcase attached, measures 28-3/4 in. x 65-15/16 in. x 35-7/8 in. (730.3 mm x 1674.8 mm x 911.2 mm).

An oak radiator cover measuring 29-7/16 in. x 65-5/16 in. x 13-5/16 in. (747.7 mm x 1658.9 mm x 338.1 mm).

Three wood framed, copper came clear glass windows with some opaque mottled green and white glass, each of which measures 47-7/16 in. x 37-5/16 in. (1204.9 mm x 947.7 mm).

Midway Gardens for Edward C. Waller, Jr. (1913)
Chicago, Illinois

A concrete building block with a geometric design measuring 17-3/4 in. x 20-9/16 in. x 2-3/4 in. (450.9 mm x 522.3 mm x 69.9 mm).

Emil Bach Residence (1915)
Chicago, Illinois

A wood framed, lead came clear glass window with some opaque white, green, and orange colored stained glass, which measures 39 in. x 30-9/16 in. (990.6 mm x 776.3 mm).

Sherman M. Booth Residence (1915)
Ravine Bluffs Development
Glencoe, Illinois

A walnut lantern measuring 16-1/16 in. x 3-7/16 in. x 6 in. (408 mm x 87.3 mm x 152.4 mm).

Imperial Hotel (1915)
Tokyo, Japan

One six-piece reissued table setting manufactured by Nippon Toki Kaisha in 1968. The setting consists of a cup measuring 3-3/8 in. (85.7 mm) in diameter and 2-3/16 in. (55.6 mm) in

height; a bowl measuring 5-1/8 in. (130.2 mm) in diameter; a
bowl measuring 5-11/16 in. (144.5 mm) in diameter; and four
plates whose diameters measure 6-3/8 in. (161.9 mm), 7-1/2 in.
(190.5 mm), 9-1/8 in. (231.8 mm), and 10-9/16 in. (268.3 mm).

S.C. Johnson and Son Administration Building (1936)
Racine, Wisconsin
    One tubular metal frame chair, painted Cherokee Red, with birch
    arms covered with formica, measuring 34-7/8 in. (885.8 mm) high
    with a 15-7/8 in. x 17 in. (403.2 mm x 431.8 mm) seat.
    One metal frame desk, painted Cherokee Red, with a formica
    top on birch wood, measuring overall 33-1/8 in. x 84 in. x
    32 in. (841.4 mm x 2133.6 mm x 812.8 mm).

C.R. Weltzheimer Residence (1948)
Oberlin, Ohio
    One redwood silhouette window measuring 11-1/4 in. x 48 in. x
    13/16 in. (285.8 mm x 1219.2 mm x 20.6 mm).

John L. Rayward Residence, "Tirranna" (1955)
New Canaan, Connecticut
    One side chair made of mahogany plywood, with a green velvet
    cover, measuring 50-1/4 in. x 20 in. x 19-1/2 in. (1276.4 mm
    x 508 mm x 495.3 mm) and having a 12-1/4-in. (311.2-mm) high
    seat.

Wallpaper and Fabric Designs for F. Schumacher and Company's
Taliesin Line (1955)
New York, New York
    One copy of the sample book, containing sample materials of the
    various fabric designs, and an authorized laminated dealer
    sign are also in the collection. (Note: This sample book
    is housed in the Art Institute's Department of Textiles.)

A10

The Albright-Knox Art Gallery
The Buffalo Fine Arts Academy
1285 Elmwood Avenue
Buffalo, New York 14222

    The Albright-Knox Art Gallery houses six Frank Lloyd Wright
designed items from the Darwin D. Martin Residence (1904) at Buffalo,
New York. These items include two identical stone bird houses, which
were formerly atop the pergola of the Martin residence, measuring
79 in. x 65 in. (2006.6 mm x 1651 mm); one wood table measuring 27 in. x
27 in. x 26-1/4 in. (685.8 mm x 685.8 mm x 666.8 mm); one straight
back wood chair measuring 32 in. x 16 in. (812.8 mm x 406.4 mm); one
oak armchair, with upholstered seat, measuring 32 in. x 23 in. 23 in.
(812.8 mm x 584.2 mm x 584.2 mm); and one stained glass "tree of life"
window pane measuring 41 in. x 25-1/2 in. (1041.4 mm x 647.7 mm).

A11

Chicago Architecture Foundation
Glessner House
1800 South Prairie Avenue
Chicago, Illinois 60616

The collection contains drawings by Frank Lloyd Wright for the
Wright designed Sherman Booth Residence in the Ravine Bluffs Development at Glencoe, Illinois, of 1915; the Thomas P. Hardy Residence at
Racine, Wisconsin, of 1905; and five drawings of the Avery Coonley
Playhouse at Riverside, Illinois, of 1912. The collection also houses
tables and chairs from several of Wright's buildings, two incomplete
sets of Wright's *Ausgeführte Bauten und Entwürfe von Frank Lloyd
Wright* (Berlin: Ernst Wasmuth, 1910), as well as an extensive amount
of material from the studio of Alphonso Iannelli, including correspondence, job order records, sketches and drawings, poster designs, and
sculptures. Among the Iannelli sculptures are a number of pieces relating to Wright's Midway Gardens for Edward C. Waller, Jr., at
Chicago, Illinois, of 1913 (now demolished); both plaster models made
for finished sculptures and fragments salvaged from Midway Gardens,
which include four plaster models measuring 10 in. (254 mm), 9-7/8 in.
(250.8 mm), 10-5/8 in. (269.9 mm), and 10-3/8 in. (263.5 mm), and a
sprite plaster model which measures 15 in. x 10 in. x 9-1/2 in. (381 mm
x 254 mm x 241.3 mm).

The collection is incompletely catalogued (as of late 1979) and
there is no set of photographs of all of the Frank Lloyd Wright items.

A12

The Arts Study Collections: Chicago Campuses
Architecture and Art Department
Chicago Circle Campus
601 South Morgan
Chicago, Illinois 60607

The Arts Study Collections at the Chicago Circle Campus has only
one Frank Lloyd Wright related manuscript, an invitation to Catherine
Lloyd Wright's wedding (Frank Lloyd Wright's daughter). However,
the collection does contain numerous pieces of Frank Lloyd Wright
designed furniture and cabinets for the Mori Oriental Art Studio of
1914. The studio, built in Chicago, has been demolished. Only these
accessories survive and were acquired by the Chicago Circle Campus in
1969. The items include:

> Two Display Cabinets (large)
>> Height: 5 ft. 6 in. (1676.4 mm)
>> Width: 4 ft. 10 in. (1473.2 mm)
>> Depth: 1 ft. 6 in. (457.2 mm)
>> These are made of oak; the upper section has a plate glass
>> top; the front, end doors, and shelves are lined with silk;
>> the lower cupboard has two panel doors.
> One Display Cabinet (small)
>> Height: 5 ft. 6 in. (1676.4 mm)
>> Width: 3 ft. 11-1/4 in. (565.2 mm)
>> Depth: 1 ft. 10-1/4 in. (565.2 mm)

This cabinet matches the two large display cabinets mentioned above. It is made of oak, with the bottom of the upper glass section lined with silk. The lower portion of the cabinet functions as a cupboard.

One Display Cabinet (deep)
  Height: 5 ft. 6 in. (1676.4 mm)
  Width: 3 ft. 8 in. (1117.6 mm)
  Depth: 2 ft. 2-1/4 in. (666.8 mm)
  The cabinet is made of oak, on an oak stand, with an inner spindled base.

One Display Cabinet (shallow)
  Height: 5 ft. 3 in. (1600.2 mm)
  Width: 3 ft. 8 in. (1117.6 mm)
  Depth: 1 ft. 6 in. (457.2 mm)
  This cabinet matches the deep display cabinet described above. It is made of oak, lined with silk, and is on an oak stand with a spindled base.

One Work/Study Table
  Height: 2 ft. 3-1/4 in. (692.2 mm)
  Width: 5 ft. 5-3/4 in. (1670.1 mm)
  Depth: 3 ft. 1/4 in (920.8 mm)
  The table is made of oak and has a lower cupboard with double doors on both the front and the back.

One Writing Table/Desk
  Height: 2 ft. 6 in. (762 mm)
  Width: 3 ft. 6 in. (1066.8 mm)
  Depth: 1 ft. 11-3/4 in. (603.3 mm)
  The desk has a stained pine top and two apron drawers.

Two Open Armchairs
  Height: 2 ft. 2-1/2 in. (673.1 mm)
  Width: 1 ft. 10 in. (558.8 mm)
  Depth: 1 ft. 5-1/2 in. (444.5 mm)
  The chairs are made of oak with pine seats and down filled seat cushions covered in green velvet.

Two Side Chairs
  Height: 3 ft. 1/4 in. (920.8 mm)
  Width: 1 ft. 4-1/2 in. (419.1 mm)
  Depth: 1 ft. 4 in. (406.4 mm)
  The chairs are made of oak, with a slatted back, and have slip seats in brown uncut velvet.

Three Stools
  Height: 1 ft. 5 in. (431.8 mm)
  Width: 1 ft. 7-1/4 in. (489 mm)
  Depth: 1 ft. 0 in. (304.8 mm)
  These stools are made of oak, with quadrangular shaped supports, and have down filled cushions covered in green velvet.

Four End Tables
  Height: 1 ft. 10 in. (558.8 mm)
  Width: 1 ft. 7-3/4 in. (501.7 mm)
  Depth: 1 ft. 0 in. (304.8 mm)
  These tables are made of oak with quadrangular shaped supports.

Six Stands
  Height: 2 ft. 6 in. (762 mm)
  Width: 1 ft. 7-3/4 in. (501.7 mm)

    Depth: 1 ft. 1/4 in. (311.2 mm)
    The stands are made of oak with quadrangular shaped supports.
One Easel Type Print Display Rack
    Height: 3 ft. 4-1/2 in. (1028.7 mm)
    Width: 3 ft. 4 in. (1016 mm)
    The stand is made of oak with quadrangular shaped supports.
One Easel Type Print Display Rack
    Height: 3 ft. 4-1/2 in. (1028.7 mm)
    Width: 2 ft. 6 in. (762 mm)
    The stand is made of oak with quadrangular shaped supports
    and is similar to the print display rack listed above.
One Window Display Case
    Height: 2 ft. 1 in. (635 mm)
    Width: 3 ft. 2-1/2 in. (977.9 mm)
    Depth: 1 ft. 4-1/4 in. (412.8 mm)
    This display case is made of oak, has a glass top and numerous
    doors on all sides. The bottom of the case is lined with silk
    and the case rests upon a platform base.

A13

The Chicago Historical Society
Clark Street at North Avenue
Chicago, Illinois 60614

    The collection of The Chicago Historical Society houses only one
manuscript from the hand of Frank Lloyd Wright. That manuscript is the
title page of *The House Beautiful* drawn with ink on paper and measures
13-1/2 in. x 11 in. (343 mm x 279 mm). *The House Beautiful* was written
by William C. Gannett in a setting designed by Frank Lloyd Wright and
printed by hand at the Auvergne Press at River Forest, Illinois, by
William Herman Winslow and Frank Lloyd Wright in 1896-1897; there were
ninety original copies printed. A facsimile edition was reprinted by
W.R. Hasbrouck at Park Forest, Illinois, in 1963.

A14

The David and Alfred Smart Gallery
Cochrane-Woods Art Center
The University of Chicago
5550 South Greenwood Avenue
Chicago, Illinois 60637

    The David and Alfred Smart Gallery, which hosted "The Decorative
Designs of Frank Lloyd Wright" exhibition from January to February
of 1979, has furniture from three Frank Lloyd Wright designed buildings.

    B. Harley Bradley Residence (1900)
    Kankakee, Illinois
      One barrel armchair measuring 27 in. x 27-1/2 in. x 28 in.
        (685.8 mm x 698.5 mm x 711.2 mm), made of oak, with an uphol-
        stered seat.
      One armchair (this item may not have been designed by Frank
        Lloyd Wright).
      One rocker chair (this may not have been designed by Frank
        Lloyd Wright).

Larkin Company Administration Building (1903)
Buffalo, New York
   Three side chairs.

Frederick G. Robie Residence (1906)
Chicago, Illinois
   Six windows of leaded glass with wood frames measuring 49 in. x
   30-1/4 in. (1245 mm x 768 mm).
   Dining table and nine side chairs made of oak, metal, glass,
   and ceramic. The table measures 55-5/8 in. x 96-1/4 in. x
   53-1/2 in. (1413 mm x 2449 mm x 1359 mm). Each side chair
   measures 52-3/8 in. x 17 in. x 19-3/4 in. (1330 mm x 432 mm x
   502 mm).
   Two side chairs.
   One set of three chairs (two side chairs and one rocking chair).
   One double bed.
   One single bed.
   One pair of chairs (armchair and rocking chair).
   One bureau with mirror.
   One side chair.
   One library table.

A15

Special Collections
Joseph Regenstein Library
The University of Chicago
1100 East 57th Street
Chicago, Illinois 60637

   The Joseph Regenstein Library of the University of Chicago contains
nine manuscripts written by Frank Lloyd Wright, housed in four different
collections: the Poetry Magazine Papers, 1912-1936, the Poetry Magazine
Papers, 1936-1953 (Series II), the Jenkin Lloyd Jones Collection, and
the Elinor Castle Nef Papers.
   The Poetry Magazine Papers, 1912-1936 has five letters written by
Frank Lloyd Wright to Harriet Monroe who had been an editor of *Poetry
Magazine* and a correspondent for *The Chicago Examiner*. These five
letters are dated April 18, 1907; April 22, 1907; April 13, 1914;
April 20, 1914; and November 18, 1924. Other materials in the collec-
tion pertaining to Wright include a copy of a letter Harriet Monroe
wrote to him dated April 1907.
   The Poetry Magazine Papers, 1936-1953 (Series II) contains two
Frank Lloyd Wright related materials. The first is a letter from
Wright to Peter De Vries of *Poetry Magazine* dated November 9, 1942,
and the second item is a letter from Eugene Masselink, Wright's
secretary, to Peter De Vries, dated December 1, 1942, arranging a
lecture by Frank Lloyd Wright.
   The Jenkin Lloyd Jones Collection contains two letters to Frank
Lloyd Wright's uncle, Jenkin Lloyd Jones, written by Frank Lloyd Wright.
One letter is dated May 15, 1894, and the other is undated (possibly
1898 or 1899?) regarding the All Souls Church Project in which Frank
Lloyd Wright had a limited involvement during its early stages.
   The Elinor Castle Nef Papers contain four Frank Lloyd Wright re-
lated materials. The first is a letter from Frank Lloyd Wright to
John U. Nef, dated May 11, 1946. The second is a letter from Olgivanna

Lloyd Wright to Elinor Castle Nef, dated June 17, 1946, regarding a
visit to Taliesin. The third is a letter from Elinor Castle Nef to
Frank Lloyd Wright, dated May 14, 1946, concerning a dinner invitation.
The fourth item is a copy of a letter from Elinor Castle Nef to
Olgivanna Lloyd Wright, dated September 7, 1946.

One may make written application for permission to examine the
manuscripts. However, permission is subject to any restrictions
imposed by the writer, the donor, or the library. Manuscripts may not
be copied unless the applicant has given written assurance that no
document or substantial portion of a document will be published or
reproduced without the permission of the writer or his legal representative and the director of the library. Copies are intended solely
for the use of the applicant.

A16

The Avery Architectural Library
Columbia University
New York, New York 10027

The Avery Architectural Library of Columbia University houses
numerous original manuscripts, drawings, and copies of drawings by
Frank Lloyd Wright. Most of these are contained in the John Lloyd
Wright Collection which was given to the Library in 1969 by John
Lloyd Wright, Frank Lloyd Wright's son, of Del Mar, California.

The John Lloyd Wright Collection contains the following original
Frank Lloyd Wright manuscripts:

> A brochure announcing Wright's practice of architecture en-
>   titled "Frank Lloyd Wright, Architect" dated 1898 with
>   handwritten revisions.
> A copy of a letter from Frank Lloyd Wright to Francis C.
>   Sullivan dated September 10, 1911.
> An article entitled "In the Cause of Architecture" dated
>   January 4, 1923.
> An article entitled "In the Cause of Architecture, He Who
>   Gets Slapped" dated January 7, 1923.
> Article entitled "In the Cause of Architecture, The Third
>   Dimension" dated February 9, 1923. There are two copies
>   of this manuscript in the collection--one copy has pencil
>   revisions in the hand of Frank Lloyd Wright and the other
>   is a typed revised draft.
> Article entitled "Taliesin III" dated June 8, 1926.
> Article for *The Dodgeville Chronicle* (Dodgeville, Wisconsin)
>   dated 1926. There are three signed copies of this manuscript
>   in the collection.
> A copy of an Academie des Beaux-Arts Award with pencil nota-
>   tions by Frank Lloyd Wright dated 1927.
> An autographed copy of Frank Lloyd Wright's *Two Lectures on
>   Architecture* published by the Art Institute of Chicago
>   dated 1931.
> A piece of sheet music signed by Frank Lloyd Wright and others
>   dated August 11, 1932, the day on which the Taliesin Fellow-
>   ship was founded.
> Article entitled "A Philosophy of Fine Art" undated (probably
>   1932).
> Address by Frank Lloyd Wright to the International Congress
>   of Architects, Rome, Italy, dated September 3, 1935.

Address entitled "An Architect Speaking for Culture" dated
   February 14, 1936.
Article entitled "Introducing a Son and a House in the Wood"
   dated July 16, 1936.
Four lectures entitled "Watson Chair Foundation of the Sulgrave
   Manor Board, The Sir George Watson Lectures for 1937, A
   Series of Four Evenings on Organic Architecture, the Archi-
   tecture of Democracy, by Frank Lloyd Wright" dated 1939.
Two copies of "Moral" by Frank Lloyd Wright dated 1939.
Text of "An Address by Frank Lloyd Wright in Connection with
   Founders Week, Florida Southern College, Lakeland, Florida"
   dated March 3, 1950.

Letters written to John Lloyd Wright by Frank Lloyd Wright contained in this collection include those dated April 30, 1928; November
8, 1928; October 5, 1929; October 24, 1929; June 2, 1930; March 7,
1932; February 9, 1934; January 23, 1937; August 27, 1938; June 14,
1939; a Christmas greeting card dated 1943; letter dated September 27,
1944; a New Year's greeting card dated 1945; letters dated March 6,
1945; February 23, 1945; June 25, 1945; a New Year's greeting card
dated January 1946; letters dated May 30, 1946; July 11, 1946; October
16, 1948; December 1, 1948; a Christmas greeting card dated 1948; letters
dated September 15, 1949; April 30, 1951; March 19, 1952; August 23,
1952; September 30, 1952; a Christmas greeting card dated 1953; a
letter dated March 13, 1955; and seven undated letters.
   Letters written to Frank Lloyd Wright by John Lloyd Wright are
also contained in the collection, including letters dated June 25,
1938; August 28, 1938 (to Frank Lloyd Wright's secretary); September
30, 1938; September 30, 1944; March 12, 1945; June 30, 1945; September
30, 1948; April 26, 1951; August 4, 1952; and August 28, 1952.
   Several other pieces of correspondence are housed in the collections
of the Avery Architectural Library which are not part of the John Lloyd
Wright Collection. These items include a letter from Frank Lloyd Wright
to Catherine Baxter, Wright's daughter, dated February 7, 1921; a
letter to Justin L. Miner dated November 9, 1929; two different telegrams to Horace Holley dated March 31, 1930; a telegram dated March
31, 1930 to Justin L. Miner; a letter to Dr. William Norman Guthrie
dated May 5, 1927; a letter to Justin L. Miner dated April 22, 1930;
a letter to Mrs. Irwin Elkins Auerbach dated January 18, 1949; and a
letter to Richard Herpers (Secretary of Columbia University) dated
March 11, 1959. The Avery collections also contain Frank Lloyd Wright's
1905 passport for a trip to Japan, Catherine Lloyd Wright's diary, and
Catherine Lloyd Wright's family records.
   The Avery Architectural Library contains the Frank Lloyd Wright
Collection of Drawings by Louis H. Sullivan totaling one hundred and
twenty-two drawings. Several of these drawings were used by Wright
in his *Genius and the Mobocracy*, published by Duell, Sloan and
Pearce, at New York in 1949 (drawings 3 through 10, 13-15, 17-22, 25,
26, 29, 32-34, 36-38, 40, 41, 43-50, and 122). Drawings 21, 25, 26,
35-40, 42, 43, 45-47, 50, 89, and 122 contain brief notes by Wright on
how they should be cropped for publication. Two of the drawings were
done by Frank Lloyd Wright--number 35, which is an ink drawing of the
Getty Tomb bronze gates designed by Louis Sullivan in 1890 and measures
23-1/2 in. x 27 in. (596.9 mm x 685.8 mm) and number 2, an ornamental
frieze study for Louis Sullivan's Getty Tomb measuring 9-1/2 in. x
8 in. (241.3 mm x 203.2 mm). An index for the collection was done by

the Frank Lloyd Wright Foundation and is to be found in the Avery Architectural Library Collection. The drawings were reproduced, in black
and white, in Paul Sprague (ed.), *The Drawings of Louis H. Sullivan:
A Catalogue of the Frank Lloyd Wright Collection at the Avery Architectural Library* (Princeton, New Jersey: Princeton University Press,
1979).

The many other Frank Lloyd Wright original drawings and copies of
drawings in the Avery Architectural Library, together with their
respective building or project, are:

> Frank Lloyd Wright Studio and Residence (1889-1911)
> Oak Park, Illinois
>> One perspective drawing in ink, pencil, and grey and white
>> wash on paper measuring 14-1/4 in. x 6 in. (362 mm x 152.4
>> mm).
>> One pencil sketch of the floor plan measuring 17-3/4 in. x
>> 9-1/2 in. (450.9 mm x 241.3 mm).
>> One perspective drawing in ink, pencil, and white wash on
>> paper measuring 14-1/4 in. x 5-1/4 in. (362 mm x 133.4 mm),
>> which was torn in half and repaired.
>> One drawing of a detail (John Lloyd Wright Collection).
>> One sketch of the studio with a detail (John Lloyd Wright
>> Collection).
>> One set of mimeographed copies of working drawings, with
>> revisions by Frank Lloyd Wright (John Lloyd Wright Collec-
>> tion).
>> One watercolor rendering of the residence (John Lloyd Wright
>> Collection).
>> One window detail of a studio window (John Lloyd Wright
>> Collection).
>> One drawing in pen and ink of an interior corner of the studio
>> (John Lloyd Wright Collection).
>> Three portions of pencil drawings on tracing paper of the
>> residence (John Lloyd Wright Collection).

> Ward W. Willits Residence (1901)
> Highland Park, Illinois
>> Detail drawing of the china cabinets in the dining room drawn
>> in pencil and yellow wash on tracing paper dated as revised
>> December 10, 1902, and January 7, 1903.

> Susan Lawrence Dana Residence (1902)
> Springfield, Illinois
>> One drawing of the dining room in pencil, pastels, and washes
>> on brown paper, measuring 25 in. x 20-5/16 in. (635 mm x
>> 516 mm).
>> Two drawings by George Niedecken of an interior perspective
>> in color and a preliminary drawing for a mural in the dining
>> room (John Lloyd Wright Collection).

> Unity Church (1905)
> Oak Park, Illinois
>> Two drawings in pencil on tracing paper of a window frame
>> detail and glass details.

> Harvey P. Sutton Residence (1905)
> McCook, Nebraska
>> One drawing in pencil on tracing paper of a detail of a

braided hip roof drawn at a scale of 1-1/2 in. = 1 ft. 0 in.
One drawing in pencil on tracing paper of a detail of the
vestibule drawn at a scale of 3/4 in. = 1 ft. 0 in.

P.D. Hoyt Residence (1906)
Geneva, Illinois
One sheet showing an elevation and a section drawn in pencil
on tracing paper.
One drawing showing a detail of a sash drawn in pencil on
tracing paper.

Frederick C. Robie Residence (1906)
Chicago, Illinois
One drawing of details of stair and chimney drawn in pencil on
tracing paper.

Avery Coonley Residence (1907)
Riverside, Illinois
One drawing of a section through the ceiling screen drawn in
pencil on tracing paper.

Fox River Country Club Remodeling (1907)
Geneva, Illinois
A pencil drawing on tracing paper of the details for a stage
and roof truss. The drawing is inscribed "Office Copy."

E.A. Gilmore Residence (1908)
Madison, Wisconsin
Two sheets of details for the porch roof drawn at a scale of
3/4 in. = 1 ft. 0 in., in pencil on tracing paper.
One drawing of the radiator screen drawn in pencil on tracing
paper.

Frank Lloyd Wright Residence/Studio Project (1910)
Viale Verdi, Fiesole, Italy
One drawing in pencil on tracing paper measuring 27-1/2 in. x
12-1/4 in. (700 mm x 310 mm) inscribed on the back "not
holograph."

Ernest Vosburgh Residence (1916)
Grand Beach, Michigan
Original pen line perspective drawing which appeared as plate
211 in Henry-Russell Hitchcock's *In the Nature of Materials:
1887-1941, the Buildings of Frank Lloyd Wright* published by
Duell, Sloan and Pearce, New York, in 1942.

Tahoe Summer Colony Project (1922)
Lake Tahoe, California
Original pencil line drawing of the plan which appeared as plate
245 in Henry-Russell Hitchcock's *In the Nature of Materials*.

St. Mark's-in-the-Bouwerie Towers Project (1927)
New York, New York
One blue line print with colored pencil of the lot plan for
the towers.
Two sheets of diagrams drawn in pencil on tracing paper showing
the proposed structure.

Poster: "Modern Concepts Concerning an Organic Architecture"
(1930)

The poster measures 33-3/4 in. x 32-3/8 in. (857.3 mm x 822.3 mm) and is inscribed "To Ely Kahn in appreciation of his quality and kindness--Frank Lloyd Wright, Taliesin, June 27, 1930."

Edgar J. Kaufmann, Sr., Residence, "Fallingwater" (1935)
Ohiopyle, Pennsylvania
  One topographic map of the building site prior to construction, dated March 1935.
  Floor plans of the first, second, and third floors, and two elevations.
  One section through the residence looking west.
  Plan of the guest wing connection.
  All of these drawings have been reproduced in Donald Hoffmann's *Frank Lloyd Wright's Fallingwater: The House and Its History*, published by Dover Publications, Inc., at New York in 1978. There is also a collection of the engineer inspections of the building at the Avery Library.

Warren Tremaine Observatory Project (1948)
Meteor Crater, Meteor, Arizona
  One black line print with colored crayon measuring 35-3/8 in. x 39-5/16 in. (900 mm x 1000 mm) of the plan inscribed "To H.R.H. from F.LL.W."
  One black line print with crayon of a perspective drawing also inscribed "To H.R.H. from F.LL.W."
  One black line print with crayon of a perspective drawing measuring 38-1/2 in. x 26-1/2 in. (977.9 mm x 673.1 mm) and is inscribed "The God-father of this scheme--from his friend--Frank Lloyd Wright, Taliesin West, Feb. 16, 50."

Irwin Auerbach Residence Project (1950)
Pleasantville, New York
  Fourteen sheets of drawings of this project at three different stages. The drawings include a plot plan, site plan, floor plans, elevations, sections through the building, mechanical and structural plans, and details. There are nine blueprints, three blue line prints, and two drawings done in pencil and colored pencil on tracing paper. The drawings date from April 1949 to April 1950.

Joseph H. Brewer Residence Project (1953)
East Fishkill, New York
  Six blue line prints including a perspective, elevations, and plans.

Point View Apartment Towers Project (1953)
Pittsburgh, Pennsylvania
  There is a total of thirteen drawings of this project in the Avery collection, including perspectives, plans, sections through the building, and elevations drawn in colored pencil, pencil, and brown ink on white paper. There are also thirty-eight blue line prints drawn with colored pencil over the blue line image.

Maximilian Hoffman Residence (1955)
Rye, New York
  Eight blue line prints of floor plans, elevations, sections, millwork, roof framing plan, and cabinet work.

Solomon R. Guggenheim Museum (1956)
New York, New York
A number of prints and drawings for this building are housed
in the Avery collections, including:

Floor plans--nine blueprints and sixteen blue line prints.
Elevations and sections--nine blueprints and three blue
    line prints.
Details--seventeen blueprints.
Structural plans--seven blueprints.
Heating, ventilating, and air conditioning (HVAC) plans--ten
    blueprints.
Electrical and plumbing plans--six blueprints.

Several other miscellaneous types of drawings by Frank Lloyd
Wright are contained in the John Lloyd Wright Collection, including
a pencil drawing made when Wright was a child, a photographic print
of shrubs dated 1895 drawn on Japanese paper, a landscape watercolor
circa 1892, three brown line prints entitled "Spring," "Summer," and
"Autumn," drawn by Wright for the poem "Stirs and Is Still" dated
1892, and a landscape watercolor signed "F.L. Wright, April 2, '92."
    There are also a number of unidentified drawings by Wright in the
Avery collections which warrant further study and investigation to
discover their identity and the building or project to which they
belong. They include:

A pencil on tracing paper drawing of "detail of stiffening
    of beams and columns 49 and 52."
Two floor plans and three elevations drawn in pencil with
    color on tracing paper.
Two floor plans of a residence drawn in pencil with color on
    tracing paper.
A floor plan drawn in pencil with color on tracing paper.
Details of a roof for a project in Japan dated October 14,
    1919, drawn with pencil on tracing paper. This drawing has
    remarks in Japanese and notes concerning the building and
    the draftsman.
"Truss to support roof over living room and terrace. Also
    construction of balcony and chandelier" drawn with pencil
    on tracing paper.
Sheet 10 of details of exterior trim drawn in pencil with
    yellow on tracing paper.
Sheet 12, "Special window frame detail; second story over
    front entrance. Used with typical second story head" drawn
    in pencil on tracing paper.
Sheet 13 of details of special window; window over front
    entrance drawn at a scale of 1-1/2 in. = 1 ft. 0 in. in
    pencil on tracing paper.
Sheet 14, details of rear doorway drawn in pencil on tracing
    paper.
Section through building and free-hand sketches in pencil on
    tracing paper.

Application must be made to the Avery Librarian for access to the
original Frank Lloyd Wright manuscripts and drawings housed in the
Avery Architectural Library collections.

A17

Oral History Research Office
Butler Library
Columbia University
New York, New York 10027

The Biographical Oral History Collection, 1948-1968 of the Butler Library contains a forty-six-page typed transcript of the 1957 interview of Frank Lloyd Wright by Mike Wallace of ABC (see "Wright to be on Wallace Show" [*The Capital Times*, Madison, Wisconsin, August 27, 1957], for a detailed account of the interview). A complete transcript of that interview was published in "Mike Wallace Program: Here's Transcript of Wright T.V. Interview," in *The Capital Times* on September 2, 1957; see also "Wallace Invites Wright Again," *The Capital Times*, September 21, 1957. A partial transcript of Wright's second interview with Wallace is in "Second Mike Wallace Interview: Wright Airs Tart Comment on Churches, Sex, Press," *The Capital Times*, September 30, 1957.

During the two interviews Wright was questioned on such topics as religion, the American Legion, mercy killing, "the common man," the Guggenheim Museum, Picasso, Salvador Dali, arrogance, Louis Sullivan, the U.S. Capitol, the "Mile-High" Illinois skyscraper project, the city, teenagers, *A Testament*, Charlie Chaplin, McCarthyism, General Douglas MacArthur, President Eisenhower, Arthur Miller and Marilyn Monroe, New York City, *An Autobiography*, Alexander Woollcott, President Franklin D. Roosevelt, government, Thomas Jefferson, Communism, the press (news media), Warren McArthur, Walt Whitman, Adlai Stevenson, Lloyd Lewis, St. Patrick's Cathedral, Elvis Presley, and "organic" architecture.

A18

Dallas Museum of Fine Arts
P.O. Box 26250
Dallas, Texas 75226

In 1974 the Dallas Museum of Fine Arts purchased, from the Metropolitan Museum of Art in New York, fourteen window panels from Frank Lloyd Wright's Francis W. Little Residence of Deephaven, Minnesota, of 1912, which was demolished. The window panels are from the Little sitting room, thirteen of which are from the north wall of that room and one from the west wall. The glass in each window measures 44-1/2 in. x 16 in. (1130.3 mm x 406.4 mm). The Dallas Museum of Fine Arts has installed twelve of the fourteen panels in the Museum's library.

A19

The Frank Lloyd Wright Archive of Published Work 1867-1959
School of Humanities
The Flinders University of South Australia
Bedford Park
South Australia 5042

   The Frank Lloyd Wright Archive of Published Work 1867-1959 began
collecting all published material about Frank Lloyd Wright and his work
in 1973. Although this archive is of published work only, in either
original or photoduplicate form, it is significant enough to include
here. The archive contains approximately 75% of the Wright items listed
in Robert L. Sweeney's *Frank Lloyd Wright: An Annotated Bibliography*
(Los Angeles: Hennessey and Ingalls, Inc., 1978), as well as many
other published materials not included in Sweeney's book. A complete
index, however, was not available during the research period. Although
the archive concentrates primarily on works about Wright published
between 1867 and 1959, they do accept post-1959 works as they come to
hand. The archive is arranged into areas such as books and articles
by Frank Lloyd Wright, books and articles about Frank Lloyd Wright,
books and articles which include other architects as well as Frank
Lloyd Wright. There is also an arrangement by decade. There is a
special section on Frank Lloyd Wright's influence on Australian architects, students, assistants, and followers, and a special section on
Walter Burley Griffin, 1876-1976. The works are mainly in the English
language but other language publications are being acquired. Newspapers and news magazines are not searched but are included fortuitously.
   The archive has been funded over the years by the Australian
Research Grants Committee, the Visual Arts Board of the Australian
Council, and Flinders University of South Australia. In 1980 the
archives experienced dramatic cuts in funding and a delay in the formal
announcement of its existence and access resulted. However, access
for study and use by the scholarly public should be announced and outlined in the very near future. Both Australasian and overseas researchers will have access through the mails as well as personal perusal.

A20

The Richard W. Bock Sculpture Collection
Greenville College
Greenville, Illinois 62246

   The Richard W. Bock Sculpture Collection at Greenville College
houses an extensive collection of archival materials relating to those
buildings and projects by Frank Lloyd Wright on which the sculptor,
Richard W. Bock, collaborated. Bock served as Wright's sculptor for
nearly twenty years, during which time they became personal friends.
The buildings and projects represented by the various items in the
collection are the Frank Lloyd Wright Studio of 1898 at Oak Park,
Illinois; the Susan Lawrence Dana Residence of 1902 at Springfield,
Illinois; the Richard Bock Ateliers/Studio/Residence Project of 1902-
1906 at Maywood, Illinois; the Larkin Company Administration Building
of 1903 at Buffalo, New York; the Scoville Park Fountain of 1903 at
Oak Park, Illinois; the Darwin D. Martin Residence, Conservatory, and
Garage of 1904 at Buffalo, New York; and the Midway Gardens for Edward
C. Waller, Jr., of 1913 at Chicago, Illinois. For a ten-year period,
beginning in 1903, Bock worked almost exclusively with Frank Lloyd
Wright and his associates. In addition to those buildings and designs
represented in this collection, major work was done by Bock for Frank
Lloyd Wright for Unity Temple of 1905 at Oak Park, Illinois, and the
City National Bank and Hotel for Blythe and Markley of 1909 at Mason
City, Iowa. After Bock's death in 1949 his son and daughter kept many

of Bock's works in storage and maintained all of his drawings, documents, and photographs. They preserved the collection because they
shared their father's dream that some day the objects would be displayed.
In 1972, they presented the Richard W. Bock Sculpture Collection to
Greenville College on the condition that the works be place on exhibition. In the fall of 1972, the first collection pieces were brought
from Los Angeles, California, to Greenville, Illinois. Many of these
art objects had been in storage since 1932. The last major shipment
of art objects arrived at Greenville College in early 1975.

The collection contains a number of original manuscripts, writings,
and letters by Bock but manuscript materials written by Frank Lloyd
Wright are limited. There are four letters by Wright in the collection,
all of which were written to Dorathi Bock Pierre, Bock's daughter:
these letters are dated August 11, 1932; August 13, 1932; December 8,
1941; and August 1, 1949. There are also two books given to Dorathi
Bock Pierre by Frank Lloyd Wright which were inscribed by him and
include *An Autobiography*, published by Longmans, Green and Company
at New York in 1932. The inscription reads, "To Dolly Bock from Frank
Lloyd Wright her 'uncle'--with love to the 'Bocks.'" Another book is
inscribed, "To Dorothy from Uncle Frank."

Other related materials by Frank Lloyd Wright in the collection
are:

> Frank Lloyd Wright Studio (1898)
> Oak Park, Illinois
>> Floor plans of the Frank Lloyd Wright Oak Park drafting rooms
>> and business office in the Rookery Building at Chicago which
>> measure 5 in. x 6 in. (127 mm x 152.4 mm).
>
> Susan Lawrence Dana Residence (1902)
> Springfield, Illinois
>> One window of leaded glass in a wood frame measuring 46-1/4
>> in. x 31-1/2 in. (1174.8 mm x 800.1 mm), executed by Linden
>> Glass Company and designed by Frank Lloyd Wright.
>> One hanging lamp made with leaded glass measuring 19 In. x
>> 23-1/2 in. (482.6 mm x 596.9 mm).
>> One 8 x 10 photograph of a drawing by Frank Lloyd Wright of
>> the interior of the Dana Residence.
>> An 8 x 10 photograph of a sketch of the round-arched entrance
>> to the Dana Residence.
>> One sketch by Richard W. Bock for the Dana Residence figure,
>> which was later titled "The Flower in the Crannied Wall."
>> The sketch is drawn with graphite and measures 6-1/2 in. x
>> 3-3/4 in. (165.1 mm x 95.3 mm). The sketch was restored in
>> 1975.
>> A sculpture by Richard Bock entitled "Moon Children," which
>> served as the fountain panel of the Dana Residence. The
>> sculpture is the original plaster model in half-moon shape.
>> It has eight figures and an urn in high relief and is set
>> in a wooden frame. It measures 26 in. x 44 in. (660.4 mm x
>> 1117.6 mm); the wooden frame measures 35 in. x 51 in.
>> (889 mm x 1295.4 mm).
>> One oak table measuring 24 in. x 24 in. x 30 in. (609.6 mm x
>> 609.6 mm x 762 mm) designed by Frank Lloyd Wright possibly
>> for the Dana Residence.

Richard Bock Ateliers/Studio/Residence Project (1902 and 1906)
Maywood, Illinois
   One graphite drawing by Frank Lloyd Wright.
   One graphite drawing by Frank Lloyd Wright showing an elevation
   of the design, measuring 10-1/4 in. x 21-1/4 in. (260.4 mm x
   539.8 mm). This drawing was restored in 1975 and is not
   signed or dated.
   One graphite drawing by Frank Lloyd Wright of the floor plan,
   measuring 10-1/4 in. x 21-1/4 in. (260.4 mm x 539.8 mm).
   This drawing was restored in 1975 and is not signed or dated.
   One 8 x 10 photograph of an original drawing by Marion Mahoney,
   from Frank Lloyd Wright's office, of the project.

Larkin Company Administration Building (1903)
Buffalo, New York
   A working drawing by Frank Lloyd Wright for the sculpture and
   and panels on the front of the Larkin Company Administration
   Building. The drawing was drawn in graphite, measures 29 in.
   x 28 in. (736.6 mm x 711.2 mm), and was restored in 1975.
   An 8 x 10 photograph of a drawing by Frank Lloyd Wright for
   the pier terminations on the front of the Larkin Company
   Administration Building.
   A graphite drawing by Richard Bock of a fireplace relief sculpture showing a figure with outstretched arms. The drawing
   measures 4-3/4 in. x 6-1/4 in. (120.7 mm x 158.8 mm). This
   drawing was restored in 1975.
   A graphite drawing by Richard Bock of a design for a light
   fixture. The drawing measures 3-1/4 in. x 5-1/4 in. (82.6 mm
   x 133.4 mm) and was restored in 1975. The light fixture was
   never executed for the building.
   A graphite drawing by Richard Bock of a design for an interior
   fireplace relief sculpture showing a figure with outstretched
   arms holding globes. The drawing measures 8 in. x 5-1/4 in.
   (203.2 mm x 133.4 mm) and was restored in 1975.
   A graphite drawing by Richard Bock of a design for the pier
   gloves and supporting figures of the building. The drawing
   measures 7-1/2 in. x 4-1/4 in. (190.5 mm x 108 mm) and was
   restored in 1975.
   A sketch by Richard Bock of a free-standing figure facing left,
   used as a building relief sculpture. The drawing measures
   6 in. x 3-3/4 in. (152.4 mm x 95.3 mm) and was restored in
   1975.
   A sketch by Richard Bock of a free-standing figure facing
   right, used as a building relief sculpture. The drawing
   measures 6 in. x 3-3/4 in. (152.4 mm x 95.3 mm) and was
   restored in 1975.
   A full-size plaster model by Richard Bock of an exterior
   relief sculpture panel for the building, measuring 12-1/4 in.
   x 7 in. (311.2 mm x 177.8 mm).
   A plaster model prototype by Richard Bock for a terracotta
   ornamental relief sculpture for the facade of the building
   measuring 17-3/4 in. x 11-3/8 in. x 1-3/8 in. (450.9 mm x
   288.9 mm x 34.9 mm).

Scoville Park Fountain (1903)
Oak Park, Illinois

A sketch in graphite by Richard Bock (possibly for Frank Lloyd
Wright's Scoville Park Fountain?), measuring 4-1/2 in. x
7 in. (114.3 mm x 177.8 mm). This drawing was restored in
1975.

Darwin D. Martin Residence, Conservatory, and Garage (1904)
Buffalo, New York
A plaster study by Richard Bock for the Martin Residence fountain entitled "Spring." The study shows five child figures
set in a rectangular block of foliage and measures 4 in. x
9 in. x 4-1/2 in. (101.6 mm x 228.6 mm x 114.3 mm).
A concrete sculpture by Richard Bock for the Martin Residence
entitled "Spring." It is signed "RWB, 1915" and measures
27 in. x 58 in. x 29 in. (685.8 mm x 1473.2 mm x 736.6 mm).
A plaster study by Richard Bock for the Martin Residence fountain entitled "Winter." It measures 9 in. x 5 in. x 4 in.
(228.6 mm x 127 mm x 101.6 mm).

Midway Gardens for Edward C. Waller, Jr. (1913)
Chicago, Illinois
A graphite drawing by Frank Lloyd Wright of the sculptured
panels for Midway Gardens measuring 16 in. x 21 in. (406.4 mm
x 533.4 mm). This drawing was restored in 1975.
A graphite drawing by Richard Bock for a head for Midway
Gardens measuring 7 in. x 4-1/2 in. (177.8 mm x 114.3 mm).
This drawing was restored in 1975.

The Richard Bock Sculpture Collection contains several other items
which, although not related to any specific buildings or projects
designed by Frank Lloyd Wright, have special significance. These items
are:

A bronze sculpture entitled "John Lloyd Wright as a Goldenrod"
designed in 1897 and finally cast in 1975. The sculpture
measures 7-1/2 in. x 7-3/4 in. (190.5 mm x 196.9 mm).
An architectural drawing of an unidentified building. The
drawing measures 18 in. x 24 in. (457.2 mm x 609.6 mm).
One mission oak table with a set of architectural blocks set
up on it which was a gift of Frank Lloyd Wright to the
Richard Bock children.
Gifts from Frank Lloyd Wright to Dorathi Bock Pierre, including
a set of German blocks, a book about Japan, a book entitled
King of the Golden River by John Ruskin, a Hillside Home
School booklet dated 1907, and a small book of Japanese poems
or songs.
Various photographs of Richard Bock's sculptures for Frank
Lloyd Wright designed buildings and of people.

The collection can be viewed and studied by obtaining permission
from the Curator of the collection.

A21

Historic American Buildings Survey
National Park Service
801 19th Street, N.W.
Washington, D.C. 20240

and/or
Historic American Buildings Survey Collection
Prints and Photographs Division
The Library of Congress
Annex Building
Room 1041
Washington, D.C. 20540

In 1933 the Historic American Buildings Survey (HABS) was initiated
and given permanence by the Historic Sites Act of 1935 which declared
as national policy the preservation of historic sites, historic
buildings, and historic objects for public use. In 1978 there were at
least twenty-nine Frank Lloyd Wright designed buildings for which
either an HABS file existed or was under preparation. These buildings
and their respective HABS file contents are outlined here:

Frank Lloyd Wright Residence and Studio (1889-1911)
Oak Park, Illinois
The following items are contained in HABS File No. ILL-1099:
Four exterior photographs.
Three interior photographs.
Fifteen data pages.

James Charnley Residence (1891)
Chicago, Illinois
The following items are contained in HABS File No. ILL-1009:
Seven Measured Drawings (1964)--
Sheet--Site plan
Sheet--First floor plan and second floor plan
Sheet--Third floor plan and molding detail
Sheet--Building section
Sheet--West elevation
Sheet--Stair hall details
Sheet--Living room bookcase door detail, soffit plan, and
cornice detail.
Three exterior photographs dated 1963 and 1964.
Three interior photographs dated 1963.
One photocopy of one view dated 1900.
Six data pages dated 1963.
Historic American Buildings Survey Inventory (HABSI) forms
dated 1957 and 1960.

George Blossom Residence (1892)
Chicago, Illinois
HABSI forms (HABS office only).

Allison Harlan Residence (1892)
Chicago, Illinois
HABSI forms (HABS office only).

Warren McArthur Residence (1892)
Chicago, Illinois
HABSI forms (HABS office only).

William H. Winslow Residence and Stable (1893)
River Forest, Illinois
The following items are contained in HABS File No. ILL-1061:
Five Measured Drawings--
Sheet--Site plan

Sheet--First floor plan
Sheet--Second floor plan
Sheet--West elevation
Sheet--Reception hall plan and wall section.
Six exterior photographs.
Five interior photographs.
Two photocopies.
Seventeen data pages.

Francis Apartments for the Terre Haute Trust Company (1895)
Chicago, Illinois
  The following items are contained in HABS File No. ILL-1076:
    Five exterior photographs.
    Four data pages.

Francisco Terrace Apartments for Edward C. Waller (1895)
Chicago, Illinois
  HABSI forms (HABS office only).

Edward C. Waller Apartments (1895)
Chicago, Illinois
  HABSI forms (HABS office only).

Isidor Heller Residence and Stable (1896)
Chicago, Illinois
  The following items are contained in HABS File No. ILL-1046:
    Four Measured Drawings--
      Sheet--Site plan
      Sheet--First and second floor plans
      Sheet--East elevation, south elevation, and building
        section
      Sheet--Four details of the staircase windows.
    Four exterior photographs.
    Three interior photographs.
    One photocopy of old view.
    Six data pages.

Abraham Lincoln Center for Reverend Mr. Jenkin Lloyd Jones (1903)
Chicago, Illinois
  HABSI forms (HABS office only).

Darwin D. Martin Residence, Conservatory, and Garage (1904)
Buffalo, New York
  The following items are contained in HABS File No. NY-5611:
    Five exterior photographs.
    Eight photocopies.
    Thirteen data pages.

E-Z Polish Factory for Darwin D. Martin and W.E. Martin (1905)
Chicago, Illinois
  HABSI forms (HABS office only).

Unity Church (1905)
Oak Park, Illinois
  The following items are contained in HABS File No. ILL-1093:
    Seven Measured Drawings--
      Sheet--Site plan
      Sheet--North elevation
      Sheet--West elevation
      Sheet--Auditorium level plan

Sheet--Ground floor plan
Sheet--Balcony level plan
Sheet--Building section (longitudinal).
Three exterior photographs.
Two interior photographs.
Thirteen data pages.
HABSI form.

Frederick G. Robie Residence (1906)
Chicago, Illinois
   The following items are contained in HABS File No. ILL-1005:
      Fourteen Measured Drawings--
         Sheet--Location map and title sheet to drawings
         Sheet--First (ground) floor plan
         Sheet--Second (main) floor plan
         Sheet--Third floor plan
         Sheet--South elevation and longitudinal section
         Sheet--West, east, and north elevations
         Sheet--Fireplace elevations (east and west)
         Sheet--Window elevation and detail window frame section
         Sheet--Second floor window elevations
         Sheet--Living room section, plan, and environmental control
            notes
         Sheet--Furniture (dresser elevations)
         Sheet--Furniture (elevations of living room chair, foot
            stool, dining room chair, and billiard room andirons)
         Sheet--Construction details of straight back chair
         Sheet--Side chair.
      Three exterior photographs.
      Two interior photographs.
      Three photocopies (1911).
      Seventeen data pages.
      One sheet of drawings at the HABS office.

E.E. Boynton Residence (1908)
Rochester, New York
   The following items are at the HABS office only:
      Two exterior photographs.
      Five interior photographs.
      Four data pages.

Meyer May Residence (1908)
Grand Rapids, Michigan
   The following items are contained in HABS File No. MICH-241 at
   the HABS office only:
      Four exterior photographs.
      One photocopy.
      Eleven data pages.

David M. Amberg Residence (1909)
Grand Rapids, Michigan
   The following items are contained in HABS File No. MICH-242
   at the HABS office only:
      Five exterior photographs.
      Eleven data pages.

Frank J. Baker Residence (1909)
Wilmette, Illinois
   HABSI forms (HABS office only).

Oscar Steffens Residence (1909)
Chicago, Illinois
  The following items are contained in HABS File No. ILL-1063:
    Six Measured Drawings--
      Sheet--Site plan, elevations, and sections
      Sheet--Ground floor plan, living room fireplace detail
      Sheet--Second floor plan, master bedroom fireplace detail,
        and other details
      Sheet--West, north, south, and east elevations
      Sheet--Building sections
      Sheet--Window details
    Two photocopies.
    Four data pages.

Reverend J.R. Ziegler Residence (1909)
Frankfort, Kentucky
  The following items are contained in HABS File No. KY-103:
    Fourteen Measured Drawings--
      Sheet--Location map
      Sheet--Basement plan and sections
      Sheet--First floor plan
      Sheet--Second floor plan
      Sheet--Roof plan
      Sheet--West elevation, fireplace elevations, and details
      Sheet--South elevation
      Sheet--East elevation, building sections, and details
      Sheet--North elevation
      Sheet--Building sections
      Sheet--Building sections
      Sheet--Cabinet sections and details
      Sheet--Window details
      Sheet--Window details.

Lake Geneva Hotel for Arthur L. Richards (1911)
Lake Geneva, Wisconsin
  The following items are at the HABS office only:
    Two exterior photographs.
    Four interior photographs.

Emil Bach Residence (1915)
Chicago, Illinois
  The following items are contained in HABS File No. ILL-1088:
    Six Measured Drawings--
      Sheet--Site plan
      Sheet--First floor plan
      Sheet--Second floor plan
      Sheet--South and west elevations
      Sheet--North and east elevations
      Sheet--Building sections.
    Two exterior photographs.
    One interior photograph.
    Eleven photocopies of original drawings.
    Seven data pages.

F.C. Bogk Residence (1916)
Milwaukee, Wisconsin
  The following items are contained in HABS File No. WIS-252:

Five exterior photographs.
Seven interior photographs.
Seven data pages.

Aline Barnsdall "Hollyhock" Residence (1917)
Los Angeles, California
The following items are contained in HABS File No. CAL-356:
Nine exterior photographs.
Four interior photographs.
Thirteen data pages.

Aline Barnsdall Studio Residence A (1920)
Los Angeles, California
The following items are contained in HABS File No. CAL-357:
Six exterior photographs.
Eight data pages.

Samuel Freeman Residence (1923)
Los Angeles, California
The following items are contained in HABS File No. CAL-1935
at the HABS office only:
Seven micromasters of F.L. Wright's plans.
Four data pages.

S.C. Johnson and Son Administration Building (1936)
Racine, Wisconsin
The following materials are at the HABS office only:
Fourteen exterior photographs.
Seventeen interior photographs.

Loren Pope Residence (1939)
Falls Church, Virginia
The following materials are contained in HABS File No. VA-638:
Nine Measured Drawings--
    Sheet--Site plan
    Sheet--Floor plan
    Sheet--East elevation
    Sheet--South elevation
    Sheet--West elevation
    Sheet--North elevation
    Sheet--Building sections
    Sheet--Building sections
    Sheet--Details.
Four exterior photographs.
Two interior photographs.
Five data pages.
Eighteen exterior photographs (at HABS office).
Eighteen interior photographs (at HABS office).
Seven photocopies of plans, clippings, and correspondence
    (at HABS office).

Reproductions of materials contained in these files may be ordered
from the Prints and Photographs Division of the Library of Congress.
However, not all file collections were housed at the Library of Congress
during the research period and these are listed as being in the HABS
files only. Files at the HABS office are typically incomplete staff
working files whereas those HABS files at the Library of Congress are
complete. Typical HABS data forms are 8-1/2 in. x 11 in. (215.9 mm x
279.4 mm) in size. It should be pointed out, however, that although

some of these buildings have Historic American Buildings Survey files, this does not mean that each of the listed structures are on the National Register of Historic Places, are National Historic Landmarks, or were properly recorded in the Historic American Buildings Survey. Those listed which are not are the George Blossom Residence, Allison Harlan Residence, Warren McArthur Residence, Francis Apartments for the Terre Haute Trust Company, Francisco Terrace Apartments for Edward C. Waller, Edward C. Waller Apartments, Abraham Lincoln Center for Reverend Mr. Jenkin Lloyd Jones, E-Z Polish Factory for Darwin D. Martin and W.E. Martin, E.E. Boynton Residence, Meyer May Residence, David M. Amberg Residence, Oscar Steffens Residence, and the Lake Geneva Hotel for Arthur L. Richards. For a complete listing of Frank Lloyd Wright designed structures which are on the National Register of Historic Places, are National Historic Landmarks, and are properly recorded in the Historic American Buildings Survey, see Patrick J. Meehan's "Frank Lloyd Wright Designed Structures Which Are on the National Register of Historic Places, National Historic Landmarks, and Recorded in the Historic American Buildings Survey" (*The Frank Lloyd Wright Newsletter* [Oak Park, Illinois], Vol. 3, No. 3, Third Quarter 1980). The appendices of this research guide designate those which are on the National Register of Historic Places.

A22

Frank Lloyd Wright Manuscript Collection
Department of Special Collections
Kenneth Spencer Research Library
University of Kansas
Lawrence, Kansas 66045

The Frank Lloyd Wright Manuscript Collection has manuscripts which date from 1925 to 1959. Approximately half the collection are letters and cards written to George and Helen Beal by the Wrights, thirteen of which were written by Frank Lloyd Wright. The remaining portion of the collection contains letters and manuscripts written by former Wright students and persons interested in Wright's work. Other holdings in the collection include typescripts, original sketches, and letters relating to Wright and *House Beautiful* magazine. The letters written by Wright to the Beals include those dated October 30, 1934; January 30, 1935; April 27, 1935; December 16, 1935; January 10, 1936; May 8, 1936; Christmas 1944; Christmas 1946; August 6, 1948; July 13, 1949; January 25, 1950; and June 4, 1952. There is also one letter to a Mr. Schlagel which is undated.

The Kenneth Spencer Research Library grants permission to examine manuscripts to qualified scholars upon submission of an application form. The library will consider, and at its discretion, grant requests for photoduplication of manuscript material with regard for the physical condition of the original manuscript and in compliance with copyright law (as interpreted by the Department of Special Collections). Written consent of the writer or the literary heirs of the writer is required by the Library before the Library will provide photoduplicates or grant permission for publication.

A23

Lawrence Institute of Technology
Southfield, Michigan 48075

The Lawrence Institute of Technology owns the Frank Lloyd Wright
designed Gregor Affleck Residence of 1940 in Bloomfield Hills,
Michigan. This researcher was unable to obtain any information from
the Institute concerning any Frank Lloyd Wright materials, other than
the house itself, which may be in their collection. An account of the
Institute's acquisition of the Affleck Residence is given in "News
Reports--LIT Architectural School Receives Usonian House as Gift"
(*Architectural Record*, Vol. 163, No. 4, April 1978), p. 37.

A24

The Manuscript Division
The Library of Congress
Thomas Jefferson Building
Third Floor, Rooms 3004 and 3005
Washington, D.C. 20540

The Manuscript Division of the Library of Congress has four
collections of manuscripts which house Frank Lloyd Wright written
manuscripts. These collections are the Ludwig Mies van der Rohe
Papers, 1921-1969, the Edmund Randolph Purves Papers, 1916-1964, the
Lawrence Edmund Spivak Papers, 1927-1960, and the Frank Lloyd Wright
Papers, 1894-1940.

The Ludwig Mies van der Rohe Papers, 1921-1969 houses six letters
and telegrams written by Frank Lloyd Wright to Mies van der Rohe, dated
August 26, 1944; November 15, 1944; August 21, 1946; October 12, 1946;
October 16, 1947; and October 25, 1947. Also in the collection are
six letters and telegrams from Mies van der Rohe to Wright dated
August 14, 1946; October 3, 1946; October 11, 1946; October 15, 1947;
October 17, 1947; and November 25, 1947. A complete search of this
collection was made and these are the only original Frank Lloyd Wright
manuscripts in the sixty-five containers of the collection.

The Edmund Randolph Purves Papers, 1916-1964 collection contains
only one letter to Edmund Purves, dated June 15, 1949, from Frank Lloyd
Wright. Edmund R. Purves was the Executive Director of the American
Institute of Architects at the time Wright wrote this letter. Wright
received the Gold Medal of the American Institute of Architects in
1949 and this letter is concerned with that honor.

The Lawrence Edmund Spivak Papers, 1927-1960 collection contains
three pieces of correspondence in Container C 1 of the *American Mercury*
File, 1927-1953, Editorial Correspondence, 1927-1953, which includes
a letter from Charles Angoff to Frank Lloyd Wright dated January 3,
1947; a letter from Frank Lloyd Wright to Charles Angoff dated January
27, 1947; and a letter from Charles Angoff to Frank Lloyd Wright
dated February 5, 1947. The letters concern Frank Lloyd Wright's
preparation of an article for *American Mercury* magazine.

The Frank Lloyd Wright Papers, 1894-1940 represents two separate
acquisitions to the Library of Congress. The first acquisition was
from Frederick A. Gutheim in 1959. The Gutheim acquisition is arranged
in two series, Series I and Series II. Series I (Box 1) consists of
duplicate copies (printed, mimeographed, carbon, typed, etc.) of
speeches and articles with corrections and modifications, in some

instances, by Frank Lloyd Wright. Series II (Box 2) consists of excerpts made at Taliesin by Frederick A. Gutheim from Frank Lloyd Wright's papers. There is much duplication in the two series. Only those manuscripts which were either written by Frank Lloyd Wright as original manuscripts or were direct copies of original manuscripts are discussed in this book. Gutheim obtained these manuscripts from Frank Lloyd Wright for Wright's *Frank Lloyd Wright on Architecture: Selected Writings, 1894-1940*, edited by Frederick A. Gutheim and published by Duell, Sloan and Pearce at New York in 1941.

The balance of this collection represents correspondence between William R. Heath, a former client, and Frank Lloyd Wright. The Heath correspondence, dating from 1904 to 1927, was acquired by the Library of Congress in 1961 from A. Wilmot Jacobsen (Elizabeth Heath Jacobsen) of Buffalo, New York.

The manuscripts contained in the collection are all typescripts unless otherwise noted and are listed as follows:

> Speech entitled "This 'Ideal' Architect (What Is Architecture)" dated 1901.
>
> Letter to William R. Heath from Frank Lloyd Wright dated December 28, 1904.
>
> Lecture entitled "Chicago Culture" dated February 7, 1918.
>
> Article entitled "The Architect and the Machine" dated prior to May 1927 (two copies).
>
> Article entitled "Three Propositions" dated November 25, 1927.
>
> Five letters to William R. Heath, some of which are handwritten and undated, but probably early 1927.
>
> Article entitled "In Ancient Yedo" dated 1927.
>
> Article entitled "A Plan for the Erection of a Model Building" dated 1927.
>
> Article entitled "In the Cause of Architecture: The Logic of the Plan," probably done in late 1927.
>
> Article entitled "In the Cause of Architecture: What 'Styles' Mean to the Architect," probably dates prior to February 1928.
>
> Article entitled "In the Cause of Architecture: The Meaning of Materials," probably dates prior to April 1928.
>
> Article entitled "In the Cause of Architecture: The Meaning of Materials--Stone," probably dates prior to April 1928.
>
> Book review of *"Toward a New Architecture*--Le Corbusier: translated by Frederick W. Etchells" dated June 1, 1928.
>
> Article entitled "In the Cause of Architecture: The Meaning of Materials--The Kiln," probably dates prior to June 1928.
>
> Article entitled "In the Cause of Architecture--The Meaning of Materials--Glass," probably dates prior to July 1928.
>
> Wedding announcement addressed to William R. Heath dated August 25, 1928.
>
> Article entitled "In the Nature of Materials--Concrete," probably dates prior to August 1928.
>
> Article entitled "The Use of Metalplates In the Art of Building," probably dates prior to October 1928.
>
> Article entitled "In the Cause of Architecture--Sheet Metal and a Modern Instance," probably dates prior to October 1928.
>
> Article entitled "In the Cause of Architecture: the Terms," probably dates prior to December 1928.

Article entitled "In the Cause of Architecture XII--Composi-
tion" dated 1928.
Article entitled "Wood" dated 1928.
Article entitled "Surface and Mass--Again" dated April 5, 1929.
Article entitled "The Profession" dated July 1, 1930.
Article entitled "Modern Concepts Concerning an Organic
Architecture from the Work Of," probably dates prior to
July 1930.
Lecture entitled "To the Young Man in Architecture--Chicago
Art Institute Lecture Afternoon Oct. 1, 1930 at Fullerton
Hall, Chicago" dated October 1, 1930.
Lecture entitled "In the Realm of Ideas--Lecture I" dated
October 1, 1930?
Lecture entitled "The New Architecture," probably dates prior
to October 1930.
Lecture entitled "Salvation by Imagination" dated 1930.
Lecture entitled "The Card-Board House" dated 1930.
Article entitled "Hell-Bent Is Eclecticism," probably dates
prior to May 1931.
Speech entitled "Address of Frank Lloyd Wright at the Annual
Banquet of the Annual Convention of the Michigan Society of
Architects and the Grand Rapids Chapter of the American
Institute of Architects" dated June 8, 1931?
Article entitled "Radio City" dated June 21, 1931.
Article entitled "The City of Tomorrow" dated 1931.
Article entitled "Brochures on Contemporary Architecture--
Published by the Whittlesey House: Raymond Hood" dated
December 13, 1931.
Article entitled "A Song to Heaven: A Sermonette" dated 1931.
Article entitled "For All May Raise the Flowers Now for All
Have Got the Seed" dated 1931.
Article entitled "What Does the Machine Mean to Life in a
Democracy" dated April 15, 1932.
Article entitled "The House on the Mesa ..." dated April 29,
1932.
Article entitled "Of Thee I Sing" dated May 9, 1932.
Article entitled "What Is the 'Modern' Idea?" dated July 24,
1932.
Article entitled "I Will" dated 1932 or 1933?
Article entitled "The Chicago World's Fair: To 'The Architects
Journal' London, England," probably dates prior to July
1933.
Article entitled "In the Show Window at Macy's" dated October
1, 1933.
Article entitled "First Answers to Questions by Pravda" dated
1933.
Article entitled "What Shall We Work For" dated December 4,
1934.
Article entitled "To Arizona" dated January 31, 1935.
Letter entitled "Robert D. Lusk: The Evening Huronite: Huron,
South Dakota" dated September 28, 1935.
Article entitled "Organic Architecture: 1. The United States
from 1893 to 1920" dated December 15, 1935.
Article entitled "Louis Sullivan's Words and Works" dated
1935?

Article entitled "An Architect Speaking for Culture" dated
    January 26, 1936.
Article entitled "At Taliesin" dated February 1936.
Article entitled "At Taliesin" dated July 29, 1936.
Article entitled "The Country Doctor" dated December 30, 1936.
Article entitled "At Taliesin" dated March 30, 1937.
Article/editorial entitled "At Taliesin: An Open Letter to
    Frank Lloyd Wright and a Reply" dated August 2, 1937.
Untitled paper dated August 1, 1937.
Article entitled "Architecture and Life in the U.S.S.R." dated
    August 31, 1937.
Editorial entitled "Editorial For 'Izvestia'" dated October 18,
    1937.
Speech or open letter entitled "My Dear Comrades ..." dated
    1937.
Article entitled "Categorical Reply to Questions by the
    'Architecture of the U.S.S.R.'" dated 1937 or 1938?
Speech entitled "From an Architect's Point of View" dated
    June 2, 1938.
Article entitled "The Man and the Issue" dated July 31, 1938.
Speech entitled "Speech to the A.F.A." dated October 25, 1938.
Speech entitled "Madison's Public Servants" dated December 4,
    1938.
Speeches entitled "The Sir George Watson Lectures for 1939:
    A Series of Four Evenings on--An Organic Architecture: The
    Architecture of Democracy" dated May 2, 4, 9, 11, and 20,
    1939.
Article entitled "To the Fifty-Eighth" dated August 1939.
Lecture entitled "Dinner Talk at Hull House" dated November 8,
    1939.
Note entitled "Notes--Frank Lloyd Wright," probably dates prior
    to 1940.
Article/letter entitled "To *The Chicago Daily News*," probably
    dates prior to 1940.
Article entitled "Article for 'The - Hour,'" probably dates
    prior to 1940.
Editorial entitled "Editorial," probably dates prior to 1940.
Article entitled "The Internationalist Style," probably dates
    prior to 1940.
Article entitled "Of Frank Lloyd Wright," probably dates prior
    to 1940.
Editorial entitled "Self Defense" dated June 15, 1940.
Graphic design for Part Two of *An Autobiography* by Frank Lloyd
    Wright drawn in ink on paper measuring 8-7/8 in. x 13-3/4 in.
    (225 mm x 349 mm).

The national manuscript collection may be consulted by any person
engaged in serious research who presents proper identification, completes the Manuscript Division's registration form, and agrees to
adhere to the Library's rules for the use of rare materials. Only in
exceptional circumstances are high school students or undergraduates
permitted to consult manuscripts. In such circumstances, students
should be introduced in person or in writing by their advisors.

The Manuscript Division has a professional staff of historians
who are available for private consultation with readers. Most manuscripts, subject to preservation and copyright restraints, may be

photocopied for research use. The Manuscript Division provides photoduplication services with a full range of copying facilities.

A25

The Municipal Arts Department
The City of Los Angeles
Room 1500
City Hall
Los Angeles, California 90012

The city of Los Angeles owns and the Municipal Arts Department
operates the Frank Lloyd Wright designed Aline Barnsdall "Hollyhock"
Residence of 1917. The Aline Barnsdall Studio Residence A of 1920
is operated by the Department of Recreation and Parks. The Los Angeles
Exhibition Pavilion of 1954 was a temporary structure which was dismantled in 1969. All of the buildings are located in Barnsdall Park
in Los Angeles. The buildings designed for Aline Barnsdall and the
grounds (approximately eleven acres) were donated to the city in 1926.

In addition to Barnsdall Park and the buildings, the Municipal
Arts Department and the Department of Recreation and Parks also house
numerous Frank Lloyd Wright drawings, blueprints, and furniture which
are associated with the Aline Barnsdall commissions. Drawings in the
collection from the office of Frank Lloyd Wright include, but are not
limited to, the following:

> Three sketch elevations drawn on one sheet of paper of Holly-
> wood Boulevard, Vermont Avenue, and Sunset Boulevard.
> "Construction Plan for Property of A. Barnsdall" which is one
> sheet showing a detailed site development plan drawn at a
> scale of 1 in. = 40 ft. and dated both December 1920 and
> March 5, 1921.
> Three conceptual sketches of the west elevation, each of which
> is on a separate sheet of paper.
> A perspective rendering of the west elevation on one sheet with
> several small detail sketches.
> A drawing of the front elevation dated 1923. This drawing is
> for the Wright designed Aline Barnsdall Residence Project
> for Beverly Hills, California, which was never executed.
> A drawing of the main floor plan for the Aline Barnsdall
> Residence Project of 1923 for Beverly Hills, California,
> which was never executed.
> A floor plan of "The Little Dipper" Barnsdall Playhouse dated
> 1923.
> A drawing of lamps showing elevation, plan, and details drawn
> in pencil on tracing paper measuring 26-5/8 in. x 34-3/8 in.
> (676 mm x 867 mm).

In December 1979 the Frank Lloyd Wright drawings and blueprints
were not catalogued and the list in this book represents only some
of the many drawings and blueprints on the Barnsdall commissions that
are in the collection. Since the blueprints are fragile, they would
not be ready for viewing or study until such time as they are photographed and mylars are made.

Furniture associated with the Barnsdall "Hollyhock" Residence include:

Six dining room side chairs with the "Hollyhock" motif backs.
Each chair is made of wood with upholstered seats and measure
45-3/4 in. x 17-3/4 in. x 20 in. (1162 mm x 451 mm x 508 mm).
One dining room table, which belongs with the six dining room
side chairs. It measures 54 in. x 29 in. (1371.6 mm x 736.6
mm).
One desk measuring 20 in. x 36 in. x 26-1/2 in. (508 mm x
914.4 mm x 673.1 mm). This is not a confirmed Frank Lloyd
Wright designed piece.
One side chair which measures 44-3/4 in. (1136.7 mm) tall.
Two side chairs which measure 32 in. (812.8 mm) tall.
Three upholstered armchairs.

In addition to the Frank Lloyd Wright designed furniture in the
collection there are three pieces designed by his son Lloyd Wright:

Two desks each of which measures 42 in. x 72 in. x 30 in.
(1066.8 mm x 1828.8 mm x 762 mm).
One desk measuring 40 in. x 54 in. x 30 in. (1016 mm x 1371.6 mm
x 762 mm).

The Aline Barnsdall "Hollyhock" Residence is open to the public
at certain times. The Frank Lloyd Wright designed furniture may be
viewed at the residence. The drawings may be viewed by appointment
with the curator of "Hollyhock" Residence.

A26

Fine Arts Collection
University Committee on Fine Arts
Marquette University
Milwaukee, Wisconsin   53233

The Fine Arts Collection of Marquette University obtained four
renderings by Frank Lloyd Wright of the motel, pavilion, and entertainment area for the Leesburg (Florida) Floating Gardens Project
of 1952 (for an account of the acquisition see James Auer's "Wright
Work Donated" [*The Milwaukee Journal*, February 28, 1978, Part 2]).
All of the drawings are done on tracing paper with colored pencil
and colored ink. The drawings were prepared for Messrs. Lawrence
Ottinger, Carl Byoir, Robert Furguson, and J.T. Claiborne, Jr., and
Co. The first two drawings are a plan of the pavilion drawn at a scale
of 1/8 in. = 1 ft. 0 in. and measure 36 in. x 49-1/2 in. (914.4 mm x
1257.3 mm); one of the two drawings is dated 1952 with Frank Lloyd
Wright's initial and the other is neither dated nor signed. The third
drawing is a perspective rendering of the project measuring 36 in. x
49-1/2 in. (914.4 mm x 1257.3 mm) which is neither dated nor signed.
The fourth drawing is a site perspective rendering of the motel,
pavilion, and entertainment area measuring 36 in. x 54-1/4 in. (914.4
mm x 1378 mm). It is dated July 20, 195- and initialed by Wright. The
drawings were donated to Marquette's collection by Kirby Raab of
Milwaukee in 1978 whose mother had obtained the drawings in trade with
Frank Lloyd Wright for stone sculptures which Mrs. Raab had had (possibly from Wright's Midway Gardens of Chicago which was demolished)
at the Dawn Manor Estate near Wisconsin Dells, Wisconsin.

A27

Maryland Historical Society Library
Maryland Historical Society
201 West Monument Street
Baltimore, Maryland 21201

The Frank Lloyd Wright Maryland Registration Papers Collection
contains eight items regarding Wright's architect registration in
Maryland. Wright was required to register as an architect during the
building of the Joseph Euchtman Residence at Baltimore, Maryland, in
1940. There are five letters from John H. Scarff, Executive Secretary
to the Maryland Board of Examiners and Registration of Architects,
to Frank Lloyd Wright on the matter of Wright's application for architect registration in Maryland dated July 2, 1940; July 30, 1940;
August 16, 1940; September 3, 1940; and November 20, 1940. Wright
filed an application with the Board on July 27, 1940 (the four-page
application is also contained in the collection), but did not remit
the required fee of $20.00. Subsequent letters to Wright from Scarff
are concerned with the payment of this fee. Wright's application was
transmitted by Eugene Masselink in a one-page letter dated July 27,
1940, which is also contained in the collection. The eighth item in
the collection is a brief memo to Scarff probably written by one of
Scarff's employees regarding Wright's contractor for the Euchtman
Residence, Leimbach and Williams.

A28

Department of American Decorative Arts
The Metropolitan Museum of Art
Fifth Avenue at 82nd Street
New York, New York 10028

The Department of American Decorative Arts houses numerous Frank
Lloyd Wright materials, most of which pertain to the Francis W. Little
Residence I and Stable at Peoria, Illinois, of 1902, and the Francis
W. Little Residence II, "Northome," originally located at Deephaven,
Minnesota, of 1912. However, the Department also houses several Frank
Lloyd Wright items related to his Ward W. Willits Residence of 1901
at Highland Park, Illinois; the Avery Coonley Playhouse of 1912 at River-
side, Illinois; and the Imperial Hotel of 1915 at Tokyo, Japan.
The Metropolitan Museum of Art acquired the Francis W. Little
Residence II, "Northome," in 1972. The residence was dismantled and
portions sold to private individuals and museums, and portions remained
in the Metropolitan Museum of Art collections, including the entire
living room of the residence. The Allentown Art Museum of Allentown,
Pennsylvania, purchased the library room. The Minneapolis Institute
of Arts purchased the east hallway. And the Dallas Museum of Fine
Arts purchased fourteen window panels from the Little sitting room.
The Metropolitan Museum of Art also purchased various other items
relating to both the Little Residence II and the Little Residence I.
These items included manuscripts, drawings, and furniture by Frank
Lloyd Wright.
The Frank Lloyd Wright/Francis Little Collection contains a total
of fourteen pieces of correspondence between Frank Lloyd Wright and
Francis Little. The letters written by Frank Lloyd Wright are dated

April 1908; September 18, 1908; November 3, 1913; and November 8, 1913.
The letters written by Francis Little addressed to Frank Lloyd Wright
are dated June 7, 1909 (telegram); February 6, 1912; two letters dated
October 8, 1912; October 11, 1912; October 20, 1912; October 30, 1912;
November 5, 1913; September 24, 1913; and April 27, 1914.
Several publications which describe and discuss the Little acquisi-
tion in detail are "19th-Century Architecture for the American Wing:
Sullivan and Wright" (*The Metropolitan Museum of Art Bulletin*, Vol.
30, June/July 1972), pp. 300-305; "Preservation: The Met to the Rescue"
(*Architectural Forum*, Vol. 136, June 1972), p. 22; Morrison Heckscher
and Elizabeth G. Miller's *An Architect and His Client: Frank Lloyd
Wright and Francis W. Little* (New York: The Metropolitan Museum of Art,
May 2, 1973); "Architect and His Client: Frank Lloyd Wright and Francis
W. Little" (*Interiors*, Vol. 132, June 1973), p. 10; Tom Martinson's
"A Loss of Consequence" (*Northwest Architect*, Vol. 37, March/April
1973), pp. 82-85; Sarah B. Sherrill's Frank Lloyd Wright: Living Room
of Northome to the Metropolitan Museum of Art" (*Antiques*, Vol. 103,
June 1973), pp. 1054, 1058; and Morrison Heckscher's Frank Lloyd Wright's
Furniture for Francis W. Little" (*Burlington Magazine*, Vol. 117,
December 1975), pp. 866, 869, 871, and 872.
The following Frank Lloyd Wright designs are represented, with the
items listed, in the Metropolitan Museum of Art collections:

Ward W. Willits Residence (1901)
Highland Park, Illinois
One tall back dining chair.

Francis W. Little Residence I and Stable (1902)
Peoria, Illinois
Four armchairs made of white oak and stained dark brown
measuring 33-1/4 in. x 37 in. x 29 in. (844.6 mm x 939.8 mm
x 736.6 mm).
One table made of white oak and stained dark brown measuring
28-1/2 in. x 155-1/2 in. (723.9 mm x 3949.7 mm).
One print table made of white oak and stained dark brown
measuring 45-3/8 in. x 37-3/8 in. x 44-1/16 in. (1152.5 mm x
949.3 mm x 1119.2 mm).
Two plant stands made of white oak and stained dark brown
measuring 35-3/4 in. x 15-1/2 in. x 15-1/2 in. (908.1 mm x
393.7 mm x 393.7 mm).
Drawing of an elevation, plan, and section for buffet and dining
room post drawn in pencil and colored pencil on paper measuring 19 in. x 40 in. (482.6 mm x 1016 mm).

Francis W. Little Residence II, "Northome" (1912)
Deephaven, Minnesota
A preliminary sketch drawn in pencil on tissue paper at a
scale of 1/8 in. = 1 ft. of the south and east elevation
measuring 23-1/4 in. x 38-1/2 in. (590.6 mm x 977.9 mm).
A preliminary sketch in pencil on tissue paper drawn at a
scale of 1/8 in. = 1 ft. of the west elevation measuring
23-1/4 in. x 42-1/2 in. (590.6 mm x 1079.5 mm).
A preliminary sketch drawn in pencil on tissue paper at a
scale of 1/8 in. = 1 ft. of a furniture plan measuring
10-1/2 in. x 36 in. (266.7 mm x 914.4 mm).
A preliminary sketch drawn in pencil on tissue paper of dining
room furniture and the buffet measuring 19-3/8 in. x 21-7/8
in. (492.1 mm x 555.6 mm).

One drawing of the billiard table and rail to the dining room
   measuring 19-1/4 in. x 40 in. (489 mm x 1016 mm).
A preliminary sketch drawn in pencil on tissue paper of the
   cue rack and wall seat in the billiard room drawn at a scale
   of 1-1/2 in. = 1 ft. and measuring 19-1/4 in. x 28-1/2 in.
   (489 mm x 723.9 mm).
A preliminary sketch of the dressing table and highboy bedroom
   furniture drawn in pencil and colored pencil on tissue paper
   at a scale of 1-1/2 in. = 1 ft. measuring 19-1/4 in. x
   40 in. (489 mm x 1016 mm).
One drawing of an elevation and plan for the dressing table
   and highboy done in pencil and colored pencil on paper measuring 19-1/2 in. x 22 in. (495.3 mm x 558.8 mm).
A preliminary sketch of the piano and bench drawn at a scale of 1-
   1/2 in. = 1 ft. in pencil on tissue paper measuring 19-3/8 in. x
   40 in. (492.1 mm x 1016 mm).
A preliminary sketch of a glass design for a living room bay
   and two in pencil on tissue paper measuring 9-5/16 in. x
   21-1/8 in. (236.5 mm x 536.6 mm).

Several items of furnishings designed by Frank Lloyd Wright for
the Littles, including the complete living room, are contained
in the collection. The furniture pieces for the Littles' "Northome" Residence include:

Doors made of oak with leaded glass measuring 77-1/4 in. x
   41-3/4 in. x 1-3/4 in. (1962.2 mm x 1060.5 mm x 44.5 mm).
One table from the library made of white oak treated with a
   clear varnish measuring 26-5/16 in. x 72 in. x 27 in.
   (668.3 mm x 1828.8 mm x 685.8 mm).
Two side chairs, each of which are made of oak and stained
   dark brown, measuring 36 in. x 23-1/2 in. x 18 in. (914.4 mm
   x 596.9 mm x 457.2 mm).
One end table made of white oak and treated with a clear
   varnish measuring 29 in. x 15-1/2 in. x 12-7/8 in. (736.6 mm
   x 395.1 mm x 327 mm).
Six standing lamps, each of which is made of oak and treated
   with a clear varnish, measuring 54-1/2 in. (1384.3 mm) in
   height.
One light fixture made of white oak and treated with clear
   varnish measuring 32 in. x 7 in. x 11 in. (812.8 mm x
   177.8 mm x 279.4 mm).

Other items in the Frank Lloyd Wright/Francis Little Collection
include a German edition of *Frank Lloyd Wright: Ausgeführte Bauten*
dated 1911 inscribed by Wright to Francis W. Little and several drawings, listed below, which relate to either the Peoria or Deephaven
Little Residences:

Roof plan drawn in pencil and ink.
Blueprint of a detail section through a window and eave.
A fragment of a drawing done in pencil on tracing paper of
   the garage downspout for the stable/gardener's cottage.
Roof plan and detailed wall section for a boat house drawn in
   pencil and ink dated July 15, 1909.
Site plan for a fern garden drawn in pencil on tracing paper.
Fireplace plans and sections drawn in pencil on white paper.
Fragment of a pencil drawing on tracing paper of a plaster
   soffit detail.

"Detail of Section A-A'" drawn with pencil and red pencil on
tracing paper.
Drawing of a window frame at Section C-C' through the garage
drawn with pencil and red pencil on tracing paper.
East elevation of stable drawn in pencil and pen on white paper.
Floor plan blueprints of the first, second, and cellar floors.
These drawings are not necessarily from Wright's office and indeed may not be Wright's designs. Further research will have to
be done to further identify them.

Avery Coonley Playhouse (1912)
Riverside, Illinois
   Three leaded (zinc came) glass windows in wood frames measuring 86-1/4 in. x 28 in. x 2 in. (2190.8 mm x 711.2 mm x
   50.8 mm) originally from the front facade of the structure.

Imperial Hotel (1915)
Tokyo, Japan
   One side chair.
   Two place settings of porcelain dinnerware.

Wallpaper and Fabric Designs for F. Schumacher and Company's
Taliesin line (1955)
New York, New York
   One sample of fabric.

Access to the Frank Lloyd Wright items at the Metropolitan Museum
of Art are granted by appointment through the Curator of the Department of American Decorative Arts. The American Wing at the Museum was
completed in 1982 and many of the Frank Lloyd Wright materials are on
view, including the living room of the Francis W. Little Residence II,
"Northome," as shown in "Frank Lloyd Wright at the Metropolitan Museum
of Art" (*The Metropolitan Museum of Art Bulletin*, Vol. 40, No. 2, Fall
1982, entire issue).

A29

The Prairie Archives
The Milwaukee Art Museum
750 North Lincoln Memorial Drive
Milwaukee, Wisconsin 53202

   The Prairie Archives of the Milwaukee Art Museum houses materials
which relate to sixteen Frank Lloyd Wright designs. The bulk of these
items are drawings by George M. Niedecken who was the interior designer
of the firm of Niedecken-Walbridge of Milwaukee, Wisconsin. The
Niedecken collection was acquired by the Prairie Archives in 1977
(see Linda Fibich's "Architect's Papers Find New Home" [*The Milwaukee
Journal*, December 14, 1977]) from Mr. and Mrs. Robert L. Jacobson--Mr.
Jacobson became a partner in the Niedecken-Walbridge firm in 1938.
Frank Lloyd Wright had collaborated with Niedecken on the furnishings
for such Wright designed buildings as the Frederick G. Robie Residence
of 1906, the Avery Coonley Residence of 1907, the F.F. Tomek Residence
of 1907, the Meyer May Residence of 1908, the David M. Amberg Residence
of 1909, the E.P. Irving Residence of 1909, the Robert Mueller Residence of 1909, the F.C. Bogk Residence of 1916, the Henry J. Allen
Residence of 1917, the Susan Lawrence Dana Residence of 1903, and
possibly the Darwin D. Martin Residence of 1904. An account of
Niedecken is given in David A. Hanks' *The Decorative Designs of Frank
Lloyd Wright* (New York: E.P. Dutton, 1979) and in the Milwaukee Art

Museum's *The Domestic Scene (1897-1927): George M. Niedecken, Interior
Architect* (Milwaukee: The Milwaukee Art Museum, 1981). Frank Lloyd
Wright related archival materials in the Prairie Archives include:

Robert W. Roloson Apartments (1894)
Chicago, Illinois
  A terra-cotta ornamental baluster measuring 16-7/8 in. x
  7-7/8 in. x 7-7/8 in. (428.6 mm x 200.1 mm x 200.1 mm).

Susan Lawrence Dana Residence (1902)
Springfield, Illinois
  Drawing of a leaded glass hanging light fixture drawn in ink
  and watercolor on paper measuring 8 in. x 7-1/2 in. (203.2 mm
  x 190.5 mm). This is a drawing by George M. Niedecken inscribed with his monograph and attributed to the Dana Residence although not labeled as such.

Larkin Company Administration Building (1903)
Buffalo, New York
  One metal side chair on rollers with original upholstery
  measuring 20-3/4 in. (527.1 mm) in height of seat from floor,
  37-3/8 in. (949.3 mm) in height of back of chair, 16 in.
  (406.4 mm) depth of seat, and 14 in. (355.6 mm) in width
  of seat.

Darwin D. Martin Residence (1904)
Buffalo, New York
  A fireplace mural study drawing done on tracing paper in
  pencil and watercolor measuring 9 in. x 12 in. (228.6 mm x
  304.8 mm). This drawing was done by George M. Niedecken and
  is only attributed to the Martin Residence but not labeled
  as such.
  "Tree of Life" stained glass window measuring 41-1/2 in. x
  22-1/2 in. (1054.1 mm x 571.5 mm). A detailed account of the
  acquisition of this window can be found in "Art Center Gets
  Wright Work" (*The Milwaukee Journal*, August 25, 1978,
  Section 2), p. 1.

Frederick G. Robie Residence (1906)
Chicago, Illinois
  A watercolor on kraft paper drawing for the living room, dining
  room, and hall rugs measuring 15-1/8± in. x 40-3/8± in.
  (380.0 mm x 1025.0 mm).
  Drawing of the dining room scheme drawn on paper with brown
  ink and measuring 23 in. x 25-1/2 in. (584.2 mm x 647.7 mm).
  Perspective drawing of andirons which is drawn with pencil on
  kraft paper measuring 8-1/2 in. x 11-3/4 in. (209.6 mm x
  298.5 mm).
  Drawing of the breakfast table, done in pencil on kraft paper
  measuring 6-1/2 in. x 8 in. (165.1 mm x 203.2 mm).
  Drawing of the living room lamp, done in pencil on tracing
  paper measuring 11-3/4 in. x 9 in. (298.5 mm x 228.6 mm).
  Presentation drawing on cardboard mount of the billiard room
  with a sketch by Frank Lloyd Wright on the reverse side. The
  presentation drawing is drawn in pencil and watercolor on
  paper measuring 10-1/4 in. x 31-1/4 in. (260.6 mm x 793.8 mm)
  with the Niedecken-Walbridge logo in the upper left corner
  of the drawing.

Primary rug design drawing done in pencil and watercolor on
kraft paper mounted on cardboard measuring 14-3/4 in. x 13-
1/2 in. (374.7 mm x 342.9 mm).

Primary rug design drawing done in pencil and watercolor on
kraft paper mounted on cardboard measuring 14-3/4 in. x
13-1/2 in. (374.7 mm x 342.9 mm).

Secondary rug design drawing, inscribed "Hall rug for Mr.
F.C. Robie, Chicago, Ill.," drawn in pencil and watercolor
on kraft paper measuring 9-3/4 in. x 13 in. (247.7 mm x
330.2 mm).

Wool color chart drawing done in pencil on kraft paper, inscribed "Rug #68-69," with sample wool swatches, measures
10-1/4 in. x 7-7/8 in. (260.6 mm x 200.1 mm).

Handwritten (not in Wright's hand) price list for furniture
to Mr. Taylor (second owner) in pencil on kraft paper
measuring 9-5/8 in. x 6-1/4 in. (244.4 mm x 158.8 mm).

Perspective drawing of andirons drawn in pencil on kraft paper
measuring 8-7/8 in. x 10-1/4 in. (225.4 mm x 260.6 mm); a
handwritten inscription in pencil reads "Andiron-Robies."

Perspective drawing of dresser, inscribed "Dresser for Robie,"
drawn in pencil on kraft paper measuring 10-1/8 in. x
8-1/8 in. (257.2 mm x 206.4 mm).

Perspective drawing of a small lamp drawn in pencil on tracing
paper and measuring 9 in. x 8-1/4 in. (228.6 mm x 209.6 mm).

Drawing of a breakfast table drawn in pencil on tracing paper
showing the side view, front view, plan, and detail measuring 10 in. x 10-1/4 in. (254.0 mm x 260.4 mm).

Perspective drawing of davenport, inscribed with handwritten
note "Hold for fututr [sic]," and drawn in pencil on tracing
paper measuring 7-1/2 in. x 13-1/4 in. (190.5 mm x 336.6 mm).

Rug layout plan for rugs #70-71-72 dated "June 14-'10," with
other pencil notations, drawn in pencil on tracing paper
measuring 17-3/4 in. x 10 in. (450.9 mm x 254.0 mm).

Layout plan for stair hall rugs, inscribed "Robie Stair Hall
Rugs," drawn in pencil on tracing paper measuring 9-5/8 in.
x 7-5/8 in. (244.4 mm x 193.7 mm).

Full-size drawings of carpet details drawn in pencil on kraft
and tracing paper.

All drawings listed for the Robie Residence were drawn by George
M. Niedecken.

Avery Coonley Residence (1907)
Riverside, Illinois

Drawing of a hall chair done in ink and watercolor on tracing
paper measuring 9-3/4 in. x 6 in. (247.7 mm x 152.4 mm).

Drawing of a hall chair done in pencil on kraft paper measuring 10-3/8 in. x 5-1/2 in. (263.5 mm x 139.7 mm).

Drawing of a desk for the rear guest room drawn in pencil on
kraft paper measuring 7-1/2 in. x 5-1/2 in. (190.5 mm x
139.7 mm).

Perspective drawing of a desk for a guest room drawn with
pencil on kraft paper measuring 10-1/4 in. x 9-3/4 in.
(273.1 mm x 247.7 mm).

Drawing of rug no. 1 done in colored pencil on tracing paper
measuring 21-1/2 in. x 31-1/4 in. (546.1 mm x 793.8 mm).

Drawing of a dining room rug done with colored pencil on tracing paper measuring 9-5/8 in. x 11-1/2 in. (244.5 mm x
292.1 mm).

Drawing for the hall rug done with colored pencil on tracing
paper measuring 8-3/8 in. x 9-1/8 in. (212.7 mm x 231.8 mm).
Perspective drawing of a table, inscribed "Coonley," drawn
in pencil on tracing paper measuring 6-3/4 in. x 4-3/4 in.
(171.4 mm x 120.7 mm).
Mechanically drawn perspective drawing of a bedroom chair,
with various notations in pencil, drawn in pencil on kraft
paper measuring 8-1/2 in. x 5-5/8 in. (215.9 mm x 142.9 mm).
Drawing for lower hall flower table, with handwritten notations, drawn in pencil on kraft paper measuring 8-1/4 in. x
7-3/8 in. (209.6 mm x 187.3 mm).
Drawing of flower table for second story hall, with written
pencil notations, drawn in pencil on kraft paper measuring
8-3/8 in. x 6-1/4 in. (212.7 mm x 158.8 mm).
Kindergarten table drawing done in pencil on kraft paper
measuring 7-1/4 in. x 11-7/8 in. (184.2 mm x 301.6 mm).
Drawing for a bedroom rocking chair, with pencil notation
"1 of these," measures 7-3/4 in. x 5-1/4 in. (196.9 mm x
133.4 mm).
Drawing of a flower table drawn in pencil on kraft paper
measuring 6-1/4 in. x 4-5/8 in. (158.8 mm x 117.5 mm).
Rear guest room double bed drawing done in pencil on kraft
paper measuring 7-1/2± in. x 13-1/2± in. (190.5± mm x
342.9± mm).
Drawing of a table done in pencil on kraft paper measuring
6-5/8 in. x 5-3/4 in. (168.3 mm x 146.1 mm).
Drawing of a table, done in pencil on tracing paper, with the
inscription "Coonley" and measuring 6-3/4 in. x 5-1/8 in.
(171.5 mm x 130.2 mm).
Drawing of a side chair drawn in pencil on kraft paper,
with pencil notations and crossed out designs on the reverse side, measuring 10-1/2 in. x 14 in. (266.7 mm x
355.6 mm).
Perspective drawing of a rocking chair, with inscription
"Coonley," drawn in pencil on kraft paper measuring 6-1/4
in. x 4-1/2 in. (158.8 mm x 114.3 mm).
Drawing of lamp designs has handwritten inscription "Coonley,"
and is drawn in pencil and colored pencil on kraft paper
measuring 6-1/4 in. x 8-1/4 in. (158.8 mm x 209.6 mm).
Detail drawing of lamp shade has pencil notation "$5.00"
on front and "Coonley" on reverse. It is drawn in pencil
and colored pencil on tracing paper measuring 15-1/2 in. x
15-1/2 in. (393.7 mm x 393.7 mm).
Drawing of a table has handwritten inscription, "Coonley,"
and is drawn in pencil on tracing paper measuring 6-1/8± in.
x 5± in. (155.6± mm x 127.0± mm).
Color swatches for wool runner rugs with notation in ink
"order'd. feb. 18, '09," mounted on Niedecken-Walbridge
stationery measuring 6-1/2 in. x 6 in. (165.1 mm x 152.4 mm).
Drawing of the main bedroom rug, with handwritten notation
at top of sheet "Avery Coonley." Drawing is done in pencil
and watercolor on tracing paper measuring 19± in. x 27± in.
(482.6± mm x 685.8± mm).
Working sketch of carpet drawn in pencil and colored pencil
on tracing paper measuring 17-1/2 in. x 16-1/4 in. (444.5
mm x 412.8 mm).

Mural design, inscribed "#244," drawn in watercolor and ink on kraft paper mounted on cardboard measuring 8-1/2 in. x 15 in. (215.9 mm x 381.0 mm).

Drawing of mural design in two pieces; inscribed on the two pieces are a pencil notation "1909" on the reverse and "#245" in the lower right corner; each drawing measures 3-1/2 in. x 15-1/4 in. (89.9 mm x 387.4 mm).

Drawing of a mural design, with George M. Niedecken's monogram and inscription, "#246," in lower right corner. Drawing is done in watercolor and ink on kraft paper mounted on cardboard measuring 9 in. x 23 in. (228.6 mm x 584.2 mm).

Eight drawings of full-size carpet details drawn in various mediums, mostly in pencil and colored pencil, on tracing paper of varying sizes.

Bedroom rug color charts, with wool samples, on kraft paper measuring 8 in. x 7 in. (203.2 mm x 177.8 mm).

Drawing of a hall rug design, with various notations, drawn in colored pencil on tracing paper measuring 8-3/4 in. x 9-1/8 in. (222.3 mm x 231.8 mm).

Various full-size cartoons for rug designs drawn in various mediums, mostly on paper.

All drawings listed for the Coonley Residence were by George M. Niedecken.

F.F. Tomek Residence (1907)
Riverside, Illinois

Drawing of two elevations of an upholstered oak armchair done in pencil and colored pencil on paper mounted on cardboard measuring 7-1/4 in. x 4-3/4 in. (184.2 mm x 120.7 mm).

Drawing of two elevations of an oak plant stand drawn in pencil and colored pencil on tracing paper mounted on cardboard measuring 7-1/8± in. x 4-3/8± in. (181.0± mm x 111.1± mm).

Drawing of two elevations of an upholstered armchair, inscribed "F.F. Tomek" in lower left corner, drawn in pencil and colored pencil on tracing paper measuring 7 in. x 4-5/8 in. (177.8 mm x 117.5 mm).

Drawing of two elevations of upholstered armchair, inscribed "F.F. Tomek" in lower left corner, drawn in pencil and colored pencil on tracing paper measuring 7-1/8 in. x 4-5/8 in. (181.0 mm x 117.5 mm).

Drawing of two elevations of a library table, inscribed "F.F. Tomek," drawn in pencil and colored pencil on tracing paper measuring 10-1/2 in. x 4-1/4 in. (266.7 mm x 108.0 mm).

Drawing of two elevations of a side chair, inscribed "F.F. Tomek" in lower left corner, drawn in pencil and colored pencil on tracing paper measuring 7-1/8 in. x 4-5/8 in. (181.0 mm x 117.5 mm).

All drawings listed for the Tomek Residence were drawn by George M. Niedecken.

Meyer May Residence (1908)
Grand Rapids, Michigan

Perspective drawing of a plant stand, initialed in pencil by Meyer May in the lower right corner, also has the design of door knobs at the top of the drawing. The drawing is done in pencil on tracing paper and measures 7-1/2 in. x 6-1/2 in. (190.5 mm x 165.1 mm).

Perspective drawing of the dining room table and three chairs,
inscribed in pencil "M.S." and "12 ch., 1 table" in lower
right corner, drawn in pencil on tracing paper measuring
6-3/4 in. x 9-3/4 in. (171.5 mm x 247.7 mm).

Perspective drawing of a table lamp, inscribed in pencil "O.K.
M.S. May," and drawn in pencil and colored pencil on tracing
paper measuring 8-1/4 in. x 5-3/4 in. (209.6 mm x 146.1 mm).

Perspective drawing of a davenport, inscribed in pencil on the
lower edge "Coppied[sic] May House, Grand Rapids, Mich."
and on the left edge "May." There is an unidentified rough
sketch, possibly a light fixture, on the reverse side of
the main part of the drawing. The drawing is done in pencil
on kraft paper and measures 10-7/8 in. x 20-5/8 in. (276.2 mm
x 523.9 mm).

Perspective drawing of a dresser and table scarf, with a
drawing of a bed and bedspread on the reverse side, done
in pencil on kraft paper measuring 10-1/2 in. x 10-7/8 in.
(266.7 mm x 276.2 mm).

Perspective drawing of a pencil tray, with pencil notations
relating to size and cost on both sides, drawn in pencil
on kraft paper measuring 7-1/4 in. x 10-1/2 in. (184.2 mm x
266.7 mm).

Perspective drawing of a footstool drawn in pencil on kraft
paper measuring 5 in. x 5 in. (127.0 mm x 127.0 mm).

Perspective drawing of dresser with mirror and table scarf.
Inscribed "OK M.S." in pencil on lower right of drawing
which is done in pencil on tracing paper measuring 10 in. x
8-3/8 in. (254.0 mm x 212.7 mm).

Perspective drawing and elevation of a plant stand, with an
inscription "May" in pencil on right of drawing. It is done
in pencil on kraft paper measuring 14 in. x 12-1/2 in.
(355.6 mm x 317.5 mm).

Perspective drawing of davenport, with Meyer May's initials
in pencil on lower right corner of drawing, done in pencil
on tracing paper measuring 8-1/4 in. x 13-3/4 in. (209.6 mm
x 349.3 mm).

Drawing of the profile of baseboard trim drawn in pencil on
bond paper measuring 13 in. x 8-1/2 in. (330.2 mm x 215.9
mm).

Perspective drawing of chair, inscribed with Meyer May's initials and "#328" and cost notes, drawn in pencil on tracing
paper measuring 8-1/2 in. x 8-1/8 in. (215.9 mmx 206.4 mm).

Perspective drawing of table with cabinet built into bottom
and table scarf. Drawing is done on tracing paper with pencil and measures 8-1/16 in. x 9-1/16 in. (204.8 mm x 230.2
mm). It is initialed by Meyer May.

Perspective drawing of a lamp with a glass shade, inscribed
"May" in blue pencil on the upper center portion of the
drawing, done in pencil on kraft paper measuring 9-3/8 in. x
7-1/2 in. (238.1 mm x 190.5 mm).

Perspective drawing of a clock drawn in pencil on kraft paper
measuring 4 in. x 5-1/2 in. (101.6 mm x 139.7 mm).

Perspective drawing of an armchair is inscribed with Meyer
May's initials and drawn in pencil on tracing paper measuring 11 in. x 13-3/4 in. (279.4 mm x 349.3 mm).

Perspective drawing of an inkwell has pencil notation "May's
Res." It is drawn on kraft paper measuring 4-3/4± in. x
10-1/2± in. (120.7± mm x 266.7± mm).

Front and side view of a living room table lamp has inscription "2 of these" in pencil notation and is drawn in pencil on
kraft paper measuring 9-1/2± in. x 8-5/8± in. (241.3± mm x
219.1± mm).

Perspective drawing of a small table, table runner design, and
chair is initialed in pencil by Meyer May and drawn in pencil and watercolor on tracing paper which measures 7-5/8 in.
x 10-1/2 in. (193.7 mm x 266.7 mm).

Perspective drawing of an upholstered chair has pencil initial
of Meyer May and is drawn in pencil on tracing paper measuring 7-1/2 in. x 7-7/8 in. (190.5 mm x 200.1 mm).

Perspective drawing of a palm stand is done in pencil on tracing paper measuring 7-1/2 in. x 6-5/8 in. (190.5 mm x 168.3
mm).

Perspective drawing of a desk lamp has inscription "OK,MM"
in pencil on the lower right corner and is drawn in pencil
on tracing paper measuring 8-1/4 in. x 9-1/4 in. (209.6 mm x
235.0 mm).

Drawing of a living room andiron design has pencil note "Ok,
M May" on the lower right corner and "May" on the reverse
side and is drawn in pencil on tracing paper measuring
20-5/8 in. x 26 in. (523.9 mm x 660.4 mm).

Drawing of a living room andiron design has inscriptions in
lower right and upper left corners "Send to Mr. Niedecken"
and in the center "Revised" and in pencil below the label
"No. 2." The drawing is done in pencil on tracing paper and
measures 21-3/4 in. x 22-1/2 in. (552.5 mm x 571.5 mm).

Perspective drawing of a rocking chair has inscription in
pencil, "O.K. M.S. May," and is drawn in pencil on tracing
paper measuring 8-1/2 in. x 6-3/8 in. (215.9 mm x 161.9 mm).

Drawing of front and side elevations of a dresser, costumer,
and twin bed with mirror is drawn in pencil on tracing paper
measuring 22-3/8 in. x 27 in. (568.3 mm x 685.8 mm). The
drawing contains revisions and notations written in blue pencil, with "May" noted on the reverse side.

Drawing of a ceiling light fixture with handwritten inscription "May" and cost notations on the lower left corner. The
drawing is done in pencil on kraft paper measuring 11-3/4
in. x 12-7/8 in. (298.5 mm x 327.1 mm).

Perspective drawing of a stamp box has a pencil notation
"May's Res." and is drawn in pencil on kraft paper measuring
5 in. x 6-3/4 in. (127.0 mm x 171.5 mm).

Wool color chart, with wool samples attached, drawn in pencil
on kraft paper measuring 10-1/2 in. x 6-3/4 in. (266.7 mm x
171.5 mm).

Rough perspective drawing of a chair with sliding arms has
pencil notation "Mr. May's Res." and is drawn in pencil on
tracing paper measuring 8-5/8 in. x 7-5/8 in. (219.1 mm x
193.7 mm).

Perspective drawing of morning room ceiling drop lamp inscribed "#315, Woodframe-glass shade" on the lower right
corner of the drawing. It is done in pencil on tracing paper
measuring 10-3/8 in. x 9 in. (263.5 mm x 228.6 mm).

Perspective drawing of a desk lamp has inscription "Desk Lamp
For Mr. May's Res. Chicago, Ill. [sic]" in lower left corner
and is drawn in pencil on tracing paper measuring 8-1/4 in.
x 5-3/8 in. (209.6 mm x 136.5 mm).
Perspective drawing of a footstool has inscription "#317.L.R.
Foot Stool For Mr. May's Res. Chicago, Ill. [sic]" in pencil
in lower left corner and is drawn in pencil on tracing paper
measuring 10-1/4 in. x 6-1/4 in. (260.4 mm x 158.8 mm).
Perspective drawing of stamp box drawn in pencil on tracing
paper measuring 6 in. x 8-1/8 in. (152.4 mm x 206.4 mm).
Perspective drawing of ink blotter drawn in pencil on tracing
paper measuring 6-1/4 in. x 8-1/2 in. (158.8 mm x 215.9 mm).
Drawing of a chair cushion design has inscription of the
Niedecken-Walbridge Co. rubber stamp in the upper left
corner and is drawn in pencil and colored pencil on tracing
paper measuring 12 in. x 14 in. (304.8 mm x 355.6 mm).
Perspective drawing of a gas log fireplace for the main bedroom has measurement notations and is drawn in pencil on
kraft paper measuring 13 in. x 11-1/2 in. (330.2 mm x
292.1 mm).
Perspective drawing of plant stand is drawn in pencil on tracing paper measuring 6-1/4 in. x 4-3/4 in. (158.8 mm x 120.7
mm).
Perspective drawing of costumer placed against a baseboard
detail has inscription "O.K. M.S. May" on the right edge and
is drawn in pencil on tracing paper measuring 11-3/4 in. x
7-5/8 in. (298.5 mm x 193.7 mm).
Perspective drawing of hall chair has May's initials in pencil
on the lower right corner of the drawing and is done in
pencil on tracing paper measuring 9-3/4 in. x 8-1/2 in.
(247.7 mm x 215.9 mm).
Drawing of a costumer design has pencil notation "to be traced
and mailed to Mr. Niedecken" and is drawn in pencil on tracing paper measuring 27 in. x 7-1/2 in. (685.8 mm x 190.5 mm).
This drawing is from the office of Frank Lloyd Wright.
Drawing of dressing table, chaise, and floor lamp designs has
inscriptions of several price and measurement notations and
is done in pencil on tracing paper measuring 27 in. x
38-1/4 in. (685.8 mm x 971.6 mm).
Drawing of a hanging morning room lamp design is inscribed
with Meyer May's initials and is drawn in pencil on tracing
paper measuring 12-1/4 in. x 8-1/2 in. (311.2 mm x 215.9 mm).
Drawing of a table plan (section through top of table) is
drawn in pencil on tracing paper measuring 4-5/8 in. x 6 in.
(117.5 mm x 152.4 mm).
Drawing of table is inscribed with May's initials and drawn
in pencil on tracing paper measuring 8 in. x 9-1/2 in.
(203.2 mm x 241.3 mm).
Drawing of a dresser design done in pencil on tracing paper
measuring 9 in. x 9-1/2 in. (228.6 mm x 241.3 mm).
Perspective drawing of gas log fireplace drawn in pencil on
tracing paper measuring 9-3/4 in. x 8-1/2 in. (247.7 mm x
215.9 mm).
Drawing of a record cabinet design has handwritten instructions
and notations and is drawn in pencil on tracing paper measuring 12-5/8 in. x 16-1/8 in. (320.7 mm x 409.6 mm).

Perspective drawing of a desk lamp with glass shade is inscribed "May" and is drawn in pencil on kraft paper measuring 4-3/4 in. x 6-7/8 in. (120.7 mm x 174.6 mm).

Perspective drawing of clothes and umbrella stand is drawn
in pencil on kraft paper measuring 14+ in. x 7-3/4+ in.
(355.6+ mm x 196.9+ mm).

Perspective drawing of an ink pad is done in pencil on kraft
paper and is inscribed with various notations regarding
measurements and materials. The drawing measures 6-3/4 in.
x 8-3/4 in. (171.5 mm x 222.3 mm).

Perspective drawing of an ink blotter is done in pencil on
kraft paper and is inscribed with various measurements,
also in pencil. The drawing measures 6 in. x 6-7/8 in.
(152.4 mm x 174.6 mm).

Perspective drawing of an inkwell drawn in pencil on tracing
paper measuring 5-7/8 in. x 7-1/2 in. (149.2 mm x 190.5 mm).

Perspective drawing of an ink pad drawn in pencil on tracing
paper measuring 5-1/4 in. x 8-3/4 in. (133.4 mm x 222.3 mm).

Perspective drawing of a pencil tray is drawn in pencil on
tracing paper measuring 5-3/4 in. x 9 in. (146.1 mm x
228.6 mm).

Drawing of the front and side views of a hanging light for a
dressing table is done in pencil and colored pencil on
tracing paper measuring 14-1/2 in. x 13-7/8 in. (368.3 mm x
352.4 mm).

Various full-size carpet details drawn in pencil and colored
pencil on kraft paper and tracing paper of various sizes.

All drawings listed for the May Residence were drawn by George
M. Niedecken unless otherwise noted.

David M. Amberg Residence (1909)
Grand Rapids, Michigan

Drawing of a plan and elevation for a fireplace design has
inscription "Amberg" in lower right corner and is drawn
with pencil and colored pencil on tracing paper measuring
8-1/4 in. x 10-1/8 in. (209.6 mm x 257.2 mm).

Drawing of a lamp design has a handwritten inscription "Amberg"
and is drawn in pencil on kraft paper measuring 7-1/4 in. x
6-1/2 in. (184.2 mm x 165.1 mm).

Perspective drawing of a chair design has pencil notation "3
rockers" and is drawn in pencil on kraft paper measuring
7-7/8 in. x 4-3/4 in. (200.1 mm x 120.7 mm).

Perspective drawing of living room wall lamp has handwritten
inscription "Amberg" and is drawn in pencil on kraft paper
measuring 7-3/8 in. x 5-5/8 in. (187.3 mm x 142.9 mm).

Perspective drawing of a living room chair has handwritten
inscription "2 chairs" in the lower right corner and is
drawn in pencil on kraft paper measuring 7-3/8 in. x
5-5/8 in. (187.3 mm x 142.9 mm).

Perspective drawing of a rocking chair is drawn in pencil on
kraft paper and measures 6-3/4 in. x 5-7/8 in. (171.5 mm x
149.2 mm).

Perspective drawing of breakfast table is drawn in pencil on
kraft paper measuring 8-1/2 in. x 7-3/4 in. (215.9 mm x
196.9 mm).

Drawing of a lamp design showing two views drawn in pencil
on tracing paper measuring 5-5/8 in. x 6-3/4 in. (142.9 mm
x 171.5 mm).
Drawing of two views of a plant stand has the inscription
"Amberg" and is drawn in pencil on tracing paper measuring
6-3/8 in. x 8-1/4 in. (161.9 mm x 209.6 mm).
Perspective drawing of a living room table and chair drawn
in pencil on kraft paper measuring 7-1/2± in. x 12± in.
(190.5± mm x 304.8± mm).
Perspective drawing of dining set drawn in pencil on kraft
paper measuring 8-1/8± in. x 13± in. (206.4± mm x 330.2±
mm).
Drawing of the front and side elevations of a mirror, sewing
cabinet, and plant stand is drawn in pencil on tracing paper
measuring 13-1/2 in. x 11-3/4 in. (342.9 mm x 298.5 mm).
Perspective drawing of a table has inscription "$21.00 each"
and is drawn in pencil on kraft paper measuring 7 in. x
3-3/4 in. (177.8 mm x 95.3 mm).
Perspective drawing of a table lamp has inscription "Amberg"
and is drawn in pencil on kraft paper measuring 8-1/8 in.
x 4-1/8 in. (206.4 mm x 104.8 mm).
Drawing of a rocking chair design has inscription "ordered
Aug. 3/11. GMN" and is drawn in pencil on tracing paper
measuring 7-5/8 in. x 9-1/8 in. (193.7 mm x 231.8 mm).
Revised perspective drawing of a rocking chair drawn with
pencil on tracing paper measuring 6-1/4 in. x 4-1/4 in.
(158.8 mm x 108.0 mm).
Drawing of revised front and side design for pier glass drawn
in pencil on tracing paper measuring 11-3/4 in. x 9-3/8
in. (298.5 mm x 238.1 mm).
Drawing of the front and side views of a rocking chair is
done in pencil on tracing paper measuring 6 in. x 8-7/8 in.
(152.4 mm x 225.4 mm).
Drawing of the front and side view of an umbrella stand has
pencil inscription "$75.00" and is drawn in pencil on trac-
ing paper measuring 11-1/2 in. x 9 in. (292.1 mm x 228.6 mm).
Perspective drawing of a rocking chair drawn in pencil on
tracing paper measuring 8-1/8 in. x 10 in. (206.4 mm x
254.0 mm).
Drawing of a desk design done in pencil on paper measuring
6-5/8 in. x 5-1/4 in. (168.3 mm x 133.4 mm).
Drawing of the front and side views of a desk design is done
in pencil on tracing paper measuring 8-5/8 in. x 9-5/8 in.
(219.1 mm x 244.5 mm).
Drawing of the wall treatment recess for hall portrait is
done in pencil on tracing paper and is inscribed "O.K.
R.A.L." The drawing measures 11-1/2 in. x 12-1/2 in.
(292.1 mm x 317.5 mm).
Drawing for a morning room rug design drawn in pencil and
watercolor on tracing paper measuring 11-1/2 in. x 10-1/2
in. (292.1 mm x 266.7 mm) with 3 in. x 3-3/4 in. (76.2 mm
x 95.3 mm) added onto the right side.
Drawing of a fireplace design has inscription "Chas. Sheam,
#565 So. Ionia Ave., Grand Rapids, Mich." and is drawn in
pencil on tracing paper measuring 9-5/8 in. x 10-1/2 in.
(244.5 mm x 266.7 mm).

Drawing of an upholstered chair drawn in pencil on tracing
paper measuring 10 in. x 11-1/8 in. (254.0 mm x 282.6 mm).
Drawing of a section, elevation, and plan of a lampshade
design measures 18-1/2 in. x 12-1/2 in. (469.9 mm x 317.5
mm).
Perspective drawing of the original rocking chair design
is drawn in pencil on tracing paper measuring 6-1/4+ in.
x 4-3/8+ in. (158.8+ mm x 111.1+ mm).
Drawing of the fireplace elevation has note "Amberg" on the
front and brown ink sketches on the back. The drawing is
done in pencil on kraft paper and measures 7-1/2 in. x
12 in. (190.5 mm x 304.8 mm).
Front and side elevations of a dresser design has note
"#333" and is drawn in pencil on tracing paper measuring
12-1/8 in. x 13 in. (308.0 mm x 330.2 mm).
Drawing of a sideboard lantern detail has cost notes on the
reverse side and is drawn in pencil on tracing paper
measuring 22-1/4 in. x 17 in. (565.2 mm x 431.8 mm).
Drawing of a table lamp design has inscriptions "Amberg" and
"one of these" and is drawn in pencil on tracing paper
measuring 9-1/2 in. x 6-1/4 in. (241.3 mm x 158.8 mm).
Drawing of front and side elevation of an upholstered armchair design is inscribed "$29.00" and drawn in pencil on
tracing paper measuring 6-7/8 in. x 11-1/8 in. (174.6 mm x
282.6 mm).
Drawing of front and side elevation of a side chair design
is inscribed "Ordered Aug. 3/11.GMN" and is done in pencil
on tracing paper measuring 8 in. x 8-1/4 in. (203.2 mm x
209.6 mm).
Drawing of the front and side views of pier glass and cabinet
design is inscribed "Amberg" in pencil and is drawn in pencil on tracing paper measuring 15 in. x 11-1/4 in. (381.0
mm x 285.8 mm).
Drawing of the front, side, and rear views of the morning
room chair design has note "#331" and is drawn in pencil
on tracing paper measuring 8-3/4 in. x 11-3/8 in. (222.3
mm x 288.9 mm).
Drawing of front and side views of a piano lamp design has
penciled note "$100.00" and is drawn in pencil on tracing
paper measuring 13-1/4 in. x 10 in. (336.6 mm x 254.0 mm).
Drawing of the front and side views of a table and lamp design has inscription "Ordered Aug 3/11. GMN" and is drawn
in pencil on tracing paper measuring 9-5/8 in. x 11-1/4 in.
(244.9 mm x 285.8 mm).
Drawing of small fixtures throughout house is done in pencil
on tracing paper measuring 13-1/4 in. x 20-1/4 in. (336.6
mm x 514.4 mm).
Drawing of bedroom furniture designs consisting of a woman's
dresser and seven double beds showing the front and side
views is drawn in pencil on tracing paper measuring 12 in.
x 24-3/4 in. (304.8 mm x 628.7 mm).
Drawing of the front and side views of a dressing table
design is drawn in pencil on tracing paper measuring
10-1/8 in. x 12-1/8 in. (257.2 mm x 308.0 mm).
Drawing of lighting and glass designs is done in pencil on
kraft paper measuring 8-7/8 in. x 9 in. (225.4 mm x 228.6 mm).

Drawing of front and side views of an umbrella stand is drawn
in pencil on tracing paper measuring 6-3/4 in. x 7-1/2 in.
(171.5 mm x 190.5 mm).
Revised perspective drawing of a straight chair is drawn in
pencil on tracing paper measuring 6-1/2 in. x 4-1/8 in.
(165.1 mm x 104.8 mm).
Drawing of a bed design is done in pencil on tracing paper
measuring 8-1/2 in. x 12-1/4 in. (215.9 mm x 311.2 mm).
Drawing of the front and side views of a double bed design
is inscribed "#326" and "Ordered Aug. 3/11. GMN" and drawn
in pencil on tracing paper measuring 10-1/8 in. x 13-1/4 in.
(257.2 mm x 336.6 mm).
Drawing of front elevation and plan for a mantel design is
done in pencil on tracing paper measuring 10-1/2 in. x 9 in.
(266.7 mm x 228.6 mm).
Drawing of a humidor design has inscription "Ordered July
19/11. GMN" and is drawn in pencil on tracing paper measuring 9-3/4 in. x 8-1/4 in. (247.7 mm x 209.6 mm).
Various full-size carpet details drawn in pencil and colored
pencil on tracing paper in varying sizes.
Wool color chart, with wool samples attached, dated "July 18,
'11" is drawn in pencil on kraft paper measuring 8-3/4 in. x
7-1/8 in. (222.3 mm x 181.0 mm).
Wool color chart, with wool samples attached, dated "GMN
June 6/11" is drawn in pencil on kraft paper measuring
9-1/4 in. x 6-3/4 in. (235.0 mm x 171.5 mm).
All drawings for the Amberg Residence were drawn by George M.
Niedecken.

E.P. Irving Residence (1909)
Decatur, Illinois
Perspective drawing of couch and easy chair has pencil notation "28. each" and is drawn in pencil on kraft paper
measuring 7 in. x 12-1/2 in. (177.8 mm x 317.5 mm).
Perspective drawing of a side chair has pencil notation
"$16." and is drawn in pencil on kraft paper measuring 7 in.
x 5-1/4 in. (177.8 mm x 133.4 mm).
Perspective drawing of a service table, table runner, and
floral design has pencil notation "$65" and is drawn in
pencil on kraft paper measuring 5-1/2 in. x 7-7/8 in.
(139.7 mm x 200.1 mm).
Perspective drawing of a rocking chair has pencil notation
"$31." and is drawn in pencil on kraft paper measuring
8 in. x 6-1/2 in. (203.2 mm x 165.1 mm).
Perspective drawing of a rocking chair has pencil notation
"$19." and is drawn in pencil on kraft paper measuring
7 in. x 5-5/8 in. (177.8 mm x 142.9 mm).
Perspective drawing of reception room and table runner has
penciled notation "35." and is drawn in pencil on kraft
paper measuring 6 in. x 5 in. (152.4 mm x 127.0 mm).
Perspective drawing of a side chair is drawn in pencil on
kraft paper and has a pencil notation "Von Holst & Fyfe"
on top of drawing which measures 5 in. x 10 in. (127.0 mm x
254.0 mm).
Perspective drawing of a table, couch, and desk with a
lighting unit is drawn in pencil on kraft paper and has

inscription "Irving" on reverse side. Drawing measures
8 in. x 12-1/8 in. (203.2 mm x 308.0 mm).

Drawing of a fragment of a corner rug detail is done in pencil
on tracing paper and has inscribed pencil notations and instructions. The drawing measures 9 in. x 7-3/4 in. (228.6
mm x 196.9 mm).

Rough sketch of views of a rocking chair drawn in pencil on
tracing paper has various notations written in pencil. The
sketch measures 12-1/8 in. x 14-3/4 in. (308.0 mm x 374.7 mm).

Guest room rug drawing, rug #130, is done in pencil and watercolor on tracing paper measuring 8-3/4 in. x 10 in. (222.3 mm
x 254.0 mm).

Perspective drawing of wrap table is drawn in pencil on kraft
paper measuring 7-3/4 in. x 8-3/8 in. (196.9 mm x 212.7 mm).
This drawing could also be for the Amberg Residence designed
by Wright.

Drawing of a rug plan for the guest room is done in pencil and
watercolor on tracing paper and has various notations in
pencil. The drawing measures 9 in. x 7-3/4 in. (228.6 mm x
196.9 mm).

Drawing of detail of trim done in pencil on tracing paper with
various inscribed pencil notations and instructions. The
drawing measures 10-5/8 in. x 9-1/2 in. (269.9 mm x 241.3 mm).
This drawing, though not specifically identified with the
Irving Residence, was with the Irving Residence materials
received from the donor of the Irving Residence drawings.

Drawing of the front and side views of a table lamp design
has notations regarding the cost of glass and is drawn in
pencil and colored pencil on tracing paper measuring 10-1/2
in. x 10-1/4 in. (266.7 mm x 260.4 mm).

Drawings of full-size carpet details done in pencil on tracing
paper of varying sizes.

Wool color chart, with wool samples attached, for stair rugs
is drawn in pencil on kraft paper measuring 9-3/8 in. x
8 in. (238.1 mm x 203.2 mm).

Wool color chart, with wool color samples attached, for main
floor and guest room rugs is drawn in pencil on kraft paper
measuring 9-1/2 in. x 8 in. (241.3 mm x 203.2 mm).

Drawings of embroidery color samples, with cotton embroidery
samples attached, for draperies and portiers are drawn in
pencil on kraft paper and are inscribed "June 19-'11" in
pencil. The drawings measure 8-1/8 in. x 4-1/4 in. (206.4
mm x 108.0 mm).

Perspective drawing of music cabinet is done in pencil on
kraft paper measuring 11 in. x 6 in. (279.4 mm x 152.4 mm).

Perspective drawing of library table is drawn in pencil on
kraft paper measuring 8-5/8 in. x 6-5/8 in. (219.1 mm x
168.3 mm).

Drawing of rug designs is done in ink and watercolor on tracing paper measuring 21 in. x 34-3/4 in. (533.4 mm x 882.7
mm).

All drawings for the Irving Residence were drawn by George M.
Niedecken.

Robert Mueller Residence (1909)
Decatur, Illinois

Drawing of a rug layout done in pencil and colored pencil on
tracing paper has several notations in pencil and measures
18-7/8 in. x 30 in. (479.4 mm x 762.0 mm). This drawing
was made by George M. Niedecken.

Imperial Hotel (1915)
Tokyo, Japan
   Dining chair made of elm recovered with naugahyde and measuring
   37-1/2 in. x 15-1/2 in. x 18 in. (952.5 mm x 393.7 mm x
   457.2 mm).

F.C. Bogk Residence (1916)
Milwaukee, Wisconsin
   Drawing of the living room interior done in colored pencil on
   tracing paper measuring 14 in. x 18 in. (355.6 mm x 457.2 mm).
   Drawing of the dining room table and chairs done in pencil on
   tracing paper measuring 18-1/4 in. x 32-1/2 in. (463.6 mm x
   825.5 mm).
   Drawing of a plan for rugs drawn in pencil on paper measuring
   30-3/4 in. x 34-1/4 in. (781.1 mm x 870.0 mm).
   Drawing of a plan for a hallway rug which is drawn in pencil
   on paper measuring 22 in. x 35 in. (558.8 mm x 889.0 mm).
   Drawing of a dining room rug detail done in colored pencil on
   tracing paper which measures 22 in. x 34-3/4 in. (558.8 mm
   x 882.7 mm).
   Drawing of the entry stairs rug detail which is drawn in
   colored pencil on tracing paper and measures 22 in. x
   34-3/4 in. (558.8 mm x 882.7 mm).
   Drawing of a hall radiator screen design done in pencil on
   tracing paper measuring 19 in. x 18 in. (482.6 mm x 457.2 mm).
   This drawing is from the office of Frank Lloyd Wright.
   Numerous wool samples for carpets.
   Drawing of a radiator screen design for the dining room is
   drawn in pencil on tracing paper measuring 15-1/2 in. x
   22 in. (393.7 mm x 558.8 mm). This drawing is from the office
   of Frank Lloyd Wright.
   Drawing of the plan for a library table done in pencil on trac-
   ing paper measuring 16-1/4 in. x 20-1/2 in. (412.8 mm x
   520.7 mm). This drawing is from the office of Frank Lloyd
   Wright.
   Drawing of a lighting fixture detail drawn in pencil on tracing paper measuring 22-1/2 in. x 26 in. (571.5 mm x 660.4 mm).
   This drawing is from the office of Frank Lloyd Wright.
   Drawing of an upholstered armchair design done in pencil on
   tracing paper measures 15 in. x 21 in. (381.0 mm x 533.4 mm).
   This drawing is from the office of Frank Lloyd Wright.
   Drawing of a detail for the mosaic edge of steps is drawn in
   pencil on tracing paper measuring 13-1/2 in. x 20-1/2 in.
   (342.9 mm x 520.7 mm). This drawing is from the office of
   Frank Lloyd Wright.
   Drawing of a bookcase design drawn in pencil on tracing paper
   measuring 24± in. x 30± in. (609.6± mm x 762.0± mm). This
   drawing is from the office of Frank Lloyd Wright.
   Drawing of rug details done in pencil and colored pencil on
   tracing paper measuring 22 in. x 34-1/4 in. (558.8 mm x
   870.0 mm). This drawing is from the office of Frank Lloyd
   Wright.

Drawing of a telephone stand and stool done in pencil on tracing paper has prices inscribed in pencil and measures 10 in. x 12 in. (254.0 mm x 304.8 mm).

Drawing of a remodeled library table is done in pencil on tracing paper measuring 14-1/4 in. x 21-3/4 in. (362.0 mm x 552.5 mm).

Drawing of a remodeled dining table is drawn in pencil on tracing paper measuring 17 in. x 17-1/4 in. (431.8 mm x 438.2 mm).

Rough sketch of fixture details drawn in pencil on tracing paper measuring 10 in. x 9 in. (254.0 mm x 228.6 mm).

Drawing of a leaf table design is inscribed "O.K. Aug. 31" and is drawn in pencil on tracing paper measuring 9 in. x 12 in. (228.6 mm x 304.8 mm).

Drawing of standard light design done in pencil on tracing paper measuring 18 in. x 12-1/4 in. (457.2 mm x 311.2 mm).

Drawing of a wood grille design done in pencil and colored pencil on tracing paper measuring 12-3/4 in. x 15 in. (323.9 mm x 381.0 mm).

Drawing of a table lamp design drawn in pencil on tracing paper measuring 15-3/4 in. x 13-1/2 in. (400.1 mm x 342.9 mm).

Drawing of a ceiling fixture design drawn in pencil on tracing paper measuring 12 in. x 8-1/2 in. (304.8 mm x 215.9 mm).

Drawing of a table scarf design for the living room done in pencil and colored pencil on tracing paper measuring 14 in. x 15 in. (355.6 mm x 381.0 mm).

Rough sketches of the front and side views of a dining room chair and plant stand design drawn in pencil on tracing paper measuring 11-1/2 in. x 10-1/2 in. (292.1 mm x 266.7 mm).

Drawing for living room andirons done in pencil on tracing paper measuring 16-1/2 in. x 18-1/4 in. (419.1 mm x 463.6 mm).

Drawing of an upholstered couch design has inscription "not ordered" and is drawn in pencil and colored pencil on tracing paper measuring 9± in. x 15± in. (228.6± mm x 381.0± mm).

Drawing of an upholstered davenport design has various pencil notations and is done in pencil on tracing paper measuring 7-1/2 in. x 11 in. (190.5 mm x 279.4 mm).

Drawing of the wall treatment is done in pencil and colored pencil on tracing paper measuring 10-1/2 in. x 14 in. (266.7 mm x 355.6 mm).

Drawing of an upholstered chair design is inscribed "Carpenter-type chair" and drawn in pencil on tracing paper measuring 8 in. x 12-1/4 in. (203.2 mm x 311.2 mm).

Drawing of a table scarf for living room is drawn in pencil and colored pencil on tracing paper measuring 14 in. x 14-1/2 in. (355.6 mm x 368.3 mm).

Drawing of a side chair is inscribed "cane in back" and is drawn in pencil on tracing paper measuring 16-1/4 in. x 6-1/4 in. (412.8 mm x 158.8 mm).

Drawing of a remodeled dining chair design drawn in pencil on tracing paper measuring 14 in. x 14 in. (355.6 mm x 355.6 mm).

Drawing of a plant stand is inscribed "not ordered" and drawn in pencil on tracing paper measuring 9 in. x 11 in. (228.6 mm x 279.4 mm).

Drawing of an upholstered armchair design is inscribed "2 of these" and drawn in pencil on tracing paper measuring 9 in. x 10 in. (228.6 mm x 254.0 mm).

Drawing of a full-size detail of the living room grille drawn
in pencil on tracing paper measuring 18 in. x 57 in. (457.2
mm x 1447.8 mm).
Drawing of a rug color chart, with wool samples attached, is
drawn in pencil on kraft paper measuring 8-1/8 in. x 4-7/8
in. (206.4 mm x 123.8 mm).
All drawings of the Bogk Residence were drawn by George M.
Niedecken unless otherwise noted.

Henry J. Allen Residence (1917)
Wichita, Kansas
Drawing of a dining room table and chairs done in pencil on
tracing paper measuring 14-1/2 in. x 17-5/8 in. (368.3 mm x
447.7 mm).
Drawing of an elevation and plan for a dining room light stand
is drawn in pencil on paper measuring 14-3/4 in. x 7-1/2
in. (374.7 mm x 190.5 mm).
Drawing of a day couch for Mrs. Allen's boudoir is done in
pencil on tracing paper measuring 14-5/8 in. x 17-3/4 in.
(371.5 mm x 450.9 mm).
Drawing of a piano bench and plant stand drawn with colored
pencil on tracing paper measuring 14-5/8 in. 17-7/8 in.
(371.5 mm x 454.0 mm).
Bedroom furniture details drawn in pencil and colored pencil
on tracing paper measuring 14-1/2 in. x 17-1/2 in. (368.3
mm x 444.5 mm). This drawing is from the office of Frank
Lloyd Wright.
Drawing of a table and chair for Mrs. Allen's boudoir done in
pencil and colored pencil on tracing paper measuring 14-1/2
in. x 17-1/2 in. (368.3 mm x 444.5 mm). This drawing is from
the office of Frank Lloyd Wright.
Drawing of a desk for Mrs. Allen's room drawn in pencil on
tracing paper measuring 7-1/4 in. x 9 in. (184.2 mm x
228.6 mm).
Drawing of Mrs. Allen's dressing table done in pencil on kraft
paper measuring 15-1/2 in. x 18-3/4 in. (393.7 mm x 476.3
mm).
Rough sketch of an upholstered armchair design measuring 10 in.
x 8 in. (254.0 mm x 203.2 mm).
Drawing of details of a hall seat done in pencil on tracing
paper measuring 18 in. x 34 in. (457.2 mm x 863.6 mm).
This drawing is from the office of Frank Lloyd Wright.
Drawing for embroidered drapes is inscribed "Embroidered drapes
for Allen's" and drawn in pencil and colored pencil on tracing paper measuring 9-1/2 in. x 10 in. (241.3 mm x 254.0 mm).
Drawing of living room furniture designs is inscribed with
various notations and drawn in pencil and colored pencil on
tracing paper measuring 9-1/2+ in. x 22+ in. (241.3 mm x
558.8+ mm).
Drawing of a living room davenport design is inscribed with
various notations in pencil and done in pencil on tracing
paper measuring 10 in. x 21-1/2 in. (254.0 mm x 546.1 mm).
Drawing of a living room table and cabinet design drawn in
pencil on tracing paper measuring 9-3/4 in. x 23 in.
(247.7 mm x 584.2 mm).

Drawing of chair and table designs for the first floor hall
drawn in pencil on tracing paper measuring 10-1/2 in. x
26-1/2 in. (266.7 mm x 673.1 mm).

Drawing of a hanging fixture done in pencil on tracing paper
measuring 11-1/2 in. x 9-3/4 in. (292.1 mm x 247.7 mm).

Three drapery schemes on drawing done in pencil and colored
pencil on tracing paper measuring 14 in. x 17 in. (355.6 mm
x 431.8 mm).

Drawing of bedroom furniture is drawn in pencil on tracing
paper measuring 12-1/4 in. x 15-1/2 in. (311.2 mm x 393.7
mm).

Drawing of a desk for Mrs. Allen is drawn in pencil on tracing
paper measuring 8-3/4 in. x 12 in. (222.3 mm x 304.8 mm).

Rough sketch of couch drawn in pencil on tracing paper measuring 8 in. x 15 in. (203.2 mm x 381.0 mm).

Drawing of a table for Mrs. Allen's room drawn in pencil and
colored pencil on tracing paper measuring 11 in. x 7-3/4 in.
(279.4 mm x 196.9 mm).

Drawing of an upholstered armchair design done in pencil on
tracing paper measuring 9 in. x 12-3/4 in. (228.6 mm x
323.9 mm).

Drawing of a living room plant stand and table with music
cabinet done in pencil on tracing paper measuring 10 in. x
19-1/4 in. (254.0 mm x 489.0 mm).

Drawing of an armchair is drawn in pencil and colored pencil
on tracing paper measuring 7-1/2 in. x 6-3/4 in. (190.5 mm x
171.5 mm).

Drawing of a ceiling fixture done in pencil and colored pencil
on tracing paper measuring 13-1/2 in. x 13-1/2 in. (342.9
mm x 342.9 mm).

Drawing of a couch design is done in pencil and colored pencil
on tracing paper measuring 13-1/4 in. x 20-1/2 in. (336.6 mm
x 520.7 mm).

Drawing of a ceiling fixture drawn in pencil and colored pencil on tracing paper measuring 8-1/2 in. x 7-1/4 in.
(215.9 mm x 184.2 mm).

Drawing of a floor lamp design drawn in pencil and colored
pencil on tracing paper measuring 19-1/2 in. x 17-1/2 in.
(495.3 mm x 444.5 mm).

Drawing of andirons for a dining room is done in pencil on
tracing paper which measures 14-1/2 in. x 17 in. (368.3 mm
x 431.8 mm).

Drawing of andirons for the living room is drawn in pencil
on tracing paper measuring 15-1/2 in. x 17-3/4 in. (393.7 mm
x 450.9 mm).

Drawing of andirons for the entrance hall fireplace done in
pencil on tracing paper measuring 12-3/4 in. x 13 in.
(323.9 mm x 330.2 mm).

Drawing of living room furniture drawn in pencil and colored
pencil on tracing paper measuring 13-1/4 in. x 16 in.
(336.6 mm x 406.4 mm).

Drawing of a window detail and bookcase in study is drawn in
pencil on tracing paper measuring 12 in. x 12 in. (304.8
mm x 304.8 mm).

Drawing of a hall seat done in pencil and colored pencil on
kraft paper measuring 15-1/2 in. x 25-1/2 in. (393.7 mm x
647.7 mm).

All drawings listed for the Allen Residence were drawn by George
M. Niedecken unless otherwise noted.

C.R. Weltzheimer Residence (1948)
Oberlin, Ohio
   Sawn redwood window panel without glass measures 11-1/8 in. x
   48 in. (282.6 mm x 1219.2 mm).

Wallpaper and Fabric Designs for F. Schumacher and Company's
Taliesin Line (1955)
New York, New York
   One wallpaper sample book without any fabric samples.
   Two fabric samples (somewhat faded).
   Catalogue of paints by Wright for the Martin-Senour Company
   to harmonize with the Taliesin Line of fabrics and wallpaper.

The general policy of the Prairie Archives, with regard to the use
of Frank Lloyd Wright related materials, requires that a researcher
make written request to them outlining the purposes, goals, and intended end product of the researcher's area of study. It should also
be noted that, in addition to the items listed above, the archives
also house the account books for the Niedecken-Walbridge firm from
1907 to circa 1925 and those include account records for several Wright
commissions for the following residences: Coonley, Bogk, Robie, Gilmore, Irving, Mueller, Tomek, Amberg, May, and Allen.

A30

The Milwaukee Public Library
The Central Library
814 West Wisconsin Avenue
Milwaukee, Wisconsin 53223

   The F. Schumacher and Company catalogue for the Taliesin Line of
Wallpaper and Interior Finishes was published by E.W. Bredemeier and
Company Sample Books at Chicago in 1955 and is housed in the collections of the Milwaukee Public Library. The book, containing many fabric
and wallpaper samples, measures 22-3/4 in. x 17-7/16 in. (578 mm x
443 mm) and is accompanied by a large box containing twenty-one
actual samples of the Frank Lloyd Wright designed fabrics. It displays
twenty-one different fabric designs in a variety of colors as well as
four wallpaper designs, three of which match three fabric designs.
The fabric and wallpaper designs were designed by Wright in conjunction with his furniture designs for Heritage-Henredon and rugs for
Karastan Rug Mills. Schumacher's Director of Design, Rene Carrillo,
worked very closely with Frank Lloyd Wright during the process of
creating the fabric and wallpaper designs and many of the fabrics
were the result of the melding of ideas of the two men; this process
took two years. In September of 1955 Virginia Connor Dick decorated
a permanent suite of five rooms at the New York Republican Club for
a complete presentation of Wright's Schumacher fabric designs and
Heritage-Henredon furniture designs. The sample catalogue sold for
$35 and was requisite to a dealership in the Taliesin Line. In 1955,
the Taliesin Line fabric prices ranged from $3.40 to $13.50 per yard
and the wallpapers from $5.95 to $7.45 per roll. A detailed description of the fabrics and wallpaper designs contained in the sample
catalogue and sample box follows:

Fabric Design No. 101
This design was available in a 50-in. (1270-mm) width and
was done on printed linen, a fabric made of smooth surface
flax fibers. The rectilinear pattern design was repeated
every 29 in. (736.6 mm). It was available in varying shades
of olive green, varying shades of old gold, copper and peach,
turquoise and blue, and wood brown and tan. A sample fabric
is in the sample book and a full-size piece of the fabric is
in the sample box.

Fabric Design No. 102
Available in a 50-in. (1270-mm) wide printed linen fabric
with a rectilinear pattern design which repeated every
28-1/2 in. (723.9 mm). The colors available for this fabric
were leaf green, old gold, coral and flame, tan and slate,
and wood brown and tan. A sample fabric is in the sample book
and full-size piece of the fabric is in the sample box.

Fabric Design No. 103
This fabric was available in a 50-in. (1270-mm) width and
has a rectilinear pattern design printed on mohair casement
which is made of 17 percent mohair, spun rayon, and cotton.
Made from the fleece of the Angora goat, mohair is a resilient
fiber which adds body to the other fabrics, and in this line
was to be used for draperies. The rectilinear pattern repeats
every 48-3/4 in. (1238.3 mm) and was available in color
patterns of tan and turquoise, green and gold, old gold and
olive, blue and midnight, slate and coral, and wood brown and
brick. A companion design of wallpaper was also offered. A
sample of the fabric and the wallpaper are contained in the
sample book; a full-size sample is in the sample box.

Fabric Design No. 104
This fabric was available in a 50-in. (1270-mm) width and
has a circular color pattern which repeats every 27 in.
(685.8 mm). It was made of printed silk and Fortisan casement.
Fortisan is the trademark for a strong regenerated cellulose
yarn produced by the Celanese Corporation of America. This
yarn is often combined with silk to be used for draperies
because it is not greatly affected by humidity. The fabric
was available in slate, willow, gold, blue, pink, white, and
wood. Samples are contained in the sample book and a full-
size sample is in the sample box.

Fabric Design No. 105
Available in a 50-in. (270-mm) width, this fabric is made of
linen and consists of a rectilinear multi-colored pattern on
a single colored background with the pattern repeating every
25 in. (635 mm). The fabric was available in soft grey and
tanager red as well as five additional color combinations.
Design No. 105 is not shown in the sample book; however, a
full-size sample is contained in the sample box. A companion
wallpaper design was also available.

Fabric Design No. 106
The fabric is made of cotton, rayon and 14 percent mohair
and was available in a 50-in. (1270-mm) width. It has a
circular multi-colored pattern which repeats every 32 in.

(812.8 mm) and was available in varying shades of cream and
tan, varying shades of olive and gold, varying shades of
tan, varying shades of blue, varying shades of grey and white,
and varying shades of grey and pink color combinations. This
design is not shown in the sample book but a full-size sample
is contained in the sample box.

Fabric Design No. 501
The fabric is a boucle damask made of rayon and cotton and
was available in a 54-in. (1371.6-mm) width. Boucle fabrics
are those woven with small regularly spaced loops and flat
irregular surfaces produced by using specially twisted yarns
and are suited for upholstery. Damask fabrics are made with
a jacquard weave, a weave with multi-colored patterns, and
are often reversible for color change. Design No. 501 is a
repetitive diamond pattern and was available in turquoise,
leaf green, gold, flame, granite, pink, willow, wood brown,
Vermont slate, olive, brick, and copper. A sample is contained in the sample book and a full-size sample is in the
sample box.

Fabric Design No. 502
This was a 50-in. (1270-mm) wide linen texture fabric in a
solid pattern available in blue, green, gold, wood rose,
natural, pink, willow, coral, brown, and oyster white. Samples
are contained in the sample book as well as a full-size one
in the sample box.

Fabric Design No. 503
The fabric was available in a 50-in. (1270-mm) width and is
a textured satin made of rayon and cotton. It was available
in gold, willow, flame, beige, blue, turquoise, slate, olive,
copper, tan, sapphire, and green. Samples are contained in
the sample book as well as a full-size one in the sample
box.

Fabric Design No. 504
The fabric is made of 41 percent wool and 59 percent rayon
which was available in 52-in. (1320.8 mm) widths. It has a
linear color pattern on a light woven background and was
available in copper, green, gold, rust, natural, blue, turquoise, flame, and black. Samples are contained in the sample
book and a full-size sample is in the sample box.

Fabric Design No. 505
Available in 48-in. (1219.2-mm) widths, the fabric is a
reversible casement made of rayon, cotton, and Lurex. Lurex
is the trademark for a nontarnishing, aluminum-base metallic
yarn and was produced by the Dobeckman Company. This fabric
was available in solid colors of natural, green, gold, wood
rose, blue, pink, white, charcoal, willow, straw, turquoise,
tea rose, beige, lavender, and brown. Samples are contained
in the sample book and a full-size one is in the sample box.

Fabric Design No. 506
A 54-in. (1371.6-mm) wide solid color rayon fabric available
in walnut, willow, desert gold, crimson, granite, midnight
blue, pink, turquoise, white, kelp brown, amethyst, old rose,

aquamarine, topaz, olive, wood brown, lime green, old gold,
copper, sand, blue, cactus green, linseed gold, cantaloupe,
nutmeg, spruce, old red, curry, orange, and birch. Samples
are contained in the sample book and there is a full-size
sample in the sample box.

Fabric Design No. 507
This is a 50-in. (1270-mm) wide chenille casement fabric
in solid colors with parallel Lurex yarn placed at regular
intervals. Chenille is a woven yarn which has a pile pro-
truding all around it at right angles to the body thread and
the fabric has a plush-like surface. The fabric was available
in willow, granite, blue, eggshell, old gold, brick, topaz,
pink, turquoise, and tan. Samples are contained in the sample
book; there is a full-size sample in the accompanying sample
box.

Fabric Design No. 508
The fabric is a 54-in. (1371.6-mm) wide rayon which was
available in solid colors of spring green, sienna, flame,
beigesand, blue, bittersweet, turquoise, claret, allspice,
leaf green, almond, parchment, sunset, mist, blue haze,
cinnamon, cornflower, crocus, bronze, bark brown, lime, gold,
brick, smoke, wood brown, and natural. The fabric was not
displayed in the sample book; however, a full-size sample
is contained in the sample box.

Fabric Design No. 510
This is a 54-in. (1371.6 mm) wide fabric made of 94 percent
cotton, and 6 percent Lurex. It was available in black with
blue, black with green, black with gold, black with old
brick, black with white, black with copper, black with tur-
qoise, black with parakeet yellow, and black with wood brown.
The fabric was not displayed in the sample book. There is,
however, a full-size sample in the sample box.

Fabric Design No. 511
Available in a 54-in. (1371.6-mm) width, the solid colored
fabric is made of rayon, 19 percent mohair, and cotton. The
color selection was sand, willow green, gold, brick, blue,
cactus, pink, turquoise, pumpkin, spring green, and bark
brown. Though this fabric was not part of the sample book,
there is a full-size sample in the sample box.

Fabric Design No. 512
The fabric is a 50-in. (1270-mm) wide mohair damask made
of rayon, 23 percent mohair, and cotton. The fabric was
available in gold, jade green, flame, fawn, blue mist, pink,
peacock blue, white, willow, and copper colors. The fabric
was not displayed in the sample book; however, a full-size
sample is in the sample box.

Fabric Design No. 513
The fabric is a damask with a triangular pattern on a colored
background made of spun rayon and cotton and was available
in a 50-in (1270-mm) width. The available colors were light
blue, willow, yellow, red, beige, cobalt blue, shell, jade,
olive green, old gold, brick, straw, turquoise, and orange.

The full-size fabric is contained in the sample box but is
not shown in the sample book.

Fabric Design No. 514
A colored textured damask fabric made of spun rayon in a
52-in. (1320.8-mm) width. The fabric was available in bis-
cuit and brown; green and turquoise; yellow; orange and
gold; grey-blue; turquoise and blue; peony; turquoise;
white; gold and green; old gold; orange; grey and turquoise;
and green and orange. The fabric is not shown in the sample
book but a full-size sample is contained in the sample box.

Fabric Design No. 705
A 48-in. (1219.2-mm) wide Fortisan printed casement in a
diamond module pattern which repeats every 10-1/2 in.
(266.7 mm). The fabric was available in champagne, willow
green, gold, pink, turquoise, granite and tan. The fabric
is shown with samples in the sample book and a full-size
piece of the fabric is contained in the sample box. This
fabric design was also represented in a companion wallpaper
design.

Fabric Design No. 706
A 36-in. (914.4-mm) wide printed duck fabric made of 100
percent cotton. The fabric consists of triangles used to
form larger triangular, rectangular, and diamond patterns
of differing colors; the pattern repeats every 8-1/2 in.
(215.9 mm). It was available in varying shades of the color
combinations of green; old gold and olive; olive and brick;
blue and granite; copper and pink; and turquoise and peach.
The fabric is represented in the sample book and a full-size
sample is contained in the sample box. A companion wallpaper of the same design is also contained in the sample
book.

Unidentified Wallpaper Design
Wallpaper with a rectilinear style design that is almost
bricklike. No companion design fabric is offered. The wallpaper design came in seven color combinations. This wallpaper uses metallic inks.

For a more detailed account of Wright's Taliesin Line for the
F. Schumacher Company, see F. Schumacher and Company, *The Taliesin
Line of Wallpaper and Interior Finishes Catalog* (Chicago: E.W.
Bredemeier and Company Sample Books, undated [1955?]; "FLLW--Frankly,
We Believe that This Will Be the Biggest Decorating News for the
Year. Watch for Details From F. Schumacher and Co." (*Interiors*, Vol.
114, No. 11, June 1955), p. 68 [advertisement]; "Frank Lloyd Wright
Projects" (*Interiors*, Vol. 114, No. 11, June 1955), p. 130; Betty
Pepis, "Conventional Furniture by Frank Lloyd Wright" (*The New York
Times*, October 18, 1955), p. 44, col. 5; "New Era for Wright at 86:
The Market Place Redeemed?" (*Architectural Record*, Vol. 118, October
1955), p. 20; "Taliesin to the Trade" (*Interiors*, Vol. 115, No. 3,
October 1955), pp. 130-133; "Frank Lloyd Wright Designs Home Furnish-
ings You Can Buy" (*House Beautiful*, Vol. 97, November 1955), pp. 282-
290; "A Master Architect Creates Fabric and Wallpaper Designs"
(*American Fabric and Fashions*, No. 35, Winter 1955-1956), pp. 50-51;
"FLLW Designs Home Furnishings" (*House and Home*, Vol. 9, January 1956),

p. 188; "New Fabrics and Rugs from Two Sources" (*Interiors*, Vol. 115, No. 10, May 1956), p. 120; "Eastern Ambience in Panels, Wallpaper" (*Interiors*, Vol. 116, No. 2, September 1956), p. 162; and David A. Hanks, *The Decorative Designs of Frank Lloyd Wright* (New York: E.P. Dutton, 1979), pp. 195-198.

A31

Department of Decorative Arts
The Minneapolis Institute of Arts
2400 Third Avenue South
Minneapolis, Minnesota 55404

The Minneapolis Institute of Arts purchased the east hallway of the now demolished Francis W. Little Residence II, "Northome," of 1912 from the Metropolitan Museum of Art of New York. The Little Residence was originally located at Deephaven, Minnesota. The hallway measures approximately 18 feet long and 6 feet wide. It contains ten leaded stained glass windows, two pairs of doors, two cupboards, and a window bench, all of which were also designed by Wright for the residence. The room is in storage awaiting a time of permanent installation in the musuem. An article which reviews this acquisition is Peg Meier's "A Gem of a Room Finds a Museum Setting" (*The Minneapolis Tribune*, August 20, 1972, Picture Section), pp. 6-13, 20.

A32

Northwest Architectural Archives
University Libraries
University of Minnesota
Minneapolis, Minnesota 55455

The University of Minnesota Library's Northwest Architectural Archives contains one letter by Frank Lloyd Wright to William Grey Purcell dated January 24, 1944. This letter is contained in the Purcell and Elmslie, Architects, Minneapolis, Minnesota Records 1855-1965 Collection.

A33

Architecture and Design Study Center
Department of Architecture and Design
The Museum of Modern Art
11 West 53rd Street
New York, New York 10019

The Department of Architecture and Design of the Museum of Modern Art houses five original Frank Lloyd Wright drawings and nine other Frank Lloyd Wright related items from various Wright designed buildings. The drawings are for the following Wright buildings and projects:

James B. Christie Residence (1940)
Bernardsville, New Jersey
    View from the east.
    View from the southeast.

Stuart Wells Residence (1944)
Minneapolis, Minnesota
    Perspective view.
    Lower level plan.
    Upper level plan.

Very little has been written on the James B. Christie Residence; however, an article entitled "The Christie House: Reassessing of Frank Lloyd Wright's Design" by Philip S. Grant, Jr., can be found in *Architecture New Jersey* ([New Jersey Society of Architects], Vol. 11, No. 1, January/February/March 1977), pp. 4-5.

Furniture in the collection designed by Frank Lloyd Wright is as listed:

Larkin Company Administration Building (1903)
Buffalo, New York
    Office armchair made of painted steel with oak seat. The chair measures 37-1/2 in. x 24-11/16 in. x 21-1/8 in. (952 mm x 627 mm x 536 mm).
    Two side chairs made of wood and leather. These chairs are a slightly changed version of a 1904 chair designed for the restaurant of the Larkin Company Administration Building; the chairs may be from Wright's 1905 Unity Church at Oak Park, Illinois. One of the two chairs measures 35-3/4 in. x 15 in. x 18-5/8 in. (908 mm x 381 mm x 473 mm); the other chair measures 35-3/8 in. x 15 in. x 18-5/8 in. (898 mm x 381 mm x 473 mm).

Darwin D. Martin Residence (1904)
Buffalo, New York
    One first floor window and frame. The window uses zinc came with clear plate glass and irridized cathedral and flashed glass. The window and frame measure 41-1/4 in. x 28-5/8 in. (1048 mm x 727 mm); the window alone measures 39 in. x 26-1/2 in. (991 mm x 660 mm).

Midway Gardens for Edward C. Waller, Jr. (1913)
Chicago, Illinois
    A precast concrete panel measuring 17-3/4 in. x 20-3/4 in. x 2-3/4 in. (450 mm x 527 mm x 70 mm).

Taliesin III for Frank Lloyd Wright (1925)
Spring Green, Wisconsin
    One armchair made of pine with plush upholstery measuring 32-3/8 in. x 20-1/2 in. x 17-3/4 in. (823 mm x 521 mm x 451 mm). This chair was given to the Museum of Modern Art by Frank Lloyd Wright in 1947. It was possibly designed for the living room at Taliesin.

S.C. Johnson and Son Administration Building (1936)
Racine, Wisconsin
    One desk made of steel and wood manufactured by Metal Office Furniture Company which is now Steelcase Business Equipment, Inc.
    One office armchair made of steel and upholstered with a foam cushion. The chair measures 35 in. x 24 in. x 18 in. (889 mm x 610 mm x 457 mm) and was also manufactured by Metal Office Furniture Company.

John L. Rayward Residence, "Tirranna" (1955)
New Canaan, Connecticut
 One straight backed chair made of wood with an upholstered
  cushion. The chair measures 50-1/4 in. x 20 in. x 22-1/4 in.
  (1276 mm x 508 mm x 565 mm).

The Frank Lloyd Wright materials are available for study by appointment only through the Curator of the Architecture and Design Study Center.

A34

The Grey Art Gallery and Study Center
New York University Art Collection
New York University
100 Washington Square East
New York, New York 10003

The Grey Art Gallery and Study Center of New York University houses one lead glass window with the frame from the Frank Lloyd Wright designed Darwin D. Martin Residence (1904) at Buffalo, New York. The window has the "tree of life" design and measures 41-1/2 in. x 26-1/4 in. (1054 mm x 667 mm).

A35

The University Archives
420 Capen Hall
State University of New York at Buffalo
Amherst, New York 14260

There are four pieces of correspondence in the Frank Lloyd Wright Collection which includes one letter from Michael Meredith Hare to Frank Lloyd Wright concerning Hare's joining the Taliesin Fellowship; one letter from William Beye Fyfe, a Taliesin apprentice, to Michael Meredith Hare; and two letters from Frank Lloyd Wright to Michael Meredith Hare dated November 8, 1933, and December 2, 1933, in response to Hare's inquiry to join the Taliesin Fellowship. A 1940 autobiographical sketch of Hare is also included in the correspondence collection.

The State University of New York at Buffalo also owns the Frank Lloyd Wright designed Darwin D. Martin Residence of 1904 located at 125 Jewett Parkway in Buffalo, New York. There are guided tours available to view the residence, which has numerous original furnishings.

The University Archives also contain many drawings and artifacts from five Frank Lloyd Wright designed buildings and projects. The designs represented in the collection are the Larkin Company Administration Building, the Darwin D. Martin Residence, the W.W. Davis Residence Project (this project does not appear in any list or publication of Frank Lloyd Wright's works), the Darwin D. Martin "Graycliff" Residence, and the Imperial Hotel. The items are listed as follows:

 The Larkin Company Administration Building (1903)
 Buffalo, New York
  Drawings (by Frank Lloyd Wright)
   One sheet of the basement plan (revised, microfilm of the
    original plan).

One sheet of the first floor plan (revised April 1, 1904,
microfilm of original).
One sheet of the second floor plan (revised April 1, 1904,
microfilm of original).
One sheet of the third floor plan (revised April 1, 1904,
microfilm of original).
One sheet of the fourth floor plan (revised April 1, 1904,
microfilm of the original).
One sheet of the fifth floor plan (revised April 1, 1904,
microfilm of the original).
One sheet of the sixth floor plan (revised April 1, 1904,
microfilm of the original).
Drawings Prepared in 1912 (probably by the Larkin Company):
One sheet of a cross-section (microfilm of original).
One sheet of sections through the stairs (microfilm of the
original).
Two sheets of drawings of the heating and ventilating systems
(microfilm of original).
One sheet of elevations, plan, and sections (microfilm of
original).
One sheet of details of heating and ventilating systems
(microfilm of original).
Four sheets of floor plans (microfilm of original).
One sheet of the plan for the locker rooms (microfilm of
original).

Darwin D. Martin Residence (1904)
Buffalo, New York
Boundary Surveys and Site Plans of the Martin Property
Sheet 1--Map of the plot surveyed by H.T. Buttolph showing
the corner of Jewett Parkway and Summit Avenue drawn in
black ink on paper dated October 3, 1903 (Collection Item
27).
Sheet 2--Map of the plot, same as above but with the plan for
the house sketched in pencil, on parchment paper (Collec-
tion Item 27).
Map of the site drawn by O.S. Lang in blueprint form dated
April 18, 1905 (Collection Item 28).
Site drawing by Frederick K. King in blueprint form dated
September 4, 1918 (Collection Item 29).
Site drawing by Krehbiel and Krehbiel, engineers, in photo-
copy form dated June 5, 1961; revised June 28, 1961; and
resurveyed February 1, 1963 (Collection Item 30).
Site Designs for the Martin Property
Planting plan blueprint by Walter Burley Griffin, dated
October 15, 1910 (Collection Item 23).
An undated blueprint of planting details by Johnson Elliott,
a landscape architect from Pittsburgh, Pennsylvania
(Collection Item 24).
Drawings of the Martin Residence by Frank Lloyd Wright--Site
Plans
Sheet 1--Plan of plantings for grounds drawn on a linen
backed original tracing and dated February 15, 1905
(Collection Item 21).
Sheet 2--Plan of planting for grounds in blueprint form and
dated February 15, 1905 (Collection Item 21).

Undated blueprint of a plan for a floral arrangement for the
residence (Collection Item 22).
Residence Plans by Frank Lloyd Wright
The following are Collection Item 1 and are all undated
blueprints mounted to board:
Sheet 1--Basement plan.
Sheet 2--First floor plan.
Sheet 3--Second floor plan.
Sheet 4--North and south elevations.
Sheet 5--East and west elevations.
Sheet 6--Sections.
Sheet 7--Frame details.
Sheet 8--Second story frames.
The following set of blueprints are also undated and are
catalogued as Collection Item 2. Item number 13 of the col-
lection is the same as Sheet 1 below; however, the plans
for the electrical system are drawn on this sheet which
are dated March 3, 1905.
Sheet 1--Basement plan.
Sheet 2--First floor plan.
Sheet 3--Second floor plan.
Sheet 4--North and south elevations.
Sheet 5--East and West elevations.
Sheet 6--Sections.
The following drawings are identified as Collection Item 8
and are undated. They are drawn in pencil on Japanese tracing paper:
Sheet 1--measuring 23-7/8 in. x 25-3/8 in. (606.4 mm x
644.5 mm)--First floor furniture arrangement.
Sheet 2--measuring 17-3/4 in. x 20-5/8 in. (450.9 mm x
523.9 mm)--Elevation and plan of the dining room table
and chairs.
Sheet 3--measuring 17-7/8 in. x 20-3/4 in. (450 mm x
527.1 mm)--Library table.
Sheet 4--measuring 23-7/8 in. x 25-3/8 in. (606.4 mm x
644.5 mm)--Elevation and plan of couch, table, chairs,
and stand.
Sheet 5--measuring 17-7/8 in. x 26-3/4 in. (450 mm x
679.5 mm)--Bedroom furniture.
Sheet 6--measuring 17-3/4 in. x 20-5/8 in. (450.9 mm x
523.9 mm)--Bedroom furniture.
Drawings of the Martin Barn and Conservatory
The following drawings are all blueprints and are identified
as Collection Item 19 dated May 7, 1904; June 1, 1904 re-
vised; and October 8, 1904, revised.
Sheet 1--Basement and foundation plan.
Sheet 2--First floor plan.
Sheet 3--Second floor plan.
Sheet 4--North and south elevations.
Sheet 5--East and west elevations.
Sheet 6--Details.
Sheet 7--Sections.
Collection Item 4 consists of drawings of alterations to the
barn and conservatory all of which are dated June 1916:
Sheet 1--Exterior view, drawn with watercolor.

Sheet 2--First floor plan of the Martin Residence, drawn
in pencil with color on tracing paper.
Sheet 3--Second floor plan of the Martin Residence, drawn
in pencil with color on tracing paper.
Sheet 4--The conservatories, drawn in pencil with color on
tracing paper.
Item 20 of the collection is a plan for new skylights for
the Martin Conservatory and is an undated drawing in red
and black on linen.
Martin Residence Gardener's Cottage Plans
Collection Item 25 consists of four blueprints all of which
are dated November 23, 1905:
Sheet 1a--Floor plans.
Sheet 1b--Floor plans, revised.
Sheet 2--Elevations.
Sheet 3--Details.
Collection Item 26 consists of three blueprints originally
dated November 29, 1905, and revised May 1, 1908:
Sheet 1--Floor plans.
Sheet 2--Elevations.
Sheet 3--Details.
Other Drawings of the Darwin D. Martin Residence in the
Collection
One blueprint dated May 15, 1905, which is the revised
Sheet 11 of the building sections (Collection Item 3).
One undated blueprint for details of a skylight (Collection
Item 10).
One undated tracing drawn in pencil of details for a fireplace
(Collection Item 11).
An undated blueprint of a detail of outside windows near
lighting fixtures (Collection Item 12).
A linen plan of the foundation which is undated (Collection
Item 14).
An undated linen plan of the plumbing and heating systems
by Foster and Glidden (Collection Item 15).
Various plans by Pierson Sefton Co. of Jersey City, New
Jersey, including a tracing in pencil dated December 5,
1904 of a plan for a stone sill, cement walk, and wall
section (Collection Item 16); a blueprint of the masonry
plan for the greenhouse dated December 5, 1904 (Collection
Item 17); and a blueprint of a plan for a bench for the
greenhouse dated December 14, 1904 (Collection Item 18).
Drawings of Alterations to the Martin Residence by Various
Other Architects
Alterations by Andrew Willatzen of Seattle, dated March 10,
1920, include two blueprints, one of the first floor and
sections and the other of the second floor (Collection
Item 5).
Alterations by S.J. Tauriello, all of which are undated--
Sheet 1 of the first floor; Sheet 2 of the second floor;
Sheet 3 of the basement on tracing paper; Sheet 4 of the
first floor on tracing paper; and Sheet 5 of the second
floor on tracing paper (Collection Item 6).
Photocopies of drawings by Edgar Tafel, who also performed
alterations, including Sheet 1 of the basement plan,
Sheet 2 of the first floor plan, Sheet 3 of the second
floor plan, Sheet 4 of the family and commercial kitchen,

Sheet 5 of the laundry room on the second floor (Collection Item 7).

Miscellaneous Items Concerning the Martin Residence
The contractor's letterbook of 290 pages dated 1905 to 1906 from O.S. Lang (Collection Item 35). Photographs of the Martin Residence and properties. Many of the photographs were taken shortly after the residence was occupied by the Martins and during construction.

Tape recordings and tape summaries of interviews with two children of Darwin D. Martin, Darwin R. Martin and Dorothy Martin Foster; Edgar Tafel; Mrs. Sebastian J. Tauriello; and Mrs. Robert L. Ketter (wife of the President of the State University of New York at Buffalo, New York).

Several fragments which were removed from the Darwin D. Martin Residence including several pieces of glass from the Martin fireplace mosaic.

W.W. Davis Residence Project (1889-1911?)
Louisville, Kentucky
The following set of blueprints is undated and has not been shown in any listing of Frank Lloyd Wright's works or projects. However, due to the title block on the sheet containing the rendering of the residence, which lists "Frank Lloyd Wright, Architect--Oak Park, Illinois," the building project can be attributed to Wright's Oak Park practice years. The set of blueprints was bought for the collection by the University of Buffalo Foundation from Mr. Carl Sperl of West Seneca, New York, and became a part of the Wright Collection in September of 1976. Drawings of the W.W. Davis Residence Project are listed as follows:
Two sheets, measuring 16-1/4 in. x 21 in. (412.8 mm x 538.4 mm), of the site plan with elevations, gas, water, and sanitary sewer.
One sheet, measuring 19-3/4 in. x 31 in. (501.7 mm x 787.4 mm), of the main floor plan showing locations of carriage house/stable, playroom, study, two guest rooms, living room, and entry foyer.
One sheet, measuring 20 in. x 33-1/2 in. (508 mm x 850.9 mm), of the lower level floor plan showing locations of laundry area, porch, kitchen and yard, servants' hall, furnace room, coal room, servants' rooms, and dining room.
One sheet, measuring 20 in. x 25-1/2 in. (508 mm x 647.7 mm), of the upper level floor plan showing upper portion of living room, childrens' suite, balcony, and another suite.
One sheet, measuring 20 in. x 38 in. (508 mm x 965.2 mm) with title block "Frank Lloyd Wright, Architect--Oak Park, Illinois," of a front view rendering.

Darwin D. Martin "Graycliff" Residence and Garage (1927)
Derby, New York
Drawings by Frank Lloyd Wright
The following drawings drawn in ink on linen and dated August 19, 1929 (Collection Item 32):
Sheet 1--Second floor.
Sheet 2--North elevation.
Sheet 3--South elevation.

Sheet 4--East and west elevations and sections.
Sheet 5--Sections and details.
The following set of blueprints all of which are dated
August 19, 1929 (Collection Item 33):
    Sheet 1--Second floor.
    Sheet 2--North elevation.
    Sheet 3--South elevation.
    Sheet 4--East and west elevations and sections.
Other "Graycliff" materials in the collection
    Blueprints, possibly shop drawings, by Jones Iron Works of
    the garage beams and columns, dated April 8, 1929 (Collec-
    tion Item 34).
    Photographs of the Darwin D. Martin Residence, "Graycliff,"
    at Derby, New York, during construction.

The Imperial Hotel (1915)
Tokyo, Japan
    The following architectural fragments were donated to the State
    University of New York at Buffalo by former Wright apprentice,
    Edgar Tafel:
        Item 1--Five square-shaped architectural blocks made of oya
        stone and off-white in color, each measuring 8± in. (203.2±
        mm) in size.
        Item 2--Five architectural blocks each measuring 8-1/2 in. x
        8 in. x 2 in. (215.9 mm x 203.2 mm x 50.8 mm) and made of
        terra-cotta.
        Item 3--Five decorative glazed tiles of a red-brown color
        measuring 7 in. x 7 in. x 1 in. (177.8 mm x 177.8 mm x
        25.4 mm).
        Item 4--Five plain tiles of a sand color measuring 9 in. x
        9 in. x 3/4 in. (228.6 mm x 228.6 mm x 19.1 mm).
        Item 5--Four decorative bricks measuring 8-1/2 in. x 2-1/2
        in. x 1-1/2 in. (215.9 mm x 63.5 mm x 38.1 mm).
        Item 6--Three bricks measuring 12 in. x 2-1/2 in. x 2 in.
        (304.8 mm x 63.5 mm x 50.8 mm).
        Item 7--Six bricks measuring 8 in. x 2 in. x 2 in. (203.2
        mm x 50.8 mm x 50.8 mm).
        Item 8--One leaded glass window in a wooden frame with clear
        and amber glass measures 34-3/8 in. x 32-3/8 in. (873.1 mm
        x 822.3 mm).
        Item 9--A portion of the copper exterior of the Imperial
        Hotel measuring 12 in. x 49 in. x 5 in. (304.8 mm x 1244.6
        mm x 127 mm).

According to the University Archivist, the Frank Lloyd Wright
Collection is available for research using microfilm copy only in the
University Archives at 420 Capen Hall on the Amherst Campus of the
State University of New York at Buffalo. Special permission must be
granted by the Archivist to use original materials.

A36

The Newberry Library
60 West Walton
Chicago, Illinois 60610

The Newberry Library of Chicago has fifteen letters written by
Frank Lloyd Wright in three different manuscript collections. The
Wallace Rice Collection has one letter to Wallace Rice dated July 14,
1915. The Lloyd Downs Lewis Papers, 1863-1949, include two letters
written by Frank Lloyd Wright to Lloyd Lewis, Wright's longtime friend
and client, one dated January 30, 1944, the other undated. The William
Kittredge Collection contains twelve letters written by Frank Lloyd
Wright to William A. Kittredge spanning the years from 1932 to 1943.
The letters are dated December 3, 1932; December 23, 1932; June 5,
1935; October 12, 1937; October 19, 1937; July 28, 1939; August 28,
1939; August 15, 1941; August 11, 1942; September 14, 1942; October
5, 1942; and March 1, 1943. The Kittredge Collection also contains a
handwritten letter from Olgivanna Lloyd Wright to Kittredge, dated
July 23, 1940, in which she thanks him for a favor.

Also in the collections of the Newberry Library is the title page
for *The Eve of St. Agnes* published by the Auvergne Press at River
Forest, Illinois, by William Winslow and Chauncey Williams. Wright
had designed this title page which measures 8 in. x 4-7/8 in. (203 mm
x 124 mm) and is drawn with black and red ink on paper.

The use of the manuscript collections at the Newberry Library
requires an application in writing for permission from the curator.
Manuscripts may not be photocopied or reproduced without the curator's
approval.

A37

Special Collections Department
Northwestern University Library
Northwestern University
Evanston, Illinois 60201

The Special Collections Department of the Northwestern University
Library houses numerous original manuscripts written by Frank Lloyd
Wright. They are located in the Frank Lloyd Wright Correspondence
with Baker Brownell, 1931 to 1939 and the Frank Lloyd Wright Corre-
spondence with E. Willis Jones, 1936 to 1959 collections. The former
collection contains eighteen pieces of correspondence written by Frank
Lloyd Wright to Baker Brownell as well as other pieces of correspondence written by associates of Frank Lloyd Wright to Baker Brownell.
Baker Brownell and Frank Lloyd Wright jointly authored the book
Architecture and Modern Life published by Harper and Brothers at New
York and London in 1937. The latter collection contains fourteen pieces
of correspondence written by Frank Lloyd Wright to E. Willis Jones
dating from 1937 to 1959. E. Willis Jones was a close friend of Wright.
This collection was purchased by Northwestern University in 1964 (for
a brief description of the acquisition, see "Wright Collection at
Northwestern" [*The Milwaukee Journal*, June 12, 1964]).

Other miscellaneous Frank Lloyd Wright original manuscripts found
in the Special Collections Department include an undated poem entitled
"Work Song"; a typescript article entitled "In the Cause of Architecture: The 'International Style'" dated 1953; a typescript speech
entitled "Dinner Talk at Hull House" dated November 8, 1939; a pen
sketch and note written by Frank Lloyd Wright pertaining to his Johnson's Wax building at Racine, Wisconsin; five Christmas cards from
Taliesin signed by Frank Lloyd Wright dated 1935, 1943, 1944, 1945,
and 1948; and one signed photostated copy of an architect's drawing
of the Herbert Johnson Residence located at Wind Point, Wisconsin.

Letters and correspondence written by Frank Lloyd Wright to Baker Brownell in the Frank Lloyd Wright Correspondence with Baker Brownell, 1931 to 1939 collection are dated May 2, 1933; July 21, 1933; December 1, 1933; December 6, 1933; February 5, 1934; February 24, 1934 (or 1936); March 30, 1934; August 6, 1934; April 28, 1935; May 11, 1935; December 16, 1935; July 24, 1936; August 18, 1936; October 10, 1936; February 14, 1937; May 22, 1937; August 11, 1937; and August 31, 1937.

There are also ten pieces of correspondence from Karl Jensen of the Taliesin Fellowship to Baker Brownell which are contained in this collection and are dated May 7, 1931; February 26, 1932; March 7, 1932; April 1, 1932; July 1, 1933; August 14, 1933; August 28, 1933; November 21, 1933; April 20, 1934; and July 16, 1934.

Seventeen pieces of correspondence from Eugene Masselink, Frank Lloyd Wright's secretary, to Baker Brownell are in this collection as well and are dated January 30, 1934; March 9, 1934; February 14, 1935; April 16, 1935; April 18, 1935; April 20, 1935; May 10, 1935; May 16, 1935; August 6, 1935; August 16, 1935; September 6, 1935; December 30, 1936; January 22, 1937; March 5, 1937; April 11, 1937; April 24, 1937; and April 1, 1939. There is also one letter from a Mr. Morgan (apprentice Charles L. Morgan?) of the Taliesin Fellowship, dated July 6, 1937, to Baker Brownell.

The Frank Lloyd Wright authored letters and correspondence to E. Willis Jones contained in the Frank Lloyd Wright Correspondence with E. Willis Jones, 1936 to 1959 collection are housed in the Special Collections Department. This correspondence is dated January 26, 1937; October 10, 1936; April 16, 1940; March 19, 1941; March 20, 1941; January 27, 1943; December 21, 1942; July 22, 1946; June 17, 1947; March 15, 1948; April 24, 1948; May 25, 1948; August 17, 1949; and April 2, 1959. One letter from E. Willis Jones to Frank Lloyd Wright dated October 2, 1936 is also contained in the collection but this letter is probably a copy of the original.

Also in this collection are fourteen letters and correspondence from Eugene Masselink, Frank Lloyd Wright's secretary. These letters and correspondence are dated March 11, 1937; April 18, 1941; February 2, 1943; February 15, 1943; July 24, 1946; August 21, 1946; November 19, 1946; January 21, 1949; June 16, 1949; October 14, 1949; September 14, 1949; August 18, 1949; September 10, 1956; and July 14, 1956.

There are four drawings by Frank Lloyd Wright in the Special Collections Department. However, these drawings are not catalogued by the Department nor were they viewed by the author.

Permission from the Department Curator is needed to study the Frank Lloyd Wright manuscripts and drawings contained in the Special Collections Department.

A38

School of Architecture Library
School of Architecture
Notre Dame University
Notre Dame, Indiana 46556

The School of Architecture at Notre Dame University has seven sheets of drawings by Frank Lloyd Wright for the 1906 design of the K.C. DeRhodes Residence at South Bend, Indiana. The drawings are:

Sheet 1--Basement plan
  One blueprint and two mylar transparencies.
Sheet 2--First floor plan
  One blueprint and two mylar transparencies.
Sheet 3--Second floor plan
  One blueprint and two mylar transparencies.
Sheet 4--North and south elevation
  One blueprint and two mylar transparencies.
Sheet 5--East elevation and west elevation
  One blueprint and two mylar transparencies.
Sheet 6--Longitudinal section/cross-section
  One blueprint and two mylar transparencies.
Sheet 7--Details
  One blueprint and two mylar transparencies.

Each of the drawings measures 36± in. x 24± in. (914.4 mm x 609.9 mm).

A39

The Oak Park Public Library
Lake Street and Grove Avenue
Oak Park, Illinois 60301

The Oak Park Public Library houses both the Grant Carpenter Manson Collection and the Unitarian Universalist Church Papers, 1906 to 1911 collection. Both of these collections contain Frank Lloyd Wright related archival materials.

Grant Carpenter Manson was the author of *Frank Lloyd Wright to 1910: The First Golden Age* (New York: Reinhold, 1958). The Grant Carpenter Manson Collection of materials was given to the Oak Park Public Library for the use of serious researchers and contains a variety of materials used by Manson for the writing of his book. They include notes, photographs, prints, drawings, correspondence, and various other printed materials. The collection contains six pieces of correspondence written by Frank Lloyd Wright to Grant Carpenter Manson dated June 18, 1953; December 25, 1953; April 30, 1953; November 16, 1957; November 27, 1957; and August 30, 1958. Other correspondence in the collection includes several letters to Manson from Eugene Masselink (Frank Lloyd Wright's secretary) and from Olgivanna Lloyd Wright.

Drawings in the Grant Carpenter Manson Collection include an original plan of the Chauncey Williams Residence at River Forest, Illinois, dated as February 1895 by a researcher at the library; an original sketch of the elevation towards the side street of the W.H. Freeman Residence at Hinsdale, Illinois; two exterior presentation renderings in gold paint, of the Robert D. Clark [sic for Clarke] Residence Project of 1904 for Moss Avenue in Peoria, Illinois, and an interior rendering in watercolor of the Clarke Residence; and an original sketch, on tracing paper, believed to be of the Larkin Building at Buffalo, New York. The collection contains several litho prints of the American Systems Built Houses for Arthur L. Richards of Milwaukee, Wisconsin, dating from 1911 to 1917. One print measuring 18-7/16 in. x 12 in. (468.3 mm x 304.8 mm) is of a single-family residence, another measuring 14-7/8 in. x 12 in. (377.8 mm x 304.8 mm) is of a four-family residence, and a third also measuring 14-7/8 in. x 12 in. (377.8 mm x 304.8 mm) is of a multi-family residence.

The Manson collection also contains a pencil drawing measuring 20-1/2 in. x 15-1/2 in. (520.7 mm x 393.7 mm), of the west elevation of the William H. Winslow Residence of 1893 at River Forest, Illinois, showing the development of the ornamentation in the frieze.

The Unitarian Universalist Church Papers, 1906 to 1911 collection of manuscripts contains eleven manuscripts written and signed by Frank Lloyd Wright. These manuscripts include a copy of a letter to the Trustees of Unity Church (Oak Park) dated July 10, 1906; a voucher dated September 8, 1906; a voucher dated September 25, 1906; a letter to Mr. E.H. Ehrmann dated March 18, 1907; a voucher dated September 12, 1907; a voucher dated September 17, 1907; a voucher dated November 30, 1907; a letter to Unity Church (Oak Park) possibly written in 1907; a letter to Mr. E.H. Ehrmann dated January 18, 1908; a letter to the Trustees of Unity Church dated March 20, 1908; and a letter to Mr. William G. Adams dated March 8, 1909. The papers generally pertain to the construction of the Frank Lloyd Wright designed Unity Church at Oak Park, Illinois, and include contract documents and other correspondence from church officers with Wright's studio and contractors. Some of the other letters in the file are signed by Isabel Roberts, William Drummond, and Francis B. ·Byrne. The papers are the property of the Unitarian Universalist Church of Oak Park.

The Oak Park Public Library also contains several other Frank Lloyd Wright related items which are of special interest. These are a letter to Mr. Elkan Allan dated February 26, 1947; a letter from Frank Lloyd Wright to William Beye Fyfe (a former Wright apprentice) dated May 5, 1933; and a drawing on thin paper applied to a linen backing with yellow wash of the William H. Winslow Stable at River Forest, Illinois, dated 1893 and measuring 17 in. x 9 in. (431.8 mm x 228.6 mm).

Several Frank Lloyd Wright first editions which are autographed by him are also in the library collections: William C. Gannett and Frank Lloyd Wright's *The House Beautiful* (River Forest, Illinois: Auvergne Press, 1896-1897), which is copy number 47 of 90 autographed by both men; Frank Lloyd Wright's *Ausgeführte Bauten und Entwürfe von Frank Lloyd Wright* (Berlin: Ernst Wasmuth, 1910), which is autographed by F.L. Wright to his son, John Lloyd Wright. And H. Th. Wijdeveld's *The Life Work of the American Architect: Frank Lloyd Wright* (Santpoort, Holland: C.A. Mees, 1926), autographed by Wright to Gilman Lane.

A40

Rijkdienst voor de Monumentenzorg
Nederlands Documentatiecentrum voor de Bouwkunst
Droogbak 1a
Amsterdam
Netherlands

The Rijkdienst voor de Monumentenzorg of the Nederlands Documentatiecentrum voor de Bouwkunst has twenty-one letters written by Frank Lloyd Wright to Dutch architects Dr. H.P. Berlage, J.J.P. Oud, H. Th. Wijdeveld, and to the American Arthur B. Gallion. The letter to Dr. H.P. Berlage is dated November 30, 1922. There are two letters to J.J.P. Oud dated November 30, 1922 and December 19, 1935. The bulk of the letters contained in the collection, a total of seventeen, were written to H. Th. Wijdeveld spanning a time period of twenty-six years. The letters to him are dated March 28, 1923; May 7, 1926;

August 6, 1930; an undated letter possibly written in 1931; August 13, 1931; July 13, 1931; September 5, 1931; September 8, 1931; January 1, 1932; April 6, 1932; February 13, 1932; March 10, 1933; April 7, 1933; October 21, 1947; April 15, 1948; February 12, 1949; and March 30, 1949. The one letter to Arthur B. Gallion is dated June 5, 1948, and concerns H. Th. Wijdeveld.

The Rijkdienst voor de Monumentenzorg also has three Frank Lloyd Wright drawings in the collection including a perspective drawing done in Chinese ink and colored pencil on paper of the Henry J. Allen Residence of 1917 at Wichita, Kansas. The drawing measures 20 in. x 29-7/8 in. (507 mm x 759 mm). The other two drawings are of a theater interior (building or project not known) drawn in black and colored pencil on paper. One of these drawings measures 7-3/4 in. x 12-1/4 in. (196 mm x 312 mm) and the other 6-1/2 in. x 11 in. (164 mm x 281 mm).

The manuscripts can be viewed at the center. Requests for copies must be made by applying to the director of the center.

A41

Rush Rhees Library
University of Rochester
Wilson Boulevard
Rochester, New York 14627

Four letters written by Frank Lloyd Wright are contained in three different collections at the Rush Rhees Library of the University of Rochester. The William Channing Gannett Papers, 1850-1944 contains two letters, one dated December 27, 1898, and the other January 30, 1899, both of which were written by Wright and addressed to William Channing Gannett. The Bragdon Family Papers, 1819-1947 has one letter written by Wright to Claude Bragdon dated May 27, 1932. The library also has a letter dated October 20, 1947, from Wright to Harry B. Harvey. The library makes available copies of manuscripts under certain conditions with application and reason for copy.

A42

Drawings Collection
The British Architectural Archives
The Royal Institute of British Architects
66 Portland Place
London WIN 4AD
England

Three drawings by Frank Lloyd Wright are in the British Architectural Archives Collection. The first is a drawing of a design for the Terre Haute Trust Company Francis Apartments dated 1894. It is drawn with brown ink on tracing paper measuring 11-3/4 in. x 17 in. (298.5 mm x 431.8 mm). The second is a brown ink on Japanese paper drawing of the Yahara Boat Club Project for Madison, Wisconsin, measuring 6-1/4 in. x 22 in. (158.8 mm x 558.8 mm). The Yahara drawing is signed by Frank Lloyd Wright in his red square, although the style of the drawing indicates that it may have been drawn by Marion Mahoney. The Third drawing is for the All Steel House Project of Los Angeles, California, of 1937, drawn on paper with pencil and measuring 15 in. x

18-1/4 in. (381 mm x 463.6 mm). The All Steel House Project was for
a prefabricated housing system of 12-in. steel channels in panel
sections. The drawing is inscribed by Frank Lloyd Wright to Russell
Hitchcock (i.e., Henry-Russell Hitchcock). The Yahara Boat Club
Project drawing and the All Steel House Project drawing were both
presented to the Royal Institute of British Architects by Henry-
Russell Hitchcock.

A43

Cooper-Hewitt Museum
The Smithsonian Institution's National Museum of Design
2 East 91st Street
New York, New York 10028

    The Imperial Hotel (1915), Tokyo, Japan, now demolished, is the
only building by Frank Lloyd Wright represented in the holdings of
the Cooper-Hewitt Museum at New York. The items from the Imperial
Hotel in the collection are two identical side chairs made of oak
with upholstered seats and backs measuring 38 in. x 16 in. x 17 in.
(965.2 mm x 406.4 mm x 431.8 mm) and a small bedroom desk/table made
of oak. However, the collection does house the sample book for Frank
Lloyd Wright's Taliesin Line of wallpapers and fabrics which were
manufactured by the F. Schumacher Company. The sample book of the
Wright designed Schumacher fabrics and wallpapers is in the Department of Textiles of the museum. A more complete description of the
Taliesin Line can be found in the discussion of the holdings of the
Milwaukee Public Library which also houses a rather complete sample
book of wallpaper and fabrics.

A44

Stanford University Archives
Stanford University
Stanford, California 94305

    The Stanford University Archives contains the Paul R. and Jean S.
Hanna "Honeycomb" Residence Papers Collection. This collection contains over 8,000 pieces of archival materials relating to Frank Lloyd
Wright and the Paul R. and Jean S. Hanna "Honeycomb" Residence which
Wright designed for the Hannas in 1936 at Stanford, California. The
archives consists of over 50 binder volumes including letters, telegrams, sketches, newspaper and periodical articles, notes, over 100
drawings, and about 500 photographs and transparencies. The entire
collection has been microfilmed for publication and distribution by
the Architectural History Foundation of New York and the MIT Press
as *The Hanna House Documents* (Cambridge: The MIT Press, 1982) and
consists of seven rolls of 35mm microfilm. Unfortunately, *The Hanna
House Documents* was not available to the author during the conduct
of the research for this book and consequently are not described.
However, the Architectural History Foundation and the MIT Press
jointly published *Frank Lloyd Wright's Hanna House: The Client's
Report*, by Paul R. and Jean S. Hanna in 1981, which reproduced twenty-
four manuscripts by Frank Lloyd Wright, including letters dated
February 11, 1936, and April 2, 1936; a "Memo of Agreement" dated

1936 (?); letters dated May 31, 1936; June 17, 1936; August 28, 1936; September 2, 1936; November 28, 1936; November 30, 1936; December 1, 1936; January 2, 1937; a telegram dated mid-January of 1937; letters dated mid-January 1937; January 26, 1937; January 27, 1937; telegrams dated February 2, 1937; February 3, 1937; letters dated February 5, 1937; April 25, 1937; a telegram dated August 6, 1937; a letter dated August 18, 1937; telegrams dated October 1, 1937; October 12, 1937; and a letter dated November of 1937. These documents are catalogued in chronological order in Part II of this research guide.

The Hanna "Honeycomb" Residence is owned by Stanford University, a gift from the Hannas. This researcher was unable to obtain a listing of the various Frank Lloyd Wright designed items contained in the residence which includes furniture. However, an urn from the Frank Lloyd Wright designed Imperial Hotel (1915) at Tokyo, Japan (now demolished), is located on the Hanna Residence property. The urn measures 94 in. (2387.6 mm) in height and 47 in. (1193.8 mm) in diameter and weighs two tons. An extensive description of the Hanna Residence can be found in "A Great Frank Lloyd Wright House" (*House Beautiful*, Vol. 105, No. 1, January 1963), pp. 6, 8, 53-113, 117-120, and the front cover, and the 1981 publication of the Hannas' *Frank Lloyd Wright's Hanna House: The Clients' Report*.

A45

The George Arents Research Library
Syracuse University
Syracuse, New York 13210

The George Arents Research Library at Syracuse University houses the Coronet Magazine Collection, 1935-1961. This collection contains four items relating to Frank Lloyd Wright and an article which Wright had written for possible publication in *Coronet Magazine* entitled "The Man who Paid Cash: A Scenario Wherein a Rich Man Meets an Artist and, for a While, Each Has His Say" (*Coronet*, January 1939), pp. 175-176. The items are a three-page galley with a typed manuscript of the article; also, three preliminary typeset printings of the article are in the collection. The library must approve photoduplicates of these materials and application for their use must be made to the library.

A46

Special Collections Department
Marriott Library
University of Utah
Salt Lake City, Utah 84112

The Taylor Woolley Archive of the Special Collections Department of the Marriott Library at the University of Utah contains the microfilm of thirteen original pieces of correspondence, eighteen Wright drawings, and twenty-five blueprints of drawings used by Wright for his famous *Ausgeführte Bauten und Entwürfe von Frank Lloyd Wright* (the Wasmuth Portfolio) among its many Prairie School related holdings. Taylor A. Woolley worked for Frank Lloyd Wright from about 1908 to about 1911, during Wright's years at the Oak Park, Illinois, prac-

tice and in the preparation of the Wasmuth Portfolio in Italy.
    The correspondence consists of a letter for Taylor A. Woolley dated
June 1909; a letter to Walter Burley Griffin dated June 10, 1910;
letters to Taylor A. Woolley dated June 16, 1910; July 20, 1910; April
6, 1911; April 22, (1911?); telegrams to Woolley dated August 31,
1911; September 12, 1911; letters to Woolley dated July 16, 1912;
September 1, (1912?); December 17, 1912; a telegram to Woolley dated
March 30, 1914; and a letter to Woolley dated January 10, 1938.
    The microfilmed items in the Taylor Woolley Archive include blue-
prints and drawings of the following buildings and projects by Frank
Lloyd Wright (the microfilm image number of each drawing follows the
description of the drawing in parenthesis):

William H. Winslow Residence (1893)
River Forest, Illinois
    One blueprint of a perspective of the facade (#193).

A.C. McAfee Residence Project (1894)
Lake Michigan at Chicago, Illinois
    One blueprint of a perspective of the facade; this is a blue-
    print of Plate 4 of the Wasmuth Portfolio (#36).

Wolf Lake Amusement Park (1895)
Wolf Lake, Illinois
    One blueprint of a general view; this is a blueprint of Plate
    6 of the Wasmuth Portfolio (#43).
    One blueprint of a site plan; this is a blueprint of Plate 7
    of the Wasmuth Portfolio (#51).
    One blueprint of an aerial perspective; this is a blueprint
    of Plate 7 of the Wasmuth Portfolio (#38).

Frank Lloyd Wright Studio (1898)
Oak Park, Illinois
    One pencil drawing similar to Wright's Oak Park Studio. This
    drawing may not be by Frank Lloyd Wright; further investiga-
    tion to properly identify the drawing is needed (#164).

River Forest Golf Club (1898)
River Forest, Illinois
    One blueprint of the perspective of the facade; this is a
    blueprint of Plate 17 of the Wasmuth Portfolio (#188).

"A Small House with Lots of Room in It"
Ladies Home Journal Project (1900)
    One blueprint of a perspective of the facade; this is a blue-
    print of Plate 14 of the Wasmuth Portfolio (#37).

F.B. Henderson Residence (1901)
Elmhurst, Illinois
    One blueprint of a perspective of the facade; this is a blue-
    print of Plate 18 of the Wasmuth Portfolio (#46).

Nell and Jane Lloyd Jones Hillside Home School II (1901)
Spring Green, Wisconsin
    One blueprint of a "bird's eye view"; this is a blueprint of
    Plate 25 of the Wasmuth Portfolio (#192).

Lexington Terrace Project (1901)
Chicago, Illinois
    One blueprint of a "bird's eye view"; this is a blueprint of
    Plate 89 of the Wasmuth Portfolio (#59).

Ward W. Willits Residence (1901)
Highland Park, Illinois
  One blueprint of a perspective of the facade; this is a blue-
    print of Plate 22 of the Wasmuth Portfolio (#191).

Walter Gerts Residence (1902)
Whitehall, Michigan
  One blueprint of a perspective of a side elevation; this is
    a blueprint of Plate 59 of the Wasmuth Portfolio (#45).

Victor Metzger Residence Project (1902)
Desbarats, Ontario, Canada
  One blueprint of a perspective of a side elevation; this is
    a blueprint of Plate 23 of the Wasmuth Portfolio (#39).
  One blueprint of a perspective of the facade; this is a blue-
    print of Plate 24 of the Wasmuth Portfolio (#194).

Yahara Boat Club Project (1902)
Madison, Wisconsin
  One blueprint of a perspective of the facade; this is a blue-
    print of Plate 28 of the Wasmuth Portfolio (#189).

Edwin H. Cheney Residence (1904)
Oak Park, Illinois
  One blueprint of a perspective of the facade; this is a blue-
    print of Plate 42 of the Wasmuth Portfolio (#49).

Robert D. Clarke Residence Project (1904)
Peoria, Illinois
  One blueprint of a "bird's eye view"; this is a blueprint of
    Plate 38 of the Wasmuth Portfolio (#52).

Burton J. Westcott Residence (1904)
Springfield, Ohio
  One perspective drawing of the facade drawn in ink over pen-
    cil; this is a drawing of Plate 75 of the Wasmuth Portfolio
    (#58).

P.A. Beachy Residence (1906)
Oak Park, Illinois
  One blueprint of a perspective of the facade (#190).

George Madison Millard Residence (1906)
Highland Park, Illinois
  One blueprint of a perspective of the facade; this is a blue-
    print of Plate 54 of the Wasmuth Portfolio (#50).

Frederick G. Robie Residence (1906)
Chicago, Illinois
  One blueprint of a perspective of the facade; this is a blue-
    print of Plate 87 of the Wasmuth Portfolio (#40).

Elizabeth Stone Residence Project (1906)
Glencoe, Illinois
  One blueprint of a "bird's eye view"; this is a blueprint of
    Plate 55 of the Wasmuth Portfolio (#44).

Avery Coonley Residence (1907)
Riverside, Illinois
  One drawing in ink of the living room (#6).
  One blueprint of a perspective of the facade; this is a blue-
    print of Plate 81 of the Wasmuth Portfolio (#185).

Browne's Bookstore (1908)
Chicago, Illinois
　　One blueprint of the interior; this is a blueprint of Plate 78
　　of the Wasmuth Portfolio (#47).

Como Orchards Summer Colony (1908)
University Heights, Darby, Montana
　　One blueprint of a perspective of the facade; this is a blue-
　　print of Plate 98 of the Wasmuth Portfolio (#187).

Horseshoe Inn for Willard Ashton (1908)
Estes Park, Colorado
　　One drawing of a "bird's eye perspective" drawn in pencil (#12).
　　One blueprint of a "bird's eye view"; this is a blueprint of
　　Plate 79 of the Wasmuth Portfolio (#186).

Frank J. Baker Residence (1909)
Wilmette, Illinois
　　One drawing of a perspective of the facade drawn in ink (#3).

Town of Bitter Root Project (1909)
Darby, Montana
　　Two drawings of a "bird's eye perspective" drawn in ink (#14
　　and #15).
　　Two site plans drawn in ink (#65 and #66).

City National Bank and Hotel for Blythe and Markley (1909)
Mason City, Iowa
　　One blueprint of a perspective of a facade of the hotel and
　　side elevation of the bank; this is a blueprint of Plate 94
　　of the Wasmuth Portfolio (#198).

Three Small Residences for Edward C. Waller Project (1909)
River Forest, Illinois
　　One blueprint of a perspective; this is a blueprint of Plate
　　91 of the Wasmuth Portfolio (#48).

Frank Lloyd Wright Residence/Studio Project (1910)
Viali Verdi, Fiesole, Italy
　　One unidentified pencil drawing of a floor plan and facade
　　perspective, possibly an early design for this project;
　　further research will have to be done to more properly
　　identify this drawing (#16).
　　One unidentified pencil drawing of the floor plan and perspec-
　　tive with "Italian Villino" and "Florence/Mar 1910" scribbled
　　in pencil at the bottom of the drawing; further research
　　will have to be done to further identify this drawing (#17).

Lake Geneva Hotel for Arthur L. Richards (1911)
Lake Geneva, Wisconsin
　　One ink and pastel drawing of a perspective of the facade (#35).

　　The following are unidentified microfilmed drawings in the collection which may be by Frank Lloyd Wright; further scholarly investigation is necessary to properly identify these drawings:

　　One blueprint of first floor plan for a residence (#197) and
　　one blueprint of second floor plan (#201). The plans are
　　cruciform in design, similar to Wright's plans for the Isabel
　　Roberts Residence and the Ward W. Willits Residence.

One pencil drawing of a perspective of a residence facade
(#1).
One pencil drawing of a design for a puppet theater (#2).

It is unfortunate that the drawings of this collection survive
only in microfilm form, but the originals have been destroyed. Research
access to the Taylor Woolley Archive can be gained by contacting the
Curator of the Special Collections Department of the Marriott Library.

A47

Department of Furniture and Woodwork
The Victoria and Albert Museum
South Kensington
London SW7 2RL
England

The Department of Furniture and Woodwork of the Victoria and
Albert Museum houses the dismantled Frank Lloyd Wright designed office
for Edgar J. Kaufmann done in 1937 which was originally built for
Kaufmann's department store in Pittsburgh, Pennsylvania. The room was
dismantled in the late 1950s and was presented to the Victoria and
Albert Museum in 1974. The room was temporarily exhibited on its
arrival at the Victoria and Albert Museum and the Museum is presently
awaiting its permanent installation--the room is in storage until then.
Due to the lack of space during its temporary exhibition, the room
could only be shown in three-quarter view.

Bebbe Klatt-Mooring, author of "What Is the Essence of the Kaufmann Office and How Does It Fit into the Development of Frank Lloyd
Wright's Ornamentation," offers, with permission, the following description of the office:

Its two perimeter glass screens measure 22 feet and 26 feet. The
room is basically rectangular, with a notched out corner, making
it slightly L-shaped. Its six walls, the ceiling and the floor
are constructed of swamp cypress plywood.... Standard plywood
sheets in America are produced to 8 feet x 4 feet. Wright has
utilized these dimensions by constructing a three dimensional
module 4 ft. x 4 ft. x 4 ft. The length of the entire sheet
becomes the room height (8 feet), while the ceiling and floor
are clad with 4 ft. x 4 ft. squares. Light from the exterior
glass screen of the two adjoining walls penetrates through
louvres, set in a 2 ft. module which are made of cypress wood
as well. On one wall the louvres extend from the ceiling down
to the top of built in cupboards, while on the other wall the
louvres run all the way down to the floor.

But the main feature of the room is the huge mural that takes
up a whole wall and extends its ornament on to four other walls.
The mural is composed of pieces of the same swamp cypress plywood and strips sawn to size on site. The pattern is geometrical,
consisting of 30-60-90 degree angles, thus forming triangles,
rhomboids or hexagonal shapes. A relief effect is achieved by
layering the plywood, and highlighted by the insertion of strips
projecting even further forward. Depth is also given by saw cuts
into the plywood. A further intensification of the pattern is
achieved by having the boards cut either perpendicularly, length-

wise or at an angle with the grain. A focal point is created by
a light fixture incorporated in the design as a triangle of
translucent glass, flush with the plywood. According to early
photographs in *In the Nature of Materials* by Hitchcock, the
original glass was divided in triangular fields by timber beads.
It has since been replaced by white perspex, without the beads.
The basic module is 3/8 in., therefore dimensions of 3/4 in.
(2 modules), 1-1/8 in. (3), 3-3/8 in. (9), 4-1/2 in. (12),
6-3/4 in. (18) are found throughout the mural. The repetition
of the module is very regular. However, occasionally Wright
extends (uses 13 modules instead of 12) or shortens (8 instead
of 9) the rhythm.... At the base of the mural is a shelf which
at one point extends into the room and forms the top of the
desk. This desk consists of two surfaces that overlap each other
and cantilever over the box-like base....

Contributing to the good look is the marvellous craftsmanship
of not only the chairs, but all joinery work, including the
mural. There was no source mentioning who was responsible for
the carpentry until I happened to find a pencil note under the
bottom of the desk reading "Manuel J. Sandoval & Ray Porraz,
March 18/37, from Nicaragua, C. America." Sandoval's name re-
appears in a list of apprentices who were chartered applicants
for the Taliesin Fellowship, October 25th, 1932.... The original
upholstery for the chairs was specially woven by Loja Saarinen
(1879-1968) in the weaving studios at Cranbrook Academy of Art,
Bloomfield Hills, Michigan.... The yarns for the covers of the
chairs are of different materials and textures. Mercerised
cotton, rayon and cotton chenille are combined in a pattern of
stripes of varying lengths. The chenille stripes, in a range
of lemon-yellow-mustard, form a relief effect against the flat
background of subtle cream-sand grey-beige ... the two original
handknotted, fitted carpets were rolled up and put in storage,
and replaced by the two pairs of different, badly matching
patterned ones.... The originals are unavailable for viewing,
but are described as having 'a flex warp, woollen pile and flax
securing weft bands. The asymmetrical pattern is formed by a
block and stripes of irregular lengths in mid-yellow and an off-
white ground'.

The inside space can be divided into decks ... this is demonstrated by the line of cupboards that run along the opposite
wall as one enters the room. The height is the same as the top
of the door, and above them louvres continue to the ceiling.
The louvres do not run above the whole length of the cupboards,
but stop before the corner. This corner is illuminated by a
concealed light on top of the ledge. The horizontal ... is
further emphasized in the office by the way the mural extends
its ornament to the adjoining walls by way of horizontal bands
that end up in one line only, on the wall furthest away ...
nothing starts or ends in the corners of the room. Where the
cupboard wall ends, the mural floats over the upper ledge, and
the shelf underneath....

Further documentation concerning the Kaufmann Office can be found
in "Strong Room" (*Architects' Journal* [England], Vol. 160, September
18, 1974), p. 655; "Not Quite Wright: Frank Lloyd Wright Interior of

1937 Office from Kaufmann Department Store in the Victoria and Albert Museum" (*Building Design* [England], No. 225, November 8, 1974), p. 9; and Toni del Renzio's "Frank Lloyd Wright and the Pop Tradition" (*Art and Artists*, Vol. 9, January 1975), pp. 28-31.

A48

The Warehouse
300 South Church Street
Richland Center, Wisconsin 53581

The Warehouse is actually the Frank Lloyd Wright designed A.D. German Warehouse of 1915 at Richland Center, Wisconsin. In the early 1970s a group of Richland County, Wisconsin, citizens joined together to form the Richland Museum, Ltd., a non-profit educational corporation. The main goal of this organization was to purchase the A.D. German Warehouse and to restore it for use as a museum and cultural center; emphasis was to be placed on Frank Lloyd Wright's works and his contributions to architecture in general. Currently, the building is being renovated taking into consideration Wright's original drawings for the building. In 1972 the A.D. German Warehouse was placed on the National Register of Historic Places.

The Warehouse collections have only three possible Frank Lloyd Wright original manuscripts and these have not been positively confirmed to have been written by him. These three manuscripts are typed, with handwritten corrections (which was very characteristic of most of Wright's original manuscripts), and have no signatures. Two of the three manuscripts appear to be rough drafts of "Letters to the Editor" (possibly to William T. Evjue, of Madison, Wisconsin's *The Capital Times* newspaper), describing the writer's (Wright's?) views on World War II and conscription. The third document (only two of the five original pages remain) discusses the rebuilding of London. There is limited discussion of these manuscripts here, because of their presently questionable authenticity, though it may be proven at a later date.

The Warehouse has a set of blueprints of the original design for the building which were reproduced from the original tracings by the Frank Lloyd Wright Foundation. Also housed in the collection are six pieces of furniture from the Frank Lloyd Wright designed Clarence Sondern Residence of 1940 at Kansas City, Missouri. These six pieces of furniture include one table made of cypress plywood measuring 26 in. x 30 in. x 24 in. (660.4 mm x 762 mm x 609.6 mm); one chair made of cypress plywood, with upholstery, measuring 29 in. x 22 in. x 25 in. (736.6 mm x 558.8 mm x 635 mm); and one chair made of cypress plywood and upholstery measuring 28 in. x 18 in. x 21 in. (711.2 mm x 457.2 mm x 533.4 mm).

Items in The Warehouse collections may be viewed with permission of the Curator. *The Milwaukee Journal* reported in early 1980 that The Warehouse had been sold to Minneapolis businessmen. According to this report, the new owners planned to restore and renovate the entire structure and lease part of it to the museum free of charge (see *The Milwaukee Journal* [April 2, 1980, Part 1], p. 2 and James Auer's "A Wright Renovation" [*The Milwaukee Journal*, August 24, 1980, Lively Arts Section, Part 5,], p. 4 for a detailed review of the alterations proposed for the building and how the museum is to be funded by other uses housed in the building).

A49

The State Historical Society of Wisconsin
816 State Street
Madison, Wisconsin 53706

   The State Historical Society of Wisconsin contains eighty-seven
manuscripts written by Frank Lloyd Wright including letters and telegrams. These manuscripts are contained in the American Council for
Judaism Papers, 1938-1953; the Don Anderson Papers Collection, 1890-
1972; the Bruce Barton Papers, 1881-1965; the August Derleth Papers;
the William Theodore Evjue Papers, 1905-1969; the First Unitarian
Society of Madison, Wisconsin Records 1878-1976; the Jane Lloyd Jones
Correspondence, 1899-1940; and the Harold M. Groves Papers, 1927-1969.
   The American Council for Judaism Papers, 1938-1953 contains only
two letters written by Wright; one of which is dated April 4, 1949,
and the other March 12, 1952. In both letters Wright expresses his
opinions on religion and Judaism in particular. The American Council
for Judaism was an anti-Zionist organization of Americans of the
Jewish faith committed to the principle that Judaism is a religion.
   The Don Anderson Papers Collection, 1890-1972 contains two letters
from Wright to Anderson, one dated August 14, 1930 and the other dated
July 3, 1954. Mr. Anderson was the publisher of *The Wisconsin State
Journal*. Researchers wanting to examine this collection must obtain
Anderson's written permission.
   The Bruce Barton Papers, 1881-1965 contains only one letter written
by Frank Lloyd Wright to Bruce Barton dated December 22, 1951. There
are also two letters from Olgivanna Lloyd Wright (Frank Lloyd Wright's
wife) to Barton, one of which requests Barton to review her book and
the other, dated April 14, 1959, invites Barton to Wright's memorial
dinner. Bruce Barton was an author, advertising executive, and a
politician.
   The August Derleth Papers Collection has four manuscripts written
by Wright. There are three letters to August Derleth dated December
22, 1942; January 5, 1943; and January 12, 1943; and one holiday greeting card dated 1944-1945.
   The William Theodore Evjue Papers, 1905-1969 contains thirty-nine
manuscripts (letters, telegrams, etc.) written by Frank Lloyd Wright.
Of the thirty-nine manuscripts, thirty-three are addressed directly
to Evjue. The others are copies to Evjue sent by Wright for Evjue's
review. William T. Evjue was the founder, editor, and publisher of
Madison, Wisconsin's *The Capital Times* newspaper. Evjue became a close
friend of Wright's in 1922 following Wright's return from Japan. The
Wright letters in the Evjue Papers collection span a period from 1926
to February 1959, the bulk of which are written in the 1950s and con-
cern the Wright proposed Monona Terrace Civic Center Project for
Madison, Wisconsin. The manuscripts in the William Theodore Evjue
Papers, 1905-1969 collection are enumerated as follows: undated telegram; undated letter written either in 1926 or 1927; letters dated
January 30, 1934; February 5, 1934; February 15, 1934; May 18, 1936;
October 7, 1940; December 11, 1942; undated letter probably of January
1 or January 2, 1943; letters dated January 8, 1943; January 22, 1943;
July 26, 1943; January 31, 1944; July 19, 1945; March 15, 1944; June
16, 1944; December 9, 1944; July 31, 1947; October 23, 1947; April
5, 1951; June 13, 1952; October 15, 1952; September 21, 1953; letter
to George Rodgerson dated October 3, 1953; letters dated June 12, 1954;

November 2, 1954; unaddressed letter dated October 22, 1954; letter
to Ivan Nestingen dated December 4, 1954; letters dated March 24,
1955; July 9, 1955; letter to Alvin Sarra dated July 14, 1955; telegram to Richard Hawley Cutting dated July 3, 1954; letter to Drew
Pearson dated October 18, 1955; letter to William Evjue dated May 11,
1956; letters dated June 18, 1956; August 22, 1958; September 18,
1958; December 17, 1958; and February 8, 1959.

The Harold M. Groves Papers, 1927-1969 houses thirty-seven original
manuscripts written by Frank Lloyd Wright which span from the early
1940s to 1958. Harold M. Groves was a noted economist and University
of Wisconsin professor. Groves met Wright in the early 1930s and was
involved with Wright's designs for the Unitarian Church at Shorewood
Hills, Wisconsin, of 1947, and the Monona Terrace Civic Center Project
for Madison, Wisconsin, of 1955. Groves' wife, Helen, was the secretary of Citizens for Monona Terrace and organized support for the
project. After passage of a referendum on the Monona Terrace Civic
Center Project, Harold M. Groves was appointed to the Monona Terrace
Civic Center Project Auditorium Committee. Original manuscripts in
this collection written by Frank Lloyd Wright are: an autographed
copy of Wright's *An Autobiography--Book Six, Broadacre City*; a letter
to Harold M. Groves dated February 11, 1946; a letter to the First
Unitarian Society of Madison dated May 29, 1947; letters to Harold M.
Groves dated June 7, 1947; and June 17, 1947; a letter to Dr. Frederic
E. Mohs dated March 10, 1948; a letter to Kenneth L. Patton dated
October 16, 1948; a letter to Mr. C. Howard King dated January 18,
1949; letters to Harold M. Groves dated February 19, 1949; August
1, 1949; September 22, 1950; October 23, 1950; and January 4, 1952;
a letter to Mr. Howard C. Custer dated February 25, 1952; Christmas
greetings to Mr. and Mrs. Harold M. Groves dated December 25, 1953;
letters to the Harold M. Groves' dated January 31, 1954; February 23,
1954; March 2, 1954 (telegram); June 12, 1954; June 23, 1954; and
June 27, 1954; an undated (November 1954?) letter to the mayor, city
council, and county board of Madison, Wisconsin, area; a letter to
Mayor Ivan A. Nestingen (Madison, Wisconsin) dated December 4, 1954;
a letter to Mr. and Mrs. Harold M. Groves dated December 21, 1954;
a copy of the Building Program Outline--Monona Terrace Civic Center
Project for Madison, Wisconsin, dated February 12, 1955; letters to
Mr. and Mrs. Harold M. Groves dated March 24, 1955 and June 14, 1955;
a letter to William T. Evjue dated July 9, 1955; a copy of the contract between Frank Lloyd Wright and Madison, Wisconsin, for architectural services relating to the Monona Terrace Civic Center Project
dated July 5, 1956; letters to Mayor Ivan A. Nestingen dated September
6, 1956; and September 10, 1956; a letter to Mr. and Mrs. Harold M.
Groves dated December 11, 1956; and December 27, 1956 telegram; a
letter to the Building Committee of the Monona Terrace Civic Center
Project dated March 20, 1957; a telegram to Harold M. Groves dated
April 15, 1957; a letter to Mayor Ivan Nestingen and the Common Council
(Madison, Wisconsin) dated November 27, 1957; and a letter to Mr. James
Marshall of the City of Madison Parks Department dated June 13, 1958.

In addition to the original manuscripts written by Frank Lloyd
Wright and Harold M. Groves, the Harold M. Groves Papers, 1927-1969
collection contains numerous other Frank Lloyd Wright related items.
Some of these items include correspondence between Harold M. Groves
or Helen Groves with Eugene Masselink, William Wesley Peters, Robert
L. Wright, Rabbi Mortimer Cohen, Herbert E. Johnson, August Derleth,

Joseph Jackson, William T. Evjue, Harold Price, Jr., Ben Raeburn,
Alicia Patterson Guggenheim, Ivan Nestingen, Edgar Kaufmann, Jr.,
William Proxmire, and Baker Brownell. There is an extensive file on
the Monona Terrace Civic Center Project which includes speeches and
notes by the Groves'; items on the Metzner Act, the case of the *Frank
Lloyd Wright Foundation* vs. *City of Madison and Attorney General* dating
from November of 1958 to April of 1959, as well as other general
correspondence pertaining to the project. Although there were several
pamphlets about the project no drawings were discovered in the Groves
collection. There is also an extensive file on the Unitarian Church
near Madison, Wisconsin, designed by Wright including general correspondence and other records.

The First Unitarian Society of Madison, Wisconsin Records 1878-
1976 contains only one letter written by Frank Lloyd Wright, an
authorization letter to pay a contractor for work done on the Unitarian
Church in Shorewood Hills, Wisconsin, designed by him. The letter
written by Wright is dated November 6, 1951. There are a number of
other letters addressed to Wright from the Unitarian Church dis-
cussing the plans for the building.

The Jane Lloyd Jones Correspondence, 1899-1940 contains only three
pages which relate to Frank Lloyd Wright. These are two pages of a
genealogy composed by one of Frank Lloyd Wright's aunts tracing
Wright's ancestry and a "To Whom It May Concern" letter written by
Wright dated February 3, 1912.

Several tape recordings on and by Frank Lloyd Wright are also
contained in the Society's holdings. There is the collection of three
phonograph records which were produced by Wright for Columbia Records
in the early 1950s. Record one is on the topic of acoustics and was
recorded at Taliesin in April of 1951. It also includes Wright's reading from Walt Whitman in August of 1951 and a few piano solos by
Wright recorded in July of 1951. Record two of this set is a talk by
Wright entitled "Man or Machine" recorded at Taliesin in July of 1951.
Record three is a lecture given by Wright to the Junior Chapter of the
American Institute of Architects at New York in June of 1952. The records
are recorded on two reels of recording tape with the Society's call
number, Tape Recording 147A.

On February 10, 1955, Frank Lloyd Wright gave a speech at a testimonial dinner organized to assist in the payment of property taxes
owed by Wright to Iowa County, Wisconsin. This speech was recorded
and given anonymously to the State Historical Society of Wisconsin
(call number, Tape Recording 537A). In this speech, Wright discusses
the need for personal architecture, the architect as visionary, and
an American architecture.

There is a tape recording (call number, Tape Recording 506A) of
Frank Lloyd Wright speaking at the Merchandise Mart in Chicago on
September 14, 1955, for the introduction of his designs for the
Heritage-Henredon Furniture Company. Introducing him on this occasion
was Elizabeth Gordon, the editor of *House Beautiful* magazine.

There is also a tape, recorded December 29, 1958, (call number,
Tape Recording 140A) of Frank Lloyd Wright on the subject of the
creative mind. The tape was sponsored by the Lowell Institute Cooperative Broadcasting Council and titled "Frank Lloyd Wright: The Architect as Creator." It is essay number two of the National Association
of Educational Broadcastors Series "The Creative Mind," produced by
WGBH radio in Boston, under a grant from the Educational Television

and Radio Center. Wright is interviewed on the tape by Dr. Lyman Bryson.

Also included in the Society's tape recording collection on Wright is an interview by Doris Platt, of the Society's staff, of Mrs. Frank Lloyd Wright (call number, Tape Recording 315A). The interview is dated September 6, 1962, and was made for broadcast over Madison's radio station WHA in their "Wisconsin Writers" series.

The Society houses one Frank Lloyd Wright drawing, that of the floor plan of the Nakoma Country Club and Winnebago Camping Ground Indian Memorial Project for Madison, Wisconsin, of 1924. The drawing is a blueprint drawn at a scale of 1/8 in. = 1 ft. 0 in. and measures 30+ in. x 24+ in. (762+ mm x 609.6+ mm). The Society call number for this drawing is WF90a, W94.

The Society will only reproduce those materials from its collections, which in the opinion of the head of the division holding custody, are properly available for duplication. The Society does not sell photo-duplicates, but merely performs the service of copying. The fees paid are exclusively for such service. All responsibility for questions which may arise in the copying of and use of copies is to be assumed by the applicant. Copyrighted material is not reproduced beyond recognized "fair use" without the authorization of the copyright owner. In the Archives Division of the Society, every researcher using the facility is requested to sign an annual registration form which includes an agreement to abide by the rules governing the use of the Division's holdings.

A50

Elvehjem Art Center
800 University Avenue
The University of Wisconsin
Madison, Wisconsin 53706

In 1924 Frank Lloyd Wright designed the Nakoma Country Club and Winnebago Camping Ground Indian Memorial Project to be located at Madison, Wisconsin. He designed monumental sculptures, for this project, called Nakoma and Nakomis, as a memorial to the Winnebago (Ojibwa) Indians who were native to the Madison area. Unfortunately, the project did not materialize into an executed building. However, miniature models of the Nakoma and Nakomis Indian figures were cast in Chicago (1927-1929); these figures were acquired by the Elvehjem Art Center. The figures are made of terracotta with platinum glaze. The Nakoma figure measures 15-3/4 in. (400 mm) high and the Nakomis figure measures 12-1/4 in. (311.2 mm) high. The Nakoma double figure is teaching his son to take the bow to the Sun God and the female Nakomis figure is a symbol of fertility.

Copies of these two sculptures were made available for sale to the general public in a limited edition. For reviews of these special sales see "FLLW Sculpture Offered in Limited Edition" (*Architectural Record*, Vol. 157, No. 2, February 1975), p. 35 and "Nakoma Warrior and Nakomis Woman (1924)" (*Art in America*, Vol. 63, No. 6, November 1975), p. 140.

A51

School of Architecture and Urban Planning
The University of Wisconsin-Milwaukee
P.O. Box 413
Milwaukee, Wisconsin 53201

   The Arthur L. Richards Lake Geneva Hotel designed by Frank Lloyd
Wright in 1911 at Lake Geneva, Wisconsin, was demolished in 1970
to make space for a new building. One hundred and seventy-two items
were removed from the structure prior to demolition and were donated
to the School of Architecture and Urban Planning of the University
of Wisconsin-Milwaukee (for a detailed discussion of the presentation
see "School Given Wright Items" [*The Milwaukee Journal*, February 21,
1971]). These items included one skylight frame; one lamp base; one
box of miscellaneous items including lead-strips, glass pieces, and
window cranks; seven panes of glass; seven window frames measuring
37-1/2 in. x 36 in. (952.5 mm x 914.4 mm); four window frames measuring
36 in. x 48 in. (952.5 mm x 1219.2 mm); two window frames measuring
7 ft. x 4 ft. (213.4 cm x 121.9cm); eighteen cracked and broken windows; and seventy-nine intact windows, several of which measure approximately 43 in. x 21 in. (1092.2 mm x 533.4 mm) and are leaded glass.

A52

The Frank Lloyd Wright Home and Studio Foundation
Chicago and Forest Avenues
Oak Park, Illinois 60302

   The Frank Lloyd Wright Home and Studio Foundation was founded in
1974 as a non-profit corporation to acquire and preserve the Frank
Lloyd Wright Home and Studio (1889-1911) located at Oak Park, Illinois.
Under the terms of the agreement finalized in August of 1975 between
the Foundation and the National Trust for Historic Preservation, the
Trust holds title to the property and leases it to the Foundation for
a nominal sum. The Foundation has responsibility for the operation
and restoration of the Frank Lloyd Wright Home and Studio. The Foundation, housed in the Frank Lloyd Wright Home and Studio, also serves
as a research center for Frank Lloyd Wright and his architecture and
houses related archival materials. Original archival materials housed
at the Home and Studio by the Foundation include one item of correspondence, a letter to Mrs. Ethel Gerts from Frank Lloyd Wright dated
September 21, 1937, and the items listed under the following Wright
designs:

   Frank Lloyd Wright Residence and Studio (1889-1911)
   Oak Park, Illinois
      Six straight back upholstered wood side chairs for the dining
         room, each of which measures 57-3/4 in. x 16 in. x 17-3/4 in.
         (1466.9 mm x 406.4 mm x 450.9 mm).
      One oak side chair, with an upholstered seat, measuring 42 in.
         x 16 in. x 16-1/4 in. (1066.8 mm x 406.4 mm x 412.8 mm); the
         seat measures 19 in. (482.6 mm) high.
      One dining table made of oak measuring 52 in. x 83 in. (1320.8
         mm x 2108.2 mm) and 28 in. (711.2 mm) high.
      One wood picture frame (gilded) measuring 31-1/2 in. x 27-1/2
         in. (800.1 mm x 698.5 mm).

One wood bed measuring 84 in. x 41 in. (2133.6 mm x 1041.4 mm)
with a headboard 60 in. (1524.0 mm) high and a footboard
30 in. (762.0 mm) high.
One oak table measuring 54 in. x 60-1/2 in. x 29 in. (1371.6 mm
x 1536.7 mm x 736.6 mm).
Two blue line working drawing prints of the basement plan of
the Frank Lloyd Wright Residence (1889) measuring 17 in. x
22 in. (431.8 mm x 558.8 mm) drawn at a scale of 1/4 in. =
1 foot.
Two blue line working drawing prints of the first floor plan
of the Frank Lloyd Wright Residence (1889) measuring 17 in. x
22 in. (431.8 mm x 558.8 mm) drawn at a scale of 1/4 in. =
1 foot.
Two blue line working drawing prints of the ground floor plan
of the Frank Lloyd Wright Residence (1889) measuring 17 in. x
22 in. (431.8 mm x 558.8 mm) drawn at a scale of 1/4 in. =
1 foot.
Two blue line working drawing prints of the north elevation of
the Frank Lloyd Wright Residence (1889) measuring 17 in. x
22 in. (431.8 mm x 558.8 mm) drawn at a scale of 1/4 in. =
1 foot.
Two blue line working drawing prints of the south elevation of
the Frank Lloyd Wright Residence (1889) measuring 17 in. x
22 in. (431.8 mm x 558.8 mm) drawn at a scale of 1/4 in. =
1 foot.
Two blue line working drawing prints of the east elevation of
the Frank Lloyd Wright Residence (1889) measuring 17 in. x
22 in. (431.8 mm x 558.8 mm) drawn at a scale of 1/4 in. =
1 foot.
Two blue line working drawing prints of the west elevation of
the Frank Lloyd Wright Residence (1889) measuring 17 in. x
22 in. (431.8 mm x 558.8 mm) drawn at a scale of 1/4 in. =
1 foot.
Two blue line working drawing prints of a building section of
the Frank Lloyd Wright Residence (1889) measuring 17 in. x
22 in. (431.18 mm x 558.8 mm) drawn at a scale of 1/4 in. =
1 foot.
In addition to these items there is also an extensive collection of paint samples from the building.

Frederick Bagley Residence (1894)
Hinsdale, Illinois
Paint samples from the building.

Chauncey L. Williams Residence (1895)
River Forest, Illinois
Paint samples from the building.

Francis W. Little Residence I and Stable (1902)
Peoria, Illinois
One wood library table measuring 88 in. x 42 in. x 28-1/2 in.
(2235.2 mm x 1066.8 mm x 723.9 mm). This table is an attribu-
tion to this residence.

Arthur Heurtley Residence (1902)
Oak Park, Illinois
Paint samples from the building.

Frederick G. Robie Residence (1906)
Chicago, Illinois
  One blue line print of the foundation plan measuring 24-1/4 in.
  x 46 in. (616.0 mm x 1168.4 mm) drawn at a scale of 1/4 in.
  = 1 foot. This is a print of the original working drawing.
  One blue line working drawing print of the ground floor plan
  measuring 24-1/4 in. x 46 in. (616.0 mm x 1168.4 mm) drawn
  at a scale of 1/4 in. = 1 foot.
  One blue line working drawing print of the first floor plan
  measuring 24-1/4 in. x 46 in. (616.0 mm x 1168.4 mm) drawn
  at a scale of 1/4 in. = 1 foot.
  One blue line print of the working drawing for the second floor
  plan measuring 24-1/4 in. x 46 in. (616.0 mm x 1168.4 mm)
  drawn at a scale of 1/4 in. = 1 foot.
  One blue line print of the working drawing of the north elevation measuring 24-1/4 in. x 46 in. (616.0 mm x 1168.4 mm)
  drawn at a scale of 1/4 in. = 1 foot.
  One blue line print of the working drawing of the south elevation of the garage and residence measuring 24-1/4 in. x
  46 in. (616.0 mm x 1168.4 mm) drawn at a scale of 1/4 in. =
  1 foot.
  One blue line print of working drawings of the east and west
  elevations measuring 24-1/4 in. x 46 in. (616.0 mm x 1168.4
  mm) drawn at a scale of 1/4 in. = 1 foot.
  One blue line print of a building section and wall section from
  the working drawings measuring 24-1/4 in. x 46 in. (616.0
  mm x 1168.4 mm) drawn at a scale of 1/4 in. = 1 foot.
  One blue line print of working drawings of various interior
  details drawn at various scales measuring 24-1/4 in. x 35 in.
  (616.0 mm x 889.0 mm).
  One blue line print of working drawings for case work and
  cabinets measuring 19-3/4 in. x 34 in. (501.7 mm x 863.6 mm)
  with no scale indicated.

K.C. DeRhodes Residence (1906)
South Bend, Indiana
  Paint samples from the building.

Avery Coonley Residence (1907)
Riverside, Illinois
  Upholstered wood easy chair/armchair measuring 33 in. x 37 in.
  x 29 in. (838.2 mm x 939.8 mm x 736.6 mm) with a 16-in.
  (406.4 mm) high seat. This item of furniture is attributed
  to the Coonley Residence.

American System Ready-Cut Houses Projects (1911)
Richards Company
Milwaukee, Wisconsin
  Two blue line prints of Design No. A-203 of the floor plan
  for a single-family residence measuring 12 in. x 18-1/4 in.
  (304.8 mm x 463.6 mm) drawn at a scale of 1/4 in. = 1 foot.
  Two blue line prints of Design No. A-203 of the basement plan
  for a single-family residence measuring 12 in. x 18-1/4 in.
  (304.8 mm x 463.6 mm) drawn at a scale of 1/4 in. = 1 foot.
  Two blue line prints of Design No. A-201 of the roof plan
  for a single-family residence measuring 12 in. x 18-1/4 in.
  (304.8 mm x 463.6 mm) with no scale indicated.

Two blue line prints of Design No. A-201 of the front and rear
elevations for a single-family residence measuring 12 in. x
18-1/4 in. (304.8 mm x 463.6 mm) with no scale indicated.
Two blue line prints of Design No. A-201 of the side and
entrance elevations for a single-family residence measuring
12 in. x 18-1/4 in. (304.8 mm x 463.6 mm) with no scale
indicated.
Two blue line prints of Design No. 401 of the interior finish
elevations for a single-family residence measuring 12 in. x
18-1/4 in. (304.8 mm x 463.6 mm) with no scale indicated.
Two blue line prints of Design No. 501 of the interior finish
elevations for a single-family residence measuring 12 in. x
18-1/4 in. (304.8 mm x 463.6 mm) with no scale indicated.
Two blue line prints of Design No. 601 showing detailed building sections measuring 12 in. x 18-1/4 in. (304.8 mm x
463.6 mm).
Two blue line prints of Design No. 301 showing building sections
measuring 12 in. x 18-1/4 in. (304.8 mm x 463.6 mm) with
no scale indicated.

Royal H. Jurgensen Residence Project (1938)
Evanston, Illinois
One blueprint of an exterior rendering measuring 15-1/2 in. x
25-1/2 in. (393.7 mm x 647.7 mm).
One reproducible black line drawing (copy of original) showing
the northeast and southwest elevations drawn a scale of
1/4 in. = 1 foot and measuring 24+ in. x 30+ in. (610+ mm x
762+ mm).
One reproducible black line drawing (copy of the original)
showing the roof framing plan drawn at a scale of 1 in. =
1 foot and a detail of the the roof. The drawing measures
24+ in. x 30+ in. (610+ mm x 762+ mm).

Frank Lloyd Wright Furniture (1955)
Designs for Heritage-Henredon
Morganton, North Carolina
Two walnut dining room cabinets with doors measuring 21-1/2
in. x 20 in. x 28-1/8 in. (546.1 mm x 508.0 mm x 714.4 mm).
One walnut dining room cabinet with drawers measuring 21-1/2
in. x 20 in. x 28-1/8 in. (546.1 mm x 508.0 mm x 714.4 mm).
One octagonally shaped walnut end table measuring 25 in.
(635.0 mm) wide and 26-1/2 in. (673.1 mm) high.
Two walnut coffee tables measuring 26-1/2 in. x 26-1/2 in.
(673.1 mm x 673.1 mm) and 12-1/2 in. (317.5 mm) high.
One walnut desk measuring 52 in. x 20 in. x 28-1/4 in. (1320.8
mm x 508.0 mm x 717.6 mm).
Two wood upholstered armchairs measuring 40 in. x 20-3/4 in. x
20 in. (1016.0 mm x 527.1 mm x 508.0 mm) with a seat 19 in.
(482.6 mm) high.
Two wood upholstered side chairs measuring 40 in. x 20-3/4 in.
x 20 in. (1016.0 mm x 527.1 mm x 508.0 mm) with a seat 19 in.
(482.6 mm) high. These chairs are of the the same style as
those mentioned above except they do not have arms.
One walnut coffee table with a round slate top measures 14-1/2
in. (368.3 mm) high and has a 22-1/2 in. (571.5 mm) wide
pedestal base.

In addition to the original archival materials outlined, the Home
and Studio also houses other Wright related materials of importance.
There are over 200 original "as built" drawings of the Home and Studio
which document all of the major additions, remodelings, and drawings
for various buildings by William Drummond, done after Drummond worked
in Wright's office.

There is also an extensive collection of black and white photos
documenting the Home and Studio from 1889 to the present. The collection includes early photographs of the Wright, Lloyd Jones, and Tobin
families; of Wright's other architectural works particularly from the
period 1887 to 1911; and of draftsmen who worked in Wright's Oak Park
Studio and of their architectural works.

Other important research materials include:

A file of Wright's buildings arranged by client.
Correspondence and interviews with Wright's children, Lloyd,
   Catherine, David, and Robert Llewellyn.
Memorabilia from the Wright Home and Studio (1889 to 1925)
   including legal papers, deeds, transfers of title, etc.
File copies of Oak Park newspaper articles on Wright and his
   family from 1892 to 1914.
File material on Oak Park, the Yaryan system of heating, etc.
Paint color analysis of the Home and Studio, keyed to the
   Munsel color notation system.
Paint color analysis of Unity Church, keyed to the Munsel
   color notation system.
Copies of all major books on Frank Lloyd Wright and all major
   periodical articles that appeared from 1936 to 1960.
An original set of Froebel blocks; original sets of Lincoln
   Logs and Wright Blocks, both of which were designed by John
   Lloyd Wright.
Various archival materials from the personal collection of John
   Lloyd Wright relating to John Lloyd Wright and his work.

The Frank Lloyd Wright Home and Studio is open for tours and the
Frank Lloyd Wright Home and Studio Foundation Research Center is open
to anyone interested in using it. Appointments to use the Research
Center should be made with the Executive Director.

A53

Archive of Contemporary History
Library
The University of Wyoming
Box 3334
Laramie, Wyoming 82071

The Oskar Stonorov Papers, 1931-1970 collection of the Archive
of Contemporary History of the University of Wyoming Library houses
a very large collection of Frank Lloyd Wright related materials. Oskar
Stonorov and Frank Lloyd Wright organized Wright's "Sixty Years of
Living Architecture" exhibition in the early 1950s which featured much
of Wright's work to that time. This collection houses correspondence
between Oskar Stonorov and Frank Lloyd Wright related to this exhibition, correspondence between Mrs. Frank Lloyd Wright and Oskar Stonorov,
several original Frank Lloyd Wright manuscripts in addition to the

letters in the collection, exhibition press releases, memorabilia, a
tape recording, magazine articles, drawings, and numerous photographs
of drawings, models, and executed buildings designed by Frank Lloyd
Wright.

Correspondence written by Frank Lloyd Wright to Oskar Stonorov
include letters dated November 9, 1949; February 15, 1950; September
2, 1950; November 29, 1950; December 19, 1950; December 21, 1950;
February 9, 1951; February 14, 1951; February 15, 1951; February 22,
1951; March 2, 1951; March 7, 1951; March 12, 1951; March 31, 1951;
April 30, 1951; May 1, 1951; August 11, 1951; December 18, 1951;
January 11, 1952; February 13, 1952; March 5, 1952; March 12, 1952;
May 1, 1952; June 13, 1952; September 29, 1952; December 8, 1952;
December 17, 1952; a December 29, 1952 letter from Eugene Masselink;
letters from Wright, to Stonorov dated March 4, 1953; May 5, 1953;
June 6, 1953; July 3, 1953; December 29, 1953; March 31, 1956; and an
undated letter. There is also one letter written to Oskar Stonorov
by Mrs. Frank Lloyd Wright which is dated August 6, 1959.

Correspondence written by Oskar Stonorov to Frank Lloyd Wright
includes letters dated June 13, 1949; June 28, 1949; August 11, 1949;
November 22, 1949; June 14, 1950; August 24, 1950; December 18, 1950;
February 6, 1951; February 14, 1951; February 16, 1951; February 22,
1951, with attachment; February 26, 1951; March 21, 1951; March 28,
1951, with attachment; April 11, 1951; April 27, 1951, with attachment; May 19, 1951; May 29, 1951; September 5, 1951; September 20,
1951, with attachment; September 21, 1951 (two copies); December 27,
1951; January 7, 1952; February 4, 1952; February 11, 1952; February
28, 1952; March 7, 1952; March 19, 1952; April 9, 1952; April 10,
1952; April 14, 1952; April 28, 1952; April 30, 1952; May 5, 1952;
May 21, 1952; June 11, 1952; June 16, 1952; July 16, 1952; July 25,
1952; August 27, 1952; October 13, 1952; January 27, 1953; April 14,
1953; December 24, 1953; September 10, 1954; and January 26, 1959.

The following buildings and projects by Frank Lloyd Wright are
represented with an extensive photograph collection as part of Wright's
"Sixty Years of Living Architecture" exhibition.

James Charnley Residence (1891)
Chicago, Illinois
   One 8 in. x 10 in. (203.2 mm x 254 mm) photograph with negative
   (Box 62).

Allison Harlan Residence (1892)
Chicago, Illinois
   Three 8 in. x 10 in. negatives (Box 62).

Romeo and Juliet Windmill for Nell and Jane Lloyd Jones (1896)
Spring Green, Wisconsin
   Two 8 in. x 10 in. negatives (Box 63).

Warren Hickox Residence (1900)
Kankakee, Illinois
   One 8 in. x 10 in. photograph with negative (Box 62).
   Two 8 in. x 10 negatives (Box 62).

Ward W. Willits Residence, Gardeners Cottage, and Stables (1901)
Highland Park, Illinois
   Two 8 in. x 10 in photographs with negatives (Box 63).

Susan Lawrence Dana Residence (1902)
Springfield, Illinois
   One 8 in. x 10 in. photograph with negative (Box 62).
   Three 8 in. x 10 in. negatives (Box 62).

Larkin Company Administration Building (1903)
Buffalo, New York
   Three 8 in. x 10 in. photographs with negatives (Box 62).
   Four 8 in. x 10 in. negatives (Box 62).

Unity Church (1905)
Oak Park, Illinois
   Three 8 in. x 10 in. photographs with negatives (Box 63).
   One 8 in. x 10 in. negative (Box 63).

Hiram Baldwin Residence (1905)
Kenilworth, Illinois
   One 8 in. x 10 in. photograph with negative (Box 62).

Frederick G. Robie Residence (1906)
Chicago, Illinois
   One 10 in. x 12 in. (254 mm x 304.8 mm) photograph (Box 63).
   One 8 in. x 10 in. photograph with negative (Box 63).
   Three 8 in. x 10 in. negatives (Box 63).

Avery Coonley Residence (1907)
Riverside, Illinois
   Two 8 in. x 10 in. photographs with negatives (Box 62).

E.A. Gilmore "Airplane House" Residence (1908)
Madison, Wisconsin
   Two 10 in. x 12 in. mounted photographs (Box 61).
   One 8 in. x 10 in. photograph with negative (Box 62).
   One 8 in. x 10 in. photograph (Box 62).

Avery Coonley Playhouse (1912)
Riverside, Illinois
   One 8 in. x 10 in. photograph with negative (Box 62).
   One 8 in. x 10 in. negative (Box 62).

Francis W. Little "Northome" Residence II (1912)
Deephaven, Minnesota
   Three 8 in. x 10 negatives (Box 62).

Midway Gardens for Edward C. Waller, Jr. (1913)
Chicago, Illinois
   One 8 in. x 10 in. negative (Box 63).

Imperial Hotel (1915)
Tokyo, Japan
   One 8 in. x 10 in. photograph with negative (Box 62).
   Thirteen 8 in. x 10 in. negatives (Box 62).

Aline Barnsdall "Hollyhock" Residence (1917)
Los Angeles, California
   One 8 in. x 10 in. photograph with negative (Box 62).
   One 8 in. x 10 in. negative (Box 62).

Charles Ennis Residence (1923)
Los Angeles, California
   One 8 in. x 10 in. negative (Box 62).

Mrs. George Madison Millard "La Miniatura" Residence (1923)
Pasadena, California
  One 8 in. x 10 in. negative (Box 63).

Gordon Strong Planetarium Project (1925)
Sugar Loaf Mountain, Maryland
  Two 8 in. x 10 in. negatives (Box 63).

Taliesin III for Frank Lloyd Wright (1925)
Spring Green, Wisconsin
  Two 8 in. x 10 in. photographs (Box 63).
  Five 8 in. x 10 in. negatives (Box 63).

St. Mark's-in-the-Bouwerie Project (1927)
New York, New York
  One 8 in. x 10 in. negative (Box 63).

"House on the Mesa" Project (1931)
Denver, Colorado
  Five 8 in. x 10 in. negatives (Box 63).

Malcolm E. Willey Residence (1933)
Minneapolis, Minnesota
  One 8 in. x 10 in. negative (Box 63).

Edgar J. Kaufmann, Sr., "Fallingwater" Residence (1935)
Ohiopyle, Pennsylvania
  Four 8 in. x 10 in. photographs with negatives (Box 62).
  Five 8 in. x 10 in. photographs (Box 62).
  Two 8 in. x 10 in. negatives (Box 62).
  Two 10 in. x 12 in. mounted photographs (Box 61).

S.C. Johnson and Son Administration Building (1936)
Racine, Wisconsin
  Three 10 in. x 12 in. mounted photographs (Box 61).
  Three 9 in. x 14 in. (228.6 mm x 355.6 mm) photographs (Box 61).
  Three 8 in. x 10 in. photographs with negatives (Box 62).
  Eight 8 in. x 10 in. photographs (Box 62).

Paul R. Hanna "Honeycomb" Residence (1936)
Stanford, California
  Three 8 in. x 10 in. photographs with negatives (Box 62).
  Nine 8 in. x 10 in. photographs (Box 62).
  Three 8 in. x 10 in. negatives (Box 62).

Herbert Jacobs Residences I and II (1936 and 1943)
Madison, Wisconsin
  Four 3 in. x 5 in. (76.2 mm x 127 mm) photographs (Box 62).
  One 4 in. x 8 in. (101.6 mm x 203.2 mm) photograph (Box 62).
  Four 8 in. x 10 in. photographs (Box 62).
  Three 8 in. x 10 in. negatives (Box 62).

Edgar J. Kaufmann, Sr., Office (1937)
Pittsburgh, Pennsylvania
  Two 10 in. x 12 in. mounted photographs (Box 61).

Taliesin West (1937)
Scottsdale, Arizona
  Six 8 in. x 10 in. photographs (Box 63).

Herbert F. Johnson "Wingspread" Residence (1937)
Wind Point, Wisconsin
    Three 8 in. x 10 in. photographs with negatives ·(Box 62).

Sidney Bazett Residence (1939)
Hillsborough, California
    One 8 in. x 10 in. photograph with negative (Box 62).

Goetsch-Winckler Residence (1939)
Okemos, Michigan
    Three 10 in. x 12 in. mounted photographs (Box 61).
    One 8 in. x 10 in. photograph with negative (Box 62).
    Four 8 in. x 10 in. negatives (Box 62).

C.D. Hause Residence Project (1939)
Usonian Development
Okemos, Michigan
    One 8 in. x 10 in. negative (Box 62).

Lloyd Lewis Residence (1939)
Libertyville, Illinois
    Two 8 in. x 10 in. photographs with two negatives (Box 62).
    Two 8 in. x 10 in. photographs (Box 62).
    Two 8 in. x 10 in. negatives (Box 62).

Sidney A. Newman Residence Project
Usonian Development
Okemos, Michigan
    One 8 in. x 10 in. negative (Box 63).

Rose Pauson Residence (1939)
Phoenix, Arizona
    One 8 in. x 10 in. negative (Box 63).

John C. Pew Residence (1939)
Shorewood Hills, Wisconsin
    One 8 in. x 10 in. photograph (Box 63).

Stanley Rosenbaum Residence (1939)
Florence, Alabama
    Two 8 in. x 10 in. negatives (Box 63).

George D. Sturges Residence (1939)
Brentwood Heights, California
    Twelve 8 in. x 10 in. photographs (Box 63).
    Five 8 in. x 10 in. negatives (Box 63).

Clarence R. Van Dusen Residence Project (1939)
Usonian Development
Okemos, Michigan
    One 8 in. x 10 in. negative (Box 63).

Clarence Sondern Residence (1940)
Kansas City, Missouri
    One 8 in. x 10 in. photograph (Box 63).

Gerald M. Loeb Residence "Pergola House" Project (1944)
Redding, Connecticut
    Two 10 in. x 12 in. mounted photographs of model (Box 61).
    Three 8 in. x 10 in. negatives of model (Box 62).

Lowell Walter Residence (1945)
Quasqueton, Iowa
   One 8 in. x 10 in. negative (Box 63).

Alexis Panshin Residence Project (1946)
State Teachers College
Lansing, Michigan
   One 8 in. x 10 in. negative (Box 63).

Huntington Hartford Project (1947)
Hollywood Hills, California
   Two 8 in. x 10 in. negatives (Box 62).

V.C. Morris Gift Shop (1948)
San Francisco, California
   Seventeen 8 in. x 10 in. photographs (Box 63).

Erling P. Brauner Residence (1948)
Okemos, Michigan
   One 8 in. x 10 in. negative (Box 62).

The New Theatre Project (1948)
Hartford, Connecticut
   Eight 8 in. x 10 in. photographs (Box 63).

Solomon R. Guggenheim Museum (1956)
New York, New York
   Three 10 in. x 12 in. mounted photographs (Box 61).
   Two 8 in. x 10 in. photographs (Box 62).

The following buildings or projects have not been specifically identified as Wright's work. Several of the names associated with the photographs in the collection cannot be found on any listings of Wright's buildings and projects. More intense research will have to be done with respect to these photographs in order to properly identify them.

Ross Residence
   One 8 in. x 10 negative (Box 63).

Roberts Residence
   One 8 in. x 10 in. photograph with negative (Box 63).

Martin Residence
   One 8 in. x 10 in. photograph with negative (Box 63).
   One 8 in. x 10 in. negative (Box 63).

Usonian Residences
   One 8 in. x 10 in. negative (Box 63).

Columbian Fair
   Eight 8 in. x 10 in. negatives (Box 62).

Guerrero Residence
   Eight 8 in. x 10 in. negatives (Box 62).

Pors Residence
   One 8 in. x 10 in. photograph with negative (Box 63).

Twenty-One Club
   Eleven 8 in. x 10 in. photographs (Box 63).

Winston Residence
   One 8 in. x 10 in. photograph with negative (Box 63).

Wooden Model
    Seven 8 in. x 10 in. photographs (Box 63).
Unidentified Photographs
    Nine 8 in. x 10 in. photographs with negatives (Box 63).
    Eight 8 in. x 10 in. photographs (Box 63).
    Eleven 8 in. x 10 in. negatives (Box 63).

The collection also houses many miscellaneous Frank Lloyd Wright
related materials, almost all of which pertain to the "Sixty Years of
Living Architecture" exhibition. These items are contained in Boxes
29, 30, 60, and 61 and the contents of each are outlined as follows:

Collection Box 29
    Thirty-two pieces of exhibition articles (Item 1).
    Nine Frank Lloyd Wright blueprints (Item 2).
    Forty-two Frank Lloyd Wright exhibition brochures for the
        "Sixty Years of Living Architecture" exhibition (Item 3).
    Twenty-two Frank Lloyd Wright exhibition drawings (Item 4).
Collection Box 30
    Fifty-four pieces pertaining to Frank Lloyd Wright's "Sixty
        Years of Living Architecture" exhibition expenses (Item 1).
    Five pieces pertaining to Frank Lloyd Wright's Strozzi
        "Sixty Years of Living Architecture" exhibition (Item 2).
    One hundred and sixteen miscellaneous pieces which pertain
        to Wright's "Sixty Years of Living Architecture" exhibi-
        tion (Item 3).
    Twenty pieces of Wright exhibition newspaper clippings
        (Item 4).
    Forty pieces of exhibition notes (probably written by
        Stonorov) (Item 5).
    Fifty-two exhibition photographs (Item 6).
    Six Wright exhibition press releases (Item 7).
    Twenty-seven Wright exhibition programs (Item 8).
    Five Wright exhibition speeches (Item 9).
    Four Wright exhibition travel schedules (Item 10).
Collection Box 60
    Seven magazine articles and booklets.
    Drawing of an elevation of a Robert L. Forest Residence
        (this building cannot be found on any listing of Wright's
        buildings or projects).
    Floor plans for the Thomas H. Gale Residence at Oak Park,
        Illinois, of 1892.
    Drawings of a Metropolitan Life Insurance Company Building
        (?) lobby (this may not be a Wright design).
    One tape recording of Frank Lloyd Wright and Oskar Stonorov
        discussing architecture and democracy and Broadacre City.
Collection Box 61
    Wright's "Sixty Years of Living Architecture" exhibition
        plans and display and lighting instructions.

In order to use these manuscripts for research purposes, the researcher must file an Application for the Use of Manuscripts with the
Division of Rare Books and Special Collections of the Library. For
permission to publish, in full or in part, written application specify-
ing the manuscript or excerpt must be directed to the Director of
the Division of Rare Books and Special Collections and the user must
abide by his or her decision. For unpublished manuscripts which are

controlled by the author, his heirs, or literary executors it will
be necessary to present written permission to publish from the legal
holders of the copyright.

A54

Wichita State University Art Collection
Wichita State University
Wichita, Kansas 67208

The Wichita State University Art Collection houses seventeen
pieces of furniture designed by Frank Lloyd Wright and George M.
Niedecken for the Wright designed Henry J. Allen Residence of 1917,
located at Wichita, Kansas. These seventeen pieces of furniture include the following:

> Dining table made of walnut and walnut wood veneer measuring
> 42 in. x 42 in. x 84 in. (106.7 cm x 106.7 cm x 213.4 cm)
> when closed and 42 in. x 42 in. x 144 in. (106.7 cm x
> 106.7 cm x 365.8 cm) when fully extended.
> Twelve dining chairs made of walnut which have been refinished
> and reupholstered. Each chair measures 40 in. x 18 in. x
> 18 in. (101.6 cm x 457.2 cm x 457.2 cm).
> One dressing table with mirror made of walnut and walnut wood
> veneer which has been refinished. The table measures 29 in. x
> 66-1/2 in. x 27 in. (73.7 cm x 168.9 cm x 68.6 cm) and the
> mirror measures 30 in. x 52 in. (76.2 cm x 132.1 cm).
> One davenport made of walnut and walnut wood veneer which has
> been refinished and reupholstered. It measures 48-1/2 in. x
> 110-1/2 in. x 37 in. (123.2 cm x 280.7 cm x 94.0 cm).
> One living room table made of walnut and walnut wood veneer
> which has been refinished and measures 30-1/2 in. x 120 in.
> x 27 in. (77.5 cm x 304.8 cm x 68.6 cm).
> One tabouret/music cabinet made of walnut and walnut wood
> veneer which has been refinished and measures 30 in. x
> 41 in. x 40-1/4 in. (76.2 cm x 104.1 cm x 102.2 cm).

A55

South Dakota Department of Education and Cultural Affairs
Historical Resource Center
Memorial Building
Pierre, South Dakota 57501

The Historical Resource Center of the South Dakota Department of
Education and Cultural Affairs contains eight pieces of correspondence
written by Frank Lloyd Wright. These eight manuscripts are housed
in the Robert Davies Lusk Correspondence, 1935-1936 file. These
pieces of correspondence are related to a potential architectural
commission for Wright to design a hotel near Sylvan Lake, South
Dakota, on publicly owned property and include two telegrams to
Senator Peter Norbeck dated July 23, 1935; and July 24, 1935; a letter
to Senator Peter Norbeck dated September 28, 1935; a letter to Robert
D. Lusk also dated September 28, 1935; a letter to Harry L. Gandy also
dated September 28, 1935; a letter to Robert D. Lusk dated October
25, 1935; a letter to Senator Peter Norbeck also dated October 25,

1935; and a letter to Harry L. Gandy dated November 8, 1935. Other letters in the file, although not from Wright, relate to both the Sylvan Lake Hotel Project and Wright's design for the Robert D. Lusk Residence at Huron, South Dakota, of 1936.

Part II
The Frank Lloyd Wright
Manuscripts

Identifying the location and extent of original Frank Lloyd Wright
manuscripts has been elusive to scholars, and discussion of Wright
manuscripts has been scarce. Several important studies of Frank Lloyd
Wright and his work discuss, but only briefly, the need for the
identification and analysis of his manuscripts and letters. James
Muggenburg in "Frank Lloyd Wright in Print, 1959-1970" (*Papers of The
American Association of Architectural Bibliographers* Vol. 9, 1972),
pp. 105 and 106, outlined briefly the existence of ten manuscript
collections which reportedly held original Frank Lloyd Wright manuscripts. Robert C. Twombly in *Frank Lloyd Wright: An Interpretive
Biography*, pp. 358 and 359, stated that there were few Wright letters
available to the public for study and he outlined very briefly five
institutions which housed original Frank Lloyd Wright manuscripts.
John Sergeant in *Frank Lloyd Wright's Usonian Houses: The Case for
Organic Architecture* (New York: Whitney Library of Design, 1976), pp.
9 and 203, reported that Frank Lloyd Wright archival material was
being lost and that it was necessary to travel far to discover collections containing letters. Sergeant added one additional collection to
Twombly's 1973 list of institutions containing Wright manuscripts.
Again, in 1979, Robert C. Twombly discussed the availability of Frank
Lloyd Wright original manuscripts for scholarly research (see Robert
C. Twombly's *Frank Lloyd Wright: His Life and His Architecture*, pp.
433 and 434) and identified seven institutions which housed original
manuscripts written by Frank Lloyd Wright, concluding that there were
a little over one hundred unpublished Frank Lloyd Wright letters
available to the public for scholarly research. Robert L. Sweeney,
In *Frank Lloyd Wright: An Annotated Bibliography* (Los Angeles: Hennessey
and Ingalls, Inc., 1978), did not address this area of research.

Part II, the guide to the Frank Lloyd Wright original manuscripts,
is intended to aid the researcher in the use of these archival materials.
It is not the purpose of this guide to serve as a substitute for the
original Frank Lloyd Wright manuscripts; for there are no substitutes,
other than in the sources referenced here in which some of the manuscripts have been previously published.

The original manuscripts of Frank Lloyd Wright, including both
published and unpublished letters housed in public archives, have
been catalogued and indexed in this part in chronological order from
the earliest discovered manuscript housed in a public archive dated
1894 to the last manuscript researched, dated April 2, 1959, only
seven days before Wright's death. This part, which represents a
catalogue and guide to some of the original Frank Lloyd Wright manuscripts housed in many of the collections discussed in Part I, is
divided into seven chapters representing seven different time periods.
These seven chapters are based on the author's interpretation of the
content of the manuscripts themselves, and on significant stages in
Wright's architectural career and life.

Each chapter includes a brief introduction to the manuscripts
of its particular time period, focusing on people and events, as
well as significant architectural contributions made by Frank Lloyd

Wright during the period. Also, extensive references, which further
elaborate upon and document subject areas discussed in the manuscripts,
are provided at the end of each chapter. These references include relevant books and periodicals, and heretofore untapped data contained in
various newspapers in which Wright had extensive coverage. These latter
include, but are not limited to, *The Capital Times* (Madison, Wisconsin),
The Milwaukee Journal, *The New York Times*, and *The London Times*. Each
of these reference sections are arranged under the headings of books,
periodicals, and newspapers; books are arranged alphabetically by
author, periodicals and newspapers are arranged chronologically.

Each manuscript is catalogued and analyzed. The cataloguing
provides, where applicable, the catalogue number,* the date the
manuscript was written, the type of manuscript (i.e., letter, telegram,
memorandum or note, article or paper, speech or text of lecture,
holiday greetings), the person to whom the manuscript is addressed
(in the case of correspondence), the archival collection in which the
manuscript is located or its appropriate source document, the medium
of the manuscript and how it was signed by Wright, its physical size,
the total number of pages of each manuscript, the number of words
it contains, a listing of descriptors and key words identifying places,
people, events, and topic areas discussed in each manuscript, and
a brief review of each manuscript which may indicate its significance
within the context of other Frank Lloyd Wright manuscripts as well as
other published texts, significant events, or significant architectural contributions by Frank Lloyd Wright. More than 500 original
manuscripts of Frank Lloyd Wright's authorship are catalogued by this
method.

The method of listing the manuscripts in chronological order will
assist the researcher in discovering relationships among Wright's
manuscripts as well as relationships among his numerous works, although
the manuscripts may be housed at different locales. The original
Frank Lloyd Wright manuscripts, available to the general scholarly
public for research purposes at the various archives, can be examined
here as a somewhat unified whole.

The photographs in Part II serve as a reference to Wright's
architectural development and to supplement the index and the manuscripts themselves.

---

*The numbering system used to catalogue each manuscript is consecutive
beginning with B1, B2, B3, B4,.... However, while this book was in
preparation, the Wright manuscripts housed in the Robert Davies Lusk
Correspondence, 1935-1936 papers, at the Historical Resource Center
of the South Dakota Department of Education and Cultural Affairs, and
the Wright manuscripts reproduced in Paul R. and Jean S. Hanna's
Frank Lloyd Wright's Hanna House: The Client's Report (Cambridge:
The M.I.T. Press, 1981) emerged. Consequently, a letter suffix has
been added to the consecutive numbering system for these manuscripts
in order to accommodate these recently discovered materials. The
recently published letters in Frank Lloyd Wright's *Letters to Apprentices* (Fresno, California: The Press at California State University,
1982) have not been referenced in this book since this publication
first became available in early 1983 and stands alone as a significant
collection and literary work.

2-1.1 Frank Lloyd Wright (circa 1910–1920). Photo by DeLonge Studio; courtesy of the State Historical Society of Wisconsin.

CHAPTER 1

THE EARLY YEARS (1894 TO 1910)

Introduction

This chapter catalogues and examines manuscripts born out of
Frank Lloyd Wright's Oak Park, Illinois, practice. Correspondence
during this period includes letters from him to several of his early
clients including Frank L. Smith and Roland S. Ludington, for whom
F.L. Wright prepared two designs for the First National Bank of Dwight,
Illinois, dated 1904 and 1905 (later, in 1906, Wright also designed
a residence for Ludington, which was not built); William R. Heath,
an executive of the Larkin Soap Company, for whom Wright had designed
a residence at Buffalo, New York, in 1904 (Wright had completed the
design for the famous Larkin Company Administration Building at
Buffalo, New York, in 1903); Francis Little, for whom Wright completed
a residence in 1902 at Peoria, Illinois; Mrs. Harvey P. Sutton, for
whom Wright had executed a residence at McCook, Nebraska, in 1905; and
the Trustees of Unity Church at Oak Park, Illinois, for whom Wright
designed Unity Church at Oak Park, Illinois, in 1905.

Other correspondence during this period includes letters to Jenkin
Lloyd Jones, Wright's uncle, who introduced Wright to architect Joseph
Lyman Silsbee (Wright's earliest Chicago employer prior to Louis
Sullivan); William Channing Gannett, who was co-author with Wright
of *The House Beautiful*, done in 1896 to 1898; letters to English architect
Charles Robert Ashbee, who introduced Wright's work and the Chicago
School of Architecture to England at the turn of the century; and a
series of correspondence with Taylor A. Woolley, a "draughtsman" with
Wright during Wright's Oak Park practice who also worked with him in
Italy during the preparation of Wright's famous Wasmuth Portfolio
(*Ausgeführte Bauten und Entwürfe von Frank Lloyd Wright*). Manuscript
collections are also identified which house the original drafts of
some of Wright's most famous speeches during this period, including
"This 'Ideal Architect' (What Is Architecture)," of 1901, and "The
Modern Home as a Work of Art (Why Architecture, Architect, and Client),"
of 1902.

From the beginning of his independent career in late 1893 through
1910, Wright did 247 designs, of which 155 were built. The number of designs during this period represents about 25 percent of all of the designs
Wright did during his lifetime. During this early period the years 1905
and 1909 brought the most work, with 24 designs in 1905 and 23 in 1909.

B1

Date:
    May 15, 1894

Type of Manuscript:
    Letter

To:
    Jenkin Lloyd Jones

From:
    Frank Lloyd Wright
    Schiller Building
    Chicago, Illinois

Collection:
    Jenkin Lloyd Jones Collection
    University of Chicago Library
    University of Chicago
    Box 4:4

Medium:
    Typed on Frank L. Wright,
    Architect, stationery, signed "Frank"

Size:
    8-1/2 in. x 11 in.; 215.9 mm x 279.4 mm

Number of Pages:
    1

Number of Words:
    87 Typed; 2 Handwritten

Descriptors:
    Jenkin Lloyd Jones, Schiller Building, Joseph Lyman Silsbee

Review:
    Wright asks his uncle, Jenkin Lloyd Jones, to consider him for a
    potential building design project rather than architect J.L.
    Silsbee, Wright's former employer. The stationery locates Wright's
    office as the Schiller Building in Chicago.

B2

Date:
    Undated (1893 or 1896?)

Type of Manuscript:
    Typescript poem

Title:
    "Work Song"

By:
    Frank Lloyd Wright

Collection:
    Frank Lloyd Wright Special Collections
    Northwestern University Archives
    Northwestern University Library

Medium:
    Typed in red and black, signed by Frank Lloyd Wright

Size:
    16-7/8 in. x 12-5/8 in; 430 mm x 320 mm

Descriptors:
  "Work Song"

Review:
  According to Wright's *An Autobiography*, "Work Song" was written
  when Wright was twenty-seven and because Wright believed he was born
  in 1869 the poem could be dated 1896. The text and music for it
  was published in *An Autobiography*. It was also reprinted in Herbert
  Jacob's "Devoted Wife Played Requiem--Wright Laid to Rest at Home
  He Loved" (*The Capital Times* [Madison, Wisconsin], April 13, 1959);
  this article also dates "Work Song" as 1896. It was later reproduced
  in Norris Kelly Smith's *Frank Lloyd Wright: A Study in Architectural
  Content* (Watkins Glen, New York: American Life Foundation and Study
  Institute, 1979), p. 71, and here, too, Smith dates it as 1896.

B3

Date:
  December 27, 1898

Type of Manuscript:
  Letter

To:
  William Channing Gannett

From:
  Frank Lloyd Wright

Collection:
  William Channing Gannett Papers, 1850-1944
  Rush Rhees Library
  University of Rochester
  Box XIV

Medium:
  Handwritten, signed "Frank Lloyd Wright"

Number of Pages:
  1

Number of Words:
  102

Descriptors:
  William Channing Gannett, *The House Beautiful*, William
  Winslow, Auvergne Press

Review:
  Wright transmits *The House Beautiful* book written by Wright and
  Gannett to Gannett and asks for his criticism of the work. Wright's
  tone in this letter strongly suggests that *The House Beautiful* was
  published and printed in 1898 rather than 1896-1897 as suggested
  by the book itself which states "Printed by Hand at the Auvergne
  Press in River Forest by William Herman Winslow and Frank Lloyd
  Wright during the Winter Months of the Year Eighteen Hundred Ninety
  Six and Seven." In Wright's letter to Gannett dated January 30,
  1899, reference is made to the book's having been in preparation
  for three years.

2-1.2 The William Winslow Stable (1893), River Forest, Illinois, where the Auvergne Press printed *The House Beautiful* by Frank Lloyd Wright and William Channing Gannett. Photo by the author.

B4

Date:
   Undated (1898 or 1899?)

Type of Manuscript:
   Letter

To:
   Jenkin Lloyd Jones

From:
   Frank Lloyd Wright
   Oak Park, Illinois

Collection:
   Jenkin Lloyd Jones Collection
   University of Chicago Library
   University of Chicago
   Box 4:4

Medium:
   Handwritten by Wright (unsigned) on Frank Lloyd
   Wright, Architect, stationery

Number of Pages:
   2

Number of Words:
   154

Descriptors:
   Jenkin Lloyd Jones, All Souls Church Project,
   Dwight Herald Perkins

Review:
   Wright asks his uncle, Jenkin Lloyd Jones, to keep things moving
   on the All Souls Church Project. Wright had prepared a building
   design for that project in 1897.

B5

Date:
   1898

Type of Manuscript:
   Announcement

Title:
   "Frank Lloyd Wright, Architect"

By:
   Frank Lloyd Wright

Collection:
   The John Lloyd Wright Collection
   The Avery Architectural Library
   Columbia University
   Folder 1

Medium:
   Typeset, with handwritten corrections by Wright

Size:
   5 in. x 5-1/2 in.; 127 mm x 139.7 mm

Number of Pages:
   4

Descriptors:
   The Rookery, Frank Lloyd Wright Home and Studio

Review:
   The full title of this promotional brochure announcing Wright's
   practice is "Frank Lloyd Wright, Architect. The Rookery, Chicago,
   Room 1119. Hours Twelve to Two. Telephone Main 2668. Draughting
   Rooms and Studio at the Corner of Forest and Chicago Avenues. Oak
   Park, Illinois. Hours Eight to Eleven a.m. Seven to Nine p.m. Telephone Oak Park." Corrections were made on this early version of the
   brochure by Wright and later reprinted as revised. The Avery Architectural Library also has the final revised printed copy as does
   the Oak Park Public Library. This manuscript was reproduced in
   Robert L. Sweeney's *Frank Lloyd Wright: An Annotated Bibliography*,
   published by Hennessey and Ingalls, Inc., at Los Angeles, in 1978,
   as Plate 2.

B6

Date:
   January 30, 1899

Type of Manuscript:
   Letter

To:
   William Channing Gannett

From:
   Frank Lloyd Wright
   Oak Park, Illinois

Collection:
   William Channing Gannett Papers, 1850-1944
   Rush Rhees Library
   University of Rochester
   A.G18

Medium:
   Handwritten on Frank Lloyd Wright, Architect, stationery, signed
   "Frank Wright"

Size:
   5-1/4 in. x 11 in.; 133.4 mm x 279.4 mm

Number of Pages:
   2

Number of Words:
   268

Descriptors:
   William Channing Gannett, *The House Beautiful*,
   William Winslow, Auvergne Press

2-1.3 Frank Lloyd Wright Studio (1895), Oak Park, Illinois. Photo by the author.

2-1.4 Frank Lloyd Wright Residence (1889), Oak Park, Illinois. Photo by the author.

Review:
Wright talks of the fine quality of the book, *The House Beautiful*, written by him and Gannett.

B7

Date:
January 30, 1901

Type of Manuscript:
Letter and sketches

To:
M.H. Lowell
Matteawan, New York

From:
Frank Lloyd Wright

Collection:
The Avery Architectural Library
Columbia University

Medium:
Typed, with sketches, on Frank Lloyd Wright/Webster
Tomlinson design stationery, signed "Frank Lloyd Wright"

Size:
8-1/8 in. x 8-3/8 in.; 206.4 mm x 212.7 mm

Number of Pages:
1

Number of Words:
110

Descriptors:
M.H. Lowell, Studio of Frank Lloyd Wright/Webster
Tomlinson Architects, Webster Tomlinson, M.H. Lowell
Studio Project

Review:
Wright submits rough sketches of his thoughts for a studio for a prospective client, M.H. Lowell, with brief cost estimates. The sketches include a rough floor plan and exterior perspective of the studio design. The letter was written during Wright's brief partnership with Webster Tomlinson (see "In General," published in *The Brickbuilder*, January 1901, for the announcement bulletin of the Wright/Tomlinson partnership). This letter was photographically reproduced in Robert C. Twombly's *Frank Lloyd Wright: His Life and His Architecture*, p. 37.

B8

Date:
1901

Type of Manuscript:
Typescript of speech

Title:
   "This 'Ideal' Architect (What Is Architecture)"

By:
   Frank Lloyd Wright

Collection:
   The Library of Congress, Manuscript Division
   The Frank Lloyd Wright Papers
   Speech and Article File, 1901 to 1918

Medium:
   Typed double spaced, with handwritten corrections by
   Wright.

Size:
   8-1/2 in. x 11-1/8 in.; 215.9 mm x 282.6 mm

Number of Pages:
   18

Descriptors:
   College Endowment Association

Review:
   The text of a speech read by Wright in 1901 at Evanston, Illinois,
   to the College Endowment Association. This speech may have originally
   been titled "What Is Architecture." The copy on file in this collection has been revised with handwritten corrections and modifications
   by Wright. He may have made these revisions prior to transmitting
   the paper to Frederick Gutheim for possible inclusion in Gutheim's
   Frank Lloyd Wright on Architecture: Selected Writings, 1894-1940.
   On this copy the typewritten title "What Is Architecture" and
   typewritten date of 1900 were changed by Wright to "This 'Ideal'
   Architect" and dated 1901. Robert C. Twombly in his *Frank Lloyd
   Wright: His Life and His Architecture,* p. 57, note 21, claims that
   there is no record of "What Is Architecture"; however, this manuscript proves otherwise. Gutheim did not use this manuscript in
   the preparation of his book. The speech is not the same as Wright's
   "The Philosophy of Fine Art," which appeared in Gutheim's book.

B9

Date:
   January 3, 1902

Type of Manuscript:
   Letter

To:
   Charles Robert Ashbee
   London, South West

From:
   Frank Lloyd Wright

Source:
   Alan Crawford
   "Ten Letters from Frank Lloyd Wright to Charles Robert
   Ashbee"

Collection:
   The Ashbee Journals
   King's College
   Cambridge, England

Number of Words:
   224

Descriptors:
   Charles Robert Ashbee, England

Review:
   An apology to Ashbee for not writing to him sooner. Wright explains
   that financially he cannot afford a trip to England to visit Ashbee and Wright conveys a mood of unhappiness with himself.

B10

Date:
   1902

Type of Manuscript:
   Typescript of lecture

Title:
   "The Modern Home as a Work of Art (Why Architecture,
   Architect and Client)"

By:
   Frank Lloyd Wright

Collection:
   The Library of Congress, Manuscript Division
   The Frank Lloyd Wright Papers
   Speech and Article File, 1901 to 1918

Medium:
   Typed double spaced, with handwritten corrections by
   Wright

Size:
   8-1/2 in. x 11-1/8 in.; 215.9 mm x 282.6 mm

Number of Pages:
   19

Descriptors:
   Chicago Women's Club, Brick, Art, Science

Review:
   The text of a lecture read before the Chicago Women's Club in
   1902 at Chicago, Illinois. A short excerpt from this lengthy
   paper was presented in *Frank Lloyd Wright on Architecture:
   Selected Writings, 1894-1940*.

B11

Date:
   December 28, 1904

Type of Manuscript:
   Letter

To:
   William R. Heath
   Larkin Soap Company
   Buffalo, New York

From:
   Frank Lloyd Wright
   Oak Park, Illinois

Collection:
   The Library of Congress, Manuscript Division
   The Frank Lloyd Wright Papers
   Letters and Notes to William R. Heath File

Medium:
   Typed on red-square design stationery, signed "Wright"

Size:
   9-5/8 in. x 8-1/4 in.; 244.5 mm x 209.6 mm

Number of Pages:
   1

Number of Words:
   206

Descriptors:
   William R. Heath, William R. Heath Residence, Catherine
   Wright

Review:
   Wright had designed a home for William R. Heath at Buffalo,
   New York. In this letter Wright explains his reasons for being
   unable to attend the house warming party at the Heaths' new
   house. This letter shows that the completion date of the Heath
   Residence was 1904 rather than 1905 as indicated in Henry-Russell
   Hitchcock's *In the Nature of Materials*, and William Allin Storrer's
   The Architecture of Frank Lloyd Wright. The residence was completed
   prior to Wright's 1905 departure for Japan.

B12

Date:
   Undated (before 1904)

Type of Manuscript:
   Genealogy of the Wright Family

Collection:
   Jane Lloyd Jones Correspondence, 1899-1940
   The State Historical Society of Wisconsin
   Wis MSS NN

Medium:
   Typed list, with handwritten chart

Size:
   8-1/2 in. x 11 in.; 215.9 mm x 279.4 mm

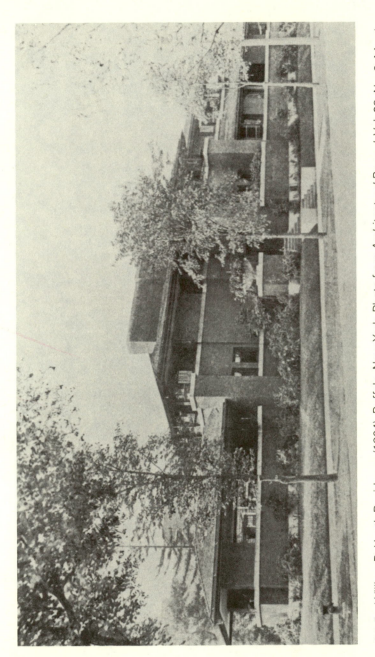

2-1.5 William R. Heath Residence (1904), Buffalo, New York. Photo from *Architectural Record*, Vol. 23, No. 3, March 1908.

Number of Pages:
    2

Number of Words:
    595 Text; 16 Names on Chart

Descriptors:
    Frank Lloyd Wright Genealogy, Wright Family, William
    C. Wright, Abbie Whitaker, Richard Lloyd Jones

Review:
    A very comprehensive and detailed listing of Wright's genealogy.
    The genealogy traces Wright's family back to A.D. 512 but more
    specific data is included after 1614. A small chart traces Wright's
    family back to Richard Lloyd Jones, F.L. Wright's grandfather.
    The list was compiled by Abbie Whitaker, who died in 1893. She
    was F.L. Wright's aunt and sister of Wright's father. The list
    shows F.L. Wright's birthday as 1867 but has him named Frank
    Lincoln, an error on Wright's aunt's part. Research into Wright's
    birthdate can be found in Thomas S. Hines' "Frank Lloyd Wright--
    The Madison Years: Records Versus Recollections," *Wisconsin Magazine
    of History*, Vol. 50, Winter 1967, pp. 109-119. Additional research
    was done on this subject by Herbert Jacobs, a former Wright client,
    which can be found in the Herbert and Katherine Jacobs Frank Lloyd
    Wright Collection at the Art Institute in Chicago. The research
    done by Jacobs uses a different approach than Hines' and also
    somewhat different data and source materials, although it reaches
    the same conclusion that Wright was indeed born in 1867.

B13

Date:
    February 9, 1905

Type of Manuscript:
    F.L. Wright's passport signed "Frank Lloyd Wright"

Collection:
    The Frank Lloyd Wright Collection
    The Avery Architectural Library
    Columbia University

Medium:
    Passport form

Descriptors:
    Passport, Japan

Review:
    A copy of this passport is in the Herbert and Katherine Jacobs
    Frank Lloyd Wright Collection at the Art Institute of Chicago.
    Wright used this passport for a trip to Japan the same year.

B14

Date:
    February 9, 1905

Type of Manuscript:
Photocopy of F.L. Wright's passport signed "Frank
Lloyd Wright"

Collection:
The Herbert and Katherine Jacobs Frank Lloyd Wright Collection
The Art Institute of Chicago
Documents, Envelope 6

Medium:
Passport form

Number of Pages:
1

Descriptors:
Passport, Japan

Review:
A photoduplicate of the original passport which is housed in the
Frank Lloyd Wright Collection of the Avery Architectural Library
at Columbia University. Wright used this passport for a trip to
Japan in the same year.

B15

Date:
November 2, 1905

Type of Manuscript:
Letter

To:
Frank L. Smith

From:
Frank Lloyd Wright

Collection:
The Frank L. Smith Bank (Dwight, Illinois) Collection
The Art Institute of Chicago
Special Case 58

Medium:
Typed, signed "Frank Lloyd Wright"

Size:
8-1/2 in. x 5± in.; 215.9 mm x 127± mm

Number of Pages:
1

Number of Words:
124

Descriptors:
Frank L. Smith, Frank L. Smith Bank, Paul F.P. Mueller

Review:
Comments from Wright on the expected completion date of the Frank
L. Smith Bank at Dwight, Illinois, and on a seemingly incompetent
contractor working on the bank.

2-1.6 Frank L. Smith–First National Bank (1905), Dwight, Illinois. Photo by Thomas A. Heinz.

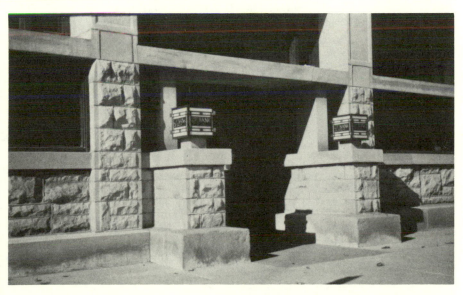

2-1.7 Close-up of entrance to Frank L. Smith–First National Bank (1905), Dwight, Illinois, showing lights. Photo by Thomas A. Heinz.

B16

Date:
January 29, 1906

Type of Manuscript:
Letter

To:
Frank L. Smith

From:
Frank Lloyd Wright

Collection:
The Frank L. Smith Bank (Dwight, Illinois) Collection
The Art Institute of Chicago
Special Case 58

Medium:
Typed, signed "Frank Lloyd Wright"

Size:
8-1/2 in. x 11 in.; 215.9 mm x 279.4 mm

Number of Pages:
1

Number of Words:
281

Descriptors:
Frank L. Smith, Frank L. Smith Bank

Review:
Wright comments on a design idea for the placement of glass
between two portions of the interior of the Frank L. Smith Bank
at Dwight, Illinois, and on Smith's choice for the door frame
for the bank vault's door. For an 83-word quotation from this
letter regarding the vault door, see David A. Hanks, *The Decorative
Designs of Frank Lloyd Wright* (New York: E.P. Dutton, 1979), p. 37.
This letter is dated January 29, 1906, rather than February 2 as
indicated by Hanks in his book.

B17

Date:
July 6, 1906

Type of Manuscript:
Letter

To:
Roland S. Ludington

From:
Frank Lloyd Wright

Collection:
The Frank L. Smith Bank (Dwight, Illinois) Collection
The Art Institute of Chicago
Special Case 58

Medium:
   Typed, signed "Frank Lloyd Wright"

Size:
   8-1/2 in. x 9-1/2 in.; 215.9 mm x 241.3 mm

Number of Pages:
   1

Number of Words:
   130

Descriptors:
   Roland S. Ludington, Frank L. Smith, Frank L. Smith Bank

Review:
   Wright is concerned over a payment problem and misunderstanding
   which has occurred regarding the stonework for the Frank L. Smith
   Bank at Dwight, Illinois.

B18

Date:
   July 10, 1906

Type of Manuscript:
   Copy of letter

To:
   Trustees of Unity Church
   Oak Park, Illinois

From:
   Frank Lloyd Wright

Collection:
   Unitarian Universalist Church Papers, 1906-1911
   The Oak Park Public Library
   Oak Park, Illinois

Medium:
   Tissue paper carbon copy of letter signed by Frank
   Lloyd Wright

Size:
   8-3/8 in. x 9-1/8 in.; 212.7 mm x 231.8 mm

Number of Pages:
   1

Descriptors:
   Unity Church (Oak Park, Illinois), Trustees of Unity Church
   (Oak Park, Illinois)

Review:
   On the exterior finish of Unity Church at Oak Park, Illinois,
   designed by Wright.

B19

Date:
   July 19, 1906

2-1.8   Unity Church (1905), Oak Park, Illinois. Photo by the author.

2-1.9   Interior of Unity Church (1905), Oak Park, Illinois. Photo by the author.

Type of Manuscript:
   Letter

To:
   Mrs. Harvey P. Sutton

From:
   Frank Lloyd Wright

Source:
   "A Wright House on the Prairie," pp. 5-19 (p. 15)

Number of Words:
   330

Descriptors:
   Mrs. Harvey P. Sutton, Harvey P. Sutton Residence

Review:
   The costs of interior finishing, windows, and doors are
   presented to Mrs. Sutton for the Harvey P. Sutton Residence.

B20

Date:
   July 30, 1906

Type of Manuscript:
   Letter

To:
   Mrs. Harvey P. Sutton

From:
   Frank Lloyd Wright

Source:
   "A Wright House on the Prairie," pp. 5-19 (p. 15)

Number of Words:
   116

Descriptors:
   Mrs. Harvey P. Sutton, Harvey P. Sutton Residence

Review:
   Estimates from Wright on the costs for construction of the
   Harvey P. Sutton Residence.

B21

Date:
   September 8, 1906

Type of Manuscript:
   Voucher

To:
   Unity Church (Oak Park, Illinois)

From:
   Frank Lloyd Wright

Collection:
   Unitarian Universalist Church Papers, 1906-1911
   The Oak Park Public Library
   Oak Park, Illinois

Medium:
   Paper form of Frank Lloyd Wright, Architect, stationery, printed
   in brown and red-orange colors and signed by Frank Lloyd
   Wright

Size:
   4-3/4 in. x 8-1/4 in.; 120.7 mm x 209.6 mm

Number of Pages:
   1

Descriptors:
   Unity Church (Oak Park, Illinois)

B22

Date:
   September 25, 1906

Type of Manuscript:
   Voucher

To:
   Unity Church (Oak Park, Illinois)

From:
   Frank Lloyd Wright

Collection:
   Unitarian Universalist Church Papers, 1906-1911
   The Oak Park Public Library
   Oak Park, Illinois

Medium:
   Paper form of Frank Lloyd Wright, Architect, stationery, printed
   in brown and red-orange colors and signed by Frank Lloyd
   Wright

Size:
   4-3/4 in. x 8-1/4 in.; 120.7 mm x 209.6 mm

Number of Pages:
   1

Descriptors:
   Unity Church (Oak Park, Illinois)

B23

Date:
   November 26, 1906

Type of Manuscript:
   Letter

To:
   Roland S. Ludington

From:
  Frank Lloyd Wright (per John)

Collection:
  The Frank L. Smith Bank (Dwight, Illinois) Collection
  The Art Institute of Chicago
  Special Case 58

Medium:
  Typed, signed "Frank Lloyd Wright per John"

Size:
  8-1/2 in. x 5± in.; 215.9 mm x 127± mm

Number of Pages:
  1

Number of Words:
  68

Descriptors:
  Roland S. Ludington, Frank L. Smith Bank

Review:
  A short not on how to clean the floors of the Frank L. Smith
  Bank at Dwight, Illinois.

B24

Date:
  January 25, 1907

Type of Manuscript:
  Letter

To:
  Roland S. Ludington

From:
  Frank Lloyd Wright

Collection:
  The Frank L. Smith Bank (Dwight, Illinois) Collection
  The Art Institute of Chicago
  Special Case 58

Medium:
  Typed, signed "Frank Lloyd Wright"

Size:
  8-1/2 in. x 9± in.; 215.9 mm x 228± mm

Number of Pages:
  1

Number of Words:
  152

Descriptors:
  Roland S. Ludington, Frank L. Smith, Frank L. Smith
  Bank, Japan

Review:
Wright informs Ludington that Wright is to leave for Japan on February 15, 1907, and offers to help on the Frank L. Smith Bank at Dwight, Illinois, before he departs.

B25

Date:
March 18, 1907

Type of Manuscript:
Letter

To:
E.H. Ehrmann

From:
Frank Lloyd Wright

Collection:
Unitarian Universalist Church Papers, 1906-1911
The Oak Park Public Library
Oak Park, Illinois

Medium:
Stationery of Frank Lloyd Wright, Architect, signed "Frank"

Size:
9-3/8 in. x 8-1/8 in.; 238.1 mm x 206.4 mm

Number of Pages:
1

Descriptors:
E.H. Ehrmann, Unity Church (Oak Park, Illinois)

Review:
A response from Wright to a request for definite and accurate information on additional work not covered by the contract for the construction of Unity Church at Oak Park, Illinois.

B26

Date:
April 9, 1907

Type of Manuscript:
Letter

To:
Mrs. Harvey P. Sutton

From:
Frank Lloyd Wright

Source:
"A Wright House on the Prairie," pp. 5-19 (p. 16)

Medium:
Typed on red-square design stationery, signed "Frank Lloyd Wright"

Number of Pages:
    1

Number of Words:
    181

Descriptors:
    Mrs. Harvey P. Sutton, Harvey P. Sutton Residence

Review:
    Wright briefly discusses minor changes for the Sutton Residence
    design and requests payment for his services.

B27

Date:
    April 18, 1907

Type of Manuscript:
    Letter

To:
    Harriet Monroe

From:
    Frank Lloyd Wright
    Oak Park, Illinois

Collection:
    Poetry Magazine Papers, 1912-1936
    University of Chicago Library
    University of Chicago
    Box 41:5

Medium:
    Type on red-square design stationery, signed "Frank Lloyd Wright"

Size:
    8-1/2 in. x 14 in.; 215.9 mm x 355.6 mm

Number of Pages:
    2

Number of Words:
    1,160

Descriptors:
    Harriet Monroe, *The Chicago Examiner*

Review:
    Wright's long letter to Monroe is very critical of her review of
    his exhibition at the Art Institute in Chicago, published in her
    article, "In the Galleries."

B28

Date:
    April 22, 1907

Type of Manuscript:
    Letter

To:
    Harriet Monroe

From:
    Frank Lloyd Wright

Collection:
    Poetry Magazine Papers, 1912-1936
    University of Chicago Library
    University of Chicago
    Box 41:5

Medium:
    Typed, signed

Descriptors:
    Harriet Monroe

Review:
    An apology from Wright.

B29

Date:
    September 12, 1907

Type of Manuscript:
    Voucher

To:
    Unity Church (Oak Park, Illinois)

From:
    Frank Lloyd Wright

Collection:
    Unitarian Universalist Church Papers, 1906-1911
    The Oak Park Public Library
    Oak Park, Illinois

Medium:
    Paper form of Frank Lloyd Wright, Architect, stationery, printed
    in brown and red-orange colors and signed by Frank Lloyd
    Wright

Size:
    4-3/4 in. x 8-1/4 in.; 120.7 mm x 209.6 mm

Number of Pages:
    1

Descriptors:
    Unity Church (Oak Park, Illinois)

B30

Date:
    September 17, 1907

Type of Manuscript:
    Voucher

To:
   Unity Church

From:
   Frank Lloyd Wright

Collection:
   Unitarian Universalist Church Papers, 1906-1911
   The Oak Park Public Library
   Oak Park, Illinois

Medium:
   Paper form of Frank Lloyd Wright, Architect, stationery, printed
   in brown and red-orange colors and signed by Frank Lloyd
   Wright

Size:
   4-3/4 in. x 8-1/4 in.; 120.7 mm x 209.6 mm

Number of Pages:
   1

Descriptors:
   Unity Church (Oak Park, Illinois)

B31

Date:
   November 30, 1907

Type of Manuscript:
   Voucher

To:
   Unity Church (Oak Park, Illinois)

From:
   Frank Lloyd Wright

Collection:
   Unitarian Universalist Church Papers, 1906-1911
   The Oak Park Public Library
   Oak Park, Illinois

Medium:
   Paper form of Frank Lloyd Wright, Architect, stationery, printed
   in brown and red-orange colors and signed by Frank Lloyd
   Wright

Size:
   4-3/4 in. x 8-1/4 in.; 120.7 mm x 209.6 mm

Number of Pages:
   1

Descriptors:
   Unity Church (Oak Park, Illinois)

B32

Date:
   Undated (1905 to 1907?)

Type of Manuscript:
    Letter

To:
    Dear Sir (Frank L. Smith?)

From:
    Frank Lloyd Wright

Collection:
    The Frank L. Smith Bank (Dwight, Illinois) Collection
    The Art Institute of Chicago
    Special Case 58

Medium:
    Typed, signed "Frank Lloyd Wright"

Size:
    8-1/2 in. x 9+ in.; 215.9 mm x 228+ mm

Number of Pages:
    1

Number of Words:
    133

Descriptors:
    Frank L. Smith, Frank L. Smith Bank, John W. Ayres

Review:
    Discussion of the design for the radiator screens of the Frank L.
    Smith Bank for Dwight, Illinois, and some problems Wright is
    having with the design.

B33

Date:
    Undated (1907?)

Type of Manuscript:
    Letter

To:
    Unity Church (Oak Park, Illinois)

From:
    Frank Lloyd Wright

Collection:
    Unitarian Universalist Church Papers, 1906-1911
    The Oak Park Public Library
    Oak Park, Illinois

Medium:
    Stationery of Frank Lloyd Wright, Architect, signed by Frank
    Lloyd Wright

Size:
    9-3/8 in. x 8-1/8 in.; 238.1 mm x 206.4 mm

Number of Pages:
    1

Descriptors:
    Unity Church (Oak Park, Illinois)

Review:
    Wright notes that Unity House is to be ready for occupancy on
    May 15, 1907, and Unity Church on September 1, 1907.

B34

Date:
    January 18, 1908

Type of Manuscript:
    Letter

To:
    E.H. Ehrmann

From:
    Frank Lloyd Wright

Collection:
    Unitarian Universalist Church Papers, 1906-1911
    The Oak Park Public Library
    Oak Park, Illinois

Medium:
    Stationery of Frank Lloyd Wright, Architect, signed by
    Frank Lloyd Wright

Size:
    9-7/16 in. x 8-1/8 in.; 239.7 mm x 206.4 mm

Number of Pages:
    1

Descriptors:
    E.H. Ehrmann, Unity Church (Oak Park, Illinois)

Review:
    Discussed are the complete costs of light fixtures for the Unity
    House portion of the Unity Church at Oak Park, Illinois.

B35

Date:
    March 20, 1908

Type of Manuscript:
    Letter

To:
    Trustees of Unity Church

From:
    Frank Lloyd Wright

Collection:
    Unitarian Universalist Church Papers, 1906-1911
    The Oak Park Public Library
    Oak Park, Illinois

Medium:
   Stationery of Frank Lloyd Wright, Architect, signed by
   Frank Lloyd Wright

Size:
   9-3/8 in. x 8-3/16 in.; 238.1 mm x 207.9 mm

Number of Pages:
   1

Descriptors:
   Unity Church (Oak Park, Illinois), Trustees of Unity
   Church (Oak Park, Illinois), Paul Mueller

Review:
   Concerning the financial situation of Paul Mueller, the general
   contractor for Unity Church.

B36

Date:
   April 1908

Type of Manuscript:
   Letter

To:
   Francis Little

From:
   Frank Lloyd Wright

Collection:
   Frank Lloyd Wright/Francis Little Collection
   The Metropolitan Museum of Art
   New York, New York

Medium:
   Signed, typed on F.L. Wright letterhead

Number of Pages:
   1

Descriptors:
   Francis Little

Review:
   Wright offers to visit the Littles.

B37

Date:
   September 18, 1908

Type of Manuscript:
   Letter

To:
   Mrs. Francis Little

From:
   Frank Lloyd Wright

Collection:
   Frank Lloyd Wright/Francis Little Collection
   The Metropolitan Museum of Art
   New York, New York

Medium:
   Typed on F.L. Wright letterhead, signed

Descriptors:
   Francis Little

Review:
   Wright expresses concern over one of the Littles' projects and
   offers to help.

B38

Date:
   October 24, 1908

Type of Manuscript:
   Letter

To:
   Charles Robert Ashbee

From:
   Frank Lloyd Wright

Source:
   Alan Crawford
   ''Ten Letters From Frank Lloyd Wright to Charles Robert
   Ashbee''

Collection:
   The Ashbee Journals
   King's College
   Cambridge, England

Number of Words:
   114

Descriptors:
   Charles Robert Ashbee

Review:
   Wright is looking forward to seeing Ashbee when Ashbee visits
   Chicago.

B39

Date:
   January 3, 1909

Type of Manuscript:
   Letter

To:
   Charles Robert Ashbee

From:
   Frank Lloyd Wright

Source:
   Alan Crawford
   "Ten Letters from Frank Lloyd Wright to Charles Robert
   Ashbee"

Collection:
   The Ashbee Journals
   King's College
   Cambridge, England

Number of Words:
   163

Descriptors:
   Charles Robert Ashbee, Lexington Terrace Apartments
   Project, City National Bank and Hotel, Sicily

Review:
   Ashbee had invited Wright to visit Sicily with him. However,
   Wright declines to go because he has a large amount of work
   in his office.

B40

Date:
   March 8, 1909

Type of Manuscript:
   Letter

To:
   William G. Adams

From:
   Frank Lloyd Wright

Collection:
   Unitarian Universalist Church Papers, 1906-1911
   The Oak Park Public Library
   Oak Park, Illinois

Medium:
   Stationery of Frank Lloyd Wright, signed by Frank Lloyd Wright

Size:
   18-7/8 in. x 8-1/4 in.; 479.4 mm x 209.6 mm

Number of Pages:
   1

Descriptors:
   William G. Adams, Unity Church (Oak Park, Illinois),
   Paul Mueller

Review:
   Concerning money owed Paul Mueller for extras for Unity Church.
   Mueller was the general contractor for the project.

B41

Date:
   June 1909

Type of Manuscript:
   Letter

To:
   "To Whom It May Concern" (for Taylor A. Woolley)

From:
   Frank Lloyd Wright
   Forest and Chicago Avenues
   Oak Park, Illinois

Collection:
   University of Utah
   Marriott Library
   Taylor Woolley Archive, Special Collections, Item 152

Medium:
   Typed on red-square design stationery, signed

Size:
   8-1/8 in. x 4-5/8 in.; 207 mm x 118 mm

Number of Pages:
   1

Descriptors:
   Taylor A. Woolley

Review:
   A letter of recommendation for Taylor A. Woolley in which Wright
   states that Woolley worked in Wright's office for one year.
   Wright speaks highly of Woolley in this letter.

B42

Date:
   September 22, 1909 (copydated April 1, 1951)

Type of Manuscript:
   Contract (copy)

Between:
   Frank Lloyd Wright and Herman von Holst

Collection:
   The Wrightiana Collection
   The Art Institute of Chicago

Medium:
   Copy of original (retyped)

Size:
   8-1/2 in. x 14 in.; 215.9 mm x 355.6 mm

Number of Pages:
   5

Descriptors:
   Herman von Holst, Wasmuth Portfolio, William Grey Purcell,
   Isabel Roberts, T.A. Woolley, J.H. Ingalls Residence, J.G.
   Melson Residence, J.R. Zeigler Residence, Mrs. Thomas Gale
   Residence, Bank and Hotel for Mason City, W.H. Copeland Altera-

tions, Hiram Baldwin Residence, F.C. Robie Residence, P.C. Stohr
Arcade Building, M.S. May Residence, G.C. Stewart Cottage, D.H.
Amberg Residence, E.P. Irving Residence, Walter Gerts Residence,
Ausgeführte Bauten und Entwürfe von Frank Lloyd Wright.

Review:
The original is contained in the Purcell and Elmslie Archives of
the University of Minnesota and this retyped copy is addressed to
William Gray Purcell. When Wright went abroad to work on the Wasmuth
Portfolio, he retained the services of Herman von Holst in his Oak
Park office. The contract outlines current projects which von Holst
would be taking over in Wright's absence, along with a short listing
of prospective projects which might develop into commissions. These
are listed in the descriptors for this manuscript.

B43

Date:
March 31, 1910

Type of Manuscript:
Letter

To:
Charleś Robert Ashbee

From:
Frank Lloyd Wright

Source:
Alan Crawford
"Ten Letters from Frank Lloyd Wright to Charles Robert
Ashbee"

Collection:
The Ashbee Journals
King's College
Cambridge, England

Descriptors:
Charles Robert Ashbee, England

Review:
Personal reasons prevent Wright from going to England to visit
Ashbee.

B44

Date:
June 10, 1910

Type of Manuscript:
Letter

To:
Walter B. Griffin
11th Floor--Steinway Hall
Chicago, Illinois
U.S.A.

2-1.10 The David M. Amberg Residence (1909), Grand Rapids, Michigan, which Herman von Holst had contracted to complete while Wright was abroad working on the Wasmuth Portfolio drawings. Photo by the author.

From:
    Frank Lloyd Wright
    Villino Belvedere
    Fiesole, Italy

Collection:
    University of Utah
    Marriott Library
    Taylor Woolley Archive, Special Collections, Item 152

Medium:
    Signed letter on red-square design stationery

Size:
    7-1/2 in. x 12 in.; 192 mm x 305 mm

Number of Pages:
    1

Descriptors:
    Walter Burley Griffin, Japanese Prints

Review:
    This letter deals with some Japanese prints which Frank Lloyd
    Wright had given to Walter Burley Griffin as payment for Griffin's
    services to Wright while Wright was abroad. Wright comments on a
    rumor which he had heard concerning Griffin's dissatisfaction over
    their mutual arrangement. Wright's tone throughout the letter is
    one of disgust. He makes the point that he doesn't have much money
    to spare, but if Griffin feels that he was treated unfairly he should
    return the prints for which Wright would pay him his money plus
    six percent interest from the time of the arrangement and a 20
    percent profit on his investment. Wright feels, however, that the
    Japanese prints are worth more. Wright closes by noting that Griffin's
    money would be available in September 1910 after Wright returns
    from Italy. This letter has a matching envelope with a red square
    and Wright's name on the back flap and is addressed to Walter B.
    Griffin but is not postmarked. It was probably never sent and was
    perhaps given to Taylor Woolley to mail which would explain its
    existence in this collection of Woolley-Wright related materials.

B45

Date:
    June 16, 1910

Type of Manuscript:
    Letter

To:
    "To Whom It May Concern" (for Taylor A. Woolley)

From:
    Frank Lloyd Wright
    Fiesole, Italy

Collection:
    University of Utah
    Marriott Library
    Taylor Woolley Archive, Special Collections, Item 152

Medium:
   Signed letter on red-square design stationery

Size:
   7-1/2 in. x 12 in.; 192 mm x 305 mm

Number of Pages:
   1

Descriptors:
   Taylor A. Woolley

Review:
   A letter of recommendation for Taylor A. Woolley in which Frank
   Lloyd Wright states that Woolley worked in Wright's office for
   two years. Wright commends Woolley for being an effective draughtsman and speaks highly of him.

B46

Date:
   July 8, 1910

Type of Manuscript:
   Letter

To:
   Charles Robert Ashbee

From:
   Frank Lloyd Wright
   Villino Belvedere
   Fiesole, Italy

Source:
   Alan Crawford
   "Ten Letters from Frank Lloyd Wright to Charles Robert Ashbee"

Collection:
   The Ashbee Journals
   King's College
   Cambridge, England

Number of Words:
   746+

Descriptors:
   Charles Robert Ashbee, Wasmuth, *Ausgeführte Bauten und Entwürfe
   von Frank Lloyd Wright*, Oak Park, Iconoclast, Fiesole, Florence,
   Italy, Italian Art

Review:
   Wright speaks of what he has learned from Ashbee and of his
   experience with Italian art while at Fiesole.

B47

Date:
   July 20, 1910

Type of Manuscript:
   Letter

To:
   Taylor A. Wooley [sic for Taylor A. Woolley]
   c/o Thos. Cook and Sons
   Avenue de l'Opera
   Paris, France

From:
   Frank Lloyd Wright
   Villino Belvedere
   Fiesole, Italy

Collection:
   University of Utah
   Marriott Library
   Taylor Woolley Archive, Special Collections, Item 152

Medium:
   Signed letter on red-square design stationery

Size:
   7-1/2 in. x 12 in.; 191 mm x 305 mm

Number of Pages:
   1

Descriptors:
   Taylor A. Woolley, Fiesole (Italy), Ernst Wasmuth, Harley Bradley
   Residence, Wasmuth Portfolio, Berlin, Potsdam, Rofaello, Paris,
   Mrs. Fleaye (?), *Ausgeführte Bauten und Entwürfe von Frank Lloyd
   Wright, Frank Lloyd Wright: Ausgeführte Bauten*

Review:
   This letter is a response to a telegram which Woolley had sent to
   Wright in Italy while Woolley was in Berlin seeing Ernst Wasmuth,
   publisher of the famous Wasmuth Portfolio, *Ausgeführte Bauten und
   Entwürfe von Frank Lloyd Wright*, and *Frank Lloyd Wright: Ausgeführte
   Bauten*. Wright informs Woolley that all of the plates for the
   Wasmuth publication are finished except those for the Harley
   Bradley Residence which Wright will do over again. He suggests
   that Woolley visit Potsdam. Wright also suggests that if Woolley
   needs more money while in Paris he wire Wright because Wright can
   now pay, since a Mrs. Fleaye (?) has paid him. Wright feels that
   early completion of the Wasmuth publication is dubious since Wasmuth
   is moving slowly. Wright concludes by informing Woolley that he
   will be stopping in England on September 10, 1910.

B48

Date:
   July 24, 1910

Type of Manuscript:
   Letter

To:
   Charles Robert Ashbee

From:
    Frank Lloyd Wright
    Villino Belvedere
    Fiesole, Italy

Source:
    Alan Crawford
    "Ten Letters from Frank Lloyd Wright to Charles Robert Ashbee"

Collection:
    The Ashbee Journals
    King's College
    Cambridge, England

Number of Words:
    722+

Descriptors:
    Charles Robert Ashbee, *Ausgeführte Bauten und Entwürfe von Frank
    Lloyd Wright*, *Frank Lloyd Wright: Ausgeführte Bauten*, Wasmuth,
    Sonderheft, Wasmuth Portfolio, Oak Park, Guthrie

Review:
    Wright goes into great detail concerning the preparation of
    Ausgeführte Bauten und Entwürfe von Frank Lloyd Wright (the
    famous Wasmuth portfolio) and *Frank Lloyd Wright: Ausgeführte
    Bauten*, for which Ashbee wrote the introduction, "Frank Lloyd
    Wright: A Study and an Appreciation."

B49

Date:
    September 26, 1910

Type of Manuscript:
    Letter

To:
    Charles Robert Ashbee

From:
    Frank Lloyd Wright

Source:
    Alan Crawford
    "Ten Letters from Frank Lloyd Wright to Charles Robert Ashbee"

Collection:
    The Ashbee Journals
    King's College
    Cambridge, England

Number of Words:
    303

Descriptors:
    Charles Robert Ashbee, *Frank Lloyd Wright: Ausgeführte Bauten*,
    Wasmuth, Japanese Art

Review:
    Comments on Ashbee's introduction to *Frank Lloyd Wright: Ausge-
    führte Bauten* entitled "Frank Lloyd Wright: A Study and an Apprecia-

tion." Wright disagrees with several of the points made by Ashbee about Wright's work, including the influence of Japanese art on his building designs.

REFERENCES

Books:

Brooks, H. Allen.
The Prairie School: Frank Lloyd Wright and His Midwest Contemporaries.
Toronto: University of Toronto Press, 1972.

Chicago Architectural Club.
Annual of the Chicago Architectural Club, Being the Book of the Thirteenth Annual Exhibition 1900. Chicago: Architectural Club, 1900.

Chicago Architectural Club.
The Chicago Architectural Annual Published by the Chicago Architectural Club: A Selection of Works Exhibited at the Art Institute in March of the Year One Thousand Nine Hundred and Two. Chicago: Architectural Club, 1902.

Clark, Robert Judson (ed.).
The Arts and Crafts Movement in America 1876-1916. Princeton: Princeton University Press, 1972.

Cowles, Linn Ann.
An Index and Guide to "An Autobiography," the 1943 Edition by Frank Lloyd Wright. Hopkins, Minnesota: Greenwich Design, 1976.

Drexler, Arthur (ed.).
The Drawings of Frank Lloyd Wright. New York: Horizon Press for the Museum of Modern Art, 1962.

Eaton, Leonard K.
Two Chicago Architects and Their Clients: Frank Lloyd Wright and Howard Van Doren Shaw. Cambridge, Massachusetts: The M.I.T. Press, 1969.

Gannett, William C., and Frank Lloyd Wright.
The House Beautiful. River Forest, Illinois: The Auvergne Press, 1896-1897 (1898).

Gannett, William C., and Frank Lloyd Wright.
The House Beautiful. Park Forest, Illinois: W.R. Hasbrouck, 1963.

Gutheim, Frederick (ed.).
Frank Lloyd Wright on Architecture: Selected Writings, 1894-1940. New York: Duell, Sloan and Pearce, 1941.

Hitchcock, Henry-Russell.
Frank Lloyd Wright. Paris: Cahiers d'Art, 1928.

Hitchcock, Henry-Russell.
  In the Nature of Materials: 1887-1941, the Buildings of Frank Lloyd Wright. New York: Duell, Sloan and Pearce, 1942.

Manson, Grant Carpenter.
  Frank Lloyd Wright to 1910: The First Golden Age. New York: Reinhold Publishing Corporation, 1958.

Minnesota Museum of Art.
  Prairie School Architecture in Minnesota, Iowa, Wisconsin. St. Paul, Minnesota: Minnesota Museum of Art, 1982.

Storrer, William Allin.
  The Architecture of Frank Lloyd Wright, a Complete Catalog, Second Edition. Cambridge, Massachusetts: The M.I.T. Press, 1978.

Twombly, Robert C.
  Frank Lloyd Wright: An Interpretive Biography. New York: Harper and Row Publishers, 1973.

Twombly, Robert C.
  Frank Lloyd Wright: His Life and His Architecture. New York: John Wiley and Sons, Inc., 1979.

Wijdeveld, H. Th. (ed.).
  The Life-Work of the American Architect, Frank Lloyd Wright. Santpoort, Holland: C.A. Mees, 1925.

Wright, Frank Lloyd.
  Frank Lloyd Wright, Architect. Chicago: Publisher Unknown, 1898.

Wright, Frank Lloyd.
  Ausgeführte Bauten und Entwürfe von Frank Lloyd Wright. Berlin: Ernst Wasmuth, 1910.

Wright, Frank Lloyd.
  Frank Lloyd Wright: Ausgeführte Bauten. Berlin: Verlegt bei Ernst Wasmuth A.G., 1911.

Wright, Frank Lloyd.
  Drawings for a Living Architecture. New York: Horizon Press for the Bear Run Foundation, Inc., and the Edgar J. Kaufmann Charitable Foundation, 1959.

Wright, Frank Lloyd.
  An Autobiography. New York: Horizon Press, 1977.

Periodicals:

Anonymous.
  "Brick and Terra-Cotta Work in American Cities, and Manufacturers' Department," *The Brickbuilder,* Vol. 7, November 1898, pp. 239-241.

Anonymous.
"Brick and Terra-Cotta Work in American and Foreign Cities, and Manufacturers' Department," *The Brickbuilder*, Vol. 8, January 1899, pp. 16-19.

Spencer, Robert C., Jr.
"The Work of Frank Lloyd Wright," *Architectural Review* (Boston), Vol. 7, June 1900, pp. 61-72.

Anonymous.
"In General," *The Brickbuilder*, Vol. 10, No. 1, January 1901, p. 20.

Anonymous.
"Residence of Wm. R. Heath, Buffalo, N.Y.," *Inland Architect and News Record*, Vol. 48, October 1906, plate.

Hitchcock, Henry-Russell, Jr.
"Notes on Wright Buildings in Buffalo," *Albright Art Gallery, Gallery Notes*, Vol. 11, June 1947, pp. 18-21.

Anonymous.
"A Wright House on the Prairie," *The Prairie School Review*, Vol. 2, No. 3, 1965, pp. 5-11.

Hines, Thomas S.
"Frank Lloyd Wright--the Madison Years: Records Versus Recollections," *Wisconsin Magazine of History*, Vol. 50, Winter 1967, pp. 109-119.

Crawford, Alan.
"Ten Letters from Frank Lloyd Wright to Charles Robert Ashbee," *Journal of the Society of Architectural Historians of Great Britain* (England), Vol. 13, 1970, pp. 64-76.

Anonymous.
"New Frank Lloyd Wright and Louis H. Sullivan Papers in the Burnham Library of Architecture," *Calendar of the Art Institute of Chicago*, Vol. 65, January 1971, pp. 6-15.

Newspapers:

Monroe, Harriet.
"In the Galleries," *The Chicago Examiner*, April 13, 1907.

2-2.1   Frank Lloyd Wright (circa 1924). Photo courtesy of the State Historical Society of Wisconsin.

CHAPTER 2

FOREIGN APPRECIATION AND PERSONAL TURMOIL
(1911 TO 1926)

Introduction

The year 1911 saw the publication of *Frank Lloyd Wright: Ausgeführte Bauten*, a photographic expansion of the earlier *Ausgeführte Bauten und Entwürfe von Frank Lloyd Wright* (Wasmuth Portfolio), published in 1910, which was already influencing European architects. During this period Wright relocated his practice from the Chicago area to Spring Green, Wisconsin, and built Taliesin. In 1914 tragedy fell upon Wright, when several persons were murdered at Taliesin by a mad chef in his employ. One of the persons murdered was Wright's mistress, Mamah Borthwick Cheney--and Taliesin was almost totally destroyed by a fire started by the madman. In late 1914 or early 1915, Wright met Maud Miriam Noel, who accompanied him to Japan. In 1922 Wright secured a divorce from his first wife, Catherine, and in late 1923 he and Maud Miriam Noel were married. The marriage to Maud Miriam Noel was ill fated and ended with divorce in 1930, after a legal and emotional battle between the two which lasted from 1924 to 1930. Further turmoil prevailed in Wright's life in April of 1925 when another extensive fire nearly destroyed all of Taliesin. However, Wright's architectural work continued to fascinate the Europeans, particularly with the publication of the Wendingen edition of his work done by H.Th. Wijdeveld.

During the period 1911 to 1926, Wright produced 145 designs of which 62 were constructed. His designs for this period represent about 15 percent of his total life work. The peak years for this period, in terms of amount of workload during one year, were 25 designs for the year 1911 and 22 designs for the year 1915. From 1915 through 1926, however, Wright experienced a large decline in his workload. This lessening of his design activity offered him the opportunity to write on architecture, as indicated by his series, "In the Cause of Architecture," for *Architectural Record* magazine.

This chapter looks at Wright's introduction to and influence upon the architects and architecture of Holland and other European countries, through the cataloguing of correspondence written by Wright to Dutch architect H. Th. Wijdeveld, who first introduced Wright's work in Holland with the publication of the famous Wendingen articles and book and whom Wright had later asked to assist in the establishment of the Taliesin Fellowship in the early 1930s. Also included are Wright's letters to Dutch architects H.P. Berlage and J.J.P. Oud. Other letters which are catalogued include correspondence to F.L. Wright's son, John Lloyd Wright, who was also an architect, and F.L. Wright's daughter, Catherine Baxter; letters to architects Charles Robert Ashbee of England who introduced Wright's work to England as

159

described earlier in Chapter 1, Francis Sullivan who collaborated
with Wright on several designs for buildings located in Canada, and
Antonin Raymond who worked with Wright in Japan on the famous Imperial
Hotel and other Japanese and American designs. There is also correspondence with Taylor A. Woolley, former Wright "draughtsman" who worked
on the Wasmuth Portfolio and who later became an architect in Salt
Lake City, Utah; Francis Little, an earlier client, for whom Wright
designed a second residence during this period; critic Harriet Monroe;
Wallace Rice; Alexander C. Goth; and the editor of *The Capital Times*
(a Madison, Wisconsin, newspaper), William T. Evjue, with whom Wright
developed a warm and long friendship which lasted until Wright's
death in April of 1959.

Three early drafts for Wright's "In the Cause of Architecture"
series for *Architectural Record* magazine are indexed, including "In
the Cause of Architecture," "In the Cause of Architecture, He Who Gets
Slapped" (from *Western Architect* magazine), and "In the Cause of
Architecture, the Third Dimension," each of which was written in
early 1923, long before the "In the Cause of Architecture" series
reappeared in *Architectural Record*, in May of 1927, with "In the
Cause of Architecture: I. The Architect and the Machine." Wright's
first article entitled "In the Cause of Architecture" done for
Architectural Record initially appeared in that magazine in March of
1908.

B50

Date:
    April 6, 1911

Type of Manuscript:
    Letter

To:
    T.A. Woolley (Taylor A. Woolley)
    Salt Lake City, Utah

From:
    Frank Lloyd Wright
    Forest and Chicago Avenues
    Oak Park, Illinois

Collection:
    University of Utah
    Marriott Library
    Taylor Woolley Archive, Special Collections, Item 152

Medium:
    Typed on red-square stationery, signed

Size:
    8-1/8 in. x 9-3/8 in.; 209 mm x 239 mm

Descriptors:
    Taylor A. Woolley, Wasmuth Portfolio, *Ausgeführte Bauten und
    Entwürfe von Frank Lloyd Wright*, Van Dort

Review:
    Wright informs Woolley that the first volume of Wright's *Ausge-
    führte und Entwürfe von Frank Lloyd Wright* (Berlin: Ernst Wasmuth,

1910) is completed and that it and about twenty plates of the
second volume are being sent to Woolley. Wright indicates that
he would like Woolley to have an inscribed copy. He also indicates
that the price of the completed work is to be $50, $15 of which
is to go to Woolley for any copies Woolley may sell for Wright.

B51

Date:
   April 22 (1911?)

Type of Manuscript:
   Letter

To:
   Taylor A. Woolley

From:
   Frank Lloyd Wright

Collection:
   University of Utah
   Marriott Library
   Taylor Woolley Archive, Special Collections, Item 152

Medium:
   Signed

Size:
   8-1/2 in. x 12-15/16 in.; 216 mm x 329 mm

Number of Pages:
   2

Descriptors:
   Taylor A. Woolley, *Ausgeführte Bauten und Entwürfe von Frank Lloyd
   Wright*, Wasmuth Portfolio, Sonderheft, Dittke, Van Dort, *Frank
   Lloyd Wright: Ausgeführte Bauten*, Ryerson, The Art Institute of
   Chicago, MacArthur (Albert Chase McArthur?), Hermann von Holst,
   Avery Coonley Residence (Riverside, Illinois), Sherman Booth
   Residence Project

Review:
   The letter is dated April 22 with no year indicated. However, it
   is believed that this letter was written in 1911 because of its
   contents in relation to other letters and the progression of the
   sale of his *Ausgeführte Bauten und Entwürfe von Frank Lloyd Wright*
   (the famous Wasmuth Portfolio) and the later *Frank Lloyd Wright:
   Ausgeführte Bauten*. Much of this letter concerns these two books.
   Wright states that there were 650 editions of the Wasmuth Portfolio
   printed to be sold at $50 each. The completion date for *Frank
   Lloyd Wright: Ausgeführte Bauten* is May 15. A first edition, which
   was not satisfactory, was sold in Europe only. Wright briefly
   mentions a new commission at Glencoe, Illinois, for a project
   similar in size to his design for the Avery Coonley Residence at
   Riverside, Illinois, of 1907 (this commission is possibly the
   Sherman Booth Residence Project of 1911). At this time Wright only
   has one assistant and is very busy but does not want any of the
   architects who had once worked for him in the past to work for him
   now and does not feel this to be a total loss.

B52

Date:
   August 31, 1911

Type of Manuscript:
   Telegram

To:
   Taylor A. Wiley [sic for Taylor A. Woolley]
   San Diego, California

From:
   Frank Lloyd Wright
   Oak Park, Illinois

Collection:
   University of Utah
   Marriott Library
   Taylor Woolley Archive, Special Collections, Item 152

Medium:
   Telegram

Size:
   7-15/16 in. x 5-1/4 in.; 202 mm x 134 mm

Number of Pages:
   1

Number of Words:
   15

Descriptors:
   Taylor A. Woolley, Lloyd Wright, Olmsted and Olmsted

Review:
   Wright asks Woolley to come to work for him at his Oak Park,
   Illinois, office. He also mentions that Lloyd Wright, his son,
   is working for Olmsted and Olmsted in San Diego.

B53

Date:
   September 10, 1911

Type of Manuscript:
   Letter (copy of original)

To:
   Francis C. Sullivan, Architect
   Canada

From:
   Frank Lloyd Wright
   Taliesin
   Spring Green, Wisconsin

Collection:
   The John Lloyd Wright Collection
   The Avery Architectural Library
   Columbia University
   Folder 14

Medium:
    Handwritten, signed "Frank Lloyd Wright"

Size:
    Two--5-1/2 in. x 8 in.; 139.7 mm x 203.2 mm
    One--8-1/2 in. x 11 in.; 215.9 mm x 279.4 mm

Number of Pages:
    3

Number of Words:
    901

Descriptors:
    Francis C. Sullivan, Arthur L. Richards Co., Lloyd Wright,
    Miriam Noel Wright, Porter Family, Lake Geneva Hotel for Arthur L.
    Richards

Review:
    The copy of this letter was obtained by John Lloyd Wright from
    Martin Birkhans of the University of Toronto. Discussed in the
    letter is Lloyd Wright's active participation in F.L. Wright's
    architectural practice. F.L. Wright had sent Lloyd to Milwaukee
    to look into the matter of the Arthur L. Richards Company; the
    elder Wright decided not to work with the company any further.
    F.L. Wright had submitted a plan for reorganization but the
    Richards Company "rejected it so I rejected them." Unfortunately,
    nowhere in this letter does Wright mention any specific project
    he was working on with the Arthur L. Richards Company. It was
    probably the Lake Geneva Hotel. Plate 47 in Arthur Drexler's
    The Drawings of Frank Lloyd Wright is an aerial perspective of
    the design for the Lake Geneva Hotel and is dated August 1911.
    Wright also explains some problems which may occur if Francis C.
    Sullivan were to join Wright's architecture practice. Apparently,
    Frank Lloyd Wright had considered having Francis C. Sullivan as
    a partner in his architectural firm. A sincere letter to a friend
    and colleague.

B54

Date:
    September 12, 1911

Type of Manuscript:
    Telegram

To:
    Taylor Wooley [sic for Taylor A. Woolley]
    1636 Monroe Street
    Chicago, Illinois

From:
    Frank Lloyd Wright
    Spring Green, Wisconsin

Collection:
    University of Utah
    Marriott Library
    Taylor A. Woolley Archive, Special Collections, Item 152

2-2.2   South facade of the Lake Geneva Hotel, for Arthur L. Richards (1911), Lake Geneva, Wisconsin. Photo by Alyn W. Hess.

2-2.3 East facade of the Lake Geneva Hotel, for Arthur L. Richards (1911), Lake Geneva, Wisconsin. Photo by Alyn W. Hess.

2-2.4 North facade of the Lake Geneva Hotel, for Arthur L. Richards (1911), Lake Geneva, Wisconsin. Photo by Alyn W. Hess.

Medium:
   Telegram

Size:
   7-15/16 in. x 5-1/4 in.; 202 mm x 134 mm

Number of Pages:
   1

Number of Words:
   11

Descriptors:
   Taylor A. Woolley, Mrs. Roberts (Isabel Roberts?)

Review:
   An invitation and instructions for Woolley to come to Spring
   Green, Wisconsin.

B55

Date:
   1911?

Type of Manuscript:
   Inscribed book

To:
   Francis W. Little

From:
   Frank Lloyd Wright

Collection:
   Frank Lloyd Wright/Francis Little Collection
   The Metropolitan Museum of Art
   New York, New York

Medium:
   Handwritten in book

Descriptors:
   Francis Little, *Frank Lloyd Wright: Ausgeführte Bauten*

Review:
   Inscription in pencil in *Frank Lloyd Wright: Ausgeführte Bauten*
   (Berlin: Ernst Wasmuth, 1911), which says "To my friend--client
   Francis W. Little--from his problematical Frank Lloyd Wright with
   real affection nevertheless."

B56

Date:
   February 3, 1912

Type of Manuscript:
   Letter (public announcement)

To:
   Whom It May Concern

From:
    Frank Lloyd Wright
    Taliesin, Spring Green

Collection:
    Jane Lloyd Jones Correspondence, 1899-1940
    The State Historical Society of Wisconsin
    Wis. MSS, NN

Medium:
    Typed and signed by Wright

Size:
    8-1/2 in. x 11 in.; 215.9 mm x 279.4 mm

Number of Pages:
    1

Number of Words:
    162

Descriptors:
    Hillside Home School, Lloyd Jones Sisters

Review:
    Frank Lloyd Wright disassociates himself from the Lloyd Jones
    Sisters who ran the Hillside Home School near Spring Green.
    The letter was sworn before a notary public at Sauk County,
    Wisconsin.

B57

Date:
    July 16, 1912

Type of Manuscript:
    Letter

To:
    Wooley [sic for Taylor A. Woolley]

From:
    Frank Lloyd Wright
    Taliesin

Collection:
    University of Utah
    Marriott Library
    Taylor Woolley Archive, Special Collections, Item 152

Medium:
    Signed

Size:
    8 in. x 4-13/16 in.; 203 mm x 122 mm

Number of Pages:
    1

Descriptors:
    Taylor A. Woolley, Taliesin, Bernhard, Gibbs, Fucher,
    Madison Hotel (Arthur L. Richards Madison Hotel Project?)

2-2.5 Nell and Jane Lloyd Jones Hillside Home School II (1901), Spring Green, Wisconsin. Photo by the author.

Review:
   A short letter informing Woolley to take his time; there is no
   hurry for him to return to Taliesin. Wright also informs Woolley
   that the Madison Hotel at Madison, Wisconsin, has been set aside
   (this could possibly be Wright's Arthur L. Richards Hotel Project
   for Madison, Wisconsin, of 1911).

B58

Date:
   September 1, 1912 (?)

Type of Manuscript:
   Letter

To:
   Taylor Woolley
   Salt Lake City, Utah

From:
   Frank Lloyd Wright and
   Edward Sanderson, Jr.
   600 to 610 Orchestra Hall
   Chicago, Illinois

Collection:
   University of Utah
   Marriott Library
   Taylor Woolley Archive, Special Collections, Item 152

Medium:
   Typed on Frank Lloyd Wright's red-square stationery, signed by
   someone other than Frank Lloyd Wright, believed to be Sanderson's
   signature

Size:
   7-1/4 in. x 8-3/8 in.; 185 mm x 213 mm

Number of Pages:
   1

Descriptors:
   Taylor A. Woolley, Edward Sanderson, Jr., Orchestra
   Hall (Chicago), Frank Lloyd Wright and Edward Sanderson,
   Jr., Partnership

Review:
   The letter is dated "1912-9-1," which could indicate that its
   true date is January 9, 1912, instead of September 1, 1912. It
   is an announcement of the dissolution of the partnership of Frank
   Lloyd Wright and Edward Sanderson by mutual agreement on the date
   shown. Wright is to continue to work at the same address. This
   is a little known partnership which should be researched and
   substantiated further. However, the letter is printed on "Frank
   Lloyd Wright, Architect" stationery, with his typical square
   symbol in raised letters.

B59

Date:
December 17, 1912

Type of Manuscript:
Letter

To:
Not shown (Taylor Woolley)

From:
Frank Lloyd Wright
New York (written at top of page next to date)
605 Orchestra Hall (office address)
Chicago

Collection:
University of Utah
Marriott Library
Taylor Woolley Archive, Special Collections, Item 152

Medium:
Signed final draft of letter and rough draft of same letter

Size:
Final Draft--6-1/16 in. x 7-3/4 in.; 154 mm x 198 mm
Rough Draft--8-1/2 in. x 5-13/16 in.; 216 mm x 148 mm

Number of Pages:
2

Descriptors:
Taylor A. Woolley, Orchestra Hall (Chicago)

Review:
Letter of recommendation for Taylor A. Woolley from Frank Lloyd
Wright.

B60

Date:
November 3, 1913

Type of Manuscript:
Letter

To:
Francis Little

From:
Frank Lloyd Wright

Collection:
Frank Lloyd Wright/Francis Little Collection
The Metropolitan Museum of Art
New York, New York

Medium:
Handwritten on grey stationery, signed "Wright"

Number of Pages:
2

Descriptors:
Francis Little, Francis W. Little Second Residence

Review:
Wright talks of the handling of the lighting in the living room
of the second Little Residence he is designing. Wright suggests
the use of colored glass panels in the area.

B61

Date:
November 8, 1913

Type of Manuscript:
Letter

To:
Francis Little

From:
Frank Lloyd Wright

Collection:
Frank Lloyd Wright/Francis Little Collection
The Metropolitan Museum of Art
New York, New York

Medium:
Handwritten with pencil on tracing paper, signed "F.L.W."

Descriptors:
Francis Little, Francis W. Little Second Residence

Review:
Wright encloses a living room design detail with the letter and
suggests that this design be used for windows elsewhere in the
residence, along with plain plate glass windows.

B62

Date:
March 30, 1914

Type of Manuscript:
Telegram

To:
Taylor Wooley [sic for Taylor A. Woolley]
439 Third East
Salt Lake, Utah

From:
Frank Lloyd Wright
Spring Green, Wisconsin

Collection:
University of Utah
Marriott Library
Taylor Woolley Archive, Special Collections, Item 152

Medium:
   Telegram

Size:
   7-15/16 in. x 5-1/4 in.; 202 mm x 134 mm

Number of Pages:
   1

Number of Words:
   15

Descriptors:
   Taylor A. Woolley

Review:
   Wright asks Woolley to come to Spring Green to assist him in
   preparing an architectural exhibition. It is probably the Art
   Institute of Chicago exhibition of 1914 (see the Art Institute
   of Chicago's *The Work of Frank Lloyd Wright*, 4pp.).

B63

Date:
   April 13, 1914

Type of Manuscript:
   Letter

To:
   Harriet Monroe

From:
   Frank Lloyd Wright
   Taliesin
   Spring Green, Wisconsin

Collection:
   Poetry Magazine Papers, 1912-1936
   University of Chicago Library
   University of Chicago
   Box 41:5

Medium:
   Handwritten, signed "Frank Lloyd Wright"

Size:
   5-1/8 in. x 7-7/8 in.; 130.2 mm x 200.0 mm

Number of Pages:
   1

Number of Words:
   217

Descriptors:
   Harriet Monroe, John Root, Architectural Club Exhibit
   (Chicago)

Review:
   John Root, architect, is spoken of highly by Wright in this
   letter to Ms. Monroe. Wright also talks about one of her recent
   reviews of his work.

B64

Date:
April 20, 1914

Type of Manuscript:
Letter

To:
Harriet Monroe

From:
Frank Lloyd Wright

Collection:
Poetry Magazine Papers, 1912-1936
University of Chicago Library
University of Chicago
Box 41:5

Medium:
Handwritten, signed "Frank Lloyd Wright"

Size:
8-1/2 in. x 11-1/2 in; 215.9 mm x 292.1 mm

Number of Pages:
1

Number of Words:
304

Descriptors:
Harriet Monroe, George Maher, Montgomery Schuyler

Review:
Wright talks of Ms. Monroe's recent review of his work and his
letter to her dated April 13, 1914. He also writes of the possible
coverage of one of his projects in a New York newspaper.

B65

Date:
July 14, 1915

Type of Manuscript:
Letter

To:
Wallace Rice

From:
Frank Lloyd Wright
Taliesin

Collection:
Wallace Rice Collection
Newberry Library
Chicago, Illinois

Medium:
Handwritten, signed "Frank Lloyd W."

Number of Pages:
  1

Number of Words:
  105

Descriptors:
  Wallace Rice, Elizabeth Bingham

Review:
  Wright invites Rice to Taliesin to play some music.

B66

Date:
  February 9, 1916

Type of Manuscript:
  Letter

To:
  Charles Robert Ashbee

From:
  Frank Lloyd Wright

Source:
  Alan Crawford
  "Ten Letters from Frank Lloyd Wright to Charles Robert
  Ashbee"

Collection:
  The Ashbee Journals
  King's College
  Cambridge, England

Descriptors:
  Charles Robert Ashbee

Review:
  Wright asks Ashbee to visit him at Taliesin near Spring Green,
  Wisconsin, and apologizes for his past actions towards Ashbee.

B67

Date:
  September 10, 1917

Type of Manuscript:
  Letter

To:
  Antonin Raymond

From:
  Frank Lloyd Wright

Source:
  Antonin Raymond
  An Autobiography, pp. 56-57

Number of Words:
    466

Descriptors:
    Antonin Raymond, Miriam Noel Wright, Noemi Raymond,
    Taliesin, David Wright, Imperial Hotel, World War I

Review:
    Wright talks of the struggles of Taliesin and briefly reflects
    on progress on the design for the Imperial Hotel. Antonin Raymond
    was drafted into the armed forces during World War I. Wright has
    been facing economic constraints in the operation of his archi-
    tectural practice.

B68

Date:
    February 7, 1918

Type of Manuscript:
    Typescript lecture

Title:
    "Chicago Culture"

By:
    Frank Lloyd Wright
    Taliesin

Collection:
    The Library of Congress, Manuscript Division
    The Frank Lloyd Wright Papers
    Speech and Article File, 1901-1918

Medium:
    Typed single spaced

Size:
    8-1/2 in. x 11-1/8 in.; 215.9 mm x 282.6 mm

Number of Pages:
    12

Descriptors:
    Chicago, Chicago Women's Aid, Charles Robert Ashbee,
    Paris, Greece, Boston, Philadelphia, New York, Gothic,
    Art Institute of Chicago, Homer, Michelangelo, Bramante
    Rodin, Carlyle, William Blake, Beethoven, Louis Sullivan,
    Dankmar Adler, Daniel Burnham, Egypt

Review:
    A very long verbal attack on Chicago. According to Wright, Chicago
    has no culture. The lecture was given to the Chicago's Women's
    Aid at the Chicago Auditorium. It was printed in *Frank Lloyd
    Wright on Architecture: Selected Writings, 1894-1940*, edited by
    Frederick Gutheim and published by Duell, Sloan and Pearce at
    New York in 1941.

2-2.6　Aerial side elevation of the main entrance lobby wing of the Imperial Hotel (1915), as reconstructed at the Museum Meiji Mura near Nagoya, Japan (1976). Photo by Juro Kikuchi.

2-2.7　Front elevation of main entrance lobby wing of the Imperial Hotel (1915), with reflecting pool in the foreground, as reconstructed at the Museum Meiji Mura near Nagoya, Japan (1976). Photo by Juro Kikuchi.

B69

Date:
   February 7, 1921

Type of Manuscript:
   Letter

To:
   Catherine and Kenneth Baxter

From:
   Frank Lloyd Wright
   The Imperial Hotel
   Tokio, Japan

Collection:
   The Frank Lloyd Wright Collection
   Avery Architectural Library
   Columbia University

Medium:
   Handwritten on Imperial Hotel design stationery,
   signed "Father"

Number of Pages:
   2

Number of Words:
   400

Descriptors:
   New York, Christmas 1920, New Year 1921, Japan, America, Taliesin,
   Imperial Hotel, Catherine and Kenneth Baxter

Review:
   Wright tells Catherine Baxter of his leaving Japan to return
   to Taliesin. There is also talk of the design for the Imperial
   Hotel at Tokyo, Japan, and a brief discussion of politics. A copy
   of this letter is at The Art Institute of Chicago in the Herbert
   and Katherine Jacobs Frank Lloyd Wright Collection.

B70

Date:
   February 7, 1921

Type of Manuscript:
   Copy of letter

To:
   Catherine and Kenneth Baxter

From:
   Frank Lloyd Wright
   The Imperial Hotel
   Tokyo, Japan

Collection:
   The Herbert and Katherine Jacobs Frank Lloyd Wright
   Collection
   The Art Institute of Chicago
   Documents, Envelope 6

Medium:
    Handwritten on Imperial Hotel design stationery,
    signed "Father"

Size:
    5 in. x 8 in.; 127.0 mm x 203.2 mm

Number of Pages:
    2

Number of Words:
    400

Descriptors:
    New York, Christmas 1920, New Year 1921, Japan, America, Taliesin,
    Imperial Hotel, Catherine and Kenneth Baxter

Review:
    Talk of the design for the Imperial Hotel at Tokyo, Japan, and of
    Christmas, and a brief discussion of politics. The original letter
    is in the Frank Lloyd Wright Collection at the Avery Architectural
    Library of Columbia University (see B69).

B71

Date:
    February 8, 1921

Type of Manuscript:
    Letter

To:
    Antonin Raymond

From:
    Frank Lloyd Wright
    Imperial Hotel
    Tokyo, Japan

Source:
    Antonin Raymond
    An Autobiography, p. 77

Number of Words:
    230

Descriptors:
    Antonin Raymond, Aisaku Hayashi, Imperial Hotel

Review:
    Wright expresses his displeasure with Raymond's work and in
    particular Raymond's decision to leave Wright's architecture
    practice. Wright's tone is very severe and degrading to Raymond.
    Raymond's *An Autobiography* goes into detail regarding this par-
    ticular incident between Wright and him.

B72

Date:
    Undated (before 1921)

Type of Manuscript:
   Wedding invitation

To:
   Adena Miller Rich
   Hull House

From:
   Mr. and Mrs. Frank Lloyd Wright

Collection:
   Arts Study Collections: Chicago Campuses
   Chicago Circle Campus
   Chicago, Illinois

Medium:
   Typeset wedding invitation

Size:
   5-1/2 in. x 8-5/8 in.; 139.7 mm x 219.1 mm

Number of Pages:
   1

Number of Words:
   42

Descriptors:
   Catherine Lloyd Wright, Kenneth Stuart Baxter, Unity
   Church (Oak Park, Illinois), Adena Miller Rich

Review:
   An invitation to Catherine Lloyd Wright's wedding, F.L. Wright's
   daughter, who married Kenneth Stuart Baxter.

B73

Date:
   November 30, 1922

Type of Manuscript:
   Letter

To:
   Dr. H.P. Berlage
   Holland

From:
   Frank Lloyd Wright
   Taliesin
   Spring Green, Wisconsin

Collection:
   Dr. H.P. Berlage Papers
   Rijksdienst voor de Monumentenzorg
   Nederlands Documentatiecentrum voor de Bouwkunst

Medium:
   Handwritten, signed "Frank Lloyd Wright"

Size:
   6-1/2 in. x 9-1/2 in.; 165.1 mm x 241.3 mm

Number of Pages:
4

Number of Words:
934

Descriptors:
Dr. H.P. Berlage, *The Life-Work of the American Architect: Frank Lloyd Wright* (The Wendingen Edition), Boschi Reitz, Robert Van't Hoff, Imperial Hotel, Aline Barnsdall "Hollyhock" Residence, Louis H. Sullivan, Metropolitan Museum of New York

Review:
This letter was written after Wright received his copy of the book. He says that he would have liked to have included some additional photographs of his later buildings and also would have liked to have responded to some of the Dutch architects. Wright sends a reprint of his 1908 "In the Cause of Architecture." Wright also sends Berlage several photographs of his Aline Barnsdall "Hollyhock" Residence and of the Imperial Hotel. Wright's tone throughout the letter is one of appreciation for the interest Berlage and Europe have shown towards his work.

B74

Date:
November 30, 1922

Type of Manuscript:
Letter

To:
J.J.P. Oud
Holland

From:
Frank Lloyd Wright
Taliesin
Spring Green, Wisconsin

Collection:
J.J.P. Oud Letters
Rijksdienst voor de Monumentenzorg
Nederlands Documentatiecentrum voor de Bouwkunst

Medium:
Handwritten, signed "Frank Lloyd Wright"

Size:
6-1/2 in. x 9-1/2 in.; 165.1 mm x 241.3 mm

Number of Pages:
3

Number of Words:
649

Descriptors:
J.J.P. Oud, Dr. H.P. Berlage, *The Life-Work of the American Architect: Frank Lloyd Wright* (Wendingen

2-2.8　Aline Barnsdall Residence (1917), Los Angeles. Photo by the author.

Edition), Boschi Reitz, Metropolitan Museum of New York,
Bedrich Feurstein

Review:
Wright thanks Oud for visiting Wright's mother in Oak Park and
sends Oud photographs of himself and of his recent work. A letter
written by Wright to Dr. H.P. Berlage dated November 30, 1922,
was enclosed with this letter to Oud (see B73).

B75

Date:
January 4, 1923

Type of Manuscript:
Typescript article

Title:
"In the Cause of Architecture"

By:
Frank Lloyd Wright

Collection:
The John Lloyd Wright Collection
The Avery Architectural Library
Columbia University
Folder 29

Medium:
Typed

Number of Pages:
8

Descriptors:
The Mainichi (Japan), Imperial Hotel, Japan, *Architectural
Record*

Review:
An article prepared by F.L. Wright for *Architectural Record*.

B76

Date:
January 7, 1923

Type of Manuscript:
Typescript article

Title:
"In the Cause of Architecture, He Who Gets Slapped"

By:
Frank Lloyd Wright

Collection:
The John Lloyd Wright Collection
The Avery Architectural Library
Columbia University
Folder 29

Medium:
  Typed

Number of Pages:
  11

Descriptors:
  Imperial Hotel, *The Mainichi* (Japan), Japan, *Western
  Architect*

Review:
  An early draft of Wright's "In the Wake of the Quake, Concerning
  the Imperial Hotel, Tokio I," and "In the Cause of Architecture:
  In the Wake of the Quake, Concerning the Imperial Hotel, Tokio."

B77

Date:
  February 9, 1923

Type of Manuscript:
  Typescript article

Title:
  "In the Cause of Archtecture, the Third Dimension"

By:
  Frank Lloyd Wright

Collection:
  The John Lloyd Wright Collection
  The Avery Architectural Library
  Columbia University
  Folder 3

Medium:
  Typed, with corrections by Wright

Number of Pages:
  18

Descriptors:
  The Third Dimension

Review:
  Not seen by author.

B78

Date:
  March 28, 1923

Type of Manuscript:
  Letter

To:
  H. Th. Wijdeveld
  Holland

From:
  Frank Lloyd Wright
  Hollywood
  Los Angeles, California

Collection:
  H. Th. Wijdeveld Papers
  Rijksdienst voor de Monumentenzorg
  Nederlands Documentatiecentrum voor de Bouwkunst

Medium:
  Typed, signed "Frank Lloyd Wright"

Size:
  6-5/8 in. x 9-1/2 in.; 168.3 mm x 241.3 mm

Number of Pages:
  2

Number of Words:
  393 Typed; 47 Handwritten

Descriptors:
  H. Th. Wijdeveld, *The Life-Work of the American Architect:*
  Frank Lloyd Wright (Wendingen Edition), Dr. H.P. Berlage,
  The Western Architect, G.R. Horton

Review:
  Wright attempts a Dutch translation of "In the Cause of Architecture" for Wijdeveld but gives up. Also, Wright sends Wijdeveld
  photographs of his work for possible future publication. Wright
  suggests that a link be made between Wijdeveld and *The Western*
  Architect magazine.

B79

Date:
  November 18, 1924

Type of Manuscript:
  Letter

To:
  Harriet Monroe

From:
  Frank Lloyd Wright

Collection:
  Poetry Magazine Papers, 1912-1936
  University of Chicago Library
  University of Chicago
  Box 41:5

Medium:
  Handwritten on red-square stationery, signed
  "Frank Lloyd Wright"

Size:
  4-5/8 in. x 6-3/8 in.; 117.5 mm x 161.9 mm

Number of Pages:
  1

Number of Words:
  127

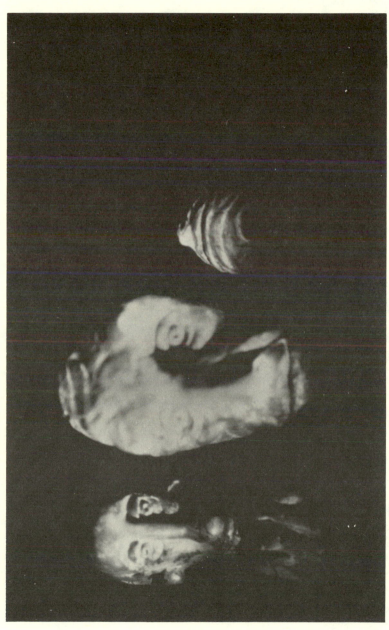

2-2.9 "Figures of dogs modelled by Frank Lloyd Wright in 1923 . . ." inscribed on back of photo. Attributed to Frank Lloyd Wright by E.B. Trimpey. Photo by E.B. Trimpey; courtesy of the State Historical Society of Wisconsin.

Descriptors:
   Harriet Monroe

Review:
   A short note wishing Ms. Monroe well during her illness.

B80

Date:
   Undated (1924?)

Type of Manuscript:
   Letter

To:
   John Lloyd Wright

From:
   Frank Lloyd Wright

Collection:
   The John Lloyd Wright Collection
   The Avery Architectural Library
   Columbia University
   Folder 13

Medium:
   Handwritten

Size:
   5-1/2 in. x 7-3/4 in.; 139.7 mm x 196.9 mm

Number of Pages:
   1

Number of Words:
   173

Descriptors:
   John Lloyd Wright, Olgivanna Lloyd Wright, Iovanna
   Lloyd Wright, Genroku (Japanese embroidered kimona),
   Nakoma Country Club and Winnebago Camping Ground Indian
   Memorial Project

Review:
   Wright sends John Lloyd a Japanese kimona for Hazel, John's
   wife, and discusses the Nakoma Country Club and Winnebago Camping
   Ground Indian Memorial Project briefly. Also, F.L. Wright invites
   John Lloyd and his family to visit him.

B81

Date:
   December 21, 1925

Type of Manuscript:
   Letter

To:
   Alexander C. Goth

From:
Frank Lloyd Wright
Taliesin
Spring Green, Wisconsin

Collection:
The John Lloyd Wright Collection
The Avery Architectural Library
Columbia University
Folder 13

Medium:
Handwritten, signed "Frank Lloyd Wright"

Size:
4-5/8 in. x 6-1/2 in.; 117.5 mm x 165.1 mm

Number of Pages:
1

Number of Words:
70

Descriptors:
Alexander C. Goth

Review:
Wright offers to talk on architecture at a meeting of architects
on the 9th of January 1926.

B82

Date:
May 7, 1926

Type of Manuscript:
Letter

To:
H. Th. Wijdeveld
Holland

From:
Frank Lloyd Wright
Taliesin
Spring Green, Wisconsin

Collection:
H. Th. Wijdeveld Papers
Rijksdienst voor de Monumentenzorg
Nederlands Documentatiecentrum voor de Bouwkunst

Medium:
Handwritten, signed "Frank Lloyd Wright"

Size:
6-1/2 in. x 9-1/4 in.; 165.1 mm x 235.0 mm

Number of Pages:
1

Number of Words:
182

Descriptors:
  H. Th. Wijdeveld, *The Life-Work of the American Architect:*
  Frank Lloyd Wright (Wendingen Edition)

Review:
  Wright invites H. Th. Wijdeveld to visit Taliesin.

B83

Date:
  October 1, 1926

Type of Manuscript:
  Listing of Japanese prints in the collection of Frank
  Lloyd Wright

Collection:
  The State Historical Society of Wisconsin
  SC
  565

Medium:
  Typed

Size:
  8-1/2 in. x 11 in.; 215.9 mm x 279.4 mm

Number of Pages:
  6

Descriptors:
  Japanese prints, Hiroshige, Anderson Galleries

Review:
  A complete listing of the Japanese prints which were in Wright's
  personal collection prior to their sale at the Anderson Galleries
  in New York (see "Japanese Art on Sale: Prints Collected by
  F.L. Wright Now on Exhibition"). The inventory was prepared for
  the transfer of the collection to the Bank of Wisconsin which
  held the prints as security (see Robert C. Twombly, *Frank Lloyd*
  Wright: An Interpretive Biography, p. 152).

B84

Date:
  1926

Type of Manuscript:
  Letter to the Editor

To:
  The Dodgeville Chronicle (Dodgeville, Wisconsin)

From:
  Frank Lloyd Wright

Collection:
  The John Lloyd Wright Collection
  The Avery Architectural Library
  Columbia University
  Folder 3

2-2.10   Taliesin sign on entrance gate, Spring Green, Wisconsin. Photo by the author.

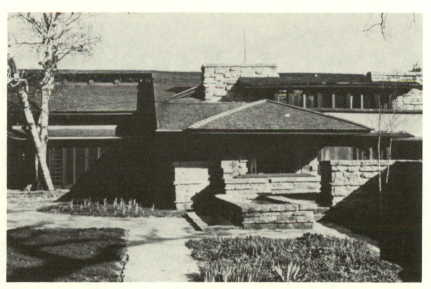

2-2.11   Exterior elevation of loggia entrance of Taliesin (1925ff) from garden court area, Spring Green, Wisconsin. Photo by the author.

2-2.12 Exterior elevation of kitchen wing of Taliesin (1925ff), Spring Green, Wisconsin. Photo
by the author.

2-2.13 Exterior view of a Taliesin (1925ff) wing, Spring Green, Wisconsin. Photo by
the author.

2-2.14 Exterior view of courtyard of Taliesin (1925ff), Spring Green, Wisconsin. Photo by the author.

2-2.15 Exterior view of Taliesin (1925ff) garage from the car court, Spring Green, Wisconsin. Photo by the author.

2-2.16   Exterior view of Taliesin (1925ff) from the work court, Spring Green, Wisconsin. Photo by the author.

2-2.17   Exterior detail view of Taliesin (1925ff) second story from courtyard, Spring Green, Wisconsin. Photo by the author.

Medium:
   Typed and signed by Wright

Number of Pages:
   4

Descriptors:
   Miriam Noel Wright, *The Dodgeville Chronicle* (Dodgeville,
   Wisconsin), Taliesin

Review:
   A reply to an attack on Wright regarding his former wife in the
   newspaper, *The Dodgeville Chronicle.*

B85

Date:
   Undated (1926 or 1927?)

Type of Manuscript:
   Letter

To:
   William T. Evjue

From:
   Frank Lloyd Wright

Collection:
   The William Theodore Evjue Papers, 1905-1969
   The State Historical Society of Wisconsin
   MSS 244, Box 155, Folder 21

Medium:
   Typed and handwritten, signed "Frank Lloyd Wright"
   and "FLW"

Size:
   8-1/2 in. x 14 in.; 215.9 mm x 355.6 mm

Number of Pages:
   2

Number of Words:
   454 Typed; 83 Handwritten

Descriptors:
   William T. Evjue, *The Capital Times*, William Dawson,
   Hearst Newspapers, Miriam Noel Wright, *Chicago Herald
   and Examiner*

Review:
   Regarding Wright's alleged statement concerning his
   former wife Miriam Noel's being supported by two Hearst
   newspapers.

B86

Date:
   Undated (1920s?)

2-2.18 Interior detail view of upper portion of Taliesin (1925ff) living room, Spring Green, Wisconsin. Photo by the author.

2-2.19 The Taliesin (1925ff) living room fireplace, Spring Green, Wisconsin. Photo by the author.

Type of Manuscript:
Letter

To:
John Lloyd Wright

From:
Frank Lloyd Wright

Collection:
The John Lloyd Wright Collection
The Avery Architectural Library
Columbia University
Folder 13

Medium:
Handwritten, signed "Dad"

Size:
6-1/8 in. x 7-3/4 in.; 155.6 mm x 196.9 mm

Number of Pages:
1

Number of Words:
48

Descriptors:
John Lloyd Wright, Miriam Noel Wright

Review:
Frank Lloyd Wright tells his son John Lloyd that he will be
glad to take care of John's dog. Also, a brief mention of
F.L. Wright's divorce from Miriam Noel Wright.

B87

Date:
Undated (1920s)

Type of Manuscript:
Letter

To:
John Lloyd Wright

From:
Frank Lloyd Wright
Taliesin
Spring Green, Wisconsin

Collection:
The John Lloyd Wright Collection
The Avery Architectural Library
Columbia University
Folder 13

Medium:
Handwritten and signed "Dad"

Size:
8-1/2 in. x 11 in.; 215.9 mm x 279.4 mm

Number of Pages:
1

Number of Words:
235

Descriptors:
John Lloyd Wright, Miriam Noel Wright, Phil La Follette, Porter
Cottage, William Weston

Review:
Brief discussion of Frank Lloyd Wright's divorce proceedings
involving Miriam Noel and on the current condition of Taliesin
at Spring Green, Wisconsin. F.L. Wright invites John Lloyd to
visit Taliesin.

REFERENCES

Books:

Akashi, Nobumichi.
  Kyu Teikoku Hoteru no Jisshoteki Kenkyu (*Frank Lloyd Wright in
  Imperial Hotel*). Tokyo: Tōkōdo Shoten, 1972.

Art Institute of Chicago.
  The Work of Frank Lloyd Wright. Chicago: The Art Institute of
  Chicago, 1914.

Cowles, Linn Ann.
  *An Index and Guide to "An Autobiography," the 1943 Edition by
  Frank Lloyd Wright*. Hopkins, Minnesota: Greenwich Design, 1976.

Drexler, Arthur (ed.).
  The Drawings of Frank Lloyd Wright. New York: Horizon Press for
  the Museum of Modern Art, 1962.

Gutheim, Frederick (ed.).
  Frank Lloyd Wright on Architecture: Selected Writings 1894-1940.
  New York: Duell, Sloan and Pearce, 1941.

Haight, Deborah S., and Peter F. Blume.
  Frank Lloyd Wright: The Library from the Francis W. Little House.
  Allentown, Pennsylvania: Allentown Art Museum, 1978.

Heckscher, Morrison, and Elizabeth G. Miller.
  *An Architect and His Client: Frank Lloyd Wright and Francis W.
  Little*. New York: The Metropolitan Museum of Art, May 2, 1973.

Hitchcock, Henry-Russell.
  *In the Nature of Materials: 1887-1941, the Buildings of Frank
  Lloyd Wright*. New York: Duell, Sloan and Pearce, 1942.

Izzo, Alberto, and Camillo Gubitosi (eds.).
  Frank Lloyd Wright, Dessins 1887-1959. Paris: C.E.R.A. Ecole
  Nationale Supérieure des Beaux-Arts, 1977.

James, Cary.
The Imperial Hotel: Frank Lloyd Wright and the Architecture of Unity. Rutland, Vermont: Charles E. Tuttle Company, 1968.

Raymond, Antonin.
An Autobiography. Rutland, Vermont: Charles E. Tuttle Company, 1973.

The Richards Company.
American System Built Houses, Designed by Frank Lloyd Wright. Milwaukee: The Richards Company, 1916?

Storrer, William Allin.
The Architecture of Frank Lloyd Wright, a Complete Catalog, Second Edition. Cambridge, Massachusetts: The M.I.T. Press, 1978.

Twombly, Robert C.
Frank Lloyd Wright: An Interpretive Biography. New York: Harper and Row, 1973.

Twombly, Robert C.
Frank Lloyd Wright: His Life and His Architecture. New York: John Wiley and Sons, Inc., 1979.

Wijdeveld, H. Th. (ed.).
The Life-Work of the American Architect: Frank Lloyd Wright. Santpoort, Holland: C.A. Mees, 1925.

Wright, Frank Lloyd.
Drawings for a Living Architecture. New York: Horizon Press for the Bear Run Foundation, Inc., and the Edgar J. Kaufmann Charitable Foundation, 1959.

Wright, Frank Lloyd.
An Autobiography. New York: Horizon Press, 1977.

Periodicals:

Wright, Frank Lloyd.
"In the Cause of Architecture," *Architectural Record*, Vol. 23, No. 3, March 1908, pp. 155-221.

Wright, Frank Lloyd.
"In the Wake of the Quake, Concerning the Imperial Hotel, Tokio, I," *Western Architect*, Vol. 32, November 1923, pp. 129-132.

Wright, Frank Lloyd.
"In the Cause of Architecture: In the Wake of the Quake, Concerning the Imperial Hotel, Tokio," *Western Architect*, Vol. 33, February 1924, pp. 17-20.

Crawford, Alan.
"Ten Letters from Frank Lloyd Wright to Charles Robert Ashbee," *Journal of the Society of Architectural Historians of Great Britain* (England), Vol. 13, 1970, pp. 64-76.

Anonymous.
"Preservation: The Met to the Rescue," *Architectural Forum*, Vol. 136, June 1972, p. 22.

Anonymous.
"19th-Century Architecture for the American Wing: Sullivan and Wright," *Metropolitan Museum of Art Bulletin*, Vol. 30, June-July 1972, pp. 300-305.

Martinson, Tom.
"A Loss of Consequence," *Northwest Architect*, Vol. 37, March-April 1973, pp. 32-85.

Anonymous.
"Architect and His Client: Frank Lloyd Wright and Francis W. Little," *Interiors*, Vol. 132, June 1973, p. 10.

Newspapers:

Wright, Frank Lloyd.
"To My Neighbors," *The Weekly Home News* (Spring Green, Wisconsin), August 20, 1914.

Anonymous.
"Wright Divorce Ends 'Love Bungalow' Romance: Architect Silent on Court Act: Frank Lloyd Wright Is Back in Seclusion as Court Here Acts," *The Capital Times* (Madison, Wisconsin), November 14, 1922, p. 1. col. 2.

Seton, Grace Thompson.
"Two Japanese Experiments in Stone and Brains," *The New York Times*, December 31, 1922, section 4, p. 12, col. 1.

Anonymous.
"$500,000 Fire in Bungalow: Wisconsin Architect Loses Home of Valuable Prints," *The New York Times*, April 22, 1925, p. 9, col. 3.

Anonymous.
"Suit Ends Wright Romance: Sculptress Who Fled with Architect to Japan Obtains Alimony," *The New York Times*, November 27, 1925, p. 3, col. 5.

Anonymous.
"F.L. Wright and Wife Drop Divorce Suits: Mutual Charges of Desertion Are Withdrawn by Architect and Sculptress," *The New York Times*, November 28, 1925, p. 3, col. 6.

Anonymous.
"Wright Divorce Trial Set," *The New York Times*, January 17, 1926, p. 6, col. 1.

Anonymous.
"Storms Taliesin in Vain: Mrs. Wright Foiled in Attempt to Take Husband's Estate," *The New York Times*, June 4, 1926, p. 9, col. 5.

Anonymous.
"Issue Warrant for Wright: Architect's Wife Seeks to Re-enter Their
Wisconsin Home," *The New York Times*, June 5, 1926, p. 6, col. 2.

Anonymous.
"Mrs. Wright Ends Siege: Architect's Wife Gets Offer of $125 a
Month to Go Away," *The New York Times*, June 7, 1926, p. 14, col. 4.

Wright, Frank Lloyd.
"To the Countryside," *The Weekly Home News* (Spring Green, Wisconsin),
June 10, 1926.

Anonymous.
"Miriam Noel Wright's Life Has Been Filled with Marital Trouble,"
The Capital Times (Madison, Wisconsin), September 1, 1926, section
2, p. 1, cols. 5, 6.

Anonymous.
"Hinzenberg Seeks Child: Divorced Husband of Frank Lloyd Wright's
Housekeeper Gets Writ," *The New York Times*, September 4, 1926,
p. 13, col. 2.

Anonymous.
"Police Search for Wright: Seek Architect and Companion on Charges
of Her Ex-Husband," *The New York Times*, September 6, 1926, p. 2,
col. 4.

Anonymous.
"Mrs. Wright Seizes Villa: Is Again in Possession of House from
Which Husband Ousted Her," *The New York Times*, September 8, 1926,
p. 4, col. 5.

Anonymous.
"Wright's Wife Joins Suit: Attorney Files Appearance in Madison
Foreclosure Action," *The New York Times*, September 29, 1926, p. 25,
col. 4.

Anonymous.
"Sues Wright for $250,000: Hinzenberg Charges the Architect
Alienated Wife and Daughter," *The New York Times*, October 10,
1926, section 2, p. 6, col. 6.

Anonymous.
"Mann Act Charge Made Against Wright: Architect and Woman in Jail,
Minneapolis Fight Wisconsin Extradition for Adultery," *The New York
Times*, October 22, 1926, p. 18, col. 3.

Anonymous.
"New Wright Case Inquiry: Estranged Wife's Attorney Probes Deaths
on Architect's Estate," *The New York Times*, October 23, 1926, p. 17,
col. 3.

Anonymous.
"Appeal for Wright to Federal Attorney: University of Chicago
Professors and Others Say Architect Is an Object of Revenge," *The
New York Times*, October 29, 1926, p. 17, col. 3.

Anonymous.
"Wright Charges Dropped: Architect and His Companion Still Face
Mann Act Prosecution," *The New York Times*, October 30, 1926, p. 21,
col. 4.

Anonymous.
"Wright in Federal Court: Architect is Held on Mann Act Charge
in Minneapolis," *The New York Times*, October 31, 1926, section 12,
p. 19, col. 3.

Anonymous.
"Frank Lloyd Wright Tells Story of Life: Years of Work, Love, and
Despair," *The Capital Times*, (Madison, Wisconsin), November 1,
1926.

Anonymous.
"Wright Companion Held for Jury," *The New York Times*, November 2,
1926, p. 17, col. 2.

Anonymous.
"Japanese Art on Sale: Prints Collected by F.L. Wright Now on
Exhibition," *The New York Times*, January 2, 1927, section 2, p.
16, col. 1.

Meier, Peg.
"A Gem of a Room Finds a Museum Setting," *The Minneapolis Tribune*,
August 20, 1972.

2-3.1 Aerial view of Taliesin (1925ff), Spring Green, Wisconsin. Photo courtesy of *The Capital Times*, Madison, Wisconsin.

CHAPTER 3

THE END OF TURMOIL/
INNOVATION IN THE CAUSE OF ARCHITECTURE
(1927 TO 1930)

Introduction

This chapter identifies fifteen original manuscripts of Wright's famous "In the Cause of Architecture" series, written for *Architectural Record*, some of which were never published and most of which were published with some modifications to Wright's original draft versions submitted to the magazine's editor. It is the carbon copies of these drafts, with handwritten notes made by Wright, which are catalogued. Eleven other original manuscripts are catalogued for this period, a period which represented a decline of building designs by Wright from previous years. During these four years Wright produced only 23 designs, of which only 6 were built.

Correspondence indexed and catalogued from this period includes letters to Dr. William Norman Guthrie, Justin L. Miner, and Horace Holley, all of whom were clients involved with the design of Wright's St. Mark's-in-the-Bouwerie Towers Project, a cluster of cantilevered skyscrapers to be built in New York in the late 1920s (this project never was executed). The design for the the St. Mark's-in-the-Bouwerie Towers Project foreshadowed Wright's executed design for the Harold Price, Sr., Company Tower at Bartlesville, Oklahoma, of 1952, by about 25 years and served as a theoretical model for Wright's later designs for other cantilevered skyscraper projects. Other correspondence catalogued for this period represent continued contact with William R. Heath, a former client for whom Wright had designed a residence in 1904; son John Lloyd Wright; and Dutch architect H. Th. Wijdeveld.

B88

Date:
May 5, 1927

Type of Manuscript:
Copy of letter

To:
Dr. William Norman Guthrie

From:
Frank Lloyd Wright
Spring Green, Wisconsin

Collection:
The Avery Architectural Library
Columbia University
DR 106.7.4

Medium:
Typed single spaced

Size:
12-3/4 in. x 8 in.; 323.9 mm x 203.2 mm

Number of Pages:
2

Number of Words:
543

Descriptors:
Dr. William Norman Guthrie, St. Mark's-in-the-Bouwerie
Towers Project, National Life Insurance Company Project,
Imperial Hotel

Review:
Wright outlines his services, pay schedule, and projected building
costs for the St. Mark's-in-the-Bouwerie Towers Project to Dr.
Guthrie. Wright points out the many innovative features of the
proposed project and their respective low costs. One of the inno-
vations was the use of cantilevered levels.

B89

Date:
1927 (prior to May 1927)

Type of Manuscript:
Typescript article

Title:
"The Architect and the Machine"

By:
Frank Lloyd Wright

Collection:
The Library of Congress, Manuscript Division
The Frank Lloyd Wright Papers
Speech and Article File, Undated

Medium:
Typed double spaced

Size:
8-1/2 in. x 11 in.; 215.9 mm x 279.4 mm

Number of Pages:
16

Descriptors:
Architectural Record, The Machine, Greece, Rome, Usonian

Review:
Typescript of "In the Cause of Architecture: I. The Architect and
the Machine," *Architectural Record*, pp. 394-396. The text of the
final published version differs slightly from this earlier draft.

2-3.2   Model of the St. Mark's-in-the-Bouwerie Towers Project (1927), New York. Photo courtesy of the State Historical Society of Wisconsin.

2-3.4 Price Company Tower for Harold Price, Sr. (1952), Bartlesville, Oklahoma, was based, in part, on the St. Mark's-in-the-Bouwerie Towers Project of 1927 for New York. Photo by the author.

2-3.3 Model of the Price Company Tower for Harold Price, Sr. (1952), Bartlesville, Oklahoma, which was based, in part, on the St. Mark's-in-the-Bouwerie Towers Project of 1927 for New York. Photo by the author.

B90

Date:
   1927 (prior to May 1927)

Type of Manuscript:
   Typescript article

Title:
   "The Architect and the Machine"

By:
   Frank Lloyd Wright

Collection:
   The Library of Congress, Manuscript Division
   The Frank Lloyd Wright Papers
   Speech and Article File, 1928

Medium:
   Typed double spaced, with handwritten corrections

Size:
   8-1/2 in. x 11 in.; 215.9 mm x 279.4 mm

Number of Pages:
   17

Descriptors:
   The Machine, *Architectural Record*, Greece, Rome, Nature

Review:
   On the use of the machine for the benefit of architecture. The
   final article was published as "In the Cause of Architecture, I:
   The Architect and the Machine," *Architectural Record*, pp. 394-396.

B91

Date:
   November 25, 1927

Type of Manuscript:
   Typescript article

Title:
   "Three Propositions"

By:
   Frank Lloyd Wright
   Taliesin
   Spring Green, Wisconsin

Collection:
   The Library of Congress, Manuscript Division
   The Frank Lloyd Wright Papers
   Speech and Article File, 1927

Medium:
   Typed double spaced

Size:
   8-1/2 in. x 11 in.; 215.9 mm x 279 mm

Number of Pages:
    4

Descriptors:
    Marriage, Democracy

Review:
    The three propositions Wright states are concerned with marriage.
    During this period, 1925 to 1928, Wright faced severe marital
    problems (see "Will Give Wright Divorce: Wife of Architect Will
    Grant Her Husband His Liberty," *The New York Times*, July 3, 1927,
    and "Mrs. Wright Releases Architect by Divorce: Latter Is Now Free
    to Marry Montenegrin Dancer as His Third Wife," *The New York Times*,
    August 27, 1927).

B92

Date:
    1927

Type of Manuscript:
    Typescript article

Title:
    "In Ancient Yedo"

By:
    Frank Lloyd Wright

Collection:
    The Library of Congress, Manuscript Division
    The Frank Lloyd Wright Papers
    Speech and Article File, 1927

Medium:
    Typed double spaced, with handwritten corrections by
    Wright

Size:
    8-1/2 in. x 11-1/8 in.; 215.9 mm x 282.6 mm

Number of Pages:
    17

Descriptors:
    Tokyo, Yedo of Shunsho, Shigemasa, Hiroshige, Hokusai,
    Alexander Woollcott, Heywood Broun

Review:
    Life and art in old Japan is the topic of Wright's article.

B93

Date:
    1927

Type of Manuscript:
    Typescript article

Title:
    "A Plan for the Erection of a Model Building"

By:
   Frank Lloyd Wright, Architect, and
   Charles L. Morgan, Associate

Collection:
   The Library of Congress, Manuscript Division
   The Frank Lloyd Wright Papers
   Speech and Article File, 1927

Medium:
   Typed double spaced

Size:
   8-1/2 in. x 11 in.; 215.9 mm x 279.4 mm

Number of Pages:
   9

Descriptors:
   Charles L. Morgan, Imperial Hotel, National Life Insurance
   Company Project, Starret Lehigh Building (New York),
   St. Mark's-in-the-Bouwerie Towers Project, Avery Brundage

Review:
   A description of the St. Mark's-in-the-Bouwerie Towers Project
   for New York City. This article was probably used as a sales device
   for Wright to sell his architectural services to the client and
   describes such areas of concern as the building project economy
   of materials as well as structure, costs, use and maintenance of
   the project, financing, ownership arrangements, and architect
   fees. Wright stresses the innovative nature of the project and
   uses his Imperial Hotel design as a working example. A few short
   excerpts from this appeared in *Frank Lloyd Wright on Architecture:
   Selected Writings, 1894-1940*.

B94

Date:
   Late 1927

Type of Manuscript:
   Typescript article

Title:
   "In the Cause of Architecture: The Logic of the Plan"

By:
   Frank Lloyd Wright

Collection:
   The Library of Congress, Manuscript Division
   The Frank Lloyd Wright Papers
   Speech and Article File, 1928

Medium:
   Typed double spaced

Size:
   8-1/2 in. x 11 in.; 215.9 mm x 279.4 mm

Number of Pages:
  14

Descriptors:
  Architectural Record, The Plan, Style, Standardization,
  Scale, Articulation, Building Methods, Materials, Avery
  Coonley Residence, Einstein Tower, Eric Mendelsohn,
  Unity Temple, Charles Ennis Residence, Greece, Darwin D.
  Martin Residence.

Review:
  Typescript of "In the Cause of Architecture: I. The Logic of the
  Plan," *Architectural Record*, pp. 49-57. The exact text is somewhat
  different than the final draft which appeared in the periodical.
  An excerpt from this early typescript version appeared in *Frank
  Lloyd Wright on Architecture: Selected Writings*.

B95

Date:
  Undated (early 1927)

Type of Manuscript:
  Letter

To:
  William R. Heath

From:
  Frank Lloyd Wright
  New York, New York

Collection:
  The Library of Congress, Manuscript Division
  The Frank Lloyd Wright Papers
  Letters and Notes to William R. Heath File

Medium:
  Handwritten on Hotel Brevoort, New York, stationery,
  signed "Frank Lloyd Wright" and "FLLW"

Size:
  9-1/2 in. x 6-1/2 in.; 241.3 mm x 165.1 mm

Number of Pages:
  2

Number of Words:
  408

Descriptors:
  William R. Heath, Darwin D. Martin, Wright Incorporated,
  Olgivanna Lloyd Wright, Iovanna Lloyd Wright

Review:
  A very sincere letter asking Heath to buy into Wright
  Incorporated and come to his financial aid.

B96

Date:
Undated (early 1927)

Type of Manuscript:
Letter

To:
William R. Heath

From:
Frank Lloyd Wright
New York, New York

Collection:
The Library of Congress, Manuscript Division
The Frank Lloyd Wright Papers
Letters and Notes to William R. Heath File

Medium:
Handwritten on Hotel Brevoort, New York, stationery,
signed "F.LL.W."

Size:
9-1/2 in. x 6-3/8 in.; 241.3 mm x 161.9 mm

Number of Pages:
1

Number of Words:
247

Descriptors:
William R. Heath, Hamlin Garland, Washington, D.C.,
Anderson Galleries, Darwin D. Martin, Alexander Davidson

Review:
Wright invites Heath to aid him in a legal matter with Hamlin
Garland at Washington, D.C. Also mentioned is a potential resi-
dence design for a Mr. Davidson, probably former client Alexander
Davidson, which probably did not materialize to a project or design.
Wright was in New York for the sale of his Japanese prints collec-
tion at the Anderson Galleries. For details on the sale of Wright's
collection see "Japanese Art on Sale: Prints Collected by F.L.
Wright Now on Exhibition," *The New York Times*, January 2, 1927,
Section 2, Page 16, Column 1; "Wife Fails to Halt Wright Art Sale...,"
The New York Times, January 7, 1927; "Backs Mrs. Wright's Claim,"
The New York Times, February 18, 1927; and "Retain Auction Proceeds,"
The New York Times, February 20, 1927.

B97

Date:
Undated (1927)

Type of Manuscript:
Letter

To:
William R. Heath

From:
  Frank Lloyd Wright

Collection:
  The Library of Congress, Manuscript Division
  The Frank Lloyd Wright Papers
  Letters and Notes to William R. Heath File

Medium:
  Handwritten, signed "Frank"

Size:
  8-1/2 in. x 11 in.; 215.9 mm x 279.4 mm

Number of Pages:
  2

Number of Words:
  392

Descriptors:
  William R. Heath, Olgivanna Lloyd Wright, Darwin D. Martin,
  Philip La Follette

Review:
  Wright expresses his feelings to Heath on a very personal basis
  regarding the various unfortunate happenings in Wright's life at
  this time. He discusses his personal feelings about Philip La
  Follette, the young Madison attorney representing him during his
  time of crisis, although Wright does not mention La Follette by
  name in the letter.

B98

Date:
  Undated (1927?)

Type of Manuscript:
  Letter

To:
  John Lloyd Wright

From:
  Frank Lloyd Wright
  Phoenix, Arizona

Collection:
  The John Lloyd Wright Collection
  The Avery Architectural Library
  Columbia University
  Folder 13

Medium:
  Handwritten, signed "Father"

Size:
  Two pages--5-1/2 in. x 6-3/4 in.; 139.7 mm x 171.5 mm
  One page--8-1/2 in. x 11 in.; 215.9 mm x 279.4 mm

Number of Pages:
  3

Number of Words:
525

Descriptors:
John Lloyd Wright, Albert Chase McArthur, Arizona
Biltmore Hotel, San Marcos-in-the-Desert Project,
Lloyd Wright, Edward H. Doheny, Barry Byrne

Review:
Wright talks of the Arizona Biltmore Hotel in Phoenix which
architect Albert Chase McArthur and he are doing together, with
Wright as a silent partner. F.L. Wright is visiting Phoenix to
start work on the San Marcos-in-the-Desert Project. F.L. Wright
seeks John Lloyd Wright's help on this project. He explains also
that Lloyd Wright is preparing some of the renderings for the
project (see Drexler, Arthur (ed.), *The Drawings of Frank Lloyd
Wright*; plates 66, 67, 68, 69, 70, 82, 87, and 88 were all from
the hand of F.L. Wright's son, Lloyd). F.L. Wright suggests to
John Lloyd that he leave the Indiana practice with Barry Byrne
upon arriving in Arizona.

B99

Date:
1927

Type of Manuscript:
Copy of award

Collection:
The John Lloyd Wright Collection
The Avery Architectural Library
Columbia University
Folder 35

Medium:
Copy of award, with handwritten comments by Wright

Number of Pages:
1

Descriptors:
Academie des Beaux-Arts Award

Review:
Notes by Wright on a copy of the Academie des Beaux-Arts Award.

B100

Date:
Undated (1927)

Type of Manuscript:
Note

To:
William R. Heath

From:
Frank Lloyd Wright

2-3.5 Warren McArthur's Arizona Biltmore Hotel and Cottages (1927), Phoenix, Arizona. Wright worked with McArthur on this building as an advisor. Photo by the author.

Collection:
   The Library of Congress, Manuscript Division
   The Frank Lloyd Wright Papers
   Letters and Notes to William R. Heath File

Medium:
   Handwritten in pencil, signed "F"

Size:
   9-1/2 in. x 5 in.; 241.3 mm x 127.0 mm

Number of Pages:
   1

Number of Words:
   66

Descriptors:
   William R. Heath, Olgivanna Lloyd Wright, Iovanna
   Lloyd Wright

Review:
   Wright allows the Heaths to take care of Iovanna Wright, then
   a baby, until he returns from a trip.

B101

Date:
   Undated (1927)

Type of Manuscript:
   Note

To:
   William R. Heath

From:
   Frank Lloyd Wright

Collection:
   The Library of Congress, Manuscript Division
   The Frank Lloyd Wright Papers
   Letters and Notes to William R. Heath File

Medium:
   Handwritten, signed "Frank"

Size:
   3-1/2 in. x 2 in.; 88.9 mm x 50.8 mm

Number of Pages:
   1

Number of Words:
   61

Descriptors:
   William R. Heath

Review:
   This note was found by the Heaths pinned on the door of their
   new residence at East Aurora, built in 1925. It was not designed
   by Wright and he is critical of it in this note. Wright had

apparently attempted to visit the Heaths while they were out. His
keen wit is displayed in this note.

B102

Date:
 1928? (prior to February 1928)

Type of Manuscript:
 Typescript article

Title:
 "In the Cause of Architecture: What 'Styles' Mean
 to the Architect"

By:
 Frank Lloyd Wright

Collection:
 The Library of Congress, Manuscript Division
 The Frank Lloyd Wright Papers
 Speech and Article File, 1928

Medium:
 Typed double spaced

Size:
 8-1/2 in. x 11 in.; 215.9 mm x 279.4 mm

Number of Pages:
 16

Descriptors:
 Architectural Record, Usonian, John Bright, Style,
 America, Greece, Unity Temple, Democracy, Character,
 Dr. Arthur Johonnot.

Review:
 Typescript of "In the Cause of Architecture: II. What 'Styles'
 Mean to the Architect," *Architectural Record*, pp. 145-151. The
 text of the final published version differs slightly from this
 early draft. A portion of this draft was printed in *Frank Lloyd
 Wright on Architecture*.

B103

Date:
 April 30, 1928

Type of Manuscript:
 Letter

To:
 John Lloyd Wright
 Michigan City, Indiana

From:
 Frank Lloyd Wright
 Phoenix, Arizona

Collection:
    The John Lloyd Wright Collection
    The Avery Architectural Library
    Columbia University
    Folder 9

Medium:
    Typed on Albert Chase McArthur, Architect,
    stationery, signed "Dad"

Size:
    8-1/2 in. x 11 in.; 215.9 mm x 279.4 mm

Number of Pages:
    1

Number of Words:
    264

Descriptors:
    John Lloyd Wright, Albert Chase McArthur, W.A. Zumphe
    Residence (John Lloyd Wright), Duke Residence (John Lloyd
    Wright), David Wright

Review:
    Discussion of John Lloyd Wright's Zumphe Residence (see "Summer
    Residence of Mr. and Mrs. W.A. Zumphe, Long Beach, Indiana," *The
    Western Architect*, plates 181-186, for a full presentation of the
    design) and his newly established practice in Indiana. Also, on
    the possibilities of John Lloyd's joining Frank Lloyd Wright in
    his practice of architecture.

B104

Date:
    1928 (prior to April 1928)

Type of Manuscript:
    Typescript article

Title:
    "In the Cause of Architecture: The Meaning of Materials"

By:
    Frank Lloyd Wright

Collection:
    The Library of Congress, Manuscript Division
    The Frank Lloyd Wright Papers
    Speech and Article File, 1928

Medium:
    Typed double spaced

Size:
    8-1/2 in. x 11 in.; 215.9 mm x 279.4 mm

Number of Pages:
    5

Descriptors:
    Architectural Record, Stone

Review:
   Introductory paragraphs for "In the Cause of Architecture: III.
   The Meaning of Materials--Stone," *Architectural Record*, pp. 350-
   356. The text is somewhat differently phrased than in the final
   version.

B105

Date:
   1928 (prior to April 1928)

Type of Manuscript:
   Typescript article

Title:
   "In the Cause of Architecture: The Meaning of Materials--
   Stone"

By:
   Frank Lloyd Wright

Collection:
   The Library of Congress, Manuscript Division
   The Frank Lloyd Wright Papers
   Speech and Article File, 1928

Medium:
   Typed double spaced

Size:
   8-1/2 in. x 11 in.; 215.9 mm x 279.4 mm

Number of Pages:
   8

Descriptors:
   Architectural Record, Madison (Wisconsin), Stone,
   Janesville (Wisconsin), Grand Canyon, Auditorium Building
   (Chicago), Bessemer Steel, Stonehenge, Druids, Byzantine,
   Maya, Egypt, China, Roman, Gothic, The Machine

Review:
   Typescript of "In the Cause of Architecture: III. The Meaning
   of Materials--Stone," *Architectural Record*, pp. 350-356. The
   text is somewhat different in this early version than that which
   finally appeared in the periodical. An excerpt from this version
   appeared in *Frank Lloyd Wright on Architecture*.

B106

Date:
   June 1, 1928

Type of Manuscript:
   Typescript of book review

Title:
   "*Towards a New Architecture*--Le Corbusier: Translated
   by Frederick W. Etchells"

By:
    Frank Lloyd Wright
    Phoenix, Arizona

Collection:
    The Library of Congress, Manuscript Division
    The Frank Lloyd Wright Papers
    Speech and Article File, 1928

Medium:
    Typed double spaced, with handwritten notes by Wright

Size:
    8-1/2 in. x 13 in.; 215.9 mm x 330.2 mm

Number of Pages:
    3

Descriptors:
    Le Corbusier, *Towards a New Architecture*, L'Art Nouveau,
    John Bright, Louis H. Sullivan, France, Germany, Austria,
    Holland, Sweden, Manhattan, Ralph Waldo Emerson, *World Unity*

Review:
    This is a book review of Le Corbusier's *Toward a New Architecture*.
    It is also an attack on Le Corbusier's architecture. There is
    a handwritten quotation from Ralph Waldo Emerson on the last page
    in Wright's hand. An excerpt from this review appeared in *Frank
    Lloyd Wright on Architecture*.

B107

Date:
    1928 (prior to June 1928)

Type of Manuscript:
    Typescript article

Title:
    "In the Cause of Architecture: The Meaning of Materials--
    The Kiln"

By:
    Frank Lloyd Wright

Collection:
    The Library of Congress, Manuscript Division
    The Frank Lloyd Wright Papers
    Speech and Article File, 1928

Medium:
    Typed double spaced

Size:
    8-1/2 in. x 11 in.; 215.9 mm x 279.4 mm

Number of Pages:
    14

Descriptors:
    Architectural Record, China, Greek, Kiln, Persia, Japan,
    Ceramics, Terracotta, Louis Sullivan, Organic, Palermo,
    Usonian

Review:
Typescript of "In the Cause of Architecture: V. The Meaning of
Materials--The Kiln." The text is somewhat differently phrased
in this early version than that which finally appeared in *Archi-
tectural Record*. An excerpt from this version was published in
Frank Lloyd Wright on Architecture.

B108

Date:
1928 (prior to July 1928)

Type of Manuscript:
Typescript article

Title:
"In the Cause of Architecture--The Meaning of Materials--
Glass"

By:
Frank Lloyd Wright

Collection:
The Library of Congress, Manuscript Division
The Frank Lloyd Wright Papers
Speech and Article File, 1928

Medium:
Typed double spaced

Size:
8-1/2 in. x 11-1/8 in.; 215.9 mm x 282.6 mm

Number of Pages:
10

Descriptors:
Architectural Record, Persia, Egypt, Glass, France, Nature,
Avery Coonley Playhouse, Susan Lawrence Dana Residence,
Frank Lloyd Wright Home and Studio.

Review:
Typescript of "In the Cause of Architecture: VI. The Meaning of
Materials--Glass," pp. 10-16. The text of the final published
version differs slightly from this earlier draft. A somewhat
lengthy excerpt from the early draft was printed in *Frank Lloyd
Wright on Architecture*.

B109

Date:
August 25, 1928

Type of Manuscript:
Wedding announcement

To:
William R. Heath

From:
  Mr. and Mrs. Frank Lloyd Wright
  Taliesin
  Wisconsin

Collection:
  The Library of Congress, Manuscript Division
  The Frank Lloyd Wright Papers
  Letters and Notes to William R. Heath File

Medium:
  Hand lettered

Size:
  5-1/2 in. x 4-1/2 in.; 139.7 mm x 114.3 mm

Number of Pages:
  1

Number of Words:
  35

Descriptors:
  Olgivanna Lloyd Wright, Iovanna Lloyd Wright, William R.
  Heath

Review:
  The wedding announcement also shows a photograph of daughter
  Iovanna Lloyd Wright.

B110

Date:
  1928 (prior to August 1928)

Type of Manuscript:
  Typescript article

Title:
  "In the Nature of Materials--Concrete"

By:
  Frank Lloyd Wright

Collection:
  The Library of Congress, Manuscript Division
  The Frank Lloyd Wright Papers
  Speech and Article File, 1928

Medium:
  Typed double spaced

Size:
  8-1/2 in. x 11-1/8 in.; 215.9 mm x 282.6 mm

Number of Pages:
  16

Descriptors:
  Architectural Record, Phoenix, Mexico, Concrete, Persia

Review:
    Typescript for "In the Cause of Architecture: VII. The Meaning
    of Materials--Concrete," *Architectural Record*, pp. 98-104. The
    text which finally appeared in *Architectural Record* was retitled
    and some of the phrasing is different in the final version. Ex-
    cerpts from this early draft were printed in *Frank Lloyd Wright
    on Architecture*.

B111

Date:
    1928 (prior to October 1928)

Type of Manuscript:
    Typescript article

Title:
    "The Use of Metalplates in the Art of Building"

By:
    Frank Lloyd Wright

Collection:
    The Library of Congress, Manuscript Division
    The Frank Lloyd Wright Papers
    Speech and Article File, 1928

Medium:
    Typed single spaced

Size:
    8-1/2 in. x 11 in.; 215.9 mm x 279.4 mm

Number of Pages:
    3

Descriptors:
    Metalplates, James A. Miller, *Architectural Record*,
    The Machine, China, Japan, "The Art and Craft of the
    Machine," Jane Addams, Louis Sullivan, Los Angeles

Review:
    An early version of "In the Cause of Architecture VIII:
    Sheet Metal and a Modern Instance," *Architectural Record*,
    pp. 334-342.

B112

Date:
    1928 (prior to October 1928)

Type of Manuscript:
    Typescript article

Title:
    "In the Cause of Architecture--Sheet Metal and the
    Modern Instance"

By:
    Frank Lloyd Wright

Collection:
The Library of Congress, Manuscript Division
The Frank Lloyd Wright Papers
Speech and Article File, 1928

Medium:
Typed double spaced

Size:
8-1/2 in. x 11 in.; 215.9 mm x 279.4 mm

Number of Pages:
1

Descriptors:
Architectural Record, The Machine, Sheet Metal, Copper,
Japan, China, James A. Miller, Miller Brothers (Chicago),
Jane Addams, Hull House, Imperial Hotel

Review:
Typescript of "In the Cause of Architecture: VIII. Sheet Metal
and a Modern Instance," *Architectural Record*, pp. 334-342. The
text of the final published version of this article differs
slightly from this early draft. A short excerpt from this early
draft was printed in *Frank Lloyd Wright on Architecture.*

B113

Date:
November 8, 1928

Type of Manuscript:
Letter

To:
John Lloyd Wright
Michigan City, Indiana

From:
Frank Lloyd Wright
Taliesin, Wisconsin

Collection:
The John Lloyd Wright Collection
The Avery Architectural Library
Columbia University
Folder 9

Medium:
Typed, with handwritten corrections and added notes
and signed "Father"

Size:
8-1/2 in. x 11 in.; 215.9 mm x 279.4 mm

Number of Pages:
1

Number of Words:
110 Typed; 21 Handwritten

Descriptors:
John Lloyd Wright, Sears and Roebucks (sic)

Review:
F.L. Wright invites John Lloyd to Taliesin for a visit. Also, a brief reply by John Lloyd dated November 13, 1928, is noted on the letter. It was possibly a carbon copy of the reply.

B114

Date:
1928 (prior to December 1928)

Type of Manuscript:
Typescript article

Title:
"In the Cause of Architecture: The Terms"

By:
Frank Lloyd Wright

Collection:
The Library of Congress, Manuscript Division
The Frank Lloyd Wright Papers
Speech and Article File, 1928

Medium:
Typed double spaced

Size:
8-1/2 in. x 11-1/8 in.; 215.9 mm x 282.6 mm

Number of Pages:
16

Descriptors:
Architectural Record, Usonian, The Machine, Carl Sandburg, Poetry of Form, Neo-Spanish, Neo-Italian, Renaissance, Tudor, Colonial, Romance, Principle

Review:
Typescript of "In the Cause of Architecture: IX. The Terms," *Architectural Record*, pp. 507-514. The text of the final published version differs slightly from this early draft. A short excerpt from this draft was printed in *Frank Lloyd Wright on Architecture*.

B115

Date:
1928

Type of Manuscript:
Typescript article

Title:
"In the Cause of Architecture XII--Composition"

By:
Frank Lloyd Wright

Collection:
    The Library of Congress, Manuscript Division
    The Frank Lloyd Wright Papers
    Speech and Article File, 1928

Medium:
    Typed double spaced

Size:
    8-1/2 in. x 11-1/8 in.; 215.9 mm x 282.6 mm

Number of Pages:
    7

Descriptors:
    Composition, *Architectural Record*

Review:
    This article was probably prepared as part of Wright's "In the
    Cause of Architecture" series for *Architectural Record* magazine
    although it never appeared in the series. However, the article
    was printed in *Frank Lloyd Wright on Architecture*.

B116

Date:
    1928

Type of Manuscript:
    Typescript article

Title:
    "Wood"

By:
    Frank Lloyd Wright

Collection:
    The Library of Congress, Manuscript Division
    The Frank Lloyd Wright Papers
    Speech and Article File, 1928

Medium:
    Typed double spaced

Size:
    8-1/2 in. x 11-1/8 in.; 215.9 mm x 282.6 mm

Number of Pages:
    18

Descriptors:
    Wood, *Architectural Record*, Japan, England, Norsemen,
    South Sea Islanders, Queen Anne, Usonian, The Machine,
    Art

Review:
    Only small portions of this article appeared in *Frank Lloyd
    Wright on Architecture*. A final version of the article appeared
    as "In the Cause of Architecture IV: The Meaning of Materials--
    Wood," *Architectural Record*, pp. 481-488.

B117

Date:
   April 5, 1929

Type of Manuscript:
   Typescript article

Title:
   "Surface and Mass,--Again"

By:
   Frank Lloyd Wright
   Chandler, Arizona

Collection:
   The Library of Congress, Manuscript Division
   The Frank Lloyd Wright Papers
   Speech and Article File, 1929

Medium:
   Typed double spaced with handwritten corrections by
   Wright

Size:
   8-1/2 in. x 12 in.; 215.9 mm x 304.8 mm

Number of Pages:
   7

Descriptors:
   Art, Douglas Haskell, Henry-Russell Hitchcock, Democracy,
   Organic Architecture, Oak Park (Illinois), New York,
   Paris, *Architectural Record*

Review:
   Criticisms of Wright's use of weight and ornament in his designs
   are answered by him in this article. It was published in *Architectural Record* in July 1929, and reprinted in *Frank Lloyd Wright
   on Architecture.*

B118

Date:
   October 5, 1929

Type of Manuscript:
   Letter

To:
   John Lloyd Wright
   Michigan City, Indiana

From:
   Frank Lloyd Wright
   Taliesin
   Spring Green, Wisconsin

Collection:
   The John Lloyd Wright Collection
   The Avery Architectural Library
   Columbia University
   Folder 9

Medium:
Typed, with handwritten corrections, signed "Father"

Size:
8-1/2 in. x 11 in.; 215.9 mm x 279.4 mm

Number of Pages:
1

Number of Words:
318 Typed; 6 Handwritten

Descriptors:
John Lloyd Wright, Europe

Review:
Talk of a recent trip to Europe by John Lloyd Wright. F.L. Wright
is a bit upset with John Lloyd concerning this trip.

B119

Date:
October 24, 1929

Type of Manuscript:
Letter

To:
John Lloyd Wright
Michigan City, Indiana

From:
Frank Lloyd Wright
Taliesin
Spring Green, Wisconsin

Collection:
The John Lloyd Wright Collection
The Avery Architectural Library
Columbia University
Folder 9

Medium:
Typed, signed "Dad"

Size:
8-1/2 in. x 11 in.; 215.9 mm x 279.4 mm

Number of Pages:
1

Number of Words:
109

Descriptors:
John Lloyd Wright, New York, Michigan City

Review:
Concerning a trip to Taliesin, Spring Green, Wisconsin, by John
Lloyd Wright.

B120

Date:
   November 9, 1929

Type of Manuscript:
   Letter

To:
   Justin L. Miner
   New York, New York

From:
   Frank Lloyd Wright
   Taliesin
   Spring Green, Wisconsin

Collection:
   The Avery Architectural Library
   Columbia University
   DR 106.6.1-2

Medium:
   Typed, signed "Frank Lloyd Wright"

Size:
   8-1/4 in. x 11 in.; 209.6 mm x 279.4 mm

Number of Pages:
   3

Number of Words:
   806 Typed; 2 Handwritten

Descriptors:
   Justin L. Miner, St. Mark's-in-the-Bouwerie Towers
   Project, Horace Holley, Warren Matthews

Review:
   Wright responds to a request by Miner and others to secure a
   patent on the construction technique Wright intends to use on
   the St. Mark's-in-the-Bouwerie Towers Project, using cantilevers
   for the first time in a skyscraper design. Wright presents the
   case against obtaining a patent on the construction technique.

B121

Date:
   March 31, 1930 (6:01 p.m.)

Type of Manuscript:
   Telegram

To:
   Justin L. Miner
   New York, New York

From:
   Frank Lloyd Wright
   Spring Green, Wisconsin

Collection:
    The Avery Architectural Library
    Columbia University
    DR 106.7.3

Medium:
    Western Union Telegram, signed "Frank Lloyd Wright"

Size:
    6-1/2 in. x 8 in.; 165.1 mm x 203.2 mm

Number of Pages:
    1

Number of Words:
    28

Descriptors:
    Justin L. Miner, St. Mark's-in-the-Bouwerie Towers Project

Review:
    Wright asks Miner for the name of a New York architect to work
    with him on the St. Mark's-in-the-Bouwerie Towers Project.

B122

Date:
    March 31, 1930 (6:18 p.m.)

Type of Manuscript:
    Telegram

To:
    Horace Holley
    New York, New York

From:
    Frank Lloyd Wright
    Spring Green, Wisconsin

Collection:
    The Avery Architectural Library
    Columbia University
    DR 106.7.1-2

Medium:
    Western Union Telegram, signed "Frank"

Size:
    8 in. x 10-1/2 in.; 203.2 mm x 266.7 mm

Number of Pages:
    1

Number of Words:
    71

Descriptors:
    Horace Holley, St. Mark's-in-the-Bouwerie Towers Project,
    National Life Insurance Company Project, Imperial Hotel,
    Justin L. Miner

Review:
    Brief discussion of Wright's innovative use of the cantilever for
    the St. Mark's-in-the-Bouwerie Towers Project and his earlier uses
    of the cantilever.

B123

Date:
    March 31, 1930 (6:25 p.m.)

Type of Manuscript:
    Telegram

To:
    Horace Holley
    New York, New York

From:
    Frank Lloyd Wright
    Spring Green, Wisconsin

Collection:
    The Avery Architectural Library.
    Columbia University
    DR 106.7.1-2

Medium:
    Western Union Telegram, signed "Frank"

Size:
    8 in. x 10-1/2 in.; 203.2 mm x 266.7 mm

Number of Pages:
    1

Number of Words:
    84

Descriptors:
    Horace Holley, St. Mark's-in-the-Bouwerie Towers Project

Review:
    Wright suggests very strongly that a Chicago builder handle the
    construction of the St. Mark's-in-the-Bouwerie Towers Project.

B124

Date:
    April 22, 1930

Type of Manuscript:
    Letter

To:
    Justin L. Miner
    New York, New York

From:
    Frank Lloyd Wright
    Taliesin
    Spring Green, Wisconsin

Collection:
   The Avery Architectural Library
   Columbia University
   DR 106.6.1-2

Medium:
   Typed on Taliesin stationery, with handwritten
   corrections, signed "Frank Lloyd Wright"

Number of Pages:
   2

Number of Words:
   374 Typed; 8 Handwritten

Descriptors:
   Justin L. Miner, St. Mark's-in-the-Bouwerie Towers
   Project, Horace Holley, Mr. Hoffmann (architect, New York),
   Princeton Lectures of 1930

Review:
   A response to Miner's selection of Mr. Hoffmann, a New York City
   architect, to be Wright's architectural contact in New York for
   the St. Mark's-in-the-Bouwerie Towers Project.

B125

Date:
   June 2, 1930

Type of Manuscript:
   Letter

To:
   John Lloyd Wright

From:
   Frank Lloyd Wright
   Taliesin

Collection:
   The John Lloyd Wright Collection
   The Avery Architectural Library
   Columbia University
   Folder 10

Medium:
   Typed, signed "Father"

Size:
   8-1/2 in. x 11 in.; 215.9 mm x 279.4 mm

Number of Pages:
   1

Number of Words:
   53

Descriptors:
   John Lloyd Wright, Architectural League Exhibition
   (New York)

Review:
   Discussion of F.L. Wright's exhibition at the Architectural League
   in New York. Also, an invitation to J.L. Wright to visit Taliesin.
   A review of the exhibition appeared as "Wright's Time," *Time*, p. 30.

B126

Date:
   July 1, 1930

Type of Manuscript:
   Typescript article

Title:
   "The Profession"

By:
   Frank Lloyd Wright
   Taliesin

Collection:
   The Library of Congress, Manuscript Division
   The Frank Lloyd Wright Papers
   Speech and Article File, 1930

Medium:
   Typed double spaced

Size:
   8-1/2 in. x 11-1/4 in.; 215.9 mm x 285.8 mm

Number of Pages:
   10

Descriptors:
   American Institute of Architects, Horace Greeley, Charles
   A. Dana, James Gordon Bennett, Marion Reedy, Henry Wattersen,
   H.H. Richardson, Louis Sullivan, John Root, Dankmar
   Adler, Graham, Anderson, Probst and White, Princeton,
   American Architect

Review:
   Wright attacks the architectural profession and the American
   Institute of Architects. This article was published in *Frank
   Lloyd Wright on Architecture*. The typescript appears to be
   an early draft of Wright's "Architecture as a Profession Is
   All Wrong," which was published in *American Architect*.

B127

Date:
   1929 or prior to July 1930

Type of Manuscript:
   Typescript article

Title:
   "Modern Concepts Concerning an Organic Architecture
   from the Work Of"

By:
Frank Lloyd Wright

Collection:
The Library of Congress, Manuscript Division
The Frank Lloyd Wright Papers
Speech and Article File, 1929

Medium:
Typed double spaced

Size:
8-1/2 in. x 13± in.; 215.9 mm x 330± mm

Number of Pages:
3

Descriptors:
Organic Architecture, *Die Form, Modern Architecture, Being the Kahn Lectures of 1930*

Review:
Principle, simplicity, growth, form, intellect, and other qualities are related to the organic architecture of Wright. Published versions of this typescript article appeared as "Modern Concepts Concerning an Organic Architecture from the Work of Frank Lloyd Wright," in *Die Form*, and as the front and back end papers of Wright's *Modern Architecture, Being the Kahn Lectures for 1930* published by Princeton University Press.

B128

Date:
August 6, 1930

Type of Manuscript:
Letter

To:
H. Th. Wijdeveld

From:
Frank Lloyd Wright
Taliesin
Spring Green, Wisconsin

Collection:
H. Th. Wijdeveld Papers
Rijksdienst voor de Monumentenzorg
Nederlands, Documentatiecentrum voor de Bouwkunst

Medium:
Typed, signed "Frank Lloyd Wright"

Size:
8-1/2 in. x 11 in.; 215.9 mm x 279.4 mm

Number of Pages:
1

Number of Words:
95

Descriptors:
H. Th. Wijdeveld, Okami San, Herr Laubi, John Lloyd
Wright

Review:
Wright is sending two students to Wijdeveld in Holland to examine
Dutch architecture.

B129

Date:
August 14, 1930

Type of Manuscript:
Letter

To:
Don Anderson
Madison, Wisconsin

From:
Frank Lloyd Wright
Taliesin
Spring Green, Wisconsin

Collection:
The Don Anderson Papers, 1890-1972
The State Historical Society of Wisconsin
U.S. MSS, 123 AF, Box 14, Folder 7

Medium:
Typed on stationery with the Taliesin square and signed

Number of Pages:
1

Number of Words:
73

Descriptors:
The Wisconsin State Journal, Stafford, Taliesin, Don
Anderson

Review:
Wright invites Anderson to Taliesin, and offers to discuss an
article by Anderson on Taliesin.

B130

Date:
October 1, 1930

Type of Manuscript:
Typescript of Lecture

Title:
"To the Young Man in Architecture--Chicago Art
Institute Lecture Afternoon October 1, 1930 at
Fullerton Hall, Chicago"

By:
Frank Lloyd Wright

Collection:
The Library of Congress, Manuscript Division
The Frank Lloyd Wright Papers
Speech and Article File, 1930

Medium:
Typed double spaced, with handwritten corrections by
Wright

Size:
8-1/2 in. x 11 in.; 215.9 mm x 279.4 mm

Number of Pages:
22

Descriptors:
Chicago Art Institute, America, Organic Architecture,
Beaux Arts, Louis Sullivan, Tudor, Colonial, American
Architecture, *Two Lectures on Architecture*

Review:
The typescript of one of Wright's most famous speeches, the
lecture was one of two presented by him at the Art Institute
of Chicago on October 1 and 2, 1930, the other lecture being
"In the Realm of Ideas." This lecture was published in Wright's
Two Lectures on Architecture and later reprinted in his *The Future
of Architecture.*

B131

Date:
October 1, 1930?

Type of Manuscript:
Typescript of Lecture

Title:
"In the Realm of Ideas--Lecture I"

By:
Frank Lloyd Wright

Collection:
The Library of Congress, Manuscript Division
The Frank Lloyd Wright Papers
Speech and Article File, 1930

Medium:
Typed double spaced

Size:
8-1/2 in. x 11 in.; 215.9 mm x 279.4 mm

Number of Pages:
15

Descriptors:
Idealism, History, America, Russia, Louis Sullivan,
skyscrapers, Pei-Woh, Chicago, Oak Park, Organic,

Plasticity, Standardization, Unity Temple, Modern
Architecture, Chicago Art Institute, *Two Lectures on
Architecture*

Review:
Typescript of one of two lectures which Wright gave at the Art
Institute of Chicago on October 1 and 2 of 1930. This lecture
was published in Wright's *Two Lectures on Architecture* and later
reprinted in *The Future of Architecture*.

B132

Date:
1930 (prior to October 1930)

Type of Manuscript:
Typescript of Lecture at Music Hall, Madison, Wisconsin

Title:
"The New Architecture"

By:
Frank Lloyd Wright

Collection:
The Library of Congress, Manuscript Division
The Frank Lloyd Wright Papers
Speech and Article File, 1930

Medium:
Typed double spaced--an incomplete draft

Size:
8-1/2 in. x 11-1/8 in.; 215.9 mm x 282.6 mm

Number of Pages:
19

Descriptors:
Modern Architecture, *Two Lectures on Architecture*

Review:
An early draft of "To the Young Man in Architecture," this was
the text of Wright's lecture at the Music Hall in Madison, Wisconsin. He gave his final version of this speech at the Chicago
Art Institute in October of 1930 and published the lecture in
Two Lectures on Architecture; it was reprinted in his *The Future
of Architecture*.

B133

Date:
1930

Type of Manuscript:
Typescript of Lecture at Madison, Wisconsin

Title:
"Salvation by Imagination"

By:
Frank Lloyd Wright

Collection:
The Library of Congress, Manuscript Division
The Frank Lloyd Wright Papers
Speech and Article File, 1930

Medium:
Typed double spaced--an incomplete draft

Size:
8-1/2 in. x 11 in.; 215.9 mm x 279.4 mm

Number of Pages:
19

Descriptors:
Organic Architecture

Review:
An incomplete draft of a lecture delivered at Madison, Wisconsin, in 1930.

B134

Date:
1930

Type of Manuscript:
Typescript lecture

Title:
"The Card-Board House"

By:
Frank Lloyd Wright

Collection:
The Library of Congress, Manuscript Division
The Frank Lloyd Wright Papers
Speech and Article File, 1930

Medium:
Typed double spaced, with handwritten notes and revisions
by Wright

Size:
8-1/2 in. x 11 in.; 215.9 mm x 279.4 mm

Number of Pages:
17

Descriptors:
William Blake, Organic, *Modern Architecture, Being the Kahn Lectures of 1930*, Simplicity, Gothic, Roycroft-Stickley-Mission Style, Jesus, Solomon, Usonian

Review:
One of six lectures Wright delivered at Princeton University in 1930. This lecture was published as *Modern Architecture, Being the Kahn Lectures for 1930* by Princeton University Press in 1931 and later reprinted in Wright's *The Future of Architecture*.

REFERENCES

Books:

Cowles, Linn Ann.
    *An Index and Guide to "An Autobiography," the 1943 Edition by
    Frank Lloyd Wright.* Hopkins, Minnesota: Greenwich Design, 1976.

Drexler, Arthur (ed.).
    The Drawings of Frank Lloyd Wright. New York: Horizon Press for
    the Museum of Modern Art, 1962.

The Frank Lloyd Wright Foundation.
    The Arizona Biltmore Hotel: History and Guide. Taliesin: The Frank
    Lloyd Wright Foundation, 1974.

Gutheim, Frederick (ed.).
    Frank Lloyd Wright on Architecture: Selected Writings, 1894-1940.
    New York: Duell, Sloan and Pearce, 1941.

Hitchcock, Henry-Russell.
    *In the Nature of Materials: 1887-1941, the Buildings of Frank Lloyd
    Wright.* New York: Duell, Sloan and Pearce, 1942.

Izzo, Alberto, and Camillo Gubitos (eds.).
    Frank Lloyd Wright, Dessins 1887-1959. Paris: C.E.R.A. Ecole
    Nationale Supérieure des Beaux-Arts, 1977.

Le Corbusier.
    Towards a New Architecture. New York: Praeger Publishers, 1960.

Storrer, William Allin.
    The Architecture of Frank Lloyd Wright, a Complete Catalog, Second
    Edition. Cambridge, Massachusetts: The M.I.T. Press, 1978.

Twombly, Robert C.
    Frank Lloyd Wright: An Interpretive Biography. New York: Harper
    and Row, 1973.

Twombly, Robert C.
    Frank Lloyd Wright: His Life and His Architecture. New York: John
    Wiley and Sons, Inc., 1979.

Wright, Frank Lloyd.
    Modern Architecture, Being the Kahn Lectures for 1930. Princeton,
    New Jersey: Princeton University Press, 1931.

Wright, Frank Lloyd.
    Two Lectures on Architecture. Chicago: The Art Institute, 1931.

Wright, Frank Lloyd.
    The Future of Architecture. New York: Horizon Press, 1953.

Wright, Frank Lloyd.
    The Story of the Tower: The Tree that Escaped the Crowded Forest.
    New York: Horizon Press, 1956.

Wright, Frank Lloyd.
Drawings for a Living Architecture. New York: Horizon Press for the
Bear Run Foundation, Inc., and the Edgar J. Kaufmann Charitable
Foundation, 1959.

Wright, Frank Lloyd.
An Autobiography. New York: Horizon Press, 1977.

Wright, Frank Lloyd.
Frank Lloyd Wright: Selected Drawings Portfolio. New York: Horizon
Press, 1977.

Periodicals:

Wright, Frank Lloyd.
"In the Cause of Architecture: I. The Architect and the Machine,"
Architectural Record, Vol. 61, May 1927, pp. 394-396.

Anonymous.
"Summer Residence of Mr. and Mrs. W.A. Zumphe, Long Beach, Indiana,"
The Western Architect, Vol. 36, No. 11, November 1927, plates 181-
186.

Wright, Frank Lloyd.
"In the Cause of Architecture: I. The Logic of the Plan," *Architectural Record,* Vol. 63, January 1928, pp. 49-57.

Wright, Frank Lloyd.
"In the Cause of Architecture: II. What 'Styles' Mean to the   ·
Architect," *Architectural Record,* Vol. 63, February 1928, pp. 145-
151.

Wright, Frank Lloyd.
"In the Cause of Architecture: III. The Meaning of Materials--
Stone," *Architectural Record,* Vol. 63, April 1928, pp. 350-356.

Wright, Frank Lloyd.
"In the Cause of Architecture IV: The Meaning of Materials--Wood,"
Architectural Record, Vol. 63, May 1928, pp. 481-488.

Wright, Frank Lloyd.
"In the Cause of Architecture: V. The Meaning of Materials--The
Kiln," *Architectural Record,* Vol. 63, June 1928, pp. 555-561.

Wright, Frank Lloyd.
"In the Cause of Architecture: VI. The Meaning of Materials--Glass,"
Architectural Record, Vol. 64, July 1928, pp. 10-16.

Wright, Frank Lloyd.
"In the Cause of Architecture: VII. The Meaning of Materials--Con-
crete," *Architectural Record,* Vol. 64, August 1928, pp. 98-104.

Wright, Frank Lloyd.
"Book Review--Towards a New Architecture," *World Unity,* Vol. 2,
September 1928, pp. 393-395.

Wright, Frank Lloyd.
"In the Cause of Architecture: VIII. Sheet Metal and a Modern Instance," *Architectural Record*, Vol. 64, October 1928, pp. 334-342.

Wright, Frank Lloyd.
"In the Cause of Architecture: IX. The Terms," *Architectural Record*, Vol. 64, December 1928, pp. 507-514.

Anonymous.
"The Arizona-Biltmore Hotel, Phoenix, Arizona. Albert Chase McArthur, Architect," *Architectural Record*, Vol. 66, July 1929, pp. 19-55.

Wright, Frank Lloyd.
"Surface and Mass--Again!" *Architectural Record*, Vol. 66, July 1929, pp. 92-94.

Anonymous.
"Wright's Pyramids," *Time*, Vol. 14, October 28, 1929, p. 62.

Anonymous.
"Modern Pyramids," *Outlook and Independent*, Vol. 153, October 30, 1929, p. 336.

Anonymous.
"What Architects Are Talking About," *American Architect*, Vol. 86, December 1929, pp. 53-54.

Anonymous.
"St. Mark's Tower--St. Mark's in the Bouwerie, New York City," *Architectural Record*, Vol. 67, January 1930, pp. 1-4.

Anonymous.
"Wright's Time," *Time*, Vol. 15, June 9, 1930, p. 30.

Wright, Frank Lloyd.
"Modern Concepts Concerning an Organic Architecture from the Work of Frank Lloyd Wright," *Die Form*, Vol. 5, July 1930, pp. 343-349.

Anonymous.
"Frank Lloyd Wright to the Fore!" *Western Architect*, Vol. 39, September 1930, p. 152.

Anonymous.
"Two Lectures," *Bulletin of the Art Institute of Chicago*, Vol. 24, October 1930, p. 91.

Wright, Frank Lloyd.
"Architecture as a Profession Is All Wrong," *American Architect*, Vol. 88, December 1930, pp. 22, 23, 84, 86, and 88.

Robertson, Howard.
"Frank Lloyd Wright: Lectures at the Art Institute of Chicago," *Architect and Building News*, Vol. 128, October 16, 1931, pp. 62-63.

McArthur, Albert Chase.
"To the Editor," *Architectural Record*, Vol. 89, June 1941, p. 7.

Anonymous.
"Frank Lloyd Wright: After 36 Years His Tower Is Completed,"
Architectural Forum, Vol. 104, February 1956, pp. 106-113.

Newspapers:

Anonymous.
"Wife Fails to Halt Wright Art Sale: Auction Goes on as Lawyers
Compromise on Attachment of Japanese Prints--Husband Now Out on
Bail--Architect Faces Mann Act Charges After Arrest in Minnesota--
$250,000 Suit Pending," *The New York Times*, January 7, 1927, p. 19,
col. 3.

Anonymous.
"$36,975 for Wright Prints: Sale of Collection, of Which Wife Is
Suing for Proceeds, Ends," *The New York Times*, January 8, 1927,
p. 12, col. 1.

Anonymous.
"Backs Mrs. Wright's Claim: Court Denies Art Galleries Plea to
Vacate Attachment of Prints," *The New York Times*, February 18,
1927, p. 44, col. 5.

Anonymous.
"Retain Auction Proceeds; Anderson Galleries Win Contest over
Wright Sale," *The New York Times*, February 20, 1927, p. 6, col. 5.

Anonymous.
"Wright Charges Dropped: Mme. Milanoff Also Escapes Mann Act
Trial in Minnesota," *The New York Times*, March 5, 1927, p. 27,
col. 4.

Anonymous.
"Miriam Take Taliesin? Smile Here at Report--Bank's Injunction
Restrains Wright's Wife from Estate," *The Capital Times*, (Madison,
Wisconsin), May 9, 1927, p. 3, col. 4.

Dawson, William, Jr.
"Wright May Soon Return to Taliesin--Extra! May Pay Him to Dwell
in Rural Villa--Architect's Friends to Incorporate Him, Buy Back
Estate--Drawing Plans in Madison--Scheme Would Bar Miriam from
Intruding upon Her Husband," *The Capital Times* (Madison, Wisconsin),
May 10, 1927, p. 1 and 12.

Anonymous.
"Wright in Madison, Sued by Miriam--Architect Is Served with
Papers Here--Estranged Wife Demands Money from Wright for Support--
Conferring with Banker--Spring Green Man Here to Discuss Incorpora-
tion Plans," *The Capital Times* (Madison, Wisconsin), May 16, 1927,
p. 1, col. 8.

Anonymous.
"Will Give Wright Divorce: Wife of Architect Will Grant Her Husband
His Liberty," *The New York Times*, July 3, 1927, section 2, p. 1,
col. 5.

Anonymous.
"Mrs. Wright Releases Architect by Divorce: Latter Is Now Free to
Marry Montenegrin Dancer as His Third Wife," *The New York Times*,
August 27, 1927, p. 17, col. 2.

Wright, Frank Lloyd.
"Letter to the Editor," *The Weekly Home News* (Spring Green,
Wisconsin), December 15, 1927.

Anonymous.
"Arrest Mrs. Wright for Raid on Husband: Jail Sentence Suspended
After She Had Smashed Rival's Furniture at San Diego," *The New
York Times*, July 15, 1928, section 1, p. 6, col. 1.

Anonymous.
"To Try Wright and Dancer: San Diego Court Will Hear Architect
on Wife's Charges," *The New York Times*, July 18, 1928, section 1,
p. 5, col. 4.

Anonymous.
"Wright Accuses Ex-Wife: Architect Gets New Warrant Charging Her
with Theft," *The New York Times*, July 20, 1928, section 1, p. 40,
col. 5.

Anonymous.
"Architect Loses Estate: Bank Forecloses on Wisconsin Property of
Frank Lloyd Wright," *The New York Times*, July 31, 1928, p. 43,
col. 2.

Anonymous.
"Wright Weds Olga Ivanova: Charges Filed by Architect's Former Wife
Still Stand in San Diego," *The New York Times*, August 27, 1928,
p. 24, col. 8.

Anonymous.
"Plans Skyscrapers as Inverted Cones: To Be Built of Glass, Copper,
and Concrete with Steel Furnishings: For St. Mark's Apartments:
Architect Says Building Will Have Abutments Giving an Overlapping
Appearance," *The New York Times*, October 18, 1929, p. 22, col. 3.

Anonymous.
"Odd-Type Buildings to Overlook Church: St. Mark's, In Erecting
Novel 'Inverted Cone' Apartments, Will Use Its Own Land," *The New
York Times*, October 19, 1929, p. 24, col. 3.

Brock, H.I.
"A Pioneer in Architecture that Is Called Modern: Frank Lloyd
Wright, Who Proposes a Glass Tower for New York, Has Adapted His
Art to the Machine Age," *The New York Times*, June 29, 1930, section
5, pp. 11, 19.

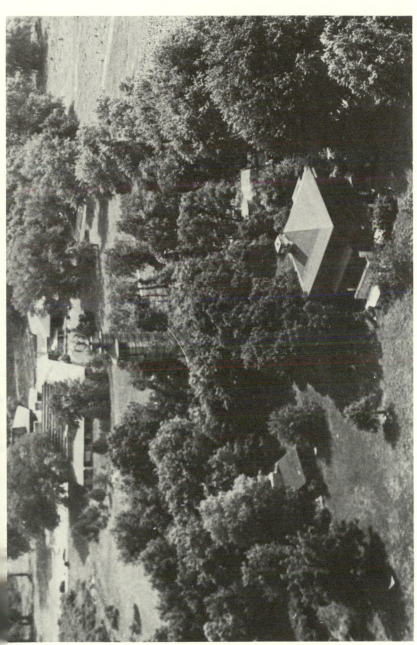

2-4.1   Aerial view of the Taliesin Fellowship Complex, 1933ff (background), the Romeo and Juliet Windmill for Nell and Jane Lloyd Jones, dated 1896 (center), and the Andrew T. Porter Residence, Tanyderi, dated 1907 (foreground), Spring Green, Wisconsin. Photo courtesy of *The Capital Times*, Madison, Wisconsin.

CHAPTER 4

THE TALIESIN FELLOWSHIP (1931 TO 1936)

Introduction

This chapter explores manuscripts from the early years of the
Taliesin Fellowship, which was formally established by Wright in
August of 1932. Correspondence catalogued during this period includes
numerous letters to architect H. Th. Wijdeveld of Holland, who Wright,
in 1931, had asked to be the director of his proposed Taliesin Fellow-
ship. Also, during this period Wright wrote *Architecture and Modern
Life* with Baker Brownell, with whom Wright had much correspondence
relating to this book. Wright continued his friendships with William
T. Evjue, editor of Madison's *The Capital Times*; architects Charles
Robert Ashbee of England and J.J.P. Oud of Holland; and Dorathi Bock
Pierre, daughter of Richard Bock, a sculptor who had assisted Wright
with the sculptural elements for some of his earlier building designs.
    Other correspondence includes letters to Senator Peter Norbeck,
author Claude Bragdon, Robert D. Lusk, publisher William A. Kittredge,
Taliesin Fellows William Beye Fyfe and Edgar Tafel, Harry L. Gandy,
Michael Meredith Hare, George Beal, E. Willis Jones, and clients
Herbert Jacobs (for whom Wright was to eventually design two residences)
and Paul R. Hanna. Additional listings have over twenty-five texts
for articles and speeches including an analysis of Rockefeller Center
at New York, entitled "Radio City," dated June 1931, in which Wright
is critical of the architectural design of the facility; a pointed
reply by Wright to criticisms of his designs made by German critics
while Wright's work was on exhibition in Berlin at the Prussian Academy
of Fine Arts in 1931; a typescript paper explaining Wright's "House
on the Mesa" Project design, dated 1931, for Denver, Colorado; a five-
page thesis on age and growing old entitled "What Shall We Work For"
written in December of 1934 when Wright was 67 years old; and the text
of an address delivered by John Lloyd Wright for his father at the
International Congress of Architects at Rome in September of 1935,
as well as other manuscripts, some of which have been published in
either edited or original form.
    The 35 designs Wright produced during this period represent only
about 4 percent of all of the designs of his lifetime; and of these
35 designs only eight were executed. However, some of Wright's most
famous works emerged from this seemingly small count, including the
Taliesin Fellowship Complex at Spring Green, Wisconsin, of 1933;
Broadacre City; the Edgar J. Kaufmann, Sr., Residence, "Fallingwater,"
at Ohiopyle, Pennsylvania, of 1935; the Paul R. Hanna "Honeycomb"
Residence at Stanford, California, of 1936; the First Residence for
Herbert Jacobs, near Madison, Wisconsin, of 1936; and the S.C. Johnson
and Son Administration Building at Racine, Wisconsin, also of 1936.

B135

Date:
   April 6, 1931

Type of Manuscript:
   Letter

To:
   H. Th. Wijdeveld
   Holland

From:
   Frank Lloyd Wright
   Taliesin
   Spring Green, Wisconsin

Collection:
   H. Th. Wijdeveld Papers
   Rijksdienst voor de Monumentenzorg
   Nederlands Documentatiecentrum voor de Bouwkunst

Medium:
   Typed and handwritten, signed "Frank Lloyd Wright"

Size:
   8-1/2 in. x 11 in.; 215.9 mm x 279.4 mm

Number of Pages:
   1

Number of Words:
   162 Typed; 70 Handwritten

Descriptors:
   H. Th. Wijdeveld, Chicago Allied Arts and Industries

Review:
   Wright asks Wijdeveld to have a Wright exhibition catalogue printed
   in Holland in several different languages for Wright's exhibition
   travels through Europe. Brief mention is made by Wright of the
   Chicago Allied Arts and Industries School for which Wright suggests
   Wijdeveld as the director and himself as chairman.

B136

Date:
   1931 (prior to May 1931)

Type of Manuscript:
   Typescript article

Title:
   "Hell-Bent Is Eclecticism"

By:
   Frank Lloyd Wright

Collection:
   The Library of Congress, Manuscript Division
   The Frank Lloyd Wright Papers
   Speech and Article File, Undated

Medium:
Typed double spaced, with handwritten corrections by Wright

Size:
8-1/2 in. x 11-1/8 in.; 215.9 mm x 282.6 mm

Number of Pages:
2

Descriptors:
Tower-Town Topics, Taste, Style, Culture, Machine,
Eclecticism

Review:
Typescript of "Eclecticism by Way of 'Taste' Is America's Substitute for Culture," *Tower Town Topics*, p. 19.

B137

Date:
June 8, 1931?

Type of Manuscript:
Typescript of text of speech

Title:
"Address of Frank Lloyd Wright at the Annual Banquet of the
Annual Convention of the Michigan Society of Architects and
the Grand Rapids Chapter of the American Institute of
Architects"

By:
Frank Lloyd Wright

Collection:
The Library of Congress, Manuscript Division
The Frank Lloyd Wright Papers
Speech and Article File, 1931

Medium:
Typed double spaced, with handwritten corrections by Wright

Size:
8-1/2 in. x 11-1/8 in.; 215.9 mm x 282.6 mm

Number of Pages:
30

Descriptors:
Michigan Society of Architects

Review:
Text of Wright's lecture at the Annual Convention of the Michigan
Society of Architects. This address was printed as "Address of
Frank Lloyd Wright at the 17th Annual Convention."

B138

Date:
June 21, 1931

Type of Manuscript:
    Typescript article

Title:
    "Radio City"

By:
    Frank Lloyd Wright
    Taliesin
    Spring Green, Wisconsin

Collection:
    The Library of Congress, Manuscript Division
    The Frank Lloyd Wright Papers
    Speech and Article File, 1931

Medium:
    Typed double spaced

Size:
    8-1/2 in. x 11-1/4 in.; 215.9 mm x 285.8 mm

Number of Pages:
    7

Descriptors:
    Radio City (New York), Rockefeller Center

Review:
    Wright talks on the design of Rockefeller Center (which has also
    been called Radio City), in New York.

B139

Date:
    July 23, 1931

Type of Manuscript:
    Typed reply to German critics

To:
    H. Th. Wijdeveld
    Holland

From:
    Frank Lloyd Wright, transmitted by letter from K.E. Jensen
    of Taliesin at Spring Green, Wisconsin, also dated
    July 23, 1931

Collection:
    H. Th. Wijdeveld Papers
    Rijksdienst voor de Monumentenzorg
    Nederlands Documentatiecentrum voor de Bouwkunst

Medium:
    Typed double spaced, with handwritten corrections, and
    signed "Frank Lloyd Wright"

Size:
    8-1/2 in. x 11 in.; 215.9 mm x 279.4 mm

Number of Pages:
    6

Descriptors:
   Erich Mendelsohn, K.E. Jensen, Heinrich Klumb,
   Frankfurter Zeitung, International Style, Walter Curt
   Behrendt

Review:
   Wright is critical of the developing German style, what will later
   be termed the "International Style," and its calculated approach
   using flat plane surfaces and box styles. He attacks the machine-
   like approach to architectural design. Wright's response to criticism may have been to an article which appeared in the *Frankfurter
   Zeitung* by Walter Curt Behrendt on June 30, 1931, concerning Wright's
   buildings. At this time several of Wright's designs were on exhibi-
   tion in Germany at the Prussian Academy of Fine Arts in Berlin.
   Reviews of this Berlin exhibition can be found in "Wright in
   Berlin," *Art Digest*, p. 12; "Frank Lloyd Wright: Ausstellung in der
   Akademie der Kunste, Berlin," *Bauwelt*, p. 914; "Ausstellugen,"
   Baugilde, p. 1190; "Models by Frank Lloyd Wright in Berlin Exhibi-
   tion," *Art News*, p. 16; Dora Landau's "An American Architect
   Exhibits in Berlin," *American Magazine of Art*, p. 165; and Harry
   Adsit Bull's "Notes of the Month," *International Studio*, p. 54.

B140

Date:
   August 13, 1931

Type of Manuscript:
   Letter

To:
   H. Th. Wijdeveld
   Holland

From:
   Frank Lloyd Wright
   Taliesin
   Spring Green, Wisconsin

Collection:
   H. Th. Wijdeveld Papers
   Rijksdienst voor de Monumentenzorg
   Nederlands Documentatiecentrum voor de Bouwkunst

Medium:
   Typed, signed "Frank Lloyd Wright"

Size:
   8-1/2 in. x 11 in.; 215.9 mm x 279.4 mm

Number of Pages:
   2

Number of Words:
   588

Descriptors:
   H. Th. Wijdeveld, Chicago Allied Arts and Industries,
   W. Ruscha, Taliesin Fellowship

Review:
Wright talks again of the possibilites of setting up a school of
architecture at Taliesin and invites Wijdeveld to become the
director of the proposed school, ultimately to be called the
Taliesin Fellowship.

B141

Date:
September 5, 1931

Type of Manuscript:
Telegram

To:
H. Th. Wijdeveld
Holland

From:
Frank Lloyd Wright
Spring Green, Wisconsin

Collection:
H. Th. Wijdeveld Papers
Rijksdienst voor de Monumentenzorg
Nederlands Documentatiecentrum voor de Bouwkunst

Medium:
Western Union Telegram

Size:
6-3/4 in. x 8-1/4 in.; 171.5 mm x 209.6 mm

Number of Pages:
1

Number of Words:
12

Descriptors:
H. Th. Wijdeveld

Review:
Wright invites Wijdeveld to visit Taliesin at Spring Green,
Wisconsin.

B142

Date:
September 8, 1931

Type of Manuscript:
Telegram

To:
H. Th. Wijdeveld
Holland

From:
Frank Lloyd Wright
Spring Green, Wisconsin

Collection:
H. Th. Wijdeveld Papers
Rijksdienst voor de Monumentenzorg
Nederlands Documentatiecentrum voor de Bouwkunst

Medium:
Western Union Telegram

Size:
6-3/4 in. x 8-1/4 in.; 171.5 mm x 209.6 mm

Number of Pages:
1

Number of Words:
16

Descriptors:
H. Th. Wijdeveld, Columbus Memorial Competition (Rio
de Janeiro).

Review:
Wright asks Wijdeveld to come to Taliesin after Novermber 10, 1931.

B143

Date:
December 13, 1931

Type of Manuscript:
Typescript article

Title:
"Brochures on Contemporary Architecture--Published by
the Whittlesey House: Raymond Hood"

By:
Frank Lloyd Wright
Taliesin
Wisconsin

Collection:
The Library of Congress, Manuscript Division
The Frank Lloyd Wright Papers
Speech and Article File, 1931

Medium:
Typed double spaced

Size:
8-1/2 in. x 11-1/8 in.; 215.9 mm x 282.6 mm

Number of Pages:
9

Descriptors:
Raymond Hood, Whittlesey House, The Chicago World's Fair
1933

Review:
Wright verbally attacks architect Raymond Hood. The text of this
article appeared in *Frank Lloyd Wright on Architecture*.

B144

Date:
  1931

Type of Manuscript:
  Typescript article

Title:
  "For All May Raise the Flowers Now for All Have Got
  the Seed"

By:
  Frank Lloyd Wright

Collection:
  The Library of Congress, Manuscript Division
  The Frank Lloyd Wright Papers
  Speech and Article File, 1931

Medium:
  Typewritten double spaced, with handwritten corrections
  by Wright

Size:
  8-1/2 in. x 11-1/8 in.; 215.9 mm x 282.6 mm

Number of Pages:
  8

Descriptors:
  Culture, America, Europe, American Art, American
  Architecture, International Style, *T-Square*, *U.S.A.*
  Tomorrow

Review:
  Imitation in American art and architecture is the topic of
  Wright's discussion. This article appeared as "For All May
  Raise the Flowers Now for All Have Got the Seed," in *T-Square*,
  and later reprinted in *U.S.A. Tomorrow* (Vol. 1, January 1955),
  pp. 8-10.

B145

Date:
  1931

Type of Manuscript:
  Typescript article

Title:
  "A Song to Heaven: A Sermonette"

By:
  Frank Lloyd Wright

Collection:
  The Library of Congress, Manuscript Division
  The Frank Lloyd Wright Papers
  Speech and Article File, 1931

Medium:
   Typed double spaced

Size:
   8-1/2 in. x 11-1/4 in.; 215.9 mm x 285.8 mm

Number of Pages:
   12

Descriptors:
   Japan

Review:
   Wright talks of one of his trips to Japan.

B146

Date:
   1931

Type of Manuscript:
   Typescript article

Title:
   "The City of To-morrow"

By:
   Frank Lloyd Wright

Collection:
   The Library of Congress, Manuscript Division
   The Frank Lloyd Wright Papers
   Speech and Article File, 1931

Medium:
   Typed double spaced

Size:
   8-1/2 in. x 11-1/8 in.; 215.9 mm x 282.6 mm

Number of Pages:
   11

Descriptors:
   The City, *Pictorial Review*

Review:
   Wright on the city. This article appeared in *Pictorial Review*.

B147

Date:
   Undated (1931?)

Type of Manuscript:
   Letter

To:
   H. Th. Wijdeveld
   Holland

From:
   Frank Lloyd Wright
   Taliesin
   Spring Green, Wisconsin

Collection:
   H. Th. Wijdeveld Papers
   Rijksdienst voor de Monumentenzorg
   Nederlands Documentatiecentrum voor de Bouwkunst

Medium:
   Typed, signed "Frank Lloyd Wright"

Size:
   8-1/2 in. x 11 in.; 215.9 mm x 279.4 mm

Number of Pages:
   3

Number of Words:
   686

Descriptors:
   H. Th. Wijdeveld, University of Wisconsin, Princeton
   University Lectures, Architectural League of New York,
   Dr. Hengerer, De Fries, St. Mark's-in-the-Bouwerie
   Towers Project

Review:
   Talk of Wright's forming a school of architecture and possibly
   having H. Th. Wijdeveld as the director; however, according to
   Wright, economics at the present time would not permit a success-
   ful school. Wright offers an exhibition of his work to travel
   in Europe.

   B148

Date:
   1931

Type of Manuscript:
   Book

Title:
   Two Lectures on Architecture

By:
   Frank Lloyd Wright

Collection:
   The John Lloyd Wright Collection
   The Avery Architectural Library
   Columbia University
   Folder 4

Medium:
   Typeset edition autographed "To John--F.LL.W."

Size:
   7-1/2 in. x 10-1/2 in.; 190.5 mm x 266.7 mm

Number of Pages:
   63

Descriptors:
   Two Lectures on Architecture, Art Institute of Chicago

Review:
   An autographed copy of *Two Lectures on Architecture* (Chicago:
   The Art Institute, 1931), which included the text of "In the
   Realm of Ideas" and "To the Young Man in Architecture," delivered
   by Wright at the Art Institute of Chicago October 1 and 2, 1930.

B149

Date:
   January 1, 1932

Type of Manuscript:
   Telegram

To:
   H. Th. Wijdeveld
   Holland

From:
   Frank Lloyd Wright
   Spring Green, Wisconsin

Collection:
   H. Th. Wijdeveld Papers
   Rijksdienst voor de Monumentenzorg
   Nederlands Documentatiecentrum voor de Bouwkunst

Medium:
   Western Union Telegram

Size:
   7 in. x 7-5/8 in.; 177.8 mm x 193.7 mm

Number of Pages:
   1

Number of Words:
   3

Descriptors:
   H. Th. Wijdeveld, New Year 1932

Review:
   New Year's greetings.

B150

Date:
   February 13, 1932

Type of Manuscript:
   Letter

To:
   H. Th. Wijdeveld
   Holland

From:
Frank Lloyd Wright

Collection:
H. Th. Wijdeveld Papers
Rijksdienst voor de Monumentenzorg
Nederlands Documentatiecentrum voor de Bouwkunst

Medium:
Typed, signed "Frank Lloyd Wright"

Size:
8-1/2 in. x 11 in.; 215.9 mm x 279.4 mm

Number of Pages:
2

Number of Words:
320

Descriptors:
H. Th. Wijdeveld, Taliesin Fellowship

Review:
Wright decides not to have Wijdeveld as his director for the
Taliesin Fellowship. His various reasons for this decision are
outlined in this letter.

B151

Date:
March 7, 1932

Type of Manuscript:
Letter

To:
John Lloyd Wright
Michigan City, Indiana

From:
Frank Lloyd Wright

Collection:
The John Lloyd Wright Collection
The Avery Architectural Library
Columbia University
Folder 10

Medium:
Typed, with handwritten notes, signed "Dad"

Size:
8-1/2 in. x 11 in.; 215.9 mm x 279.4 mm

Number of Pages:
1

Number of Words:
269 Typed; 47 Handwritten

Descriptors:
John Lloyd Wright, Cinema and Shops Project (with
John Lloyd Wright)

Review:
  An in-depth discussion of a project in which Frank Lloyd Wright
  and John Lloyd Wright collaborated, the Cinema and Shops Project
  for Michigan City, Indiana.

B152

Date:
  April 15, 1932

Type of Manuscript:
  Typescript article

Title:
  "What Does the Machine Mean to Life in a Democracy"

By:
  Frank Lloyd Wright

Collection:
  The Library of Congress, Manuscript Division
  The Frank Lloyd Wright Papers
  Speech and Article File, 1932

Medium:
  Typed double spaced, with handwritten corrections by Wright

Size:
  8-1/2 in. x 11-1/16 in.; 215.9 mm x 281.0 mm

Number of Pages:
  6

Descriptors:
  Organic Architecture, The Machine, *Pictorial Review*,
  Democracy

Review:
  On organic architecture, this article first appeared in *Pictorial
  Review* of September 1932 and was later reprinted in Frederick
  Gutheim's *Frank Lloyd Wright on Architecture*.

B153

Date:
  April 29, 1932

Type of Manuscript:
  Typescript article

Title:
  "The House on the Mesa ..."

By:
  Frank Lloyd Wright

Collection:
  The Library of Congress, Manuscript Division
  The Frank Lloyd Wright Papers
  Speech and Article File, 1932

Medium:
  Typed double spaced with handwritten corrections by
  Wright

Size:
  8-1/2 in. x 11-1/16 in.; 215.9 mm x 281.0 mm

Number of Pages:
  6

Descriptors:
  Fortune Magazine, House on the Mesa Project

Review
  Wright prepared this article for *Fortune Magazine*. The typescript
  article by Wright explains in detail his concepts for the design
  of the "House on the Mesa" Project at Denver, Colorado, of 1931.
  Six drawings of this project can be found in Arthur Drexler's
  The Drawings of Frank Lloyd Wright, plates 126 through 131.

B154

Date:
  May 9, 1932

Type of Manuscript:
  Typescript article

Title:
  "Of Thee I Sing"

By:
  Frank Lloyd Wright

Collection:
  The Library of Congress, Manuscript Division
  The Frank Lloyd Wright Papers
  Speech and Article File, 1932

Medium:
  Typed double spaced with brief handwritten note signed
  "Frank Lloyd Wright"

Size:
  8-1/2 in. x 11-1/8 in.; 215.9 mm x 282.6 mm

Number of Pages:
  6

Descriptors:
  International Exhibition of the Museum of Modern Art
  (New York), *Shelter*, *New Humanist*

Review:
  Wright prepared this article and sent copies to various architectural magazines. The article was printed in *Shelter* and in
  New Humanist. The copy at the Library of Congress may be a
  reworked paper of the original which had appeared in *Shelter* and
  New Humanist or the April issue of *Shelter* may have been late in
  publication.

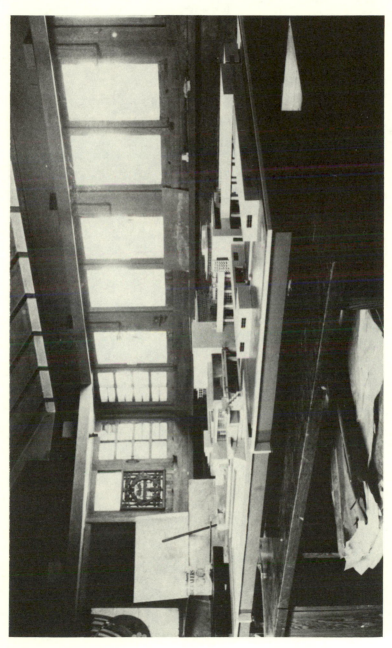

2-4.2 Model of the "House of the Mesa" Project (1931), Denver, Colorado. Photo courtesy of the State Historical Society of Wisconsin.

B155

Date:
   May 27, 1932

Type of Manuscript:
   Letter

To:
   Claude Bragdon
   New York, New York

From:
   Frank Lloyd Wright
   Taliesin
   Spring Green, Wisconsin

Collection:
   Bragdon Family Papers, 1819-1947
   Rush Rhees Library
   University of Rochester
   A. B81, Box 1

Medium:
   Typed on Taliesin-design stationery, signed
   "Frank Lloyd Wright"

Size:
   8-1/2 in. x 9-1/2 in.; 215.9 mm x 241.3 mm

Number of Pages:
   1

Number of Words:
   223

Descriptors:
   Claude Bragdon, Louis H. Sullivan, *The Saturday Review
   of Literature, The Frozen Fountain* by Claude Bragdon

Review:
   Wright talks of an article which may have appeared in *The
   Saturday Review of Literature* that may have been critical
   of Bragdon or Bragdon's work. A book review written by Wright
   of Bragdon's *The Frozen Fountain* appeared as "A Treatise on
   Ornament," in *The Saturday Review of Literature.*

B156

Date:
   July 24, 1932

Type of Manuscript:
   Typescript article

Title:
   "What Is the 'Modern' Idea?"

By:
   Frank Lloyd Wright
   Taliesin
   Spring Green, Wisconsin

Collection:
    The Library of Congress, Manuscript Division
    The Frank Lloyd Wright Papers
    Speech and Article File, 1932

Medium:
    Typed double spaced

Size:
    8-1/2 in. x 11-1/8 in.; 215.9 mm x 282.6 mm

Number of Pages:
    7

Descriptors:
    Columbian Fair, Chicago Progress Fair of 1933, *Liberty*

Review:
    Wright's philosophy of what "modern" is. This article was later
    printed as "What Is the Modern Idea?" in *Liberty*.

B157

Date:
    August 11, 1932

Type of Manuscript:
    Letter

To:
    Dorathi Bock Pierre

From:
    Frank Lloyd Wright

Collection:
    The Richard W. Bock Sculpture Collection
    Greenville College

Medium:
    Signed "Uncle Frank"

Descriptors:
    Dorathi Bock Pierre, *An Autobiography*

Review:
    Wright discusses his *An Autobiography*.

B158

Date:
    August 11, 1932

Type of Manuscript:
    Sheet Music

Collection:
    The John Lloyd Wright Collection
    The Avery Architectural Library
    Columbia University
    Folder 22

Medium:
   Autographed with signatures listed in
   Descriptors, including F.L. Wright

Number of Pages:
   1

Descriptors:
   Svetlana Wright, Rudolph Mock, Vischer Boyd, Yen Liang,
   Samuel Ratesky, Hail Brolter, James T. Drought, Jr.

Review:
   Sheet music autographed on the day the Taliesin Fellowship
   was founded.

B159

Date:
   August 13, 1932? (postmark)

Type of Manuscript:
   Letter

To:
   Dorathi Bock Pierre

From:
   Frank Lloyd Wright

Collection:
   The Richard W. Bock Sculpture Collection
   Greenville College

Descriptors:
   Dorathi Bock Pierre, The Taliesin Fellowship

Review:
   Included in this letter is an application for the Taliesin
   Fellowship, a drawing of an aerial view of Taliesin, a plan
   of the buildings, and a four-page outline of the requirements,
   living conditions, etc.

B160

Date:
   September 22, 1932

Type of Manuscript:
   Telegram

To:
   Edgar Tafel
   New York

From:
   Frank Lloyd Wright
   Spring Green, Wisconsin

Source:
   Edgar Tafel
   Apprentice to Genius: Years with Frank Lloyd Wright, p. 16

2-4.3   Exterior view of drafting studio of the Taliesin Fellowship Complex (1933ff),
Spring Green, Wisconsin. Photo by the author.

2-4.4   Exterior detail of the Taliesin Fellowship Complex (1933ff), Spring Green,
Wisconsin. Photo by the author.

2-4.5　Interior of the assembly hall of the Taliesin Fellowship Complex (1933ff), which was formerly the living room pavilion of the Hillside Home School (1901), Spring Green, Wisconsin. Photo by the author.

2-4.6　Exterior view of the two-story assembly hall wing (background) and drafting studio (foreground) of the Taliesin Fellowship Complex (1933ff), Spring Green, Wisconsin. These areas were formerly of the Hillside Home School (1901). Photo by the author.

2-4.8 Interior of the theater of the Taliesin Fellow-ship Complex (1933ff), Spring Green, Wisconsin. Photo by the author.

2-4.7 Interior detail of windows below the balcony of the assembly hall of the Taliesin Fellowship Complex (1933ff), which was formerly the living room pavilion of the Hillside Home School (1901), Spring Green, Wisconsin. Photo by the author.

Medium:
Western Union Telegram

Number of Pages:
1

Number of Words:
40

Descriptors:
Edgar Tafel, Percival Goodman, The Taliesin Fellowship

Review:
Tafel photographically reproduces the original telegram F.L.
Wright sent to invite Tafel to join the Taliesin Fellowship
in response to Tafel's application. He later became an apprentice
to Wright as a Taliesin Fellow.

B161

Date:
December 3, 1932

Type of Manuscript:
Letter

To:
William A. Kittredge
The Lakeside Press
Chicago, Illinois

From:
Frank Lloyd Wright
Taliesin
Spring Green, Wisconsin

Collection:
William Kittredge Collection
Newberry Library
Chicago, Illinois

Medium:
Typed on Taliesin design stationery, signed
"Frank Lloyd Wright"

Size:
8-1/2 in. x 11 in.; 215.9 mm x 279.4 mm

Number of Pages:
1

Number of Words:
407 Typed; 20 Handwritten

Descriptors:
William A. Kittredge, The Taliesin Fellowship, The
Lakeside Press, *An Autobiography*

Review:
Kittredge had some stationery printed for Frank Lloyd Wright
and Wright inquires about having Kittredge print some copies
of *An Autobiography*.

B162

Date:
December 22, 1932

Type of Manuscript:
Inscribed book

To:
Edgar Tafel

From:
Frank Lloyd Wright
Taliesin

Source:
Edgar Tafel
Apprentice to Genius: Years with Frank Lloyd Wright, p. 133

Medium:
Inscribed copy of *Modern Architecture, Being the Kahn
Lectures for 1930* by Frank Lloyd Wright

Size:
10-5/8 in. x 8-1/4 in.; 269 mm x 210 mm

Number of Words:
15

Descriptors:
Edgar Tafel, *Modern Architecture, Being the Kahn Lectures
for 1930*

Review:
The inscription in Tafel's copy of *Modern Architecture* reads
"To Edgar Tafel 'a young man in architecture' Frank Lloyd Wright,
Taliesin, December 22, 1932." Tafel was then a Taliesin Fellow.

B163

Date:
December 23, 1932

Type of Manuscript:
Letter

To:
William A. Kittredge
Lakeside Press
Chicago, Illinois

From:
Frank Lloyd Wright
Taliesin
Spring Green, Wisconsin

Collection:
William Kittredge Collection
Newberry Library
Chicago, Illinois

Medium:
   Typed on Taliesin-design stationery, signed
   "Frank Lloyd Wright"

Size:
   8-1/2 in. x 11 in.; 215.9 mm x 279.4 mm

Number of Pages:
   1

Number of Words:
   369

Descriptors:
   William A. Kittredge, *An Autobiography*, The Lakeside
   Press, Taliesin Fellowship

Review:
   Times are hard at Taliesin and Wright is short of money to cover
   some expenses for printing. Wright is thankful for help from
   Kittredge.

B164

Date:
   Undated (1932 or 1933?)

Type of Manuscript:
   Typescript article

Title:
   "I Will"

By:
   Frank Lloyd Wright
   Taliesin
   Spring Green, Wisconsin

Collection:
   The Library of Congress, Manuscript Division
   The Frank Lloyd Wright Papers
   Speech and Article File, 1932

Medium:
   Typed double spaced, with handwritten corrections by Wright

Size:
   8-1/2 in. x 11 in.; 215.9 mm x 279.4 mm

Number of Pages:
   2

Descriptors:
   Chicago World's Fair of 1933, Columbian Fair, Skyscrapers,
   Organic Architecture, American Culture

Review:
   Wright talks of the Chicago World's Fair of 1933 and the possible
   effects on American culture due to the Fair's bad design. He makes
   brief reference to a (recent?) meeting he attended in New York
   concerning the Fair. Because of articles in *The New York Times*
   of February 26, 1931, and February 27, 1931, this probably dates

the manuscript as 1931 (see "Fight Ban on Wright as Architect for Fair" and "Architects Debate on Chicago's Fair"). Wright's tone in the article is one of bitterness.

B165

Date:
Undated (1932?)

Type of Manuscript:
Typescript article

Title:
"A Philosophy of Fine Art"

By:
Frank Lloyd Wright

Collection:
The John Lloyd Wright Collection
The Avery Architectural Library
Columbia University
Folder 8

Medium:
Typed, with handwritten corrections by Wright

Size:
8-1/2 in. x 9-1/2 in.; 215.9 mm x 241.3 mm

Number of Pages:
16

Descriptors:
Fine Art

Review:
Not seen by author.

B166

Date:
March 10, 1933

Type of Manuscript:
Letter

To:
H. Th. Wijdeveld
Holland

From:
Frank Lloyd Wright
Taliesin
Spring Green, Wisconsin

Collection:
H. Th. Wijdeveld Papers
Rijksdienst voor de Monumentenzorg
Nederlands Documentatiecentrum voor de Bouwkunst

Medium:
   Typed on Taliesin red-square design stationery, signed
   "Frank Lloyd Wright"

Size:
   8-1/2 in. x 11 in.; 215.9 mm x 279.4 mm

Number of Pages:
   1

Number of Words:
   159

Descriptors:
   H.Th. Wijdeveld, Taliesin Fellowship

Review:
   Wright again asks Wijdeveld to come to Taliesin to work with him.
   This is a somewhat different mood than expressed in his letter
   of February 13, 1932 (B150), in which he asked Wijdeveld not to
   come. The Taliesin Fellowship at this time has been established
   and Wright encloses a prospectus on the school.

B167

Date:
   April 7, 1933

Type of Manuscript:
   Letter

To:
   H. Th. Wijdeveld
   Holland

From:
   Frank Lloyd Wright
   Taliesin
   Spring Green, Wisconsin

Collection:
   H. Th. Wijdeveld Papers
   Rijksdienst voor de Monumentenzorg
   Nederlands Documentatiecentrum voor de Bouwkunst

Medium:
   Typed, signed "Frank Lloyd Wright"

Size:
   8-1/2 in. x 11 in.; 215.9 mm x 279.4 mm

Number of Pages:
   2

Number of Words:
   406

Descriptors:
   H. Th. Wijdeveld, Taliesin Fellowship

Review:
   Again, Wright offers the directorship of the Taliesin Fellowship
   to Wijdeveld, for he has had no response from Wijdeveld since his

letter of March 10, 1933 (B166). A detailed outline of Wright's plan
for the Taliesin Fellowship director's position is given by Wright.
Wright seems to be very sincere in his offer to Wijdeveld.

B168

Date:
   May 2, 1933

Type of Manuscript:
   Letter

To:
   Baker Brownell
   Northwestern University
   Evanston, Illinois

From:
   Frank Lloyd Wright
   Taliesin
   Spring Green, Wisconsin

Collection:
   Frank Lloyd Wright Correspondence with Baker Brownell,
   1931-1939
   Northwestern University Archives
   Northwestern University Library

Medium:
   Typed, signed "Frank Lloyd Wright"

Size:
   8-1/2 in. x 11 in.; 215.9 mm x 279.4 mm

Number of Pages:
   1

Number of Words:
   124

Descriptors:
   Baker Brownell, Samuel Johnson

Review:
   Wright speaks of the prices paid to him for lectures and also
   invites Brownell to visit Taliesin.

B169

Date:
   May 5, 1933

Type of Manuscript:
   Letter

To:
   William Beye Fyfe
   Oak Park, Illinois

From:
   Frank Lloyd Wright
   Taliesin
   Spring Green, Wisconsin

Collection:
   Frank Lloyd Wright Files
   General Articles, Volume 1
   The Oak Park Public Library
   Oak Park, Illinois

Medium:
   Typed on Taliesin design stationery, signed
   "F.LL.W."

Size:
   8-1/2 in. x 11 in.; 215.9 mm x 279.4 mm

Number of Pages:
   1

Number of Words:
   88

Descriptors:
   William Beye Fyfe

Review:
   Wright comments on Fyfe and his work, but the general subject
   matter of the letter is not fully disclosed. Fyfe was a Wright
   apprentice.

B170

Date:
   July 21, 1933

Type of Manuscript:
   Letter

To:
   Baker Brownell
   Northwestern University
   Evanston, Illinois

From:
   Frank Lloyd Wright
   Taliesin
   Spring Green, Wisconsin

Collection:
   Frank Lloyd Wright Correspondence with Baker Brownell,
   1931-1939
   Northwestern University Archives
   Northwestern University Library

Medium:
   Typed on Taliesin design stationery, signed
   "Frank Lloyd Wright"

Size:
   8-1/2 in. x 11 in.; 215.9 mm x 279.4 mm

Number of Pages:
   1

Number of Words:
    89

Descriptors:
    Baker Brownell

Review:
    Wright invites Brownell to Taliesin for a visit.

B171

Date:
    Undated (probably 1933 prior to July)

Type of Manuscript:
    Article

Title:
    "The Chicago World's Fair: To 'The Architects Journal'
    London, England"

By:
    Frank Lloyd Wright

Collection:
    The Library of Congress, Manuscript Division
    The Frank Lloyd Wright Papers
    Speech and Articles File, 1933

Medium:
    Typed double spaced

Size:
    8-1/2 in. x 11-1/8 in.; 215.9 mm x 282.6 mm

Number of Pages:
    5

Descriptors:
    Chicago Progress Fair of 1933, Columbian Fair, Dawes
    Family, City of Chicago, *The Architects' Journal* (England)

Review:
    The failures of the Chicago Progress Fair of 1933 are pointed
    out by Wright. This article was printed as "The Chicago World's
    Fair."

B172

Date:
    October 1, 1933

Type of Manuscript:
    Article

Title:
    "In the Show Window at Macy's"

By:
    Frank Lloyd Wright
    Taliesin
    Spring Green, Wisconsin

Collection:
    The Library of Congress, Manuscript Division
    The Frank Lloyd Wright Papers
    Speech and Articles File, 1933

Medium:
    Typed double spaced with handwritten corrections by
    Wright

Size:
    8-1/2 in. x 11-3/8 in.; 215.9 mm x 288.9 mm

Number of Pages:
    5

Descriptors:
    New York City, Philip Johnson, skyscraper, *Architectural
    Forum*

Review:
    Wright reviews a recent architecture exhibition in New York and
    is highly critical of it. This article was printed in *Architectural
    Forum.*

B173

Date:
    November 8, 1933

Type of Manuscript:
    Letter

To:
    Michael Meredith Hare

From:
    Frank Lloyd Wright

Collection:
    Frank Lloyd Wright Collection
    The University Archives
    State University of New York at Buffalo

Medium:
    Typed, signed

Number of Pages:
    2

Descriptors:
    Michael Meredith Hare, Taliesin Fellowship, Beaux Arts,
    Yale University

Review:
    Wright talks of the Taliesin Fellowship to Hare, who had inquired
    about joining, and Wright comments on the Beaux Arts program at
    Yale University.

B174

Date:
December 1, 1933

Type of Manuscript:
Telegram

To:
Baker Brownell
Chicago, Illinois

From:
Frank Lloyd Wright
Spring Green, Wisconsin

Collection:
Frank Lloyd Wright Correspondence with Baker Brownell,
1931-1939
Northwestern University Archives
Northwestern University Library

Medium:
Western Union Telegram

Size:
6-1/2 in. x 8 in.; 165.1 mm x 203.2 mm

Number of Pages:
1

Number of Words:
16

Descriptors:
Baker Brownell

Review:
Wright invites Mr. and Mrs. Brownell to visit Taliesin, Spring
Green, Wisconsin.

B175

Date:
December 2, 1933

Type of Manuscript:
Letter

To:
Michael Meredith Hare

From:
Frank Lloyd Wright

Collection:
Frank Lloyd Wright Collection
The University Archives
State University of New York at Buffalo

Medium:
Typed, signed

Number of Pages:
1

Descriptors:
Michael Meredith Hare, Taliesin Fellowship, Architect
Licensing

Review:
Wright comments on college degrees and on the licensing of architects. Hare had asked Wright about joining the Taliesin Fellowship
in a letter.

B176

Date:
December 6, 1933

Type of Manuscript:
Letter

To:
Baker Brownell
Chicago, Illinois

From:
Frank Lloyd Wright
Taliesin
Spring Green, Wisconsin

Collection:
Frank Lloyd Wright correspondence with Baker Brownell,
1931-1939
Northwestern University Archives
Northwestern University Library

Medium:
Typed on Taliesin design stationery, signed
"Frank Lloyd Wright"

Size:
8-1/2 in. x 11 in.; 215.9 mm x 279.4 mm

Number of Pages:
1

Number of Words:
70

Descriptors:
Baker Brownell

Review:
Wright thanks Brownell for a recent visit Brownell made to
Taliesin.

B177

Date:
1933

Type of Manuscript:
   Typescript article

Title:
   "First Answers to Questions by Pravda"

By:
   Frank Lloyd Wright
   Taliesin
   Spring Green, Wisconsin

Collection:
   The Library of Congress, Manuscript Division
   The Frank Lloyd Wright Papers
   Speech and Article File, Undated

Medium:
   Typed double spaced

Size:
   8-1/2 in. x 11-1/8 in.; 215.9 mm x 282.6 mm

Number of Pages:
   2

Descriptors:
   Pravda, U.S.S.R., Depression

Review:
   Half of this text was printed on page 171 of *Frank Lloyd Wright
   on Architecture*.

B178

Date:
   January 30, 1934

Type of Manuscript:
   Letter

To:
   William T. Evjue
   Madison, Wisconsin

From:
   Frank Lloyd Wright
   Taliesin
   Spring Green, Wisconsin

Collection:
   The William Theodore Evjue Papers, 1905-1969
   The State Historical Society of Wisconsin
   MSS 244, Box 155, Folder 21

Medium:
   Typed on Taliesin design stationery and signed
   "Frank Lloyd Wright"

Size:
   8-1/2 in. x 11 in.; 215.9 mm x 279.4 mm

Number of Pages:
   1

Number of Words:
    179

Descriptors:
    William T. Evjue, *The Capital Times*, "Taliesin" Newspaper
    Column

Review:
    Discussion of Wright's proposed series of news columns entitled
    "Taliesin" for the Madison, Wisconsin, newspaper *The Capital Times*.

B179

Date:
    February 5, 1934

Type of Manuscript:
    Letter

To:
    Baker Brownell
    Evanston, Illinois

From:
    Frank Lloyd Wright
    Taliesin
    Spring Green, Wisconsin

Collection:
    Frank Lloyd Wright Correspondence with Baker Brownell,
    1931-1939
    Northwestern University Archives
    Northwestern University Library

Medium:
    Typed on Taliesin design stationery, signed
    "Frank Lloyd Wright"

Size:
    8-1/2 in. x 11 in.; 215.9 mm x 279.4 mm

Number of Pages:
    1

Number of Words:
    157

Descriptors:
    Baker Brownell

Review:
    Wright sends Brownell literature on his newly established
    Taliesin Fellowship and asks for Brownell's support.

B180

Date:
    February 5, 1934

Type of Manuscript:
    Letter

To:
   William T. Evjue
   Madison, Wisconsin

From:
   Frank Lloyd Wright
   Taliesin
   Spring Green, Wisconsin

Collection:
   The William Theodore Evjue Papers, 1905-1969
   The State Historical Society of Wisconsin
   MSS 244, Box 155, Folder 21

Medium:
   Typed on Taliesin design stationery and signed "F L L W "

Size:
   5-1/2 in. x 8-1/2 in.; 139.7 mm x 215.9 mm

Number of Pages:
   1

Number of Words:
   89

Descriptors:
   William T. Evjue, *The Capital Times*, "Taliesin" Newspaper
   Column, Glenn Frank

Review:
   On Glenn Frank and an article Wright wrote concerning him.

B181

Date:
   February 9, 1934

Type of Manuscript:
   Letter

To:
   John Lloyd Wright

From:
   Frank Lloyd Wright

Collection:
   The John Lloyd Wright Collection
   The Avery Architectural Library
   Columbia University
   Folder 22

Medium:
   Signed by F.L. Wright

Descriptors:
   The Taliesin Fellowship, John Lloyd Wright

Review:
   Wright transmits a copy of *The Taliesin Fellowship* prospectus
   dated December 1933 to his son.

B182

Date:
    February 15, 1934

Type of Manuscript:
    Letter

To:
    William T. Evjue
    Madison, Wisconsin

From:
    Frank Lloyd Wright
    Taliesin
    Spring Green, Wisconsin

Collection:
    The William Theodore Evjue Papers, 1905-1969
    The State Historical Society of Wisconsin
    MSS 244, Box 155, Folder 21

Medium:
    Typed on Taliesin design stationery and signed "FLLW"

Size:
    5-1/2 in. x 8-1/2 in.; 139.7 mm x 215.9 mm

Number of Pages:
    1

Number of Words:
    78

Descriptors:
    William T. Evjue, *The Capital Times*, "Taliesin" Newspaper
    Column

Review:
    Transmittal letter for a "Taliesin" column article to be printed
    in *The Capital Times* and for the design drawing of the "Taliesin"
    column heading.

B183

Date:
    February 24, 1934 (or 1936?)

Type of Manuscript:
    Letter

To:
    Baker Brownell
    Chicago, Illinois

From:
    Frank Lloyd Wright
    Taliesin
    Spring Green, Wisconsin

Collection:
    Frank Lloyd Wright Correspondence with Baker Brownell,
    1931-1939

Northwestern University Archives
Northwestern University Library

Medium:
Typed on Taliesin design stationery, signed
"Frank Lloyd Wright"

Size:
8-1/2 in. x 11 in.; 215.9 mm x 279.4 mm

Number of Pages:
1

Number of Words:
184 Typed; 15 Handwritten

Descriptors:
Baker Brownell, The University of Wisconsin, *The Cardinal*

Review:
Wright forwards some literature to Brownell to read to one of
Brownell's classes at the university. Also, Wright invites
Brownell to Taliesin for a visit.

B184

Date:
March 30, 1934

Type of Manuscript:
Letter

To:
Baker Brownell
Chicago, Illinois

From:
Frank Lloyd Wright
Taliesin
Spring Green, Wisconsin

Collection:
Frank Lloyd Wright Correspondence with Baker Brownell,
1931-1939
Northwestern University Archives
Northwestern University Library

Medium:
Typed on Taliesin design stationery, signed
"Frank Lloyd Wright"

Size:
5-1/2 in. x 8-3/8 in.; 139.7 mm x 212.7 mm

Number of Pages:
1

Number of Words:
39

Descriptors:
Baker Brownell

Review:
Wright sets a date to visit Brownell in this brief letter.

B185

Date:
August 6, 1934

Type of Manuscript:
Letter

To:
Baker Brownell
Chicago, Illinois

From:
Frank Lloyd Wright
Taliesin
Spring Green, Wisconsin

Collection:
Frank Lloyd Wright Correspondence with Baker Brownell,
1931-1939
Northwestern University Archives
Northwestern University Library

Medium:
Typed on Taliesin design stationery, signed
"Frank Lloyd Wright"

Size:
8-1/2 in. x 11 in.; 215.9 mm x 279.4 mm

Number of Pages:
1

Number of Words:
41

Descriptors:
Baker Brownell

Review:
Brownell has sent Wright a small present and Wright invites Brownell
to Taliesin for a visit.

B186

Date:
October 30, 1934

Type of Manuscript:
Letter

To:
George Beal

From:
Frank Lloyd Wright
Taliesin

Collection:
    Frank Lloyd Wright Collection
    Kenneth Spencer Research Library
    University of Kansas

Medium:
    Typed on Taliesin design stationery and signed

Size:
    Letter--8-3/8 in. x 10-3/4 in.; 212 mm x 272 mm
    Enclosure--8-1/2 in. x 11 in.; 216 mm x 279 mm

Number of Pages:
    Letter--1; Enclosure--2

Number of Words:
    Letter--193; Enclosure--212

Descriptors:
    Walter Gropius, Louis Sullivan, *Kindergarten Chats*, George Elmslie,
    Claude Bragdon, George Beal, Yen, China

Review:
    Wright enclosues a Taliesin editorial on Gropius' dissertation
    and Louis Sullivan's *Kindergarten Chats*; says Elmslie and Bragdon
    were not respected by Louis Sullivan and Yen is to go to China
    for a wife but plans on returning to Taliesin.

B187

Date:
    December 4, 1934

Type of Manuscript:
    Typescript article

Title:
    "What Shall We Work For"

By:
    Frank Lloyd Wright
    Taliesin
    Spring Green, Wisconsin

Collection:
    The Library of Congress, Manuscript Division
    The Frank Lloyd Wright Papers
    Speech and Article File, 1934

Medium:
    Typed double spaced

Size:
    8-1/2 in. x 13 in.; 215.9 mm x 330.2 mm

Number of Pages:
    5

Descriptors:
    Taliesin, Chicago Progress Fair, Age, Internationalists,
    Immortality, China, Japan, New York City, Youth

Review:
    Wright talks of age and growing old and achieving immortality.
    The quality of youth is also explored.

B188

Date:
    December 25, 1934

Type of Manuscript:
    Inscribed Japanese Print

To:
    Edgar Tafel

From:
    Frank Lloyd Wright

Source:
    Edgar Tafel
    Apprentice to Genius: Years with Frank Lloyd Wright, p. 101

Medium:
    Handwritten, signed "FLLW"

Number of Words:
    7

Descriptors:
    Edgar Tafel, Japanese Prints, Christmas 1934

Review:
    A Japanese print inscribed "To Edgar, Christmas '34--FLLW and
    Olgivanna" is reproduced photographically in the text of Tafel's
    book.

B189

Date:
    1934 (Undated)

Type of Manuscript:
    Handwritten note in Wright's *An Autobiography*

To:
    Charles Robert Ashbee

From:
    Frank Lloyd Wright

Source:
    Alan Crawford
    "Ten Letters From Frank Lloyd Wright to Charles Robert
    Ashbee"

Collection:
    The Ashbee Journals
    King's College
    Cambridge, England

Medium:
Handwritten in 1932 edition of Wright's *An Autobiography*

Number of Words:
106

Descriptors:
Charles Robert Ashbee, Taliesin Fellowship

Review:
A copy of the Taliesin Fellowship prospectus and Wright's *An Autobiography* are given to Ashbee. Wright wants to continue to be Ashbee's friend.

B190

Date:
1934 (undated)

Type of Manuscript:
Inscribed book

To:
Edgar Tafel

From:
Frank Lloyd Wright
Taliesin

Source:
Edgar Tafel
Apprentice to Genius: Years with Frank Lloyd Wright, p. 141

Size:
11-3/8 in. x 8-3/4 in.; 288 mm x 224 mm

Medium:
Inscribed copy of H. de Fries' *Frank Lloyd Wright: Aus dem Lebenswerke eines Architekten*

Number of Words:
35

Descriptors:
Edgar Tafel, *Frank Lloyd Wright: Aus dem Lebenswerke eines Architekten*, H. de Fries

Review:
Tafel's inscribed copy of H. de Fries' *Frank Lloyd Wright: Aus dem Lebenswerke eines Architekten* is signed "Frank Lloyd Wright." Wright wishes Tafel to become a great architect. Tafel was then a Taliesin Fellow.

B191

Date:
January 30, 1935

Type of Manuscript:
Letter

To:
  George and Helen Beal

From:
  Frank Lloyd Wright
  Taliesin

Collection:
  Frank Lloyd Wright Collection
  Kenneth Spencer Research Library
  University of Kansas

Medium:
  Typed on Taliesin design stationery and signed

Size:
  8-3/8 in. x 10-3/4 in.; 212 mm x 272 mm

Number of Pages:
  2

Number of Words:
  72

Descriptors:
  George Beal, Helen Beal

Review:
  Wright thanks the Beals for their hospitality during a trip
  he made to Arizona.

B192

Date: .
  January 31, 1935

Type of Manuscript:
  Typescript article

Title:
  "To Arizona"

By:
  Frank Lloyd Wright
  La Hacienda
  Chandler, Arizona

Collection:
  The Library of Congress, Manuscript Division
  The Frank Lloyd Wright Papers
  Speech and Article File, 1935

Medium:
  Typed double spaced

Size:
  8-1/2 in. x 11-1/8 in.; 215.9 mm x 282.6 mm

Number of Pages:
  6

Descriptors:
  America, Arizona, Nature, La Hacienda (Chandler, Arizona)

Review:
Wright reflects upon Arizona and its beauty. Wright feels that the Arizona beauty should be protected by the government.

B193

Date:
April 27, 1935

Type of Manuscript:
Letter

To:
George and Helen Beal

From:
Frank Lloyd Wright
Taliesin

Collection:
Frank Lloyd Wright Collection
Kenneth Spencer Research Library
University of Kansas

Medium:
Typed on Taliesin design stationery and signed

Size:
8-3/8 in. x 10-3/4 in; 212 mm x 272 mm

Number of Pages:
1

Number of Words:
24

Descriptors:
George Beal, Helen Beal, Broadacre City, Taliesin

Review:
Wright asks the Beals to join him at Taliesin for the summer at a cost of $100. Wright explains to Beal that he is trying to borrow money to finance his Broadacre City designs.

B194

Date:
April 28, 1935

Type of Manuscript:
Letter

To:
Baker Brownell
Northwestern University
Evanston, Illinois

From:
Frank Lloyd Wright
Taliesin
Spring Green, Wisconsin

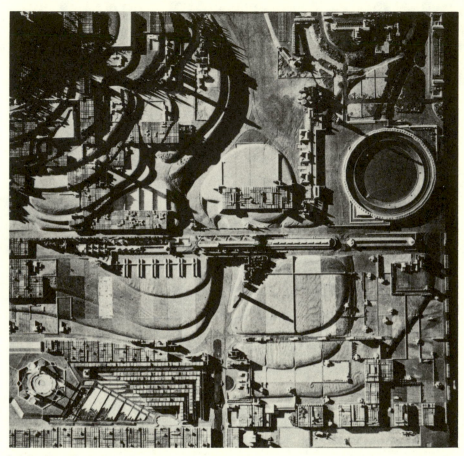

2-4.9 Broadacre City Project (1934). Model of a portion of the Broadacre City Project. This photograph was taken at La Hacienda, Arizona, prior to the construction of Wright's Taliesin West. The Taliesin Fellowship used La Hacienda as temporary quarters while working on the model. Photo courtesy of the State Historical Society of Wisconsin.

Collection:
   Frank Lloyd Wright Correspondence with Baker Brownell,
   1931-1939
   Northwestern University Archives
   Northwestern University Library

Medium:
   Typed on Taliesin design stationery, signed "F.L.L.W."

Size:
   8-1/2 in. x 11 in.; 215.9 mm x 279.4 mm

Number of Pages:
   1

Number of Words:
   56

Descriptors:
   Baker Brownell

Review:
   Wright speaks of payment for a lecture and invites Brownell to
   visit him at Taliesin, Spring Green, Wisconsin.

B195

Date:
   May 11, 1935

Type of Manuscript:
   Telegram

To:
   Baker Brownell
   Chicago, Illinois

From:
   Frank Lloyd Wright
   Spring Green, Wisconsin

Collection:
   Frank Lloyd Wright Correspondence with Baker Brownell,
   1931-1939
   Northwestern University Archives
   Northwestern University Library

Medium:
   Western Union Telegram

Size:
   6-1/2 in. x 8 in.; 165.1 mm x 203.2 mm

Number of Pages:
   1

Number of Words:
   17

Descriptors:
   Baker Brownell

Review:
    On an undisclosed topic.

B196

Date:
    June 5, 1935

Type of Manuscript:
    Letter

To:
    William A. Kittredge
    Lakeside Press
    Chicago, Illinois

From:
    Mr. and Mrs. Frank Lloyd Wright
    Taliesin
    Spring Green, Wisconsin

Collection:
    William Kittredge Collection
    Newberry Library
    Chicago, Illinois

Medium:
    Typed on Taliesin design stationery, unsigned

Size:
    8-1/2 in. x 11 in.; 215.9 mm x 279.4 mm

Number of Pages:
    1

Number of Words:
    339

Descriptors:
    William A. Kittredge, The Lakeside Press, Broadacre
    City, State Historical Society (Wisconsin), Taliesin
    Fellowship

Review:
    Kittredge is invited to a private showing of Wright's Broadacre
    City Model on June 9, 1935, at the State Historical Society in
    Madison. However, the word "cancelled" is printed over the
    invitation.

B196a

Date:
    July 23, 1935

Type of Manuscript:
    Telegram

To:
    Senator Peter Norbeck

From:
    Frank Lloyd Wright
    Spring Green, Wisconsin

Collection:
    Robert Davies Lusk Correspondence, 1935-1936
    South Dakota Department of Education and Cultural Affairs
    Historical Resource Center

Medium:
    Copy of Western Union Telegram, signed "Frank Lloyd Wright"

Size:
    8-1/2 in. x 7 in.; 215.9 mm x 177.8 mm

Number of Pages:
    1

Number of Words:
    64

Descriptors:
    Senator Peter Norbeck, Government Architect, Government,
    Sylvan Lake Hotel Project (South Dakota), South Dakota

Review:
    Wright tells of his feelings regarding the "government architect."
    This telegram was sent by Wright regarding a potential commission
    for the proposed Sylvan Lake Hotel in South Dakota. The project
    ultimately was not designed by him.

B196b

Date:
    July 24, 1935

Type of Manuscript:
    Telegram

To:
    Senator Peter Norbeck

From:
    Frank Lloyd Wright
    Spring Green, Wisconsin

Collection:
    Robert Davies Lusk Correspondence, 1935-1936
    South Dakota Department of Education and Cultural Affairs
    Historical Resource Center

Medium:
    Copy of Western Union Telegram, signed "Frank Lloyd Wright"

Size:
    8-1/2 in. x 7 in.; 215.9 mm x 177.8 mm

Number of Pages:
    1

Number of Words:
    40

Descriptors:
  Senator Peter Norbeck, Sylvan Lake Hotel Project (South Dakota),
  South Dakota

Review:
  Wright tells Norbeck that he is willing to go to South Dakota
  if he has been selected as the Sylvan Lake Hotel Project architect.

B197

Date:
  September 3, 1935

Type of Manuscript:
  Typescript speech

Title:
  "To the International Congress of Architects, Rome,
  Italy, September, 1935"

By:
  Frank Lloyd Wright

Collection:
  The John Lloyd Wright Collection
  The Avery Architectural Library
  Columbia University
  Folder 5

Medium:
  Manuscript, with handwritten note, signed by Wright

Descriptors:
  International Congress of Architects, Rome

Review:
  This speech was delivered at the International Congress of
  Architects at Rome in September of 1935 by John Lloyd Wright;
  F.L. Wright was unable to attend.

B198

Date:
  September 28, 1935

Type of Manuscript:
  Letter

Title:
  "Robert D. Lusk: The Evening Huronite: Huron,
  South Dakota"

By:
  Frank Lloyd Wright
  Taliesin
  Spring Green, Wisconsin

Collection:
  The Library of Congress, Manuscript Division

The Frank Lloyd Wright Papers
Speech and Article File, 1935

Medium:
Typed double spaced

Size:
8-1/2 in. x 11-1/8 in.; 215.9 mm x 282.6 mm

Number of Pages:
9

Descriptors:
Robert D. Lusk, *The Evening Huronite* (Huron, South Dakota),
Paul Bellamy, Bad Lands (Dakotas), Rapid City (South Dakota),
Harold Spitznagel, Sylvan Lake (South Dakota), Ted Lusk,
Gutzon Borglum, Harry Gandy, Sylvan Lake Hotel Project

Review:
Wright goes into fine detail on a trip he made through South
Dakota during this period.

B198a

Date:
September 28, 1935

Type of Manuscript:
Letter

To:
Robert D. Lusk
The Evening Huronite
Huron, South Dakota

From:
Frank Lloyd Wright
Taliesin
Spring Green, Wisconsin

Collection:
Robert Davies Lusk Correspondence, 1935-1936
South Dakota Department of Education and Cultural Affairs
Historical Resource Center

Medium:
Typed, signed "Frank Lloyd Wright"

Size:
8-1/2 in. x 11 in.; 215.9 mm x 279.4 mm

Number of Pages:
9

Number of Words:
2,366

Descriptors:
The Evening Huronite, Robert D. Lusk, Harold Spitznagel,
Bad Lands (Dakotas), Black Hills (South Dakota),
Spearfish Canyon (South Dakota), South Dakota, Paul Bellamy,
Egyptian, Mayan, Ted Lusk, Gutzon Borglum, Harry L. Gandy,

Rapid City (South Dakota), Sylvan Lake Hotel Project (South
Dakota)

Review:
Wright speaks of his recent trip to South Dakota to visit the
proposed site of the Sylvan Lake Hotel Project. The letter is
very detailed and gives a very vivid picture of how Wright felt
about South Dakota and the Bad Lands. This letter may have been
intended as a short article for Lusk's newspaper. This manuscript
is identical to that of B198; B198 is probably the copy.

B198b

Date:
September 28, 1935

Type of Manuscript:
Letter

To:
Harry L. Gandy
Rapid City, South Dakota

From:
Frank Lloyd Wright
Taliesin
Spring Green, Wisconsin

Collection:
Robert Davies Lusk Correspondence, 1935-1936
South Dakota Department of Education and Cultural Affairs
Historical Resource Center

Medium:
Typed copy, signed "Frank Lloyd Wright"

Size:
8 in. x 10-1/2 in.; 203.2 mm x 266.7 mm

Number of Pages:
2

Number of Words:
507

Descriptors:
Harry L. Gandy, Black Hills (South Dakota), Senator Peter
Norbeck, Sylvan Lake Hotel Project (South Dakota), South
Dakota, Gutzon Borglum

Review:
Wright outlines his proposed architectural fees for the design
of the Sylvan Lake Hotel Project in South Dakota. Wright's
philosophy, with respect to competing for architectural jobs,
is given.

B198c

Date:
September 28, 1935

Type of Manuscript:
   Letter

To:
   Senator Peter Norbeck
   Rapid City, South Dakota

From:
   Frank Lloyd Wright
   Taliesin
   Spring Green, Wisconsin

Collection:
   Robert Davies Lusk Correspondence, 1935-1936
   South Dakota Department of Education and Cultural Affairs
   Historical Resource Center

Medium:
   Typed copy, signed "Frank Lloyd Wright"

Size:
   8 in. x 10-1/2 in.; 203.2 mm x 266.7 mm

Number of Pages:
   1

Number of Words:
   73

Descriptors:
   Senator Peter Norbeck, Paul Bellamy, Robert D. Lusk,
   Harry L. Gandy, Sylvan Lake Hotel Project (South Dakota),
   South Dakota

Review:
   A letter informing Norbeck that Wright had recently visited
   South Dakota and had sent a brief article about it to Robert
   D. Lusk (see B198a). Wright had visited South Dakota regarding
   a potential commission to do the Sylvan Lake Hotel Project.

B198d

Date:
   October 25, 1935

Type of Manuscript:
   Letter

To:
   Robert D. Lusk
   The Evening Huronite
   Huron, South Dakota

From:
   Frank Lloyd Wright
   Spring Green, Wisconsin

Collection:
   Robert Davies Lusk Correspondence, 1935-1936
   South Dakota Department of Education and Cultural Affairs
   Historical Resource Center

Medium:
   Typed, signed "F.L.L W."

Size:
   8-1/2 in. 11 in.; 215.9 mm x 279.4 mm

Number of Pages:
   1

Number of Words:
   137

Descriptors:
   The Evening Huronite, Robert D. Lusk, Sylvan Lake Hotel
   Project (South Dakota), Harold Spitznagel

Review:
   Wright discusses his feelings regarding the loss of the Sylvan
   Lake Hotel Project in South Dakota. Wright did not want to compete
   with other architects in order to get the project.

B198e

Date:
   October 25, 1935

Type of Manuscript:
   Letter

To:
   Senator Peter Norbeck
   Rapid City, South Dakota

From:
   Frank Lloyd Wright
   Taliesin
   Spring Green, Wisconsin

Collection:
   Robert Davies Lusk Correspondence, 1935-1936
   South Dakota Department of Education and Cultural Affairs
   Historical Resource Center

Medium:
   Typed copy, signed "Frank Lloyd Wright"

Size:
   8-1/2 in. x 11 in.; 215.9 mm x 279.4 mm

Number of Pages:
   1

Number of Words
   109

Descriptors:
   Senator Peter Norbeck, Sylvan Lake Hotel Project (South
   Dakota), South Dakota, Harry L. Gandy

Review:
   Wright informs Norbeck that the potential commission for the
   Sylvan Lake Hotel Project is now lost to Wright.

B198f

Date:
November 8, 1935

Type of Manuscript:
Letter

To:
Harry L. Gandy
Boston, Massachusetts

From:
Frank Lloyd Wright
Taliesin
Spring Green, Wisconsin

Collection:
Robert Davies Lusk Correspondence, 1935-1936
South Dakota Department of Education and Cultural Affairs
Historical Resource Center

Medium:
Typed copy, signed "FLLW"

Size:
8-1/2 in. x 11 in.; 215.9 mm x 279.4 mm

Number of Pages:
1

Number of Words:
373

Descriptors:
Harry L. Gandy, Sylvan Lake Hotel Project (South Dakota),
Robert D. Lusk, Ray Milliken

Review:
Wright outlines his position as an architect regarding the Sylvan
Lake Hotel Project design competition which Gandy expects Wright
to enter. Wright declines to enter based upon his ideals as an
architect.

B199

Date:
December 15, 1935

Type of Manuscript:
Typescript article

Title:
"Organic Architecture: 1. The United States from 1893
to 1920"

By:
Frank Lloyd Wright

Collection:
The Library of Congress, Manuscript Division
The Frank Lloyd Wright Papers
Speech and Article File, 1935

Medium:
   Typed double spaced, with handwritten corrections by
   Wright

Size:
   8-1/2 in. x 13 in.; 215.9 mm x 330.2 mm

Number of Pages:
   19

Descriptors:
   Organic Architecture, Adler and Sullivan, Oak Park,
   Wainwright Building, Schiller Building, Herman Winslow,
   Louis Sullivan, Charnley House, Winslow House, Larkin
   Building, Unity Temple, International Style, Albert
   Einstein, Nature, Organic Architecture, Imperial Hotel,
   Hull House, "The Art and Craft of the Machine,"
   C.R. Ashbee, Kuno Francke, *Architectural Record*,
   Midway Gardens

Review:
   Wright reviews his years as an architect between 1893 and 1920.
   He reflects upon the impact of some of his more famous designs
   on world architecture and the development of world architecture
   in the modern era. This is an important paper because a history
   of modern architecture, or at least a history of early twentieth-
   century modern architecture as Wright perceives it, is given. An
   early draft of Frank Lloyd Wright's "Recollections--The United
   States, 1893-1920."

B200

Date:
   December 16, 1935

Type of Manuscript:
   Letter

To:
   Baker Brownell
   Northwestern University
   Evanston, Illinois

From:
   Frank Lloyd Wright
   Taliesin
   Spring Green, Wisconsin

Collection:
   Frank Lloyd Wright Correspondence with Baker Brownell,
   1931-1939
   Northwestern University Archives
   Northwestern University Library

Medium:
   Typed, signed "F.L.L.W."

Size:
   8-1/2 in. x 11 in.; 215.9 mm x 279.4 mm

Number of Pages:
1

Number of Words:
43 Typed; 2 Handwritten

Descriptors:
Baker Brownell

Review:
Wright asks Brownell to bring someone to Taliesin with him when he visits.

B201

Date:
December 16, 1935

Type of Manuscript:
Letter

To:
George and Helen Beal

From:
Frank Lloyd Wright

Collection:
Frank Lloyd Wright Collection
Kenneth Spencer Research Library
University of Kansas

Medium:
Typed on onion skin paper and signed

Size:
8-3/8 in. x 12-7/8 in.; 213 mm x 327 mm

Number of Pages:
1

Number of Words:
60

Descriptors:
George Beal, Helen Beal, Taliesin, Christmas 1935

Review:
An invitation to the Beals to spend the Christmas holidays at Taliesin, Spring Green, Wisconsin.

B202

Date:
December 19, 1935

Type of Manuscript:
Christmas card

To:
J.J.P. Oud
Holland

From:
    Frank Lloyd Wright
    Spring Green, Wisconsin

Collection:
    J.J.P. Oud Papers
    Rijksdienst voor de Monumentenzorg
    Nederlands Documentatiecentrum voor de Bouwkunst

Medium:
    Taliesin Fellowship Christmas card

Size:
    6-3/4 in. x 18 in.; 171.5 mm x 457.2 mm

Number of Pages:
    1

Descriptors:
    Christmas 1935, Taliesin Fellowship, J.J.P. Oud

Review:
    Christmas greetings to J.J.P. Oud.

B203

Date:
    Christmas 1935

Type of Manuscript:
    Christmas card

Collection:
    Special Collections Department
    Northwestern University Library
    Northwestern University

Medium:
    Printed and signed Taliesin Fellowship Christmas card

Size:
    6-3/4 in. 18 in.; 171.5 mm x 457.2 mm

Number of Pages:
    1

Descriptors:
    Christmas 1935, Taliesin Fellowship

Review:
    Christmas greetings.

B204

Date:
    Undated (1935?)

Type of Manuscript:
    Typescript article

Title:
    "Louis Sullivan's Words and Work"

By:
Frank Lloyd Wright

Collection:
The Library of Congress, Manuscript Division
The Frank Lloyd Wright Papers
Speech and Article File, 1935

Medium:
Typed double spaced, with handwritten corrections by
Wright

Size:
8-1/2 in. x 11-1/8 in.; 215.9 mm x 282.6 mm

Number of Pages:
3

Descriptors:
Louis Sullivan

Review:
A eulogy for Louis Sullivan by Wright.

B205

Date:
January 10, 1936

Type of Manuscript:
Telegram

To:
George Beal

From:
Frank Lloyd Wright

Collection:
Frank Lloyd Wright Collection
Kenneth Spencer Research Library
University of Kansas

Medium:
Western Union Telegram

Size:
6-1/2 in. 8 in.; 165 mm x 203 mm

Number of Pages:
1

Number of Words:
30

Descriptors:
Lawrence, Kansas, George Beal

Review:
Wright plans to visit Lawrence, Kansas, on January 11,
1936.

B206

Date:
    January 26, 1936

Type of Manuscript:
    Typescript article

Title:
    "An Architect Speaking for Culture"

By:
    Frank Lloyd Wright
    Arizona Camp

Collection:
    The Library of Congress, Manuscript Division
    The Frank Lloyd Wright Papers
    Speech and Article File, 1936

Medium:
    Typed double spaced, with handwritten corrections
    by Wright

Size:
    8-1/2 in. x 13 in.; 215.9 mm x 330.2 mm

Number of Pages:
    13

Descriptors:
    Culture, Government, Alexander Woollcott

Review:
    Wright on culture and on American governmental buildings. Wright
    provides two endings to this article. See also B207.

B206a

Date:
    February 11, 1936

Type of Manuscript:
    Letter

To:
    Paul R. Hanna

From:
    Frank Lloyd Wright
    Chandler, Arizona

Source:
    Paul R. and Jean S. Hanna
    Frank Lloyd Wright's Hanna House: The Clients' Report, pp. 19-20

Number of Words:
    49

Descriptors:
    Paul R. Hanna, Paul R. Hanna Residence, Chandler (Arizona),
    La Hacienda, Leland Stanford

Review:
  Wright invites Paul R. Hanna to view some houses on which Wright
  is working.

B207

Date:
  February 14, 1936

Type of Manuscript:
  Typescript speech

Title:
  "An Architect Speaking for Culture"

By:
  Frank Lloyd Wright

Collection:
  The John Lloyd Wright Collection
  The Avery Architectural Library
  Columbia University
  Folder 5

Medium:
  Typed

Number of Pages:
  7

Descriptors:
  Third Annual Woman's Congress, Palmer House (Chicago), *The
  Chicago Tribune*

Review:
  Wright's speech was delivered to the Third Annual Woman's Congress
  at Palmer House in Chicago. See also B206.

B208

Date:
  February 1936 (February 1937?)

Type of Manuscript:
  Typescript of newspaper article

Title:
  "At Taliesin"

By:
  Frank Lloyd Wright

Collection:
  The Library of Congress, Manuscript Division
  The Frank Lloyd Wright Papers
  Speech and Article File, 1936

Medium:
  Typed double spaced

Size:
   8-1/2 in. x 13 in.; 215.9 mm x 330.2 mm

Number of Pages:
   3

Descriptors:
   The Realtor, Cemeteries, Blue Sky Mausoleum Project,
   Getty Tomb (Graceland Cemetery), Ryerson Tomb (Graceland
   Cemetery), Wainwright Tomb (St. Louis), Louis H. Sullivan,
   "Revolutionists" (Soviet film)

Review:
   This is a portion of a lecture given by Wright at a convention
   of the Memorial Craftsmen Union of America. Wright discusses, at
   length, his concept of cemetery design. The article was prepared
   for publication in *The Capital Times* of Madison, Wisconsin.
   The "At Taliesin" column was a regular feature of the newspaper
   during that period. Also, Wright announces that the Soviet film
   "Revolutionists" is to be shown at the Taliesin Playhouse on
   February 28. This article appeared in the "At Taliesin" column
   of *The Capital Times* on February 26, 1937, which strongly suggests
   that the date of this article is February 1937 rather than February
   1936 as noted in pencil on the original document.

B208a

Date:
   April 2, 1936

Type of Manuscript:
   Letter

To:
   Paul R. Hanna

From:
   Frank Lloyd Wright

Source:
   Paul R. and Jean S. Hanna
   Frank Lloyd Wright's Hanna House: The Clients' Report, pp. 20-21

Number of Words:
   357

Descriptors:
   Paul R. Hanna, Paul R. Hanna Residence

Review:
   Wright explains his design for the Paul R. Hanna Residence to
   Hanna.

B209

Date:
   May 8, 1936

Type of Manuscript:
   Letter

To:
George Beal

From:
Frank Lloyd Wright

Collection:
Frank Lloyd Wright Collection
Kenneth Spencer Research Library
University of Kansas

Medium:
Typed on onion skin paper and signed

Size:
8-3/8 in. x 12-7/8 in.; 213 mm x 328 mm

Number of Pages:
1

Number of Words:
67

Descriptors:
George Beal

Review:
Wright comments on an article which Beal has written. Wright
invites Beal to spend the summer at Taliesin near Spring Green.

B210

Date:
May 18, 1936

Type of Manuscript:
Letter

To:
William T. Evjue
Madison, Wisconsin

From:
Frank Lloyd Wright
Taliesin
Spring Green, Wisconsin

Collection:
The William Theodore Evjue Papers, 1905-1969
The State Historical Society of Wisconsin
MSS 244, Box 155, Folder 21

Medium:
Typed and signed "F.L.LW."

Number of Pages:
1

Number of Words:
57

Descriptors:
William T. Evjue, *The Capital Times*, "At Taliesin" Newspaper
Column

Review:
   Several articles written by Wright did not appear in the weekly
   "At Taliesin" column of *The Capital Times* and Wright asks Evjue why
   they did not.

B210a

Date:
   May 31, 1936

Type of Manuscript:
   Letter

To:
   Paul R. Hanna

From:
   Frank Lloyd Wright

Source:
   Paul R. and Jean S. Hanna
   Frank Lloyd Wright's Hanna House: The Clients' Report, pp. 23-24

Number of Words:
   79

Descriptors:
   Paul R. Hanna, Paul R. Hanna Residence

Review:
   Wright sends Hanna his first bill for architectural services
   rendered for the Paul R. Hanna Residence.

B210b

Date:
   June 17, 1936

Type of Manuscript:
   Letter

To:
   Paul R. Hanna

From:
   Frank Lloyd Wright

Source:
   Paul R. and Jean S. Hanna
   Frank Lloyd Wright's Hanna House: The Clients' Report, pp. 24-25

Number of Words:
   549

Descriptors:
   Paul R. Hanna, Paul R. Hanna Residence, Edgar Kaufmann
   "Fallingwater" Residence, Mrs. Abby Beecher Roberts Resi-
   dence, Robert D. Lusk Residence Project, Palo Alto, Jean Hanna

Review:
   Frank Lloyd Wright explains his fee schedule for the architectural
   work for the design of the Paul R. Hanna Residence.

B211

Date:
July 16, 1936

Type of Manuscript:
Typescript article

Title:
"Introducing a Son and a House in the Wood"

By:
Frank Lloyd Wright

Collection:
The John Lloyd Wright Collection
The Avery Architectural Library
Columbia University
Folder 5

Medium:
Typed with handwritten corrections by Wright

Review:
The text of this article was reproduced in John Lloyd Wright's
My Father Who Is on Earth, (New York: G.P. Putnam's Sons, 1946),
pp. 114-116.

B212

Date:
July 24, 1936

Type of Manuscript:
Telegram

To:
Baker Brownell
Chicago, Illinois

From:
Frank Lloyd Wright

Collection:
Frank Lloyd Wright Correspondence with Baker Brownell,
1931-1939
Northwestern University Archives
Northwestern University Library

Medium:
Western Union Telegram

Size:
6-1/2 in. x 8 in.; 165.1 mm x 203.2 mm

Number of Pages:
1

Number of Words:
21

Descriptors:
Baker Brownell

Review:
  Wright invites Brownell to visit Taliesin at Spring Green, Wisconsin.

B213

Date:
  July 29, 1936

Type of Manuscript:
  Typescript of newspaper article

Title:
  "At Taliesin"

By:
  Frank Lloyd Wright
  Taliesin

Collection:
  The Library of Congress, Manuscript Division
  The Frank Lloyd Wright Papers
  Speech and Article File, 1936

Medium:
  Typed double spaced

Size:
  8-1/2 in. x 11-1/8 in.; 215.9 mm x 282.6 mm

Number of Pages:
  2

Descriptors:
  Taliesin, Guy Tugwell, "The Plow that Broke the Plains" (film),
  Pare Lorentz, Virgil Thompson, Thomas Chalmer, Russian Movies,
  Hollywood, Peter Lorre, Madeleine Carroll, W. Somerset Maugham,
  "Secret Agent" (film)

Review:
  This article was prepared for publication in *The Capital Times*
  of Madison, Wisconsin. The "At Taliesin" column was a regular
  feature of that newspaper at the time. Also, Wright reviews a
  film entitled "The Plow that Broke the Plains" which had recently
  played at Taliesin Playhouse.

B214

Date:
  August 18, 1936

Type of Manuscript:
  Telegram

To:
  Baker Brownell
  Chicago, Illinois

From:
  Frank Lloyd Wright
  Spring Green, Wisconsin

Collection:
    Frank Lloyd Wright Correspondence with Baker Brownell,
    1931-1939
    Northwestern University Archives
    Northwestern University Library

Medium:
    Western Union Telegram

Size:
    6-1/2 in. x 8 in.; 165.1 mm x 203.2 mm

Number of Pages:
    1

Number of Words:
    15

Descriptors:
    Baker Brownell

Review:
    Wright invites Brownell to visit Taliesin at Spring Green.

B214a

Date:
    August 28, 1936

Type of Manuscript:
    Letter

To:
    Paul R. and Jean S. Hanna

From:
    Frank Lloyd Wright

Source:
    Paul R. and Jean S. Hanna
    Frank Lloyd Wright's Hanna House: The Clients' Report, pp. 27-28

Number of Words:
    202

Descriptors:
    Paul R. Hanna, Paul R. Hanna Residence, Jean S. Hanna

Review:
    Wright discusses the costs of earth filling at the site of the
    Paul R. Hanna Residence which would be necessary in order to
    construct the terraces on the sloping site.

B214b

Date:
    September 2, 1936

Type of Manuscript:
    Probably a telegram (not clear in source)

To:
    Paul R. Hanna

From:
    Frank Lloyd Wright

Source:
    Paul R. and Jean S. Hanna
    Frank Lloyd Wright's Hanna House: The Clients' Report, pp. 28

Number of Words:
    36

Descriptors:
    Paul R. Hanna, Paul R. Hanna Residence

Review:
    Wright tells Hanna that he can make a model of the Paul R. Hanna
    Residence in winter.

B215

Date:
    October 10, 1936

Type of Manuscript:
    Letter

To:
    Baker Brownell
    Fort Meyers, Florida

From:
    Frank Lloyd Wright

Collection:
    Frank Lloyd Wright Correspondence with Baker Brownell,
    1931-1939
    Northwestern University Archives
    Northwestern University Library

Medium:
    Typed, signed "F.L.W."

Size:
    8-1/2 in. x 8-1/2 in.; 215.9 mm x 215.9 mm

Number of Pages:
    1

Number of Words:
    57

Descriptors:
    Baker Brownell, *Architecture and Modern Life*

Review:
    Wright signs the contract to co-author *Architecture and Modern
    Life* with Brownell. A brief statement is made by Wright on his
    feelings concerning whose name should be placed first as author
    of the book. The book was published in 1937 under Baker Brownell
    and Frank Lloyd Wright.

B216

Date:
 October 10, 1936

Type of Manuscript:
 Letter

To:
 E. Willis Jones
 Chicago, Illinois

From:
 Frank Lloyd Wright
 Taliesin
 Spring Green, Wisconsin

Collection:
 Frank Lloyd Wright Correspondence with E. Willis Jones,
 1936-1959
 Special Collections Department
 Northwestern University Library

Medium:
 Typed, signed "F.L.W."

Size:
 8-1/2 in. x 11 in.; 215.9 mm x 279.4 mm

Number of Pages:
 1

Number of Words:
 37

Descriptors:
 E. Willis Jones

Review:
 Wright invites Jones to visit Taliesin at Spring Green.

B217

Date:
 November 15, 1936

Type of Manuscript:
 Building Contract for Architectural Services

For:
 Herbert Jacobs First Residence at Madison, Wisconsin

Collection:
 The Herbert and Katherine Jacobs Frank Lloyd Wright
 Collection
 The Art Institute of Chicago
 Documents, Box 1

Medium:
 Handwritten, signed "Frank Lloyd Wright"

Size:
 8-1/2 in. x 11 in.; 215.9 mm x 279.4 mm

Number of Pages:
1

Descriptors:
Herbert Jacobs, Herbert Jacobs First Residence

Review:
A very brief contract for Wright's services for the design of
the First Herbert Jacobs Residence. The contract was handwritten
by Mrs. Herbert Jacobs and signed by Frank Lloyd Wright. The
contract is photographically reproduced on page 19 of Herbert
and Katherine Jacobs' *Building with Frank Lloyd Wright: An
Illustrated Memoir*.

B218

Date:
November 28, 1936

Type of Manuscript:
Cancelled bank check

To:
Frank Lloyd Wright

From:
Herbert Jacobs

Collection:
The Herbert and Katherine Jacobs Frank Lloyd Wright
Collection
The Art Institute of Chicago
Documents, Box 1

Medium:
Bank check, signed "Frank Lloyd Wright"

Number of Pages:
1

Descriptors:
Herbert Jacobs, Herbert Jacobs First Residence

Review:
Probably a payment to Wright for services on Jacobs's first
residence.

B218a

Date:
November 28, 1936

Type of Manuscript:
Probably a telegram (not clear in source)

To:
Paul R. Hanna

From:
Frank Lloyd Wright

Source:
Paul R. and Jean S. Hanna
Frank Lloyd Wright's Hanna House: The Clients' Report, p. 31.

Number of Words:
4

Descriptors:
Paul R. Hanna, Paul R. Hanna Residence

Review:
Wright is preparing the construction specifications for the Paul R. Hanna Residence.

B218b

Date:
November 30, 1936

Type of Manuscript:
General Instructions to Builder

To:
Paul R. Hanna

From:
Frank Lloyd Wright
Taliesin
Spring Green, Wisconsin

Source:
Paul R. and Jean S. Hanna
Frank Lloyd Wright's Hanna House: The Clients' Report, pp. 34-37

Descriptors:
Paul R. Hanna, Paul R. Hanna Residence

Review:
Wright's "General Instructions to Builder" for the construction of the Paul R. Hanna Residence.

B218c

Date:
December 1, 1936

Type of Manuscript:
Letter

To:
Paul R. Hanna

From:
Frank Lloyd Wright

Source:
Paul R. and Jean S. Hanna
Frank Lloyd Wright's Hanna House: The Clients' Report, pp. 33-34

Number of Words:
118

Descriptors:
    Paul R. Hanna, Paul R. Hanna Residence, Stanford University

Review:
    Wright transmits the specifications for the Paul R. Hanna Residence
    to Hanna.

B218d

Date:
    Undated (1936?)

Type of Manuscript:
    Memo of Agreement (contract)

Between:
    Paul R. Hanna and Frank Lloyd Wright

Source:
    Paul R. and Jean S. Hanna
    Frank Lloyd Wright's Hanna House: The Clients' Report, p. 23

Medium:
    Handwritten note by Frank Lloyd Wright

Number of Pages:
    1

Number of Words:
    109

Descriptors:
    Paul R. Hanna, Paul R. Hanna Residence, Stanford University

Review:
    The contract for architectural services for the Paul R. Hanna
    Residence between Frank Lloyd Wright as architect and Paul R.
    Hanna as owner.

B219

Date:
    December 30, 1936

Type of Manuscript:
    Typescript article

Title:
    "The Country Doctor"

By:
    Frank Lloyd Wright
    Taliesin

Collection:
    The Library of Congress, Manuscript Division
    The Frank Lloyd Wright Papers
    Speech and Article File, 1936

Medium:
    Typed double spaced, with handwritten corrections by
    Wright

Size:
  8-1/2 in. x 11-1/8 in.; 215.9 mm x 282.6 mm

Number of Pages:
  2

Descriptors:
  Dr. Ochner, Ian McLaren, Alexander Woollcott, Doctors

Review:
  The value of rural doctors is evaluated by Wright after his
  recovery from a severe illness.

REFERENCES

Books:

Brownell, Baker, and Frank Lloyd Wright.
  Architecture and Modern Life. New York: Harper and Brothers
  Publishers, 1937.

Cowles, Linn Ann.
  *An Index and Guide to "An Autobiography," the 1943 Edition by
  Frank Lloyd Wright.* Hopkins, Minnesota: Greenwich Design, 1976.

Drexler, Arthur (ed.).
  The Drawings of Frank Lloyd Wright. New York: Horizon Press for
  the Museum of Modern Art, 1962.

Fries, H. de (ed.).
  Frank Lloyd Wright: Aus dem Lebenswerke eines Architekten. Berlin:
  Verlag Ernst Pollak, 1926.

Gutheim, Frederick (ed.).
  Frank Lloyd Wright on Architecture: Selected Writings, 1894-1940.
  New York: Duell, Sloan and Pearce, 1941.

Hanna, Paul R. and Jean S. Hanna.
  Frank Lloyd Wright's Hanna House: The Clients' Report. Cambridge:
  Massachusetts, The M.I.T. Press, 1981.

Hitchcock, Henry-Russell.
  *In the Nature of Materials: 1887-1941, the Buildings of Frank
  Lloyd Wright.* New York: Duell, Sloan and Pearce, 1942.

Izzo, Alberto, and Camillo Gubitos (eds.).
  Frank Lloyd Wright, Dessins 1887-1959. Paris: C.E.R.A. Ecole
  Nationale Supérieure des Beaux-Arts, 1977.

Jacobs, Herbert, and Katherine Jacobs.
  Building with Frank Lloyd Wright: An Illustrated Memoir. San
  Francisco: Chronicle Books, 1978.

Storrer, William Allin.
  The Architecture of Frank Lloyd Wright, a Complete Catalog, Second
  Edition. Cambridge, Massachusetts: The M.I.T. Press, 1978.

Tafel, Edgar.
Apprentice to Genius: Years with Frank Lloyd Wright. New York: McGraw-Hill, Inc., 1979.

Twombly, Robert C.
Frank Lloyd Wright: An Interpretive Biography. New York: Harper and Row, 1973.

Twombly, Robert C.
Frank Lloyd Wright: His Life and His Architecture. New York: John Wiley and Sons, Inc., 1979.

Wright, Frank Lloyd.
The Hillside Home School of the Allied Arts: Why We Want This School. Taliesin: The Taliesin Fellowship, October 1931.

Wright, Frank Lloyd.
Modern Architecture, Being the Kahn Lectures for 1930. Princeton, New Jersey: Princeton University Press, 1931.

Wright, Frank Lloyd.
An Autobiography. New York: Longmans, Green and Company, 1932.

Wright, Frank Lloyd.
The Disappearing City. New York: William Farquhar Payson, 1932.

Wright, Frank Lloyd.
The Taliesin Fellowship. Taliesin: The Taliesin Fellowship, January 1, 1933.

Wright, Frank Lloyd.
The Taliesin Fellowship. Taliesin: The Taliesin Fellowship, December 1933.

Wright, Frank Lloyd (ed.).
Taliesin I, No. 1. Taliesin: The Taliesin Fellowship, 1934.

Wright, Frank Lloyd.
Taliesin I, No. 1. Taliesin: The Taliesin Fellowship, October 1940.

Wright, Frank Lloyd.
When Democracy Builds. Chicago: University of Chicago Press, 1945.

Wright, Frank Lloyd.
The Living City. New York: Horizon Press, 1958.

Wright, Frank Lloyd.
Drawings for a Living Architecture. New York: Horizon Press for the Bear Run Foundation, Inc., and the Edgar J. Kaufmann Charitable Foundation, 1959.

Wright, Frank Lloyd.
An Autobiography. New York: Horizon Press, 1977.

Periodicals:

Wright, Frank Lloyd.
"Eclecticism by Way of 'Taste' Is America's Substitute for Culture,"
Tower-Town Topics, Vol. 2, May 1931, p. 19.

Behrendt, Walter Curt.
"Frank Lloyd Wright," *Frankfurter Zeitung*, June 30, 1931.

Anonymous.
"Wright in Berlin," *Art Digest*, Vol. 5, July 1, 1931, p. 12.

Anonyous.
"Frank Lloyd Wright: Ausstellung in der Akademie der Kunste,
Berlin," *Bauwelt*, Vol. 22, July 2, 1931, p. 914.

Anonymous.
"Ausstellungen," *Baugilde*, Vol. 13, July 25, 1931, p. 1190.

Wright, Frank Lloyd.
"Address of Frank Lloyd Wright at the 17th Annual Convention,"
The Michigan Society of Architects Journal, July 1931.

Anonymous.
"Models by Frank Lloyd Wright in Berlin Exhibition," *Art News*,
Vol. 29, August 15, 1931, p. 16.

Bull, Harry Adsit.
"Notes of the Month," *International Studio*, Vol. 89, August 1931,
p. 54.

Landau, Dora.
"An American Architect Exhibits in Berlin," *American Magazine of
Art*, Vol. 23, August 1931, p. 165.

Anonymous.
"Frank Lloyd Wright Tells of the Broadacre City," *Bulletin of the
City Club of Chicago*, Vol. 25, February 15, 1932, pp. 27, 29.

Wright, Frank Lloyd.
"For All May Raise the Flowers Now for All Have Got the Seed,"
T-Square, Vol. 2, February 1932, pp. 6-8.

Wright, Frank Lloyd.
"O Thee I Sing," *Shelter*, Vol. 2, April 1932, pp. 10-12.

Wright, Frank Lloyd.
"A Treatise on Ornament," *The Saturday Review of Literature*, Vol.
8, May 21, 1932, p. 744.

Wright, Frank Lloyd.
"Of Thee I Sing," *New Humanist*, Vol. 5, May/June 1932, pp. 1-5.

Wright, Frank Lloyd.
"The City of To-morrow," *Pictorial Review*, Vol. 34, March 1933,
pp. 4, 61.

Wright, Frank Lloyd.
"The Chicago World's Fair," *The Architects' Journal* (England),
Vol. 78, July 13, 1933, pp. 36, 45-47.

Wright, Frank Lloyd.
"In the Show Window at Macy's," *Architectural Forum*, Vol. 59,
November 1933, pp. 419-420.

Wright, Frank Lloyd.
"What Is the Modern Idea?" *Liberty*, Vol. 11, February 10, 1934,
p. 49.

Wright, Frank Lloyd.
"The Taliesin Fellowship," *Wisconsin Alumni Magazine*, Vol. 35,
March 1934, pp. 152-153, 176.

Anonymous.
"An Architect Visualizes 'Broadacre City,'" *American City*, Vol. 50,
No. 4, April 1935, pp. 85, 87.

Wright, Frank Lloyd.
"Broadacre City: A New Community Plan," *Architectural Record*, Vol.
77, April 1935, pp. 243-254.

Anonymous.
"Broadacre City: Frank Lloyd Wright, Architect," *American Architect*,
Vol. 146, May 1935, pp. 55-62.

Alexander, Stephen.
"Frank Lloyd Wright's Utopia," *New Masses*, Vol. 15, June 18, 1935,
p. 28.

Wright, Frank Lloyd.
"Freedom Based on Form," *New Masses*, Vol. 16, July 23, 1935, pp.
23-24.

Wright, Frank Lloyd.
"Taliesin: Our Cause," *Professional Art Quarterly*, Vol. 2, No. 3,
March 1936, pp. 6, 7, and 24.

Wright, Frank Lloyd.
"Recollections--The United States, 1893-1920," *The Architects'
Journal* (England), Vol. 84, July 16, 23, 30, and August 6, 1936,
pp. 76-78, 111-112, 141-142, and 173-174.

Wright, Frank Lloyd.
"Apprenticeship--Training for the Architect," *Architectural Record*,
Vol. 80, September 1936, pp. 179, 207-210.

Anonymous.
"Sandbags in Racine," *Inland Architect*, Vol. 13, August/September
1969, pp. 18-19.

Crawford, Alan.
"Ten Letters from Frank Lloyd Wright to Charles Robert Ashbee,"
Journal of the Society of Architectural Historians of Great Britain
(England), Vol. 13, 1970, pp. 64-76.

Grabow, Stephen.
"Frank Lloyd Wright and the American City: The Broadacre Debate,"
Journal of the American Institute of Planners, Vol. 18, April
1977, pp. 115-124.

Newspapers:

Anonymous.
"Fight Ban on Wright as Architect for Fair: Adherents of Modernism
to Meet Here Tonight to Discuss Action by Chicago," *The New York
Times*, February 26, 1931, p. 17, col. 5.

Anonymous.
"Architects Debate on Chicago's Fair: Leaving F.L. Wright off of
Planning Board Termed an 'Insult' at Meeting Here," *The New York
Times*, February 27, 1931, p. 13, col. 5.

Anonymous.
"Frank Lloyd Wright Sails--Architect Will Join Jury to Make
$1,500,000 Santo Domingo Award," *The New York Times*, September 20,
1931, p. 31, col. 4.

Anonymous.
"Briton's Design Wins for Columbus Crypt: J.L. Gleave Plan for
Lighthouse of Santo Domingo Chosen, F.L. Wright Reveals," *The New
York Times*, November 7, 1931, p. 15, col. 2.

Wright, Frank Lloyd.
"Broadacre City: An Architect's Vision--Spread Wide and Integrated,
It Will Solve the Traffic Problem and Make Life Richer, Says Frank
Lloyd Wright," *The New York Times Magazine*, March 20, 1932, section
5, pp. 8 and 9.

Anonymous.
"F.L. Wright to Open a Bookless School: Architect to Have Students
Learn His Profession by Doing Actual Building: Physical Labor
Required: Those Attending to be Known as 'Apprentices,' Will Also
Take up the Arts and Industry," *The New York Times*, August 19,
1932, p. 10, col. 3.

Anonymous.
"Wisconsin Architect Defies the Depression: Apprentices Cut Rock,
Fell Trees and Raise Food on Frank Lloyd Wright's Project," *The
Milwaukee Journal* (Milwaukee, Wisconsin), September 4, 1932.

Anonymous.
"Unique Theatre Opening at Taliesin," *The Capital Times*, (Madison,
Wisconsin), November 1, 1932.

Anonymous.
"Financial Aid for Students: Allied Arts School in Wisconsin Has
a Plan for Marketing the Products of Pupils," *The New York Times*,
November 6, 1932, section 8, p. 5, col. 5.

Anonymous.
"Wright Students Cut Dreams in Hard Stone," *The Milwaukee Journal*
(Milwaukee, Wisconsin), November 25, 1934.

Anonymous.
"Architect Models New Type of City: Frank Lloyd Wright to Show at
Exposition Here Plan for Self-Contained Group: 1,400 Families
to be Unit: Small Farms and Factories and Home Industries Are Held
to be Ideal for Future," *The New York Times*, March 27, 1935,
p. 16, col. 1.

Anonymous.
"Exhibit Model City: Design by F.L. Wright on View in Rockefeller
Center," *The New York Times*, April 14, 1935, sections 10, 11, p.
2, col. 2.

CHAPTER 5

USONIA (1937 TO 1942)

Introduction

During this period Wright produced 88 designs, representing about 9 percent of all his lifetime work. Of these 88 designs 54 were single-family residences, including, to mention only a few, the Herbert F. Johnson "Wingspread" Residence at Wind Point, Wisconsin, of 1937; the Ben Rebhuhn Residence at Great Neck Estates, New York, of 1937; the Joseph Euchtman Residence at Baltimore, Maryland, of 1939; the Goetsch-Winckler Residence at Okemos, Michigan, of 1939; the Lloyd Lewis Residence at Libertyville, Illinois, of 1939; the George D. Sturges Residence at Brentwood Heights, California, of 1939; the Loren Pope Residence, originally at Falls Church, Virginia, of 1939; and the Gregor Affleck Residence at Bloomfield Hills, Michigan, of 1940.

Wright's earliest works for his Usonian home concepts are examined through documents concerning the First Residence for Herbert Jacobs near Madison, Wisconsin, the Loren Pope Residence at Falls Church, Virginia (both of which introduced new construction techniques for moderately priced dwellings), and the Paul R. Hanna "Honeycomb" Residence. General correspondence indexed from Wright during this time includes letters to E. Willis Jones; Baker Brownell; William A. Kittredge; Charles Robert Ashbee; Taliesin Fellows Gordon Chadwick and Edgar Tafel; William T. Evjue, Paul R. Hanna, Dorathi Bock Pierre; John Lloyd Wright; Peter DeVries, editor of *Poetry Magazine*; and Taylor A. Woolley.

More than twenty original typescript articles and speeches are located and catalogued, including Wright's famous series of lectures entitled "Watson Chair Foundation of the Sulgrave Manor Board, The Sir George Watson Lectures for 1939, A Series of Four Evenings on An Organic Architecture, The Architecture of Democracy," delivered by Wright in England in May of 1939.

B219a

Date:
   January 2, 1937

Type of Manuscript:
   Letter

To:
   Paul R. Hanna

From:
   Frank Lloyd Wright

Source:
    Paul R. and Jean S. Hanna
    Frank Lloyd Wright's Hanna House: The Clients' Report, pp. 40-41

Number of Words:
    218

Descriptors:
    Paul R. Hanna, Paul R. Hanna Residence, Harold Turner

Review:
    Wright talks of the price of the Paul R. Hanna Residence and
    mentions that he has just overcome an illness.

B220

Date:
    January 23, 1937

Type of Manuscript:
    Letter

To:
    John Lloyd Wright
    Michigan City, Indiana

From:
    Frank Lloyd Wright
    Taliesin
    Spring Green, Wisconsin

Collection:
    The John Lloyd Wright Collection
    The Avery Architectural Library
    Columbia University
    Folder 10

Medium:
    Typed, signed "Dad"

Size:
    8-1/2 in. x 11 in.; 215.9 mm x 279.4 mm

Number of Pages:
    1

Number of Words:
    44

Descriptors:
    John Lloyd Wright

Review:
    Frank Lloyd Wright invites John Lloyd to visit him at Taliesin,
    Spring Green, Wisconsin.

B221

Date:
    January 25, 1937

Type of Manuscript:
    Cancelled bank check

To:
    Frank Lloyd Wright

From:
   Herbert Jacobs

Collection:
   The Herbert and Katherine Jacobs Frank Lloyd Wright Collection
   The Art Institute of Chicago
   Documents, Box 1

Medium:
   Bank check, signed "Frank Lloyd Wright"

Number of Pages:
   1

Descriptors:
   Herbert Jacobs, Herbert Jacobs First Residence

Review:
   Payment to Wright probably for Wright's architectural services
   on the Herbert Jacobs First Residence at Madison, Wisconsin.

B222

Date:
   January 26, 1937

Type of Manuscript:
   Letter

To:
   E. Willis Jones
   Chicago, Illinois

From:
   Frank Lloyd Wright
   Taliesin
   Spring Green, Wisconsin

Collection:
   Frank Lloyd Wright Correspondence with E. Willis Jones,
   1936-1959
   Special Collections Department
   Northwestern University Library

Medium:
   Typed, signed "F.L. W."

Size:
   8-1/2 in. x 11 in.; 215.9 mm x 279.4 mm

Number of Pages:
   1

Number of Words:
   70

Descriptors:
   E. Willis Jones, Montgomery Ward

Review:
   Talk of a possible Montgomery Ward building project?

B222a

Date:
    January 26, 1937

Type of Manuscript:
    Telegram

To:
    Paul R. Hanna

From:
    Frank Lloyd Wright

Source:
    Paul R. and Jean S. Hanna
    Frank Lloyd Wright's Hanna House: The Clients' Report, p. 48

Number of Words:
    135

Descriptors:
    Paul R. Hanna, Paul R. Hanna Residence

Review:
    Wright discusses design details regarding the Paul R. Hanna
    Residence.

B222b

Date:
    January 27, 1937

Type of Manuscript:
    Letter

To:
    Paul R. Hanna

From:
    Frank Lloyd Wright

Source:
    Paul R. and Jean S. Hanna
    Frank Lloyd Wright's Hanna House: The Clients' Report, pp. 50-52

Number of Words:
    925

Descriptors:
    Paul R. Hanna, Paul R. Hanna Residence, Imperial Hotel,
    Simmons Factory

Review:
    Wright discusses, at length, design details of the Paul R. Hanna
    Residence.

B222c

Date:
    Mid-January 1937

Type of Manuscript:
   Telegram

To:
   Paul R. Hanna

From:
   Frank Lloyd Wright

Source:
   Paul R. and Jean S. Hanna
   Frank Lloyd Wright's Hanna House: The Clients' Report, p. 44

Number of Words:
   5

Descriptors:
   Paul R. Hanna, Paul R. Hanna Residence

Review:
   Wright sends Hanna the blueprints for the Paul R. Hanna Residence.

B222d

Date:
   Mid-January 1937

Type of Manuscript:
   Letter

To:
   Paul R. Hanna

From:
   Frank Lloyd Wright

Source:
   Paul R. and Jean S. Hanna
   Frank Lloyd Wright's Hanna House: The Clients' Report, p. 44

Number of Words:
   61

Descriptors:
   Paul R. Hanna, Paul R. Hanna Residence

Review:
   Wright sends a brief note along with a bill for architectural
   services rendered for the Paul R. Hanna Residence.

B222e

Date:
   February 2, 1937

Type of Manuscript:
   Telegram

To:
   Paul R. Hanna

From:
   Frank Lloyd Wright

Source:
Paul R. and Jean S. Hanna
Frank Lloyd Wright's Hanna House: The Clients' Report, p. 54

Number of Words:
16

Descriptors:
Paul R. Hanna, Paul R. Hanna Residence

Review:
Wright wants to make some design changes to the Paul R. Hanna Residence.

B222f

Date:
February 3, 1937

Type of Manuscript:
Telegram

To:
Paul R. Hanna

From:
Frank Lloyd Wright

Source:
Paul R. and Jean S. Hanna
Frank Lloyd Wright's Hanna House: The Clients' Report, p. 55

Number of Words:
16

Descriptors:
Paul R. Hanna, Paul R. Hanna Residence

Review:
Wright is to send revised detailed drawings regarding the design of the Paul R. Hanna Residence.

B222g

Date:
February 5, 1937

Type of Manuscript:
Letter

To:
Paul R. Hanna

From:
Frank Lloyd Wright

Source:
Paul R. and Jean S. Hanna
Frank Lloyd Wright's Hanna House: The Clients' Report, p. 56

Number of Words:
236

Descriptors:
    Paul R. Hanna, Paul R. Hanna Residence, Electro-gas
    Company

Review:
    Wright discusses the basement of the Paul R. Hanna Residence and
    its heating system.

B223

Date:
    February 14, 1937

Type of Manuscript:
    Letter

To:
    Baker Brownell
    Northwestern University
    Evanston, Illinois

From:
    Frank Lloyd Wright
    Taliesin
    Spring Green, Wisconsin

Collection:
    Frank Lloyd Wright Correspondence with Baker Brownell,
    1931-1939
    Northwestern University Archives
    Northwestern University Library

Medium:
    Typed on Taliesin design stationery, signed "F.L. W "

Size:
    8 in. x 10-1/8 in.; 203.2 mm x 257.2 mm

Number of Pages:
    1

Number of Words:
    70

Descriptors:
    Baker Brownell, *Architecture and Modern Life*

Review:
    Concerning preliminary draft of *Architecture and Modern Life*.
    Wright also invites Brownell to visit him at Taliesin. The book,
    co-authored by Brownell and Wright, was published by Harper and
    Brothers, New York, in 1937.

B224

Date:
    March 30, 1937

Type of Manuscript:
    Typescript of article

Title:
   "At Taliesin"

By:
   Frank Lloyd Wright

Collection:
   The Library of Congress, Manuscript Division
   The Frank Lloyd Wright Papers
   Speech and Article File, 1937

Medium:
   Typed double spaced

Size:
   8-1/2 in. x 13 in.; 215.9 mm x 330.2 mm

Number of Pages:
   3

Descriptors:
   J. Russell Pope, Thomas Jefferson, Washington, D.C.,
   Lincoln Memorial (Washington, D.C.), Congressional Library
   (Washington, D.C.), Union Station (Washington, D.C.), Taliesin
   Playhouse

Review:
   A protest of Washington, D.C., architecture. Also, an announcement
   concerning what will be playing at the Taliesin Playhouse on
   April 4, 1937.

B224a

Date:
   April 25, 1937

Type of Manuscript:
   Handwritten note

To:
   Paul R. Hanna

From:
   Frank Lloyd Wright

Source:
   Paul R. and Jean S. Hanna
   Frank Lloyd Wright's Hanna House: The Clients' Report, p. 65

Medium:
   Handwritten, signed "FLlW"

Number of Pages:
   1

Number of Words:
   154

Descriptors:
   Paul R. Hanna, Paul R. Hanna Residence

Review:
   The note has a rough design sketch of a detail for the structural
   support system of the Paul R. Hanna Residence design.

B225

Date:
    May 22, 1937

Type of Manuscript:
    Telegram

To:
    Baker Brownell
    Northwestern University
    Evanston, Illinois

From:
    Frank Lloyd Wright
    Spring Green, Wisconsin

Collection:
    Frank Lloyd Wright Correspondence with Baker Brownell,
    1931-1939
    Northwestern University Archives
    Northwestern University Library

Medium:
    Western Union Telegram

Size:
    6-1/2 in. x 8 in.; 165.1 mm x 203.2 mm

Number of Pages:
    1

Number of Words:
    50

Descriptors:
    Baker Brownell, *Architecture and Modern Life*

Review:
    Wright threatens to stop working on *Architecture and Modern Life*
    because of Brownell's revisions of Wright's writings for the book.
    It was finally published by Harper and Brothers in 1937.

B226

Date:
    July 31, 1937

Type of Manuscript:
    Letter

To:
    Herbert Jacobs
    Madison, Wisconsin

From:
    Frank Lloyd Wright
    Taliesin
    Spring Green, Wisconsin

Collection:
    The Herbert and Katherine Jacobs Frank Lloyd Wright
    Collection

The Art Institute of Chicago
Documents, Box 1

Medium:
Typed on Taliesin design stationery with handwritten
corrections, signed "F.L. W"

Size:
10 in. x 12 in.; 254.0 mm x 304.8 mm

Number of Pages:
1

Number of Words:
119 Typed; 16 Handwritten

Descriptors:
Herbert Jacobs, Herbert Jacobs First Residence

Review:
About the construction materials of the Herbert Jacobs First
Residence at Madison, Wisconsin.

B227

Date:
August 1, 1937

Type of Manuscript:
Typescript paper

Title:
Untitled paper

By:
Frank Lloyd Wright
Taliesin

Collection:
The Library of Congress, Manuscript Division
The Frank Lloyd Wright Papers
Speech and Article File, 1937

Medium:
Typed double spaced

Size:
8-1/2 in. x 11-1/8 in.; 215.9 mm x 282.6 mm

Number of Pages:
4

Descriptors:
Capitalism, Russia, U.S.A., Unions, Fascism, Labor

Review:
Wright talks of labor unions, capitalism, and the Soviet Union.

B228

Date:
August 2, 1937

Type of Manuscript:
   Typescript article/editorial

Title:
   "At Taliesin: An Open Letter to Frank Lloyd Wright and
   a Reply"

By:
   Frank Lloyd Wright

Collection:
   The Library of Congress, Manuscript Division
   The Frank Lloyd Wright Papers
   Speech and Article File, 1937

Medium:
   Typed double spaced

Size:
   8-1/2 in. x 11-1/8 in.; 215.9 mm x 282.6 mm

Number of Pages:
   5

Descriptors:
   Capitalism, Russia, University of Wisconsin Faculty
   Branch of Communist Party, *The Capital Times*, American
   Communist Party, Republican, Socialist, Democrat

Review:
   Wright responds to a letter from the University of Wisconsin
   Faculty Branch of the Communist Party. A series of six articles
   appeared in *The Capital Times* (Madison, Wisconsin) regarding
   Wright and his trip to Soviet Russia in 1937 and the experiences
   he encountered with American Communists upon his return. These
   articles are "Architect Wright Is Soviet Guest for World Conven-
   tion" in the June 6, 1937, issue; "Wright Regrets Russia Is Using
   U.S. as Model for Architecture--Raps Communists of University as
   Racketeers After Trip" in the July 22, 1937, issue; "US, USSR
   are the Two Greatest Hopes for Better Life and Democracy, FLW
   Declares" dated August 1, 1937; "Communists Ask Wright to Explain
   Slap: Protest Charge by Architect That 'American Communists are
   Racketeers'" in the August 3, 1937, issue; Ruben Levin's article
   "Wright Lists 'Testament' of Beliefs After Visit to Russia" in
   the August 3, 1937, issue; and the reprint of the letter written
   by Wright, contained in this file, to the University of Wisconsin
   Faculty Branch of the Communist Party in an article entitled
   "Wright Denies He Said Communists Racketeers" in the August 5,
   1937, issue.

B228a

Date:
   August 6, 1937

Type of Manuscript:
   Telegram

To:
   Paul R. Hanna

From:
  Frank Lloyd Wright

Source:
  Paul R. and Jean S. Hanna
  Frank Lloyd Wright's Hanna House: The Clients' Report, p. 66

Number of Words:
  10

Descriptors:
  Paul R. Hanna, Paul R. Hanna Residence

Review:
  Wright transmits further drawings to Hanna of the residence
  which Wright designed for him.

B229

Date:
  August 11, 1937

Type of Manuscript:
  Telegram

To:
  Baker Brownell
  Chicago, Illinois

From:
  Frank Lloyd Wright
  Spring Green, Wisconsin

Collection:
  Frank Lloyd Wright Correspondence with Baker Brownell,
  1931-1939
  Northwestern University Archives
  Northwestern University Library

Medium:
  Western Union Telegram

Size:
  6-1/2 in. x 8 in.; 165.1 mm x 203.2 mm

Number of Pages:
  1

Number of Words:
  17

Descriptors:
  Baker Brownell, *Architecture and Modern Life*

Review:
  Concerns the proof sheets for Brownell's and Wright's *Architecture
  and Modern Life*.

B230

Date:
August 13, 1937

Type of Manuscript:
Telegram

To:
Baker Brownell
Chicago, Illinois

From:
Frank Lloyd Wright
Spring Green, Wisconsin

Collection:
Frank Lloyd Wright Correspondence with Baker Brownell,
1931-1939
Northwestern University Archives
Northwestern University Library

Medium:
Western Union Telegram

Size:
6-1/2 in. x 8 in.; 165.1 mm x 203.2 mm

Number of Pages:
1

Number of Words:
18

Descriptors:
Baker Brownell, *Architecture and Modern Life*

Review:
On the manuscript for *Architecture and Modern Life*.

B230a

Date:
August 18, 1937

Type of Manuscript:
Letter

To:
Paul R. Hanna

From:
Frank Lloyd Wright

Source:
Paul R. and Jean S. Hanna
Frank Lloyd Wright's Hanna House: The Clients' Report, p. 70

Number of Words:
446

Descriptors:
Paul R. Hanna, Paul R. Hanna Residence, Alice Millard

Review:
Wright is disappointed about the cost overruns during the
building of the Paul R. Hanna Residence.

B231

Date:
August 31, 1937

Type of Manuscript:
Typescript of article

Title:
"Architecture and Life in the U.S.S.R."

By:
Frank Lloyd Wright

Collection:
The Library of Congress, Manuscript Division
The Frank Lloyd Wright Papers
Speech and Article File, 1937

Medium:
Typed with handwritten notations by Wright

Size:
8-1/2 in. x 11 in.; 215.9 mm x 279.4 mm

Number of Pages:
14

Descriptors:
Soviet Russia, *Architectural Record*, *Soviet Russia
Today*

Review:
The complete text of this manuscript appeared in both *Architectural
Record* and *Soviet Russia Today*. The manuscript in this Library of
Congress file is noted as "Copy 2."

B232

Date:
September 21, 1937

Type of Manuscript:
Letter

To:
Ethel Gerts
Fairhope, Alabama

From:
Frank Lloyd Wright
Taliesin
Spring Green, Wisconsin

Collection:
The Frank Lloyd Wright Home and Studio Foundation
Oak Park, Illinois

Medium:
    Typed on Taliesin red-square design stationery,
    signed "Frank"

Size:
    10 in. x 12 in.; 254.0 mm x 304.8 mm

Number of Pages:
    1

Number of Words:
    59

Descriptors:
    Mrs. Ethel Gerts, Walter Gerts, *House Beautiful*

Review:
    Wright thanks Mrs. Gerts for sending him a copy of *House Beautiful*
    for the library at Taliesin.

B232a

Date:
    October 1, 1937

Type of Manuscript:
    Telegram

To:
    Paul R. Hanna

From:
    Frank Lloyd Wright

Source:
    Paul R. and Jean S. Hanna
    Frank Lloyd Wright's Hanna House: The Clients' Report, p. 74

Number of Words:
    11

Descriptors:
    Paul R. Hanna, Paul R. Hanna Residence

Review:
    Brief note regarding Wright's forthcoming trip to Palo Alto,
    California.

B233

Date:
    October 12, 1937

Type of Manuscript:
    Letter

To:
    William A. Kittredge
    The Lakeside Press
    Chicago, Illinois

From:
Frank Lloyd Wright
Taliesin
Spring Green

Collection:
William Kittredge Collection
Newberry Library
Chicago, Illinois

Medium:
Typed on Taliesin design stationery, signed "F.L.W."

Size:
4 in. x 8-1/2 in.; 101.6 mm x 215.9 mm

Number of Pages:
1

Number of Words:
65

Descriptors:
William Kittredge, George Switzer

Review:
Wright invites Kittredge and friends to Taliesin.

B233a

Date:
October 12, 1937

Type of Manuscript:
Telegram

To:
Paul R. Hanna

From:
Frank Lloyd Wright

Source:
Paul R. and Jean S. Hanna
Frank Lloyd Wright's Hanna House: The Clients' Report, p. 74

Number of Words:
38

Descriptors:
Paul R. Hanna, Paul R. Hanna Residence

Review:
Wright reports that he is ill and that he would like the Hannas
to visit him at Taliesin, Spring Green, Wisconsin.

B234

Date:
October 18, 1937

Type of Manuscript:
  Typescript editorial

Title:
  "Editorial for 'Izvestia'"

By:
  Frank Lloyd Wright
  Taliesin

Collection:
  The Library of Congress, Manuscript Division
  The Frank Lloyd Wright Papers
  Speech and Article File, 1937

Medium:
  Typed double spaced

Size:
  8-1/2 in. x 11-1/8 in.; 215.9 mm x 282.6 mm

Number of Pages:
  5

Descriptors:
  Russia, Capitalism, Facism, Democracy, *Izvestia*
  (Soviet publication)

Review:
  Wright writes an editorical on his views of the Soviet Union
  and their art for a Soviet publication. The editorial was
  written following a trip by Wright to the Soviet Union in 1937.

B235

Date:
  October 19, 1937

Type of Manuscript:
  Letter

To:
  William A. Kittredge
  The Lakeside Press
  Chicago, Illinois

From:
  Frank Lloyd Wright
  Taliesin
  Spring Green, Wisconsin

Collection:
  William Kittredge Collection
  Newberry Library
  Chicago, Illinois

Medium:
  Typed on Taliesin design stationery, signed "F.L W"

Size:
  4-1/8 in. x 8-1/2 in.; 104.8 mm x 215.9 mm

Number of Pages:
   1

Number of Words:
   106

Descriptors:
   William Kittredge, Moholy-Nagy, Tavern Club

Review:
   Wright informs Kittredge of his earlier than planned departure
   for Taliesin West and asks Kittredge to visit the following year
   when he is back at Spring Green, Wisconsin.

B235a

Date:
   November 1937

Type of Manuscript:
   Letter

To:
   Paul R. Hanna

From:
   Frank Lloyd Wright
   Jokake Inn
   Jokake, Arizona

Source:
   Paul R. and Jean S. Hanna
   Frank Lloyd Wright's Hanna House: The Clients' Report, pp. 74-75

Medium:
   Handwritten on Jokake Inn (Jokake, Arizona) stationery,
   signed "FLlW"

Number of Words:
   366

Descriptors:
   Paul R. Hanna, Paul R. Hanna Residence, Jokake Inn (Jokake,
   Arizona), Harold Turner

Review:
   Wright talks about his recent trip to visit the Hannas and
   suggests some minor changes to the design of the Hanna house.

B236

Date:
   Undated (1937 or 1938?)

Type of Manuscript:
   Typescript of article

Title:
   "Categorical Reply to Questions on the 'Architecture in the
   U.S.S.R.'"

By:
Frank Lloyd Wright

Collection:
The Library of Congress, Manuscript Division
The Frank Lloyd Wright Papers
Speech and Article File, 1937

Medium:
Typed double spaced, with handwritten corrections by
Wright

Size:
8-1/2 in. x 11 in.; 215.9 mm x 279.4 mm

Number of Pages:
3

Descriptors:
Soviet Russia, Design, Drawing, Architectural History,
Painting, Sculpture, Construction, Composition,
Architectural Collaboration, Problem Solutions

Review:
A basic outline of Wright's design process and underlying
philosophy used to design his buildings is uncovered through
his answers to questions on "Architecture in the U.S.S.R." Nine
very important points are made regarding problem solving in
building design, composition, drawing, architectural history,
architectual collaboration, painting and sculpture, finalizing
building design, construction, and corrections to plans.

B237

Date:
1937

Type of Manuscript:
Typescript open letter or speech

Title:
"My Dear Comrades: ..."

By:
Frank Lloyd Wright

Collection:
The Library of Congress, Manuscript Division
The Frank Lloyd Wright Papers
Speech and Article File, 1937

Medium:
Typed double spaced

Size:
8-1/2 in. x 13 in.; 215.9 mm x 330.2 mm

Number of Pages:
4

Descriptors:
U.S.S.R., U.S.A., Broadacre City, The Kremlin, Culture,
American Building

Review:
  Text of a speech which may have been presented when Wright
  visited the Soviet Union in 1937. Wright discusses the lack
  of culture in American building and architectural design.

B238

Date:
  January 10, 1938

Type of Manuscript:
  Letter

Title:
  "To the Young Man in Architecture--A Challenge"

To:
  Woolley and Evans, Architects
  724 McIntyre Building
  Salt Lake City, Utah

From:
  Frank Lloyd Wright
  Taliesin
  Spring Green, Wisconsin

Collection:
  University of Utah
  Marriott Library
  Taylor Woolley Archive, Special Collections, Item 152

Medium:
  Signed form letter

Size:
  11-7/8 in. x 10 in.; 303 mm x 254 mm

Number of Pages:
  2

Descriptors:
  Taylor A. Woolley; Woolley and Evans, Architects;
  Architectural Forum

Review:
  A form letter which states Wright's purpose for writing and
  editing *Architectural Forum*, Vol. 68, January 1938, supplement,
  pp. 1-102.

B239

Date:
  January 12, 1938

Type of Manuscript:
  Telegram

To:
  Herbert Jacobs
  Madison, Wisconsin

2-5.1 Sign directing visitors to Taliesin West (1937), Scottsdale, Arizona. Photo by the author.

2-5.2 Entrance court to Taliesin West (1937ff), Scottsdale, Arizona. Photo by the author.

2-5.3 Workroom terrace and broad steps (background), with reflecting pool (foreground), of Taliesin West (1937ff), Scottsdale, Arizona. Photo by the author.

2-5.4   Exterior terrace view of Taliesin West (1937ff), Scottsdale, Arizona. Photo by the author.

2-5.5   Exterior view of terrace near the entrance court of Taliesin West (1937ff), Scottsdale, Arizona. Photo by the author.

From:
Frank Lloyd Wright
Arizona

Collection:
The Herbert and Katherine Jacobs Frank Lloyd Wright
Collection
The Art Institute of Chicago
Documents, Box 1

Medium:
Western Union Telegram

Number of Pages:
1

Number of Words:
31

Descriptors:
Groves (Harold M. Groves?), Herbert Jacobs, Herbert Jacobs
First Residence

Review:
On the payment of a bill, probably in conjunction with the
Herbert Jacobs First Residence.

B240

Date:
June 2, 1938

Type of Manuscript:
Typescript of speech

Title:
"From an Architect's Point of View"

By:
Frank Lloyd Wright

Collection:
The Library of Congress, Manuscript Division
The Frank Lloyd Wright Papers
Speech and Article File, 1938

Medium:
Typed double spaced, with handwritten corrections by Wright

Size:
8-1/2 in. x 11 in.; 215.9 mm x 279.4 mm

Number of Pages:
9

Descriptors:
Chicago Real Estate Board, General Housing Conference
of 1938, Progress, Inventions

Review:
Excerpts from an address given by Frank Lloyd Wright at a banquet
of the Chicago Real Estate Board on the occasion of the General

Housing Conference on the evening of June 2, 1938. Wright talks of progress and inventions.

B241

Date:
July 31, 1938

Type of Manuscript:
Typescript article

Title:
"The Man and the Issue"

By:
Frank Lloyd Wright
Taliesin

Collections:
The Library of Congress, Manuscript Division
The Frank Lloyd Wright Papers
Speech and Article File, 1938

Medium:
Typed double spaced, with handwritten corrections by
Wright

Size:
8-1/2 in. x 11-1/8 in.; 215.9 mm x 282.6 mm

Number of Pages:
3

Descriptors:
Broadacre City, American Politicians, Franklin D. Roosevelt,
Tom Amlie

Review:
Political backing for Tom Amlie, a member of Congress at the
time. An article was featured in the August 11, 1938, issue of
The Capital Times (Madison, Wisconsin) entitled "Architect
Wright Boosts Tom Amlie for Senate; Calls Him 'Like FDR.'"

B242

Date:
October 25, 1938

Type of Manuscript:
Typescript of speech

Title:
"Speech to the A.F.A."

By:
Frank Lloyd Wright

Collection:
The Library of Congress, Manuscript Division
The Frank Lloyd Wright Papers
Speech and Article File, 1938

Medium:
   Typed manuscript

Size:
   8-1/2 in. x 11-1/8 in.; 215.9 mm x 282.6 mm

Number of Pages:
   14

Descriptors:
   American Federal Architect, *Federal Architect*

Review:
   Original typescript article of Wright's speech to the A.F.A.
   meeting at the Hotel Mayflower in Washington, D.C., on October
   25, 1938, which 600 Federal architects attended. The text of
   this speech later appeared in *Federal Architect.*

B243

Date:
   November 9, 1938

Type of Manuscript:
   Letter

To:
   Herbert Jacobs

From:
   Frank Lloyd Wright and others from the Taliesin Fellowship
   Spring Green, Wisconsin

Collection:
   The Herbert and Katherine Jacobs Frank Lloyd Wright Collection
   The Art Institute of Chicago
   Documents, Box 1

Medium:
   Signed letter on Taliesin design stationery

Number of Pages:
   1

Descriptors:
   Herbert Jacobs, Herbert Jacobs First Residence, Edgar
   Tafel, John Howe, Kevin Lynch

Review:
   A thank-you note for dinner signed "F.LL.W.," together with
   sixteen other signatures, including those of Edgar Tafel, John
   Howe, and Kevin Lynch, all Wright apprentices at the time.

B244

Date:
   December 4, 1938

Type of Manuscript:
   Typescript of speech

Title:
   "Madison's Public Servants ..."

By:
   Frank Lloyd Wright
   Taliesin, Spring Greeen

Collection:
   The Library of Congress, Manuscript Division
   The Frank Lloyd Wright Papers
   Speech and Article File, 1938

Medium:
   Typed double spaced

Size:
   8-1/2 in. x 11 in.; 215.9 mm x 279.4 mm

Number of Pages:
   2

Descriptors:
   Madison (Wisconsin), Unitarian Church (Madison, Wisconsin)

Review:
   Wright speaks at the Unitarian Church in Madison, Wisconsin,
   against the building of an office building by the city of
   Madison.

B245

Date:
   December 25, 1938

Type of Manuscript:
   Inscribed Japanese Print

To:
   Edgar Tafel (Edgar Tafel's mother)

From:
   Frank Lloyd Wright

Source:
   Edgar Tafel
   Apprentice to Genius: Years with Frank Lloyd Wright, p. 13

Medium:
   Handwritten, signed "FLLW"

Number of Words:
   6

Descriptors:
   Edgar Tafel, Japanese Prints, Christmas 1938

Review:
   Japanese print inscribed "To Mother Tafel, Xmas '38 FLLW" is
   shown in Tafel's book.

B246

Date:
  Undated (Fall 1938)

Type of Manuscript:
  Ditto copy of manuscript

Title:
  "Unconnected Notes on the Lecture on the Jacobs House
  by Frank Lloyd Wright"

By:
  Frank Lloyd Wright

Collection:
  The Herbert and Katherine Jacobs Frank Lloyd Wright Collection
  The Art Institute of Chicago
  Documents, Box 1

Medium:
  Typed single spaced ditto copy

Size:
  8-1/2 in. x 11 in.; 215.9 mm x 279.4 mm

Number of Pages:
  4

Descriptors:
  Herbert Jacobs, Herbert Jacobs First Residence

Review:
  Wright talks of the Herbert Jacobs First Residence.

B247

Date:
  January 19, 1939

Type of Manuscript:
  Letter

To:
  Herbert Jacobs
  Madison, Wisconsin

From:
  Frank Lloyd Wright
  Phoenix, Arizona

Collection:
  The Herbert and Katherine Jacobs Frank Lloyd Wright Collection
  The Art Institute of Chicago
  Documents, Box 1

Medium:
  Typed, signed "F.LL.W"

Size:
  10 in. x 12 in.; 254.0 mm x 304.8 mm

Number of Pages:
  1

Number of Words:
203

Descriptors:
Groves (Harold M. Groves?), Herbert Jacobs, Herbert Jacobs First Residence

Review:
Talk of the construction of the Herbert Jacobs First Residence at Madison, Wisconsin.

B248

Date:
January 22, 1939

Type of Manuscript:
Letter

To:
Edgar Tafel
1000 Sixteenth Street
Racine, Wisconsin

From:
Frank Lloyd Wright
Taliesin
Phoenix, Arizona

Source:
Edgar Tafel
Apprentice to Genius: Years with Frank Lloyd Wright, p. 190

Medium:
Typed on red-square stationery, signed "F.LL.W."

Number of Pages:
1

Number of Words:
44

Descriptors:
Edgar Tafel, Bernard Schwartz Residence

Review:
Wright instructs Tafel to look for a site for the residence to be designed for Bernard Schwartz at Two Rivers, Wisconsin. The letter is photographically reproduced in Tafel's book *Apprentice to Genius*.

B249

Date:
May 2, 4, 9, 11, and 20, 1939

Type of Manuscript:
Typescript Speeches

2-5.6 Bernard Schwartz Residence (1939), Two Rivers, Wisconsin. Photo by the author.

Title:
  "The Sir George Watson Lectures for 1939: A Series
  of Four Evenings on--An Organic Architecture: The
  Architecture of Democracy"

By:
  Frank Lloyd Wright
  London

Collection:
  The Library of Congress, Manuscript Division
  The Frank Lloyd Wright Papers
  Speech and Article File, 1939

Medium:
  Typed double spaced with handwritten corrections by
  Wright

Size:
  8-1/2 in. x 12-1/2 in.; 215.9 mm x 317.5 mm

Number of Pages:
  67

Descriptors:
  Sir George Watson Lectures for 1939, London, *An Organic
  Architecture: The Architecture of Democracy*

Review:
  The complete typescript of Wright's Sulgrave Manor Board lectures
  of 1939 in London. The final version of these lectures has been
  printed three times, the first and second by Lund Humphries of
  London in 1939 and 1941, and, in 1970, by the M.I.T. Press at
  Cambridge, Massachusetts as *An Organic Architecture: The Architecture of Democracy* (see also B250).

B250

Date:
  May 2, 4, 9, 11, and 20, 1939

Type of Manuscript:
  Typescript Speeches

Title:
  "Watson Chair Foundation of the Sulgrave Manor
  Board, The Sir George Watson Lectures for 1939, A
  Series of Four Evenings on an Organic Architecture,
  The Architecture of Democracy"

By:
  Frank Lloyd Wright

Collection:
  The John Lloyd Wright Collection
  The Avery Architectural Library
  Columbia University
  Folder 6

Medium:
  Typed with handwritten notes by Wright encased in yellow covers

Size:
    8-1/2 in. x 13 in.; 215.9 mm x 330.2 mm

Number of Pages:
    67

Descriptors:
    Sir George Watson Lectures for 1939, London, *An Organic Architecture: The Architecture of Democracy*

Review:
    The complete typescript of Wright's Sulgrave Manor Board lectures of 1939 in London. The final version of these lectures was printed by Lund Humphries of London in 1939 and 1941, and by the M.I.T. Press in 1970. Copies of these manuscripts are also in The Frank Lloyd Wright Papers Collection of the Library of Congress Manuscript Division (see B249).

B251

Date:
    May 11, 1939

Type of Manuscript:
    Letter

To:
    Charles Robert Ashbee

From:
    Frank Lloyd Wright
    England

Source:
    Alan Crawford
    "Ten Letters From Frank Lloyd Wright to Charles Robert Ashbee"

Collection:
    The Ashbee Journals
    King's College
    Cambridge
    England

Number of Words:
    132

Descriptors:
    Charles Robert Ashbee, England, *An Organic Architecture: The Architecture of Democracy*, Sir George Watson Lectures of the Sulgrave Manor, London, Paris, Dalmatia, Sir Edwin L. Lutyens, C.F.A. Voysey, Olgivanna Lloyd Wright, Iovanna Lloyd Wright.

Review:
    This letter was written during Wright's "Sir George Watson Lectures of the Sulgrave Manor Board." The lectures were later printed and published as *An Organic Architecture: The Architecture of Democracy* by Lund Humphries of London in 1939. Several articles on Wright's lectures were run in the *Times* of London: "Announcement of 'Exhibi-

tion' of Photographs of Buildings by Frank Lloyd Wright in London";
"A Vision of England"; and "An American View of Architecture."
Wright thanks Ashbee for a recent visit Wright made to Ashbee's
home and says that the lectures are tiring him out. Wright has
seen both Voysey and Lutyens while in England.

B252

Date:
   June 14, 1939

Type of Manuscript:
   Letter

To:
   John Lloyd Wright
   Michigan City, Indiana

From:
   Frank Lloyd Wright
   Taliesin

Collection:
   The John Lloyd Wright Collection
   The Avery Architectural Library
   Columbia University
   Folder 10

Medium:
   Typed on Taliesin design stationery and signed "Father"

Size:
   8-1/2 in. x 11 in.; 215.9 mm x 279.4 mm

Number of Pages:
   1

Number of Words:
   81

Descriptors:
   John Lloyd Wright, England, France

Review:
   On a family matter.

B253

Date:
   July 28, 1939

Type of Manuscript:
   Letter

To:
   William A. Kittredge
   The Lakeside Press
   Chicago, Illinois

From:
   Frank Lloyd Wright

Collection:
 William Kittredge Collection
 Newberry Library
 Chicago, Illinois

Medium:
 Typed on Taliesin design stationery, signed "Frank Lloyd
 Wright"

Size:
 7-1/2 in. x 8-1/2 in.; 190.5 mm x 215.9 mm

Number of Pages:
 1

Number of Words:
 93

Descriptors:
 William Kittredge

Review:
 Wright thanks Kittredge for a gift.

B254

Date:
 August 28, 1939

Type of Manuscript:
 Letter

To:
 William A. Kittredge
 The Lakeside Press
 Chicago, Illinois

From:
 Frank Lloyd Wright

Collection:
 William Kittredge Collection
 Newberry Library
 Chicago, Illinois

Medium:
 Typed on Taliesin design stationery, signed "F.LL.W"

Size:
 7-3/8 in. x 8-1/2 in.; 187.3 mm x 215.9 mm

Number of Pages:
 1

Number of Words:
 35

Descriptors:
 William Kittredge

Review:
 Brief note asking Kittredge to read something.

B255

Date:
   August 1939

Type of Manuscript:
   Typescript article

Title:
   "To the Fifty-Eighth"

By:
   Frank Lloyd Wright
   Taliesin
   Spring Green, Wisconsin

Collection:
   The Library of Congress, Manuscript Division
   The Frank Lloyd Wright Papers
   Speech and Article File, 1939

Medium:
   Typed double spaced

Size:
   8-1/2 in. x 11-1/8 in.; 215.9 mm x 282.6 mm

Number of Pages:
   5

Descriptors:
   London, Taliesin, Modern European Architecture

Review:
   The faults of modern European architecture are pointed out by
   Wright.

B256

Date:
   September 2, 1939

Type of Manuscript:
   Letter

To:
   Loren Pope
   East Falls Church, Virginia

From:
   Frank Lloyd Wright

Source:
   Ellen Beasley
   "Documents," p. 15

Number of Words:
   37

Descriptors:
   Loren Pope, Loren Pope Residence, Ed Rowan

Review:
   Wright agrees to design a house for Pope.

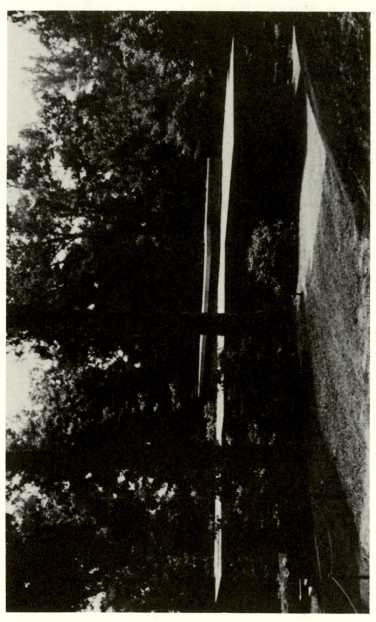

2-5.7 Approach view of the Loren Pope Residence (1939), Mount Vernon, Virginia (relocated from Falls Church). Photo by the author.

2-5.8 West portion of the exterior south elevation of the Loren Pope Residence (1939), Mount Vernon, Virginia (relocated from Falls Church). Photo by the author.

2-5.9 Exterior view looking east along the south elevation of the Loren Pope Residence (1939), with the sanctum room in the foreground, Mount Vernon, Virginia (relocated from Falls Church). Photo by the author.

2-5.10   Interior of the Loren Pope Residence (1939), Falls Church, Virginia (later relocated to Mount Vernon, Virginia). Photo by the author.

2-5.11   Dining room table and chairs for the Loren Pope Residence (1939), Falls Church, Virginia (later relocated to Mount Vernon, Virginia). Photo by the author.

B257

Date:
September 13, 1939

Type of Manuscript:
Telegram

To:
Herbert Jacobs
The Capital Times
Madison, Wisconsin

From:
Frank Lloyd Wright

Collection:
The Herbert and Katherine Jacobs Frank Lloyd Wright
Collection
The Art Institute of Chicago
Documents, Box 1

Medium:
Western Union Telegram

Number of Pages:
1

Number of Words:
43

Descriptors:
Herbert Jacobs, Herbert Jacobs First Residence

Review:
Wright invites Jacobs to Taliesin to discuss construction details
of the Herbert Jacobs First Residence.

B258

Date:
October 9, 1939

Type of Manuscript:
Letter

To:
Herbert Jacobs
Madison, Wisconsin

From:
Frank Lloyd Wright

Collection:
The Herbert and Katherine Jacobs Frank Lloyd Wright
Collection
The Art Institute of Chicago
Documents, Box 1

Medium:
Typed on Taliesin design stationery, signed
"F.LL.W"

Size:
  8-1/2 in. x 11 in.; 215.9 mm x 279.4 mm

Number of Pages:
  1

Number of Words:
  54

Descriptors:
  Herbert Jacobs, Herbert Jacobs First Residence

Review:
  On the construction details of the Jacobs First Residence.

B259

Date:
  October 16, 1939

Type of Manuscript:
  Letter

To:
  Katherine and Herbert Jacobs

From:
  Mr. and Mrs. Frank Lloyd Wright

Collection:
  The Herbert and Katherine Jacobs Frank Lloyd Wright
  Collection
  The Art Institute of Chicago
  Documents, Box 1

Medium:
  Typed on Taliesin design stationery, signed
  "F.LL.W." and "Olgivanna"

Size:
  8-1/2 in. x 11 in.; 215.9 mm x 279.4 mm

Number of Pages:
  1

Number of Words:
  127

Descriptors:
  Taliesin, Halloween 1939, Herbert Jacobs

Review:
  Invitation to a Halloween party at Taliesin.

B260

Date:
  November 8, 1939

Type of Manuscript:
  Text of speech/lecture

Title:
  "Dinner Talk at Hull House"

By:
  Frank Lloyd Wright

Collection:
  The Wrightiana Collection
  The Art Institute of Chicago

Medium:
  Typed double spaced mimeograph

Size:
  8-1/2 in. x 11 in.; 215.9 mm x 279.4 mm

Number of Pages:
  17

Descriptors:
  Hull House (Chicago), William Deknatel, Arts and Crafts
  Society (Chicago), Ruskin and Morris, Jane Addams, Julia
  Lathrop, Florence Kelly, Charles Zeublin, Professor Oscar
  Lovell Triggs, Nature, Royal Institute of British Architects,
  Broadacre City, Usonia

Review:
  Text of Wright's address at the Hull House in Chicago in 1939. A
  copy of this address is also housed in the Frank Lloyd Wright
  Papers Collection of the Library of Congress at Washington, D.C.
  Wright speaks of his association with the Arts and Crafts Society
  of Chicago, his Sir George Watson Chair lectures in England in
  1939, art, architecture, decentralization of the city, Broadacre
  City, The Chicago World's Fair, and Usonia (see B261).

B261

Date:
  November 8, 1939

Type of Manuscript:
  Typescript of lecture

Title:
  "Dinner Talk at Hull House"

By:
  Frank Lloyd Wright
  Hull House
  Chicago, Illinois

Collection:
  The Library of Congress, Manuscript Division
  The Frank Lloyd Wright Papers
  Speech and Article File, 1939

Medium:
  Typed double spaced

Size:
  8-1/2 in. x 11 in.; 215.9 mm x 279.4 mm

Number of Pages:
  14

Descriptors:
  Hull House (Chicago), William Deknatel, Arts and Crafts
  Society (Chicago), Ruskin and Morris, Jane Addams, Julia
  Lathrop, Florence Kelly, Charles Zeublin, Professor Oscar
  Lovell Triggs, Nature, Royal Institute of British
  Architects, Broadacre City, Usonia

Review:
  Text of Wright's address at the Hull House in Chicago in 1939.
  A copy of this address is also housed in the Wrightiana Collection
  of The Art Institute of Chicago (see B260). Wright speaks of his
  association with the Arts and Crafts Society of Chicago, his Sir
  George Watson Chair lectures in England in 1939, art, architecture,
  decentralization of the city, Broadacre City, the Chicago World's
  Fair, and Usonia.

B262

Date:
  November 28, 1939

Type of Manuscript:
  Letter

To:
  Loren Pope
  East Falls Church (Virginia)

From:
  Frank Lloyd Wright

Source:
  Ellen Beasley
  "Documents," p. 22

Number of Words:
  81

Descriptors:
  Loren Pope, Loren Pope Residence

Review:
  Wright sends the plans and specifications for the Pope Residence
  so that Pope may make application for a loan to build the house.

B263

Date:
  Undated (1930s)

Type of Manuscript:
  Letter

To:
  John Lloyd Wright
  Long Beach, Indiana

From:
    Frank Lloyd Wright

Collection:
    The John Lloyd Wright Collection
    The Avery Architectural Library
    Columbia University
    Folder 13

Medium:
    Typed on Taliesin design stationery, signed "Dad"

Size:
    8-1/2 in. x 11 in.; 215.9 mm x 279.4 mm

Number of Pages:
    1

Number of Words:
    53 Typed; 5 Handwritten

Descriptors:
    John Lloyd Wright

Review:
    Frank Lloyd Wright invites his son John Lloyd to visit him.

B264

Date:
    Undated (1939?)

Type of Manuscript:
    Letter

To:
    Edgar Tafel

From:
    Frank Lloyd Wright
    Sante Fe Chief (between Chicago and Phoenix)

Source:
    Edgar Tafel
    Apprentice to Genius: Years with Frank Lloyd Wright, pp. 192-193

Medium:
    Handwritten on Sante Fe Chief stationery,
    signed "F.LL.W"

Size:
    6 in. x 4 in.; 152.4 mm x 101.6 mm

Number of Pages:
    2

Number of Words:
    168

Descriptors:
    Edgar Tafel, The Sante Fe Chief, Taliesin, Herbert Jacobs
    First Residence, Hillside Home School, Bernard Schwartz Residence

Review:
Wright gives Tafel various instructions for the maintenance of
Taliesin as well as the supervision of several projects, including
the Herbert Jacobs First Residence and the Bernard Schwartz Residence. Wright also diagrams a rough detail of a folding screen
design for Tafel. This manuscript is photographically reproduced
in Tafel's book *Apprentice to Genius*.

B265

Date:
Undated (1939?)

Type of Manuscript:
Construction Specification Sheet

For:
Lloyd Lewis Residence
Libertyville, Illinois

By:
Frank Lloyd Wright

Source:
Edgar Tafel
Apprentice to Genius: Years with Frank Lloyd Wright, p. 193

Medium:
Typed, with handwritten corrections by Frank Lloyd Wright

Number of Pages:
1

Descriptors:
Lloyd Lewis Residence

Review:
One sheet of specifications for concrete work for the Lloyd
Lewis Residence at Libertyville, Illinois, is photographically
reproduced in Tafel's *Apprentice to Genius*.

B266

Date:
1939?

Type of Manuscript:
Note

To:
John Lloyd Wright

From:
Frank Lloyd Wright

Collection:
The John Lloyd Wright Collection
The Avery Architectural Library
Columbia University
Folder 10

Medium:
  Handwritten on Taliesin design stationery, signed "F.LL.W."

Size:
  8-1/2 in. x 11 in.; 215.9 mm x 279.4 mm

Number of Pages:
  1

Number of Words:
  16

Descriptors:
  John Lloyd Wright, Morale

Review:
  On morale.

B267

Date:
  1939?

Type of Manuscript:
  Note

To:
  John Lloyd Wright

From:
  Frank Lloyd Wright

Collection:
  The John Lloyd Wright Collection
  The Avery Architectural Library
  Columbia University
  Folder 10

Medium:
  Handwritten on Taliesin design stationery
  and signed "F.LL.W."

Size:
  8-1/2 in. x 11 in.; 215.9 mm x 279.4 mm

Number of Pages:
  1

Number of Words:
  8

Descriptors:
  John Lloyd Wright, Morale

Review:
  On morale.

B268

Date:
  February 13, 1940

Type of Manuscript:
   Letter

To:
   Herbert Jacobs
   Madison, Wisconsin

From:
   Frank Lloyd Wright
   Taliesin West
   Phoenix, Arizona

Collection:
   The Herbert and Katherine Jacobs Frank Lloyd Wright Collection
   The Art Institute of Chicago
   Documents, Box 1

Medium:
   Typed and handwritten on Taliesin West design
   stationery, signed "F.LLW."

Number of Pages:
   1

Number of Words:
   29 Typed; 20 Handwritten

Descriptors:
   Herbert Jacobs, Herbert Jacobs First Residence

Review:
   On the construction details of the First Jacobs Residence.

B269

Date:
   March 18, 1940

Type of Manuscript:
   Letter

To:
   Loren Pope
   East Falls Church, Virginia

From:
   Frank Lloyd Wright
   Taliesin
   Phoenix, Arizona

Source:
   Ellen Beasley
   "Documents," p. 25

Number of Words:
   65

Descriptors:
   Loren Pope, Loren Pope Residence

Review:
   Discussion of the construction costs to build the Loren Pope
   Residence.

B270

Date:
   March 31, 1940

Type of Manuscript:
   Letter

To:
   Loren Pope
   Washington

From:
   Frank Lloyd Wright
   Taliesin West
   Phoenix, Arizona

Source:
   Ellen Beasley
   "Documents," p. 26

Number of Words:
   53

Descriptors:
   Loren Pope, Loren Pope Residence, Gordon Chadwick

Review:
   Wright will send Taliesin apprentice, Gordon Chadwick, to supervise construction of the Pope Residence.

B271

Date:
   April 16, 1940

Type of Manuscript:
   Letter

To:
   E. Willis Jones
   Chicago, Illinois

From:
   Frank Lloyd Wright
   Taliesin West
   Phoenix, Arizona

Collection:
   Frank Lloyd Wright Correspondence with E. Willis Jones,
   1936-1959
   Special Collections Department
   Northwestern University Library

Medium:
   Typed on Taliesin West design stationery, signed
   "F.L. L.W."

Size:
   8-1/2 in. x 11 in.; 215.9 mm x 279.4 mm

Number of Pages:
   1

Number of Words:
   61

Descriptors:
   E. Willis Jones

Review:
   Talk of a Mr. Smith (a possible Wright client?).

B272

Date:
   April 24, 1940

Type of Manuscript:
   Letter

To:
   Loren Pope
   East Falls Church, Virginia

From:
   Frank Lloyd Wright

Source:
   Ellen Beasley
   "Documents," p. 28

Number of Words:
   47

Descriptors:
   Loren Pope, Loren Pope Residence, Gordon Chadwick

Review:
   Wright to send Gordon Chadwick, Taliesin apprentice, to supervise
   construction of the Pope Residence.

B273

Date:
   June 15, 1940

Type of Manuscript:
   Typescript editorial

Title:
   "Self Defense"

By:
   Frank Lloyd Wright
   Taliesin
   Spring Green, Wisconsin

Collection:
   The Library of Congress, Manuscript Division
   The Frank Lloyd Wright Papers
   Speech and Article File, 1940

Medium:
   Typed double spaced, with handwritten corrections by Wright

Size:
8-1/2 in. x 13 in.; 215.9 mm x 330.2 mm

Number of Pages:
4

Descriptors:
Hitler, Sir George Watson Chair (London), England,
Democracy, Usonian, U.S. Congress, Will Allen White,
Washington, D.C., World War II

Review:
The danger of Germany during this period is commented on by
Wright and the similarity between the United States and Britain
is also discussed. However, Wright claims that the neutral
position of the United States is not characteristic of a true
democracy.

B274

Date:
June 30, 1940

Type of Manuscript:
Telegram

To:
Edgar Tafel
Libertyville, Illinois

From:
Frank Lloyd Wright
Spring Green, Wisconsin

Source:
Edgar Tafel
Apprentice to Genius: Years with Frank Lloyd Wright, p. 142

Medium:
Western Union Telegram

Number of Pages:
1

Number of Words:
62

Descriptors:
Edgar Tafel, Taliesin

Review:
Wright wants Tafel to return to Taliesin. This document is
photographically reproduced in Tafel's book, *Apprentice to Genius.*

B275

Date:
July 9, 1940

Type of Manuscript:
Letter

To:
  Loren Pope
  East Falls Church, Virginia

From:
  Frank Lloyd Wright

Source:
  Ellen Beasley
  "Documents," p. 31

Number of Words:
  51

Descriptors:
  Loren Pope, Loren Pope Residence

Review:
  Wright forwards a copy of the proposed site plan for the Loren
  Pope Residence to Loren Pope.

B276

Date:
  July 10, 1940

Type of Manuscript:
  Letter

To:
  Gordon Chadwick
  East Falls Church, Virginia

From:
  Frank Lloyd Wright

Source:
  Ellen Beasley
  "Documents," p. 32

Number of Words:
  66

Descriptors:
  Gordon Chadwick, Loren Pope, Loren Pope Residence,
  Joseph Euchtman Residence, Howard C. Rickert

Review:
  Wright instructs Chadwick, Taliesin apprentice in charge of
  construction supervision of the Loren Pope Residence, to sign
  a contract with contractor Howard C. Rickert. Brief mention of
  the Joseph Euchtman Residence designed by Wright at Baltimore,
  Maryland, in 1939.

B277

Date:
  July 10, 1940

Type of Manuscript:
  Recollections by Wright

2-5.12 Joseph Euchtman Residence (1939), Baltimore, Maryland. Photo by the author.

Title:
  "The Auditorium Building and Its Architects"

By:
  Frank Lloyd Wright

Collection:
  The Wrightiana Collection
  The Art Institute of Chicago

Medium:
  Typed on Taliesin design stationery, signed "Frank Lloyd
  Wright"

Size:
  8-1/2 in. x 11 in.; 215.9 mm x 279.4 mm

Number of Pages:
  3

Descriptors:
  Auditorium Building (Chicago), Adler and Sullivan, Dankmar
  Adler, Louis Sullivan, H.H. Richardson, Orchestra Hall
  (Chicago), Theodore Thomas

Review:
  Wright gives short personality profiles of Dankmar Adler and
  Louis Sullivan. Wright attributes various portions of the
  Auditorium to Adler (plan), Sullivan (interior), and Richardson
  (exterior). Wright concludes that the building is one of the
  best for opera.

B278

Date:
  July 27, 1940

Type of Manuscript:
  Preprinted "Application for Registration" (Architect)

Collection:
  The Frank Lloyd Wright Maryland Registration Papers
  Maryland Historical Society

Medium:
  "Application for Registration" signed by Frank Lloyd Wright
  and notarized

Size:
  8-1/2 in. x 11 in.; 215.9 mm x 279.4 mm

Number of Pages:
  4

Number of Words:
  77 Handwritten on a preprinted form

Descriptors:
  State of Maryland Board of Examiners and Registration
  of Architects, Joseph Euchtman Residence

Review:
  Wright's application for Maryland architect registration. Wright
  answers all questions on the application very briefly and in

some instances humorously. The application seems to be nothing
more than another formality for Wright. Wright applied for architect registration in order to build the Joseph Euchtman Residence
in Baltimore.

B279

Date:
   October 7, 1940

Type of Manuscript:
   Letter

To:
   William T. Evjue
   Madison, Wisconsin

From:
   Frank Lloyd Wright

Collection:
   The William Theodore Evjue Papers, 1905-1969
   The State Historical Society of Wisconsin
   MSS 244, Box 155, Folder 21

Medium:
   Typed on Taliesin design stationery and signed "Frank"

Size:
   8-1/2 in. x 11 in.; 215.9 mm x 279.4 mm

Number of Pages:
   1

Number of Words:
   144

Descriptors:
   William T. Evjue, *The Capital Times*, Taliesin Chorus

Review:
   Wright asks Evjue to have the Taliesin chorus sing on a
   Madison-based radio station.

B280

Date:
   December 7, 1940

Type of Manuscript:
   Letter

To:
   Herbert Jacobs
   Madison, Wisconsin

From:
   Frank Lloyd Wright
   Taliesin
   Spring Green, Wisconsin

Collection:
The Herbert and Katherine Jacobs Frank Lloyd Wright
Collection
The Art Institute of Chicago
Documents, Box 1

Medium:
Typed on Taliesin design stationery, signed
"F.LL.W."

Size:
8-1/2 in. x 11 in.; 215.9 mm x 279.4 mm

Number of Pages:
1

Number of Words:
112

Descriptors:
Herbert Jacobs, Jeff Baker, *The Capital Times*, C.F.A. Voysey,
Charles Rennie Mackintosh.

Review:
Brief remarks on an article which had appeared in *The Capital
Times*.

B281

Date:
Undated (prior to 1940)

Type of Manuscript:
Typescript article

Title:
"Of Frank Lloyd Wright"

By:
Frank Lloyd Wright

Collection:
The Library of Congress, Manuscript Division
The Frank Lloyd Wright Papers
Speech and Article File, Undated

Medium:
Typed double spaced

Size:
8-1/2 in. x 11-3/4 in.; 215.9 mm x 298.5 mm

Number of Pages:
1

Descriptors:
Organic Architecture, Architecture

Review:
A philosophical argument on what architecture is.

B282

Date:
Undated (prior to 1940)

Type of Manuscript:
Typescript article

Title:
"The Internationalist Style"

By:
Frank Lloyd Wright

Collection:
The Library of Congress, Manuscript Division
The Frank Lloyd Wright Papers
Speech and Article File, Undated

Medium:
Typed double spaced, with handwritten corrections by Wright

Size:
8-1/2 in. x 11 in.; 215.9 mm x 279.4 mm

Number of Pages:
2

Descriptors:
International Style, Le Corbusier, Eclecticism

Review:
Le Corbusier and the International Style of architecture are criticized.

B283

Date:
Undated (prior to 1940)

Type of Manuscript:
Typescript editorial

Title:
"Editorial"

By:
Frank Lloyd Wright

Collection:
The Library of Congress, Manuscript Division
The Frank Lloyd Wright Papers
Speech and Article File, Undated

Medium:
Typed double spaced

Size:
8-1/2 in. x 13 in.; 215.9 mm x 330.2 mm

Number of Pages:
2

Descriptors:
    Le Corbusier, Museum of Modern Art (New York), Style, U.S.A.

Review:
    Le Corbusier is attacked as an architect. And comments are made
    concerning the design of the Museum of Modern Art at New York.
    Wright is very critical of both.

B284

Date:
    Undated (prior to 1940)

Type of Manuscript:
    Typescript article

Title:
    "Article for 'The Hour'"

By:
    Frank Lloyd Wright

Collection:
    The Library of Congress, Manuscript Division
    The Frank Lloyd Wright Papers
    Speech and Article File, Undated

Medium:
    Typed double spaced

Size:
    8-1/2 in. x 11 in.; 215.9 mm x 279.4 mm

Number of Pages:
    3

Descriptors:
    Capitalism, *The Hour*, The Machine, Style, Sears-Roebuck,
    Prefabrication, Housing

Review:
    Intense research investigation has not discovered if this article
    was ever published by Wright. In it he is critical of the tastes
    of Americans in housing. Although the article is in Gutheim's
    collection at the Library of Congress, this manuscript was not
    used in his *Frank Lloyd Wright On Architecture*.

B285

Date:
    July 26, ? (prior to 1940)

Type of Manuscript:
    Typescript article/letter

Title:
    "To the *Chicago Daily News*"

By:
    Frank Lloyd Wright
    Taliesin

Collection:
   The Library of Congress, Manuscript Division
   The Frank Lloyd Wright Papers
   Speech and Article File, Undated

Medium:
   Typed double spaced, with handwritten corrections by
   Wright

Size:
   8-1/2 in. x 11 in.; 215.9 mm x 279.4 mm

Number of Pages:
   2

Descriptors:
   Chicago Daily News, Chicago Art Institute, Holabird and
   Root, Chicago, Sir Joseph Duveen

Review:
   A protest letter to the *Chicago Daily News* concerning the new
   design for the Chicago Art Institute.

B286

Date:
   Undated (1938 to 1940)

Type of Manuscript:
   Letter

To:
   Taliesin Fellowship

From:
   Frank Lloyd Wright
   Apache Hotel
   Las Vegas, Nevada

Source:
   Edgar Tafel
   Apprentice to Genius: Years with Frank Lloyd Wright, p. 198

Medium:
   Handwritten on Apache Hotel stationery, signed
   "Frank Lloyd Wright"

Size:
   3-1/8 in. x 7-1/4 in.; 79.4 mm x 184.2 mm

Number of Pages:
   1

Number of Words:
   13

Descriptors:
   Edgar Tafel, Apache Hotel (Las Vegas, Nevada), Taliesin
   West

Review:
   Brief note photographically reproduced in Tafel's *Apprentice to
   Genius*. Wright was in transit between the two Taliesins when he
   wrote it.

B287

Date:
   Undated (1938 to 1940)

Type of Manuscript:
   Letter

To:
   Taliesin Fellowship

From:
   Frank Lloyd Wright
   Apache Hotel
   Las Vegas, Nevada

Source:
   Edgar Tafel
   Apprentice to Genius: Years with Frank Lloyd Wright, p. 199

Medium:
   Handwritten on Apache Hotel stationery, signed
   "FLLW"

Size:
   7 in. x 8-3/4 in.; 177.8 mm x 222.3 mm

Number of Pages:
   1

Number of Words:
   60

Descriptors:
   Edgar Tafel, Apache Hotel (Las Vegas, Nevada), Taliesin
   West

Review:
   Wright discusses his trip between the two Taliesins. The letter
   is photographically reproduced in Tafel's *Apprentice to Genius*.

B288

Date:
   Undated (prior to 1940)

Type of Manuscript:
   Inscribed photograph

Of:
   Edgar Tafel

By:
   Frank Lloyd Wright

Source:
   Edgar Tafel
   Apprentice to Genius: Years with Frank Lloyd Wright, p. 160

Medium:
   Photograph with handwriting

Number of Words:
   12

Descriptors:
    Edgar Tafel, Taliesin Lime Kiln

Review:
    Brief comment by Wright made on a photo of Tafel tending a fire
    at the Taliesin lime kiln. The photograph, as well as Wright's
    note, are reproduced in Tafel's book *Apprentice to Genius*.

B289

Date:
    Undated (prior to 1940)

Type of Manuscript:
    Typescript Notes

Title:
    "Notes--Frank Lloyd Wright"

By:
    Frank Lloyd Wright

Collection:
    The Library of Congress, Manuscript Division
    The Frank Lloyd Wright Papers
    Speech and Article File, Undated

Medium:
    Typed single spaced, with handwritten corrections by Wright

Size:
    8-1/2 in. x 11-1/8 in.; 215.9 mm x 282.6 mm

Number of Pages:
    2

Descriptors:
    R. Buckminster Fuller, International Style, Spinoza,
    Organic Architecture, John Kwait

Review:
    A series of short quotations by Wright on various topics
    including the International Style of architecture.

B290

Date:
    Undated (Fall of 1939 or Spring of 1940)

Type of Manuscript:
    Note

To:
    Herbert Jacobs

From:
    Frank Lloyd Wright

Collection:
    The Herbert and Katherine Jacobs Frank Lloyd Wright
    Collection
    The Art Institute of Chicago
    Documents, Box 1

Medium:
  Handwritten on a Canton Lumber Sales Receipt (Minneapolis,
  Minnesota), signed "F.LL.W."

Size:
  5-1/2 in. x 8-1/2 in.; 139.7 mm x 215.9 mm

Number of Pages:
  1

Descriptors:
  Herbert Jacobs, Herbert Jacobs First Residence, Canton
  Lumber (Minneapolis, Minnesota).

Review:
  On the construction costs of the First Jacobs Residence.

B291

Date:
  March 19, 1941

Type of Manuscript:
  Telegram

To:
  E. Willis Jones
  Chicago, Illinois

From:
  Frank Lloyd Wright
  Phoenix, Arizona

Collection:
  Frank Lloyd Wright Correspondence with E. Willis Jones,
  1936-1959
  Special Collections Department
  Northwestern University Library

Medium:
  Western Union Telegram

Size:
  5-3/4 in. x 8 in.; 146.1 mm x 203.2 mm

Number of Pages:
  1

Number of Words:
  53

Descriptors:
  E. Willis Jones, Art Directors Club of Chicago

Review:
  Talk of the Art Directors Club of Chicago.

B292

Date:
  March 20, 1941

Type of Manuscript:
   Letter

To:
   E. Willis Jones

From:
   Frank Lloyd Wright
   Taliesin West
   Phoenix, Arizona

Collection:
   Frank Lloyd Wright Correspondence with E. Willis Jones,
   1936-1959
   Special Collections Department
   Northwestern University Library

Medium:
   Typed on Taliesin West design stationery,
   signed "F.L.L.W"

Size:
   8-1/2 in. x 11 in.; 215.9 mm x 279.4 mm

Number of Pages:
   1

Number of Words:
   103

Descriptors:
   E. Willis Jones, The Chicago Theological Seminary,
   Robie House, Albert W. Palmer, Art Directors of Chicago

Review:
   Wright requests that Jones write a letter to help save the
   Robie House from possible destruction. Wright designed the
   Frederick Robie Residence at Chicago in 1906.

   B293

Date:
   August 15, 1941

Type of Manuscript:
   Letter

To:
   William A. Kittredge
   Chicago, Illinois

From:
   Frank Lloyd Wright

Collection:
   William Kittredge Collection
   Newberry Library
   Chicago, Illinois

Medium:
   Typed on Taliesin design stationery,
   signed "F.Ll.W."

2-5.13 Frederick Robie Residence (1906), Chicago, Illinois. Photo by the author.

Size:
    7-1/2 in. x 8-1/2 in.; 190.5 mm x 215.9 mm

Number of Pages:
    1

Number of Words:
    23

Descriptors:
    William Kittredge

Review:
    A very brief note of thanks.

B294

Date:
    December 8, 1941

Type of Manuscript:
    Letter

To:
    Dorathi Bock Pierre

From:
    Frank Lloyd Wright

Collection:
    The Richard W. Bock Sculpture Collection
    Greenville College

Descriptors:
    Dorathi Bock Pierre

Review:
    Wright asks Dorathi Bock Pierre to excuse him for being busy.

B295

Date:
    August 11, 1942

Type of Manuscript:
    Letter

To:
    William A. Kittredge

From:
    Frank Lloyd Wright

Collection:
    William Kittredge Collection
    Newberry Library
    Chicago, Illinois

Medium:
    Typed on Taliesin design stationery, signed "Frank"

Size:
    7-1/2 in. x 8-1/2 in.; 190.5 mm x 215.9 mm

Number of Pages:
  1

Number of Words:
  69

Descriptors:
  William Kittredge

Review:
  Wright invites Kittredge to Taliesin for a visit.

B296

Date:
  September 14, 1942

Type of Manuscript:
  Letter

To:
  William A. Kittredge

From:
  Frank Lloyd Wright

Collection:
  William Kittredge Collection
  Newberry Library
  Chicago, Illinois

Medium:
  Typed on Taliesin design stationery, signed
  "F.LL.W"

Size:
  7-1/2 in. x 8-1/2 in.; 190.5 mm x 215.9 mm

Number of Pages:
  1

Number of Words:
  57 Typed; 10 Handwritten

Descriptors:
  William Kittredge, Lloyd Downs Lewis

Review:
  Wright offers the services of some of his Taliesin apprentices
  to help Kittredge on a project.

B297

Date:
  October 5, 1942

Type of Manuscript:
  Letter

To:
  Mrs. William A. Kittredge
  Evanston, Illinois

From:
   Frank Lloyd Wright

Collection:
   William Kittredge Collection
   Newberry Library
   Chicago, Illinois

Medium:
   Typed on Talisin design stationery, signed
   "Frank Lloyd Wright"

Size:
   7-1/2 in. x 8-1/2 in.; 190.5 mm x 215.9 mm

Number of Pages:
   1

Number of Words:
   37

Descriptors:
   Mrs. William Kittredge, William Kittredge

Review:
   A brief note of sympathy.

B298

Date:
   November 9, 1942

Type of Manuscript:
   Letter

To:
   Peter DeVries
   Poetry Magazine
   Chicago, Illinois

From:
   Frank Lloyd Wright
   Taliesin
   Spring Green, Wisconsin

Collection:
   Poetry Magazine Papers, 1936-1953 (Series II)
   University of Chicago Library
   University of Chicago
   Box 11:8

Medium:
   Typed on Taliesin design stationery, signed
   "Frank Lloyd Wright"

Size:
   8-1/2 in. x 11 in.; 215.9 mm x 279.4 mm

Number of Pages:
   1

Number of Words;
   81

Descriptors:
Peter DeVries, *Poetry Magazine*

Review:
On DeVries' asking Wright to visit Chicago.

B299

Date:
November 30, 1942

Type of Manuscript:
Letter

To:
Whom It May Concern (for Edgar Tafel)

From:
Frank Lloyd Wright
Taliesin
Spring Green, Wisconsin

Source:
Edgar Tafel
Apprentice to Genius: Years with Frank Lloyd Wright, p. 206

Medium:
Typed on Taliesin design stationery, signed "Frank Lloyd
Wright"

Number of Pages:
1

Number of Words:
54

Descriptors:
Edgar Tafel, Taliesin Fellowship

Review:
A letter of reference for Edgar Tafel from Wright. The letter is
reproduced in Tafel's *Apprentice to Genius*.

B300

Date:
December 11, 1942

Type of Manuscript:
Letter

To:
William T. Evjue

From:
Frank Lloyd Wright

Collection:
The William Theodore Evjue Papers, 1905-1969
The State Historical Society of Wisconsin
MSS 244, Box 155, Folder 21

Medium:
Typed on Taliesin design stationery, signed
"F.L.L.W"

Size:
8-1/2 in. x 11 in.; 215.9 mm x 279.4 mm

Number of Pages:
1

Number of Words:
51

Descriptors:
William T. Evjue, Shridharani, Asia, Foreign Policy

Review:
Wright discusses a political book he has just read.

B301

Date:
December 21, 1942

Type of Manuscript:
Letter

To:
E. Willis Jones
Chicago, Illinois

From:
Frank Lloyd Wright

Collection:
Frank Lloyd Wright Correspondence with E. Willis Jones,
1936-1959
Special Collections Department
Northwestern University Library

Medium:
Typed on Taliesin design stationery, signed
"F.L.L.W."

Size:
7-1/2 in. x 8-1/2 in.; 190.5 mm x 279.4 mm

Number of Pages:
1

Number of Words:
42 Typed; 7 Handwritten

Descriptors:
E. Willis Jones

Review:
Wright is to visit Chicago.

B302

Date:
December 22, 1942

Type of Manuscript:
  Letter

To:
  August Derleth

From:
  Frank Lloyd Wright
  Taliesin
  Spring Green, Wisconsin

Collection:
  The August Derleth Papers
  The State Historical Society of Wisconsin

Medium:
  Typed on Taliesin design stationery, signed "F.LL.W"

Size:
  10 in. x 12 in.; 254 mm x 304.8 mm

Number of Pages:
  1

Number of Words:
  397 Typed; 3 Handwritten

Descriptors:
  August Derleth, Nature, Polity, Economics, *Scribner's
  Commentator*, Russia, England, France, South America,
  Japan, Wendell Willkie, Franklin D. Roosevelt, Pacifism,
  Isolationism, Truth, Democracy, Axis, World War II,
  Bureaucracy

Review:
  Wright comments on World War II and his feelings towards the
  politics of the time in general. During this period Wright was
  not in favor of World War II and his, as well as his apprentices',
  activities were much publicized in *The Capital Times* in articles
  such as "Federal Judge Patrick T. Stone Charged Wright Was
  'Poisoning the Minds' of His Apprentices Against the Draft";
  "Taliesin Men Demand Stone Retract Words: Call Court's Remarks
  on Fellowship, Wright 'Libelous'"; "Judge Sends Letter to
  Fellowship: Replies to Students Who Protested Attack on Frank
  Lloyd Wright"; and "Students Deny Influence Try in Weston Case:
  Reply to Judge Stone's Letter--Demand Apology to Frank Lloyd
  Wright."

REFERENCES

Books:

Bullock, Helen Duprey, and Terry B. Morton (eds.).
  The Pope-Leighey House. Washington, D.C.: National Trust for
  Historic Preservation, 1969.

Cowles, Linn Ann.
  An Index and Guide to "An Autobiography," the 1943 Edition by

Frank Lloyd Wright. Hopkins, Minnesota: Greenwich Design, 1976.

Drexler, Arthur (ed.).
The Drawings of Frank Lloyd Wright. New York: Horizon Press for the Museum of Modern Art, 1962.

Gutheim, Frederick (ed.).
Frank Lloyd Wright on Architecture: Selected Writings, 1894-1940. New York: Duell, Sloan and Pearce, 1941.

Hanna, Paul R. and Jean S. Hanna.
Frank Lloyd Wright's Hanna House: The Clients' Report. Cambridge: The M.I.T. Press, 1981.

Hitchcock, Henry-Russell.
In the Nature of Materials: 1887-1941, the Buildings of Frank Lloyd Wright. New York: Duell, Sloan and Pearce, 1942.

Izzo, Alberto, and Camillo Gubitosi (eds.).
Frank Lloyd Wright, Dessins 1887-1959. Paris: C.E.R.A. Ecole Nationale Supérieure des Beaux-Arts, 1977.

Jacobs, Herbert.
Frank Lloyd Wright: America's Greatest Architect. New York: Harcourt, Brace, and World, Inc., 1965.

Jacobs, Herbert, and Katherine Jacobs.
Building with Frank Lloyd Wright: An Illustrated Memoir. San Francisco: Chronicle Books, 1978.

Sergeant, John.
Frank Lloyd Wright's Usonian Houses: The Case for Organic Architecture. New York: Whitney Library of Design, 1976.

Storrer, William Allin.
The Architecture of Frank Lloyd Wright, a Complete Catalog, Second Edition. Cambridge, Massachusetts: The M.I.T. Press, 1978.

Tafel, Edgar.
Apprentice to Genius: Years with Frank Lloyd Wright. New York: McGraw-Hill, Inc., 1979.

Twombly, Robert C.
Frank Lloyd Wright: An Interpretive Biography. New York: Harper and Row, 1973.

Twombly, Robert C.
Frank Lloyd Wright: His Life and His Architecture. New York: John Wiley and Sons, Inc., 1979.

Wright, Frank Lloyd.
An Organic Architecture: The Architecture of Democracy. London: Lund Humphries and Co., 1939.

Wright, Frank Lloyd.
The Natural House. New York: Horizon Press, 1954.

Wright, Frank Lloyd.
Drawings for a Living Architecture. New York: Horizon Press for the Bear Run Foundation, Inc., and the Edgar J. Kaufmann Charitable Foundation, 1959.

Wright, Frank Lloyd.
An Autobiography. New York: Horizon Press, 1977.

Periodicals:

Wright, Frank Lloyd.
"Architecture and Life in the U.S.S.R.," *Architectural Record,* Vol. 82, No. 4, October 1937, pp. 57-63.

Wright, Frank Lloyd.
"Architecture and Life in the U.S.S.R.," *Soviet Russia Today,* Vol. 6, No. 8, October 1937, pp. 14-19.

Wright, Frank Lloyd.
"Speech to the A.F.A.: 600 Federal Architects Assembled in the Ball Room of the Mayflower Hotel at Washington, D.C. October 25, 1938," *Federal Architect,* Vol. 9, January 1939, pp. 20-23.

Anonymous.
"Frank Lloyd Wright," *Builder,* Vol. 156, April 28, 1939, p. 789.

Anonymous.
"Frank Lloyd Wright, Architecture Club Dinner," *Builder,* Vol. 156, May 5, 1939, p. 855.

Wright, Frank Lloyd.
"Organic Architecture, Mr. Lloyd Wright's First-Fourth 'Watson' Lectures," *Builder,* Vol. 156, May 5, 12, 19, 1939, pp. 856, 907, 909-910, 932, 951-954.

Anonymous.
"Mr. Frank Lloyd Wright," *Journal of the Royal Institute of British Architects,* Vol. 46, May 8, 1939, p. 643.

Anonymous.
"Frank Lloyd Wright," *Architects' Journal,* Vol. 89, May 11, 1939, pp. 756-757.

Anonymous.
"Lloyd Wright," *Architect and Building News,* Vol. 158, May 12, 1939, p. 141.

Anonymous.
"Frank Lloyd Wright," *Journal of the Royal Institute of British Architects,* Vol. 46, May 22, 1939, p. 700.

Morley-Horder, P.
    "Mr. Frank Lloyd Wright's Visit," *Journal of the Royal Institute of British Architects*, Vol. 46, May 22, 1939, p. 743.

Wright, Frank Lloyd.
    "To the Fifty-Eighth," *Journal of the Royal Institute of British Architects*, Vol. 46, October 16, 1939, pp. 1005-1006.

Abercrombie, Patrick.
    "Frank Lloyd Wright," *Journal of the Royal Institute of British Architects*, Vol. 47, December 11, 1939, p. 44.

Pope, Loren.
    "The Love Affair of a Man and His House," *House Beautiful*, Vol. 90, August 1948, pp. 32-34, 80, 90.

Kaufmann, Edgar, Jr.
    "The Usonian Pope-Leighey House," *Historic Preservation*, Vol. 17, May/June 1965, pp. 96-97.

Pope, Loren.
    "Twenty-Five Years Later: Still a Love Affair," *Historic Preservation*, Vol. 17, May/June 1965, pp. 98-101.

Morton, Terry Brust.
    "Wright's Pope-Leighey House," *The Prairie School Review*, Vol 4, No. 4, 1967, pp. 20-26.

Beasley, Ellen.
    "Documents," *Historic Preservation*, Vol. 21, Nos. 2-3, April/September 1969, pp. 9-33.

Crawford, Alan.
    "Ten Letters from Frank Lloyd Wright to Charles Robert Ashbee," *Journal of the Society of Architectural Historians of Great Britain* (England), Vol. 13, 1970, pp. 64-76.

Jacobs, Herbert.
    "Our Wright Houses," *Historic Preservation*, Vol. 28, July/September 1976, pp. 9-13.

Newspapers:

Anonymous.
    "Architect Wright Is Soviet Guest for World Convention," *The Capital Times* (Madison, Wisconsin), June 6, 1937.

Anonymous.
    "Wright Regrets Russia Is Using U.S. as Model for Architecture--Raps Communists of University as Racketeers After Trip," *The Capital Times* (Madison, Wisconsin), July 22, 1937.

Anonymous.
    "U.S., U.S.S.R. Are the Two Greatest Hopes for Better Life and Democracy, FLW Declares," *The Capital Times* (Madison, Wisconsin), August 1, 1937.

Anonymous.
"Communists Ask Wright to Explain Slap: Protest Charge by Architect
that 'American Communists are Racketeers,'" *The Capital Times*
(Madison, Wisconsin), August 3, 1937.

Levin, Ruben.
"Wright Lists 'Testament' of Beliefs After Visit to Russia, Lauds
Stalin, Famed Architect Says He'd Like to See U.S. 'Unionized to
Hilt': Raps Press for Distorted Articles Concerning Soviet," *The
Capital Times* (Madison, Wisconsin), August 3, 1937.

Anonymous.
"Wright Denies He Said Communists Racketeers: Famed Architect
Replies to U.W. Group's Letter," *The Capital Times*, (Madison,
Wisconsin), August 5, 1937.

Anonymous.
"Radical Interior Changes Feature of Jacobs House," *The Capital
Times* (Madison, Wisconsin), January 14, 1938.

Anonymous.
"Architect Wright Boosts Tom Amlie for Senate: Calls Him 'Like
FDR,'" *The Capital Times* (Madison, Wisconsin), August 11, 1938.

Anonymous.
"Jacobs Home by Wright Shown in Display at Union," *The Capital
Times* (Madison, Wisconsin), March 26, 1939.

Anonymous.
"Wright to Give Four Lectures to British Builders," *The Capital
Times* (Madison, Wisconsin), April 2, 1939.

Anonymous.
"Announcement of 'Exhibition' of Photographs of Buildings by
Frank Lloyd Wright in London," *The Times* (London), May 4, 1939,
p. 14, col. 5.

Anonymous.
"A Vision of England: When Factories Would Add to Beauty," *The
Times* (London), May 6, 1939, p. 10, col. 2.

Anonymous.
"An American View of Architecture: Harmony with Nature," *The Times*
(London), May 11, 1939, p. 12, col. 5.

Baker, Geoffrey.
"Wright as Iconoclast: Contribution of Architect to Our Age as
Set Fourth at Museum of Modern Art," *The New York Times*, November
24, 1940, section 9, p. 10, col. 1.

Jacobs, Herbert.
"A Client to the Rescue," *The New York Times*, December 8, 1940,
section 10, p. 13, col. 3.

Baker, Geoffrey.
    "By Mail: Further Comment on Frank Lloyd Wright," *The New York Times*, December 15, 1940, section 10, p. 11, col. 7.

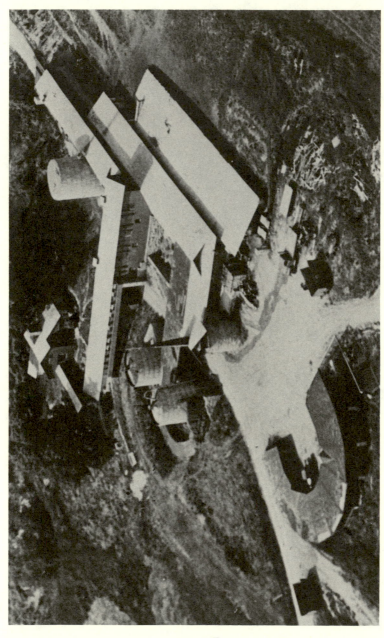

2-6.1　Aerial view of the Taliesin Midway Barns and Dairy and Machine Sheds (1938–1947), Spring Green, Wisconsin. Photo courtesy of *The Capital Times*, Madison, Wisconsin.

CHAPTER 6

NEW FORMS AND OLD FRIENDSHIPS
(1943 TO 1949)

Introduction

A review of Wright's years of continuing friendship with William
T. Evjue, E. Willis Jones, William A. Kittredge, Lloyd Downs Lewis,
Dorathi Bock Pierre, George and Helen Beal, and Dutch architect H. Th.
Wijdeveld is provided through the cataloguing and indexing of cor-
respondence from Wright to these persons. Important new building
forms were also developing during this period, such as the Second
Residence for Herbert Jacobs, the famous Solomon R. Guggenheim
Museum at New York, and the Unitarian Church at Shorewood Hills,
Wisconsin, near Madison; each of which is represented by the indexed
manuscripts, thus offering new insights into these works. World War
II and the reluctance of some members of the Taliesin Fellowship to
participate in the war caused Wright to seriously think about machines,
man, and politics. His son, John Lloyd, decides to write *My Father
Who Is on Earth*, and a series of letters between father and son
commenced on the merits of such a book. Several items of correspondence
from Wright to Ludwig Mies van der Rohe are indexed, offering some
insights into the relationship between the two, each with different,
sometimes opposing, philosophies of modern architecture.

Other correspondence located and catalogued for this period in-
clude letters to architect William Grey Purcell; City of New York
Parks Commissioner Robert Moses; John U. Nef; client Solomon R.
Guggenheim; Charles Angoff, the editor of *American Mercury*; Elkan
Allan; Harry B. Harvey; Arthur B. Gallion; client Mrs. Irwin Elkans
Auerbach, for whom Wright designed a residence which was never executed;
Elmer Berger; Edmund R. Purves, the Director of the American Institute
of Architects; architect Oskar Stonorov; and Harold M. Groves, a
famous economist who later became a backer of Wright's proposed Monona
Terrace Civic Center Project for Madison, Wisconsin. Manuscripts for
lectures and articles written during this period include "Address at
Princeton University Bicentennial Conference--Planning Man's Physical
Environment" of March 1947 and "In the Realm of Ideas," for the Society
of Contemporary American Art at Orchestra Hall, Chicago, in October
of 1948.

Wright's workload for this period increased tremendously from
previous periods. From 1943 to 1949 inclusive, he did 134 designs,
representing about 14 percent of all of the designs of his lifetime,
of which 50 were executed. In 1948 he did 41 designs, representing
the second busiest year of his architectural career with respect to
total number of designs for one year. Wright's busiest year with
respect to total number of designs was 1957, with a total of 43
designs.

B303

Date:
Undated (probably either January 1 or 2, 1943)

Type of Manuscript:
Letter

To:
William T. Evjue

From:
Frank Lloyd Wright

Collection:
The William Theodore Evjue Papers, 1905-1969
The State Historical Society of Wisconsin
MSS 244, Box 155, Folder 21

Medium:
Handwritten on Taliesin design stationery, signed "F.LL.W."

Size:
4 in. x 8-1/2 in.; 101.6 mm x 215.9 mm

Number of Pages:
1

Number of Words:
68

Descriptors:
William T. Evjue, Judge Patrick T. Stone, Military Draft,
The Capital Times

Review:
A brief note transmitting a letter to William T. Evjue from
Judge Stone who opposed Wright's students' views of the draft
during World War II. The transmitted letter was printed in *The
Capital Times* as "Judge Sends Letter to Fellowship: Replies to
Students Who Protested Attack on Frank Lloyd Wright."

B304

Date:
January 5, 1943

Type of Manuscript:
Letter

To:
August Derleth

From:
Frank Lloyd Wright
Taliesin
Spring Green, Wisconsin

Collection:
The August Derleth Papers
The State Historical Society of Wisconsin

Medium:
Typed on Taliesin design stationery, signed "F.LLW."

Size:
    8-1/2 in. x 11 in.; 215.9 mm x 279.4 mm

Number of Pages:
    1

Number of Words:
    118 Typed; 19 Handwritten

Descriptors:
    August Derleth, Vickers, Reality, Great Britain, World War II,
    Silvio Gesell's *Natural Economic Order* (book)

Review:
    Wright sends Derleth some reading materials on Great Britain with
    this transmittal letter.

B305

Date:
    January 8, 1943

Type of Manuscript:
    Letter

To:
    William T. Evjue

From:
    Frank Lloyd Wright

Collection:
    The William Theodore Evjue Papers, 1905-1969
    The State Historical Society of Wisconsin
    MSS 244, Box 155, Folder 21

Medium:
    Typed on Taliesin design stationery and signed "F.LL.W."

Size:
    7-1/2 in. x 8-5/8 in.; 190.5 mm x 219.1 mm

Number of Pages:
    2

Number of Words:
    245 Typed; 27 Handwritten

Descriptors:
    William T. Evjue, August Derleth, Clarence Darrow,
    Judge Patrick T. Stone

Review:
    Probably on Wright's problems with Judge Patrick T. Stone. The
    Judge Stone problem was given coverage by *The Capital Times* in
    "Federal Judge Patrick T. Stone Charged Wright Was 'Poisoning
    the Minds' of His Apprentices Against the Draft"; "Taliesin Men
    Demand Stone Retract Words: Call Court's Remarks on Fellowship,
    Wright 'Libelous'"; "Judge Sends Letter to Fellowship: Replies
    to Students Who Protested Attack on Frank Lloyd Wright"; and
    "Students Deny Influence Try in West Case: Reply to Judge Stone's
    Letter--Demand Apology to Frank Lloyd Wright."

B306

Date:
   January 12, 1943

Type of Manuscript:
   Letter

To:
   August Derleth

From:
   Frank Lloyd Wright
   Taliesin
   Spring Green, Wisconsin

Collection:
   The August Derleth Papers
   The State Historical Society of Wisconsin

Medium:
   Typed on Taliesin design stationery, signed "F.LL.W."

Size:
   8-1/2 in. x 11 in.; 215.9 mm x 279.4 mm

Number of Pages:
   1

Number of Words:
   53

Descriptors:
   August Derleth, August Derleth's *The Wisconsin: River
   of a Thousand Isles* (book)

Review:
   Wright comments on August Derleth's chapter, "The Shining Brow,"
   in his *The Wisconsin: River of a Thousand Isles* (New York: Farrar
   and Rinehart Inc., 1942, pp. 301-308); it offers a description
   of Wright.

B307

Date:
   January 22, 1943

Type of Manuscript:
   Letter

To:
   William T. Evjue

From:
   Frank Lloyd Wright

Collection:
   The William Theodore Evjue Papers, 1905-1969
   The State Historical Society of Wisconsin
   MSS 244, Box 155, Folder 21

Medium:
   Typed on Taliesin design stationery and signed "F.LL.W."

Size:
  7-1/2 in. x 8-5/8 in.; 190.5 mm x 219.1 mm

Number of Pages:
  1

Number of Words:
  39 Typed; 7 Handwritten

Descriptors:
  William T. Evjue

Review:
  Wright sends Evjue two articles to read.

B308

Date:
  January 27, 1943

Type of Manuscript:
  Telegram

To:
  E. Willis Jones
  Chicago, Illinois

From:
  Frank Lloyd Wright
  Spring Green, Wisconsin

Collection:
  Frank Lloyd Wright Correspondence with E. Willis Jones,
  1936-1959
  Special Collections Department
  Northwestern University Library

Medium:
  Western Union Telegram

Size:
  5-3/4 in. x 8 in.; 146.1 mm x 203.2 mm

Number of Pages:
  1

Number of Words:
  29

Descriptors:
  E. Willis Jones

Review:
  Wright is to visit Chicago.

B309

Date:
  March 1, 1943

Type of Manuscript:
  Letter

To:
   William A. Kittredge

From:
   Frank Lloyd Wright

Collection:
   William Kittredge Collection
   Newberry Library
   Chicago, Illinois

Medium:
   Typed on Taliesin design stationery, signed "Frank"

Size:
   7-1/2 in. x 8-1/2 in.; 190.5 mm x 215.9 mm

Number of Pages:
   1

Number of Words:
   53

Descriptors:
   William Kittredge

Review:
   Wright invites the Kittredges to visit Taliesin.

B310

Date:
   April 8, 1943

Type of Manuscript:
   Letter

To:
   Herbert Jacobs

From:
   Frank Lloyd Wright
   Taliesin
   Spring Green, Wisconsin

Collection:
   The Herbert and Katherine Jacobs Frank Lloyd Wright
   Collection
   The Art Institute of Chicago
   Documents, Box 1

Medium:
   Typed on Taliesin design stationery and signed "F.LL.W"

Size:
   4 in. x 8-1/2 in.; 101.6 mm x 215.9 mm

Number of Pages:
   1

Number of Words:
   100

Descriptors:
Herbert Jacobs, *An Autobiography*

Review:
Wright invites Jacobs to Taliesin to visit with him. This letter
has been photographically reproduced in Herbert and Katherine
Jacobs's *Building with Frank Lloyd Wright: An Illustrated Memoir*,
p. 74.

B311

Date:
July 26, 1943

Type of Manuscript:
Letter

To:
William T. Evjue

From:
Frank Lloyd Wright
Taliesin
Spring Green, Wisconsin

Collection:
The William Theodore Evjue Papers, 1905-1969
The State Historical Society of Wisconsin
MSS 244, Box 155, Folder 21

Medium:
Typed on Taliesin design stationery and signed "F.LL.W."

Size:
8-1/2 in. x 11 in.; 215.9 mm x 279.4 mm

Number of Pages:
1

Number of Words:
66

Descriptors:
William T. Evjue, *An Autobiography*, *The Hartford
Courant* (Newspaper)

Review:
Wright sends a review of his book, *An Autobiography*, to Evjue.
The review might be the one printed by Evjue in *The Capital Times*
entitled "Publish Autobiography of Frank Lloyd Wright."

B312

Date:
December 11, 1943

Type of Manuscript:
Letter

To:
Herbert and Katherine Jacobs

From:
   Frank Lloyd Wright
   Taliesin
   Spring Green, Wisconsin

Collection:
   The Herbert and Katherine Jacobs Frank Lloyd Wright Collection
   The Art Institute of Chicago
   Documents, Box 1

Medium:
   Typed on Taliesin design stationery and signed
   "F.LL.W"

Size:
   8-1/2 in. x 11 in.; 215.9 mm x 279.4 mm

Number of Pages:
   2

Number of Words:
   234

Descriptors:
   Herbert Jacobs, Festus Jones, Herbert Jacobs Second
   Residence

Review:
   Discussion of Jacobs' needs in a house. This letter is photograph-
   ically reproduced in Herbert and Katherine Jacobs's *Building with
   Frank Lloyd Wright*, p. 80.

B313

Date:
   December 30, 1943

Type of Manuscript:
   Letter

To:
   Herbert Jacobs
   Middleton, Wisconsin

From:
   Frank Lloyd Wright
   Taliesin
   Spring Green, Wisconsin

Collection:
   The Herbert and Katherine Jacobs Frank Lloyd Wright Collection
   The Art Institute of Chicago
   Documents, Box 1

Medium:
   Typed on Taliesin design stationery, signed "F.LL.W"

Size:
   8-1/2 in. x 11 in.; 215.9 mm x 279.4 mm

Number of Pages:
   1

Number of Words:
38

Descriptors:
Herbert Jacobs, Herbert Jacobs Second Residence

Review:
News of Jacobs's new house design. The text of this letter was reproduced in Herbert and Katherine Jacobs' *Building With Frank Lloyd Wright*, p. 81.

B314

Date:
1943

Type of Manuscript:
Autographed book

To:
Harold M. Groves

By:
Frank Lloyd Wright

Collection:
The Harold M. Groves Papers, 1927-1969
The State Historical Society of Wisconsin
MSS 272, Box 24, Folder 5

Medium:
Book signed "To Harold Groves with thanks
Frank Lloyd Wright"

Size:
8-7/16 in. x 8-7/16 in.; 214.3 mm x 214.3 mm

Number of Pages:
30

Descriptors:
Harold M. Groves, *An Autobiography*, Broadacre City

Review:
An autographed copy of Frank Lloyd Wright's *An Autobiography, Book Six: Broadacre City*, Taliesin, 1943.

B315

Date:
New Year 1944

Type of Manuscript:
New Year's card

To:
John Lloyd Wright

From:
Frank Lloyd Wright
Taliesin

2-6.2   The earth bermed, north facing exterior elevation of the Second Residence for Herbert Jacobs (1943), Middleton, Wisconsin. Photo by the author.

2-6.3   Exterior side elevation of the Second Residence for Herbert Jacobs (1943), Middleton, Wisconsin. Photo by the author.

2-6.4 The glass door walled exterior south elevation of the Second Residence for Herbert Jacobs (1943), Middleton, Wisconsin. Photo by the author.

2-6.5　Interior view, looking west, of the ground level living room area of the Second Residence for Herbert Jacobs (1943), Middleton, Wisconsin. Photo by the author.

2-6.6　Interior view, looking northeast, of the ground level living room area, with the fireplace in the background, of the Second Residence for Herbert Jacobs (1943), Middleton, Wisconsin. Photo by the author.

Collection:
    The John Lloyd Wright Collection
    The Avery Architectural Library
    Columbia University
    Folder 11

Medium:
    Greeting card of Taliesin design

Size:
    6-1/2 in. x 14 in.; 165.1 mm x 355.6 mm

Number of Pages:
    1

Number of Words:
    38 Printed

Descriptors:
    John Lloyd Wright, New Year 1944, Organic Commandments

Review:
    New Year's greetings with the four organic commandments written
    by Wright.

B316

Date:
    New Year 1944

Type of Manuscript:
    New Year's card

Collection:
    Special Collections Department
    Northwestern University Library
    Northwestern University

Medium:
    Greeting card of Taliesin design, signed by Wright

Size:
    6-1/2 in. x 14 in.; 165.1 mm x 355.6 mm

Number of Pages:
    1

Number of Words:
    38 Printed

Descriptors:
    New Year 1944, Organic Commandments

Review:
    New Year's greetings with the four organic commandments written
    by Wright.

B317

Date:
    January 24, 1944

Type of Manuscript:
  Letter

To:
  William Grey Purcell
  Pasadena, California

From:
  Frank Lloyd Wright
  Taliesin
  Spring Green, Wisconsin

Collection:
  Purcell and Elmslie, Architects, Minneapolis, Minnesota
  Records, 1855-1965
  The University of Minnesota Library
  Architectural History Archives

Medium:
  Typed on Taliesin design stationery and signed "F.L.L.W."

Size:
  8-1/2 in. x 11 in.; 215.9 mm x 279.4 mm

Number of Pages:
  1

Number of Words:
  96

Descriptors:
  William Grey Purcell, Louis H. Sullivan, Albert Kahn

Review:
  Talk of Louis H. Sullivan and Albert Kahn.

B318

Date:
  January 30, 1944

Type of Manuscript:
  Proposed newspaper article

To:
  Lloyd Downs Lewis

From:
  Frank Lloyd Wright
  Taliesin

Collection:
  Lloyd Downs Lewis Papers, 1863-1949
  The Newberry Library
  Chicago, Illinois

Medium:
  Typed, with brief handwritten note, signed "Frank"

Size:
  8-1/2 in. x 13 in.; 215.9 mm x 330.2 mm

Number of Pages:
3

Number of Words:
811 Typed, 19 Handwritten

Descriptors:
Lloyd Downs Lewis, William Allen White, Robert Browning,
Elizabeth Barrett, Chauncey Williams, Iovanna Lloyd Wright,
Sally White, Mary White, Governor Henry Allen

Review:
A short story about William and Sally White written by Wright
and submitted to Lloyd Downs Lewis for possible publication.
Wright had also sent a copy of this article to William T. Evjue,
the editor of *The Capital Times* (see B319, Wright's letter to
William T. Evjue dated January 31, 1944). Evjue printed the
article in *The Capital Times* as "Frank Lloyd Wright in Tribute
to Will and Sally (Allen White)." It is not presently known
whether Lewis ever used Wright's article for publication. William
Allen White was the editor of the *Emporia Gazette* (Kansas).

B319

Date:
January 31, 1944

Type of Manuscript:
Letter

To:
William T. Evjue

From:
Frank Lloyd Wright

Collection:
The William Theodore Evjue Papers, 1905-1969
The State Historical Society of Wisconsin
MSS 244, Box 155, Folder 21

Medium:
Handwritten, signed "Frank"

Size:
2-1/4 in. x 8-1/2 in.; 57.2 mm x 215.9 mm

Number of Pages:
1

Number of Words:
44

Descriptors:
William T. Evjue, Will White

Review:
Wright is sending an article for publication in *The Capital
Times* to Evjue for his review with this transmittal letter.
Evjue published the short article in *The Capital Times* as "Frank
Lloyd Wright in Tribute to Will and Sally (Allen White)" on

February 1, 1944. Wright had also transmitted this same article
to Lloyd Downs Lewis (see B318, F.L. Wright's letter to Lloyd
Downs Lewis dated January 30, 1944). William Allen White was the
editor of the *Emporia Gazette* (Kansas).

B320

Date:
   February 8, 1944

Type of Manuscript:
   Letter

To:
   Herbert Jacobs

From:
   Frank Lloyd Wright
   Taliesin

Collection:
   The Herbert and Katherine Jacobs Frank Lloyd Wright Collection
   The Art Institute of Chicago
   Documents, Box 1

Medium:
   Typed of Taliesin design stationery, signed "F.LL.W"

Size:
   8-1/2 in. x 11 in.; 215.9 mm x 279.4 mm

Number of Pages:
   1

Number of Words:
   63 Typed; 4 Handwritten

Descriptors:
   Herbert Jacobs, Herbert Jacobs Second Residence

Review:
   More news on Wright's design for the second Herbert Jacobs
   Residence. This letter was photographically reproduced in
   Herbert and Katherine Jacobs's *Building With Frank Lloyd Wright*,
   p. 82.

B321

Date:
   March 15, 1944

Type of Manuscript:
   Letter

To:
   William T. Evjue

From:
   Frank Lloyd Wright

Collection:
   The William Theodore Evjue Papers, 1905-1969

The State Historical Society of Wisconsin
MSS 244, Box 155, Folder 21

Medium:
Typed on Taliesin design stationery, signed "Frank"

Size:
8-1/2 in. x 11 in.; 215.9 mm x 279.4 mm

Number of Pages:
1

Number of Words:
174

Descriptors:
William T. Evjue, Winston Churchill, Franklin Roosevelt,
World War II

Review:
Wright offers to write an editorial for Evjue's *The Capital
Times* newspaper on politics during World War II.

B322

Date:
March 21, 1944

Type of Manuscript:
Letter

To:
Herbert Jacobs

From:
Frank Lloyd Wright
Taliesin

Collection:
The Herbert and Katherine Jacobs Frank Lloyd Wright
Collection
The Art Institute of Chicago
Documents, Box 1

Medium:
Typed on Taliesin design stationery and signed "F.LL.W."

Size:
8-1/2 in. x 11 in.; 215.9 mm x 279.4 mm

Number of Pages:
1

Number of Words:
51

Descriptors:
Herbert Jacobs, Herbert Jacobs Second Residence

Review:
A bill to Jacobs for Wright's architectural services in the
design of the second Herbert Jacobs Residence.

B323

Date:
March 22, 1944

Type of Manuscript:
Cancelled bank check

To:
Frank Lloyd Wright

From:
Herbert Jacobs

Collection:
The Herbert and Katherine Jacobs Frank Lloyd Wright Collection
The Art Institute of Chicago
Documents, Box 1

Medium:
Bank check signed "Frank Lloyd Wright"

Number of Pages:
1

Descriptors:
Herbert Jacobs, Herbert Jacobs Second Residence

Review:
Payment to Wright from Jacobs for design work on Jacobs's
second residence.

B324

Date:
June 16, 1944

Type of Manuscript:
Letter

To:
William T. Evjue

From:
Frank Lloyd Wright

Collection:
The William Theodore Evjue Papers, 1905-1969
The State Historical Society of Wisconsin
MSS 244, Box 155, Folder 21

Medium:
Handwritten and signed "Frank"

Size:
8-1/2 in. x 14 in.; 215.9 mm x 355.6 mm

Number of Pages:
1

Number of Words:
248

Descriptors:
   William T. Evjue, World War II, Machines, *The Capital
   Times*

Review:
   Wright discusses the war at great length and in particular
   the role of machines in the war. Wright suggests that Evjue
   write an editorial for *The Capital Times* on the topic.

B325

Date:
   August 26, 1944

Type of Manuscript:
   Letter

To:
   Unknown (possibly Ludwig Mies van der Rohe)

From:
   Frank Lloyd Wright
   Taliesin

Collection:
   The Library of Congress, Manuscript Division
   Ludwig Mies van der Rohe Papers, 1921-1969
   Container 60 (General Office File)

Medium:
   Typed on Taliesin design stationery, signed
   "F.LL.W"

Number of Pages:
   1

Number of Words:
   45 Typed; 9 Handwritten

Descriptors:
   Baldinger, Ludwig Mies van der Rohe

Review:
   Humorous talk of Ludwig Mies van der Rohe visiting Wright.

B326

Date:
   September 27, 1944

Type of Manuscript:
   Letter

To:
   John Lloyd Wright

From:
   Frank Lloyd Wright

Collection:
   The John Lloyd Wright Collection
   The Avery Architectural Library

Columbia University
Folder 11

Medium:
Typed on Taliesin design stationery, signed "DAD"

Size:
8-1/2 in. x 11 in.; 215.9 mm x 279.4 mm

Number of Pages:
1

Number of Words:
50

Descriptors:
John Lloyd Wright, *My Father Who Is on Earth*

Review:
On John Lloyd's writing the book *My Father Who Is on Earth*,
a biography of F.L. Wright. It was published in 1946.

B327

Date:
September 29, 1944

Type of Manuscript:
Letter

To:
Robert Moses

From:
Frank Lloyd Wright
Taliesin
Spring Green, Wisconsin

Source:
Robert Moses
Public Works: A Dangerous Trade, p. 858

Number of Words:
164

Descriptors:
Robert Moses, Broadacre City, Aymar Embury II, Eliel
Saarinen, *Magazine of Art, The New York Times Magazine,
A Taliesin Square-Paper: A Nonpolitical Voice from Our
Democratic Minority*

Review:
Friendly comments regarding an article featuring Robert Moses'
comments: "Mr. Moses Dissects the 'Long-Haired Planners,'" in
which Moses described Wright as another "brilliant but erratic
architect and planner." Wright also with a published response
entitled "Viewpoints: To the Mole." Wright also had "To the
Mole" printed in his *A Taliesin Square-Paper: A Nonpolitical
Voice from Our Democratic Minority*. A very strong response to
Moses' article was presented by H.L. Brock entitled "In Defense
of City Planners--Mr. Moses' Sharp Attack on "Revolutionary
Sophisticates' Brings out a Vigorous Defense."

B328

Date:
November 15, 1944

Type of Manuscript:
Letter

To:
Ludwig Mies van der Rohe

From:
Frank Lloyd Wright

Collection:
The Library of Congress, Manuscript Division
Ludwig Mies van der Rohe Papers, 1921-1969
Container 60 (General Office File)

Medium:
Typed on Taliesin design stationery, signed
"F.LL.W"

Number of Pages:
1

Number of Words:
26 Typed; 6 Handwritten

Descriptors:
Ludwig Mies van der Rohe, Thanksgiving 1944

Review:
An invitation for Mies van der Rohe to spend Thanksgiving with
Wright.

B329

Date:
December 9, 1944

Type of Manuscript:
Letter

To:
Robert Moses

From:
Frank Lloyd Wright

Source:
Robert Moses
Public Works: A Dangerous Trade, pp. 858-859

Number of Words:
316

Descriptors:
Robert Moses, Solomon R. Guggenheim Museum, Starrett
Company, *The New York Times Magazine*, Harry F. Guggenheim

Review:
Wright feels that Moses' article which appeared in *The New York
Times Magazine* entitled "Mr. Moses Dissects the 'Long-Haired

2-6.7 Exterior view, looking south, of the Solomon R. Guggenheim Museum (1956), New York. Photo by the author.

2-6.8 Exterior view of the main entrance to the Solomon R. Guggenheim Museum (1956), New York. Photo by the author.

2-6.9 Interior view, showing second and third levels of ramp, of the Solomon R. Guggenheim Museum (1956), New York. Photo by the author.

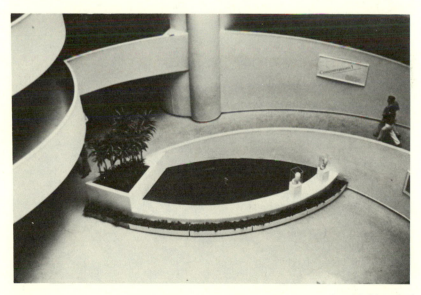

2-6.10 Interior view of ground level pool from the ramp at the third level of the Solomon R. Guggenheim Museum (1956), New York. Photo by the author.

Planners'" may harm Wright's efforts to build the Solomon R.
Guggenheim Museum in New York. And, Wright asks for Moses's
assistance.

B330

Date:
   December 9, 1944

Type of Manuscript:
   Letter

To:
   William T. Evjue
   Madison, Wisconsin

From:
   Frank Lloyd Wright

Collection:
   The William Theodore Evjue Papers, 1905-1969
   The State Historical Society of Wisconsin
   MSS 244, Box 155, Folder 21

Medium:
   Typed on Taliesin design stationery and signed "Frank"

Size:
   7-1/4 in. x 8-1/2 in.; 184.2 mm x 215.9 mm

Number of Pages:
   1

Number of Words:
   65

Descriptors:
   William T. Evjue, World War II, *The Capital Times*,
   Pearl Harbor

Review:
   Wright congratulates Evjue for a recent article in *The Capital
   Times* on World War II.

B331

Date:
   New Year 1945

Type of Manuscript:
   New Year's card and note

To:
   John Lloyd Wright

From:
   Frank Lloyd Wright
   Taliesin

Collection:
   The John Lloyd Wright Collection
   The Avery Architectural Library

Columbia University
Folder 11

Medium:
Greeting card (Taliesin design), with handwritten note,
signed "F.LL.W."

Size:
6-1/2 in. x 14 in.; 165.1 mm x 355.6 mm

Number of Pages:
1

Number of Words:
15 Handwritten; 38 Printed

Descriptors:
John Lloyd Wright, New Year 1945, Organic Commandments

Review:
New Year's greetings from Frank Lloyd Wright. The card contains
the four organic commandments written by him. A photoreproduction
of both the card and note written were reproduced in John Lloyd
Wright's *My Father Who Is on Earth*, p. 127.

B332

Date:
New Year 1945

Type of Manuscript:
New Year's card

To:
George and Helen Beal

From:
Frank Lloyd Wright

Collection:
Frank Lloyd Wright Collection
Kenneth Spencer Research Library
University of Kansas

Medium:
Printed on white paper, with autographed letter, and signed

Size:
4-3/4 in. x 24-7/8 in.; 120 mm x 631 mm

Number of Pages:
2

Number of Words:
38 Printed; 6 Handwritten

Descriptors:
George Beal, Christmas 1944, Organic Commandments

Review:
Holiday greetings from Wright with the four organic commandments
written by him.

B333

Date:
New Year 1945

Type of Manuscript:
New Years card and note

To:
August Derleth

From:
Frank Lloyd Wright
Taliesin

Collection:
The August Derleth Papers
The State Historical Society of Wisconsin

Medium:
Printed, with brief handwritten note signed "F.LLW"

Size:
6-1/2 in. x 25 in.; 165.1 mm x 635 mm

Number of Pages:
1

Number of Words:
38 Printed; 12 Handwritten

Descriptors:
New Year 1945, Organic Commandments, August Derleth,
Taliesin Fellowship

Review:
Holiday greetings with a brief note concerning the Taliesin
Fellowship.

B334

Date:
New Year 1945

Type of Manuscript:
New Year's card

From:
Frank Lloyd Wright

Collection:
Special Collections Department
Northwestern University Library
Northwestern University

Medium:
Printed

Size:
6-1/2 in. x 25 in.; 165.1 mm x 635 mm

Number of Pages:
1

Number of Words:
   38 Printed

Descriptors:
   New Year 1945, Organic Commandments

B335

Date:
   February 23, 1945

Type of Manuscript:
   Letter   -

To:
   John Lloyd Wright

From:
   Frank Lloyd Wright
   Taliesin West
   Scottsdale, Arizona

Collection:
   The John Lloyd Wright Collection
   The Avery Architectural Library
   Columbia University
   Folder 11

Medium:
   Typed on Taliesin design stationery, signed "Father"

Size:
   8-1/2 in. x 11 in.; 215.9 mm x 279.4 mm

Number of Pages:
   1

Number of Words:
   25

Descriptors:
   John Lloyd Wright

Review:
   Frank Lloyd Wright wants to know where his son John Lloyd is
   located.

B336

Date:
   March 6, 1945

Type of Manuscript:
   Letter

To:
   John Lloyd Wright

From:
   Frank Lloyd Wright
   Taliesin West
   Scottsdale, Arizona

Collection:
   The John Lloyd Wright Collection
   The Avery Architectural Library
   Columbia University
   Folder 11

Medium:
   Typed on Taliesin design stationery and signed
   "F.LL. W. your Dad"

Size:
   8-1/2 in. x 11 in.; 215.9 mm x 279.4 mm

Number of Pages:
   1

Number of Words:
   57

Descriptors:
   John Lloyd Wright, *My Father Who Is on Earth*, David Wright

Review:
   Frank Lloyd asks his son not to write a book on him. John Lloyd
   was then in the process of writing *My Father Who Is on Earth*.

B337

Date:
   March 8, 1945

Type of Manuscript:
   Letter

To:
   Robert Moses

From:
   Frank Lloyd Wright
   Taliesin West
   Scottsdale, Arizona

Source:
   Robert Moses
   Public Works: A Dangerous Trade, pp. 859-860

Number of Words:
   1972

Descriptors:
   Robert Moses, Olgivanna Lloyd Wright, *Magazine of Art*,
   *A Taliesin Square-Paper: A Nonpolitical Voice from Our
   Democratic Minority*, Mary Moses

Review:
   Discussion of Wright's "Viewpoints: To the Mole" in *Magazine
   of Art* and "To the Mole" in *A Taliesin Square-Paper*. Also, Wright
   is to visit New York. A friendly letter.

B338

Date:
June 25, 1945

Type of Manuscript:
Letter

To:
John Lloyd Wright

From:
Frank Lloyd Wright

Collection:
The John Lloyd Wright Collection
The Avery Architectural Library
Columbia University
Folder 11

Medium:
Typed on Taliesin design stationery, signed "Dad"

Size:
8-1/2 in. x 11 in.; 215.9 mm x 279.4 mm

Number of Pages:
1

Number of Words:
33

Descriptors:
John Lloyd Wright, *My Father Who Is on Earth*

Review:
A friendly note on publicity.

B339

Date:
July 19, 1945

Type of Manuscript:
Letter

To:
William T. Evjue

From:
Frank Lloyd Wright

Collection:
The William Theodore Evjue Papers, 1905-1969
The State Historical Society of Wisconsin
MSS 244, Box 155, Folder 21

Medium:
Handwritten and signed "Frank"

Size:
6-1/4 in. x 6-3/4 in.; 158.8 mm x 171.5 mm

Number of Pages:
1

Number of Words:
    53

Descriptors:
    William T. Evjue, *The Capital Times*

Review:
    Wright comments on a recent article about him in *The Capital Times*.

B340

Date:
    September 14, 1945

Type of Manuscript:
    Letter

To:
    Herbert Jacobs

From:
    Frank Lloyd Wright
    Taliesin

Collection:
    The Herbert and Katherine Jacobs Frank Lloyd Wright Collection
    The Art Institute of Chicago
    Documents, Box 1

Medium:
    Typed on Taliesin design stationery, signed "F.LL.W."

Size:
    8-1/2 in. x 11 in.; 215.9 mm x 279.4 mm

Number of Pages:
    1

Number of Words:
    17

Descriptors:
    Herbert Jacobs

Review:
    Wright to visit Jacobs.

B341

Date:
    New Year 1946

Type of Manuscript:
    New Year's card

To:
    John Lloyd Wright

From:
    Frank Lloyd Wright
    Taliesin

Collection:
    The John Lloyd Wright Collection
    The Avery Architectural Library
    Columbia University
    Folder 11

Medium:
    Greeting card of Taliesin design

Number of Pages:
    1

Number of Words:
    7 Handwritten

Descriptors:
    John Lloyd Wright, New Year 1946

Review:
    New Year's greetings from the F.L. Wrights to the J.L. Wrights.

B342

Date:
    New Year 1946

Type of Manuscript:
    New Year's Card/Christmas Card

To:
    Edgar Tafel

From:
    Frank Lloyd Wright
    Taliesin

Source:
    Edgar Tafel
    Apprentice to Genius: Years with Frank Lloyd Wright, p. 19

Medium:
    Greeting Card of Taliesin design

Number of Pages:
    1

Number of Words:
    7

Descriptors:
    Edgar Tafel, New Year 1946

Review:
    New Year's greetings from the F.L. Wrights to Edgar Tafel.
    The card is photographically reproduced in Tafel's book. It is
    the same design as the one Wright sent to his son John Lloyd
    that year (see B341).

B343

Date:
    New Year 1946

Type of Manuscript:
New Year's card

From:
Frank Lloyd Wright

Collection:
Special Collections Department
Northwestern University Library
Northwestern University

Medium:
Greeting card of Taliesin design and signed

Number of Pages:
1

Descriptors:
New Year 1946

B344

Date:
January 31, 1946

Type of Manuscript:
Letter

To:
Herbert and Katherine Jacobs

From:
Frank Lloyd Wright
Taliesin

Collection:
The Herbert and Katherine Jacobs Frank Lloyd Wright Collection
The Art Institute of Chicago
Documents, Box 1

Medium:
Typed on Taliesin design stationery, signed "F.LL.W."

Size:
8-1/2 in. x 11 in.; 215.9 mm x 279.4 mm

Number of Pages:
1

Number of Words:
23

Descriptors:
Herbert Jacobs

Review:
A brief personal note.

B345

Date:
February 11, 1946

Type of Manuscript:
Letter

To:
Harold Groves

From:
Frank Lloyd Wright
Taliesin West
Scottsdale, Arizona

Collection:
The Harold M. Groves Papers, 1927-1969
The State Historical Society of Wisconsin
MSS 272, Box 13, Folder 11

Medium:
Typed on red-square design stationery, signed
"F.LL.W"

Size:
8-1/2 in. x 11± in.; 215.9 mm x 279.4± mm

Number of Pages:
1

Number of Words:
96 Typed; 2 Handwritten

Descriptors:
Harold M. Groves, Unitarian Church (Shorewood Hills, Wisconsin)

Review:
Wright talks of the need for a topographic map of the proposed site of the Unitarian Church at Shorewood Hills, Wisconsin which he is to design. Groves was a member and representative of the First Unitarian Society in Madison, and assisted Wright during the design and ultimate construction of the building.

B346

Date:
February 23, 1946

Type of Manuscript:
Letter

To:
Herbert Jacobs

From:
Frank Lloyd Wright
Taliesin West

Collection:
The Herbert and Katherine Jacobs Frank Lloyd Wright Collection
The Art Institute of Chicago
Documents, Box 1

Medium:
Typed on Taliesin red-square stationery, signed "F.LL.W"

2-6.11 Aerial view of the Unitarian Church (1947) under construction at Shorewood Hills, Wisconsin. Photo by John Newhouse; courtesy of the State Historical Society of Wisconsin.

2-6.12 The Unitarian Church (1947) under construction at Shorewood Hills, Wisconsin. Photo by John Newhouse; courtesy of the State Historical Society of Wisconsin.

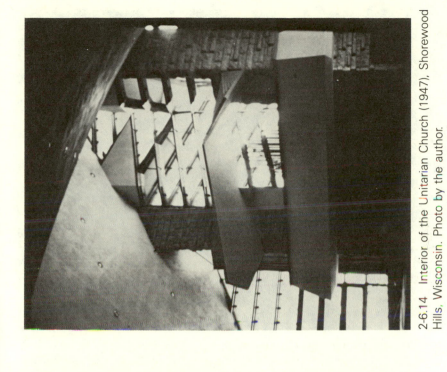

2-6.14 Interior of the Unitarian Church (1947), Shorewood Hills, Wisconsin. Photo by the author.

2-6.13 Roof framing of the Unitarian Church (1947) under construction, Shorewood Hills, Wisconsin. Photo by John Newhouse; courtesy of the State Historical Society of Wisconsin.

2-6.15 Unitarian Church (1947), Shorewood Hills, Wisconsin, under construction. Photo by John Newhouse; courtesy of the State Historical Society of Wisconsin.

2-6.16 Exterior elevation of the entrance hall (left) and rostrum of the Unitarian Church (1947), Shorewood Hills, Wisconsin. Photo by the author.

2-6.17 Exterior detailed view of the pitched roof and glass area of the rostrum of the Unitarian Church (1947), Shorewood Hills, Wisconsin. Photo by the author.

Size:
    8-1/2 in. x 11 in.; 215.9 mm x 279.4 mm

Number of Pages:
    1

Number of Words:
    27

Descriptors:
    Herbert Jacobs

Review:
    Wright to visit the Jacobses in Wisconsin.

B347

Date:
    May 11, 1946

Type of Manuscript:
    Letter

To:
    John U. Nef
    University of Chicago
    Chicago, Illinois

From:
    Frank Lloyd Wright

Collection:
    Box 11:9
    Elinor Castle Nef Papers
    University of Chicago Library
    University of Chicago

Medium:
    Typed on Taliesin design stationery, signed
    "Frank Lloyd Wright"

Size:
    8-1/2 in. x 11 in.; 215.9 mm x 279.4 mm

Number of Pages:
    1

Number of Words:
    44

Descriptors:
    John U. Nef, The University of Chicago

Review:
    Wright is to go to dinner with Mr. Nef.

B348

Date:
    May 30, 1946

Type of Manuscript:
    Letter

To:
   John Lloyd Wright

From:
   Frank Lloyd Wright

Collection:
   The John Lloyd Wright Collection
   The Avery Architectural Library
   Columbia University
   Folder 11

Medium:
   Typed on Taliesin design stationery and signed "Dad"

Size:
   8-1/2 in. x 11 in.; 215.9 mm x 279.4 mm

Number of Pages:
   1

Number of Words:
   120

Descriptors:
   John Lloyd Wright, Taliesin West, Phoenix, Arizona,
   Biltmore Hotel, Arcadia (Phoenix), Blaine Drake, David Wright

Review:
   John Lloyd intends to visit Arizona and Wright offers him
   advice on where to stay while there.

B349

Date:
   July 11, 1946

Type of Manuscript:
   Letter

To:
   John Lloyd Wright

From:
   Frank Lloyd Wright
   Taliesin

Collection:
   The John Lloyd Wright Collection
   The Avery Architectural Library
   Columbia University
   Folder 11

Medium:
   Typed on Taliesin design stationery, signed "Father"

Size:
   8-1/2 in. x 11 in.; 215.9 mm x 279.4 mm

Number of Pages:
   1

Number of Words:
   33

Descriptors:
   John Lloyd Wright, *The House Beautiful* (by Frank Lloyd Wright and
   W.C. Gannett), W.C. Gannett, W.H. Winslow

Review:
   Brief discussion of *The House Beautiful* by Frank Lloyd Wright and
   W.C. Gannett. Apparently John Lloyd had asked his father about
   the early Wright publication. The book had been printed and
   published in River Forest, Illinois, at the Auvergne Press by
   William Herman Winslow in 1896-1897. John Lloyd wrote a biography
   of F.L. Wright, *My Father Who Is on Earth*, in which the text of
   The House Beautiful was reproduced.

B350

Date:
   July 22, 1946

Type of Manuscript:
   Letter

To:
   E. Willis Jones

From:
   Frank Lloyd Wright

Collection:
   Frank Lloyd Wright Correspondence with E. Willis Jones,
   1936-1959
   Special Collections Department
   Northwestern University Library

Medium:
   Typed on Taliesin design stationery, signed "F.L.L.W."

Size:
   7-1/2 in. x 8-1/2 in.; 190.5 mm x 215.9 mm

Number of Pages:
   1

Number of Words:
   41

Descriptors:
   E. Willis Jones, David Jones, Taliesin Fellowship

Review:
   Jones is invited to bring David (his son?) to the Taliesin
   Fellowship.

B351

Date:
   July 25, 1946

Type of Manuscript:
   Letter

To:
   Herbert Jacobs

From:
   Frank Lloyd Wright

Collection:
   The Herbert and Katherine Jacobs Frank Lloyd Wright Collection
   The Art Institute of Chicago
   Documents, Box 1

Medium:
   Typed on Taliesin design stationery, signed "F.LL.W"

Size:
   8-1/2 in. x 11 in.; 215.9 mm x 279.4 mm

Number of Pages:
   1

Number of Words:
   57

Descriptors:
   Herbert Jacobs, Herbert Jacobs Second Residence

Review:
   Word from Wright on the progress of his plans for the second
   Herbert Jacobs Residence.

B352

Date:
   August 14, 1946

Type of Manuscript:
   Letter

To:
   Solomon R. Guggenheim

From:
   Frank Lloyd Wright

Source:
   Solomon R. Guggenheim Foundation
   *The Solomon R. Guggenheim Museum, Frank Lloyd Wright,
   Architect*

Number of Words:
   294

Descriptors:
   Solomon R. Guggenheim, Solomon R. Guggenheim Museum

Review:
   Wright describes in detail the characteristics of his Solomon R.
   Guggenheim Museum design to Mr. Guggenheim. The letter appears
   to be a portion of a larger text which was not printed in the
   source book.

B353

Date:
   August 21, 1946

Type of Manuscript:
   Letter

To:
   Edward V. Olencki
   Joe Fujikama
   Edward A. Duckett
   M. Goldsmith
   Mies van der Rohe

From:
   Frank Lloyd Wright

Collection:
   The Library of Congress, Manuscript Division
   Ludwig Mies van der Rohe Papers, 1921-1969
   Container 60 (General Office File)

Medium:
   Typed on Taliesin design stationery, signed "F.LL.W"

Number of Pages:
   1

Number of Words:
   61

Descriptors:
   Edward V. Olencki, Joe Fujikama, Edward A. Duckett,
   M. Goldsmith, Ludwig Mies van der Rohe

Review:
   Response to a request from friends of Mies van der Rohe to visit
   Wright at Taliesin at Spring Green, Wisconsin.

B354

Date:
   October 12, 1946

Type of Manuscript:
   Letter

To:
   Ludwig Mies van der Rohe

From:
   Frank Lloyd Wright
   Taliesin

Collection:
   The Library of Congress, Manuscript Division
   Ludwig Mies van der Rohe Papers, 1921-1969
   Container 60 (General Office File)

Medium:
   Typed on Taliesin design stationery, signed "Frank"

Size:
8-1/2 in. x 11 in.; 215.9 mm x 279.4 mm

Number of Pages:
1

Number of Words:
31

Descriptors:
Ludwig Mies van der Rohe, Helene Buchwieser

Review:
Invitation for Mies van der Rohe to visit Wright at Taliesin.

B355

Date:
Christmas 1946

Type of Manuscript:
Christmas card

To:
George and Helen Beal

From:
Frank Lloyd Wright

Collection:
Frank Lloyd Wright Collection
Kenneth Spencer Research Library
University of Kansas

Medium:
Christmas card, heavy beige paper; printed design
possibly by Gene Masselink; embossed "Taliesin to 1946"

Size:
8-1/16 in. x 11 in.; 204 mm x 279 mm

Number of Pages:
1

Number of Words:
8 Handwritten; 3 Embossed

Descriptors:
George Beal, Christmas 1946, Eugene Masselink

Review:
Holiday greetings to the Beals from Wright.

B356

Date:
January 27, 1947

Type of Manuscript:
Letter

To:
Charles Angoff
New York, New York

From:
  Frank Lloyd Wright
  Taliesin

Collection:
  The Library of Congress, Manuscript Division
  Lawrence Edmund Spivak Papers, 1927-1960
  The *American Mercury* File, 1927-1953, Editorial Correspondence
  Container C1

Medium:
  Typed on Taliesin design stationery, signed
  "Frank Lloyd Wright"

Size:
  8-1/2 in. x 11 in.; 215.9 mm x 279.4 mm

Number of Pages:
  1

Number of Words:
  33

Descriptors:
  Charles Angoff, *American Mercury*

Review:
  Wright is to prepare an article for *American Mercury* magazine.
  Research into this has not shown if Wright indeed ever wrote
  an article for *American Mercury*.

B357

Date:
  February 26, 1947

Type of Manuscript:
  Letter

To:
  Elkan Allan
  Hutchinson and Co.
  London

From:
  Frank Lloyd Wright
  Taliesin West

Collection:
  The Oak Park Public Library
  Oak Park, Illinois

Medium:
  Typed on Taliesin design stationery, signed
  "Frank Lloyd Wright"

Size:
  8-1/2 in. x 11 in.; 215.9 mm x 279.4 mm

Number of Pages:
  1

Number of Words:
  40

Descriptors:
  Elkan Allan, Hutchinson and Co.

Review:
  Brief note on an undisclosed subject.

B358

Date:
  March 5-6, 1947

Type of Manuscript:
  Text of speech

Title:
  "Address at Princeton University Bicentennial Conference--
  Planning Man's Physical Environment"

By:
  Frank Lloyd Wright

Collection:
  The Wrightiana Collection
  The Art Institute of Chicago

Medium:
  Mimeographed and typed single spaced

Size:
  8-1/2 in. x 11 in.; 215.9 mm x 279.4 mm

Number of Pages:
  4

Descriptors:
  Planning Man's Physical Environment (Princeton University)
  Conference, Arizona, United Nations, Education, Art, Religion,
  Democracy

Review:
  Wright speaks on education, ethics, American cities, and
  labor unions in this relatively short address.

B359

Date:
  March 18, 1947

Type of Manuscript:
  Letter

To:
  Robert Moses

From:
  Frank Lloyd Wright

Source:
  Robert Moses
  Public Works: A Dangerous Trade, p. 860

Number of Words:
   249

Descriptors:
   Robert Moses, Mary Moses, Solomon R. Guggenheim Museum,
   Aymar Embury II, Eclecticism

Review:
   Discussion of a recent speech made by Moses and of Moses's
   dislike for the design of the Solomon R. Guggenheim Museum.

B360

Date:
   April 4, 1947

Type of Manuscript:
   Letter

To:
   Robert Moses

From:
   Frank Lloyd Wright

Source:
   Robert Moses
   Public Works: A Dangerous Trade, pp. 861-862

Number of Words:
   372

Descriptors:
   Robert Moses, Carlyle, Hitler, Stalin, Eclecticism,
   Princeton University, New York, South America, Mexico,
   Great Britain, France, Italy, Japan, China, Sweden, Norway,
   Solomon R. Guggenheim Museum, Mary Moses, Pittsburgh Point
   Park Project

Review:
   Wright talks of the architecture of New York and his design
   for the Solomon R. Guggenheim Museum. Wright, apparently, is
   trying to sell Moses on his design for the Guggenheim Museum
   in a friendly sort of way. Also, a brief note on Wright's
   Pittsburgh Point Park Project.

B361

Date:
   April 15, 1947

Type of Manuscript:
   Letter

To:
   Robert Moses
   New York

From:
   Frank Lloyd Wright
   Taliesin West
   Scottsdale, Arizona

Source:
    Robert Moses
    Public Works: A Dangerous Trade, p. 863

Number of Words:
    70

Descriptors:
    Robert Moses, Nature, Pittsburgh Point Park Project,
    Solomon R. Guggenheim Museum

Review:
    A note on Moses's comments on both the Solomon R. Guggenheim
    Museum and the Pittsburgh Point Park designs by Wright. Wright
    concedes that Moses will never think differently about these
    two projects.

B362

Date:
    May 29, 1947

Type of Manuscript:
    Letter on statement of architectural services

To:
    First Unitarian Society of Madison

From:
    The Frank Lloyd Wright Foundation (Frank Lloyd Wright)
    Taliesin
    Spring Green, Wisconsin

Collection:
    The Harold M. Groves Papers, 1927-1969
    The State Historical Society of Wisconsin
    MSS 272, Box 13, Folder 11

Medium:
    Typed on a copy of "The Personal Architectural Services
    of Frank Lloyd Wright," unsigned

Size:
    8-1/2 in. x 10-15/16± in.; 215.9 mm x 277.8± mm

Number of Pages:
    1

Number of Words:
    37 (cover letter, excluding typeset materials)

Descriptors:
    First Unitarian Society (Madison, Wisconsin), Unitarian
    Church (Shorewood Hills, Wisconsin)

Review:
    An outline of "The Personal Architectural Services of Frank
    Lloyd Wright" covering Frank Lloyd Wright's proposed fee schedule
    for his anticipated work on the Unitarian Church at Shorewood
    Hills, Wisconsin, which he ultimately designed.

B363

Date:
June 7, 1947

Type of Manuscript:
Letter

To:
Harold M. Groves

From:
Frank Lloyd Wright

Collection:
The Harold M. Groves Papers, 1927-1969
The State Historical Society of Wisconsin
MSS 272, Box 13, Folder 11

Medium:
Typed on red-square design stationery, signed
"Frank Lloyd Wright"

Size:
Page 1--8-1/2 in. x 7-1/4± in.; 215.9 mm x 184.2± mm
Page 2--8-1/2 in. x 10-15/16± in.; 215.9 mm x 277.8± mm

Number of Pages:
2

Number of Words:
259

Descriptors:
Harold M. Groves, Unitarian Church (Shorewood Hills,
Wisconsin)

Review:
Regarding the matter of payment to Frank Lloyd Wright for
architectural services rendered by him during the design of the
Unitarian Church at Shorewood Hills, Wisconsin. Wright's tone
is one of anger as he discusses the relationship between architect and client as he perceives it to be.

B364

Date:
June 17, 1947

Type of Manuscript:
Letter

To:
Harold M. Groves
Madison, Wisconsin

From:
Frank Lloyd Wright

Collection:
The Harold M. Groves Papers, 1927-1969
The State Historical Society of Wisconsin
MSS 272, Box 13, Folder 11

Medium:
Typed on red-square design stationery,
signed "F.L.L.W"

Size:
8-1/2 in. x 10-15/16± in.; 215.9 mm x 277.8± mm

Number of Pages:
1

Number of Words:
69

Descriptors:
Harold M. Groves, Unitarian Church (Shorewood Hills,
Wisconsin)

Review:
Frank Lloyd Wright acknowledges receipt of payment for
architectural services rendered for his design of the
Unitarian Church at Shorewood Hills, Wisconsin.

B365

Date:
July 28, 1947

Type of Manuscript:
Letter

To:
Robert Moses
New York, New York

From:
Frank Lloyd Wright

Source:
Robert Moses
Public Works: A Dangerous Trade, p. 863

Number of Words:
69

Descriptors:
Robert Moses, Eclecticism

Review:
Wright speaks of his strange friendship with Moses.

B366

Date:
July 31, 1947

Type of Manuscript:
Letter

To:
William T. Evjue

From:
Frank Lloyd Wright

Collection:
   The William Theodore Evjue Papers, 1905-1969
   The State Historical Society of Wisconsin
   MSS 244, Box 155, Folder 21

Medium:
   Typed on Taliesin design stationery, signed "Frank"

Size:
   7-1/2 in. x 8-1/2 in.; 190.5 mm x 215.9 mm

Number of Pages:
   1

Number of Words:
   68

Descriptors:
   William T. Evjue, *The Capital Times*

Review:
   Wright thanks Evjue for a recent feature on Wright which
   appeared in *The Capital Times*.

B367

Date:
   October 3, 1947

Type of Manuscript:
   Letter

To:
   William T. Evjue

From:
   Frank Lloyd Wright

Collection:
   The William Theodore Evjue Papers, 1905-1969
   The State Historical Society of Wisconsin
   MSS 244, Box 155, Folder 21

Medium:
   Typed on Taliesin design stationery and signed "F.LL.W."

Size:
   7-1/2 in. x 8-1/2 in.; 190.5 mm x 215.9 mm

Number of Pages:
   1

Number of Words:
   62

Descriptors:
   William T. Evjue, Taliesin Fellowship, *The Capital Times*

Review:
   Wright thanks Evjue for a recent article in *The Capital Times*
   and invites him to visit Taliesin.

B368

Date:
   October 16, 1947

Type of Manuscript:
   Telegram

To:
   Ludwig Mies van der Rohe
   Illinois Institute of Technology

From:
   Frank Lloyd Wright
   Spring Green, Wisconsin

Collection:
   The Library of Congress, Manuscript Division
   Ludwig Mies van der Rohe Papers, 1921-1969
   Container 60 (General Office File)

Medium:
   Western Union Telegram

Size:
   5-5/8 in. x 8 in.; 142.9 mm x 203.2 mm

Number of Pages:
   1

Number of Words:
   32

Descriptors:
   Ludwig Mies van der Rohe, Mrs. Theo van Doesburg

Review:
   Mrs. Theo van Doesburg is to visit Taliesin at Spring Green,
   Wisconsin.

B369

Date:
   October 20, 1947

Type of Manuscript:
   Letter

To:
   Harry B. Harvey
   New York, New York

From:
   Frank Lloyd Wright

Collection:
   A. H34
   Rush Rhees Library
   University of Rochester

Medium:
   Typed on Taliesin design stationery, signed
   "Frank LL. W."

Size:
   8-1/2 in. x 11 in.; 215.9 mm x 279.4 mm

Number of Pages:
   1

Number of Words:
   36

Descriptors:
   Harry B. Harvey, Danny Deever, The Plaza Hotel (New York)

Review:
   Brief note of Wright's upcoming visit to New York on October 23,
   1947.

B370

Date:
   October 21, 1947

Type of Manuscript:
   Letter

To:
   H. Th. Wijdeveld
   Holland

From:
   Frank Lloyd Wright

Collection:
   H. Th. Wijdeveld Papers
   Rijkdienst voor de Monumentenzorg
   Nederlands Documentatiecentrum voor de Bouwkunst

Medium:
   Typed on Taliesin design stationery, signed "Frank
   Lloyd Wright"

Size:
   8-1/2 in. x 11 in.; 215.9 mm x 279.4 mm

Number of Pages:
   3

Number of Words:
   530

Descriptors:
   H. Th. Wijdeveld, Taliesin Fellowship

Review:
   Wijdeveld had asked Wright if he might join Wright's
   architectural practice and fellowship. This letter is Wright's
   reply. Wright feels that he owes Wijdeveld for help he received
   from him many years earlier but he does not know how to repay
   him. A very long personal letter giving insights into Wright's
   feelings towards Wijdeveld.

B371

Date:
   October 25, 1947

Type of Manuscript:
   Letter

To:
   Ludwig Mies van der Rohe

From:
   Frank Lloyd Wright

Collection:
   The Library of Congress, Manuscript Division
   Ludwig Mies van der Rohe Papers, 1921-1969
   Container 60 (General Office File)

Medium:
   Typed with handwritten corrections by Wright, signed
   "Frank Lloyd Wright"

Size:
   7-1/4 in. x 8-1/2 in.; 184.2 mm x 215.9 mm

Number of Pages:
   2

Number of Words:
   283

Descriptors:
   Ludwig Mies van der Rohe, Barcelona Pavilion, Modern
   Architecture

Review:
   Discussion of comments made by Wright at an exhibition of Mies
   van der Rohe's work in 1947. Wright invites Mies to visit and
   talk. Wright's tone is somewhat apologetic.

B372

Date:
   March 10, 1948

Type of Manuscript:
   Letter

To:
   Dr. Frederic E. Mohs
   Wisconsin General Hospital
   Madison, Wisconsin

From:
   Frank Lloyd Wright

Collection:
   The Harold M. Groves Papers, 1927-1969
   The State Historical Society of Wisconsin
   MSS 272, Box 13, Folder 11

Medium:
    Typed on red-square design stationery, signed
    "Frank Lloyd Wright"

Size:
    8-1/2 in. x 10-15/16± in.; 215.9 mm x 277.8± mm

Number of Pages:
    1

Number of Words:
    88

Descriptors:
    Dr. Frederic E. Mohs, Unitarian Church (Shorewood Hills,
    Wisconsin)

Review:
    Mohs, apparently a member of the Unitarian Society of Madison
    for which Wright had designed the Unitarian Church at Shorewood
    Hills, Wisconsin, is given a building cost estimate for that
    structure of $75,000. Wright further indicates that the working
    drawing production for the building is under way.

B373

Date:
    March 15, 1948

Type of Manuscript:
    Letter

To:
    E. Willis Jones
    Chicago, Illinois

From:
    Frank Lloyd Wright

Collection:
    Frank Lloyd Wright Correspondence with E. Willis Jones,
    1936-1959
    Special Collections Department
    Northwestern University Library

Medium:
    Typed on Taliesin design stationery, signed
    "F.L.L.W"

Size:
    7-1/4 in. x 8-1/2 in.; 184.2 mm x 215.9 mm

Number of Pages:
    1

Number of Words:
    59 Typed; 6 Handwritten

Descriptors:
    E. Willis Jones, David Jones

Review:
Brief note concerning David, a possible student of the Taliesin Fellowship and relation of Jones.

B374

Date:
April 15, 1948

Type of Manuscript:
Letter

To:
H. Th. Wijdeveld
New York, New York

From:
Frank Lloyd Wright

Collection:
H. Th. Wijdeveld Papers
Rijksdienst voor de Monumentenzorg
Nederlands Documentatiecentrum voor de Bouwkunst

Medium:
Typed on Taliesin design stationery and signed "F.LL.W"

Size:
8-1/2 in. x 11 in.; 215.9 mm x 279.4 mm

Number of Pages:
1

Number of Words:
56

Descriptors:
H. Th. Wijdeveld

Review:
Wright invites Wijdeveld to visit Taliesin at Spring Green, Wisconsin.

B375

Date:
April 24, 1948

Type of Manuscript:
Telegram

To:
E. Willis Jones
Chicago, Illinois

From:
Frank Lloyd Wright
Phoenix, Arizona

Collection:
Frank Lloyd Wright Correspondence with E. Willis Jones, 1936-1959

Special Collections Department
Northwestern University Library

Medium:
Western Union Telegram

Size:
5-3/4 in. x 8 in.; 146.1 mm x 203.2 mm

Number of Pages:
1

Number of Words:
25

Descriptors:
E. Willis Jones

Review:
Wright is to visit Chicago and announces his coming to Jones.

B376

Date:
May 25, 1948

Type of Manuscript:
Letter

To:
E. Willis Jones

From:
Frank Lloyd Wright

Collection:
Frank Lloyd Wright Correspondence with E. Willis Jones,
1936-1959
Special Collections Department
Northwestern University Library

Medium:
Typed on Taliesin design stationery, signed "F.LL.W"

Size:
7-1/4 in. x 8-1/2 in.; 184.2 mm x 215.9 mm

Number of Pages:
1

Number of Words:
79

Descriptors:
E. Willis Jones

Review:
Wright apologizes for something he said to Jones and invites the
Joneses to visit.

B377

Date:
   June 5, 1948

Type of Manuscript:
   Letter (copy)

To:
   Arthur B. Gallion
   Los Angeles, California

From:
   Frank Lloyd Wright

Collection:
   H. Th. Wijdeveld Papers
   Rijksdienst voor de Monumentenzorg
   Nederlands Documentatiecentrum voor de Bouwkunst

Medium:
   Copy of typed letter, not signed

Size:
   8-1/2 in. x 11 in.; 215.9 mm x 279.4 mm

Number of Pages:
   3

Number of Words:
   441

Descriptors:
   Arthur B. Gallion, University of Southern California,
   Lloyd Wright, H. Th. Wijdeveld, Lewis Mumford, Dr. H.P.
   Berlage, Eric Mendelsohn, Walter Gropius

Review:
   Wright addresses this letter of recommendation for H. Th. Wijdeveld
   to Arthur B. Gallion, the Dean of the College of Architecture at
   the University of Southern California. Wijdeveld was to become
   a professor there.

B378

Date:
   August 6, 1948

Type of Manuscript:
   Letter

To:
   George Beal

From:
   Frank Lloyd Wright
   Taliesin

Collection:
   Frank Lloyd Wright Collection
   Kenneth Spencer Research Library
   University of Kansas

Medium:
   Typed and signed on Taliesin stationery, with envelope

Size:
   8-1/2 in. x 11 in.; 215.9 mm x 279.4 mm

Number of Pages:
   1

Number of Words:
   21

Descriptors:
   George Beal

Review:
   Brief note to Beal from Wright.

B379

Date:
   October 5, 1948

Type of Manuscript:
   Text of speech

Title:
   "In the Realm of Ideas"

By:
   Frank Lloyd Wright

Collection:
   The Wrightiana Collection
   The Art Institute of Chicago

Medium:
   Typed double spaced

Size:
   8-1/2 in. x 11 in.; 215.9 mm x 279.4 mm

Number of Pages:
   28

Descriptors:
   Society of Contemporary American Art, Samuel A. Marx,
   Picasso, Karl Marx, Organic Architecture, Theodore Thomas,
   Daniel Burnham, Democracy, International Style, Communism,
   Fascism, Socialism, Thomas Jefferson, Jesus, Germany, Broadacre
   City, Howard Meyers, Princeton

Review:
   An address given by Wright at the Society for Contemporary American
   Art, Orchestra Hall, Chicago. Wright's broad topic is the failure
   of today's architecture and of a need for organic architecture.
   Several members of the audience were allowed to ask Wright questions
   and the texts of these are also included in the manuscript.

B380

Date:
   October 16, 1948

Type of Manuscript:
   Letter

To:
   John Lloyd Wright
   Del Mar, California

From:
   Frank Lloyd Wright

Collection:
   The John Lloyd Wright Collection
   The Avery Architectural Library
   Columbia University
   Folder 11

Medium:
   Typed on Taliesin design stationery, signed "Father"

Size:
   8-1/2 in. x 11 in.; 215.9 mm x 279.4 mm

Number of Pages:
   1

Number of Words:
   37

Descriptors:
   John Lloyd Wright, English Acedes (Car)

Review:
   Brief note on F.L. Wright's car and on J.L. Wright's car.
   Also, an invitation to visit Taliesin West in winter of 1949.

B381

Date:
   October 16, 1948

Type of Manuscript:
   Letter and statement of architectural services

To:
   Kenneth L. Patton
   First Unitarian Society
   Madison, Wisconsin

From:
   Frank Lloyd Wright

Collection:
   The Harold M. Groves Papers, 1927-1969
   The State Historical Society of Wisconsin
   MSS 272, Box 13, Folder 11

Medium:
   Cover letter on Taliesin red-square stationery, signed
   "F.LL.W," with a copy of "The Personal Architectural
   Services of Frank Lloyd Wright"

Size:
    8-7/16 in. x 10-15/16± in.; 214.3 mm x 277.8± mm

Number of Pages:
    2

Number of Words:
    56 (cover letter only)

Descriptors:
    Kenneth L. Patton, Unitarian Church (Shorewood Hills,
    Wisconsin)

Review:
    Concerning a bill for work performed by Wright for his Unitarian
    Church design at Shorewood Hills, Wisconsin. Attached to the cover
    letter is a printed statement entitled "The Personal Architectural
    Services of Frank Lloyd Wright," signed "FW." Wright's total fee
    is ten percent of the total building cost no matter how large or
    small the building project is.

B382

Date:
    November 20, 1948

Type of Manuscript:
    Cancelled bank check

To:
    Frank Lloyd Wright

From:
    Herbert Jacobs

Collection:
    The Herbert and Katherine Jacobs Frank Lloyd Wright
    Collection
    The Art Institute of Chicago
    Documents, Box 1

Medium:
    Bank check, signed "Frank Lloyd Wright"

Number of Pages:
    1

Descriptors:
    Herbert Jacobs, Herbert Jacobs Second Residence

Review:
    Probably payment for work done on the Jacobses' second residence.

B383

Date:
    December 1, 1948

Type of Manuscript:
    Letter

To:
    John Lloyd Wright
    Del Mar, California

From:
    Frank Lloyd Wright

Collection:
    The John Lloyd Wright Collection
    The Avery Architectural Library
    Columbia University
    Folder 11

Medium:
    Typed on Taliesin design stationery, signed "Dad"

Size:
    8-1/2 in. x 11 in.; 215.9 mm x 279.4 mm

Number of Pages:
    1

Number of Words:
    21

Descriptors:
    John Lloyd Wright, Motion Pictures

Review:
    Very brief note about motion pictures.

B384

Date:
    Christmas 1948

Type of Manuscript:
    Christmas card

From:
    Frank Lloyd Wright

Collection:
    Special Collections Department
    Northwestern University Library
    Northwestern University

Descriptors:
    Christmas 1948

B385

Date:
    January 18, 1949

Type of Manuscript:
    Letter

To:
    Mrs. Irwin Elkus Auerbach
    New York

From:
    Frank Lloyd Wright
    Taliesin West

Collection:
    The Avery Architectural Library
    Columbia University

Medium:
    Typed on Taliesin West design stationery, signed
    "Frank Lloyd Wright"

Size:
    8-1/2 in. x 11 in.; 215.9 mm x 279.4 mm

Number of Pages:
    1

Number of Words:
    34

Descriptors:
    Mrs. Irwin Elkus Auerbach, Irwin Auerbach Residence Project

Review:
    Wright's acceptance of the Irwin Auerbach Residence Project
    commission of 1950. It was designed but never executed.

B386

Date:
    January 18, 1949

Type of Manuscript:
    Letter

To:
    C. Howard King
    Chairman of the Board
    First Unitarian Society
    Madison, Wisconsin

From:
    Frank Lloyd Wright

Collection:
    The Harold M. Groves Papers, 1927-1969
    The State Historical Society of Wisconsin
    MSS 272, Box 13, Folder 11

Medium:
    Typed, signed "F.LLW"

Size:
    8-1/2 in. x 10-15/16± in.; 215.9 mm x 277.8± mm

Number of Pages:
    1

Number of Words:
    46 Typed; 7 Handwritten

Descriptors:
C. Howard King, First Unitarian Society (Madison, Wisconsin),
Unitarian Church (Shorewood Hills, Wisconsin)

Review:
Wright informs King, Chairman of the Board of the First Unitarian
Society of Madison, Wisconsin, that he will receive cost estimates
for the construction of the Wright designed Unitarian Church at
Shorewood Hills, Wisconsin.

B387

Date:
February 12, 1949

Type of Manuscript:
Letter

To:
H. Th. Wijdeveld

From:
Frank Lloyd Wright

Collection:
H. Th. Wijdeveld Papers
Rijksdienst voor de Monumentenzorg
Nederlands Documentiecentrum voor de Bouwkunst

Medium:
Typed on Taliesin design stationery,
signed "F.LL.W."

Size:
8-1/2 in. x 11 in.; 215.9 mm x 279.4 mm

Number of Pages:
1

Number of Words:
52

Descriptors:
H. Th. Wijdeveld

Review:
Wright invites Wijdeveld to Taliesin West.

B388

Date:
February 19, 1949

Type of Manuscript:
Letter

To:
Harold M. Groves
The University of Wisconsin
Department of Economics
Madison, Wisconsin

From:
    Frank Lloyd Wright
    Taliesin West

Collection:
    The Harold M. Groves Papers, 1927-1969
    The State Historical Society of Wisconsin
    MSS 272, Box 13, Folder 11

Medium:
    Typed on Taliesin West design stationery,
    signed "Frank Lloyd Wright"

Size:
    8-1/2 in. x 10-15/16± in.; 215.9 mm x 277.8± mm

Number of Pages:
    1

Number of Words:
    112

Descriptors:
    Harold M. Groves, Unitarian Church (Shorewood Hills,
    Wisconsin)

Review:
    Wright is to get back to work on his design for the Unitarian
    Church at Shorewood Hills, Wisconsin, in May after he returns
    from Taliesin West in Scottsdale, Arizona. Wright sounds as
    though he was not totally satisfied with the final design for
    the church.

B389

Date:
    March 30, 1949

Type of Manuscript:
    Letter

To:
    H. Th. Wijdeveld
    Los Angeles, California

From:
    Frank Lloyd Wright

Collection:
    H. Th. Wijdeveld Papers
    Rijksdienst voor de Monumentenzorg
    Nederlands Documentatiecentrum voor de Bouwkunst

Medium:
    Typed on Taliesin design stationery,
    signed "F.LL.W"

Size:
    8-1/2 in. x 11 in.; 215.9 mm x 279.4 mm

Number of Pages:
    1

Number of Words:
   38 Typed; 4 Handwritten

Descriptors:
   H. Th. Wijdeveld

Review:
   Brief note of welcome to Wijdeveld.

B390

Date:
   April 4, 1949

Type of Manuscript:
   Letter

To:
   Elmer Berger
   The American Council for Judaism
   New York

From:
   Frank Lloyd Wright
   Taliesin West

Collection:
   The American Council for Judaism Papers, 1938-1953
   The State Historical Society of Wisconsin
   U.S. MSS BJ, Box 2

Medium:
   Typed on Taliesin stationery and signed

Size:
   8-1/2 in. x 11 in.; 215.9 mm x 279.4 mm

Number of Pages:
   2

Number of Words:
   236

Descriptors:
   Elmer Berger, The American Council for Judaism, Judaism,
   Quakerism, Methodism, Jerusalem, Wales, Race, Democracy,
   Catholic, Brahmin, Buddhist

Review:
   Wright describes his views on religion generally and on Judaism
   in particular.

B391

Date:
   June 15, 1949

Type of Manuscript:
   Letter

To:
Edmund R. Purves, Executive Director
American Institute of Architects
Washington, D.C.

From:
Frank Lloyd Wright
Taliesin

Collection:
The Library of Congress, Manuscript Division
Edmund Randolph Purves Papers, 1916-1964
General Correspondence, Container 2

Medium:
Typed on Taliesin design stationery, signed
"Frank Lloyd Wright"

Size:
8-1/2 in. x 11 in.; 215.9 mm x 279.4 mm

Number of Pages:
1

Number of Words:
67

Descriptors:
Edmund R. Purves, American Institute of Architects,
Journal of the American Institute of Architects

Review:
Invitation for Purves to visit Taliesin. Also, thanks him for
their meeting at Washington, D.C. For a detailed account of this
meeting see "Frank Lloyd Wright's Honor Guest in Washington,"
The Capital Times.

B392

Date:
July 13, 1949

Type of Manuscript:
Letter

To:
George Beal

From:
Frank Lloyd Wright
Taliesin

Collection:
Frank Lloyd Wright Collection
Kenneth Spencer Research Library
University of Kansas

Medium:
Typed on Taliesin designed stationery and signed

Size:
8-1/2 in. x 11 in.; 215.9 mm x 279.4 mm

Number of Pages:
  1

Number of Words:
  46

Descriptors:
  George Beal

Review:
  The Bealses will be visiting Taliesin on August 6, 1949.

B393

Date:
  August 1, 1949

Type of Manuscript:
  Letter

To:
  Dorathi Bock Pierre

From:
  Frank Lloyd Wright

Collection:
  The Richard W. Bock Sculpture Collection
  Greenville College

Descriptors:
  Dorathi Bock Pierre, Richard W. Bock

Review:
  On the death of Richard W. Bock.

B394

Date:
  August 1, 1949

Type of Manuscript:
  Letter

To:
  Harold M. Groves
  First Unitarian Society
  Madison, Wisconsin

From:
  Frank Lloyd Wright

Collection:
  The Harold M. Groves Papers, 1927-1969
  The State Historical Society of Wisconsin
  MSS 272, Box 13, Folder 11

Medium:
  Typed on red-square design stationery, signed "FLLW"

Size:
  8-1/2 in. x 10-15/16± in.; 215.9 mm x 277.8± mm

Number of Pages:
   1

Number of Words:
   76 Typed; 7 Handwritten

Descriptors:
   Harold M. Groves, First Unitarian Society (Madison,
   Wisconsin), Unitarian Church (Shorewood Hills, Wisconsin),
   A.I.A. Contracts

Review:
   Wright is ready to proceed with the construction of the Unitarian
   Church he designed at Shorewood Hills, Wisconsin. He suggests
   to Groves that A.I.A. construction contract documents be used.

B395

Date:
   August 17, 1949

Type of Manuscript:
   Letter

To:
   E. Willis Jones
   Glencoe, Illinois

From:
   Frank Lloyd Wright

Collection:
   Frank Lloyd Wright Correspondence with E. Willis Jones,
   1936-1959
   Special Collections Department
   Northwestern University Library

Medium:
   Typed

Size:
   5-1/2 in. x 8-1/2 in.; 139.7 mm x 215.9 mm

Number of Pages:
   1

Number of Words:
   44 Typed; 3 Handwritten

Descriptors:
   E. Willis Jones, Eugene Masselink

Review:
   Brief thank-you note.

B396

Date:
   September 15, 1949

Type of Manuscript:
   Letter

To:
   John Lloyd Wright

From:
   Frank Lloyd Wright

Collection:
   The John Lloyd Wright Collection
   The Avery Architectural Library
   Columbia University
   Folder 11

Medium:
   Typed on Taliesin design stationery, signed "Dad"

Size:
   8-1/2 in. x 11 in.; 215.9 mm x 279.4 mm

Number of Pages:
   1

Number of Words:
   57

Descriptors:
   John Lloyd Wright, American Institute of Architects
   Gold Medal

Review:
   Concerning a gift John L. Wright sent to his father for his
   eightieth birthday and on F.L. Wright's A.I.A. Gold Medal award.

B397

Date:
   November 9, 1949

Type of Manuscript:
   Letter

To:
   Oskar Stonorov
   Philadelphia, Pennsylvania

From:
   Frank Lloyd Wright
   Taliesin
   Spring Green, Wisconsin

Collection:
   The Oskar Stonorov Collection
   Archive of Contemporary History
   The University of Wyoming

Medium:
   Typed on Taliesin West design stationery, signed
   "F.LL.W."

Size:
   8-1/2 in. x 11 in.; 215.9 mm x 279.4 mm

Number of Pages:
   1

Number of Words:
   181

Descriptors:
   Oskar Stonorov, Arthur Kaufmann, Gimbels Exhibition,
   "Sixty Years of Living Architecture" exhibition

Review:
   Wright states the conditions for the showing of his Gimbels
   Exhibition in Philadelphia.

B398

Date:
   Undated (1940s?)

Type of Manuscript:
   Questions and answers

Collection:
   The Herbert and Katherine Jacobs Frank Lloyd Wright
   Collection
   The Art Institute of Chicago
   Documents, Envelope 6

Medium:
   Typed and handwritten document

Size:
   8-1/2 in. x 11 in.; 215.9 mm x 279.4 mm

Number of Pages:
   4

Descriptors:
   Herbert Jacobs, Unitarian Church

Review:
   Questions (typed by Herbert Jacobs) and answers (handwritten
   by F.L. Wright) regarding the design of the Unitarian Church.
   Jacobs apparently had acted as an intermediary between the
   Unitarian Church and Wright prior to execution of the church
   project.

B399

Date:
   Undated (prior to 1949)

Type of Manuscript:
   Note

To:
   Lloyd Downs Lewis

From:
   Frank Lloyd Wright

Collection:
   Lloyd Downs Lewis Papers, 1863-1949
   The Newberry Library
   Chicago, Illinois

2-6.18 Frank Lloyd Wright's famous red-square tile symbol, signed "FLLW,"
attached to the entrance of a building he designed. Photo by the author.

Medium:
  Handwritten, signed "Frank"

Size:
  7-1/4 in. x 10 in.; 184.2 mm x 254 mm

Number of Pages:
  1

Number of Words:
  75

Descriptors:
  Lloyd Downs Lewis, Hiroshige

Review:
  Wright transmits a wedding present to Lloyd Lewis of several
  Japanese prints.

                              REFERENCES

Books:

Drexler, Arthur (ed.).
  The Drawings of Frank Lloyd Wright. New York: Horizon Press for
  the Museum of Modern Art, 1962.

Gannett, William C., and Frank Lloyd Wright.
  The House Beautiful. River Forest, Illinois: The Auvergne Press,
  1896-1897 (1898).

Izzo, Alberto, and Camillo Gubitosi (eds.).
  Frank Lloyd Wright, Dessins 1887-1959. Paris: C.E.R.A. Ecole
  Nationale Supérieure des Beaux-Arts, 1977.

Jacobs, Herbert, and Katherine Jacobs.
  Building with Frank Lloyd Wright: An Illustrated Memoir. San
  Francisco: Chronicle Books, 1978.

Moses, Robert
  Public Works: A Dangerous Trade. New York: McGraw-Hill Book, Co.,
  1970.

Sergeant, John.
  *Frank Lloyd Wright's Usonian Houses: The Case for Organic Archi-
  tecture*. New York: Whitney Library of Design, 1976.

The Solomon R. Guggenheim Foundation.
  The Solomon R. Guggenheim Museum, Frank Lloyd Wright, Architect.
  New York: The Solomon R. Guggenheim Foundation, 1975.

Storrer, William Allin.
  The Architecture of Frank Lloyd Wright. a Complete Catalog,
  Second Edition. Cambridge, Massachusetts: The M.I.T. Press, 1978.

Tafel, Edgar.
   Apprentice to Genius: Years with Frank Lloyd Wright. New York:
   McGraw-Hill, Inc., 1979.

Twombly, Robert C.
   Frank Lloyd Wright: An Interpretive Biography. New York: Harper
   and Row, 1973.

Twombly, Robert C.
   Frank Lloyd Wright: His Life and His Architecture. New York: John
   Wiley and Sons, Inc., 1979.

Wright, Frank Lloyd.
   Drawings for a Living Architecture. New York: Horizon Press for
   the Bear Run Foundation, Inc., and the Edgar J. Kaufmann Charitable
   Foundation, 1959.

Wright, Frank Lloyd.
   An Autobiography. New York: Horizon Press, 1977.

Wright, John Lloyd.
   My Father Who Is on Earth. New York: G.P. Putnam's Sons, 1946.

Periodicals:

Anonymous.
   "New York Discovers an Architect," *Architectural Forum*, Vol. 80,
   April 1944, p. 70.

Anonymous.
   "Frank Lloyd Wright Is Designing Building for Guggenheim Collection,"
   Architect and Engineer, Vol. 157, June 1944, p. 4.

Wright, Frank Lloyd.
   "To the Mole," *A Taliesin Square-Paper: A Nonpolitical Voice from
   Our Democratic Minority*, No. 7, August 14, 1944.

Wright, Frank Lloyd.
   "Viewpoints: To the Mole," *Magazine of Art*, Vol. 37, December 1944,
   pp. 310, 312-315.

Anonymous.
   "Frank Lloyd Wright," *Architectural Record*, Vol. 101, April 1947,
   p. 98.

Anonymous.
   "Planners' Platform," *Architectural Forum*, Vol. 86, April 1947,
   p. 13.

Wright, Frank Lloyd.
   "Planning Man's Physical Environment," *Berkeley, A Journal of
   Modern Culture*, No. 1, 1947, pp. 5, 7.

Wright, Frank Lloyd.
"A Four-Color Portfolio of the Recent Work of the Dean of Con-
temporary Architects with His Own Commentary on Each Building,"
Architectural Forum, Vol. 94, January 1951, pp. 73-108.

Hallmark, Donald P.
"Richard W. Bock, Sculptor, Part II: The Mature Collaborations,"
The Prairie School Review, No. 2, 1971, pp. 5-29.

Jacobs, Herbert.
"Our Wright Houses," *Historic Preservation*, Vol. 28, July/September
1976, pp. 9-13.

Newspapers:

Anonymous.
"Federal Judge Patrick T. Stone Charged Wright Was 'Poisoning the
Minds' of His Apprentices Against the Draft," *The Capital Times*
(Madison, Wisconsin), December 20, 1942.

Anonymous.
"Taliesin Men Demand Stone Retract Words: Call Court's Remarks on
Fellowship, Wright 'Libelous,'" *The Capital Times* (Madison,
Wisconsin), December 23, 1942.

Anonymous.
"Judge Sends Letter to Fellowship: Replies to Students Who Pro-
tested Attack on Frank Lloyd Wright," *The Capital Times* (Madison,
Wisconsin), January 3, 1943.

Anonymous.
"Students Deny Influence Try in Weston Case: Reply to Judge Stone's
Letter--Demand Apology to Frank Lloyd Wright," *The Capital Times*
(Madison, Wisconsin), January 4, 1943.

Anonymous.
"Publish Autobiography of Frank Lloyd Wright," *The Capital Times*
(Madison, Wisconsin), June 3, 1943.

Wright, Frank Lloyd.
"Frank Lloyd Wright in Tribute to Will and Sally (Allen White),"
The Capital Times (Madison, Wisconsin), February 1, 1944.

Anonymous.
"Mr. Moses Dissects the 'Long-Haired Planners': The Park Commissioner
Prefers Common Sense to Their Revolutionary Theories," *The New
York Times Magazine*, June 25, 1944, section 6, p. 38, col. 4.

Brock, H.L.
"In Defense of City Planners--Mr. Moses' Sharp Attack on Revolution-
ary Sophisticates Brings Out a Vigorous Defense," *The New York
Times Magazine*, July 9, 1944, section 6, pp. 20, 21, and 35.

Anonymous.
"Museum Building to Rise as Spiral--New Guggenheim Structure

Designed by F.L. Wright Is Called First of Kind," *The New York Times*, July 10, 1945, p. 11, col. 3.

Anonymous.
"Model Is Unveiled of New Museum Here," *The New York Times*, September 21, 1945, p. 38, col. 2.

Anonymous.
"Wright Will Design Unitarian Church--Site Near F-P Lab," *The Capital Times* (Madison, Wisconsin), January 26, 1946.

Anonymous.
"Frank Lloyd Wright's Honor Guest in Washington," *The Capital Times* (Madison, Wisconsin), June 6, 1949.

Anonymous.
"Exhibition for Italy of Wright Art Hailed," *The New York Times*, August 1, 1949, p. 17, col. 2.

Anonymous.
"The Jacobs Home Goes in Circles for a Purpose," *The Capital Times* (Madison, Wisconsin), December 14, 1949.

CHAPTER 7

THE LAST GOLDEN YEARS (1950 TO 1959)

Introduction

The manuscripts listed for Wright's last years of practice take
an in-depth look into the "Sixty Years of Living Architecture" exhibition, which toured Europe as well as the United States in the early
1950s. Oskar Stonorov, a Philadelphia architect, worked closely with
Wright in setting up the exhibition of Wright's work--first for a
showing at Gimbels in Philadelphia, then to be seen abroad, and then
back in the United States. A long series of correspondence on this
exhibition, from F.L. Wright to Stonorov, is catalogued in this
chapter. Also, during this period Wright continued his efforts, which
he originally began in 1938, towards the design of a civic center for
Madison, Wisconsin, called the Monona Terrace Civic Center Project.
Much of Wright's time during the last years of his life was spent in
political battles over this project which was never built. Much
correspondence from Wright to various people involved with the
Monona Terrace Civic Center Project was developed during this period.
The project continued to be a major issue in Madison long after
Wright's death on April 9, 1959; although this interest was revitalized
by Madison in 1967 and again in 1973 the matter of a Frank Lloyd Wright
designed civic center seems to have been permanently put to rest in
1980 with the remodeling of an existing downtown facility for that
purpose by the architectural firm of Hardy Holzman Pfeiffer Associates
(see Louise Kenngott's "Renaissance at Madison," [*The Milwaukee Journal*,
February 17, 1980, Lively Arts Section, part 5], pp. 1 and 3; James
Auer's "Art Center's in a Class Itself," [*The Milwaukee Journal*,
February 17, 1980, Lively Arts Section, part 5], p. 3; and Mildred F.
Schmertz's "The New Madison Civic Center by Hardy Holzman Pfeiffer
Associates," [*Architectural Record*, Vol. 168, No. 1, July 1980],
pp. 77-86, for reviews and photographs of Madison's new facility).
Wright's work on the controversial Solomon R. Guggenheim Museum in
New York also took up much of his time in his last years.
      Correspondence catalogued in this chapter includes letters to
George Beal; poet and critic John Gould Fletcher; William T. Evjue;
John Lloyd Wright; H.C. Custer, of the First Unitarian Society of
Madison; Bruce Barton; Lessing Rosenwald, of the American Council
for Judaism; Douglas Moore, President of the National Institute of
Arts and Letters; Ralph Walker, of the National Institute of Arts and
Letters; Marc Connelly, of the National Institute of Arts and Letters;
critic Emily Genauer; Grant Carpenter Manson, author of *Frank Lloyd
Wright to 1910: The First Golden Age*; George E. Rodgerson and Don
Anderson, of *The Wisconsin State Journal* of Madison, Wisconsin; Dan
Cotten Rich; Madison Mayor Ivan Nestingen; Richard Hawley Cutting;
Alvin A. Sarra; City of New York Parks Commissioner Robert Moses;
Drew Pearson; former client Herbert Jacobs; Richard Herpers, Secretary

of Columbia University; E. Willis Jones; and Harold M. Groves, who was a backer of the Monona Terrace Civic Center Project as well as a famous economist.

Wright's designs for this period and thereafter (some were executed posthumously) numbered 284, representing almost 30 percent of all of the work of his lifetime; this is quite amazing considering that Wright was over 80 years old during this time. Of these 284 designs, 131, or about 46 percent, were executed.

B400

Date:
    January 25, 1950

Type of Manuscript:
    Letter

To:
    George and Helen Beal

From:
    Frank Lloyd Wright
    Taliesin West

Collection:
    Frank Lloyd Wright Collection
    Kenneth Spencer Research Library
    University of Kansas

Medium:
    Typed on Taliesin stationery and signed

Size:
    8-3/8 in. x 10-1/2 in.; 213 mm x 267 mm

Number of Pages:
    1

Number of Words:
    33 Typed; 3 Handwritten

Descriptors:
    George Beal, Christmas 1949

Review:
    A thank-you note for a gift from Beal.

B401

Date:
    February 3, 1950

Type of Manuscript:
    Letter

To:
    John Gould Fletcher
    Tucson, Arizona

From:
    Frank Lloyd Wright

Collection:
    John Gould Fletcher Papers, 1881-1960
    Special Collections
    University of Arkansas Library
    Fayetteville, Arkansas

Medium:
    Typed on Taliesin design stationery, signed "F.LL W."

Size:
    5-3/8 in. x 8-1/2 in.; 136.5 mm x 215.9 mm

Number of Pages:
    1

Number of Words:
    89

Descriptors:
    John Gould Fletcher

Review:
    Wright invites Fletcher to Taliesin West in this brief note.
    Fletcher was an Arkansas poet, author, and critic.

B402

Date:
    February 15, 1950

Type of Manuscript:
    Letter

To:
    Oskar Stonorov
    Philadelphia, Pennsylvania

From:
    Frank Lloyd Wright

Collection:
    The Oskar Stonorov Collection
    Archive of Contemporary History
    The University of Wyoming

Medium:
    Typed, signed "F.LL.W."

Number of Pages:
    1

Number of Words:
    56

Descriptors:
    Oskar Stonorov, Gimbels Exhibition (Philadelphia), "Sixty Years
    of Living Architecture" Exhibition

Review:
    Wright discusses his positive attitude regarding an exhibition
    of his work at Gimbels (Philadelphia) and abroad.

B403

Date:
March 3, 1950

Type of Manuscript:
Typescript speech

Title:
Untitled

By:
Frank Lloyd Wright

Collection:
The John Lloyd Wright Collection
The Avery Architectural Library
Columbia University
Folder 7

Medium:
Typed

Descriptors:
Florida Southern College, Lakeland (Florida)

Review:
Text of a speech Wright made in 1950 during Founder's Week at
Florida Southern College in Lakeland.

B404

Date:
Undated (early 1950)

Type of Manuscript:
Autographed Restaurant Menu, signed "Frank Lloyd Wright"

Collection:
The Oskar Stonorov Collection
Archive of Contemporary History
The University of Wyoming
Box 29, Item 3

Descriptors:
Oskar Stonorov, Restaurant Lucas Carton, "Sixty Years of
Living Architecture" Exhibition

Review:
Signed sometime during the early 1950s when Wright's "Sixty Years
of Living Architecture" exhibition was at various galleries in its
tour of the world.

B405

Date:
September 2, 1950

Type of Manuscript:
Letter

To:
   Oskar Stonorov
   Philadelphia, Pennsylvania

From:
   Frank Lloyd Wright

Collection:
   The Oskar Stonorov Collection
   Archive of Contemporary History
   The University of Wyoming

Medium:
   Typed on Taliesin design stationery, signed "F.LL.W."

Number of Pages:
   1

Number of Words:
   21

Descriptors:
   Oskar Stonorov

Review:
   Very brief note, the subject matter of which cannot be determined
   from the text.

B406

Date:
   September 22, 1950

Type of Manuscript:
   Letter

To:
   Harold M. Groves

From:
   Frank Lloyd Wright

Collection:
   The Harold M. Groves Papers, 1927-1969
   The State Historical Society of Wisconsin
   MSS 272, Box 13, Folder 11

Medium:
   Typed on Taliesin embossed stationery, signed "F.LL.W"

Size:
   Page 1--8-7/16 in. x 8-7/8± in.; 214.3 mm x 225.4± mm
   Page 2--8-7/16 in. x 5-1/2± in.; 214.3 mm x 139.7± mm

Number of Pages:
   2

Number of Words:
   218 Typed; 6 Handwritten

Descriptors:
   Harold M. Groves, Unitarian Church (Shorewood Hills, Wisconsin),
   Marshall Erdman, Forest Products Laboratory, Insulation

Review:
   Wright is upset with the way the insulation of the Unitarian Church
   at Shorewood Hills, Wisconsin, is being installed by the contractor
   and he conveys this thought in this strongly worded letter to
   Groves.

B407

Date:
   October 23, 1950

Type of Manuscript:
   Letter

To:
   Harold M. Groves

From:
   Frank Lloyd Wright

Collection:
   The Harold M. Groves Papers, 1927-1969
   The State Historical Society of Wisconsin
   MSS 272, Box 13, Folder 11

Medium:
   Typed on red-square design stationery, signed
   "F.LL.W"

Size:
   8-7/16 in. x 10-7/8± in.; 214.3 mm x 276.2± mm

Number of Pages:
   1

Number of Words:
   75

Descriptors:
   Harold M. Groves, Unitarian Church (Shorewood Hills,
   Wisconsin), Forest Products Laboratory, Marshall Erdman,
   Insulation

Review:
   Since Wright's design for the Unitarian Church at Shorewood
   Hills, Wisconsin, had been altered by the contractor with respect
   to insulating the building, he does not accept responsibility for
   heating conditions which may develop. This letter elaborates on
   the earlier one Wright wrote to Groves dated September 22, 1950
   (B406).

B408

Date:
   February 9, 1951

Type of Manuscript:
   Letter

To:
   Oskar Stonorov

From:
   Frank Lloyd Wright

Collection:
   The Oskar Stonorov Collection
   Archive of Contemporary History
   The University of Wyoming

Medium:
   Typed on Taliesin design stationery, signed "F.LL.W."

Size:
   8-1/2 in. x 11 in.; 215.9 mm x 279.4 mm

Number of Pages:
   2

Number of Words:
   319 Typed; 11 Handwritten

Descriptors:
   Oskar Stonorov, John Hill, Gimbels Exhibition (Philadelphia),
   Museum of Modern Art, Frank Lloyd Wright Foundation, Jim
   Davis, Broadacre City, Midway Gardens, Arthur Kaufmann,
   "Sixty Years of Living Architecture" Exhibition.

Review:
   Wright invites Stonorov to Taliesin. He discusses the possibility
   of making private movies of the exhibition of his work at Gimbels
   in Philadelphia. Also, Wright details his ideas on how the portion
   of the exhibition on his Broadacre City project should be set up
   and displayed.

B409

Date:
   February 14, 1951

Type of Manuscript:
   Letter

To:
   Oskar Stonorov

From:
   Frank Lloyd Wright

Collection:
   The Oskar Stonorov Collection
   Archive of Contemporary History
   The University of Wyoming

Medium:
   Typed on Taliesin design stationery

Number of Pages:
   1

Number of Words:
   84

Descriptors:
   Oskar Stonorov, Gimbels Exhibition (Philadelphia), "Sixty
   Years of Living Architecture" Exhibition

Review:
   Wright indicates he will send someone to Stonorov to take
   photographs of the "Sixty Years of Living Architecture" exhibition
   at Gimbels in Philadelphia.

B410

Date:
   February 15, 1951

Type of Manuscript:
   Letter

To:
   Oskar Stonorov

From:
   Frank Lloyd Wright

Collection:
   The Oskar Stonorov Collection
   Archive of Contemporary History
   The University of Wyoming

Medium:
   Typed on Taliesin design stationery and signed "F.LL.W."

Size:
   8-1/2 in. x 11 in.; 215.9 mm x 279.4 mm

Number of Pages:
   1

Number of Words:
   150

Descriptors:
   Oskar Stonorov, Gimbels Exhibition (Philadelphia), "Sixty
   Years of Living Architecture" Exhibition

Review:
   Wright suggests to Stonorov that a private movie be made of
   Wright's exhibition of work at Gimbels in Philadelphia.

B411

Date:
   February 22, 1951

Type of Manuscript:
   Letter

To:
   Oskar Stonorov

From:
   Frank Lloyd Wright

Collection:
  The Oskar Stonorov Collection
  Archive of Contemporary History
  The University of Wyoming

Medium:
  Typed on Taliesin design stationery and signed "F.LL.W."

Size:
  8-1/2 in. x 11 in.; 215.9 mm x 279.4 mm

Number of Pages:
  1

Number of Words:
  115

Descriptors:
  Oskar Stonorov, Strozzi Exhibition, Arthur C. Kaufmann,
  "Sixty Years of Living Architecture" Exhibition

Review:
  Problems develop with Wright's exhibition and he requests
  that the exhibition be handled from Taliesin.

B412

Date:
  March 2, 1951

Type of Manuscript:
  Letter

To:
  Oskar Stonorov

From:
  Frank Lloyd Wright

Collection:
  The Oskar Stonorov Collection
  Archive of Contemporary History
  The University of Wyoming

Medium:
  Typed on Taliesin design stationery, signed "F.LL.W."

Size:
  8-1/2 in. x 11 in.; 215.9 mm x 279.4 mm

Number of Pages:
  1

Number of Words:
  235

Descriptors:
  Oskar Stonorov, Strozzi Exhibition, "Sixty Years of Living
  Architecture" Exhibition

Review:
  Oskar Stonorov is to coordinate the putting together of Wright's
  Strozzi Exhibition at Taliesin.

B413

Date:
   March 7, 1951

Type of Manuscript:
   Letter

To:
   Oskar Stonorov
   Philadelphia, Pennsylvania

From:
   Frank Lloyd Wright

Collection:
   The Oskar Stonorov Collection
   Archive of Contemporary History
   The University of Wyoming

Medium:
   Typed on Taliesin design stationery, signed
   "F.LL.W."

Size:
   8-1/2 in. x 11 in.; 215.9 mm x 279.4 mm

Number of Pages:
   3

Number of Words:
   554

Descriptors:
   Oskar Stonorov, Arthur C. Kaufmann, Strozzi Exhibition,
   Museum of Modern Art, Frank Lloyd Wright Foundation, "Sixty
   Years of Living Architecture" Exhibition

Review:
   Wright expresses his concern over the responsibilities involved
   in the sending of his exhibition, "Sixty Years of Living Architecture" abroad.

B414

Date:
   March 12, 1951

Type of Manuscript:
   Letter

To:
   Oskar Stonorov

From:
   Frank Lloyd Wright

Collection:
   The Oskar Stonorov Collection
   Archive of Contemporary History
   The University of Wyoming

Medium:
    Typed on Taliesin design stationery, signed
    "F.LL W."

Size:
    8-1/2 in. x 11 in.; 215.9 mm x 279.4 mm

Number of Pages:
    1

Number of Words:
    162 Typed; 9 Handwritten

Descriptors:
    Oskar Stonorov, Strozzi Exhibition, "Sixty Years of
    Living Architecture" Exhibition

Review:
    Wright offers suggestions to Stonorov on several items to include
    in the Strozzi Exhibition and asks for Stonorov's opinion.

B415

Date:
    March 31, 1951

Type of Manuscript:
    Letter

To:
    Oskar Stonorov

From:
    Frank Lloyd Wright

Collection:
    The Oskar Stonorov Collection
    Archive of Contemporary History
    The University of Wyoming

Medium:
    Typed on Taliesin design stationery, signed
    "F.L L W."

Size:
    8-1/2 in. x 11 in.; 215.9 mm x 279.4 mm

Number of Pages:
    1

Number of Words:
    40 Typed; 41 Handwritten

Descriptors:
    Oskar Stonorov, Strozzi Exhibition, "Sixty Years of
    Living Architecture" Exhibition

Review:
    Brief note on the preparations for Wright's "Sixty Years of
    Living Architecture" exhibition at the Strozzi in Florence.

B416

Date:
   April 5, 1951

Type of Manuscript:
   Letter and enclosure

To:
   William T. Evjue

From:
   Frank Lloyd Wright

Collection:
   The William Theodore Evjue Papers, 1905-1969
   The State Historical Society of Wisconsin
   MSS 244, Box 155, Folder 22

Medium:
   Typed on Taliesin design stationery and signed "F.L L W."

Size:
   8-1/2 in. x 11 in.; 215.9 mm x 279.4 mm

Number of Pages:
   1 and 1 Enclosure

Number of Words:
   29

Descriptors:
   William T. Evjue, *The Capital Times*, Senator Joseph
   McCarthy, Communism, *The Milwaukee Journal*

Review:
   Wright sends Evjue a copy of an article which appeared in
   The Milwaukee Journal on the charge, by Senator Joseph McCarthy,
   of un-Americanism on Wright's part (see Wright, Frank Lloyd,
   "Frank Lloyd Wright on Americanism"). Evjue printed the article
   in *The Capital Times* (see also "Frank Lloyd Wright Reply to the
   Un-American Activities Group Charge").

B417

Date:
   April 30, 1951

Type of Manuscript:
   Letter

To:
   John Lloyd Wright

From:
   Frank Lloyd Wright

Collection:
   The John Lloyd Wright Collection
   The Avery Architectural Library
   Columbia University, Folder 12

Medium:
   Typed, signed "Dad"

Size:
   5-3/8 in. x 6-1/8 in.; 136.5 mm x 155.6 mm

Number of Pages:
   1

Number of Words:
   98

Descriptors:
   John Lloyd Wright, Taliesin Fellowship

Review:
   John Lloyd feels that his father may have offended some friends
   of the younger Wright who wanted to join the Taliesin Fellowship
   and were apparently not allowed to. The note is Frank Lloyd's
   response to his son's allegation.

B418

Date:
   April 30, 1951

Type of Manuscript:
   Letter

To:
   Oskar Stonorov

From:
   Frank Lloyd Wright

Collection:
   The Oskar Stonorov Collection
   Archive of Contemporary History
   The University of Wyoming

Medium:
   Typed on Taliesin design stationery, with handwritten
   notes, signed "F.L L W."

Size:
   8-1/2 in. x 11 in.; 215.9 mm x 279.4 mm

Number of Pages:
   5

Number of Words:
   986 Typed; 108 Handwritten

Descriptors:
   Oskar Stonorov, Arthur Kaufmann, Gimbels Exhibition
   (Philadelphia), Strozzi Exhibition, Frank Lloyd Wright
   Foundation, Bruno Zevi, State University of Venice,
   Werner Moser, "Sixty Years of Living Architecture"
   Exhibition

Review:
   Wright discusses Arthur Kaufmann's role in the exhibition of his
   work shown in Gimbels and explains to Stonorov his letdown over

the problems encountered in the exhibition. Wright also discusses
the future of his exhibition at the Strozzi and elsewhere abroad.

B419

Date:
   May 1, 1951

Type of Manuscript:
   Letter

To:
   Oskar Stonorov

From:
   Frank Lloyd Wright

Collection:
   The Oskar Stonorov Collection
   Archive of Contemporary History
   The University of Wyoming

Medium:
   Typed on Taliesin design stationery, signed
   "F L L.W."

Size:
   8-1/2 in. x 11 in.; 215.9 mm x 279.4 mm

Number of Pages:
   1

Number of Words:
   36

Descriptors:
   Oskar Stonorov, *Architectural Forum*, Ezra Stoller

Review:
   Brief talk of payment to Ezra Stoller, photographer, for
   something published in *Architectural Forum*.

B420

Date:
   August 11, 1951

Type of Manuscript:
   Letter

To:
   Oskar Stonorov

From:
   Frank Lloyd Wright

Collection:
   The Oskar Stonorov Collection
   Archive of Contemporary History
   The University of Wyoming

Medium:
Typed on Taliesin design stationery, signed
"F. L L W."

Size:
8-1/2 in. x 11 in.; 215.9 mm x 279.4 mm

Number of Pages:
1

Number of Words:
28 Typed; 5 Handwritten

Descriptors:
Oskar Stonorov

Review:
Wright invites Stonorov and family to visit Taliesin.

B421

Date:
August 21, 1951

Type of Manuscript:
Copy of speech, "Architecture as Religion"

To:
Unitarian Church
Madison, Wisconsin

From:
Frank Lloyd Wright

Collection:
The Herbert and Katherine Jacobs Frank Lloyd Wright
Collection
The Art Institute of Chicago
Documents, Envelope 6

Medium:
Typed double spaced, unsigned

Size:
8-1/2 in. x 11 in.; 215.9 mm x 279.4 mm

Number of Pages:
2

Descriptors:
Unitarian Church, Religion, Thomas Jefferson, Davy
Crockett

Review:
"Architecture as Religion" was delivered by Wright at the
Unitarian Church which he designed near Madison, Wisconsin.
For an account of Wright's deliverance of this speech see
"Architect Speaks at Church He Designed--Search for Beautiful
Should Be Life's Greatest End: Wright," *The Capital Times*,
August 30, 1951.

B422

Date:
   November 6, 1951

Type of Manuscript:
   Letter

To:
   H.C. Custer
   The First Unitarian Society
   Madison, Wisconsin

From:
   Frank Lloyd Wright

Collection:
   The First Unitarian Society of Madison, Wisconsin, Records,
   1878-1976
   The State Historical Society of Wisconsin
   MSS 297, Box 7, Folder 6

Medium:
   Typed on Taliesin stationery and signed

Size:
   8-1/2 in. x 11 in.; 215.9 mm x 279.4 mm

Number of Pages:
   1

Number of Words:
   38

Descriptors:
   H.C. Custer, The First Unitarian Society, Norberg Electric
   Company, Unitarian Church (Madison, Wisconsin)

Review:
   Authorization to pay a contractor, Norberg Electric Company,
   an amount of money; probably for the Unitarian Church designed
   by Wright near Madison, Wisconsin.

B423

Date:
   December 18, 1951

Type of Manuscript:
   Letter

To:
   Oskar Stonorov

From:
   Frank Lloyd Wright

Collection:
   The Oskar Stonorov Collection
   Archive of Contemporary History
   The University of Wyoming

Medium:
   Typed, signed "F.L L W."

Number of Pages:
1

Number of Words:
176

Descriptors:
Oskar Stonorov, "Sixty Years of Living Architecture"
Exhibition

Review:
Wright asks Stonorov what is happening with respect to his
"Sixty Years of Living Architecture" Exhibition abroad.

B424

Date:
December 22, 1951

Type of Manuscript:
Letter

To:
Bruce Barton
New York

From:
Frank Lloyd Wright

Collection:
The Bruce Barton Papers, 1881-1965
The State Historical Society of Wisconsin
U.S. MSS 44, Box 73

Medium:
Typed and signed "Frank Lloyd Wright"

Size:
5-3/8 in. x 8-5/8 in.; 136.5 mm x 219.1 mm

Number of Pages:
1

Number of Words:
65

Descriptors:
Bruce Barton

Review:
A brief letter of sympathy to Barton.

B425

Date:
January 4, 1952

Type of Manuscript:
Letter

To:
Mr. and Mrs. Harold M. Groves

From:
   Frank Lloyd Wright

Collection:
   The Harold M. Groves Papers, 1927-1969
   The State Historical Society of Wisconsin
   MSS 272, Box 13, Folder 11

Size:
   8-1/2± in. x 10-1/4± in.; 215.9± mm x 260.4± mm

Number of Pages:
   1

Number of Words:
   14 Typed; 5 Handwritten

Descriptors:
   Harold M. Groves

Review:
   A note of optimism from Wright to the Groveses regarding an
   undisclosed subject.

   B426

Date:
   January 8, 1952

Type of Manuscript:
   Letter

To:
   Oskar Stonorov

From:
   Frank Lloyd Wright

Collection:
   The Oskar Stonorov Collection
   Archive of Contemporary History
   The University of Wyoming

Medium:
   Typed on Taliesin design stationery, signed
   "F.L L W."

Size:
   8-1/2 in. x 11 in.; 215.9 mm x 279.4 mm

Number of Pages:
   1

Number of Words:
   76 Typed; 3 Handwritten

Descriptors:
   Oskar Stonorov, Werner Moser, "Sixty Years of Living
   Architecture" Exhibition, Milan

Review:
   Wright questions Stonorov on how his "Sixty Years of Living
   Architecture" exhibition got to Milan.

B427

Date:
   January 11, 1952

Type of Manuscript:
   Letter

To:
   Oskar Stonorov

From:
   Frank Lloyd Wright
   Taliesin West

Collection:
   The Oskar Stonorov Collection
   Archive of Contemporary History
   The University of Wyoming

Medium:
   Typed on Taliesin West design stationery, signed
   "F.L L W."

Size:
   8-1/2 in. x 11 in.; 215.9 mm x 279.4 mm

Number of Pages:
   1

Number of Words:
   77 Typed; 8 Handwritten

Descriptors:
   Oskar Stonorov, "Sixty Years of Living Architecture"
   Exhibition, Milan

Review:
   Wright again questions Stonorov on how his "Sixty Years of
   Living Architecture" exhibition got to Milan (see B426,
   his letter to Stonorov dated January 8, 1952).

B428

Date:
   February 13, 1952

Type of Manuscript:
   Letter

To:
   Oskar Stonorov

From:
   Frank Lloyd Wright

Collection:
   The Oskar Stonorov Collection
   Archive of Contemporary History
   The University of Wyoming

Medium:
   Typed on Taliesin design stationery, signed "F. L L W."

Size:
    8-1/2 in. x 11 in.; 215.9 mm x 279.4 mm

Number of Pages:
    1

Number of Words:
    41

Descriptors:
    Oskar Stonorov, Lawrence S. Morris, "Sixty Years of
    Living Architecture" Exhibition, Paris

Review:
    Wright invites Stonorov to Taliesin for a meeting. Also,
    progress on the Paris showing of Wright's "Sixty Years of
    Living Architecture" exhibition is discussed.

B429

Date:
    February 25, 1952

Type of Manuscript:
    Letter

To:
    Howard C. Custer
    Treasurer
    First Unitarian Society of Madison

From:
    Frank Lloyd Wright
    Taliesin West

Collection:
    The Harold M. Groves Papers, 1927-1969
    The State Historical Society of Wisconsin
    MSS 272, Box 13, Folder 11

Medium:
    Typed on Taliesin West design stationery, signed
    "F.LlW."

Size:
    8-1/2 in. x 11 in.; 215.9 mm x 279.4 mm

Number of Pages:
    1 with 2 attachments

Number of Words:
    47

Descriptors:
    Howard C. Custer, First Unitarian Society (Madison, Wis-
    consin), Unitarian Church (Shorewood Hills, Wisconsin),
    Norberg Electric Supply Company (Madison, Wisconsin)

Review:
    Wright transmits, with this cover letter, two bills from
    the electrical contractor, Norberg Electric Supply Company,
    for work done on the Unitarian Church designed by Wright at

Shorewood Hills, Wisconsin. The first statement is dated
October 2, 1951, and is for work done on August 20, 28 and
31 of 1951, and the second statement is dated January 31,
1952. Wright advises payment of these bills in the cover
letter.

B430

Date:
   March 5, 1952

Type of Manuscript:
   Letter

To:
   Oskar Stonorov

From:
   Frank Lloyd Wright

Collection:
   The Oskar Stonorov Collection
   Archive of Contemporary History
   The University of Wyoming

Medium:
   Typed on Taliesin West design stationery, signed
   "F.L L W."

Size:
   8-1/2 in. x 11 in.; 215.9 mm x 279.4 mm

Number of Pages:
   1

Number of Words:
   49

Descriptors:
   Oskar Stonorov, Iovanna Lloyd Wright, "Sixty Years of
   Living Architecture" Exhibition, Paris

Review:
   Wright plans to go to France for the Paris showing of his
   "Sixty Years of Living Architecture" exhibition.

B431

Date:
   March 12, 1952

Type of Manuscript:
   Letter

To:
   Oskar Stonorov

From:
   Frank Lloyd Wright

Collection:
    The Oskar Stonorov Collection
    Archive of Contemporary History
    The University of Wyoming

Medium:
    Typed on Taliesin design stationery, signed "F.L L W."

Size:
    8-1/2 in. x 11 in.; 215.9 mm x 279.4 mm

Number of Pages:
    1

Number of Words:
    217 Typed; 17 Handwritten

Descriptors:
    Oskar Stonorov, Ezra Stoller, S.C. Johnson and Son
    Company, "Sixty Years of Living Architecture" Exhibition

Review:
    Discussion of a payment to Ezra Stoller, photographer, for
    photographs taken for Wright's "Sixty Years of Living
    Architecture" exhibition.

B432

Date:
    March 12, 1952

Type of Manuscript:
    Letter

To:
    Lessing Rosenwald
    The American Council for Judaism
    New York

From:
    Frank Lloyd Wright

Collection:
    The American Council for Judaism Papers, 1938-1953
    The State Historical Society of Wisconsin
    U.S. MSS BJ, Box 3

Medium:
    Typed

Size:
    8-1/2 in. x 11 in.; 215.9 mm x 279.4 mm

Number of Pages:
    1

Number of Words:
    136

Descriptors:
    Lessing J. Rosenwald, The American Council for Judaism,
    Solomon R. Guggenheim, Guggenheim Museum, Religion, Judaism,
    Race

Review:
   Wright describes his views on Judaism.

B433

Date:
   March 19, 1952

Type of Manuscript:
   Letter

To:
   John Lloyd Wright
   Del Mar, California

From:
   Frank Lloyd Wright
   Taliesin West

Collection:
   The John Lloyd Wright Collection
   The Avery Architectural Library
   Columbia University
   Folder 12

Medium:
   Typed, with handwritten note, signed "Dad"

Size:
   8-1/2 in. x 11 in.; 215.9 mm x 279.4 mm

Number of Pages:
   1

Number of Words:
   40 Typed; 10 Handwritten

Descriptors:
   John Lloyd Wright, "Sixty Years of Living Architecture"
   Exhibition

Review:
   Frank Lloyd asks John Lloyd not to visit him until the senior
   Wright returns from Paris. F.L. Wright was in Paris for his
   "Sixty Years of Living Architecture" exhibition.

B434

Date:
   May 1, 1952

Type of Manuscript:
   Letter

To:
   Oskar Stonorov
   Philadelphia, Pennsylvania

From:
   Frank Lloyd Wright
   Taliesin
   Spring Green, Wisconsin

Collection:
The Oskar Stonorov Collection
Archive of Contemporary History
The University of Wyoming

Medium:
Typed, signed "F.L L W."

Number of Pages:
2

Number of Words:
99

Descriptors:
Oskar Stonorov, Le Corbusier, Werner Moser

Review:
Some rather interesting comments are made by Wright concerning
Le Corbusier. Comparisons are made between him and Le Corbusier.

B435

Date:
June 4, 1952

Type of Manuscript:
Letter

To:
George Beal

From:
Frank Lloyd Wright
Taliesin

Collection:
Frank Lloyd Wright Collection
Kenneth Spencer Research Library
University of Kansas

Medium:
Typed on Taliesin stationery and signed, with envelope

Size:
8-1/2 in. x 11 in.; 215.9 mm x 279.4 mm

Number of Pages:
1

Number of Words:
228

Descriptors:
George Beal, Iowa County (Wisconsin)

Review:
Wright requests that Beal write a letter to the Iowa County,
Wisconsin, Board regarding his non-profit Taliesin Fellowship
program.

B436

Date:
  June 13, 1952

Type of Manuscript:
  Letter

To:
  Oskar Stonorov

From:
  Frank Lloyd Wright

Collection:
  The Oskar Stonorov Collection
  Archive of Contemporary History
  The University of Wyoming

Medium:
  Typed on Taliesin design stationery, signed "F.L L W."

Size:
  8-1/2 in. x 11 in.; 215.9 mm x 279.4 mm

Number of Pages:
  3

Number of Words:
  517

Descriptors:
  Oskar Stonorov, Metropolitan Museum of Art, Olgivanna
  Lloyd Wright, Ezra Stoller, Brigitte D'Ortschy, "Sixty
  Years of Living Architecture" Exhibition

Review:
  Wright talks of his trip to Paris and future showings of his
  "Sixty Years of Living Architecture" exhibition. He also mentions
  to Stonorov the significant number of times Stonorov has run
  into financial problems with respect to Wright's exhibition.

B437

Date:
  June 13, 1952

Type of Manuscript:
  Letter

To:
  William T. Evjue

From:
  Frank Lloyd Wright
  Taliesin

Collection:
  The William Theodore Evjue Papers, 1905-1969
  The State Historical Society of Wisconsin
  MSS 244, Box 155, Folder 22

Medium:
   Typed on Taliesin design stationery and signed "Frank"

Size:
   8-1/2 in. x 11 in.; 215.9 mm x 279.4 mm

Number of Pages:
   1

Number of Words:
   205

Descriptors:
   William T. Evjue, Iowa County Board (Wisconsin)

Review:
   Wright asks Evjue for a letter to the Board of Iowa County
   concerning the school status of the Taliesin Fellowship for
   tax purposes.

B438

Date:
   Undated (June or July 1952)

Type of Manuscript:
   Letter

To:
   Oskar Stonorov
   Philadelphia, Pennsylvania

From:
   Frank Lloyd Wright

Collection:
   The Oskar Stonorov Collection
   Archive of Contemporary History
   The University of Wyoming

Medium:
   Typed on Taliesin design stationery, signed "F.L L W."

Size:
   8-1/2 in. x 11 in.; 215.9 mm x 279.4 mm

Number of Pages:
   1

Number of Words:
   109

Descriptors:
   Oskar Stonorov, "Sixty Years of Living Architecture"
   Exhibition

Review:
   Discussion of airplane tickets Wright has from a past trip
   to Europe during which he visited his "Sixty Years of Living
   Architecture" exhibition at Munich.

B439

Date:
   August 23, 1952

Type of Manuscript:
   Letter

To:
   John Lloyd Wright

From:
   Frank Lloyd Wright
   Taliesin

Collection:
   The John Lloyd Wright Collection
   The Avery Architectural Library
   Columbia University
   Folder 12

Medium:
   Typed on Taliesin design stationery, signed "Dad"

Size:
   8-1/2 in. x 11 in.; 215.9 mm x 279.4 mm

Number of Pages:
   1

Number of Words:
   20

Descriptors:
   John Lloyd Wright

Review:
   A brief note on a project which J.L. Wright was concerned about.

B440

Date:
   September 29, 1952

Type of Manuscript:
   Letter

To:
   Oskar Stonorov?

From:
   Frank Lloyd Wright
   Taliesin

Collection:
   The Oskar Stonorov Collection
   Archive of Contemporary History
   The University of Wyoming

Medium:
   Typed on Taliesin design stationery, signed
   "Frank Lloyd Wright"

Size:
    8-1/2 in. x 11 in.; 215.9 mm x 279.4 mm

Number of Pages:
    1

Number of Words:
    122

Descriptors:
    Oskar Stonorov, Grover Cleveland, Adlai Stevenson

Review:
    Wright gives his political support to Adlai Stevenson during
    the 1952 Presidential election.

B441

Date:
    September 30, 1952

Type of Manuscript:
    Letter

To:
    John Lloyd Wright

From:
    Frank Lloyd Wright
    Taliesin

Collection:
    The John Lloyd Wright Collection
    The Avery Architectural Library
    Columbia University
    Folder 12

Medium:
    Typed on Taliesin design stationery, signed "Dad"

Size:
    8-1/2 in. x 11 in.; 215.9 mm x 279.4 mm

Number of Pages:
    1

Number of Words:
    18

Descriptors:
    John Lloyd Wright, *An Autobiography*, Midway Gardens

Review:
    John Lloyd has questioned Frank Lloyd on the Midway Gardens
    and his father responds here.

B442

Date:
    October 15, 1952

Type of Manuscript:
    Letter

To:
    William T. Evjue

From:
    Frank Lloyd Wright

Collection:
    The William Theodore Evjue Papers, 1905-1969
    The State Historical Society of Wisconsin
    MSS 244, Box 155, Folder 2

Medium:
    Typed on Taliesin design stationery, signed
    "F.L L W."

Size:
    8-1/2 in. x 11 in.; 215.9 mm x 279.4 mm

Number of Pages:
    1

Number of Words:
    73

Descriptors:
    William T. Evjue, Adlai Stevenson

Review:
    Wright thanks Evjue for his aid.

B443

Date:
    December 8, 1952

Type of Manuscript:
    Letter

To:
    Oskar Stonorov

From:
    Frank Lloyd Wright
    Taliesin West

Collection:
    The Oskar Stonorov Collection
    Archive of Contemporary History
    The University of Wyoming

Medium:
    Typed on Taliesin West design stationery, signed
    "F.L L.W."

Size:
    8-1/2 in. x 11 in.; 215.9 mm x 279.4 mm

Number of Pages:
    1

Number of Words:
    48

Descriptors:
  Oskar Stonorov, "Sixty Years of Living Architecture"
  Exhibition

Review:
  Wright's exhibition is returning to Taliesin at Spring Green,
  Wisconsin.

B444

Date:
  December 17, 1952

Type of Manuscript:
  Letter

To:
  Oskar Stonorov

From:
  Frank Lloyd Wright
  Taliesin West

Collection:
  The Oskar Stonorov Collection
  Archive of Contemporary History
  The University of Wyoming

Medium:
  Typed on Taliesin West design stationery

Size:
  8-1/2 in. x 11 in.; 215.9 mm x 279.4 mm

Number of Pages:
  2

Number of Words:
  480

Descriptors:
  Oskar Stonorov, "Sixty Years of Living Architecture"
  Exhibition, Brigitte D'Ortschy, Walter Gropius, William
  Wesley Peters, Strozzi Exhibition, Bruno Zevi, Giuseppe Samonà

Review:
  Wright wants one of his "Sixty Years of Living Architecture"
  exhibition drawings returned to Taliesin at Wisconsin in this
  note of apparent unhappiness on the exhibition and its travels.

B445

Date:
  January 22, 1953

Type of Manuscript:
  Letter

To:
  Douglas Moore, President
  National Institute of Arts and Letters
  New York, New York

From:
    Frank Lloyd Wright
    Taliesin West

Collection:
    Correspondence Collections
    American Academy and Institute of Arts and Letters
    New York

Medium:
    Typed on Taliesin West design stationery, signed
    "Frank Lloyd Wright"

Size:
    8-1/2 in. x 11 in.; 215.9 mm x 279.4 mm

Number of Pages:
    1

Number of Words:
    56

Descriptors:
    Douglas Moore, Gold Medal for Architecture--National
    Institute for Arts and Letters, National Institute
    for Arts and Letters

Review:
    A discussion of the ceremony for Wright's acceptance of the
    Gold Medal for Architecture of the National Institute for
    Arts and Letters scheduled for May 27, 1953.

B446

Date:
    1953 (February 1953?)

Type of Manuscript:
    Typescript article

Title:
    "In the Cause of Architecture: The 'International Style'"

By:
    Frank Lloyd Wright
    Taliesin West

Collection:
    Frank Lloyd Wright Special Collections
    Northwestern University Archives
    Northwestern University Library

Medium:
    Typed

Number of Pages:
    8

Descriptors:
    International Style, *Taliesin Square-Paper*

Review:
    Probably issue number 17 of the *Taliesin Square-Paper* in which
    Wright attacks the International Style of architecture.

B447

Date:
   March 4, 1953

Type of Manuscript:
   Letter

To:
   Oskar Stonorov
   Philadelphia, Pennsylvania

From:
   Frank Lloyd Wright
   Taliesin West

Collection:
   The Oskar Stonorov Collection
   Archive of Contemporary History
   The University of Wyoming

Medium:
   Typed on Taliesin West design stationery,
   signed "F.L L.W."

Size:
   8-1/2 in. x 11 in.; 215.9 mm x 279.4 mm

Number of Pages:
   1

Number of Words:
   95 Typed; 33 Handwritten

Descriptors:
   Oskar Stonorov, Bob Hutchins, "Sixty Years of Living
   Architecture" Exhibition

Review:
   Wright has been contacted by Japan and the Philippines to send
   his exhibition to those two countries and he talks of this matter
   to Stonorov.

B448

Date:
   March 12, 1953

Type of Manuscript:
   Copy of letter

To:
   Ralph Walker
   National Institute of Arts and Letters

From:
   Frank Lloyd Wright
   Taliesin West

Collection:
   Correspondence Collections
   American Academy and Institute of Arts and Letters
   New York

Medium:
   Typed, signed "Frank"

Number of Pages:
   1

Number of Words:
   87 Typed; 22 Handwritten

Descriptors:
   Ralph Walker, Gold Medal Award for Architecture--National
   Institute for Arts and Letters, National Institute for Arts
   and Letters

Review:
   Wright transmits materials to Walker and also talks of his
   acceptance of the National Institute for Arts and Letters Gold
   Medal Award for Architecture. The letter has a brief personal
   note to Walker as a postscript.

B449

Date:
   March 16, 1953

Type of Manuscript:
   Letter

To:
   Marc Connelly
   National Institute of Arts and Letters
   New York, New York

From:
   Frank Lloyd Wright
   Taliesin West

Collection:
   Correspondence Collections
   American Academy and Institute of Arts and Letters
   New York

Medium:
   Typed on Taliesin West design stationery, signed
   "Frank"

Size:
   8-1/2 in. x 11 in.; 215.9 mm x 279.4 mm

Number of Pages:
   1

Number of Words:
   55

Descriptors:
   Marc Connelly, Gold Medal Award for Architecture--National
   Institute for Arts and Letters, National Institute for
   Arts and Letters

Review:
Wright is to transmit an acceptance speech for the Gold Medal
Award for Architecture of the National Institute for Arts and
Letters to the Institute. The medal was presented to him on
May 27, 1953, at New York.

B450

Date:
May 5, 1953

Type of Manuscript:
Letter

To:
Oskar Stonorov
Philadelphia, Pennsylvania

From:
Frank Lloyd Wright
Taliesin West

Collection:
The Oskar Stonorov Collection
Archive of Contemporary History
The University of Wyoming

Medium:
Typed on Taliesin West design stationery,
signed "F.L L.W."

Size:
8-1/2 in. x 11 in.; 215.9 mm x 279.4 mm

Number of Pages:
1

Number of Words:
51

Descriptors:
Oskar Stonorov, *House Beautiful*, Solomon R. Guggenheim
Museum, "Sixty Years of Living Architecture" Exhibition

Review:
A brief note on Wright's touring exhibition "Sixty Years of
Living Architecture."

B451

Date:
May 5, 1953

Type of Manuscript:
Letter

To:
Elizabeth ? (This letter is not to Emily Genauer)

From:
Frank Lloyd Wright
Taliesin West

Collection:
The Emily Genauer Papers, 1930-1957
Archives of American Art
Microfilm #NG 1

Medium:
Typed on Taliesin West design stationery, signed
"Frank Lloyd Wright"

Size:
8-1/2 in. x 11 in.; 215.9 mm x 279.4 mm

Number of Pages:
1

Number of Words:
250

Descriptors:
Strozzi Exhibition, Museum of Modern Art, Oskar Stonorov,
Olgivanna Lloyd Wright, Solomon R. Guggenheim Museum,
"Sixty Years of Living Architecture" Exhibition

Review:
Wright proposes to have his "Sixty Years of Living Architecture"
exhibition displayed in New York City.

B452

Date:
May 27, 1953

Type of Manuscript:
Text of speech

To:
National Institute of Arts and Letters
New York, New York

From:
Frank Lloyd Wright

Collection:
Correspondence Collections
American Academy and Institute of Arts and Letters
New York

Medium:
Typed manuscript

Size:
8-1/2 in. x 11 in.; 215.9 mm x 279.4 mm

Number of Pages:
5

Descriptors:
Gold Medal Award for Architecture, National Institute
for Arts and Letters, Artists, Creativity

Review:
Text of a speech which Wright prepared, although not used, for
his acceptance of the National Institute for Arts and Letters

Gold Medal Award for Architecture on May 27, 1953. In this speech
he talks of artists and of creativity.

B453

Date:
    May 27, 1953

Type of Manuscript:
    Text of speech

To:
    National Institute of Arts and Letters
    New York, New York

From:
    Frank Lloyd Wright

Collection:
    Correspondence Collections
    American Academy and Institute of Arts and Letters
    New York

Medium:
    Typed manuscript

Size:
    8-1/2 in. x 11 in.; 215.9 mm x 279.4 mm

Number of Pages:
    2

Descriptors:
    Gold Medal Award for Architecture--National Institute for
    Arts and Letters, Ralph Walker, National Institute for
    Arts and Letters

Review:
    The text of the speech which Wright delivered at the ceremony
    for his acceptance of the Gold Medal Award for Architecture from
    the National Institute of Arts and Letters. Wright's topic was
    architecture. *The New York Times* published several articles on
    this event including: "Famed Architect to Get Medal of Arts
    Institute"; Aline B. Loucheim's "Wright Analyzes Architects
    Need: Philosophy, Not Esthetics, Is a 'Must' Now, He Holds--
    His Show Opens Tomorrow"; "Wright Honored, Voices 'Humility':
    Institute of Arts and Letters Awards Medals to Architect and
    Marianne Craig Moore"; and "Individual Architect: Frank Lloyd
    Wright Show Reveals Many Facets."

B454

Date:
    June 2, 1953

Type of Manuscript:
    Letter

To:
    Emily Genauer
    Herald-Tribune
    New York

From:
Frank Lloyd Wright
The Plaza
New York

Collection:
The Emily Genauer Papers, 1930-1957
Archives of American Art
Microfilm #NG1

Medium:
Handwritten on The Plaza, New York, stationery,
signed "F.L.L.W."

Size:
Not determined

Number of Pages:
1

Number of Words:
30

Descriptors:
Emily Genauer, Strozzi Exhibition, The Plaza Hotel, *The
New York Herald-Tribune*, "Sixty Years of Living Architecture"
Exhibition

Review:
Wright thanks Genauer for a recent article she wrote and he
hints of the "Sixty Years of Living Architecture" exhibition.

B455

Date:
June 18, 1953

Type of Manuscript:
Letter

To:
Grant Carpenter Manson

From:
Frank Lloyd Wright

Collection:
The Grant Carpenter Manson Collection
The Oak Park Public Library
Oak Park, Illinois

Medium:
Typed on Taliesin design stationery

Size:
8-1/2 in. x 11 in.; 215.9 mm x 279.4 mm

Number of Pages:
1

Number of Words:
224

Descriptors:
  Grant Carpenter Manson, *Architectural Review*, Froebel
  Education, Minnesota University, Dimitris Tselos

Review:
  Wright comments and offers his opinion on Manson's article
  "Wright in the Nursery: The Influence of Froebel Education
  on His Work," *Architectural Review*. Manson later wrote
  Frank Lloyd Wright to 1910: The First Golden Age in 1958.

B456

Date:
  July 3, 1953

Type of Manuscript:
  Letter

To:
  Oskar Stonorov

From:
  Frank Lloyd Wright
  Taliesin

Collection:
  The Oskar Stonorov Collection
  Archive of Contemporary History
  The University of Wyoming

Medium:
  Typed on Taliesin design stationery, signed
  "F.L L.W."

Size:
  8-1/2 in. x 11 in.; 215.9 mm x 279.4 mm

Number of Pages:
  1

Number of Words:
  72 Typed; 14 Handwritten

Descriptors:
  Oskar Stonorov, "Sixty Years of Living Architecture"
  Exhibition, Usonian House

Review:
  A brief note to Stonorov on Wright's proposed mockup of a
  Usonian House to be displayed in New York with his touring
  exhibition "Sixty Years of Living Architecture." A more detailed
  account of the model Usonian House can be found in: "Wright's
  Pavilion to Open Thursday: Volunteers Helping to Prepare Exhibit
  of Architect's Work at 5th Avenue Site"; "House of Wright Is
  Previewed Here: Architect Shows First Guest Through 'Usonian Home'--
  Opening Due Tomorrow"; and "Throngs Inspect Wright's Exhibit:
  Visitors Marvel at Architect's Display of Work in House near
  Guggenheim Museum."

2-7.1   Frank Lloyd Wright points to his model of the Price Company Tower for Harold Price, Sr. (1952) at the preview of his Usonian House exhibition, featured in the "Sixty Years of Living Architecture" exhibition of his work in New York on October 21, 1953. Photo courtesy of *The Capital Times*, Madison, Wisconsin.

B457

Date:
September 21, 1953

Type of Manuscript:
Letter

To:
William T. Evjue

From:
Frank Lloyd Wright

Collection:
The William Theodore Evjue Papers, 1905-1969
The State Historical Society of Wisconsin
MSS 244, Box 156, Folder 1

Medium:
Typed, signed "Frank Lloyd Wright"

Size:
7 in. x 8-1/2 in.; 177.8 mm x 215.9 mm

Number of Pages:
1

Number of Words:
221

Descriptors:
William T. Evjue, *The Capital Times*, Monona Terrace Civic
Center Project

Review:
Wright reminds Evjue that the Monona Terrace Civic Center
Project for Madison, Wisconsin, does not need the support
of *The Capital Times* but will stand on its own merit. An
important letter considering all of the support *The Capital
Times* gave the project in its pages through the efforts of
Wright's longtime friend, William T. Evjue.

B458

Date:
October 3, 1953

Type of Manuscript:
Letter (copy of original)

To:
George E. Rodgerson
The Wisconsin State Journal

From:
Frank Lloyd Wright
Taliesin

Collection:
The William Theodore Evjue Papers, 1905-1969
The State Historical Society of Wisconsin
MSS 244, Box 156, Folder 1

Medium:
   Typed copy on Taliesin design stationery, unsigned

Size:
   8-1/2 in. x 11 in.; 215.9 mm x 279.4 mm

Number of Pages:
   1

Number of Words:
   179

Descriptors:
   George E. Rodgerson, *The Wisconsin State Journal,* Monona
   Terrace Civic Center Project

Review:
   Wright feels the city of Madison will be helped by his Monona
   Terrace Civic Center Project.

B459

Date:
   December 25, 1953

Type of Manuscript:
   Small booklet entitled "Taliesin Tract," a Christmas greeting

To:
   Grant Carpenter Manson

From:
   Frank Lloyd Wright

Collection:
   The Grant Carpenter Manson Collection
   The Oak Park Public Library
   Oak Park, Illinois

Medium:
   Small booklet, typeset and hand signed "F.L L.W."

Size:
   6± in. x 8± in.; 152± mm x 203± mm

Number of Pages:
   Foldout

Descriptors:
   Grant Carpenter Manson, Christmas 1953

Review:
   Christmas greetings to Grant Manson from Wright. Manson
   was the author of *Frank Lloyd Wright to 1910: The First
   Golden Age.*

B460

Date:
   December 25, 1953

Type of Manuscript:
   Christmas greetings

To:
   Dan Catton Rich

From:
   Frank Lloyd Wright

Collection:
   The Wrightiana Collection
   The Art Institute of Chicago

Medium:
   Typeset and inscribed "F.L L.W."

Descriptors:
   Christmas 1953, Dan Catton Rich

Review:
   The title of this greeting is "Taliesin Tract Number One: Man."

B461

Date:
   December 25, 1953

Type of Manuscript:
   Christmas greetings

To:
   John Lloyd Wright

From:
   Frank Lloyd Wright

Collection:
   The John Lloyd Wright Collection
   The Avery Architectural Library
   Columbia University
   Folder 12

Medium:
   Typeset

Size:
   5-3/4 in. x 37-1/2 in.; 146.1 mm x 952.5 mm

Number of Pages:
   2

Number of Words:
   536

Descriptors:
   John Lloyd Wright, Christmas 1953

Review:
   Wright's philosophy of architecture is expressed in this
   Christmas greeting to his son and family.

B462

Date:
   December 25, 1953 (1954?)

Type of Manuscript:
   Christmas greetings

To:
   Mr. and Mrs. Harold M. Groves

From:
   Frank Lloyd Wright

Collection:
   The Harold M. Groves Papers, 1927-1969
   The State Historical Society of Wisconsin
   MSS 272, Box 14, Folder 6

Medium:
   Typeset, signed "F.LLW to the Groves' Affection. /54"

Size:
   5-11/16 in. 37-1/2 in.; 144.5 mm x 952.5 mm

Number of Pages:
   2

Number of Words:
   536

Descriptors:
   Harold M. Groves, Helen Groves, Christmas 1953

Review:
   The title of this Christmas greeting is "Taliesin Tract
   Number 1: Man."

B463

Date:
   December 29, 1953

Type of Manuscript:
   Letter

To:
   Oskar Stonorov
   Philadelphia, Pennsylvania

From:
   Frank Lloyd Wright
   Taliesin West

Collection:
   The Oskar Stonorov Collection
   Archive of Contemporary History
   The University of Wyoming

Medium:
   Typed on Taliesin West design stationery, not signed

Size:
   8-1/2 in. x 11 in.; 215.9 mm x 279.4 mm

Number of Pages:
   1

Number of Words:
   79

Descriptors:
   Oskar Stonorov, Rabbi Cohen, Beth Sholom Synagogue

Review:
   Preliminary discussion with Stonorov on Wright's doing design
   work on a building for Rabbi Cohen. This is probably the Beth
   Sholom Synagogue designed and built some years later by Wright
   at Elkins Park, Pennsylvania, a suburb of Philadelphia.

B464

Date:
   Undated (early 1950s)

Type of Manuscript:
   Corrected paper to document Wright's Broadacre City design
   in the traveling exhibition of the early 1950s entitled
   "Sixty Years of Living Architecture"

Collection:
   The Oskar Stonorov Collection
   Archive of Contemporary History
   The University of Wyoming
   Box 29, Item 3

Medium:
   Typed, with corrections in Wright's handwriting

Size:
   8-1/2 in. x 11 in.; 215.9 mm x 279.4 mm

Number of Pages:
   6 (first draft); 13 (second draft)

Descriptors:
   Oskar Stonorov, Broadacre City, "Sixty Years of Living
   Architecture" Exhibition

Review:
   Text of an interview of Frank Lloyd Wright by Oskar Stonorov
   on Wright's Broadacre City design. The text was typed and
   written from the interview and corrected with additions and
   modifications by F.L. Wright in two rough drafts, both of which
   are contained in the Oskar Stonorov Collection. A final printed
   text formed a portion of the brochure which was used by Stonorov
   for Wright's "Sixty Years of Living Architecture" exhibition which
   toured abroad and was featured in New York and Philadelphia during
   the early 1950s.

B465

Date:
   January 31, 1954

Type of Manuscript:
   Letter

2-7.2   Beth Sholom Synagogue (1954), Elkins Park, Pennsylvania. Photo by the author.

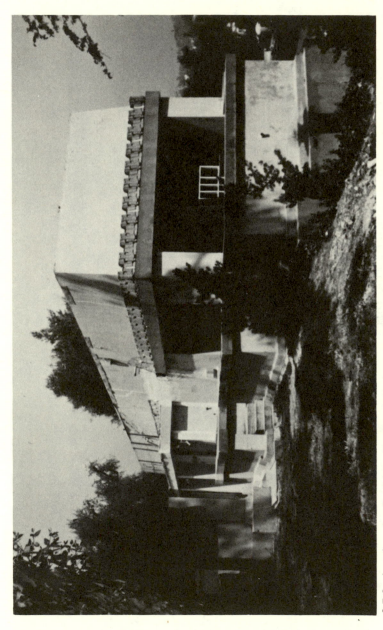

2-7.3 Los Angeles Exhibition Pavilion (1954), designed by Frank Lloyd Wright for use during the exhibition of his "Sixty Years of Living Architecture" show at Los Angeles. Photo by the author.

To:
  Mr. and Mrs. Harold M. Groves

From:
  Frank Lloyd Wright
  Taliesin West

Collection:
  The Harold M. Groves Papers, 1927-1969
  The State Historical Society of Wisconsin
  MSS 272, Box 8, Folder 5

Medium:
  Typed on Taliesin West design stationery,
  signed "F.LL.W"

Size:
  8-7/16 in. x 10-15/16 in.; 214.3 mm x 277.8 mm

Number of Pages:
  1

Number of Words:
  138 Typed; 13 Handwritten

Descriptors:
  Harold M. Groves, Helen Groves, William T. Evjue,
  Ted Boyle, *The Capital Times* (Madison, Wisconsin), Monona
  Terrace Civic Center Project, First Unitarian Church (Madison,
  Wisconsin)

Review:
  Wright is to forward some presentation drawings of his Monona
  Terrace Civic Center Project design to the Groveses.

B466

Date:
  February 23, 1954

Type of Manuscript:
  Letter

To:
  Helen Groves

From:
  Frank Lloyd Wright
  Taliesin West

Collection:
  The Harold M. Groves Papers, 1927-1969
  The State Historical Society of Wisconsin
  MSS 272, Box 8, Folder 5

Medium:
  Typed on Taliesin West design stationery, signed
  "F.L.L.W"

Size:
  8-7/16 in. x 10-15/16 in.; 214.3 mm x 277.8 mm

Number of Pages:
    1

Number of Words:
    54

Descriptors:
    Helen Groves, William T. Evjue, Ted Boyle, Madison (Wisconsin),
    Milwaukee (Wisconsin), Monona Terrace Civic Center Project

Review:
    Brief note on William T. Evjue, editor of *The Capital Times*,
    and the Monona Terrace Civic Center Project for Madison,
    Wisconsin, designed by Wright.

B467

Date:
    March 2, 1954

Type of Manuscript:
    Telegram (photocopy of original)

To:
    Harold M. Groves
    Madison, Wisconsin

From:
    Frank Lloyd Wright
    Phoenix, Arizona

Collection:
    The Harold M. Groves Papers, 1927-1969
    The State Historical Society of Wisconsin
    MSS 272, Box 7, Folder 7

Medium:
    Western Union Telegram, signed Frank Lloyd Wright; the
    original not housed in this collection

Size:
    Size of the original is not known

Number of Pages:
    2

Number of Words:
    82

Descriptors:
    Harold M. Groves, Eduardo Torroja, Monona Terrace Civic
    Center Project, Roger Corbetta, Corbetta Construction (New York)

Review:
    Wright indicates that cost estimates for the Monona Terrace
    Civic Center Project at Madison, Wisconsin, will be from 17
    to 20 million dollars. Wright also discusses possible consulta-
    tions with Eduardo Torroja, the famous Spanish engineer, and
    Roger Corbetta, of Corbetta Construction of New York.

B468

Date:
June 12, 1954

Type of Manuscript:
Letter

To:
William T. Evjue

From:
Frank Lloyd Wright

Collection:
The William Theodore Evjue Papers, 1905-1969
The State Historical Society of Wisconsin
MSS 244, Box 156, Folder 1

Medium:
Typed on Taliesin design stationery and signed "F.L L.W."

Size:
8-1/2 in. x 11 in.; 215.9 mm x 279.4 mm

Number of Pages:
1

Number of Words:
71

Descriptors:
William T. Evjue, *The Capital Times*, Monona Terrace Civic
Center Project

Review:
Wright thanks Evjue for recently printing an article he had
written for *The Capital Times*.

B469

Date:
June 12, 1954

Type of Manuscript:
Letter

To:
Mr. and Mrs. Harold M. Groves

From:
Frank Lloyd Wright
Taliesin

Collection:
The Harold M. Groves Papers, 1927-1969
The State Historical Society of Wisconsin
MSS 272, Box 8, Folder 5

Medium:
Typed on Taliesin design stationery, signed "F.LL.W"

Size:
8-7/16 in. x 10-15/16 in.; 214.3 mm x 277.8 mm

Number of Pages:
   1

Number of Words:
   40

Descriptors:
   Harold M. Groves, Helen Groves, Monona Terrace Civic
   Center Project

Review:
   A brief message on the cost estimates for the Monona Terrace
   Civic Center Project at Madison, Wisconsin.

B470

Date:
   June 23, 1954

Type of Manuscript:
   Letter

To:
   Mr. and Mrs. Harold M. Groves

From:
   Frank Lloyd Wright
   Taliesin

Collection:
   The Harold M. Groves Papers, 1927-1969
   The State Historical Society of Wisconsin
   MSS 272, Box 8, Folder 5

Medium:
   Typed on Taliesin design stationery, signed "F.LL.W"

Size:
   8-7/16 in. x 10-15/16 in.; 214.3 mm x 277.8 mm

Number of Pages:
   1

Number of Words:
   50 Typed; 2 Handwritten

Descriptors:
   Harold M. Groves, Helen Groves, Monona Terrace Civic Center
   Project, Roger Corbetta, Corbetta Construction (New York)

Review:
   Wright, apparently having received a cost estimate for his
   design for the Monona Terrace Civic Center Project at Madison,
   Wisconsin, from Roger Corbetta of Corbetta Construction, conveys
   Corbetta's thoughts on this matter to the Groveses.

B471

Date:
   June 27, 1954

Type of Manuscript:
   Letter

To:
   Helen Groves

From:
   Frank Lloyd Wright
   Taliesin

Collection:
   The Harold M. Groves Papers, 1927-1969
   The State Historical Society of Wisconsin
   MSS 272, Box 8, Folder 5

Medium:
   Typed on Taliesin design stationery, signed "F.LLW"

Size:
   8-7/16 in. x 10-15/16 in.; 214.3 mm x 277.8 mm

Number of Pages:
   1

Number of Words:
   34

Descriptors:
   Helen Groves

Review:
   A brief note on a subject matter which cannot be determined by
   the contents of the letter.

B472

Date:
   July 3, 1954

Type of Manuscript:
   Letter

To:
   Don Anderson
   Madison, Wisconsin

From:
   Frank Lloyd Wright
   Taliesin

Collection:
   The Don Anderson Papers, 1890-1972
   The State Historical Society of Wisconsin
   U.S. MSS 123AF, Box 14, Folder 7

Medium:
   Typed on Taliesin stationery, with written comments
   and signed

Size:
   8-1/2 in. x 11 in.; 215.9 mm x 279.4 mm

Number of Pages:
   1

Number of Words:
  29 Typed; 5 Handwritten

Descriptors:
  Don Anderson, Newspapers, *The Wisconsin State Journal*
  (Madison, Wisconsin)

Review:
  Wright would like to talk to Anderson. A possible topic for
  that conversation may have been Anderson's unfavorable views
  toward the building of the Monona Terrace Civic Center Project
  in Madison, Wisconsin. Anderson was a strong force behind the
  Madison newspaper, *The Wisconsin State Journal*, which opposed
  the Wright designed Monona Terrace Civic Center Project.

B473

Date:
  July 4, 1954

Type of Manuscript:
  Telegram

To:
  Don Anderson
  The Wisconsin State Journal
  Madison, Wisconsin

From:
  Frank Lloyd Wright

Source:
  "An Exchange of Telegrams"
  The Capital Times (Madison, Wisconsin), November 20, 1961

Medium:
  Western Union Telegram, signed "Frank"

Number of Pages:
  1

Number of Words:
  42

Descriptors:
  Monona Terrace Civic Center Project, Don Anderson,
  The Wisconsin State Journal (Madison, Wisconsin)

Review:
  Wright accuses Anderson of playing politics with respect to
  The Wisconsin State Journal's not backing the Monona Terrace
  Civic Center Project designed by him.

B474

Date:
  October 22, 1954

Type of Manuscript:
  Letter (copy of original)

To:
   Unknown

From:
   Frank Lloyd Wright
   Taliesin

Collection:
   The William Theodore Evjue Papers, 1905-1969
   The State Historical Society of Wisconsin
   MSS 244, Box 156, Folder 1

Medium:
   Typed and signed copy on Taliesin design stationery

Size:
   8-1/2 in. x 11 in.; 215.9 mm x 279.4 mm

Number of Pages:
   1

Number of Words:
   176

Descriptors:
   Dr. Eduardo Torroja, Monona Terrace Civic Center Project

Review:
   Wright speaks of Dr. Eduardo Torroja reviewing his plan for the
   Monona Terrace Civic Center Project at Madison, Wisconsin. The
   letter is not addressed to anyone.

B475

Date:
   October 25, 1954

Type of Manuscript:
   Building program outline

By:
   Frank Lloyd Wright
   Taliesin

Source:
   "In His Own Hand Lettering"
   The Capital Times (Madison, Wisconsin), October 26, 1954

Medium:
   Hand lettered note signed "Frank Lloyd Wright"

Number of Pages:
   1

Number of Words:
   112

Descriptors:
   Monona Terrace Civic Center Project

Review:
   A rough outline of the building program for the Monona Terrace
   Civic Center Project with area and space requirements given for

functions such as parking, offices, auditorium, and exterior
court and garden areas.

B476

Date:
November 2, 1954

Type of Manuscript:
Letter

To:
William T. Evjue

From:
Frank Lloyd Wright

Collection:
The William Theodore Evjue Papers, 1905-1969
The State Historical Society of Wisconsin
MSS 244, Box 156, Folder 1

Medium:
Typed on Taliesin design stationery, signed "Frank"

Size:
7-1/4 in. x 8-1/2 in. 184.2 mm x 215.9 mm

Number of Pages:
1

Number of Words:
60 Typed; 18 Handwritten

Descriptors:
William T. Evjue, Taliesin West

Review:
Wright sends Evjue a copy of a recent book and invites him to
Taliesin West for a visit.

B477

Date:
November 1954

Type of Manuscript:
Rough draft of letter

To:
Mayor, City Council, and County Board (Madison, Wisconsin)

By:
Frank Lloyd Wright and Harold M. Groves?

Collection:
The Harold M. Groves Papers, 1927-1969
The State Historical Society of Wisconsin
MSS 272, Box 24, Folder 11

Medium:
Typed on yellow paper, with handwritten corrections
in pencil, and signed "FLW"

Size:
    8-3/8 in. x 10-7/8 in.; 212.7 mm x 276.2 mm

Number of Pages:
    2

Number of Words:
    449 Typed; 116 Handwritten

Descriptors:
    Harold M. Groves, Helen Groves, Monona Terrace Project,
    Mayor and Common Council of the City of Madison (Wisconsin)

Review:
    A letter of thanks to the voters of Madison, Wisconsin, who
    voted for a referendum which would enable the construction of
    the Wright designed Monona Terrace Civic Center Project at
    Madison. The letter is a rough draft apparently written by
    Harold M. Groves on behalf of the Committee for the Monona
    Terrace Referendum, with corrections, additions, deletions,
    and a personal note to Helen and Harold M. Groves written by
    Wright in pencil as he reviewed this draft for Groves and the
    Committee.

B478

Date:
    December 4, 1954

Type of Manuscript:
    Letter (copy of original)

To:

Original to	Copy to
Ivan A. Nestingen, Chairman	William T. Evjue
Municipal Auditorium Committee	(initialed by Wright)
Madison, Wisconsin	

From:
    Frank Lloyd Wright

Collection:
    The William Theodore Evjue Papers, 1905-1969
    The State Historical Society of Wisconsin
    MSS 244, Box 156, Folder 1

Medium:
    Typed (copy to Evjue initialed by Wright)

Size:
    8-1/2 in. x 11 in.; 215.9 mm x 279.4 mm

Number of Pages:
    3

Number of Words:
    1,014 Typed; 3 Handwritten

Descriptors:
    Ivan A. Nestingen, Monona Terrace Civic Center Project,
    John M. Olin

Review:
  Wright states his case for building the Monona Terrace Civic
  Center at Madison, Wisconsin, and outlines some important aspects
  which must be considered (see B479).

B479

Date:
  December 4, 1954

Type of Manuscript:
  Letter (copy of original)

To:

Original to   Copy to
Ivan A. Nestingen, Chairman   Mr. and Mrs. Harold M. Groves
Municipal Auditorium Committee   (initialed by Wright)
Madison, Wisconsin

From:
  Frank Lloyd Wright

Collection:
  The Harold M. Groves Papers, 1927-1969
  The State Historical Society of Wisconsin
  MSS 272, Box 8, Folder 5

Medium:
  Copy of original, signed "Copy to the Groves-et al F.LLW"

Size:
  8-1/2 in. x 11 in.; 215.9 mm x 279.4 mm

Number of Pages:
  3

Number of Words:
  1,014 Typed; 7 Handwritten

Descriptors:
  Ivan A. Nestingen, Monona Terrace Civic Center Project,
  John M. Olin

Review:
  This is the same as the copy which Frank Lloyd Wright sent
  to William T. Evjue as described in B478. In this letter
  Wright states his case for the building of the Monona Terrace
  Civic Center at Madison, Wisconsin, which he designed and he
  outlines some important aspects which should be considered.

B480

Date:
  December 21, 1954

Type of Manuscript:
  Letter

To:
  Mr. and Mrs. Harold M. Groves

From:
    Frank Lloyd Wright
    Taliesin West

Collection:
    The Harold M. Groves Papers, 1927-1969
    The State Historical Society of Wisconsin
    MSS 272, Box 8, Folder 5

Medium:
    Typed on Taliesin West design stationery, signed
    "F. LL.W"

Size:
    8-1/2 in. x 11 in.; 215.9 mm x 279.4 mm

Number of Pages:
    1

Number of Words:
    47 Typed; 9 Handwritten

Descriptors:
    Harold M. Groves, Helen Groves, Ivan Nestingen, Monona
    Terrace Civic Center Project

Review:
    A brief letter discussing the time for the presentation of the
    Monona Terrace Civic Center Project at Madison, Wisconsin.
    Wright indicates that he is working on a model of the proposed
    complex.

B481

Date:
    February 12, 1955

Type of Manuscript:
    Building Program Outline--Monona Terrace Civic Center
    Project for Madison, Wisconsin

By:
    Frank Lloyd Wright

Collection:
    The Harold M. Groves Papers, 1927-1969
    The State Historical Society of Wisconsin
    MSS 272, Box 7, Folder 8

Medium:
    Photoduplicate of original typed text

Size:
    8-1/2 in. x 11 in.; 215.9 mm x 279.4 mm

Number of Pages:
    10

Descriptors:
    Monona Terrace Civic Center Project

Review:
    The title of this manuscript is "Outline Areas, Uses, and Location
    of Various Parts of the Proposed Monona Terrace Development,
    Frank Lloyd Wright, Architect, As Referred to the Program Therefor.
    February 12, 1955." This program may have been an attachment to a
    contract for the proposed architectural services of Frank Lloyd
    Wright.

B482

Date:
    March 13, 1955

Type of Manuscript:
    Letter

To:
    John Lloyd Wright
    Del Mar, California

From:
    Frank Lloyd Wright
    Taliesin West

Collection:
    The John Lloyd Wright Collection
    The Avery Architectural Library
    Columbia University
    Folder 12

Medium:
    Typed on Taliesin design stationery, signed "Father"

Size:
    8-1/2 in. x 11 in.; 215.9 mm x 279.4 mm

Number of Pages:
    1

Number of Words:
    43

Descriptors:
    John Lloyd Wright, San Diego (California)

Review:
    Frank Lloyd Wright to visit son John and go to San Diego,
    California, to deliver a lecture.

B483

Date:
    March 24, 1955

Type of Manuscript:
    Letter

To:
    William T. Evjue

2-7.4   Aerial view, looking north from above Lake Monona, of the model of the Monona Terrace Civic Center Project, with towers (February 1955), Madison, Wisconsin. Photo by Richard Vesey; courtesy of the State Historical Society of Wisconsin.

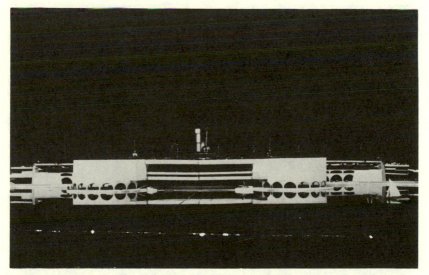

2-7.5   View from Lake Monona of the southeast elevation of the model of the Monona Terrace Civic Center Project (February 1955), Madison, Wisconsin. Photo by Richard Vesey; courtesy of the State Historical Society of Wisconsin.

2-7.6   Aerial view of model, looking northwest from above Lake Monona, of the Monona Terrace Civic Center Project, without towers (February 1955), Madison, Wisconsin. Photo by Richard Vesey; courtesy of the State Historical Society of Wisconsin.

2-7.7   Aerial view of model, looking south from above Wilson Street at Olin Terrace (foreground) and Civic Center (background), of the Monona Terrace Civic Center Project, without towers (February 1955), Madison, Wisconsin. Photo by Richard Vesey; courtesy of the State Historical Society of Wisconsin.

2-7.8 Aerial view of model, looking south at the proposed main civic center plaza, of the Monona Terrace Civic Center Project (February 1955), Madison, Wisconsin. Photo by Richard Vesey; courtesy of the State Historical Society of Wisconsin.

2-7.9 Aerial view looking down at model, with towers, of the Monona Terrace Civic Center Project (February 1955), Madison, Wisconsin. Photo by Richard Vesey; courtesy of the State Historical Society of Wisconsin.

2-7.11 Aerial view of model, with roof removed, showing the interior spaces of the Monona Terrace Civic Center Project (February 1955), Madison, Wisconsin. Photo by Richard Vesey; courtesy of the State Historical Society of Wisconsin.

2-7.10 Detailed aerial view of one of the towers for the Monona Terrace Civic Center Project (February 1955), Madison, Wisconsin. Photo by Richard Vesey; courtesy of the State Historical Society of Wisconsin.

From:
    Frank Lloyd Wright
    Taliesin West

Collection:
    The William Theodore Evjue Papers, 1905-1969
    The State Historical Society of Wisconsin
    MSS 244, Box 156, Folder 2

Medium:
    Typed on Taliesin West design stationery, signed
    "Frank"

Size:
    8-1/2 in. x 11 in.; 215.9 mm x 279.4 mm

Number of Pages:
    1

Number of Words:
    47

Descriptors:
    William T. Evjue

Review:
    Wright asks Evjue for his opinion regarding an undisclosed
    matter.

B484

Date:
    March 24, 1955

Type of Manuscript:
    Letter

To:
    Sister and Brother (Helen and Harold M. Groves)

From:
    Frank Lloyd Wright
    Taliesin West

Collection:
    The Harold M. Groves Papers, 1927-1969
    The State Historical Society of Wisconsin
    MSS 272, Box 14, Folder 5

Medium:
    Typed on Taliesin West design stationery,
    signed "F.LL.W"

Size:
    8-1/2 in. x 11 in.; 215.9 mm x 279.4 mm

Number of Pages:
    1

Number of Words:
    32

Descriptors:
   Harold M. Groves, Helen Groves, Frank Lloyd Wright Foundation,
   Monona Terrace Civic Center Project

Review:
   Wright transmits some data to the Groveses on the Frank Lloyd
   Wright Foundation with this short cover letter.

B485

Date:
   June 14, 1955

Type of Manuscript:
   Letter

To:
   Mr. and Mrs. Harold M. Groves?
   Madison, Wisconsin

From:
   Frank Lloyd Wright
   Taliesin
   Spring Green, Wisconsin

Collection:
   The Harold M. Groves Papers, 1927-1969
   The State Historical Society of Wisconsin
   MSS 272, Box 8, Folder 5

Medium:
   Typed letter, unsigned

Size:
   8-7/16 in. x 11-1/16 in.; 214.3 mm x 281.0 mm

Number of Pages:
   2

Number of Words:
   384

Descriptors:
   Harold M. Groves, Helen Groves, Monona Terrace Civic
   Center•Project

Review:
   The text of this letter is on cut carbon tissue paper mounted
   with glue on looseleaf paper. It is probably a copy of an original
   which Wright wrote to someone else. In it he discusses and is
   critical of the premature nature of the estimates on cost for the
   construction of his design for the Monona Terrace Civic Center
   Project at Madison, Wisconsin.

B486

Date:
   July 3, 1954? (probably 1955)

Type of Manuscript:
   Telegram (copy of original)

To:
   Richard Hawley Cutting (copy to William Evjue)
   Cleveland, Ohio

From:
   Frank Lloyd Wright

Collection:
   The William Theodore Evjue Papers, 1905-1969
   The State Historical Society of Wisconsin
   MSS 244, Box 156, Folder 2

Medium:
   Typed copy of Western Union Telegram, with handwritten note
   to Evjue, signed "Frank"

Size:
   8 in. x 10 in.; 203.2 mm x 254.0 mm

Number of Pages:
   1

Number of Words:
   229 Typed; 24 Handwritten

Descriptors:
   William T. Evjue, Richard Hawley Cutting, Air Force Academy
   Competition, U.S. Air Force, The Kitty Hawk Associates

Review:
   Wright refuses, on a philosophical basis, to compete with other
   architects for the Air Force Academy design at Colorado Springs,
   Colorado. The project was ultimately designed by Skidmore, Owings
   and Merrill. A short handwritten note by Wright transmits this
   copy of the telegram to William T. Evjue. This item was probably
   incorrectly dated by Wright; Wright withdrew from the competition
   in 1955 (see B489, letter dated July 14, 1955, to Mr. Alvin A.
   Sarra).

B487

Date:
   July 9, 1955

Type of Manuscript:
   Letter

To:
   William T. Evjue

From:
   Frank Lloyd Wright
   Taliesin

Collection:
   The William Theodore Evjue Papers, 1905-1969
   The State Historical Society of Wisconsin
   MSS 244, Box 156, Folder 2

Medium:
   Typed on Taliesin design stationery and signed "Frank"

Size:
    8-1/2 in. x 11 in.; 215.9 mm x 279.4 mm

Number of Pages:
    1

Number of Words:
    166

Descriptors:
    William T. Evjue, *The Capital Times*, Monona Terrace
    Civic Center Project

Review:
    Wright suggests that Evjue print his (Wright's) opinion on an
    aspect of the Monona Terrace Civic Center Project for Madison,
    Wisconsin, in *The Capital Times* (see also B488).

B488

Date:
    July 9, 1955

Type of Manuscript:
    Letter (copy of original)

To:
    William T. Evjue

From:
    Frank Lloyd Wright
    Taliesin

Collection:
    The Harold M. Groves Papers, 1927-1969
    The State Historical Society of Wisconsin
    MSS 272, Box 7, Folder 7

Medium:
    Typed copy of original

Size:
    8-1/2 in. x 11 in.; 215.9 mm x 279.4 mm

Number of Pages:
    1

Number of Words:
    166

Descriptors:
    William T. Evjue, *The Capital Times* (Madison, Wisconsin),
    Monona Terrace Civic Center Project

Review:
    Copy of letter to William T. Evjue dated July 9, 1955, described
    above (see B487). Wright suggests that William T. Evjue print his
    (Wright's) opinion on an aspect of the Monona Terrace Civic Center
    Project for Madison, Wisconsin in *The Capital Times*.

B489

Date:
   July 14, 1955

Type of Manuscript:
   Letter (copy of original)

To:
   Alvin A. Sarra (copy to William Evjue)
   Henry J. Kaufmann and Associates
   Washington, D.C.

From:
   Frank Lloyd Wright

Collection:
   The William Theodore Evjue Papers, 1905-1969
   The State Historical Society of Wisconsin
   MSS 244, Box 156, Folder 2

Medium:
   Typed copy, unsigned

Size:
   8 in. x 7-1/2 in.; 203.2 mm x 190.5 mm

Number of Pages:
   1

Number of Words:
   137

Descriptors:
   Alvin A. Sarra, Henry J. Kaufmann and Associates, Air
   Force Academy Competition, The Kitty Hawk Associates,
   Skidmore, Owings and Merrill, Richard Hawley Cutting

Review:
   Wright does not care to compete with other architects
   for the Air Force Academy to be located at Colorado
   Springs, Colorado. Included with this letter is a copy
   of Wright's telegram (see B486) dated July 3, 1954 (1955?),
   to Richard Hawley Cutting in which he withdraws from consideration for competition for the Air Force Academy design.

B490

Date:
   October 6, 1955

Type of Manuscript:
   Letter

To:
   Robert Moses

From:
   Frank Lloyd Wright

Source:
   Robert Moses
   Public Works: A Dangerous Trade, pp. 864-866

Number of Words:
   976

Descriptors:
   Robert Moses, Mary Moses, Olgivanna Lloyd Wright,
   Solomon R. Guggenheim Museum, Euclid Contracting Company,
   Dr. Feld, New York Building Code, Harry F. Guggenheim,
   George N. Cohen, New York, Skidmore, Owings and Merrill,
   Air Force Academy, U.S. Congress, Plaza Hotel (New York)

Review:
   Wright gives a brief history of the problems he encountered
   for the approval of plans for the Guggenheim Museum by New
   York City building officials. Wright's tone is one of a mild
   plea for aid from Moses.

B491

Date:
   October 18, 1955

Type of Manuscript:
   Letter (copy of original)

To:
   Drew Pearson
   Washington, D.C.

From:
   Frank Lloyd Wright

Collection:
   The William T. Evjue Papers, 1905-1969
   The State Historical Society of Wisconsin
   MSS 244, Box 156, Folder 2

Medium:
   Typed copy, unsigned

Size:
   8-1/2 in. x 11 in.; 215.9 mm x 279.4 mm

Number of Pages:
   1

Number of Words:
   277

Descriptors:
   Drew Pearson, Air Force Academy Competition, *The
   Congressional Record*

Review:
   Wright talks of a newspaper article concerning his opinions
   of the Air Force Academy design which was printed in a Colorado
   Springs, Colorado, newspaper (Wright is probably referring to his
   "Letter to the Editor," printed in the May 27, 1955, issue of
   the Colorado Springs *Free Press* and later made a part of *The
   Congressional Record*, [84th Congress, 1st Session, 101, Pt.
   7:8781]).

B492

Date:
    March 31, 1956

Type of Manuscript:
    Letter

To:
    Oskar Stonorov

From:
    Frank Lloyd Wright

Collection:
    The Oskar Stonorov Collection
    Archive of Contemporary History
    The University of Wyoming

Medium:
    Typed on Taliesin design stationery, signed
    "F. LL.W."

Size:
    8-1/2 in. x 11 in.; 215.9 mm x 279.4 mm

Number of Pages:
    2

Number of Words:
    317

Descriptors:
    Oskar Stonorov, Lloyd Lewis, Ludwig Mies van der Rohe,
    Walter Gropius

Review:
    Wright responds negatively to a request by Stonorov to
    have a Wright exhibition in Germany. The letter includes
    a very personal note to Stonorov reflecting Wright's feelings
    on his past relationships with Stonorov.

B493

Date:
    May 11, 1956

Type of Manuscript:
    Letter

To:
    William T. Evjue

From:
    Frank Lloyd Wright

Collection:
    The William T. Evjue Papers, 1905-1969
    The State Historical Society of Wisconsin
    MSS 244, Box 156, Folder 2

Medium:
    Typed on Taliesin design stationery, signed "F.L L.W."

Size:
   7-1/4 in. x 8-1/2 in.; 184.2 mm x 215.9 mm

Number of Pages:
   1

Number of Words:
   169

Descriptors:
   William T. Evjue, *The Capital Times*, Monona Terrace
   Civic Center Project

Review:
   Wright apologizes for not having read some recent articles
   Evjue wrote for *The Capital Times* regarding several of Wright's
   projects, in particular the Monona Terrace Civic Center Project
   for Madison, Wisconsin. Wright's reasons for not reading these
   articles are based on his busy schedule and fatigue due to a
   heavy workload.

B494

Date:
   June 18, 1956

Type of Manuscript:
   Letter

To:
   William T. Evjue

From:
   Frank Lloyd Wright

Collection:
   The William T. Evjue Papers, 1905-1969
   The State Historical Society of Wisconsin
   MSS 244, Box 156, Folder 2

Medium:
   Typed on Taliesin design stationery, signed
   "F.L L.W."

Size:
   7-1/4 in. x 8-1/2 in.; 184.2 mm x 215.9 mm

Number of Pages:
   1

Number of Words:
   188

Descriptors:
   William T. Evjue, Monona Terrace Civic Center Project,
   Mr. Woodburn

Review:
   Wright discusses a Mr. Woodburn with respect to the Monona
   Terrace Civic Center Project for Madison, Wisconsin.

B495

Date:
    July 5, 1956

Type of Manuscript:
    Construction Contract for Architectural Services

Between:
    The Frank Lloyd Wright Foundation
    (Frank Lloyd Wright, President)
    and
    The City of Madison, Wisconsin

Collection:
    The Harold M. Groves Papers, 1927-1969
    The State Historical Society of Wisconsin
    MSS 272, Box 23, Folder 10

Medium:
    Tissue paper copy

Size:
    8-1/2 in. x 12-7/8 in.; 215.9 mm x 227.0 mm

Number of Pages:
    9

Descriptors:
    Monona Terrace Civic Center Project; Frank Lloyd Wright
    Foundation; City of Madison (Wisconsin); Ivan A. Nestingen;
    A. Bareis; Harold E. Hanson; Arthur, Dewa, Tomlinson and
    Thomas, Attorneys at Law

Review:
    The construction contract for architectural services to be
    provided by the Frank Lloyd Wright Foundation (Frank Lloyd
    Wright, President) for the construction of the Monona Terrace
    Civic Center Project at Madison, Wisconsin.

B496

Date:
    September 6, 1956

Type of Manuscript:
    Typed copy of letter

To:
    Original to   Copy to
    Ivan A. Nestingen, Mayor   Mr. and Mrs. Harold M. Groves
    City of Madison, Wisconsin

From:
    Frank Lloyd Wright
    Taliesin

Collection:
    The Harold M. Groves Papers, 1927-1969
    The State Historical Society of Wisconsin
    MSS 272, Box 8, Folder 5

Medium:
   Typed (copy to Mr. and Mrs. Harold M. Groves)

Size:
   8-7/16 in. x 10-15/16 in.; 214.3 mm x 277.8 mm

Number of Pages:
   2

Number of Words:
   567

Descriptors:
   Harold M. Groves, Helen Groves, Ivan Nestingen,
   Monona Terrace Civic Center Project

Review:
   Wright responds to some Monona Terrace Civic Center Project
   building program changes made by the city of Madison with respect
   to the addition of a basketball court, a second auditorium to
   handle an additional sports crowd of 3,500 persons, and additional
   parking to serve these additional facilities.

B497

Date:
   September 10, 1956

Type of Manuscript:
   Carbon copy of letter

To:
   Original to   Copy to
   Ivan A. Nestingen, Mayor   Mr. and Mrs. Harold M. Groves
   City of Madison, Wisconsin

From:
   Frank Lloyd Wright
   Taliesin

Collection:
   The Harold M. Groves Papers, 1927-1969
   The State Historical Society of Wisconsin
   MSS 272, Box 8, Folder 5

Medium:
   Typed on Taliesin design
   stationery

Size:
   8-7/16 in. x 10-15/16 in.; 214.3 mm x 277.8 mm

Number of Pages:
   2

Number of Words:
   505 Typed; 4 Handwritten

Descriptors:
   Harold M. Groves, Helen Groves, Ivan A. Nestingen,
   Monona Terrace Civic Center Project

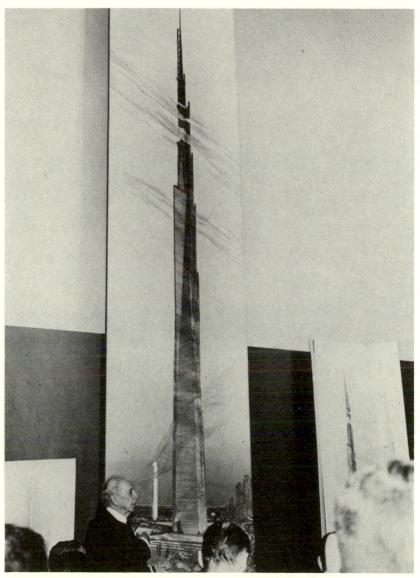

2-7.12　Frank Lloyd Wright presents his design for "The Illinois" Mile-High Skyscraper at his Testimonial Dinner at Chicago on December 7, 1956. Photo courtesy of *The Capital Times*, Madison, Wisconsin.

Review:
    Wright outlines some changes regarding a sports arena to be
    incorporated into his design for the Monona Terrace Civic Center
    at Madison, Wisconsin.

B498

Date:
    December 11, 1956

Type of Manuscript:
    Letter

To:
    Mr. and Mrs. Harold M. Groves

From:
    Frank Lloyd Wright
    Taliesin West

Collection:
    The Harold M. Groves Papers, 1927-1969
    The State Historical Society of Wisconsin
    MSS 272, Box 8, Folder 5

Medium:
    Typed on Taliesin West design stationery, signed
    "F.LLW."

Size:
    8-1/2 in. x 11 in.; 215.9 mm x 279.4 mm

Number of Pages:
    2

Number of Words:
    290 Typed; 68 Handwritten

Descriptors:
    Harold M. Groves, Helen Groves, Monona Terrace Civic
    Center Project

Review:
    Wright discusses and reviews the excellent load bearing
    capabilities of the soils on the site of the proposed Monona
    Terrace Civic Center at Madison, Wisconsin.

B499

Date:
    December 27, 1956

Type of Manuscript:
    Telegram

To:
    Mr. and Mrs. Harold M. Groves
    Madison, Wisconsin

From:
    Frank and Olgivanna Lloyd Wright
    Phoenix, Arizona

Collection:
    The Harold M. Groves Papers, 1927-1969
    The State Historical Society of Wisconsin
    MSS 272, Box 14, Folder 6

Medium:
    Western Union Telegram--"Holiday Greetings by Western Union"

Size:
    6-3/16 in. x 8 in.; 157.2 mm x 203.2 mm

Number of Pages:
    1

Number of Words:
    5 (message)

Descriptors:
    Harold M. Groves, Helen Groves, Olgivanna Lloyd Wright,
    Christmas 1956

Review:
    Christmas greetings to the Groves family from the Wright family.

B500

Date:
    January 7, 1957

Type of Manuscript:
    Letter

To:
    Emily Genauer

From:
    Frank Lloyd Wright
    Taliesin West

Collection:
    The Emily Genauer Papers, 1930-1957
    Archives of American Art
    Microfilm #NG 1

Medium:
    Typed on Taliesin West design stationery, signed
    "Frank Lloyd Wright"

Size:
    8-1/2 in. x 11 in.; 215.9 mm x 279.4 mm

Number of Pages:
    1

Number of Words:
    140

Descriptors:
    Emily Genauer, *The New York Herald-Tribune*, Solomon
    R. Guggenheim

Review:
    Wright thanks Emily Genauer for a recent article on him in
    The New York Herald-Tribune.

B501

Date:
   March 18, 1957

Type of Manuscript:
   Memorandum

To:
   Herbert Jacobs
   The Capital Times
   Madison, Wisconsin

From:
   Frank Lloyd Wright
   Hotel Loraine
   Madison, Wisconsin

Collection:
   The Herbert and Katherine Jacobs Frank Lloyd Wright
   Collection
   The Art Institute of Chicago
   Documents, Envelope 6

Medium:
   Handwritten in pen and ink and hand lettered in pencil
   on Hotel Loraine (Madison, Wisconsin) stationery

Size:
   9-1/2± in. x 5± in.; 241± mm x 127± mm

Number of Pages:
   5

Descriptors:
   Herbert Jacobs, *The Capital Times*, Monona Terrace Civic Center
   Project

Review:
   This note was written after a meeting with the Madison City
   Council Committee regarding Wright's proposed design for the
   Monona Terrace Civic Center Project. The notes are in pencil,
   hand lettered by Wright, presenting some facts and figures on
   the project.

B502

Date:
   March 20, 1957

Type of Manuscript:
   Letter

To:
   Building Committee--Monona Terrace Project for the City
   of Madison

From:
   Frank Lloyd Wright

Collection:
   The Harold M. Groves Papers, 1927-1969

The State Historical Society of Wisconsin
MSS 272, Box 7, Folder 8

Medium:
   Carbon copy of letter, unsigned

Size:
   8-1/2 in. x 11 in.; 215.9 mm x 279.4 mm

Number of Pages:
   5

Number of Words:
   1,173

Descriptors:
   Building Committee--Monona Terrace Civic Center Project,
   Monona Terrace Civic Center Project, Mayor George Forster
   (Madison, Wisconsin), Mayor Ivan A. Nestingen (Madison,
   Wisconsin)

Review:
   Wright apologizes for remarks he made to the Building Committee
   of the Monona Terrace Civic Center Project at a recent meeting
   he had attended with the group. He lists building items which
   he feels were unfairly included by the City of Madison in his
   contract for the design of the Monona Terrace Civic Center
   Project, adding extra costs to it which were not initially fore-
   seen by him. Wright feels that he should protect his client,
   the citizens of Madison, from the unwarranted extras included in
   the recent cost estimate of the facility.

B503

Date:
   April 15, 1957

Type of Manuscript:
   Telegram

To:
   Harold M. Groves
   Madison, Wisconsin

From:
   Frank Lloyd Wright
   Phoenix, Arizona

Collection:
   The Harold M. Groves Papers, 1927-1969
   The State Historical Society of Wisconsin
   MSS 272, Box 8, Folder 5

Medium:
   Copy of Western Union Telegram

Size:
   8-1/2 in. x 11 in.; 215.9 mm x 279.4 mm

Number of Pages:
   1

Number of Words:
   77

Descriptors:
   Harold M. Groves, Monona Terrace Civic Center Project,
   State of Wisconsin

Review:
   Comments by Wright on the State of Wisconsin's interference over
   the use of a portion of Lake Monona at Madison for the building
   of the Monona Terrace Civic Center Project.

B504

Date:
   April 30, 1957

Type of Manuscript:
   Letter

To:
   Grant Carpenter Manson
   School of Fine Arts and History of Art
   University of Pennsylvania

From:
   Frank Lloyd Wright
   Taliesin West

Collection:
   The Grant Carpenter Manson Collection
   The Oak Park Public Library
   Oak Park, Illinois

Medium:
   Typed on Taliesin West designed stationery, signed
   "F.Ll. W."

Size:
   8-1/2 in. x 11 in.; 215.9 mm x 279.4 mm

Number of Pages:
   1

Number of Words:
   132

Descriptors:
   Grant Carpenter Manson, *Frank Lloyd Wright to 1910: The
   First Golden Age*, Henry-Russell Hitchcock

Review:
   Wright offers the use of the archives at Taliesin for Manson's
   research work on the book *Frank Lloyd Wright to 1910: The First
   Golden Age.*

B505

Date:
   November 16, 1957

2-7.13 Frank Lloyd Wright at his desk at Taliesin in August of 1957. Photo by Richard Vesey; courtesy of the State Historical Society of Wisconsin.

Type of Manuscript:
  Letter

To:
  Grant Carpenter Manson

From:
  Frank Lloyd Wright

Collection:
  The Grant Carpenter Manson Collection
  The Oak Park Public Library
  Oak Park, Illinois

Medium:
  Typed on Taliesin design stationery,
  signed "F.Ll.W."

Size:
  8-1/2 in. x 11 in.; 215.9 mm x 279.4 mm

Number of Pages:
  1

Number of Words:
  153

Descriptors:
  Grant Carpenter Manson, *Frank Lloyd Wright to 1910:*
  The First Golden Age, Harlan Residence, Louis H. Sullivan,
  Charnley Summer Cottage, Wainwright Tomb, Stock Exchange,
  Schiller Meyer Building, J.L. Silsbee, Cecil Corwin

Review:
  Wright reviews Manson's *Frank Lloyd Wright to 1910: The First*
  Golden Age and offers constructive criticism on several items
  which Wright had problems with. Wright talks of early influence
  on his design talents.

B506

Date:
  Undated (envelope postmarked November 27, 1957)

Type of Manuscript:
  Letter

To:
  Grant Carpenter Manson

From:
  Frank Lloyd Wright

Collection:
  The Grant Carpenter Manson Collection
  The Oak Park Public Library
  Oak Park, Illinois

Medium:
  Typed on Taliesin design stationery, signed
  "F.Ll. W.," with envelope

Size:
   8-1/2 in. x 11 in.; 215.9 mm x 279.4 mm

Number of Pages:
   3

Number of Words:
   382

Descriptors:
   Grant Carpenter Manson, Henry-Russell Hitchcock,
   A Testament, International Style, Lewis Mumford,
   Maginel Wright Barney, *An Autobiography*, *An American
   Architecture*, Eugene Masselink, *Frank Lloyd Wright to
   1910: The First Golden Age*

Review:
   Wright discusses at some length Henry-Russell Hitchcock's
   book review of Wright's *A Testament*. Wright disagrees with
   Hitchcock's comments concerning his date of birth as 1867.
   Also, Wright talks of his views of critics. Manson's book
   is also mentioned.

B507

Date:
   November 27, 1957

Type of Manuscript:
   Letter

To:
   Ivan A. Nestingen and Common Council (Mayor and Common
   Council of the City of Madison, Wisconsin)

From:
   Frank Lloyd Wright, President
   Frank Lloyd Wright Foundation

Collection:
   The Harold M. Groves Papers, 1927-1969
   The State Historical Society of Wisconsin
   MSS 272, Box 23, Folder 10

Medium:
   Typed tissue paper copy of Arthur, Dewa, Tomlinson,
   and Thomas, Attorneys at Law, stationery

Size:
   8-7/16 in. x 11 in.; 214.3 mm x 279.4 mm

Number of Pages:
   2

Number of Words:
   524

Descriptors:
   Ivan A. Nestingen; Common Council of Madison (Wisconsin);
   William C. Sachtjan; Monona Terrace Civic Center Project;
   Metzner Act; Arthur, Dewa, Tomlinson and Thomas, Attorneys
   at Law

Review:
A legal letter to the city of Madison from Wright in which he
reminds the city of its legal obligations to him as architect
under their executed contract regarding the fees for architectural
services performed in conjunction with the Monona Terrace Civic
Center Project.

B508

Date:
1957

Type of Manuscript:
Inscribed photograph

Source:
Edgar Tafel
Apprentice to Genius: Years with Frank Lloyd Wright, p. 209

Medium:
Photograph, with inscription "Frank Lloyd Wright"

Descriptors:
Edgar Tafel, Plaza Hotel (New York)

Review:
Wright inscribes a photograph of himself--"To Edgar the Tafel--
affection and hope--Frank Lloyd Wright." The inscribed photograph
is reproduced in Tafel's book.

B509

Date:
May 28, 1958

Type of Manuscript:
Letter

To:
The University of Wichita

From:
Frank Lloyd Wright

Source:
Olgivanna Lloyd Wright
The Shining Brow: Frank Lloyd Wright, pp. 151-152

Number of Words:
469

Descriptors:
Juvenile Cultural Study Center Project for the University
of Wichita, Education, Gothic, Paris Beaux Arts, American
Architecture, American Universities, Government, Organic
Architecture, Culture

Review:
Wright speaks on the relations between architecture, education,
and government. He had recently finished design work for a complex

2-7.14 Juvenile Cultural Study Center at Wichita State University (1957), Wichita, Kansas. Photo by the author.

of buildings for the University of Wichita and this letter is one
of optimism for the success of the project.

B510

Date:
   June 13, 1958

Type of Manuscript:
   Letter

To:
   James Marshall
   Parks Department
   City of Madison, Wisconsin

From:
   Frank Lloyd Wright

Collection:
   The Harold M. Groves Papers, 1927-1969
   The State Historical Society of Wisconsin
   MSS 272, Box 8, Folder 1

Medium:
   Typed carbon copy, dictated by telephone from
   Eugene Masselink, Frank Lloyd Wright's secretary

Size:
   8-1/2 in. x 11 in.; 215.9 mm x 279.4 mm

Number of Pages:
   1

Number of Words:
   225

Descriptors:
   James Marshall, Parks Department (Madison, Wisconsin),
   Monona Terrace Civic Center Project, Eugene Masselink,
   William T. Evjue, Metzner Bill, Citizens for Monona Terrace
   Committee, Olin Terrace, Taliesin Fellowship, Police
   Department (Madison, Wisconsin)

Review:
   Frank Lloyd Wright offers the model for his design of the
   Monona Terrace Civic Center Project for public display at
   Madison, Wisconsin. Wright suggests a method by which it
   could be shown to the citizens of Madison.

B511

Date:
   August 22, 1958

Type of Manuscript:
   Letter

To:
   William T. Evjue

From:
    Frank Lloyd Wright
    Taliesin

Collection:
    The William Theodore Evjue Papers, 1905-1969
    The State Historical Society of Wisconsin
    MSS 244, Box 156, Folder 3

Medium:
    Typed on Taliesin design stationery, signed
    "F.L L.W."

Size:
    8-1/2 in. x 11 in.; 215.9 mm x 279.4 mm

Number of Pages:
    1

Number of Words:
    57

Descriptors:
    William T. Evjue, *The Capital Times*, Antonin Raymond,
    Imperial Hotel, *Mainchi*

Review:
    Wright asks Evjue to print in *The Capital Times* "Frank Lloyd
    Wright and Imperial Hotel," an article written by Antonin Raymond
    which appeared in the August 15, 1958, issue of *Mainchi* (Tokyo),
    a Japanese periodical. Raymond worked under Wright during the
    design and construction of the Imperial Hotel at Tokyo.

B512

Date:
    August 30, 1958

Type of Manuscript:
    Letter

To:
    Grant Carpenter Manson

From:
    Frank Lloyd Wright

Collection:
    The Grant Carpenter Manson Collection
    The Oak Park Public Library
    Oak Park, Illinois

Medium:
    Typed on Taliesin design stationery,
    signed "F.Ll. W."

Size:
    8-1/2 in. x 11 in.; 215.9 mm x 279.4 mm

Number of Pages:
    1

Number of Words:
    72

Descriptors:
    Grant Carpenter Manson, *Frank Lloyd Wright to 1910:*
    The First Golden Age

Review:
    Wright praises Manson's work on the book, *Frank Lloyd Wright to*
    1910: The First Golden Age.

B513

Date:
    September 18, 1958

Type of Manuscript:
    Letter

To:
    William T. Evjue

From:
    Frank Lloyd Wright
    Taliesin

Collection:
    The William Theodore Evjue Papers, 1905-1969
    The State Historical Society of Wisconsin
    MSS 244, Box 156, Folder 3

Medium:
    Typed on Taliesin design stationery, signed
    "Frank"

Size:
    8-1/2 in. x 11 in.; 215.9 mm x 279.4 mm

Number of Pages:
    1

Number of Words:
    33

Descriptors:
    William T. Evjue, Monona Terrace Civic Center Project,
    Carroll Metzner

Review:
    A short note to Evjue on Wright's optimism to build the
    Monona Terrace Civic Center Project for Madison, Wisconsin.

B514

Date:
    December 17, 1958

Type of Manuscript:
    Letter

To:
    William T. Evjue

From:
    Frank Lloyd Wright
    Taliesin West

Collection:
    The William Theodore Evjue Papers, 1905-1969
    The State Historical Society of Wisconsin
    MSS 244, Box 156, Folder 3

Medium:
    Typed on Taliesin design stationery, signed
    "Frank"

Size:
    8-1/2 in. x 11 in.; 215.9 mm x 279.4 mm

Number of Pages:
    3

Number of Words:
    360

Descriptors:
    William T. Evjue, The Frank Lloyd Wright Foundation,
    United States Information Agency, Metropolitan Museum
    of Art, Robie House

Review:
    Wright outlines in detail the goals of The Frank Lloyd Wright
    Foundation and presents Evjue with a listing of current projects
    which Wright is working on. Evjue printed a long listing of
    current Frank Lloyd Wright projects in "Record Number of Wright
    Projects 'On the Boards' at Taliesin West" in *The Capital Times*
    of January 16, 1959.

B515

Date:
    February 8, 1959

Type of Manuscript:
    Letter (copy of original)

To:
    William T. Evjue

From:
    Frank Lloyd Wright
    Taliesin West

Collection:
    The William Theodore Evjue Papers, 1905-1969
    The State Historical Society of Wisconsin
    MSS 244, Box 156, Folder 3

Medium:
    Typed on Taliesin West design stationery, unsigned copy

Size:
    8-1/2 in. x 11 in.; 215.9 mm x 279.4 mm

Number of Pages:
    3

Number of Words:
   406

Descriptors:
   William T. Evjue, American Legion, Joseph R. McCarthy,
   Carroll Metzner, Monona Terrace Center Project, Marin
   County Civic Center, Franklin Roosevelt, Communism,
   Russia, Architects World-Congress, J.W. Jackson,
   McCarthyism

Review:
   Wright has obtained a dossier from Carroll Metzner on his
   McCarthy alleged Communist activities at a meeting for the
   Marin County Civic Center. Wright informs Evjue that all the
   allegations in the dossier are lies and suggests that Evjue
   print them to show the public. Detailed information on this
   particular issue can be found in "Raise Red Cry Against Wright:
   J.W. Jackson Stirs Issue at Hearing on Metzner Act," written
   by Aldric Revell in *The Capital Times*, and a history of the
   "red scare" issue in Wright's career is outlined in Robert C.
   Twombly's *Frank Lloyd Wright: An Interpretive Biography*, pp.
   270-272.

B516

Date:
   March 11, 1959

Type of Manuscript:
   Letter

To:
   The Secretary of Columbia University (Richard Herpers)
   New York

From:
   Frank Lloyd Wright
   Taliesin West

Collection:
   The Avery Architectural Library
   Columbia University

Medium:
   Typed on Taliesin West design stationery and signed
   "Frank Lloyd Wright"

Size:
   8-1/2 in. x 11 in.; 215.9 mm x 279.4 mm

Number of Pages:
   1

Number of Words:
   66

Descriptors:
   Columbia University, James W. Elmore, McKim Fellowship,
   Richard Herpers

2-7.15 Marin County Civic Center (1957), San Raphael, California, under construction in May of 1961. Photo courtesy of *The Capital Times*, Madison, Wisconsin.

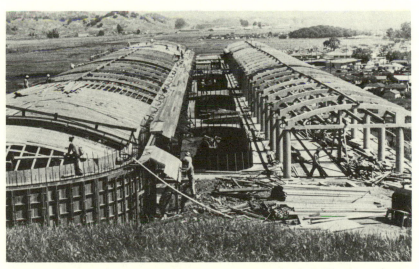

2-7.16 Marin County Civic Center (1957), San Raphael, California, under construction in June of 1961. Photo courtesy of *The Capital Times*, Madison, Wisconsin.

Review:
A letter of reference for James W. Elmore to Columbia University.

B517

Date:
April 2, 1959

Type of Manuscript:
Letter

To:
E. Willis Jones

From:
Frank Lloyd Wright
Taliesin West

Collection:
Frank Lloyd Wright Correspondence with E. Willis Jones,
1936-1959
Special Collections Department
Northwestern University Library

Medium:
Typed on Taliesin West design stationery, signed
"F.L.L.W."

Size:
8-1/2 in. x 11 in.; 215.9 mm x 279.4 mm

Number of Pages:
1

Number of Words:
26

Descriptors:
E. Willis Jones

Review:
Wright asks Jones to visit Taliesin West to discuss plans
for a residence for Jones which Wright would design. This
letter is one the last letters written by Frank Lloyd Wright
before his death on April 9, 1959. The letter shows Wright
still actively planning new building projects.

REFERENCES

Books:

Academie van Beeldende Kunsten en Technishe Wetenschappen, Rotterdam.
Frank Lloyd Wright. Rotterdam: Ahoy'-gebouw, 1952.

Drexler, Arthur (ed.).
The Drawings of Frank Lloyd Wright. New York: Horizon Press for
the Museum of Modern Art, 1962.

2-7.17 Frank Lloyd Wright's last resting place near Taliesin, Spring Green, Wisconsin. Photo by the author.

Ecole Nationale Supérieure des Beaux-Arts, Paris.
Exposition de l'oeuvre de Frank Lloyd Wright. Paris: Ecole
Nationale Supérieure des Beaux-Arts, April 1952.

First Unitarian Society, Committee on Publications and Publicity.
Meeting House of the First Unitarian Society of Madison, Wisconsin.
Madison, Wisconsin: First Unitarian Society, 1951.

Gimbel Brothers, Philadelphia.
To Meet the Great American Architect Frank Lloyd Wright.
Philadelphia: Gimbel Brothers, January 25, 1951.

Gimbel Brothers, Philadelphia.
Catalog of Frank Lloyd Wright Exhibition. New York: Architectural
Forum, 1951.

Haus der Kunst, Munich.
Frank Lloyd Wright: 60 Jahre Architektur. Munich: Veranstalter,
Haus der Kunst, June 1952.

Izzo, Alberto, and Camillo Gubitos (eds.).
Frank Lloyd Wright, Dessins 1887-1959. Paris: C.E.R.A. Ecole
Nationale Supérieure des Beaux-Arts, 1977.

Manson, Grant Carpenter.
Frank Lloyd Wright to 1910: The First Golden Age. New York:
Reinhold Publishing Corporation, 1958.

Moser, Werner M.
*Frank Lloyd Wright: Sechzig Jahre lebendige Architektur: Sixty
Years of Living Architecture*. Winterthur: Verlag Buchdruckerei
Winterthur AG, 1952.

Moses, Robert.
Public Works: A Dangerous Trade. New York: McGraw-Hill Book
Company, 1970, pp. 864-866.

Palazzo Strozzi of Florence, Italy.
Mostra di Frank Lloyd Wright, Catalogo itinerario. Florence:
Palazzo Strozzi, June 24-September 1951.

Stonorov, Oskar.
*On the Occasion of Gimbel Brothers Preview of the Italian Exhibition
at the Palazzo Strozzi, Florence, of the Life Work of the American
Architect Frank Lloyd Wright*. Philadelphia: Gimbel Brothers,
January 25, 1951.

Storrer, William Allin.
The Architecture of Frank Lloyd Wright, a Complete Catalog, Second
Edition. Cambridge, Massachusetts: The M.I.T. Press, 1978.

Tafel, Edgar.
Apprentice to Genius: Years with Frank Lloyd Wright. New York:
McGraw-Hill, Inc., 1979.

Twombly, Robert C.
Frank Lloyd Wright: An Interpretive Biography. New York: Harper and Row, 1973.

Twombly, Robert C.
Frank Lloyd Wright: His Life and His Architecture. New York: John Wiley and Sons, Inc., 1979.

Wright, Frank Lloyd.
Sixty Years of Living Architecture. New York: Guggenheim Museum, 1953.

Wright, Frank Lloyd.
Sixty Years of Living Architecture. Los Angeles: The Municipal Art Patrons and Art Commission of Los Angeles, May 1954.

Wright, Frank Lloyd.
An American Architecture. New York: Horizon Press, 1955.

Wright, Frank Lloyd.
A Testament. New York: Horizon Press, 1957.

Wright, Frank Lloyd.
Drawings for a Living Architecture. New York: Horizon Press for the Bear Run Foundation, Inc., and the Edgar J. Kaufmann Charitable Foundation, 1959.

Wright, Frank Lloyd, and Oskar Stonorov.
Mostra di Frank Lloyd Wright--Dialogo: "Broadacre City," Firenze, Italy: Studio Italiano di Storia dell'arte, May 15, 1951.

Wright, Olgivanna Lloyd.
The Shining Brow. New York: Horizon Press, 1960.

Periodicals:

Wright, Frank Lloyd.
"An Adventure in the Human Spirit," *Motive*, Vol. 11, November 1950, pp. 30-31.

Anonymous.
"Business and Culture," *Newsweek*, Vol. 37, February 5, 1951, p. 76.

Talbot, Hamlin.
"Frank Lloyd Wright in Philadelphia," *Nation*, Vol. 172, February 10, 1951, pp. 140-141.

Anonymous.
"Architect F.L. Wright," *Art Digest*, Vol. 25, February 15, 1951, p. 16.

Kaufmann, Edgar, Jr.
"Frank Lloyd Wright at the Strozzi," *Magazine of Art*, Vol. 44, May 1951, pp. 190-192.

Anonymous.
"Frank Lloyd Wright," *Arts* (Paris), No. 321, July 27, 1951, p. 8.

Anonymous.
"Frank Lloyd Wright in Italia," *Urbanistica*, Vol. 21, No. 7, 1951, p. 57.

Anonymous.
"Frank Lloyd Wright: Zürich," *Werk*, Vol. 39, March 1952, pp. 26-28.

Martinie, A.H.
"Frank Lloyd Wright, inventeur de la maison dans l'espace triomphe à Paris," *Arts* (Paris), No. 355, April 17-23, 1952, p. 7.

Anonymous.
"Frank Lloyd Wright à Paris," *Architecture d'Aujourd'hui*, Vol. 22, April 1952, p. xxxiii.

Eckstein, Hans.
"Zu den F.L. Wright-Ausstellungen in Europa," *Bauen und Wohnen*, No. 3, June 1952, p. 159.

Schelling, H.G.J.
"Tentoonstelling Frank Lloyd Wright te Rotterdam," *Bouwkundig Weekblad*, Vol. 70, July 22, 1952, pp. 231-232.

Reed, Henry H., Jr.
"Frank Lloyd Wright Conquers Paris and Visa Versa," *Architectural Record*, Vol. 112, July 1952, p. 22.

Carlo, Giancarlo de.
"Wright e l'Europa," *Sele Arte*, Vol. 1, September/October 1952, pp. 17-24.

Anonymous.
"First Unitarian Church, Madison, Wisconsin--Frank Lloyd Wright, Architect," *Architectural Forum*, Vol. 97, December 1952, pp. 85-92.

Anonymous.
"Frank Lloyd Wright," *Architecture Francaise*, Vol. 13, Nos. 123-124, 1952, pp. 3-72.

Champigneulle, Bernard.
"Frank Lloyd Wright à Paris," *Art et Décoration*, No. 28, 1952, pp. 21-24.

Manson, Grant Carpenter.
"Wright in the Nursery: The Influence of Froebel Education on His Work," *Architectural Review*, Vol. 113, No. 678, June 1953, pp. 349-351.

Anonymous.
"Another Gold Medal for Wright," *Architectural Record*, Vol. 114, July 1953, p. 16.

Anonymous.
"Frank Lloyd Wright Receives National Institute's Medal," *Architect and Engineer*, Vol. 194, July 1953, p. 5.

Anonymous.
"Wright, Continued," *The New Yorker*, Vol. 29, October 31, 1953, pp. 25-27.

Anonymous.
"Frank Lloyd Wright Exhibits 60 Years' Work," *Architectural Forum*, Vol. 99, October 1953, p. 45.

Anonymous.
"Exhibition at Guggenheim Museum," *Art News*, Vol. 52, October 1953, p. 44.

Anonymous.
"Wright Makes New York!" *Architectural Record*, Vol. 114, October 1953, p. 20.

Anonymous.
"Wright's Might," *Time*, Vol. 62, November 9, 1953, p. 74.

Brett, Lionel.
"Wright in New York," *The New Republic*, Vol. 129, November 16, 1953, pp. 19-20.

Anonymous.
"'Sixty Years of Living Architecture'--the Word of Frank Lloyd Wright," *Architectural Forum*, Vol. 99, November 1953, pp. 152-155.

Anonymous.
"Frank Lloyd Wright Completes a Long, Low Industrial Arts Building for Florida Southern University ... and Begins a Civic Center for the Capital of His Home State," *Architectural Forum*, Vol. 102, April 1955, pp. 114-121.

Anonymous.
"Spite Bill Hits at FLlW Madison Civic Center," *Architectural Forum*, Vol. 107, August 1957, p. 7.

Anonymous.
"Wisconsin Governor Signs Spite Bill that Kills Frank Lloyd Wright's Madison Civic Center," *Architectural Forum*, Vol. 107, November 1957, pp. 7, 9.

Anonymous.
"Frank Lloyd Wright: A Selection of Current Work," *Architectural Record*, Vol. 123, May 1958, pp. 167-190.

Newspapers:

Jacobs, Herbert.
"Wright Pleads for Civic Center on Lake Monona, Warns City to 'Wake Up.' Noted Architect in Attack on City-County Bldg. Plan." *The Capital Times* (Madison, Wisconsin), September 28, 1938.

Anonymous.
"FLW Offers Lake Monona Development Plan for Public Buildings,"
The Capital Times (Madison, Wisconsin), November 2, 1938.

O'Brien, J. Paul.
"Wright Attack Big Factor in Defeat of City-County Project. One
Vote Margin Beats Building; Stewart Machine Triumphs: Revival Plan
Before Board Tonight," *The Capital Times* (Madison, Wisconsin),
November 3, 1938.

Anonymous.
"Dual Building Plans Dead, ... Board Refuses to Revive Project,"
The Capital Times (Madison, Wisconsin), November 4, 1938.

Anonymous.
"Wright Urges Citizens to Push Civic Center Plan. 300 at Church
Hear Architect Hit Dual Building Plan," *The Capital Times* (Madison,
Wisconsin), December 5, 1938.

Anonymous.
"Ordinance Auditorium Bond Issue Is Passed," *The Capital Times*
(Madison, Wisconsin), March 29, 1941.

Anonymous.
"Famed Architect Has Plans for $800,000 Auditorium Over Lake:
Ultimate Aim is 7 Acre Area with City-County Building, Union
Station; Total Cost $3,250,000," *The Capital Times* (Madison,
Wisconsin), June 4, 1941.

Jacobs, Herbert.
"Civic Center Project Needs Youth, Citizens' Group for Success:
Wright. Noted Architect Talks to 600 at Union Theater," *The Capital
Times* (Madison, Wisconsin), October 15, 1941.

Revell, Aldric.
"Wright Envisions Huge Civic Center on Monona, Urges Youth to
Back Plan. All City, County Buildings, Rail," *The Capital Times*
(Madison, Wisconsin), May 31, 1946.

Anonymous.
"F.L. Wright's Work Seen: Exhibition of Noted Architect's Creations
Held in Philadelphia," *The New York Times*, January 26, 1951, p. 2,
col. 2.

Wright, Frank Lloyd.
"Frank Lloyd Wright on Americanism," *The Milwaukee Journal* (Milwaukee, Wisconsin), April 20, 1951, editorial page.

Anonymous.
"Frank Lloyd Wright Reply to the Un-American Activities Group
Charge," *The Capital Times* (Madison, Wisconsin), April 21, 1951.

Anonymous.
"Italy Decorates U.S. Architect," *The New York Times*, June 25,
1951, p. 12, col. 5.

Anonymous.
"New Wright Church Has Admirers, Critics: Crowds of Curious Are
Quite a Problem to a Madison Unitarian Congregation," *The Milwaukee
Journal* (Milwaukee, Wisconsin), July 22, 1951.

Anonymous.
"Many Hands Join Labor of Love," *The Capital Times* (Madison,
Wisconsin), August 1, 1951.

Anonymous.
"F.L.W. Hits McCarthyism: Sees Need for a New Third Party," *The
Capital Times* (Madison, Wisconsin), August 21, 1951.

Anonymous.
"Unitarian Building 'Makes Music--Is Itself a Form of Prayer'
Wright Says," *The Capital Times* (Madison, Wisconsin), August 22,
1951.

Anonymous.
"Architect Speaks at Church He Designed--Search for Beautiful Should
be Life's Greatest End--Wright," *The Capital Times* (Madison, Wisconsin), August 30, 1951.

Anonymous.
"Unitarians Answer Critics of Wright Meeting House," *The Capital
Times* (Madison, Wisconsin), January 1, 1953.

Anonymous.
"Unitarian Structure Wins New Plaudits," *The Capital Times* (Madison,
Wisconsin), January 6, 1953.

Anonymous.
"Famed Architect to Get Medal of Arts Institute," *The New York
Times*, May 14, 1953, p. 28, col. 5.

Loucheim, Aline B.
"Wright Analyzes Architects Needs: Philosophy, Not Esthetics,
Is a 'Must' Now, He Holds--His Show Opens Tomorrow," *The New York
Times*, May 26, 1953, p. 23, col. 1.

Anonymous.
"Wright Honored, Voices 'Humility': Institute of Arts and Letters
Awards Medals to Architect and Marianne Craig Moore," *The New
York Times*, May 28, 1953, p. 28, col. 5.

Anonymous.
"Individual Architect: Frank Lloyd Wright Show Reveals Many Facets,"
May 31, 1953, section 2, p. 7, col. 6.

Anonymous.
"Lake Edge Development Proposed--Wright's Civic Center Plans,"
The Capital Times (Madison, Wisconsin), July 7, 1953; July 8,
1953; July 9, 1953; and July 10, 1953.

Anonymous.
"City Civic Center Talked--Urge 'Memorial' Auditorium Plans,"
The Capital Times (Madison, Wisconsin), July 30, 1953.

Anonymous.
"To Push for Civic Center on Radio," *The Capital Times* (Madison,
Wisconsin), August 5, 1953.

Anonymous.
"Auditorium Committee Lists Plans," *The Capital Times* (Madison,
Wisconsin), August 12, 1953.

Anonymous.
"Mayor Again Hits Wright's Civic Plan," *The Capital Times* (Madison,
Wisconsin), August 17, 1953.

Anonymous.
"Forster Repeats Opposition, Civic Center Can Be Built 'Part at
Time,' Wright Says," *The Capital Times* (Madison, Wisconsin), August
24, 1953.

Anonymous.
"Voice of the People--Urge Referendum on Wright Plan," *The Capital
Times* (Madison, Wisconsin), August 24, 1953.

Anonymous.
"Supervisors Urge Study, Wright Center Plan Gets Backing," *The
Capital Times* (Madison, Wisconsin), August 31, 1953.

Anonymous.
"Referendum on Center Is Urged," *The Capital Times* (Madison, Wisconsin), September 1, 1953.

Loucheim, Aline B.
"Architect Planning Edifice for His Art: Architect Designs a
Pavilion Near Guggenheim Museum to Feature Old Drawings," *The New
York Times*, September 3, 1953, p. 23, col. 2.

Anonymous.
"Says Wright Plan Not Most Costly," *The Capital Times* (Madison,
Wisconsin), September 7, 1953.

Anonymous.
"Wright Will Tell of Civic Center Plan," *The Capital Times* (Madison,
Wisconsin), September 8, 1953.

Marcus, Herbert.
"Architect Defends Idea at Meeting--Council Agrees to Study Wright
Plan," *The Capital Times* (Madison, Wisconsin), September 9, 1953.

Anonymous.
"Seek Center Cost Data," *The Capital Times* (Madison, Wisconsin),
September 10, 1953.

Anonymous.
"Committees Act--Ask Wright to Explain Center Plan," *The Capital Times* (Madison, Wisconsin), September 12, 1953.

Anonymous.
"To Prove His Estimate--Wright Offers to Pay Survey Cost," *The Capital Times* (Madison, Wisconsin), September 15, 1953.

Anonymous.
"Forster for Wright Cost Study Plan," *The Capital Times* (Madison, Wisconsin), September 17, 1953.

Anonymous.
"Prepare to Quiz Architect Wright," *The Capital Times* (Madison, Wisconsin), September 19, 1953.

Anonymous.
"$15,000 Sum Approved Auditorium Site Cash Test Ok'd," *The Capital Times* (Madison, Wisconsin), September 23, 1953.

Anonymous.
"Council OKs Tests, But: Favors Law Park Auditorium Site," *The Capital Times* (Madison, Wisconsin), September 25, 1953.

Anonymous.
"Satisfaction Greater than Anticipated--Unitarians Answer Critics of Wright Meeting House," *The Capital Times* (Madison, Wisconsin), October 1, 1953.

McMillin, Miles.
"Unitarian Lauds Wright Structure," *The Capital Times* (Madison, Wisconsin), October 3, 1953.

Anonymous.
"Wright Not Interested in Auditorium," *The Capital Times* (Madison, Wisconsin), October 3, 1953.

Anonymous.
"Wright to Talk Before Dane Group," *The Capital Times* (Madison, Wisconsin), October 6, 1953.

Anonymous.
"Ask Wright to Discuss Civic Plan," *The Capital Times* (Madison, Wisconsin), October 15, 1953.

Anonymous.
"Plan Vote on Auditorium," *The Capital Times* (Madison, Wisconsin), October 17, 1953.

Anonymous.
"Wright's Pavilion to Open Thursday: Volunteers Helping to Prepare Exhibit of Architect's Work at 5th Avenue Site," *The New York Times*, October 18, 1953, p. 121, col. 5.

Anonymous.
"House of Wright Is Previewed Here: Architect Shows First Guests Through 'Usonian' Home--Opening Due Tomorrow," *The New York Times*, October 21, 1953, p. 35, col. 1.

Anonymous.
"Throngs Inspect Wright's Exhibit: Visitors Marvel at Architect's Display of Work in House near Guggenheim Museum," *The New York Times*, October 23, 1953, p. 34, col. 2.

Anonymous.
"Wright Presents Building Plans," *The Capital Times* (Madison, Wisconsin), October 27, 1953.

Anonymous.
"Committee Is Hostile--500 Hear Wright Explain 'Center,'" *The Capital Times* (Madison, Wisconsin), October 30, 1953.

Anonymous.
"25 Citizens Sign Petition--Ask Further Study on Wright Plan," *The Capital Times* (Madison, Wisconsin), December 10, 1953.

Anonymous.
"Auditorium Vote Delayed," *The Capital Times* (Madison, Wisconsin), December 18, 1953.

Anonymous.
"'Hidden Costs' Cited--Wright Plan Would Save $4,400,000 Local Group Says," *The Capital Times* (Madison, Wisconsin), January 25, 1954.

Anonymous.
"Shelve Study of Wright Center Plan," *The Capital Times* (Madison, Wisconsin), March 12, 1954.

Schleck, Leo P.
"Many Previous Opportunities Lost--Schleck Cites 50-Year History of Monona Plans," *The Capital Times* (Madison, Wisconsin), March 13, 1954.

Anonymous.
"An Editorial--Madison Is Missing a Good Business Deal," *The Capital Times* (Madison, Wisconsin), April 24, 1954.

Anonymous.
"An Editorial--Here's Plan for a United Madison Behind a Civic Center and Auditorium," *The Capital Times* (Madison, Wisconsin), May 26, 1954.

Anonymous.
"FLW Discusses Plan for New Civic Center," *The Capital Times* (Madison, Wisconsin), May 27, 1954.

Anonymous.
"Monona Cost $10-20 Million," *The Capital Times* (Madison, Wisconsin), June 29, 1954.

Anonymous.
"'Very High' in Design, Spanish Engineer Lauds Wright Plan," *The Capital Times* (Madison, Wisconsin), October 26, 1954.

Anonymous.
"An Editorial: Madison Now Has Chance to Win National Admiration on Civic Center," *The Capital Times* (Madison, Wisconsin), November 5, 1954.

Anonymous.
"Story of Scare on Parking Isn't Supported: Do Businessmen Fear Wright Plan? No! And Here Are Names to Prove It," *The Capital Times* (Madison, Wisconsin), November 19, 1954, p. 12.

Anonymous.
"To Estimate Terrace Costs: Wright Flatly Bars Any 'Unrelated' Auditorium Plan," *The Capital Times* (Madison, Wisconsin), November 20, 1954.

Anonymous.
"Wright Suggestion Due Jan. 10," *The Capital Times* (Madison, Wisconsin), December 8, 1954.

Anonymous.
"Wright Seeks Delay on Plans," *The Capital Times* (Madison, Wisconsin), December 24, 1954.

Anonymous.
"To Have Auditorium Model: Wright to Keep City Date February 7," *The Capital Times* (Madison, Wisconsin), January 19, 1955.

Anonymous.
"'Breathtaking Project': Architect Frank Lloyd Wright ...," *The Capital Times* (Madison, Wisconsin), February 7, 1955.

Anonymous.
"Explains Plan to Officials: This Scale Model Shows ...," *The Capital Times* (Madison, Wisconsin), February 8, 1955.

Anonymous.
"2,500 Inspect Wright Model," *The Capital Times* (Madison, Wisconsin), February 26, 1955.

Anonymous.
"8 Percent of Project Cost--Auditorium Group Votes $320,000 Wright Contract," *The Capital Times* (Madison, Wisconsin), March 4, 1955.

Anonymous.
"Move to Avoid Legal Snarls--Set Up Program on Wright Plan," *The Capital Times* (Madison, Wisconsin), March 18, 1955.

Oshiki, Kaz.
"Support Five for Council--Wright Backers Endorse Forster Unanimously," *The Capital Times* (Madison, Wisconsin), March 22, 1955.

Anonymous.
"Group Moves to Speed Work--Urge 3 Steps on Wright Project," *The Capital Times* (Madison, Wisconsin), April 1, 1955.

Anonymous.
"Wright Model at City Hall Now," *The Capital Times* (Madison, Wisconsin), April 16, 1955.

Wright, Frank Lloyd.
"Cites Advantages to City--Wright Says Civic Auditorium Can Be Built in 2 Years," *The Capital Times* (Madison, Wisconsin), April 21, 1955.

Anonymous.
"Wright to Receive Degree," *The New York Times*, May 8, 1955, p. 26, col. 7.

Anonymous.
"Bill Introduced in Assembly--To Settle Legality of Wright Plan," *The Capital Times* (Madison, Wisconsin), May 16, 1955.

Wright, Frank Lloyd.
"Letter to the Editor," *The Free Press* (Colorado Springs, Colorado), May 27, 1955.

Anonymous.
"Wright Scores Designs: Architect Calls Plans for Air Academy 'Half-Baked,'" *The New York Times*, July 8, 1955, p. 4, col. 6.

Anonymous.
"New Academy Plans Expected Monday," *The New York Times*, July 16, 1955, p. 16, col. 5.

Anonymous.
"Architecture in the Air," *The New York Times*, July 17, 1955, section 4, p. 8, col. 3.

Anonymous.
"Congress as Art Critic," *The New York Times*, July 17, 1955, section 4, p. 7, col. 3.

Anonymous.
"City Officials Hear High Praise of Wright's Work," *The Capital Times* (Madison, Wisconsin), July 23, 1955.

Anonymous.
"Rothschild Sees Wright Plan as Dead," *The Capital Times* (Madison, Wisconsin), December 14, 1955.

Anonymous.
"Talk Pact with Wright Thursday," *The Capital Times* (Madison, Wisconsin), July 3, 1956.

Anonymous.
"Terrace Pact Signed by Wright," *The Capital Times* (Madison, Wisconsin), July 6, 1956.

Marcus, Herbert.
"Provides Parking Space for 1,200 Cars--Wright Unveils His First
Plans for Civic Center," *The Capital Times* (Madison, Wisconsin),
August 17, 1956.

Anonymous.
"Three Estimates Back Wright," *The Capital Times* (Madison, Wisconsin), February 22, 1957.

Anonymous.
"Wright Agrees to Conference," *The Capital Times* (Madison, Wisconsin), March 2, 1957.

Anonymous.
"Bold Action to Save Cities--Say Terrace Plan 'Master Stroke' in
Space Creation"; *The Capital Times* (Madison, Wisconsin), March 19,
1957.

Jacobs, Herbert.
"Many 'Come Back for More'--Big Business Clients Find Wright 'Good
Investment,' Answer to His Critics, 'Terrace' to Bring Visitors
to City," *The Capital Times* (Madison, Wisconsin), March 19, 1957,
p. 6.

Anonymous.
"Wright to Redraft Plans--Architect in 'Walk-Out'; At 88, He Has
Tens of Millions in Jobs Going," *The Capital Times* (Madison, Wis-
consin), March 19, 1957.

Anonymous.
"Wright Apologizes to City--Writes to Terrace Group Says Cost
Within Money Available," *The Capital Times* (Madison, Wisconsin),
March 25, 1957.

Anonymous.
"Statesmanship Loses Out--Senators Voted for Spite and Not on
Principle: Wright," *The Capital Times* (Madison, Wisconsin), June
28, 1957.

Anonymous.
"Wright Agreeable to Conference," *The Capital Times* (Madison,
Wisconsin), August 8, 1957.

Anonymous.
"Metzner Bill Action Near," *The Capital Times* (Madison, Wisconsin),
September 21, 1957.

Anonymous.
"Mayor Asks Terrace Suit," *The Capital Times* (Madison, Wisconsin),
September 23, 1957.

Anonymous.
"Metzner Law Test Planned--Wright Rejects Site Other than Monona
Terrace," *The Capital Times* (Madison, Wisconsin), October 3, 1957.

Hitchcock, Henry-Russell.
"Architecture and the Architect," *The New York Times Book Review*, November 17, 1957, p. 44.

Anonymous.
"Urges Metzner Law Action--Wright Threatens Suit Against City on Terrace Contract," *The Capital Times* (Madison, Wisconsin), November 29, 1957.

Custer, Frank.
"Constitution Breach Charged--Metzner Act Test Suit Is Filed Here," *The Capital Times* (Madison, Wisconsin), February 27, 1958.

Anonymous.
"Summer Showing Approved--Wright Model to Be Displayed at Terrace," *The Capital Times* (Madison, Wisconsin), June 12, 1958.

Anonymous.
"Wright Center Model on Exhibit," *The Capital Times* (Madison, Wisconsin), July 28, 1958.

Anonymous.
"Cool Weather Blamed--Display of Civic Center Model to End on Wednesday," *The Capital Times* (Madison, Wisconsin), September 29, 1958.

Hippenmeyer, Charles.
"Terrace Planning Revived--2 Groups to Meet in Week, City Prepares for Metzner Act Repeal," *The Capital Times* (Madison, Wisconsin), November 6, 1958.

Anonymous.
"Opposes Further Delay--Journal Urges City Get at Building Wright Auditorium," *The Capital Times* (Madison, Wisconsin), November 12, 1958.

Anonymous.
"Hopeful of Metzner Act Repeal--Auditorium Group Resumes Its Work on Terrace Plans," *The Capital Times* (Madison, Wisconsin), December 16, 1958.

Anonymous.
"Record Number of Wright Projects 'On the Boards' at Taliesin West," *The Capital Times* (Madison, Wisconsin), January 16, 1959.

Hunter, John Patrick.
"Six Assembly Sponsors Both Houses Get Bills to Wipe Out Ban on Terrace," *The Capital Times* (Madison, Wisconsin), January 21, 1959.

Revell, Aldric.
"Raise 'Red' Cry Against Wright--J.W. Jackson Stirs Issue at Hearing on Metzner Act," *The Capital Times* (Madison, Wisconsin), February 12, 1959.

Anonymous.
"Terrace Space Study Promised," *The Capital Times* (Madison, Wisconsin), February 25, 1959.

Anonymous.
"Metzner Law Repeal Gets Final Legislative Approval," *The Capital Times* (Madison, Wisconsin), March 11, 1959.

Anonymous.
"Wright Submits His First Bill," *The Capital Times* (Madison, Wisconsin), March 16, 1959.

Anonymous.
"Copies Ordered for Council--Auditorium Plans Given to Mayor," *The Capital Times* (Madison, Wisconsin), March 17, 1959.

Anonymous.
"Before Offering Plans--Auditorium Group Asks Wright Talk," *The Capital Times* (Madison, Wisconsin), March 27, 1959.

Wright, Frank Lloyd.
"Announces His Position--Wright Replies to Group Seeking to Stall on Terrace," *The Capital Times* (Madison, Wisconsin), April 6, 1959.

Anonymous.
"Cities Foundation Contract--Terrace Can Still Be Built: Mayor," *The Capital Times* (Madison, Wisconsin), April 9, 1959.

Anonymous.
"'Some Delay' Seen on Terrace Project," *The Capital Times* (Madison, Wisconsin), April 10, 1959.

Anonymous.
"New Council Hears Plea for Terrace--Mayor Calls for Go-Ahead--Says Wright's Death Shouldn't Halt Plan," *The Capital Times* (Madison, Wisconsin), April 21, 1959.

Anonymous.
"Action by Council ...: Foe of Terrace Asks Cancellation of City Contract," *The Capital Times* (Madison, Wisconsin), April 24, 1959.

Anonymous.
"Wright Unit Asks Fee for Plans," *The Capital Times* (Madison, Wisconsin), April 28, 1959.

Anonymous.
"Wright Death No Bar to Terrace--Hanson Ruling Is Issued. Contract Valid, Attorney Finds," *The Capital Times* (Madison, Wisconsin), May 4, 1959.

Marcus, Herb.
"Peters Would Be Architect--City Acts to Speed Final Terrace Plan," *The Capital Times* (Madison, Wisconsin), May 14, 1959.

Anonymous.
  "Wright Suit Against City Is Dropped," *The Capital Times* (Madison, Wisconsin), May 21, 1959.

Anonymous.
  "Architect Fee Eyed: Amend Auditorium Proposal to Insure Against Delay," *The Capital Times* (Madison, Wisconsin), May 23, 1959.

Anonymous.
  "Terrace Plans Win Council Test--Approval Expected Thursday. Foundation Due to Get Go-Ahead," *The Capital Times* (Madison, Wisconsin), May 27, 1959.

Marcus, Herb.
  "Longtime Wright Foe--Jackson Says He'll File Suit to Halt Terrace Project," *The Capital Times* (Madison, Wisconsin), May 28, 1959.

Anonymous.
  "Joe Jackson Starts Stalling Suit, Then 'Goes Fishing,'" *The Capital Times* (Madison, Wisconsin), May 29, 1959.

Marcus, Herbert.
  "50 Years Toward an Auditorim #1," *The Capital Times* (Madison, Wisconsin), June 1, 1959.

Anonymous.
  "Terrace Plan Wins Council Test," *The Capital Times* (Madison, Wisconsin), June 10, 1959.

Hoffmann, Mack.
  "Council Takes Action--Terrace Plans Are Approved, 13 to 7," *The Capital Times* (Madison, Wisconsin), June 12, 1959.

Anonymous.
  "Councilmen Not Liable--City Attorney Says No Statue Bars Wright Pay," *The Capital Times* (Madison, Wisconsin), June 26, 1959.

Anonymous.
  "Funds Asked for Terrace. Mayor's Program Goes Before Council Tonight," *The Capital Times* (Madison, Wisconsin), July 9, 1959.

Anonymous.
  "Set Terrace Suit Trial for Sept. 14," *The Capital Times* (Madison, Wisconsin), July 23, 1959.

Anonymous.
  "Who Is Responsible for Increased Auditorium Costs?" *The Capital Times* (Madison, Wisconsin), August 5, 1959.

Anonymous.
  "Three Obstacles Eliminated--City and Railroad Reach Terrace Site Agreement," *The Capital Times* (Madison, Wisconsin), September 3, 1959.

Anonymous.
"Briefs Due by Sept. 28--Testimony Closes in Terrace Suit," *The Capital Times* (Madison, Wisconsin), September 16, 1959.

Marcus, Herbert.
"Asks Wright Fee Be Paid: City Auditorium Group Moves for Speed on Terrace," *The Capital Times* (Madison, Wisconsin), January 28, 1960.

Hoffman, Mack.
"Council Votes Wright Pay--Opponents Won't Quit. Terrace Is Advanced by Three 16-5 Votes," *The Capital Times* (Madison, Wisconsin), February 12, 1960, p. 1.

Anonymous.
"City Pays Wright Group $122,500--Path Free for Final Planning Follows Terms of Terrace Contract," *The Capital Times* (Madison, Wisconsin), February 23, 1960.

Marcus. Herbert.
"Committee Takes Big Step--Order Working Plans for Monona Terrace," *The Capital Times* (Madison, Wisconsin), June 23, 1960.

Anonymous.
"Terrace Bids $9.6 Million: Perini Company Is Lowest," *The Capital Times* (Madison, Wisconsin), March 7, 1961.

Anonymous.
"Rush to Terminate the Terrace Contract Faces Rough Water," *The Capital Times* (Madison, Wisconsin), June 15, 1961.

UNDATED FRANK LLOYD WRIGHT MANUSCRIPTS

B518

Date:
Undated

Type of Manuscript:
Announcement

Title:
"Frank Lloyd Wright Builder, Philosopher, Master of
Modern Architecture"

By:
Frank Lloyd Wright

Collection:
The Wrightiana Collection
The Art Institute of Chicago

Review:
The announcement of Wright's availability as a lecturer.

B519

Date:
Undated

Type of Manuscript:
Letter

To:
John Lloyd Wright
Long Beach, Indiana

From:
Frank Lloyd Wright

Collection:
The John John Wright Collection
The Avery Architectural Library
Columbia University
Folder 13

Medium:
Typed and signed "Father"

Size:
8-1/2 in. x 11 in.; 215.9 mm x 279.4 mm

Number of Pages:
1

Number of Words:
144

Descriptors:
John Lloyd Wright

Review:
Frank Lloyd invites John Lloyd to work at Taliesin and to leave Long Beach, Indiana.

B520

Date:
Undated

Type of Manuscript:
Letter

To:
John Lloyd Wright

From:
Frank Lloyd Wright

Collection:
The John Lloyd Wright Collection
The Avery Architectural Library
Columbia University
Folder 13

Medium:
Handwritten on Taliesin design stationery, signed "Father"

Size:
4-3/4 in. x 8-1/2 in.; 120.7 mm x 215.9 mm

Number of Pages:
1

Number of Words:
49

Descriptors:
John Lloyd Wright

Review:
Frank Lloyd invites John Lloyd and his family to visit.

B521

Date:
Undated

Type of Manuscript:
Telegram

To:
Mr. and Mrs. William T. Evjue
Madison, Wisconsin

From:
    Frank Lloyd Wright
    Phoenix, Arizona

Collection:
    The William Theodore Evjue Papers, 1905-1969
    The State Historical Society of Wisconsin
    MSS 244, Box 156, Folder 1

Medium:
    Typed "New Year's Greetings by Western Union" telegram

Size:
    6-1/4 in. x 8 in.; 158.8 mm x 203.2 mm

Number of Pages:
    1

Number of Words:
    28

Descriptors:
    William T. Evjue

Review:
    New Year greetings.

B522

Date:
    Undated

Type of Manuscript:
    Letter

To:
    Mr. Schlagel
    Superintendent of Public Schools
    Kansas City

From:
    Frank Lloyd Wright (copy made by George Beal)

Collection:
    Frank Lloyd Wright Collection
    Kenneth Spencer Research Library
    University of Kansas

Medium:
    In George Beal's handwriting, on white paper

Size:
    8-1/2 in. x 11 in.; 215.9 mm x 279.4 mm

Number of Pages:
    1

Number of Words:
    144

Descriptors:
    Mr. Schlagel (Superintendent of Schools, Kansas City),
    Education, George Beal

Review:
  Remarks on education.

B523

Date:
  Subsequent to 1932

Type of Manuscript:
  Book revisions

Source:
  Frank Lloyd Wright
  The Industrial Revolution Runs Away. New York: Horizon
  Press, 1969

By:
  Frank Lloyd Wright

Medium:
  Photographic reproductions of pages from a book showing
  handwritten revisions by Wright

Reproduction Size:
  8-3/4 in. x 8-3/4 in.; 222.3 mm x 222.3 mm

Book Size:
  13-1/4 in. x 10-1/4 in.; 336.6 mm x 260.4 mm

Number of Pages of Reproduced Original Manuscript:
  90

Number of Total Book Pages:
  187

Descriptors:
  *The Industrial Revolution Runs Away, The Disappearing
  City,* The City

Review:
  This volume represents a new edition of Wright's *The
  Disappearing City* originally published at New York by
  William Farquhar Payson in 1932. The original *Disappearing
  City* measured 8-1/4 in. x 8-1/4 in. (209 mm x 209 mm) and
  had ninety pages. This edition includes a facsimile of each
  page of the original *Disappearing City* with photographic
  reproductions of each page showing revisions made by Wright.
  This edition was limited to 1,250 copies, of which 250
  were not for sale. The changing style of Wright's writing
  for the notes and revisions on each page indicates that the
  revisions were made by him over a long period of time.

B524

Date:
  Subsequent to 1943

Type of Manuscript:
  Book page revisions (facsimile)

Source:
   Frank Lloyd Wright
   An Autobiography. New York: Horizon Press, 1977,
   inside front cover

By:
   Frank Lloyd Wright

Medium:
   Photographic reproduction of one page from book showing
   handwritten revisions by Wright

Reproduction Size:
   7-3/4 in. x 8-1/2 in.; 196.9 mm x 215.9 mm

Book Size:
   6-5/8 in. x 9-1/2 in.; 168.3 mm x 241.3 mm

Number of Pages:
   1

Descriptors:
   An Autobiography

Review:
   The book represents Wright's final revisions of his *An
   Autobiography*, originally published in New York by Duell,
   Sloan and Pearce in 1943. According to Horizon Press,
   Wright had worked on these revisions for sixteen years after
   the 1943 second edition (see "Story Behind the Book: An
   Autobiography," *Publishers Weekly* [Vol. 212, No. 4, July 25,
   1977], p. 55). Prior to his death in 1959, Wright had given
   his copy of the reworked book to Horizon Press. In this 1977
   edition, only one facsimile page showing Wright's handwritten
   revisions is photographically reproduced and it appears on the
   inside front cover of the book.

APPENDIX B

COMPILED CHRONOLOGY OF BUILDINGS, DESIGNS, AND PROJECTS OF FRANK LLOYD WRIGHT

Notes on the Compilation Procedure

History of Dating Frank Lloyd Wright's
Executed Designs and Projects

Of the many reference sources researched, five served as the basis for the compilation of the chronological listing of Frank Lloyd Wright's executed designs and projects. These five basic sources were Henry-Russell Hitchcock's *In the Nature of Materials: The Buildings of Frank Lloyd Wright, 1887-1941* (New York: Duell, Sloan and Pearce, 1942, pp. 105-130); *Frank Lloyd Wright: Writings and Buildings* (New York: Horizon Press, 1960, pp. 331-346) edited by Edgar Kaufmann and Ben Raeburn, with a list of executed designs prepared by Bruce Radde; Olgivanna Lloyd Wright's *Frank Lloyd Wright: His Life, His Work, His Words* (New York: Horizon Press, 1966, pp. 205-222), edited by Bruce Brooks Pfeiffer; and both editions of William Allin Storrer's *The Architecture of Frank Lloyd Wright: A Complete Catalog* (Cambridge, Massachusetts: The M.I.T. Press, 1974 and 1978). Each of these five sources offered a methodology or technique for the dating of Wright's executed designs and projects. By "executed designs" I mean those Wright designs which were built and by "projects" those Wright designs which were not built.

In his *In the Nature of Materials: The Buildings of Frank Lloyd Wright* Hitchcock used several methods for indicating dates for Wright's designs, including the date on which the building permit was issued for a design, the term of the construction period, when it extended for several years, and the contemporary inscription placed upon the drawing. Hitchcock warns, however, that "there is always a possibility of error in mistaking for contemporary ones approximate dates added later to the drawings." Wright's later dating and modifications to existing dates on his drawings have been alluded to by several individuals familiar with him including Edgar Tafel, a former apprentice, who said "Mr. Wright constantly changed the dates of drawings" (see Tafel's *Apprentice to Genius: Years with Frank Lloyd Wright*, New York: McGraw-Hill, Inc., 1979, p. 144). It is interesting to note that Tafel had assisted Wright in readying drawings for Henry-Russell Hitchcock's review while Hitchcock was preparing his book on Wright. Hitchcock also indicated some certain uncertainties regarding several dates of designs and in some instances dated designs on the basis of early design publication, design exhibition, or the first appearance of the client's name in a directory at the given address of the design. Hitchcock's dating methodology used the best data available at the time of his research and his dates are very well documented.

Bruce F. Radde's list of Wright's executed designs in *Frank Lloyd Wright: Writings and Buildings* dated Wright's executed buildings "final design dates" and "dates of completion." However, Radde did not define what he meant by "final design date" and "dates of completion" or explain how they were derived.

The dating of Wright's executed designs and projects compiled by Bruce Brooks Pfeiffer for *Frank Lloyd Wright: His Life, His Work, His Words* was based on Wright's first recorded conception of a design for which drawings and sketches were prepared and dated. The list was an extension of Hitchcock's earlier one in that it provided a listing of Wright's executed designs and projects after 1941, in addition to his earlier works. Many of these dates were determined by examination of the archival materials contained in the Frank Lloyd Wright Memorial Foundation Archives at Taliesin West.

William Allin Storrer, in both editions of his *Architecture of Frank Lloyd Wright*, "lists the earliest known date for Wright's concept of the project" (i.e., "executed designs" in Storrer's use of the term) and "where a more consistent picture of the chronological development of Wright's designs may be obtained, the construction date, representing all changes in the original design, is given instead of the concept date." Unfortunately, very seldom in Storrer's texts does he indicate whether the dates given for a particular design are "conception" dates or "construction" dates.

In 1979, *The Frank Lloyd Wright Newsletter* of Oak Park, Illinois, adopted a policy for dating a Wright designed structure in the *Newsletter* by using the last date of the working drawings or the initial construction date. If the working drawings are known to exist, the last revision date and the initial construction date are to be used (see Thomas A. Heinz's "Dating of Frank Lloyd Wright Buildings," *The Frank Lloyd Wright Newsletter* [Vol. 2, No. 3, Second Quarter 1979], p. 10). Other less ambitious attempts have been made to date specific types of Wright designs and list them chronologically and these are not reviewed here.

The Author's Compilation Methodology

In addition to the five basic reference sources mentioned above, I also used many others, including published drawings, books, periodicals, newspapers, and original manuscripts and correspondence as a basis for compiling Appendix B. Like Hitchcock's list of Wright's buildings and projects from 1887 to 1941, this listing also represents an attempt at the impossible. Newly discovered executed works and projects by Wright have been added to the list, as well as executed designs and projects in which Wright had substantial involvement while working in the architectural offices of Joseph Lyman Silsbee and Louis H. Sullivan. In instances where more than one date has appeared for those designs by Wright listed in the basic reference sources, I have usually used the earliest date. The list of Wright's executed designs and projects is chronological, beginning with the year 1885. Under each of the years listed, as in Hitchcock's and Pfeiffer's procedure, executed designs are listed first and projects are listed second; both are in alphabetical order. When a project has the same name as an executed design, the project is usually of a different design character.

Suggestions for a Refined Building Design Dating Methodology

The American Institute of Architects (AIA) has identified five sequential phases of architectural services for providing building design and construction administration (see American Institute of Architects "Chapter 11--Project Procedures" in *Architect's Handbook of Professional Practice*, Washington, D.C.: American Institute of Architects, 1969). These five basic sequential phases are the schematic design phase, design development phase, construction documents phase, bidding or negotiations phase, and administration of the construction contract phase. Perhaps one of the most accurate means of dating Frank Lloyd Wright designed buildings would be to use these phases of architectural services as a foundation upon which to base a precise dating system. I will briefly discuss each of these phases of architectural services to show how they might be used to date Wright designs.

The objectives of the schematic design phase are to assist the client in determining the scope of the project's feasibility, and to assist in illustrating possible solutions to the specific design problem. Products of this schematic design phase can include preliminary studies of the building and its relationship to the site, preliminary sketches, preliminary cost analyses, preliminary models, and building programming and site analyses.

The general purposes of the second phase, the design development phase, are to fix and describe the size and character of the project, including restudying the design and preparing drawings illustrating the plan and site development, determining the type of construction materials and mechanical equipment, and revising the statement of probable construction costs. General products of this phase can include site plans indicating the location and nature of site improvements, building plans, elevations, sections, schedules, notes, and outline specifications for the project.

The third phase, construction documents, is the phase in which the architect develops the preliminary drawings, which were part of the design development phase, into working drawings, including all technical information required to bid for and build the project. These documents can include but are not limited to working drawings of plumbing, ventilating, air-conditioning, electrical and mechanical systems and of site improvements. They can also include the specifications, including the general conditions of the contract, and finishing schedules. The AIA's fourth phase, the bidding/negotiation phase, can be grouped into this third phase when dating Wright buildings, since bidding generally indicates completed construction documents such as working drawings and construction specifications.

The last phase, the administration of the construction contract, would include the preparation of shop drawings, supplemental drawings, construction commencement, inspections, lists of subcontractors, materials tests, architect field reports, payment records, as well as other miscellaneous documents. Using these phases as a foundation for Wright designs would clarify many of the existing inconsistencies which have developed over the years. Each of Wright's designs, whether executed or not, could be assigned a maximum of four dates for each of the four phases outlined above. The designs would, however, have to be more thoroughly researched and documented than previous research efforts to be able to assign these very specific dates; they may indicate not only the year but also the precise day and month of the design.

This appendix is intended to serve both as a stimulus for further research efforts in this area and to further assist the researcher in the use of the Frank Lloyd Wright archival research materials described in this guide. The compiled listing of Frank Lloyd Wright's designs contained here is also intended to serve as a structuring device for the voluminous amount of research material presented. The compilation is by no means intended to be the "last word."

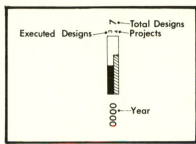

Executed Designs — Total Designs — Projects — Year

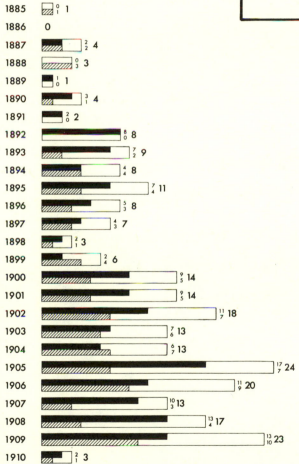

1885 0 / 1 1
1886 0
1887 2 / 2 4
1888 0 / 3 3
1889 1 / 0 1
1890 3 / 1 4
1891 2 / 0 2
1892 8 / 0 8
1893 7 / 2 9
1894 4 / 4 8
1895 7 / 4 11
1896 5 / 3 8
1897 4 / 3 7
1898 2 / 1 3
1899 2 / 4 6
1900 9 / 5 14
1901 9 / 5 14
1902 11 / 7 18
1903 7 / 6 13
1904 6 / 7 13
1905 17 / 7 24
1906 11 / 9 20
1907 10 / 3 13
1908 13 / 4 17
1909 13 / 10 23
1910 2 / 1 3

B-1   Frank Lloyd Wright's buildings, projects, and designs by year from 1885 to 1978 on this and following two pages. Chart and compilation by author.

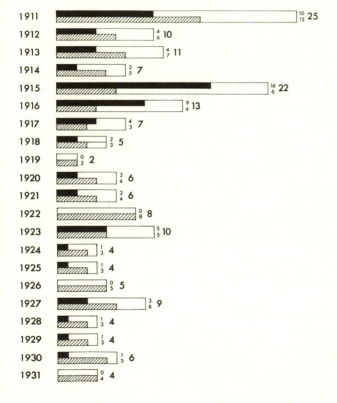

1911	10/15 25
1912	4/6 10
1913	4/7 11
1914	2/5 7
1915	16/6 22
1916	9/4 13
1917	4/3 7
1918	2/3 5
1919	0/2 2
1920	2/4 6
1921	2/4 6
1922	0/8 8
1923	5/5 10
1924	1/3 4
1925	1/3 4
1926	0/5 5
1927	3/6 9
1928	1/3 4
1929	1/3 4
1930	1/5 6
1931	0/4 4

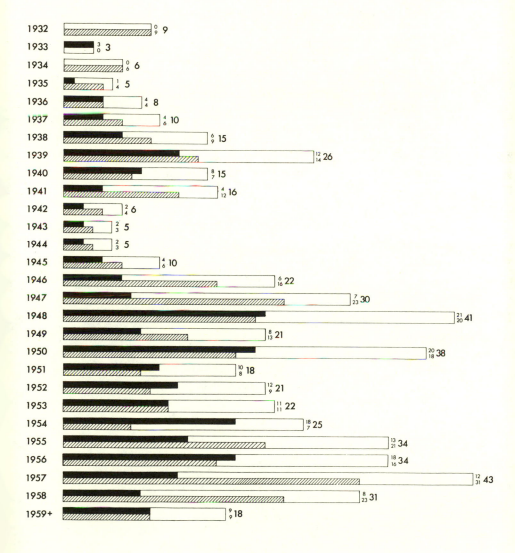

An asterisk indicates that the structure was on the National Register of Historic Places or within a historic district which was on the National Register of Historic Places as of January 1, 1981. This data was derived and compiled, in part, from "Part II: Department of the Interior: Heritage Conservation and Recreation Service: National Register of Historic Places: Annual Listing of Historic Properties," *Federal Register*, February 6, 1979, pp. 7416-7649; "Part II: Department of the Interior: National Register of Historic Places: Annual Listing of Historic Properties," *Federal Register*, March 18, 1980, pp. 17446-17488; Patrick J. Meehan's "Frank Lloyd Wright Designed Structures Which are on the National Register of Historic Places, National Historic Landmarks, and Recorded in the Historic American Buildings Survey," *The Frank Lloyd Wright Newsletter* (Oak Park, Illinois), Vol. 3, No. 3, Third Quarter 1980; and "Part II: Department of the Interior: Heritage Conservation and Recreation Service: National Register of Historic Places: Annual Listing of Historic Properties," *Federal Register*, February 3, 1981, pp. 10622-10679.

1885

    PROJECT
        University Avenue Power House[1]
        Madison, Wisconsin

1887

    EXECUTED DESIGNS
        Nell and Jane Lloyd Jones Hillside Home School #1
        Spring Green, Wisconsin

        *Unity Chapel[2]
        Helena, Wisconsin (near Spring Green)

    PROJECTS
        Misses Lloyd Jones Residence I
        Helena Valley, Spring Green, Wisconsin

        Unitarian Chapel[3]
        Sioux City, Iowa

1888

    PROJECTS
        J.L. Cochran Residence--First Design[4]
        Edgewater, Illinois(?)

        J.L. Cochran Residence--Second Design[5]
        Edgewater, Illinois

        William Waller Residences[6]
        Chicago, Illinois

1889

EXECUTED DESIGN
*Frank Lloyd Wright Residence
Oak Park, Illinois

1890

EXECUTED DESIGNS
James Charnley Summer Residence and Guest House
Ocean Springs, Mississippi

Victor Falkenau Residences[7]
Chicago, Illinois

Louis Sullivan Summer Residence and Stables
Ocean Springs, Mississippi

PROJECT
Henry N. Cooper Residence and Stable
La Grange, Illinois

1891

EXECUTED DESIGNS
*James Charnley Residence
Chicago, Illinois

W.S. MacHarg Residence
Chicago, Illinois

1892

EXECUTED DESIGNS
George Blossom Residence
Chicago, Illinois

Robert G. Emmond Residence
La Grange, Illinois

*Thomas H. Gale Residence
Oak Park, Illinois

Allison Harlan Residence
Chicago, Illinois

Warren McArthur Residence
Chicago, Illinois

*R.P. Parker Residence
Oak Park, Illinois

Albert Sullivan Residence
Chicago, Illinois

Victoria Hotel Remodeling
Chicago Heights, Illinois

1893

EXECUTED DESIGNS
W.I. Clark Residence
La Grange, Illinois

*Walter M. Gale Residence
Oak Park, Illinois

Robert M. Lamp Cottage "The Rocky Roost"
Governor's Island, Lake Mendota, Wisconsin

Municipal Boathouse for the Madison Improvement Association
Madison, Wisconsin

*William H. Winslow Residence and Stable
River Forest, Illinois

*Francis Wooley Residence
Oak Park, Illinois

*Frank Lloyd Wright Residence Playroom Addition
Oak Park, Illinois

PROJECTS
Boathouse
Lake Monona, Madison, Wisconsin

Library and Museum for the City of Milwaukee Competition
Milwaukee, Wisconsin

1894
EXECUTED DESIGNS
Frederick Bagley Residence
Hinsdale, Illinois

Dr. H.W. Bassett Residence Remodeling
Oak Park, Illinois

Peter Goan Residence
La Grange, Illinois

*Robert W. Roloson Apartments
Chicago, Illinois

PROJECTS
Concrete Monolithic Bank
Spring Green, Wisconsin?

Orrin S. Goan Residence
La Grange, Illinois

A.C. McAfee Residence
Lake Michigan at Chicago, Illinois

James L. McAfee Residence
Lake Michigan at Chicago, Illinois

1895
EXECUTED DESIGNS
Francis Apartments for the Terre Haute Trust Company
Chicago, Illinois

Francisco Terrace Apartments for Edward C. Waller
Chicago, Illinois

*Nathan G. Moore Residence and Stable
Oak Park, Illinois

Edward C. Waller Apartments
Chicago, Illinois

*Chauncey L. Williams Residence
River Forest, Illinois

*Frank Lloyd Wright Residence Addition
Oak Park, Illinois

*H.R. Young Alterations to Residence
Oak Park, Illinois

PROJECTS
Jesse Baldwin Residence
Oak Park, Illinois

Luxfer Prism Company Skyscraper
Chicago, Illinois

Residence[8]
Location Unknown

Wolf Lake Amusement Park
Wolf Lake, Illinois

1896

EXECUTED DESIGNS
*H.C. Goodrich Residence
Oak Park, Illinois

*Isidor Heller Residence and Stable
Chicago, Illinois

*Charles E. Roberts Residence and Stables Remodeling
Oak Park, Illinois

*Romeo and Juliet Windmill for Nell and Jane Lloyd Jones
Spring Green, Wisconsin

George W. Smith Residence
Oak Park, Illinois

PROJECTS
Mrs. David Devin Residence
Lake Michigan at Chicago, Illinois

Robert Perkins Apartments
Chicago, Illinois

Charles E. Roberts Four Residences
Ridgeland, Illinois

1897

EXECUTED DESIGNS
*George Furbeck Residence
Oak Park, Illinois

*Rollin Furbeck Residence
Oak Park, Illinois

Henry Wallis Boathouse
Delavan Lake, Wisconsin

Catherine M. White Residence[9]
Evanston, Illinois

PROJECTS
All Souls Building
Chicago, Illinois

Design for a Motion Picture Theatre
Los Angeles, California?

Factory Building for Chicago Screw Co.
Chicago, Illinois

1898

EXECUTED DESIGNS
River Forest Golf Club
River Forest, Illinois

*Frank Lloyd Wright Studio
Oak Park, Illinois

PROJECT
Mozart Garden Remodeling for David Meyer
Chicago, Illinois

1899

EXECUTED DESIGNS
Joseph Husser Residence
Chicago, Illinois

Edward C. Waller Residence Remodeling
River Forest, Illinois

PROJECTS
Cheltenham Beach Resort
Lake Michigan at Chicago, Illinois

Robert Eckart Residence
River Forest, Illinois

Residence[8]
Location Unknown

Edward C. Waller Residence
River Forest, Illinois

1900

EXECUTED DESIGNS
Jesse Adams Residence[10]
Chicago, Illinois

B. Harley Bradley Residence "Glenlloyd" and Stable
Kankakee, Illinois

S.A. Foster Residence and Stable
Chicago, Illinois

*Warren Hickox Residence
Kankakee, Illinois

*E.R. Hills Residence
Oak Park, Illinois

Warren McArthur Residence Remodeling
Chicago, Illinois

Warren McArthur Stable
Chicago, Illinois

E.H. Pitkin Residence
Sapper Island, Desbarats, Ontario, Canada

Henry Wallis Summer Residence
Delavan Lake, Wisconsin

PROJECTS
"A Home in a Prairie Town" for
Ladies Home Journal[11]
No Location

Francis W. Little Residence--First Design
Peoria, Illinois

Motion Picture Theater
Los Angeles, California

School House
Crosbyton, Texas

"A Small House with Lots of Room in It" for *Ladies Home Journal*[12]
No Location

1901

EXECUTED DESIGNS
*E. Arthur Davenport Residence
River Forest, Illinois

*William G. Fricke Residence
Oak Park, Illinois

F.B. Henderson Residence
Elmhurst, Illinois

*Nell and Jane Lloyd Jones Hillside Home School II
Spring Green, Wisconsin

River Forest Golf Club Addition
River Forest, Illinois

*Frank Thomas Residence "The Harem"
Oak Park, Illinois

Universal Portland Cement Company Exposition Pavilion
Buffalo, New York

Edward C. Waller Gates and Stables
River Forest, Illinois

T.E. Wilder Stable
Elmhurst, Illinois

PROJECTS
Lexington Terrace Apartments--First Design
Chicago, Illinois

Abraham Lincoln Center
Chicago, Illinois

M.H. Lowell Studio[13]
Matteawan, New York

"A Village Bank Cast in Concrete"[14]
No location

Henry Wallis Residence Remodeling
Delavan Lake, Wisconsin

1902

EXECUTED DESIGNS
  *Susan Lawrence Dana Residence
  Springfield, Illinois

  Flower Stand Series for James A. Miller
  Chicago, Illinois

  George Gerts Double Residence "Bridge Cottage"
  Whitehall, Michigan

  Walter Gerts Residence
  Whitehall, Michigan

  *Arthur Heurtley Residence
  Oak Park, Illinois

  Arthur Heurtley Summer Residence Remodeling
  Les Cheneaux Club, Marquette Island, Michigan

  Francis W. Little Residence I and Stable
  Peoria, Illinois

  *W.E. Martin Residence
  Oak Park, Illinois

  Charles S. Ross Residence
  Delavan Lake, Wisconsin

  George W. Spencer Residence
  Delavan Lake, Wisconsin

  Ward W. Willits Residence, Gardener's Cottage, and Stable
  Highland Park, Illinois

PROJECTS
  Richard Bock Ateliers--First Design
  Maywood, Illinois

  Delavan Lake Yacht Club
  Delavan Lake, Wisconsin

  Victor Metzger Residence
  Desbarats, Ontario, Canada

  John A. Mosher Residence
  Location Unknown

  Residence
  Oak Park, Illinois

  Edward C. Waller Residence--First Design
  Charlevoix, Michigan

  Yahara Boat Club
  Madison, Wisconsin

1903

EXECUTED DESIGNS

George Barton Residence
Buffalo, New York

W.H. Freeman Residence
Hinsdale, Illinois

*Fred B. Jones Residence, Gate, Lodge, Barn, Stables, and
    Boathouse
Delavan Lake, Wisconsin

Larkin Company Administration Building
Buffalo, New York

Abraham Lincoln Center for Reverend Mr. Jenkin Lloyd Jones
Chicago, Illinois

*Scoville Park Fountain
Oak Park, Illinois

J.J. Walser, Jr., Residence
Chicago, Illinois

PROJECTS

Chicago and Northwestern Railway Station
Oak Park, Illinois

Robert M. Lamp Residence--First Design
Madison, Wisconsin

Residence
Location Unknown

Charles E. Roberts Residences
Oak Park, Illinois

Edward C. Waller Residence--Second Design
Charlevoix, Michigan

Frank Lloyd Wright Studio/Residence (1 Story)
Oak Park, Illinois

1904

EXECUTED DESIGNS

*Edwin H. Cheney Residence
Oak Park, Illinois

*Mrs. Thomas H. Gale Residence
Oak Park, Illinois

William R. Heath Residence[15]
Buffalo, New York

*Robert M. Lamp Residence
Madison, Wisconsin

*Darwin D. Martin Residence, Conservatory, and Garage
Buffalo, New York

*Burton J. Westcott Residence
Springfield, Ohio

PROJECTS
Hiram Baldwin Residence--First Design
Kenilworth, Illinois

Robert D. Clarke Residence
Peoria, Illinois

Larkin Company Workmen's Rowhouses
Buffalo, New York

Residence
Highland Park, Illinois

J.A. Scudder Residence
Campement d'Ours Island,
Desbarats, Ontario, Canada

Frank L. Smith Bank--First Design
Dwight, Illinois

H.J. Ullman Residence
Oak Park, Illinois

1905

EXECUTED DESIGNS
Mary M.W. Adams Residence
Highland Park, Illinois

Hiram Baldwin Residence--Second Design
Kenilworth, Illinois

Charles E. Brown Residence
Evanston, Illinois

E.W. Cummings Real Estate Office
River Forest, Illinois

E-Z Polish Factory for Darwin D. Martin and W.E. Martin
Chicago, Illinois

Mrs. Thomas H. Gale Summer Residence
Whitehall, Michigan

Mrs. Thomas H. Gale Duplicate I Summer Residence
Whitehall, Michigan

Mrs. Thomas H. Gale Duplicate II Summer Residence
Whitehall, Michigan

W.A. Glasner Residence
Glencoe, Illinois

*Thomas P. Hardy Residence
Racine, Wisconsin

A.P. Johnson Residence
Delavan Lake, Wisconsin

*Susan Lawrence Memorial Library
Springfield, Illinois

Darwin D. Martin Gardener's Cottage
Buffalo, New York

*Rookery Building Remodeling of the Entryway and Lobby
Chicago, Illinois

Frank L. Smith Bank--First National Bank of Dwight--Second
    Design
Dwight, Illinois

*Harvey P. Sutton Residence--Second Design
McCook, Nebraska

*Unity Church
Oak Park, Illinois

PROJECTS
Charles W. Barnes Residence
McCook, Nebraska

Concrete Apartment Building for Warren McArthur
Chicago, Illinois

T.E. Gilpin Residence
Oak Park, Illinois

Lake Residence
Location Unknown

Nathan Moore Pergola and Pavilion
Oak Park, Illinois

Harvey P. Sutton Residence--First Design
McCook, Nebraska

Varnish Factory for Darwin D. Martin
Location Unknown

1906

EXECUTED DESIGNS
*P.A. Beachy Residence
Oak Park, Illinois

K.C. DeRhodes Residence
South Bend, Indiana

Grace Fuller Residence
Glencoe, Illinois

A.W. Gridley Residence and Barn
Batavia, Illinois

P.D. Hoyt Residence
Geneva, Illinois

George Madison Millard Residence
Highland Park, Illinois

Frederick Nicholas Residence
Flossmoor, Illinois

*W.H. Pettit Mortuary Chapel
Belvedere, Illinois

*River Forest Tennis Club
River Forest, Illinois

>   *Frederick G. Robie Residence
>   Chicago, Illinois
>
>   C. Thaxter Shaw Residence Remodeling
>   Montreal, Quebec, Canada

PROJECTS
>   Richard Bock Studio/Residence--Second Design
>   Maywood, Illinois
>
>   Alexander Davidson Residence--First Design
>   Buffalo, New York
>
>   Mrs. David Devin Residence
>   Eliot, Maine
>
>   "A Fireproof House for $5,000" for *The Ladies Home Journal*[16]
>   No Location
>
>   Walter Gerts Residence
>   Glencoe, Illinois
>
>   R.S. Ludington Residence
>   Dwight, Illinois
>
>   Warren McArthur Apartments
>   Chicago, Illinois
>
>   C. Thaxter Shaw Residence
>   Montreal, Canada
>
>   Elizabeth Stone Residence
>   Glencoe, Illinois

1907

EXECUTED DESIGNS
>   George Blossom Garage
>   Chicago, Illinois
>
>   *Avery Coonley Residence
>   Riverside, Illinois
>
>   Colonel George Fabyan Fox River Country Club Remodeling
>   Geneva, Illinois
>
>   Colonel George Fabyan Game Preserve Residence Remodeling
>   Geneva, Illinois
>
>   Stephen M.B. Hunt Residence I
>   La Grange, Illinois
>
>   Jamestown Exhibition Pavilion for the Larkin Company
>   Sewell Point, Norfolk, Virginia
>
>   *Emma Martin Alterations to the William G. Fricke Residence
>   and New Garage
>   Oak Park, Illinois
>
>   Pebbles and Balch Shop
>   Oak Park, Illinois
>
>   *Andrew T. Porter Residence "Tanyderi"
>   Spring Green, Wisconsin

F.F. Tomek Residence
Riverside, Illinois

PROJECTS
Sherman Booth's Municipal Art Gallery
Chicago, Illinois

Harold McCormick Residence
Lake Forest, Illinois

Andrew T. Porter Residence--Second Design
Near Spring Green, Wisconsin

1908

EXECUTED DESIGNS
Bitter Root Inn
Stevensville, Montana

E.E. Boynton Residence
Rochester, New York

Browne's Bookstore
Chicago, Illinois

Como Orchards Summer Colony
University Heights, Darby, Montana

*William H. Copeland Garage
Oak Park, Illinois

Alexander Davidson Residence--Second Design
Buffalo, New York

Robert W. Evans
Chicago, Illinois

*E.A. Gilmore Residence "Airplane House"
Madison, Wisconsin

L.K. Horner Residence
Chicago, Illinois

Horseshoe Inn for Willard Ashton
Estes Park, Colorado

Meyer May Residence
Grand Rapids, Michigan

*Isabel Roberts Residence[17]
River Forest, Illinois

*G.C. Stockman Residence
Mason City, Iowa

PROJECTS
E.D. Brigham Stables
Location Unknown

William Norman Guthrie Residence
Sewanee, Tennessee

Francis W. Little Residence II--First Design
Wayzata, Minnesota

J.G. Melson Residence
Mason City, Iowa

1909

EXECUTED DESIGNS

David M. Amberg Residence
Grand Rapids, Michigan

*Frank J. Baker Residence[18]
Wilmette, Illinois

*City National Bank and Motel for Blythe and Markley
Mason City, Iowa

Robert Clarke Additions to the Francis Little Residence I
Peoria, Illinois

*William H. Copeland Residence Alterations
Oak Park, Illinois

*J. Kibben Ingalls Residence
River Forest, Illinois

E.P. Irving Residence
Decatur, Illinois

Robert Mueller Residence
Decatur, Illinois

Oscar Steffens Residence
Chicago, Illinois

George C. Stewart Residence
Montecito, California

Peter C. Stohr Arcade Building
Chicago, Illinois

Thurber Art Gallery
Chicago, Illinois

*Reverend J.R. Ziegler Residence
Frankfort, Kentucky

PROJECTS

Harry E. Brown Residence
Geneva, Illinois

City Dwelling with Glass Front
Location Unknown

Larwill Residence
Muskegon, Michigan

Lexington Terrace Apartments--Second Design
Chicago, Illinois

Lawton Parker Studio Remodeling
Location Unknown

Mrs. Mary Roberts Residence
River Forest, Illinois

Town Hall for Sherman Booth
Glencoe, Illinois

Town of Bitter Root
Darby, Montana

Three Small Residences for Edward C. Waller
River Forest, Illinois

Edward C. Waller Bathing Pavilion
Charlevoix, Michigan

1910

EXECUTED DESIGNS
*Blythe and Markley Law Offices Remodeling
Mason City, Iowa

Universal Portland Cement Company
New York City Exhibition
New York, New York

PROJECT
Frank Lloyd Wright Residence/Studio
Viale Verdi, Fiesole, Italy

1911

EXECUTED DESIGNS
American System Ready-Cut Houses[19]
Richards Company
Milwaukee, Wisconsin

Herbert Angster Residence
Lake Bluff, Illinois

*O.B. Balch Residence
Oak Park, Illinois

Banff National Park Pavilion[20]
Alberta, Canada

Sherman Booth Summer Cottage[21]
Glencoe, Illinois

*Avery Coonley Coach House
Riverside, Illinois

*Avery Coonley Gardener's Cottage
Riverside, Illinois

Lake Geneva Hotel for Arthur L. Richards
Lake Geneva, Wisconsin

Taliesin I for Frank Lloyd Wright
Spring Green, Wisconsin

*Frank Lloyd Wright Residence Addition
Oak Park, Illinois

PROJECTS
Harry S. Adams Residence
Oak Park, Illinois

Sherman M. Booth Residence
Glencoe, Illinois

Christian Catholic Church
Zion, Illinois

Avery Coonley Kindergarten
Riverside, Illinois

Avery Coonley Greenhouse
Riverside, Illinois

Arthur M. Cutten Residence
Downer's Grove, Illinois

E. Esbenshade Residence
Milwaukee, Wisconsin

Walter Gerts Remodeling
River Forest, Illinois

W.R. Heath Garage and Stables
Buffalo, New York

North Shore Electric Waiting Station for Sherman Booth
Chicago, Illinois

Andrew T. Porter Residence--Third Design
Spring Green, Wisconsin

Arthur L. Richards Hotel
Madison, Wisconsin

Richards Co. American Systems Ready-Cut
Standardized Residences
Milwaukee, Wisconsin

Edward Schroeder Residence
Milwaukee, Wisconsin

Frank Lloyd Wright Residence
Goethe Street
Chicago, Illinois

UNDATED 1889 to 1911?
    PROJECT
        W.W. Davis Residence Project[22]
        Louisville, Kentucky

1912
    EXECUTED DESIGNS
        Avery Coonley Playhouse
        Riverside, Illinois

        William B. Greene Residence
        Aurora, Illinois

        Francis W. Little Residence II "Northome"--Second Design
        Deephaven, Minnesota

        Park Ridge Country Club Clubhouse Remodeling
        Park Ridge, Illinois

    PROJECTS
        Dress Shop
        Oak Park, Illinois

        Kehl Dance Academy with Shops and Residence
        Madison, Wisconsin

Press Building for Spreckels Estate
San Francisco, California

Schoolhouse
La Grange, Illinois

Small Town Residence
Location Unknown

Two Taliesin Cottages
Near Spring Green, Wisconsin

1913

EXECUTED DESIGNS
*Harry S. Adams Residence
Oak Park, Illinois

M.B. Hilly Residence
Brookfield, Illinois

William Louis Koehne Residence
Palm Beach, Florida

Midway Gardens for Edward C. Waller, Jr.
Chicago, Illinois

PROJECTS
Art Museum
Location Unknown

Carnegie Library
Ottawa, Ontario, Canada

Double Residence
Ottawa, Ontario, Canada

J.W. Kellogg Residence
Milwaukee, Wisconsin

Jerome Mendelson Residence
Albany, New York

Post Office
Ottawa, Ontario, Canada

Row Houses for Edward C. Waller
Chicago, Illinois

1914

EXECUTED DESIGNS
Mori Oriental Art Studio
Chicago, Illinois

Taliesin II for Frank Lloyd Wright
Spring Green, Wisconsin

PROJECTS
"Garden Project" Concert Gardens
Chicago, Illinois

State Bank
Spring Green, Wisconsin

Three Residences for Honoré J. Jaxon
Location Unknown

U.S. Embassy
Tokyo, Japan

John Vogelsang Dinner Gardens and Residence
Chicago, Illinois

1915

EXECUTED DESIGNS
American Systems Ready-Cut Residence (1915?)[23]
Lake Bluff, Illinois

American Systems Ready-Cut Residence (1915?)[24]
Wilmette, Illinois

*Emil Bach Residence
Chicago, Illinois

E.D. Brigham Residence
Glencoe, Illinois

*A.D. German Warehouse
Richland Center, Wisconsin

Glass Designs for Leerdam Glassworks
Holland

Imperial Hotel
Tokyo, Japan

Sherman M. Booth Residence
Ravine Bluffs Development
Glencoe, Illinois

William F. Kier Residence
Ravine Bluffs Development
Glencoe, Illinois

Lute F. Kissam Residence
Ravine Bluffs Development
Glencoe, Illinois

Charles R. Perry Residence
Ravine Bluffs Development
Glencoe, Illinois

*Ravine Bluffs Development Bridge for Sherman M. Booth
Glencoe, Illinois

Ravine Bluffs Development Plan for Sherman M. Booth
Glencoe, Illinois

Ravine Bluffs Development Sculptures for Sherman M. Booth
Glencoe, Illinois

Hollis R. Root Residence
Ravine Bluffs Development
Glencoe, Illinois

William F. Ross Residence
Ravine Bluffs Development
Glencoe, Illinois

PROJECTS
Imperial Hotel Preliminary Design
Tokyo, Japan

A Lake Shore Residence
Location Unknown

Model Quarter Section Development
Chicago, Illinois

Arthur L. Richards Chinese Restaurant
Milwaukee, Wisconsin

Rockefeller Foundation Chinese Hospital
Location Unknown

Wood Residence
Decatur, Illinois

1916

EXECUTED DESIGNS
Joseph J. Bagley Residence
Grand Beach, Michigan

*F.C. Bogk Residence
Milwaukee, Wisconsin

Bungalow for Arthur L. Richards
American Systems Ready-Cut
Milwaukee, Wisconsin

W.S. Carr Residence
Grand Beach, Michigan

Imperial Hotel Annex
Tokyo, Japan

Arthur Munkwitz Apartments
American Systems Ready-Cut
Milwaukee, Wisconsin

Arthur L. Richards Duplex Apartments
American Systems Ready-Cut
Milwaukee, Wisconsin

Small House for Arthur L. Richards
American Systems Ready-Cut
Milwaukee, Wisconsin

Ernest Vosburgh Residence
Grand Beach, Michigan

PROJECTS
Miss Behn-Voight Residence
Grand Beach, Michigan

Clarence Converse Residence
Palisades Park, Michigan

Small Urban Town House
Location Unknown

William Allen White Residence Remodeling
Emporia, Kansas

1917

EXECUTED DESIGNS

*Henry J. Allen Residence
Wichita, Kansas

*Aline Barnsdall "Hollyhock" Residence
Los Angeles, California

Aisaku Hayashi Residence
Tokyo, Japan

Stephen M.B. Hunt Residence II
American Systems Ready-Cut
Oshkosh, Wisconsin

PROJECTS

Aline Barnsdall Residence and Theater
Los Angeles, California

Odawara Hotel
Nagoya, Japan

William Powell Residence
Wichita, Kansas

1918

EXECUTED DESIGNS

Arinobu Fukuhara Residence
Hakone, Japan

Tazaemon Yamamura Residence
Ashiya, Japan

PROJECTS

Count Immu Residence
Tokyo, Japan

Viscount Inouye Residence
Tokyo, Japan

Movie Theater
Tokyo, Japan

1919

PROJECTS

Thomas P. Hardy Monolith Homes
Racine, Wisconsin

W.S. Spaulding Gallery
Boston, Massachusetts

1920

EXECUTED DESIGNS

Aline Barnsdall Little Dipper Kindergarten
Los Angeles, California

*Aline Barnsdall Studio Residence A
Los Angeles, California

PROJECTS

Automobile with Cantilevered Top

Aline Barnsdall Theater, Shops, Residences
Los Angeles, California

Cantilevered Concrete Skyscraper
No Location

W.J. Weber Residence
Location Unknown

1921

EXECUTED DESIGNS
Aline Barnsdall Studio Residence B
Los Angeles, California

Jiyu Gakuen Girls' School
Tokyo, Japan

PROJECTS
Cement Block Residence
Los Angeles, California

Edward H. Doheny Ranch Development
Near Los Angeles, California

Glass and Copper Skyscraper
Location Unknown

Baron Goto Residence
Tokyo, Japan

1922

PROJECTS
Desert Compound and Shrine for A.M. Johnson
Death Valley, California

G.P. Lowes Residence
Eagle Rock, California

Merchandising Building
Los Angeles, California

Arthur Sachse Residence
Mojave Desert, California

Tahoe Barge, Family Type
Tahoe Summer Colony
Lake Tahoe, California

Tahoe Summer Colony
Lake Tahoe, California

Tahoe Summer Colony Cabins
Lake Tahoe, California

Tahoe Summer Colony Floating Cabins
Lake Tahoe, California

1923

EXECUTED DESIGNS
*Charles Ennis Residence
Los Angeles, California

*Samuel Freeman Residence
Los Angeles, California

*Mrs. George Madison Millard Residence
"La Miniatura"
Pasadena, California

*Nathan G. Moore Residence II[25]
Oak Park, Illinois

*John Storer Residence
Hollywood, California

PROJECTS
Aline Barnsdall Residence
Beverly Hills, California

Concrete Block Residence
Los Angeles, California

Daughter of Darwin D. Martin Residence
Buffalo, New York

Tahoe Summer Colony Cabin
Lake Tahoe, California

Tahoe Summer Colony Hunting Lodge
Lake Tahoe, California

1924

EXECUTED DESIGN
Sculptures--Nakoma Warrior and Nakomis Woman

PROJECTS
Mrs. Samuel William Gladney Residence
Fort Worth, Texas

Nakoma Country Club and Winnebago Camping Ground Indian
Memorial
Madison, Wisconsin

National Life Insurance Company Skyscraper
Chicago, Illinois

1925

EXECUTED DESIGN
*Taliesin III for Frank Lloyd Wright
Spring Green, Wisconsin

PROJECTS
Mrs. George Millard Gallery
Pasadena, California

Phi Gamma Delta Fraternity House
Madison, Wisconsin

Gordon Strong Planetarium
Sugar Loaf Mountain, Maryland

1926

PROJECTS
Concrete and Copper Gasoline Stations
Locations Unknown

Liberty Magazine Cover Designs
(Designs Not Used by *Liberty*)

Skyscraper Regulations
Chicago, Illinois

Six Oak Park Playground Association Playhouses
Oak Park, Illinois

Steel Cathedral for William Norman Guthrie
New York, New York

1927

EXECUTED DESIGNS
Beach Cottages
Dumyat, Egypt

Darwin D. Martin Residence "Graycliff" and Garage
Derby, New York

Warren McArthur's Arizona Biltmore Hotel and Cottages[26]
Phoenix, Arizona

PROJECTS
Dr. Alexander Chandler Residences
Chandler, Arizona

Dr. Alexander Chandler San Marcos-in-the-Desert Winter Resort
Chandler, Arizona

Dr. Alexander Chandler San Marcos Water Gardens
Chandler, Arizona

Wellington and Ralph Cudney Residence
Chandler, Arizona

St. Mark's-in-the-Bouwerie Towers
New York, New York

Owen D. Young Residence
Chandler, Arizona

1928

EXECUTED DESIGN
Frank Lloyd Wright's Ocatillo Desert Camp
Chandler, Arizona

PROJECTS
Gasoline Stations
Location Unknown

Darwin D. Martin Blue Sky Mausoleum
Buffalo, New York

Rosenwald Foundation School for Negro Children
La Jolla, California

1929

EXECUTED DESIGN
Richard Lloyd Jones Residence "Westhope"
Tulsa, Oklahoma

PROJECTS
Richard Lloyd Jones Residence--Preliminary Design
Tulsa, Oklahoma

Elizabeth Noble Apartment
Los Angeles, California

Tea Cup and Saucer Designs

1930

EXECUTED DESIGN
Vases and Glass Objects for Leerdam Glass
Holland

PROJECTS
Apartment Towers
Chicago, Illinois

Automobile Design

Cabins for Desert or Woods for Chicago YMCA
Location Unknown

Designs for Tableware

Memorial Chapel
Location Unknown

1931

PROJECTS
Capital Journal Building
Salem, Oregon

"House on the Mesa"
Denver, Colorado

Skyscraper
Chicago, Illinois

Three Designs for "A Century of Progress"
(1933 World's Fair)
Chicago, Illinois

1932

PROJECTS
Automobile and Airplane Filling and Service Stations
Location Unknown

Cinema and Shops[27]
Michigan City, Indiana
(with John Lloyd Wright)

Conventional House
Location Unknown

Walter Davidson Prefab Farm Units
Location Unknown

Walter Davidson Prefab Markets
Location Unknown

Highway Overpass Design
Location Unknown

New Theater
Location Unknown

Pre-Fabricated Residence
Location Unknown

Dean Malcolm M. Willey Residence--First Design
Minneapolis, Minnesota

1933

EXECUTED DESIGNS
Hillside Home School Theater Curtain
Spring Green, Wisconsin

*Taliesin Fellowship Complex
Spring Green, Wisconsin

Malcolm E. Willey Residence--Second Design
Minneapolis, Minnesota

1934

PROJECTS
Broadacre City Project

Heliocopter[28]

A.D. German Warehouse Remodeling
Richland Center, Wisconsin

Road Machine (Motor City)[28]

Train

Zoned House No. 1[28]
Location Unknown

1935

EXECUTED DESIGN
*Edgar J. Kaufmann, Sr., Residence "Fallingwater"
Ohiopyle, Pennsylvania

PROJECTS
City Zoned House[28]
Location Unknown

Country Zoned House[28]
Location Unknown

Stanley Marcus Residence
Dallas, Texas

Suburban Zoned House[28]
Location Unknown

1936

EXECUTED DESIGNS
*Paul R. Hanna Residence "Honeycomb"
Stanford, California

*Herbert Jacobs First Residence
Madison, Wisconsin

*S.C. Johnson and Son Administration Building
Racine, Wisconsin

Mrs. Abby Beecher Roberts Residence
Marquette, Michigan

PROJECTS
Dr. Alexander Chandler Hotel Remodeling
Chandler, Arizona

Dr. Alexander Chandler Little San Marcos-in-the-Desert
Chandler, Arizona

H.C. Hoult Residence
Wichita, Kansas

Robert D. Lusk Residence
Huron, South Dakota

1937

EXECUTED DESIGNS
*Herbert F. Johnson Residence "Wingspread"
Wind Point, Wisconsin

Edgar J. Kaufmann, Sr., Office
Pittsburgh, Pennsylvania
(relocated to the Victoria and Albert Museum in London)

Ben Rebhuhn Residence--First Design
Great Neck Estates, New York

*Taliesin West
Scottsdale, Arizona

PROJECTS
"All Steel" Houses Development
Los Angeles, California

Gutson Borglum Studio
Black Hills, South Dakota

Leo Bramson Dress-Shop Reconstruction
Oak Park, Illinois

"Memorial to the Soil" Chapel
Southern Wisconsin

Hulda and Louise Notz Residence
Pittsburgh, Pennsylvania

George Parker Garage
Janesville, Wisconsin

1938

EXECUTED DESIGNS
*Florida Southern College Development Plan[29]
Lakeland, Florida

*Edgar J. Kaufmann, Sr., "Fallingwater" Guest House
Ohiopyle, Pennsylvania

Charles L. Manson Residence
Wausau, Wisconsin

*Annie Merner Pfeiffer Chapel
Florida Southern College
Lakeland, Florida

Suntop Homes for Otto Mallery of Tod Company
Ardmore, Pennsylvania

*Taliesin Midway Barns for Frank Lloyd Wright
Spring Green, Wisconsin

PROJECTS
Edith Carlson Residence
Superior, Wisconsin

Florida Southern College Campus Plans (with 16 buildings)[29]
Lakeland, Florida

"House for a Family of $5000-$6000 Income" for *Life* Magazine[30]
No Location

Ralph Jester Residence[31]
Palos Verdes, California

Herbert F. Johnson, Jr., Gatehouse and Farm Group
Wind Point, Racine, Wisconsin

Royal H. Jurgensen Residence
Evanston, Illinois

Madison Civic Center--Monona Terrace
Madison, Wisconsin

George Bliss McCallum Residence
Northampton, Massachusetts

E.A. Smith Residence "Pinetree House"
Piedmont Pines, California

1939
EXECUTED DESIGNS
Andrew F.H. Armstrong Residence
Ogden Dunes, Indiana

Sidney Bazett Residence
Hillsborough, California

Joseph Euchtman Residence
Baltimore, Maryland

Goetsch-Winckler Residence
Okemos, Michigan

Lloyd Lewis Residence
Libertyville, Illinois

Rose Pauson Residence
Phoenix, Arizona

John C. Pew Residence
Shorewood Hills, Wisconsin

*Loren Pope Residence
Falls Church, Virginia
(Later Relocated to Mount Vernon)

Stanley Rosenbaum Residence
Florence, Alabama

Bernard Schwartz Residence
Two Rivers, Wisconsin

C. Leigh Stevens Residence, Two Cottages, Guest House,
    Stables with Kennels, and Barn "The Auld Brass Plantation"
Yemassee, South Carolina

George D. Sturges Residence
Brentwood Heights, California

PROJECTS
Lewis N. Bell Residence[32]
Los Angeles, California

Front Gates
Taliesin, Spring Green, Wisconsin

Gordon Lowenstein Residence
Mason City, Iowa

Edgar A. Mauer Residence
Los Angeles, California

Martin J. Pence Residence[33]
Hilo, Hawaii

Ludd M. Spivey Residence
Fort Lauderdale, Florida

Usonia I Development Site Plan for Seven Residences
Okemos, Michigan

Usonian Development--Erling B. Brauner Residence
Okemos, Michigan

Usonian Development--Caretaker and·Farm Unit
Okemos, Michigan

Usonian Development--J.J. Garrison Residence
Okemos, Michigan

Usonian Development--C.D. Hause Residence
Okemos, Michigan

Usonian Development--Sidney H. Newman Residence
Okemos, Michigan

Usonian Development--Alexis J. Panshin Residence
Okemos, Michigan

Usonian Development--Clarence R. Van Dusen Residence
Okemos, Michigan

1940
EXECUTED DESIGNS
Gregor Affleck Residence--First Design
Bloomfield Hills, Michigan

Theodore Baird Residence
Amherst, Massachusetts

James B. Christie Residence
Bernardsville, New Jersey

Kansas City Community Christian Church
Kansas City, Missouri

Arch Obler Gatehouse
Malibu, California

Rainbow Springs Lodge[34]
East Troy, Wisconsin

Clarence Sondern Residence
Kansas City, Missouri

*Three Seminar Buildings
Florida Southern College
Lakeland, Florida

PROJECTS
Crystal Heights Hotel Theater, Shops
Washington, D.C.

Methodist Church
Spring Green, Wisconsin

Model House[35]
Museum of Modern Art Exhibition
New York, New York

John Nesbitt Residence
Carmel Bay, California

Arch Oboler Residence "Eaglefeather"--First Design
Los Angeles, California

Frank A. Rentz Residence
Madison, Wisconsin

Franklin Watkins Studio
Barnegat City, New Jersey

1941
EXECUTED DESIGNS
*Florida Southern College Library
Lakeland, Florida

Arch Obler Retreat
Malibu, California

Stuart Richardson Residence
Glen Ridge, New Jersey

Carlton David Wall Residence "Snowflake"
Plymouth, Michigan

PROJECTS
John Barton Residence
Pine Bluff, Wisconsin

Lloyd Burlingham Residence
El Paso, Texas

Walter Dayer Music Studio
Detroit, Michigan

Alfred H. Ellinwood Residence
Deerfield, Illinois

Parker B. Field Residence
Peru, Illinois

William Guenther Residence
East Caldwell, New Jersey

Roy Petersen Residence
Racine, Wisconsin

Margaret Schevill Residence
Tucson, Arizona

Sigma Chi Fraternity House
Hanover, Indiana

U.S. Government Cloverleaf Quadruple Housing
Pittsfield, Massachusetts

Vigo Sundt Residence
Madison, Wisconsin

Mary Waterstreet Studio
Spring Green, Wisconsin

1942

EXECUTED DESIGNS
  *Florida Southern College Industrial Arts Building
  Lakeland, Florida

  Lincoln Continental Alterations (Frank Lloyd Wright Owned
    Automobile)

PROJECTS
  Circle Pines Center
  Cloverdale, Michigan

  Cooperative Homesteads
  Detroit, Michigan

  Clark Foreman Residence
  Washington, D.C.

  M.N. Hein Residence
  Chippewa Falls, Wisconsin

1943

EXECUTED DESIGNS
  *Herbert Jacobs Second Residence
  Middleton, Wisconsin

  Lloyd Lewis Farm Unit
  Libertyville, Illinois

PROJECTS
  T.L. McDonald Residence
  Washington, D.C.

  V.C. Morris Residence--First Design
  San Francisco, California

  Glen Richardson Restaurant and Service Station
  Spring Green, Wisconsin

1944

EXECUTED DESIGNS
*S.C. Johnson and Son Research Tower
Racine, Wisconsin

Arch Obler Residence Addition #1
Malibu, California

PROJECTS
P.K. Harlan Residence
Omaha, Nebraska

Gerald M. Loeb Residence "Pergola House"
Redding, Connecticut

Stuart Wells Residence
Minneapolis, Minnesota

1945

EXECUTED DESIGNS
*Florida Southern College Administration Building
Lakeland, Florida

Arnold Friedman Residence "The Fir Tree"
Pecos, New Mexico

*Taliesin Dams
Spring Green, Wisconsin

Lowell Walter Residence
Quasqueton, Iowa

PROJECTS
Elizabeth Arden Resort Hotel
Phoenix, Arizona

George Berdan Residence
Ludington, Michigan

Glass House for *Ladies Home Journal*, Opus 497

Stuart Haldorn Residence "The Wave"
Carmel, California

William R. Slater Residence
Warwick, Rhode Island

Stamm Residence
Delavan Lake, Wisconsin

1946

EXECUTED DESIGNS
*Florida Southern College Esplanades
Lakeland, Florida

Douglas Grant Residence
Cedar Rapids, Iowa

Chauncey Griggs Residence
Tacoma, Washington

*Alvin Miller Residence
Charles City, Iowa

Arch Obler Residence Addition #2
Malibu, California

Melvyn Maxwell Smith Residence
Bloomfield Hills, Michigan

PROJECTS
Benjamin Adelman Laundry
Milwaukee, Wisconsin

Calico Mills Office Building
Ahmedabad, India

Malcolm Dana Residence
Olivet College, Olivet, Michigan

Walter Dayer Residence and Music Pavilion
Bloomfield Hills, Michigan

Huntington Hartford Reunion Tract[36]
Los Angeles, California

Huntington Hartford Outpost Club[36]
Hollywood, California

Thomas E. Keys Residence--First Design
Rochester, Minnesota

Rogers Lacy Hotel
Dallas, Texas

V.C. Morris Residence--Second Design
San Francisco, California

Joe Munroe Residence
Knox County, Ohio

Arch Obler Studio
Los Angeles, California

Alexis Panshin Residence
State Teachers College
Lansing, Michigan

William Pinderton Residence
Cambridge, Massachusetts

W.M. Pinkerton Residence
Fairfax County, Virginia

Sarabhi Administration Building and Store
Ahmedabad, India

State Teachers College Housing
Lansing, Michigan

1947
EXECUTED DESIGNS
Amy Alpaugh Residence
Northport, Michigan

A.H. Bulbulian Residence
Rochester, Minnesota

Galesburg Country Homes Development Plan
Galesburg, Michigan

Parkwyn Village Development Plan
Kalamazoo, Michigan

*Taliesin Dairy and Machine Sheds
Spring Green, Wisconsin

*Unitarian Church
Shorewood Hills, Wisconsin

Usonia Homes, Inc., Development Plan ʔ
Pleasantville, New York

PROJECTS
Dr. Charles Bell Residence
East St. Louis, Illinois

Marden B. Black Residence
Rochester, Minnesota

Jorgine Boomer Residence--First Design
Phoenix, Arizona

Concrete "Butterfly" Bridge, Wisconsin River
Spring Green, Wisconsin

Depot for San Antonio Transit Company
San Antonio, Texas

Vito Grieco Residence
Andover, Massachusetts

Berta Hamilton Residence
Brookline, Vermont

Huntington Hartford Play Resort--Cottage Group Center
Hollywood Hills, California

Huntington Hartford Play Resort--Sports Club
Hollywood Hills, California

Huntington Hartford Residence
Hollywood Hills, California

Walter S. Houston Residence
Schuyler County, Illinois

R.H. Keith Residence
Oakland County, Michigan? or Arlington, New Jersey?

E.L. Marting Residence
Akron, Ohio

Dr. Paul Palmer Residence
Phoenix, Arizona

John J. Pike Residence
Los Angeles, California

Point Park Community Center--First Design
Pittsburgh, Pennsylvania

Self-Service Garage
Pittsburgh, Pennsylvania

Twin Suspension Bridges, Point Park
Pittsburgh, Pennsylvania

Ayn Rand Residence
Hollywood, California

Valley National Bank of Phoenix Branch Bank
Tucson, Arizona

Roy Wetmore Auto Display Room and Workshop
Detroit, Michigan

Frank G. Wheeler Residence
Hinsdale, Illinois

Donald Wilkie Residence
Hennepin County, Minnesota

1948

EXECUTED DESIGNS
Albert Adelman Residence
Fox Point, Wisconsin

Arnold Adler Addition to the Clarence Sondern Residence
Kansas City, Missouri

Carroll Alsop Residence
Oskaloosa, Iowa

Erling P. Brauner Residence
Okemos, Michigan

Maynard P. Buehler Residence
Orinda, California

Samuel Eppstein Residence
Galesburg Country Homes Development
Galesburg, Michigan

Sol Friedman Residence
Usonia Homes, Inc., Development
Pleasantville, New York

J. Willis Hughes Residence "Fountainhead"
Jackson, Mississippi

*Edgar J. Kaufmann, Sr., Residence "Fallingwater" Guesthouse
     Alterations
Ohiopyle, Pennsylvania

Jack Lamberson Residence
Oskaloosa, Iowa

Robert Levin Residence
Parkwyn Village Development
Kalamazoo, Michigan

Curtis Meyer Residence
Galesburg Country Homes Development
Galesburg, Michigan

V.C. Morris Gift Shop
San Francisco, California

Herman T. Mossberg Residence
South Bend, Indiana

Eric Pratt Residence
Galesburg Country Homes Development
Galesburg, Michigan

Stanley Rosenbaum Residence Addition
Florence, Alabama

*Taliesin West Sun Cottage
Scottsdale, Arizona

Mrs. Clinton Walker Residence
Carmel, California

Lowell Walter River Pavilion
Quasqueton, Iowa

David I. Weisblat Residence
Galesburg Country Homes Development
Galesburg, Michigan

C.R. Weltzheimer Residence
Oberlin, Ohio

PROJECTS

Benjamin Adelman Residence--First Design
Fox Point, Wisconsin

Maginel Wright Barney Cottage
Spring Green, Wisconsin

Alfred Bergman Residence
St. Petersburg, Florida

Walter Bimson Penthouse
Phoenix, Arizona

Nicholas P. Daphne Funeral Chapels
San Francisco, California

Nicholas Daphne Residence
San Francisco, California

Henry Ellison Residence
Bridgewater Township, New Jersey

Ben Feenberg Residence
Fox Point, Wisconsin

George Hageman Residence
Peoria, Illinois

Dr. Frederick Margolis Residence
Kalamazoo, Michigan

Glenn McCord Residence
North Arlington, New Jersey

Sidney Miller Residence
Pleasantville, New York

C.W. Muehlberger Residence
East Lansing, Michigan

The New Theatre
Hartford, Connecticut

Point Park Community Center--Second Design
Pittsburgh, Pennsylvania

George M. Prout Residence
Columbus, Indiana

Vincent Scully Residence
Woodbridge, Connecticut

Talbot Smith Residence
Ann Arbor, Michigan

Warren Tremaine Observatory
Meteor Crater, Meteor, Arizona

Valley National Bank and Shopping Center
Sunnyslope, Arizona

1949

EXECUTED DESIGNS
Howard Anthony Residence
Benton Harbor, Michigan

Eric V. Brown Residence
Parkwyn Village Development
Kalamazoo, Michigan

James Edwards Residence
Okemos, Michigan

Kenneth Laurent Residence
Rockford, Illinois

Ward McCartney Residence and Alterations
Parkwyn Village Development
Kalamazoo, Michigan

Henry J. Neils Residence
Minneapolis, Minnesota

Edward Serlin Residence
Usonia Homes Inc. Development
Pleasantville, New York

*Taliesin West Cabaret Theater
Scottsdale, Arizona

PROJECTS
L.A. Bloomfield Residence
Tucson, Arizona

Charles Dabney Residence
Chicago, Illinois

Concrete Bridge, San Francisco Bay Bridge Southern Crossing
San Francisco, California

Alan Drummond Residence
Sante Fe, New Mexico

Goetsch-Winckler Residence--Second Design
Okemos, Michigan

George Griswold Residence
Greenwich, Connecticut

Huntington Hartford Theatre Square[36]
Hollywood, California

Harry G. John Residence
Oconomowoc, Wisconsin

Thomas C. Lea Residence
Asheville, North Carolina

Robert Publicker Residence
Haverford, Pennsylvania

Self-Service Garage for Edgar J. Kaufmann
Pittsburgh, Pennsylvania

Robert Windfohr Residence
Fort Worth, Texas

Y.W.C.A.
Racine, Wisconsin

1950
EXECUTED DESIGNS
Robert Berger Residence
San Anselmo, California

Raymond Carlson Residence
Phoenix, Arizona

John O. Carr Residence
Glenview, Illinois

Richard Davis Residence
Marion, Indiana

S.P. Elam Residence
Austin, Minnesota

John A. Gillan Residence
Dallas, Texas

Ina Moriss Harper Residence
Saint Joseph, Michigan

Thomas E. Keys Residence
Rochester, Minnesota

Arthur C. Mathews Residence
Atherton, California

Robert Muirhead Residence
Plato Center, Wisconsin

William Palmer Residence
Ann Arbor, Michigan

Wilbur C. Pearce Residence
Bradbury, California

Donald Schaberg Residence--Second Design
Okemos, Michigan

Seamour Shaven Residence
Chattanooga, Tennessee

*Richard Smith Residence
Jefferson, Wisconsin

Karl A. Staley Residence
North Madison, Ohio

J.A. Sweeton Residence
Cherry Hill, New Jersey

Robert D. Winn Residence
Parkwyn Village Development
Kalamazoo, Michigan

David Wright Residence
Phoenix, Arizona

Isadore J. Zimmerman Residence
Manchester, New Hampshire

PROJECTS
Harold Achuff Residence
Wauwatosa, Wisconsin

Irwin Auerbach Residence
Pleasantville, New York

Robert N. Bush Residence
Arkansas

Thomas Carroll Residence
Wauwatosa, Wisconsin

A.K. Chahroudi Residence--First Design
Lake Mahopac, New York

Tom D. Conklin Residence
Ulm, Minnesota

Donald Grove Residence
Syracuse, New York

Kenneth Hargrove Residence
Berkeley, California

Arnold Jackson Residence--First Design
Madison, Wisconsin

George Jacobsen Residence
Montreal, Quebec, Canada

George Montooth Residence
Rushville, Illinois

Dale O'Donnell Residence
East Lansing, Michigan

Brainerd Sabin Residence
Battle Creek, Michigan? or Memphis, Tennessee?

Donald Schaberg Residence--First Design
Okemos, Michigan

Dr. Leon Small Residence
West Orange, New Jersey

Arthur J. Stevens Residence
Park Ridge, Illinois

Lawrence Strong Residence
Kalamazoo, Michigan

William S. Wassel Residence
Philadelphia, Pennsylvania

1951

EXECUTED DESIGNS
Benjamin Adelman Residence--Second Design
Phoenix, Arizona

Gabrielle and Charlcey Austin Residence
Greenville, South Carolina

A.K. Chahroudi Residence--Second Design
Lake Mahopac, New York

W.L. Fuller Residence
Pass Christian, Mississippi

Charles F. Glore Residence
Lake Forest, Illinois

Patrick Kinney Residence
Lancaster, Wisconsin

Russell W.M. Kraus Residence
Kirkwood, Missouri

Roland Reisley Residence
Usonia Homes, Inc., Development
Pleasantville, New York

Nathan Rubin Residence
Canton, Ohio

Roy Wetmore Auto Service Station Remodeling
Ferndale, Michigan

PROJECTS
Bridge Design[37]
Echo Point, Wisconsin Dells, Wisconsin

George Clark Cottage
Carmel, California

Louis B. Hall Residence
Ann Arbor, Michigan

John P. Haynes Residence
Fort Wayne, Indiana

Huntington Hartford Vine Street Theatre[36]
Hollywood, California

Edgar Kaufmann, Jr., Residence
Palm Springs, California

Margaret Schevill Studio
Tucson, Arizona

Southwest Christian Seminary University[38]
Phoenix, Arizona

1952
  EXECUTED DESIGNS
    Anderton Court Shops
    Beverly Hills, California

    Quintin Blair Residence
    Cody, Wyoming

    Ray Brandes Residence
    Issaquah, Washington

    *Hillside Home School II Reconstruction
    Spring Green, Wisconsin

    Hillside Home School II Theater Curtain--Second Design
    Spring Green, Wisconsin

    *George Lewis Residence
    Tallahassee, Florida

    R.W. Lindholm Residence
    Cloquet, Minnesota

    Louis Marden Residence
    McLean, Virginia

    Arthur Pieper Residence
    Paradise Valley, Arizona

    *Price Company Tower for Harold Price, Sr.
    Bartlesville, Oklahoma

    Frank S. Sander Residence
    Stamford, Connecticut

    Archie Boyd Teater Residence
    Bliss, Idaho

  PROJECTS
    Lee Ackerman Project "Paradise on Wheels"
    Paradise Valley, Arizona

    Gregor Affleck Residence--Second Design
    Bloomfield Hills, Michigan

    Raoul Baillereres' Residence
    Acapulco, Mexico

    William Clifton Residence
    Oakland, New Jersey

    Motel, Pavilion, Entertainment Area at Leesburg Floating
       Gardens
    Leesburg, Florida

    Lawrence Sturtevant Residence
    Oakland, California

    Lawrence Swan Residence
    Detroit, Michigan

    Alexis Wainer Residence
    Valdosta, Georgia

    Zeta Beta Tau Fraternity House
    Gainesville, Florida

1953

    EXECUTED DESIGNS

        Jorgine Boomer Residence--Second Design
        Phoenix, Arizona

        Andrew B. Cooke Residence--First Design
        Virginia Beach, Virginia

        John J. Dobkins Residence
        Canton, Ohio

        Lewis H. Goddard Residence
        Plymouth, Michigan

        New York Usonian Exhibition House and Pavilion
        New York City, New York

        Louis Penfield Residence
        Willoughby Hills, Ohio

        Harold Price, Jr., Residence
        Bartlesville, Oklahoma

        Riverview Terrace Restaurant "The Spring Green"
        Spring Green, Wisconsin

       *Science and Cosmography Building
        Florida Southern College
        Lakeland, Florida

       *Taliesin West Sign
        Scottsdale, Arizona

        Robert Llewellyn Wright Residence
        Bethesda, Maryland

    PROJECTS

        Joseph H. Brewer Residence
        East Fishkill, New York

        Gift Booth Design for Frances Wright
        Location Unknown

        Huntington Hartford Fine Arts Galleries, Outdoor Theatre and
            Sculpture Gardens[36]
        Hollywood, California

        Edgar S. Lee Residence
        Midland, Michigan

        Masieri Memorial
        Venice, Italy

        V.C. Morris Residence "Sea Cliff"--Second Design
        San Francisco, California

        Pieper and Montooth Office Building
        Scottsdale, Arizona

        Point View Apartment Towers
        Pittsburgh, Pennsylvania

        William B. Proxmire FM Radio Station
        Jefferson, Wisconsin

Restaurant
Yosemite National Park, California

"Rhododendron" Chapel for Edgar Kaufmann
Bear Run, Connellsville, Pennsylvania

1954

EXECUTED DESIGNS
E. Clarke Arnold Residence
Columbus, Wisconsin

Beth Sholom Synagogue
Elkins Park, Pennsylvania

Cedric G. Boulter Residence
Cincinnati, Ohio

John E. Christian Residence
West Lafayette, Indiana

*Danforth Chapel (Minor Chapel)
Florida Southern College
Lakeland, Florida

Ellis A. Feiman Residence
Canton, Ohio

Louis B. Frederick Residence
Barrington Hills, Illinois

Dr. Maurice Greenberg Residence
Dousman, Wisconsin

I.N. Hagan Residence
Chalkhill, Pennsylvania

Hoffman Auto Showroom
New York, New York

Willard H. Keland Residence
Racine, Wisconsin

*Los Angeles Exhibition Pavilion
Los Angeles, California

Harold Price, Sr., Residence
Paradise Valley, Arizona

William L. Thaxton Residence
Bunker Hill, Texas

Gerald B. Tonkens Residence
Amberley Village, Ohio

Abraham Wilson Residence
Millstone, New Jersey

David Wright Guesthouse
Phoenix, Arizona

Frank Lloyd Wright's Hotel Plaza Apartment Remodeling
New York, New York

PROJECTS
Barnsdall Park Municipal Gallery
Los Angeles, California

Christian Science Reading Room
Riverside, Illinois

Gibbons Cornwall Residence
West Goshen, Pennsylvania

Freund and Co. Department Store[39]
San Salvador, El Salvador

Ben Rebhuhn Residence
Fort Meyers, Florida

Roger Schwenn Residence
Verona, Wisconsin

Dr. Alfons Tipshus Clinic
Stockton, California

1955

EXECUTED DESIGNS
Dallas Theater Center
Dallas, Texas

Randall Fawcett Residence
Los Banos, California

Maximillian Hoffman Residence
Rye, New York

Toufic H. Kalil Residence
Manchester, New Hampshire

Karl Kundert Medical Clinic
San Luis Obispo, California

*T.A. Pappas Residence
Saint Louis, Missouri

John L. Rayward Residence "Tirranna"
New Canaan, Connecticut

*Warren Scott Remodeling of the Isabel Roberts Residence
River Forest, Illinois

Robert H. Sunday Residence
Marshalltown, Iowa

W.B. Tracy Residence
Normandy Park, Washington

Dorothy H. Turkel Residence
Detroit, Michigan

Wallpaper and Fabric Designs for F. Schumacher and Company
    Taliesin Line
New York, New York

Frank Lloyd Wright Furniture Designs for Heritage-Henredon
Morganton, North Carolina

PROJECTS
Benjamin Adelman Residence--Third Design
Whitefish Bay, Wisconsin

A.D. Barton Residence[39]
Downers Grove, Illinois

Mel Blumberg Residence
Des Moines, Iowa

William Boswell Residence--First Design[39]
Cincinnati, Ohio

Christian Science Church
Bolinas, Marin County, California

Robert Coats Residence
Hillsborough, California

Andrew B. Cooke Residence--Second Design
Virginia Beach, Virginia

George Dlesk Residence[40]
Manistee, Michigan

John Gillan Residence
Hollywood, California

Leonard Jankowski Residence
Oakland County, Michigan

Korrick's Department Store Alterations
Phoenix, Arizona

Lenkurt Electric Co. Administration-Manufacturing Building
San Mateo, California

Oscar Miller Residence[39]
Milford Village, Michigan

Monona Terrace Civic Center--Second Design
Madison, Wisconsin

Mrs. V.C. Morris "Seadrift" Guest House[39]
San Francisco, California

"Neuroseum" Hospital and Clinic for the Wisconsin Neurological
    Society
Madison, Wisconsin

Arch Obler Residence--Second Design
Los Angeles, California

"One Room House" (Usonian)
Location Unknown

C.R. Pieper Residence
Phoenix, Arizona

Gerald Sussman Residence
Rye, New York

Daniel Wieland Motor Hotel[39]
Hagerstown, Maryland

1956
    EXECUTED DESIGNS
      *Annunciation Greek Orthodox Church
      Wauwatosa, Wisconsin

Frank Bott Residence
Kansas City, Missouri

William Cass Residence
Marshall Erdman Company Prefab #1
Richmond, New York

Allan Friedman Residence
Bannockburn, Illinois

Solomon R. Guggenheim Museum
New York, New York

Frank Iber Residence
Marshall Erdman Company Prefab #1
Stevens Point, Wisconsin

Arnold Jackson Residence--Second Design
Marshall Erdman Company Prefab #1
Madison, Wisconsin

Kenneth Laurent Residence Addition
Rockford, Illinois

R.W. Lindholm Automobile Service Station
Cloquet, Minnesota

Kenneth L. Meyers Medical Clinic
Dayton, Ohio

Joseph Mollica Residence
Marshall Erdman Company Prefab #1
Bayside, Wisconsin

*Clyde Nooker Restoration of the Frank Lloyd Wright Studio
Oak Park, Illinois

Carl Post Residence
Marshall Erdman Company Prefab #1
Barrington Hills, Illinois

Rose Parade Float for the Phoenix Junior Chamber of Commerce
Pasadena, California

Dudley W. Spencer Residence
Wilmington, Delaware

*Taliesin Music Pavilion
Scottsdale, Arizona

Paul J. Trier Residence
Des Moines, Iowa

Eugene Van Tamelen Residence
Marshall Erdman Company Prefab #1
Madison, Wisconsin

Wyoming Valley Grammar School
Wyoming Valley, Wisconsin

PROJECTS
Robert Boebel Residence[39]
Boscobel, Wisconsin

Freeman Bramlett Motor Hotel
Memphis, Tennessee

"The Golden Beacon" Skyscraper
Chicago, Illinois

Nelson G. Gross Residence
Hackensack, New Jersey

David Hunt Residence
Scottsdale, Arizona

"The Illinois" Mile-High Skyscraper
Chicago, Illinois

Bradford Mills Residence--First Design
Princeton, New Jersey

Mrs. V.C. Morris Residence "Quietwater"
Stinson Beach, California

Dr. Arthur O'Keefe Residence[39]
Santa Barbara, California

Jay Roberts Residence
Seattle, Washington

Victoria Schuck Residence[39]
South Hadley, Massachusetts

Sports Pavilion at Belmont[39]
Long Island, New York

Calvin Stillman Residence[39]
Cornwall-on-Hudson, New York

Gerald Tonkins Loan Office[39]
Cincinnati, Ohio

"Usonian Automatic" Houses Designs
Locations Unknown

J.J. Vallarino Residence[39]
Panama City, Panama

1957

EXECUTED DESIGNS
"Airhouse" Air Structure--U.S. Rubber Company
International Home Exposition
New York, New York

William P. Boswell Residence--Second Design
Indian Hill (near Cincinnati), Ohio

*Herman T. Fasbender Medical Clinic
Hastings, Minnesota

C.E. Gordon Residence
Aurora, Oregon

Juvenile Cultural Study Center for Wichita State University
Wichita, Kansas

Sterling Kinney Residence
Amarillo, Texas

Marin County Post Office, Administration Building, and Hall
    of Justice
San Raphael, California

James B. McBean Residence
Marshall Erdman Company Prefab #2
Rochester, Minnesota

Walter Rudin Residence
Marshall Erdman Company Prefab #2
Madison, Wisconsin

Carl Schultz Residence
Saint Joseph, Michigan

Robert G. Walton Residence
Modesto, California

Duey Wright Residence
Wausau, Wisconsin

PROJECTS
Lee Adams Residence[39]
St. Paul, Minnesota

Arizona State Capital "Oasis"
Phoenix, Arizona

Baghdad Art Museum
Baghdad, Iraq

(Baghdad) Plan for Greater Baghdad
Baghdad, Iraq

Baghdad Post and Telegraph Building[39]
Baghdad, Iraq

Baghdad Opera House and Gardens
Baghdad, Iraq

Baghdad University Complex and Gardens
Baghdad, Iraq

Walter Bimson Residence
Usonian Automatic
Phoenix, Arizona

Robert Brooks Residence[39]
Middleton, Wisconsin

First Christian Church Master Plan
Phoenix, Arizona

Jesse Fisher Housing Project
Whiteville, North Carolina

Stanley Hartman Residence
Lansing, Michigan

Jack P. Hennesy Two Residences
Smoke Rise, New Jersey

Robert Herberger Residence
Maricopa County, Arizona

Highway Motel for Marshall Erdman and Associates
Madison, Wisconsin

Carl Hoyer Residence[39]
Maricopa County, Arizona

Juvenile Cultural Study Center for University of Wichita,
    Building B
Wichita, Kansas

Edgar Kaufmann Gate Lodge and Buildings[39]
Bear Run, Pennsylvania

Joyce and Darryl L. McKinney Residence[39]
Cloquet, Minnesota

Arthur Miller and Marilyn Monroe Residence[39]
Roxburg, Connecticut

Bradford Mills Residence--Second Design[39]
Princeton, New Jersey

Ralph Moreland Residence
Austin, Texas

Nezam's Private Palace[39]
Tehran, Iran

Post Office
Spring Green, Wisconsin

Schanbacher and Son Interior Decorators
Springfield, Illinois

Wilton Shelton Residence
Long Island, New York

Mrs. Helen Sottil Residence
Cuernavaca, Mexico

Dr. Victor W. Stracke Residence[39]
Appleton, Wisconsin

Wedding Chapel, Claremont Hotel
Berkeley, California

Henry T. Wilson Residence
Morganton, North Carolina

Allen Zieger Residence[39]
Grosse Isle, Michigan

1958
    EXECUTED DESIGNS
        George Ablin Residence
        Bakersfield, California

        Robert Berger Dog House
        San Anselmo, California

        Cedric G. Boulter Residence Addition
        Cincinnati, Ohio

        Lockridge Medical Clinic
        Whitefish, Montana

        Paul Olfelt Residence
        Saint Louis Park, Minnesota

        *Seth Petersen Residence
        Lake Delton, Wisconsin

Pilgrim Congregational Church
Redding, California

Don M. Stromquist Residence
Bountiful, Utah

PROJECTS
Freeman Bramlett Midway Gardens[39]
Memphis, Tennessee

Ralph Colegrove Residence[39]
Hamilton, Ohio

Community Center[39]
Spring Green, Wisconsin

Lillian Crosby-Lambert Residence[39]
Colbert County, Alabama

Marshall Erdman Prefab #3
Madison, Wisconsin

Marshall Erdman Prefab #4
Madison, Wisconsin

Florida Southern College Music Building[39]
Lakeland, Florida

Jesse Franklin Residence[39]
Louisville, Kentucky

Dr. James F. Guttierez Residence
Albuquerque, New Mexico

Pat Hanley Airplane Hanger, Classroom, Chapel[39]
Benton Harbor, Michigan

Helicopter

Hungarian Freedom Fighters Memorial
Manville, New Jersey

Frank Lagomarsino Residence
San Jose, California

Dr. Jarvis Leuchauer Clinic
Fresno, California

Wesley Libbey Residence
Grand Rapids, Michigan

Don Lovness Cottages[41]
Stillwater, Minnesota

Motor Car (Road Machine)

Dudley Spencer Residence[39]
Delaware

Spring Green Auditorium
Spring Green, Wisconsin

Michael Todd Universal Theater[39]
Los Angeles, California

Trinity Chapel
University of Oklahoma
Norman, Oklahoma

Unity Chapel
Taliesin Valley, Spring Green, Wisconsin

William Zeckendorf 300 Unit Motel and Restaurant[39]
New York, New York

1959

EXECUTED DESIGNS
Grady Gammage Memorial
Auditorium for Arizona State University
Tempe, Arizona

Norman Lykes Residence
Phoenix, Arizona

*Taliesin Enclosed Garden
Spring Green, Wisconsin

PROJECTS
Art Gallery for Arizona State University
Tempe, Arizona

Christian Science Church[39]
Chicago, Illinois

Mrs. D.J. Donahoe Residence "Triptych"[42]
Phoenix, Arizona

Harvey Furgatch Residence
San Diego, California

Greek Orthodox Church[39]
San Francisco, California

Dr. John H. Mann Residence
Putnam County, New York

Louis Penfield Residence--Second Design
Willoughby, Ohio

Daniel Wieland Residence
Hagerstown, Maryland

Gilbert Wieland Residence
Hagerstown, Maryland

1971

EXECUTED DESIGN
First Christian Church[43]
Phoenix, Arizona

1974

EXECUTED DESIGN
Arthur and Bruce Brooks Pfeiffer Residence[44]
Scottsdale, Arizona

1976

EXECUTED DESIGNS
Hilary and Joe Feldman Residence[45]
Berkeley, California

Donald Lovness Guest House[46]
Stillwater, Minnesota

1978
    EXECUTED DESIGN
        First Christian Church Belltower[43]
        Phoenix, Arizona

UNDATED
    EXECUTED DESIGN
        Residence Remodeling[47]
        Oak Park, Illinois

NOTES

1. With Alan D. Conover for whom Wright was working as a draftsman
    in Madison, Wisconsin.

2. This building was designed by J.L. Silsbee under whom Wright was
    working as a draftsman. Wright prepared a drawing of this build-
    ing which appeared in "Unity Chapel, Helena, Wis.," *All Souls
    Church* (Chicago), 1887, p. 33. Wright had substantial involvement
    in the construction of this small building.

3. A J.L. Silsbee design drawn and signed by Wright which appeared
    in "Unitarian Chapel for Sioux City, Iowa," *Inland Architect and
    News Record*, Vol. 9, June 1887, plate.

4. A J.L. Silsbee design for which a drawing and plan drawn and
    signed by Wright appeared in "Residence for J.L. Cochrane, Esq.,
    J.L. Silsbee, Architect," *Inland Architect and News Record*, Vol.
    11, March 1888, plate.

5. A second design by J.L. Silsbee for Cochran, a drawing signed by
    Wright appeared in "Residence for J.L. Cochran, Edgewater, Ill.
    J.L. Silsbee, Architect," *Inland Architect and News Record*, Vol.
    11, July 1888, plate.

6. Another design by J.L. Silsbee; however, a rendering by Wright
    appeared in "Houses for William Waller, Chicago, J.L. Silsbee,
    Architect," *Inland Architect and News Record*, Vol. 11, May 1888,
    plate.

7. This building is attributed to Louis H. Sullivan; however, a
    drawing of the Falkenau Residence signed by Wright appeared in
    "Houses for Victor Falkenau, Chicago, Adler and Sullivan, Archi-
    tects, Chicago," *Inland Architect and News Record*, Vol. 11,
    June 1888, plate. This would indicate that Wright may have had
    substantial involvement in the building.

8. See Robert C. Spencer, Jr., "The Work of Frank Lloyd Wright,"
    Architectural Review (Boston), Vol. 7, June 1900, pp. 61-72.

9. This is a residence by architect Myron Hunt whom Wright had
    assisted during the design of the building. The residence is

located at 1313 and 1319 Ridge Avenue, Evanston, Illinois. For
more details on this design see H. Allen Brooks, *The Prairie School:
Frank Lloyd Wright and His Midwest Contemporaries*, New York: W.W.
Norton and Co., Inc., 1972, p. 32.

10. Taliesin lists state that both a William Adams and a Jesse Adams
     Residence were built; however, William Allin Storrer in his *The
     Architecture of Frank Lloyd Wright, a Complete Catalog*, Second
     Edition, Cambridge: The M.I.T. Press, 1978, p. 48, claims that
     the William Adams Residence was mistitled and really was the Jesse
     Adams Residence based upon inspection of the city building records.

11. See Frank Lloyd Wright, "A Home in a Prairie Town," *Ladies' Home
     Journal*, Vol. 18, February 1901, p. 17.

12. See Frank Lloyd Wright, "A Small House with 'Lots of Room in It,'"
     Ladies' Home Journal, Vol. 18, July 1901, p. 15.

13. This design was presented to M.H. Lowell with a letter from Wright
     dated January 30, 1901, and hitherto was an unknown project. The
     letter, with the sketches drawn directly upon the letter (per-
     spective and plan), is contained in the collections of the Avery
     Architectural Library of Columbia University at New York.

14. See Frank Lloyd Wright, "The 'Village Bank' Series V," *Brick-
     builder*, Vol. 10, August 1901, pp. 160-161.

15. In a letter dated December 28, 1904, to William R. Heath from
     Frank Lloyd Wright, certain information is contained there to more
     accurately date this house as being completed in 1904 rather than
     1905 as was thought by most scholars who have attempted to date
     this residence. The letter is in the Frank Lloyd Wright Papers at
     the Library of Congress.

16. See Frank Lloyd Wright, "A Fireproof House for $5000," *Ladies'
     Home Journal*, Vol. 24, April 1907, p. 24.

17. Same design as the J.G. Melson Residence Project at Mason City,
     Iowa, of 1908.

18. Same design as the William Norman Guthrie Residence Project at
     Sewanee, Tennessee, of 1908.

19. Thirty-eight designs were made, some of which were constructed
     in 1915? and 1916. These are listed as both projects and executed
     designs.

20. In collaboration with Francis C. Sullivan, Architect.

21. Located at 239 Franklin Street at Glencoe, Illinois.

22. This project has not been listed in any publication of Wright's
     work. Six blueprints of the project are housed in the Frank Lloyd
     Wright Collection of the University Archives of The State Uni-
     versity of New York at Buffalo, New York.

23. Located at 231 Prospect Avenue at Lake Bluff, Illinois.

24. Located at 330 Gregory Street at Wilmette, Illinois.

25. Wright designed this residence in 1895; however, the building caught fire in 1922 and Moore commissioned Wright to rebuild the area above the first floor.

26. With Albert McArthur, Architect.

27. With F.L. Wright's son, John Lloyd Wright.

28. Probably for the Broadacre City design.

29. The entire plan was not executed. Only portions of it were built.

30. See "Frank Lloyd Wright, Architect: House for $5000-$6000 Income," *Architectural Forum*, Vol. 69, November 1938, pp. 331-335, and *"Life* Presents in Collaboration with the *Architectural Forum* Eight Houses for Modern Living Especially Designed by Famous American Architects for Four Representative Families Earning $2,000 to $10,000 a Year," *Life*, Vol. 5, September 26, 1938, pp. 45-65.

31. This residence was later built for Arthur and Bruce Brooks Pfeiffer at Scottsdale, Arizona, in 1974.

32. This residence was later built for Hilary and Joe Feldman at Berkeley, California, in 1976.

33. The date of this project is confirmed by an article entitled "Buildings: Pence Project, Hilo, Hawaii," *The Frank Lloyd Wright Newsletter* (The Frank Lloyd Wright Association, Oak Park), Vol. 1, No. 4, July-August 1978, pp. 1-2.

34. This structure was largely destroyed by fire in February of 1958. For more detailed information on the fire see "Wright Designed Lodge Burns Up," *The Capital Times* (Madison, Wisconsin), February 14, 1958.

35. A review of Wright's exhibition appeared in Geoffrey Baker's "Wright as Iconoclast: Contribution of Architect to Our Age as Set Forth at Museum of Modern Art," *The New York Times*, November 24, 1940, section 9, p. 10, col. 1.

36. With F.L. Wright's son, Lloyd Wright, of Los Angeles, California.

37. See "Kohler Aide Meets with Wright: Wright Dells Bridge Will Be Built if 'A Benefit to State,'" *The Capital Times* (Madison, Wisconsin), November 1, 1951, for a description of this project.

38. This project later developed into the First Christian Church at Phoenix, Arizona, constructed by Taliesin Associated Architects in 1971, 1977, and the bell tower in 1978.

39. Announced in "Record Number of Wright Projects 'On the Boards' at Taliesin West," *The Capital Times* (Madison, Wisconsin), January 16, 1959.

40. This residence was announced by F.L. Wright as being completed in "Record Number of Wright Projects 'On the Boards' at Taliesin West," *The Capital Times* (Madison, Wisconsin), January 16, 1959.

41. This project was finally built by Taliesin Associated Architects in 1976.

42. According to Mrs. Wright, this was the last project F.L. Wright had worked on before his death on April 9, 1959. See Mrs. Frank Lloyd Wright, "Our House," *The Capital Times* (Madison, Wisconsin), September 18, 1959.

43. From Wright's plans for the Southwest Christian Seminary University Project of 1951.

44. From Wright's plans for the Ralph Jester Residence Project of 1938.

45. From Wright's plans for the Lewis N. Bell Residence Project of 1939.

46. From Wright's 1958 plans for the Don Lovness Cottages Project.

47. At 338 North Kenilworth Avenue at Oak Park, Illinois. A more complete account of this discovery can be found in Thomas A. Heinz, "Frank Lloyd Wright Remodelling Discovered," *The Frank Lloyd Wright Newsletter* (Oak Park, Illinois), Vol. 2, No. 3, Second Quarter 1979, p. 20, with photograph of building.

Riverside, Illinois, *see* Coonley, Avery, Playhouse; Coonley, Avery,
     Residence; Tomek, F.F., Residence
Roberts, Mrs. Abby Beecher, Residence (Marquette, Michigan)   B210b
Roberts, Charles E., Residence and Stables Remodeling (Oak Park,
     Illinois)   A9
Robie, Frederick G., Residence (Chicago, Illinois)   A9, A14, A16,
     A21, A29, A46, A52, A53, B42, B292, B514
Rochester, New York, *see* Boynton, E.E., Residence
Rockefeller Center (New York, New York)   B138
Roloson, Robert W., Apartments (Chicago, Illinois)   A9, A29,
Rome, Italy   B89, B90, B197
Romeo and Juliet Windmill for Nell and Jane Lloyd Jones (Spring Green,
     Wisconsin)   A53
Rookery Building and Remodeling (Chicago, Illinois)   A9, B5
Rosenbaum, Stanley, Residence (Florence, Alabama)   A53
Russia   B131, B177, B227, B228, B231, B234, B236, B237, B302, B515
Rye, New York, *see* Hoffman, Maximilian, Residence

San Diego, California   B482
San Francisco, California, *see* Morris, V.C., Gift Shop
San Raphael, California, *see* Marin County Civic Center
The Santa Fe Chief (train)   B264
Schiller Building (Chicago, Illinois; Adler and Sullivan, architects)
     B1, B199, B505
Schumacher, F., and Company, Wallpaper and Fabric Designs, Taliesin
     Line (New York, New York)   A4, A7, A9, A28, A29, A30, A43
Schwartz, Bernard, Residence (Two Rivers, Wisconsin)   B248, B264
Scottsdale, Arizona, *see* Taliesin West
Scoville Park Fountain (Oak Park, Illinois)   A20
Shorewood Hills, Wisconsin, *see* Pew, John C., Residence; Unitarian
     Church
Sicily   B39
Smith, Frank L., Bank (Dwight, Illinois)   A9, B15, B16, B17, B23,
     B24, B32
Smith, Melvyn Maxwell, Residence (Bloomfield Hills, Michigan)   A9
Sondern, Clarence, Residence (Kansas City, Missouri)   A48, A53
South America   B302, B360
South Bend, Indiana, *see* DeRhodes, K.C., Residence
South Dakota   B196a, B196b, B198a, B198b, B198c, B198e
     See also Bad Lands; Black Hills; Rapid City; Spearfish Canyon;
     Sylvan Lake
Spain, *see* Barcelona
Spearfish Canyon, South Dakota   B198a
Springfield, Illinois, *see* Dana, Susan Lawrence, Residence
Springfield, Ohio, *see* Westcott, Burton J., Residence
Spring Green, Wisconsin, *see* Hillside Home School II for Nell and
     Jane Lloyd Jones; Porter, Andrew T., "Tanyderi" Residence;
     Romeo and Juliet Windmill for Nell and Jane Lloyd Jones;
     Taliesin
"Spring, Summer, and Autumn" Prints   A16
Stanford, California, *see* Hanna, Paul R., "Honeycomb" Residence
Stanford University (Stanford, California)   B218c, B218d
Starret Lehigh Building (New York, New York)   B93
Steffens, Oscar, Residence (Chicago, Illinois)   A21
Stewart, George C., Residence (Monticeto, California)   B42

INDEX OF NAMES, TITLES, AND TOPICS

INDEX OF CORRESPONDENTS

B220, B252, B263, B266, B267,
B315, B326, B331, B335, B336,
B338, B341, B348, B349, B380,
B383, B396, B417, B433, B439,
B441, B461, B482, B519, B520

INDEX OF ARCHIVES AND COLLECTIONS